Clipped Wings

Corporate social and environmental
responsibility in the airline industry

Deborah Ancell

Routledge
Taylor & Francis Group

LONDON AND NEW YORK

First published 2017
by Routledge
2 Park Square, Milton Park, Abingdon, Oxon OX14 4RN

and by Routledge
711 Third Avenue, New York, NY 10017

Routledge is an imprint of the Taylor & Francis Group, an informa business

British Library Cataloguing in Publication Data
A catalogue record for this book is available from the British Library

Library of Congress Cataloging in Publication Data
Names: Ancell, Deborah, author.
Title: Clipped wings : challenges facing the airline industry / Deborah Ancell.
Description: Abingdon, Oxon ; New York, NY : Routledge, 2017.
Identifiers: LCCN 2016022081| ISBN 9781472477736 (hardback) |
ISBN 9781315572437 (ebook)
Subjects: LCSH: Airlines--Management.
Classification: LCC HE9780 .A495 2017 | DDC 387.7--dc23
LC record available at https://lccn.loc.gov/2016022081

ISBN: 978-1-4724-7773-6 (hbk)
ISBN: 978-1-315-57243-7 (ebk)

Typeset in Bembo
by Florence Production Ltd, Stoodleigh, Devon, UK

MIX
Paper from
responsible sources
FSC
www.fsc.org   FSC® C013056

Printed and bound in Great Britain by
TJ International Ltd, Padstow, Cornwall

Clipped Wings

Within the developed world, airlines have responded to the advice of advocates for corporate social and environmental responsibility (CSER) to use the intertwined dimensions of economics, society and environment to guide their business activities. However, disingenuously, the advocates and regulators frequently pay insufficient attention to the economics which are critical to airlines' sustainability and profits. This omission pushes airlines into the unprofitable domain of CSERplus.

The author identifies alleged market inefficiencies and failures, examines CSERplus impacts on international competition and assesses the unintended consequences of the regulations. She also provides innovative ideas for future-proofing airlines.

Clipped Wings is a treatise for business professionals featuring academic research as well as industry anecdotes. It is written for airlines (including their owners, employees, passengers and suppliers), airports, trade associations, policy makers, educators, students, consultants, CSERplus specialists and anyone who is concerned about the future of competitive airlines.

Deborah Ancell had a long career in the airline industry covering customer service, construction and sustainability. During her tenure, she observed the effects of social and environmental legislation implemented without economic impact assessments. This became a research field and her employers in the airline industry supported her by sponsoring MSc and PhD studies in economics and innovation. Subsequently, she became a university academic teaching economics in transport and construction at the University of Westminster, UK. Her research interests are wide-ranging, from buildings and education through to transport and airline sustainability.

Contents

Figures

Tables

Preface

Aviation is one of the most socially and environmentally responsible industries. It cannot be compared to any of the socially and environmentally exploitive industries which treat society or the environment contemptuously as they conduct their operations in multiple locations. Airlines face many unique challenges which this book examines through the lens of corporate social and environmental responsibility (CSER) with its intertwined dimensions of economics, society and the environment. CSER's advocates pursue ill-defined 'social justice' which usually requires private enterprises either to donate to their causes or to go beyond rational economics into a new domain to supply economically deficient public goods and services free of charge. This domain is 'CSERplus'. As I sought for the economics that were initially believed to have supported the CSER ideals it became apparent that the advocates' concerns were usually only for the social or environmental dimensions. These they incorrectly treated as separate, distinctive and dislocated from economics – hence 'CSERplus'. This discovery completely changed the original perspective of the book.

The airline industry has had to overcome volatile fuel prices, economic recessions, wars and invasions, natural disasters, health epidemics, security threats and imperfect competition while profits rose and fell, airlines survived or failed and new entrants came and went. In an increasingly litigious society, airlines are under continual scrutiny because of changes in legislation and regulations, rise of the compensation culture, increasing openness through digital media and the shifting of power from airlines to their customers. The aviation market has been affected by inefficiencies including lack of competition which was resolved by the liberalisation of nationalised airlines and airports. Theoretical causes of further market inefficiencies include the identification of formerly 'missing' markets, assignment of property rights to environmentally detrimental externalities, use of imperfect knowledge, presence of the principal-agent problem, publicly funded provision, and the presence of free riders, moral hazards and moral panic. These could make advanced-world international airlines uncompetitive compared to those from advancing nations with airlines unfettered by the encumbrances of higher overheads and the costs of CSERplus. It would be the advanced-world shareholders, employees and customers who would ultimately bear the costs of these inefficiencies. Besides, if these inefficiencies are embedded either only nationally or regionally they could have a damaging effect on internationally competing, advanced-world airlines which have accepted and accommodated the shifting focus on social and environmental issues at the expense of economics. In the long run this situation is not sustainable. Furthermore, the advocates for CSERplus frequently claim credit for many activities and regulations which did not evolve from their lobbying. Instead, these outcomes are the result of an entrepreneurial and responsible industry focussed on safety, customer experience, competitiveness and profitability.

Sustainable airline management decisions are based in economics and not in compassion or in the environment – the two domains favoured by CSERplus' advocates. Economics supported by impartial and complete knowledge is fundamental to sustainable airline decisions. The risk of reputational damage is enhanced by any decisions which affect the three dimensions and which are reliant on asymmetric (i.e. partisan) knowledge. Consequently, sustainability-thinking – considering the potential economic, social and environmental impacts during decision-making (the governance process) – has to be an integral part of the core business. Sustainability-thinking is not complicated and does not require specialist skills or explanations. It requires only the use of every-day language within a culture of openness and challenge. In contrast, because of political sensitivities, many of the CSERplus issues are not openly discussed and are therefore unchallenged.

This examination of the airline industry would appear to be the first to assess the potential effects of CSERplus on international competitiveness. In the spirit of challenge which sustainability-thinking encourages, many questions have arisen for which it would appear that there are no obvious answers other than 'politics vs airline economics'. This book took many years to produce and knowledge changed in all the dimensions as it was being written. Any book on the expanding, emerging and evolving CSERplus dimensions will never be finished and it will therefore be easy for detractors to identify where changes have occurred and any omissions. What has resulted is provocative and is, in parts, possibly not even politically correct (although it is not meant to offend). The book was described by one reviewer as 'special pleading for the airline industry' and by another as 'defensive' – descriptions which could possibly resonate with some readers. However, the issues described could apply equally to any industry which has unthinkingly subscribed to CSERplus without determining the economic elements. The book seeks to open debate about the economic effects of well-meaning but often misguided CSERplus social and environmental activities on the airline industry. The CSERplus advocates need to engage in the debate and explain the lack of economics, deficiency of information, distortion of data and the ominous silencing of public scrutiny in their pursuit of ill-defined 'social justice'.

This treatise is a study of the four CSER dimensions using them as a framework without endorsing them. It is a combination of treatise, textbook and (since it is peppered with industry anecdotes) storybook. It combines economic theory, industry research and informed opinions from multiple sources. Opinions provide the context to overcome the absence of data and information which should have been available from preliminary economic impact analyses and post-implementation assessments, many of which were, unfortunately, never executed. Writing it was a journey where I discovered that some regulations and policies even allowed passengers' rights to become airlines' responsibilities. Where I lacked the knowledge I satisfied my curiosity by researching documentation and interviewing passengers, aviation industry specialists (including airline representatives), civil servants, academics and managers from charities and non-governmental organisations (NGOs). Their contributions have been anonymised and I thank them for their honesty, openness and trust (behaviours which epitomise sustainability-thinking). The result is a text which interprets the CSERplus dimensions as challenges for the industry and as triggers for potential market inefficiencies and possible failures. While this study cannot hope to cover every possible concern in all the dimensions, it still raises many issues which have previously been considered settled, unimportant or too politically sensitive to discuss openly. It is an exposure of ill-conceived short-term interventions in national, regional or international airline markets which have had, and could still have, unintended, long-term, negative consequences for competitive international airlines. Could the omission of economics from the CSERplus advocates' demands make airline markets inefficient or could it eventually result in their failure?

Deborah Ancell
BCA MSc(Dist) PhD
April 2016

NB: foreign exchange conversions took place on different days at different rates.

Acknowledgements

This book had the support of many individuals to whom I am extremely grateful. In particular I owe much gratitude to Professor David Henderson, CMG, whose work has provided a scaffold for this book, whose comments have been invaluable and whose generosity with his time has been much appreciated. I am also deeply indebted to Gary Gray, whose advice, encouragement and support put the wings under this project and helped it to fly, to Jayne Simms for her reading, feedback, wisdom and insights, and to Dominic Lawson for his original article which opened the possibility of this treatise. Many others have contributed with comments, calculations, reviews and challenges including Wendy Bishop, Caroline Bonavia, Robin Crompton, David Deakin, Professor Bill Durodié, Sandra Dearden, Nigel Dennis, Stephanie Devine, Professor Christopher Essex, Dr Vincent Gray, Dr Stephen Gruneberg, Rob Jones, Stephen Payne and Dr Benny Peiser.

Special thanks for permissions also go to the Institute for Economic Affairs, International Air Transport Association and the Global Warming Policy Foundation, as well as to the anonymous interviewees and reviewers whose judgement helped to reshape the numerous drafts.

Abbreviations

AA	AccountAbility
AAU	assigned amount units
ACAA	Air Carrier Access Act 1986
ACARE	Advisory Council for Aeronautics Research in Europe
AGM	annual general meeting
AISI	Airline Industry Sustainability Index
APD	air passenger duty (UK)
APIS	advanced passenger information system
ASK	available seat kilometre
ATAG	Air Transport Advisory Group
ATC	Air Traffic Control
ATK	available tonne per kilometre
BBC	British Broadcasting Corporation
BiTC	Business in the Community
BLND	passenger is visually impaired
bn	billion
BSCI	Business Social Compliance Initiative
CAA	Civil Aviation Authority (UK)
CCC	Committee on Climate Change (UK)
CCI	corporate community investment
CFC	chlorofluorocarbons
CHP	combined heat and power
CICA	Convention on International Civil Aviation
CITES	Convention on International Trade in Endangered Species
CNG	carbon neutral growth
CO_2	carbon dioxide
COP	Conference of the Parties
CRS	Customer Reservation System
CSER	corporate social and environmental responsibility
CSERplus	beyond economically viable corporate social and environmental responsibility
CSF	critical success factor
CSR	Corporate Social Responsibility

DDA	Disabilities Discrimination Act (1996)
DEC	Disasters Emergency Committee (UK)
DETR	Department of Environment, Transport and the Regions (UK)
DfID	Department for International Development (UK)
DJSI	Dow Jones Sustainability Index
ECAC	European Civil Aviation Conference
ECJ	European Court of Justice
EHIC	European Health Insurance Card
EMAS	Eco-Management Audit Scheme
EMS	environmental management system
EPA	Environmental Protection Act (USA)
ETI	Ethical Trading Initiative
ETS	Emissions Trading Scheme
EU	European Union
EU ETS	European Union Emissions Trading Scheme
FAA	Federal Aviation Administration (USA)
FTSE	Financial Times Stock Exchange
FTSE4Good	Financial Times Stock Exchange 4 Good Index
GDP	gross domestic product
GHG	greenhouse gas
GM	genetically modified (foods)
GRI	Global Reporting Initiative
GSCP	Global Social Compliance Programme
GWPF	Global Warming Policy Foundation
HIV-AIDS	human immunodeficiency virus – acquired immune deficiency syndrome
HR	Human Resources
HSE	Health and Safety Executive (UK)
HSR	High Speed Rail
IAIA	International Association for Impact Assessment
IAPA	International Air Passenger Association
IATA	International Air Transport Association
ICAO	International Civil Aviation Organisation
IDS	Income Data Services
ILO	International Labour Organisation
IPCC	Intergovernmental Panel on Climate Change (under the auspices of the United Nations)
ISO	International Standards Organisation
ITC	Information Technology and Communications
JV	joint venture
KPI	key performance indicator
MBM	market-based measure
m	million
MNE	multi-national enterprise
n/a	not available

n.d.	no date
NED	Non-executive Director
NGO	Non-Governmental Organisation
NHS	National Health Service (UK)
NOAA	National Oceanic Atmospheric Administration (USA)
n.p.	no page
OCAI	organisational cultural assessment indicator
ODI	Office for Disability Issues
OECD	Organisation for Economic Cooperation and Development
OFT	Office of Fair Trading (UK)
ONS	Office of National Statistics (UK)
PBC	performance-based contract
PBS	performance-based specification
PDI	power-distance index
PESTLE	political, economic, social, technological, legal and environmental
PESTTLE	political, economic, social, technological, time, legal and environmental
PETA	People for the Ethical Treatment of Animals
PHOH	passenger is hard of hearing
ppm	parts per million (of CO_2)
PR	Public Relations Department
PRM	passenger with reduced mobility
RICO	Racketeer Influenced and Corrupt Organizations Act (USA)
RPK	revenue passenger kilometres
RRR	reputational risk register
SBU	strategic business unit
SLA	service-level agreement
SLF	self-loading freight
SMART	specific, measurable, achievable, relevant and timebound
SPAD	Special Adviser (to UK Labour Government)
SRI	Socially Responsible Investment
SSR	special service request
SSSI	site of special scientific interest
SUV	sports utility vehicle
SWOT	strengths, weaknesses, opportunity, threats
tba	to be arranged
tbd	to be decided
TSA	Transportation Security Agency (USA)
TUPE	Transfer and Undertakings (Protection of Employment) (TUPE) Regulations 2006 (UK)
UMs	unaccompanied minors
UN	United Nations
UNFAO	United Nations Food and Agricultural Organisation
UNFCCC	United Nations Framework Convention on Climate Change

UNGC	United Nations Global Compact
UNGP	United Nations Global Principles on Business and Human Rights
UNICEF	United Nations International Children's Emergency Fund
UNWCED	United Nations World Commission on Environment and Development
UNWTO	United Nations World Travel Organisation
UK	United Kingdom
USA	United States of America
VAT	value-added tax
VFR	visiting friends and relations
VIPs	very important passengers
V-VIPs	very-very important passengers
WBCSD	World Business Council for Sustainable Development
WCHC	passenger is unable to be independently mobile
WCHR	passenger cannot walk long distances
WCHS	passenger cannot use stairs (e.g. aircraft steps)
WEF	World Economic Forum
WHO	World Health Organisation
WTC	World Trade Centre, New York, USA

Part I

Sustainability economics

The first of the intertwined dimensions of airline sustainability is **economics** – the social science which is concerned with the production, distribution and consumption of services and products.

Chapter 1: Introduction to economic airline sustainability outlines the economic challenges which are prevalent in sustainable airlines. It introduces the indicators of market inefficiencies or failures which could be either triggered or solved by interventions from legislators and regulators. These inefficiencies include lack of competition, development of missing markets, assignment of property rights to negative externalities, presence of imperfect knowledge, activation of the principal-agent problem, government provision replacing the private market, subsidised consumption inequalities, free riders taking advantage and frequent manifestations of the principles of moral hazard and moral panic. However, legislating politicians frequently omit preliminary economic impact analyses and post-implementation assessments in order to pursue their social and environmental political aims. This leads to unresolved conflicts involving airlines and the non-governmental organisations (NGOs) which promote corporate social and environmental responsibility (CSER) over and above what is economically justified (i.e. CSERplus). CSERplus is a confluence of ideas based around the dimensions of society and the environment which frequently ignores the economics of efficient resource allocation. Economics should be the basis of sustainability-thinking, decision-making and future-proofing. It provides the context with which to identify the benefits of using sustainability-thinking including reputational risk protection, resilience against volatility in markets, prediction of future government interventions and improved market intelligence. It also provides a lens through which to identify previously unidentified (and therefore unacknowledged) subsidies given by the airline industry in return for market liberalisation.

1 Introduction to economic airline sustainability

1.1 THE AIRLINE INDUSTRY IN CONTEXT

Introduction

The earliest airline entrepreneurs could not have foreseen just how successful their idea would become. The oldest airline (KLM Royal Dutch Airlines, The Netherlands) was established in the northern hemisphere in 1919; the second oldest (Qantas, Australia) was established in the southern hemisphere in 1920. Flying between The Netherlands and Australia could take weeks – changing planes, hopping over vast continents, landing and taking off from one hewn airstrip to another. In those early decades, flying was a luxury and an aspiration. Since then, technology has progressed so that the same journey can be completed in a little over 24 hours with one stop in between, and what was once the preserve of the adventurous, famous and rich has now become the travel of the masses. Democratised air travel has arrived.

The aviation industry is now integral to the world's economies and requires the construction, equipping and maintenance of aircraft and infrastructure in order to provide its services. Airlines and their airports are *big* business integrated by economics, i.e. the social science concerned with production, consumption and distribution of scarce resources, goods and services. At its core is the optimal allocation of resources to satisfy customers' wants and needs and the concept of the market where suppliers and buyers meet and are able and willing to transact. Markets, using price as the mechanism for coordinating suppliers' and buyers' actions, have a spontaneity which evolves over time and any interference, such as that from governments, can distort their efficient operation. However, markets are also dependent on the protection of the legal system for contract enforcement and non-confiscation of private property, both of which are in the power of governments. Economists believe that the value of goods and services 'depends crucially on the "bundle of legal rights" transferred with them' (Veljanovski, 2006: 34–35). 'Today there is a greater awareness of the benefits of private property rights and markets, and the disadvantages and inefficiency of bureaucracy and regulation as means of coordinating the economy' (Veljanovski, 2006: 21). Furthermore, because markets are the outcomes of decisions made by human beings, they do not always operate as theory would suggest, which frequently provides governments with justification for interventions to correct the market inefficiencies or 'failings'.

Markets aim for productive efficiency with many competing sellers producing at lowest cost, which enables buyers to transact at market-clearing prices. If airlines' prices are too high, passengers could boycott, leaving seats and freight space unsold, both of which are inefficient outcomes. These would force airlines to reduce capacity so that resources (including aircraft and employees) could be redeployed more efficiently elsewhere. Airlines use many resources, including people, time and assets such as aircraft, ground equipment and buildings. In 2012, worldwide, the airline industry supported 56.6 million jobs, was responsible for $US2.2 trillion of global expenditure, spent $US140bn on fuel, carried 35% of world trade by value and handled 48 million tonnes of freight according to its trade body, the International Air Transport Association (IATA) (IATA, 2012). IATA (2013a) predicted passenger numbers could rise to 3.91 billion by 2017.

Airlines are, however, constrained by external geopolitical and regulatory, macro-economic factors, which are beyond their control, and micro-economic human, natural, social, financial and manufactured resources, over which they have only limited sway. However, while the 'rest of the air transport value chain continues to make money' (IATA, 2013b: 41) with fuel suppliers as the major beneficiaries, airline investors' rewards for the financial risks are proving harder to obtain with net profit per passenger of only $US2.56 (IATA, 2013b). This is despite rising demand from advancing nations, i.e. countries which are either developing (illustrated by a low standard of living) or emerging (increasing their indus-trialisation). The next most profitable part of the value chain is distribution, with customer reservations systems (CRS) and data suppliers averaging a return of 20% and freight forwarders 15% (IATA, 2013b). In contrast, the airlines currently yield 1–2%. This affects the economic sustainability of the entire airline industry, including its supply chain. Airlines have many costs to cover before they can show a return on assets, including paying interest on debt and surplus profit as dividends to the owners (the shareholders). Although airlines have significantly improved their efficiency over the last 50 years and halved the costs of air transport in real terms, these gains have only lowered transport costs and fares rather than increased shareholders' returns or employees' rewards. In fact, some privately owned airlines stopped paying dividends to preserve cash when the industry took one of its many downturns. In other words, the customers and suppliers have benefitted but investors – on whom airlines rely for capital – have not. Airlines do, however, make many other industries profitable.

Since 2000, major United Kingdom (UK) carriers have had some lean years (Figure 1.1) which mirrored significant world events, including economic recessions and threats such as those posed by terrorism, wars and health epidemics. The UK industry upswing began around 2002 and continued until the banking crisis of 2008 combined with high fuel prices caused a sharp downturn in recovering profits. This was followed by dramatic improvement in 2012 when volatile jet fuel prices (approximately 2004 to 2008) were decreasing.

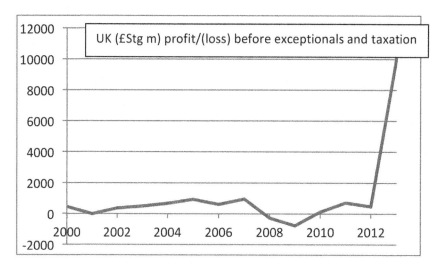

Figure 1.1 Major UK airlines profit and loss account summary 2006–2013
(adapted from Civil Aviation Authority, 2014)

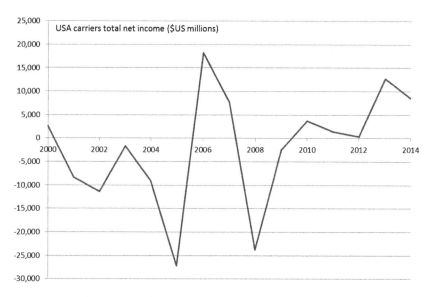

Figure 1.2 All USA carriers (all regions) net income ($USm) 2000–2014
(adapted from United States Department of Transportation, 2015)

American carriers had a similar financial profile, and although the statistics are not directly comparable their industry suffered more volatility (Figure 1.2) starting with the dramatic jump in jet fuel prices in January 2000 which 'led to a drop in operating profits, although net profits were maintained largely due to the sale of aircraft and non-core investments such as holdings in IT and communications companies' (Morrell, 2013: 5). Similarly, the volatile fuel prices of 2004 to 2008 are also reflected in total net income. During these periods, several USA carriers entered into (and some emerged from) Chapter 11 bankruptcy protection, which affords affected companies a buffer from creditors while they reorganise their businesses (*The Economist*, 2015).

CSER and CSERplus

Airlines exhibit corporate social and environmental responsibility (CSER) and are under greater scrutiny than ever because of challenges from CSER advocates concerned about rogue enterprises ruthlessly exploiting societies and environmental resources in their pursuit of profit. However, although airlines are not of that ilk, they have been swept into the CSER movement which now urges legislators, regulators and industries to go beyond CSER to pursue welfare or environmental policies which are often the remit of the State. In doing so they are invoking CSERplus (both terms will be used throughout this book). The interventions of CSERplus' advocates in the airline market have provided challenges and produced unexpected consequences because they were usually based on incomplete or zero cost-benefit data and information. This meant that regulators ultimately relied on advocacy and opinions. CSERplus' advocates often claim that their involvement in any industry (and not just aviation) leads to innovation, improved costs and social and environmental benefits. However, the aviation industry has always pursued innovation, lowered costs, increased safety, improved productivity, widened markets and enhanced environmental performance in the course of responsible and efficient business management intent on creating shareholder value. The spur was competition in the marketplace. Airlines know that displeasing regulators will incur fines, dissatisfied customers will travel with rivals, unsafe practices could ground the fleet and careless financial management could close the business. The industry did not need CSERplus interventions unsupported by economic analyses to remind them of good business practices.

Definition of sustainability

Full sustainability is bigger than the environmental or social issues to which CSER is often ascribed. It is also greater than philanthropy, charity, corporate community investment (CCI), corporate responsibility, community relations, corporate citizenship or any of the other socially aligned terms by which it is often inappropriately labelled. Over the past 20 years sustainability has also 'often been compartmentalized as an environmental issue' (Drexhage and Murphy, 2010: 2). The role of economics as the integrating force has been largely ignored and yet

'Most of the aspects that are labelled "environmental" or "social" are economic issues for which economic analysis and criteria offer a means to integration' (Henderson, 2004: 98). In the airline industry, the three best-known CSER dimensions are never independent. For example, low fares enabling democratised consumption (a social issue) are supported by sales of inflight catering (an economic issue). If the catering is too expensive, passengers might not purchase and it becomes food waste with high disposal costs (an economic-environmental issue). Consequently, reduced inflight catering sales might lead to increased seat prices. Airfares which incorporate any government's air tax are an economic, social and environmental issue.

'Sustainability' with its economic basis should not be confused with 'sustainable development' with which many CSER researchers and advocates muddle it. Sustainable development – defined as 'development that meets the needs of the present without compromising the ability of future generations to meet their own needs' (UN World Commission on Environment and Development (UNWCED), 1987: 16) – tends to give weight to social and environmental issues and not the integrating economics. The focus for this text – and without implying endorsement of the CSER ideology – will be on economics as the integrating factor for social and environmental issues. The 'triumvirate' of economics, society and environment will be used as a framework with governance (as the decision-making process) wrapping the three dimensions together (see Figure 7.2 in Chapter 7). Economic sustainability in this text will be broader than just financial sustainability, and because it concerns resource allocation, it will concern the responsible stewardship of the shareholders' assets to maintain all types of capital. This includes natural (renewable and non-renewable), social (including intellectual and cultural capital), human (such as labour and education) and manufactured (e.g. buildings and aeroplanes) as well as the financial capital. The sustainability intention is to live off the 'interest' rather than dip into the various capital bases. Shortages have different meanings in the natural world from the manufactured world. A shortage in natural world products often means increased exploitation without replacement so living off the 'interest' is sometimes not possible. In the manufactured world shortages could trigger increased production.

Airline industry background

In the 1970s, United States' (USA) President Jimmy Carter (1977–1981) deregulated American air carriers, thereby opening markets for airlines to compete. His successor (1981–1989), the late Ronald Reagan, was a free-market supporter who believed that government was a problem for markets in general and sought to reduce much of its interference. At a White House Conference on Small Business (1986) he is reported to have said: 'Government's view of the economy could be summed up in a few short phrases: if it moves, tax it; if it keeps moving, regulate it. And if it stops moving, subsidize it.' (BBC, 2004). Subsequently, other governments (e.g. UK, Germany and Australia) decided to divest themselves of their uneconomic, uncompetitive, State-owned air carriers and allow them to compete. Prior to these decisions, these airlines had been included in the national borrowing requirements and their growth had been restricted by the political priorities of the time. After this privatisation, those carriers which could compete in the marketplace survived the upheaval, but some were left with massive liabilities (especially the legacy carriers with insufficiently funded pension schemes) which have proved to be an economic deadweight. The privatised air carriers' inheritance from public ownership was uncompetitive wage rates, a civil service mentality rather than entrepreneurship, inflexible working rules and a risk-neutral/risk-averse culture since all risks had previously been government-backed. IATA (2013b) noted that 75% of the worldwide commercial airline industry is now majority-owned by the private sector, mostly in democracies. Democracy is one of the tenets of free-market capitalism.

Operations

In order to remain competitive, the carriers began cutting operating costs by shedding excess employees and outsourcing peripheral activities such as catering, logistics, baggage handling and CRS. Deregulation meant lower barriers to entry and increased competitive risk. Once airline markets were deregulated, many European and USA carriers examined their flying patterns. Some carriers preferred the point-to-point model, flying from origin to destination and return (Southwest Airlines, USA was the pioneer and exemplar which many airlines eventually emulated). Others preferred the hub-and-spoke model, flying from origin to destination with a connecting hub in between which attracted transit traffic. This model relied on short connections for time-sensitive passengers; however, it also meant charging high fares to cover a disproportionate share of fixed costs emanating from the hub-and-spoke operation itself.

Time-sensitive business travellers, with their higher-priced, flexible fares, covered a disproportionate share of the overheads and were highly prized by airline competitors. Non-business travellers were able to fill the empty seats when airlines priced fares sufficiently low to encourage travel at off-peak times. Empty seats on a flight are a 'perishable' product and cannot be sold once the flight has departed. Airlines realised that these seats could be priced at just above the marginal cost (i.e. the increase in total costs of servicing one extra passenger). What was unpredicted at the time hub-and-spoke was in vogue was that flight schedulings had to be tightly bunched at popular times so airports became extremely congested and passengers began to resent the wasted waiting time. The high fixed costs caused by the increased congestion had to be absorbed at a time of threat from the expanding no-frills, low-cost carriers which began operations when the industry was liberalised. Unfavourable congestion was reduced by making hub connections less convenient and cutting simultaneous arrivals and departures. This changed the airline operation yet again and the gap between the time-sensitive and the time-insensitive travellers began to widen. However, by this time, the time-sensitive business travellers (essential to meeting airline fixed costs) had the internet to help them challenge airlines' prices and to find departure times which suited their budgets and diaries. The market was in a state of flux as carriers began transacting with an entrepreneurial outlook rather than the risk-averse thinking which preceded their privatisation.

The concept of hub-to-hub has been growing and has spurred the growth of long-haul passenger traffic models in which the Middle East airports are now market leaders (*Oxford Economics*, 2013). Unfortunately, in a threat to economic airline competitiveness, many advanced-world airports simply do not have the capacity to match destinations in the advancing-world with less strict planning requirements and fewer land space constraints. Furthermore, airlines in democracies face many more regulatory hurdles than those in non-democratic regimes which support authoritarian, State-sponsored – rather than free enterprise – capitalism.

Industry organisation

Loosely defined, there are four economically sustainable core airline types for passengers and/or freight. The first model is that of the full-service carriers, many of which have a legacy of State ownership and are now mostly privatised, e.g. Lufthansa (Germany) and Air France (which in 2003 merged with The Netherlands' KLM). They usually have an all-in fare price that includes food, pillows, blankets and other passenger comforts. They fly passengers and freight from major airports, have often inherited a mixed fleet (which can reduce economic efficiency) and offer a range of prices to suit customers' budgets and schedules. Their passage to economic sustainability has been threatened by the arrival of the second model which appeared around 1978 when the industry was deregulated. These are the privately owned, no-frills, low-cost, low-fare carriers flying mostly short-haul routes from secondary airports. These carriers (also known as 'budget carriers') can offer lower fares than full-service carriers because they have lower costs per available seat kilometres (ASKs) (the standard industry measure of unit costs, which means that one seat is flown one kilometre). Their lower costs come from higher productivity, while their business model is predominantly short-haul using a limited range of types of young aircraft (less expensive to maintain) and reliant on high load factors, direct sales and no connections. They also unbundle the airfare into its component parts. At one extreme, unbundling involves charging for every aspect of the transaction including printing a boarding card, changing a misspelled passenger name, priority boarding, reserving a seat or an exit row seat, carrying luggage, consuming food/beverages/blankets and/or pillows – and (tongue in cheek) it has even been suggested that such ancillary charges might eventually even be levied for using the on-board lavatory (Gordon, 2010). Growth in these ancillary revenues has been 1,200% in seven years (*Ideaworks*, 2014) to $US16 per passenger. These carriers have increased tourist destinations through the use of secondary airports and their pricing means that their passenger traffic is smoother rather than having the seasonal and weekly peaks and troughs which marked many of the full-service carriers. However, nearer to departure time, many low-cost carriers offer prices which are closer to those of the full-schedule carriers. Low-cost carriers are predicted to expand their market share particularly with the emergent middle classes in advancing nations (*Oxford Economics*, 2013).

The third model describes the non-scheduled charter airlines which are usually hired or owned by a single organisation to ferry passengers and/or freight. Many are now offering scheduled passenger flights in an attempt to compete with the full-service and low-cost carriers. The fourth model covers the regional carriers operating short-haul feeder routes.

The first three models are now becoming less distinctive as the full-service carriers begin to unbundle their services and products (e.g. food, beverages, wash bags, eye masks etc.) and some carriers are now drip-charging passengers for what was previously included in airfares. Carriers are also contracting out some of their services to third-party suppliers (e.g. cabin and cockpit crew, interior cleaning, aircraft maintenance, de-icing etc.) or market testing their in-house costs. Similarly, the low-cost carriers are increasing their offerings to loosely resemble their full-service rivals' products and services. Although there will continue to be a trade-off between price and service, some low-cost carriers have also begun to ramp up their fares to almost full-schedule level on the more popular routes at favourable times.

Costs and taxes

Airlines must keep overheads low so they can compete internationally, particularly with the advancing nations of Asia Pacific and their lower labour costs. Wages generally comprise around 20% to 30% of operating costs (Table 1.1) with Asia Pacific carriers having the lowest labour costs (14.7% of operating costs). In 2008 fuel alone was responsible for 32.3% of operating costs across all major airlines. High fuel costs and the severe financial pressures from 2001 onwards necessitated improved efficiency and labour productivity (as measured by employees per available tonne kilometre (ATK)) which improved 42% over the seven years to 2008 (IATA, 2010a). As a result, labour's share of total operating costs fell from 28.3% in 2001 to 20.1% in 2008. (Asia Pacific carriers' lower wage costs were somewhat neutralised by higher fuel charges during that period.) The outlook in 2008 was for minimal increase in wages (due to higher unemployment in the recession of 2008 to 2013); however, it was forecast that the labour share of total costs might increase as passenger demand rose and rehiring commenced.

Table 1.1 Percentage share of airline operating costs, by region of airline registration

	North America		Europe		Asia Pacific		All major airlines	
	2001	*2008*	*2001*	*2008*	*2001*	*2008*	*2001*	*2008*
Labour	36.2%	21.5%	27.2%	24.8%	17.2%	14.7%	28.3%	20.1%
Fuel	13.4%	34.2%	12.2%	25.3%	15.7%	36.7%	13.6%	32.3%

Table 1.2 Labour tax and contributions as % of profit (2011–2015) (adapted from The World Bank, 2015)

North America		Europe		Middle East		Asia Pacific	
Canada	12.7	Finland	24.8	Israel	5.6	Australia	21.1
USA	n/a	France	53.5	Jordan	14.4	Fiji	10.4
		Germany	21.2	Kuwait	13.0	Hong Kong (SAR China)	5.2
		Greece	29.3	Oman	11.8	Korea Republic	13.8
		Ireland	12.1	Qatar	11.3	Malaysia	16.4
		Italy	43.4	Saudi Arabia	12.8	New Zealand	2.7
		Netherlands	20.2	United Arab Emirates	14.1	Philippines	8.7
		Spain	35.9			Samoa	6.8
		Sweden	35.4			Singapore	15.3
		Switzerland	17.7			Thailand	5.4
		Turkey	19.9				
		United Kingdom	11.2				

According to The World Bank (2015) (Table 1.2), the labour tax and contributions as a percentage of commercial profit (i.e. the amount of taxes and mandatory contributions on labour paid by businesses) would be higher for any European enterprise (including airlines) compared to those in Asia Pacific (with the exception of Australia) with their much lower levels of labour taxation. These taxes affect international competition since they must be covered in the prices charged. Therefore, competing successfully with Asia Pacific carriers (with lower wage costs and labour taxes) presents a significant challenge to North American and European international carriers.

Aircraft procurement

Delivery times for new aircraft have been reduced despite the fact that parts are now made globally and often flown between assembly plants (Boeing assembling in USA and soon, China; Airbus in France and sourcing throughout Europe; Bombardier in Canada, USA, UK and Mexico; Embraer in Brazil, Portugal, USA and China). Aircraft manufacturers are sensitive to changes in world economic performance. Synchronising aircraft arrival (supply) with market need (demand) is a competitive issue. Competition between the world's two largest aircraft manufacturers (Airbus and Boeing) is ferocious and each chose to pursue a different market for their last models. Boeing chose the smaller hub-to-hub with its 787 model, promising 20% less fuel consumed and 20% fewer emissions discharged than similarly sized aircraft; Airbus preferred the quieter, fuel efficient, hub-to-hub, super-sized mass carrier, the A380. Each manufacturer has a variety of aircraft sizes making up their fleet family. However, at the time of publication, Airbus was to launch an aircraft to compete with Boeing's 787 in the long-range, mid-sized, wide-bodied, twin-engine jet market and Boeing was about to launch a competitor to the Airbus A380 double-deck, wide-bodied, four-engine aircraft. Aircraft operating and procurement costs depend on the intended routes, business model and seating configurations. Long-haul passengers tend to want legroom comfort; short-haul passengers are inclined to sustain some discomfort in cramped seating. These decisions are among many which will ultimately decide the economic sustainability of the respective airlines.

Economic symbiosis – airlines and airports

Airlines and airports have a symbiotic economic relationship governed by contracts and service-level agreements (SLAs) between the two parties. Airports provide the physical space for tightly timed slots for aircraft to land and depart on runways, to dwell at jetties and on stands and for passengers and freight to be processed in terminal facilities. Disruptions (such as late passengers or bad weather) alter the rhythm and create confusion, complication and increased costs, all of which undermine airline economic viability. In general, the airport operators profit from disruptions because delays on the ground mean increased passenger spend in the terminal, but the airlines lose because their aircraft and crews are out of position and must be realigned to the timetable (often at great expense).

Slots

Airport slots used for landings and take-offs are a tradeable resource which makes them valuable. They can be used, bartered or retained unexploited as assets for future use (the latter being a potential market inefficiency). Existing carriers in these markets are often ineligible to purchase available slots because they are bound by competition legislation designed to prevent monopolies (where single sellers dominate a market) which indicate an imperfect market. At older airports the slots were often allocated on a 'grandfather' basis to the State-owned airlines which had historically accessed them. This system, however, distorted the market by impeding competition and contributing to airport congestion. Uncongested airports have more potential flying, hence the popularity of smaller airports for the low-cost carriers.

Passengers prefer to travel at times that suit their day, which creates a market where slots at peak times (e.g. 0800 hrs) are worth more than slots at off-peak times (e.g. 0100 hrs). Popular slots are also under pressure at certain times of the year, such as public holidays when airports work to maximum capacity. Many budget or non-scheduled carriers take advantage of the lower-cost off-peak times in order to keep their costs down. Using slots efficiently can also mean that a carrier has the freedom to alter the purpose of its slots, e.g. swapping domestic flights in favour of international routes to increase revenue. Slots are vulnerable to pressure from local airport residents to restrict the hours of operation because of environmental and social issues (such as pollution from air, lighting and noise) which also add to congestion at some airports. However, if the local residents' problems are solved, the solutions can create challenges elsewhere including affecting competition between airports (a trade-off between society and airline economics). Single-issue groups only rarely understand the concept of trade-off.

Stand allocation and competition

Airport stand allocation is a competitive issue: the quicker passengers can be disembarked, the sooner the aircraft can be turned around and the jetty freed for the next flight. Furthermore, stand allocation can be an issue of fairness at some airports with the home nation's aircraft receiving priority allocation at stands near the passenger concourse rather than on remote stands which require transfers by coach or train. Some passengers avoid certain airports because they do not like the facilities or the transport access (among other dislikes). Passengers also prefer direct access to the terminal rather than a journey by transfer vehicle and the more transactions involved in moving them between aircraft and terminal, the more complexity is introduced into the process. Complexity affects resource allocation by adding costs and time – and it can also add to, or detract from, the passenger experience.

Capacity

Airport capacity is a constraint for sustainable airlines. Growth is a combination of many factors, including available land (for runways and buildings), local neighbourhood pressure and government permission. Solutions vary from creating artificial islands (Hong Kong and Japan), extending runways and building new terminals (Frankfurt, Germany and Beijing, China) or increasing terminal capacity alone (London, UK). Airport expansion (or compression) has significant social and environmental impacts and in many democracies it is a thorny political issue which pits economics, society (e.g. airport neighbours and politicians), environmentalism and airlines against each other. In the mid-1960s, Japanese farmers protested against government plans to seize their lands to build Narita Airport. Over ensuing decades, the objections continued, resulting in protestor deaths and injuries. The airport was finally opened in 1978 and a new series of protests began against the extension of two runways (Haberman, 1986). Such protests continue in different countries today.

Airport facilities

Where airport facilities fail, airline customer service often has to intervene and absorb the costs (i.e. airport infrastructure costs vs airline operating costs). This is particularly true for disabled passengers (see Chapter 5). They frequently need airline assistance such as provision of personal guides, or motorised or manually powered mobility equipment to overcome terminal building inadequacies. Furthermore, inadequate wayfinding (the means of facilitating independent movement through the airport using terminal signs) can mean that the airline loses passengers, and lost passengers cause delays which increase flight costs. One stressed Customer Service Agent at the UK's Heathrow Airport was overheard saying 'If it wasn't for the passengers we'd be on time, every time. . .'.

In a 'silent terminal' with no broadcast announcements, passengers can become distracted by the offerings in the airport shopping concessions or by the hospitality available in the airline lounges and either miss or delay their flights while they are located. Delayed flights inconvenience all other passengers and the aircraft could miss the allocated take-off slot (contributing to even more delay). At the extreme, delay can place the crew out of hours and the flight will not leave until a new crew has been rostered and delivered to the aircraft, which adds even more to the unanticipated costs.

Airport environmental standards

Airports set their environmental performance based on international standards including those of the International Civil Aviation Organisation (ICAO) (a United Nations (UN) agency which sets and ensures airport and ground handling standards). Environmental challenges cover noise, water, air, lighting, land, flora and fauna and are governed by SLAs with critical success factors (CSFs) monitored by numerical key performance indicators (KPIs). At some airports SLAs often require early-morning or late-night aircraft arrivals to turn off their engines and wait for a tow so they can minimise the ground noise for neighbouring residents. These SLAs are strictly monitored with penalties paid if they are breached. The difficulty comes with unscheduled arrivals, such as those for emergencies or aircraft trying to get back onto timetables after major disruption. In the UK, such breaches give ammunition to airport objectors to oppose planning applications. Society, through the airport neighbours and local politicians, is often pitted against sustainable airline economics.

1.2 ECONOMIC EFFICIENCY

Context

Free-market capitalism encourages innovation, economic and allocative efficiencies and is essential for national economic growth. In democracies, such capitalism is based on equal rights, rule of law, risk-taking, security of property and freedom of choice. The ultimate outcome will be private profits or private losses for the producers. Consumers have sovereignty over the market and can choose which commercial organisation they support, and in turn successful producers can choose how they would spend their rewards (possibly on an airline seat). Free-market capitalism, with its focus on supplying markets, has been the incubator for national success. Real markets thrive under this system, whereby a nation's productive resources, distribution systems and trade mechanisms are managed by private owners seeking profits. In contrast, under socialism these same resources would be owned by governments on behalf of their nations without profit as a motivator, which could deliver shortages or surpluses. Governments, however, are not good at economic efficiency and in fact are renowned for wasting taxpayers' money when they intervene. One of the worst aviation examples is the international 'ghost airport' in Cuidad Real, Spain which was opened in 2008 and closed in 2012. This cost €1bn (£Stg760m or $US1.1bn) to build and was finally sold at auction in 2015 for €10,000 (£Stg7,600 or $US10,900) to a Chinese consortium which intended to use it as a spearhead for cargo into Europe (Fenton, 2015).

Capitalism flexes and evolves in response to changing economic conditions. In 'managerial capitalism' (approximately 1950 to 1970) big firms dominated industries and managers were primarily responsible to the shareholders as the providers of corporate risk capital. Managerial capitalism morphed into 'investor capitalism' in the 1980s when venture capitalists purchased shareholdings to influence the management and increase corporate profitability and ultimately investors' returns. From around 1990s onwards, investor capitalism evolved into CSER capitalism (i.e. CSERplus) with its focus on stakeholders requiring industry to provide or supplement many of the State's welfare conditions. Throughout the decades there has been a thread of opportunistic, crony capitalism ('cronyism') marked by a close relationship between business and government and where an entrenched few acted in their own interests and accumulated disproportionate power and influence while often enriching their friends and associates as well. Cronyism appears in many guises, such as the award of government grants or contracts for influential politicians' enterprises and the appointment to high office of friends of the government (both of which occur in democracies (e.g. USA, India and UK) and in authoritarian, State-sponsored capitalistic regimes (e.g. Russia and China) (*The Economist*, 2014)). It has also become more obvious since advances in communication connectivity and privatisations in former communist nations (e.g. Russia).

However, irrespective of which type of capitalism prevailed, governments have assigned many social responsibilities to airlines without the corresponding rights or subsidies which were allocated to privatised and other privately owned ground transport providers (see Chapter 5). Subsidies can lead to the inefficient allocation of resources and can take many forms at the level of the industry or the firm (Tretheway and Andriulaitis, 2015). Many subsidies are often unidentified and therefore remain unacknowledged. The social responsibilities assigned to airlines were either in the form of 'unfunded mandates' (where the State requires action but will not provide the funds) or 'boondoggles' (legislation that wastes resources but continues because of vested, asymmetric (i.e. biased) political and economic influences). Before politicians support any such regulations, their civil servants should provide them with impartial advice derived from preliminary economic impact analyses. Any failure to be so advised would mean that regulations would be formed on biased information, data and opinions and possibly even based on the advocacy of CSERplus lobby groups. However, mandating bodies often tend to only focus on the benefits and not the costs of their decisions. Such asymmetry in information and data can have unforeseen consequences, which will be explored in the following chapters.

Assessing economic impacts

The UK government policy is that where regulation is needed it 'should have a light touch with the right balance struck between under-regulation (so failing to protect the public) and over-regulating (so creating excessive bureaucracy)' (Comptroller and Auditor General, 2001: 1). Any such impact analysis is supposed to investigate all the benefits and costs including any indirect costs. It should also consult with all the stakeholders who could be affected by the proposals.

In Europe, the European Union (EU) (European Union, 2014a) (a bundling of 28 countries with different welfare, monetary and fiscal policies) requires an impact analysis before regulating to evaluate the 'potential economic, social and environmental impact', to ensure that decision-makers are informed and to assess alternatives before considering legislation, non-legislative proposals and implementations of any activity. This would include a rigorous cost-benefit analysis which involved all the interested stakeholders.

> An impact assessment gives decision-makers evidence regarding the need for EU [European Union] action and the advantages and disadvantages of alternative policy choices. It may also find that no action should be taken at EU level. Impact assessments are prepared for Commission initiatives expected to have significant direct economic, social or environmental impacts. These can be:

- legislative proposals
- non-legislative initiatives (white papers, action plans, financial programmes, negotiating guidelines for international agreements) that define future policies
- implementing measures and delegated acts

Stakeholders are *consulted* on all key aspects of impact assessments and final impact assessment reports are *public.* . .

(© European Union, 2014a. Author's emphasis.)[1]

Costs and benefits can be appraised in economic, social and environmental terms and should consider the strengths and weaknesses of a proposal. However, the EU has not always been rigorous in consulting airlines to seek the costs of its proposals, preferring instead to focus on the social or environmental benefits only (see Chapter 5 and Chapter 6).

Capitalism and remuneration

Employees are usually one of the biggest costs in airlines. In the UK, the providers of risk capital (i.e. the shareholders) have had low returns at a time when the median earnings of the Chief Executives of their investments have soared by 278% (Income Data Services (IDS), 2014). These Chief Executives now earn 120 times the average employee pay – this in a time when average UK earnings rose at less than 1% p.a. and real wages (inflation adjusted) were less than those in 2008 (IDS, 2014). These disparities have been defended because of the global employment market and the need to pay high rewards to those who make high-risk decisions. However, awareness of these disparities has only heightened calls by social justice advocates for government legislation to make income redistribution fairer. Social justice would appear to have two components: social equality (where consumers have equal access to the goods and services they need) and social equity (where people have equal opportunities of all types). However, it should be the shareholders exercising their rights by voting on executives' increased remuneration which determines the worthiness of such rewards because it is their potential income which is being redistributed in executive pay. In an example of the economic concept of the free rider (where consumers have not paid for something they use) many shareholders do not exercise their rights preferring to let others discharge their responsibilities for them. Individual, smaller shareholders tend to have a short-term relationship with their investments and often fail to exercise the voting rights available under democratic capitalism. Their apathy is a challenge for corporate organisations in democracies and the gap they leave is sometimes filled by the CSERplus social justice campaigners.

Competition

In theory, free markets should facilitate the efficient allocation of resources to enable the exchange of goods and services. Free markets constantly seek to achieve equilibrium where supply and demand meet at market-clearing prices. Pricing is an efficient mechanism for distribution and resource allocation. Markets thrive when there is competition (with minimal regulation) and allocated property rights which can be protected by the law (Veljanovski, 2006) and not undermined, for example, by governments levying retrospective taxes which would amount to property confiscation.

Perfect competition is characterised by low barriers to entry, full knowledge for all the transacting parties and homogeneous products supplied by many different firms which cannot control their markets. In a freely competitive market there are a large number of firms, none of which has any economic power over the others, although some are more successful than rivals because of management quality, purchasing power, innovations and ultimately customer satisfaction. On the other hand, competitors in imperfectly competitive markets (e.g. monopolies or monopolistic competition where products are not quite perfect substitutes) are likely to charge higher prices in the short-term when they might be able to earn abnormally high profits. This would encourage new entrants to the industry and competition will commence (as happened after deregulation of the airline industry). A freely competitive market has many sellers as rivals who attract customers by competing on price, services and/or products. In the airline industry, such competition drives down costs and fares while simultaneously offering increasingly better services and products. This drive towards profits makes airlines economically sustainable.

In contrast, a single seller – a monopolist – has no competition and can control the market by restricting supply, which enables them to extract above normal profits. Likewise, a small number of sellers – oligopolists – can also control the market. In both cases, consumers will lose from reduced competition and higher prices.

Competitors

Economic airline sustainability is reliant on outcompeting rivals. Airline competitiveness can be measured by the economic criteria of its costs, prices and productivity, and the social parameters of service quality and management. A sustainable airline is aware of the competition and is agile at predicting its behaviour. Sometimes competitors' behaviour can impact upon the airline industry and result in changes in regulations if governments feel that the market is not performing as it should. This was the case with Ryanair, the biggest low-cost carrier in Europe. Ryanair's handling of physically disabled passengers resulted in the former UK airlines' responsibility for disabled passenger ground handling being transferred to UK airports (see *Ross v Ryanair*, 2004, and Chapter 5). (In the UK, disabled passenger handling is now an airport service which is paid by the airlines from a surcharge on all passengers.) By such regulations, the public (social) benefits become supported by private costs. This undermines the market.

Anticipating airline competitors' behaviour comes from watching them and as far as possible, from 'flying on their wings'. The internet enables low search costs so airlines can offer passengers comparative information about fares and services, which bolsters consumer buying power. With the technology available, much competitive information is available for customers and for the competing airlines. Furthermore, reading competitors' sustainability reports (available on the internet) gives a strong indication of what frightens them. These reports also reveal much competitive information as they try to fulfil the CSERplus social and environmental reporting requirements (see Lufthansa, 2014, as one of the most informative examples).

Fare pricing is a critical factor in competitiveness and is one of the key factors of passenger choice. Airline fares have many characteristics including advance purchase requirements, cabin (class), day and time of departure and return, refundability and stay restrictions (e.g. must stay a Saturday night). Fares must entice passengers to fill the aircraft to cover costs and allow for profits. The sophisticated pricing schemes and sensitivity of intelligent revenue management systems allow for fares to change depending on the flight booking profile. Airlines use a form of price discrimination 'to charge lower fares for observably similar tickets based on the day-of-week purchase' (Puller and Taylor, 2012: 802). For example, restricted condition fares purchased on a weekend were found to be 5% lower than those purchased during the week (Puller and Taylor, 2012). Even with reduced prices, the passengers who have taken advantage of the lower price receive the same service as others on the flight who might have paid more (or perhaps even less). All these aspects have to be managed by the economically sustainable airline against the threat of competition.

Traditional carriers have long-term strategic prices which dominate their pricing strategy. In the short-term, these are used as guides for the price setting of the charter and low-cost carriers. Fares fluctuate according to circumstances such as the exchange rate, fuel prices, departure times and season. Again, the influence of the market spurs competition, not just for the airlines but also for their suppliers.

Airline competitors are not always in the aviation industry themselves. The push from environmental campaigning groups for environmentally sustainable transport encourages non-air alternatives where possible. Domestic air travel is under competition from high speed rail, coaches, motor vehicles and the increasing popularity of tele-presencing.

Imperfect competition

The competition from and with the low-cost newer entrants (particularly from the advancing-world) has threatened the survival of the legacy carriers. All carriers have national and international government interference in their marketplace, products, pricing and compensation structures. However, legacy carriers from the advanced economies with inherited higher overheads have been additionally hampered in their ability to compete.

Since 2004, airlines have had to cope with increased competition – particularly from low-cost carriers – as well as internal cost-cutting and adapting schedules to the demands of the changing market. This has heightened the vulnerability of older, established carriers, particularly in the USA because they carry 75% domestic passengers. In contrast, the European airlines carry around 75% international passengers, so they can spread their risks and more easily withstand shocks.

The newer carriers from the oil-and-gas-rich Middle East (with what is claimed to be their access to low-cost funding for new aircraft and airports, and lower-cost fuel) are perceived as a threat to older, legacy carriers, some of which are complaining of unfair competition. Emirates Airlines (Dubai), Etihad Airways (Abu Dhabi) and Qatar Airways (Qatar) are claimed by three USA carriers (Delta, United and American Airways) to have access to $US42.3bn (€38bn or £Stg29.4bn) in subsidies in various forms (including equity transferrals, interest-free loans and debt guarantees). The Gulf carriers' counter claim is that the USA carriers have received at least $US71.5bn (€64.1bn or £Stg49.7bn) in assorted benefits including pro-tection under the USA's Chapter 11 bankruptcy restructuring provisions (*The Economist*, 2015). Governments have often been asked to intervene to level the markets, but such intervention often tackles the symptoms and not the causes of any trading inequalities. Protesting airlines must ask themselves if they are asking the *right* questions (see Chapter 7).

Airline markets and government intervention

Governments have the power to intervene in markets by legislating, taxing, subsidising or even providing the goods or services themselves if they believe the market is not working efficiently. In democracies, government market intervention should support free enterprise, with its competition for consumers' spending and decentralised decision-making; however, the allocations of productive resources are ultimately decided by the countless decisions of individual consumers. The more resources commercial organisations spend in the pursuit of non-productive activities (such as complying with boondoggles), the fewer resources they have to increase profitability and reward the shareholders. Free markets operating within a framework of appropriate legislation create a prosperous nation; however, some nations do not have a clear policy on aviation. Some categorise it as essential national infrastructure which requires high-level support in order to push through its development; others categorise it as a luxury or alternatively harmful (like tobacco and alcohol) and tax it accordingly as a 'sin' (see Chapter 6). In both examples, governments intervene in the market to maximise what they perceive as the optimal social benefit; however, sometimes these interventions (such as badly drafted legislation or overprotective State interventions (see Chapter 5 and Chapter 6)) have unintended consequences, which could reduce efficiency, and at the extreme, trigger market failures.

Theories of alleged 'market failure'

Airlines have homogeneous products which they try to differentiate either by branding, or by enhancing or reducing their offerings as a spur to competition. However, markets can often be perceived to 'fail' when they deviate from the ideal of perfect competition and produce an inefficient outcome. This deviation is a market 'failure' and triggers inefficient allocation of resources. Resource allocation is sometimes imperfect because providers either over- or under-allocate which then delivers an excuse for government intervention with remedial regulation. However:

> the normal pattern is that market failure provides the rationale for the introduction of regulation, but the scope of regulation is then extended to a wide range of matters which are the subject of general or sectional interests, regardless of whether there is any element of market failure or not.
>
> (Kay and Vickers, 2015: 626)

Theoretical markets are used by economists as a framework for research and are useful for explaining the operation of real markets such as those entered by airlines and their customers for seats or freight. Symptoms of alleged airline market inefficiency or failure abound. In the short-term, rising seat prices could deter passengers from purchasing leaving the airlines with an oversupply of unsold seats; conversely, price reductions might stimulate excess passenger demand. If either the oversupply or the excess demand persists in the long-term the market could fail to efficiently distribute seats (or freight space). Preventing or correcting market failure should be the only trigger for government intervention because when resources are allocated to the highest-value users, welfare is optimised. Unfortunately, many interventions have actually had unintended consequences and undermined the airline market (see Table 8.1 in Chapter 8).

However, markets do not always behave perfectly, and any misbehaviour gives justification to governments to intervene to correct the imperfections. Some of these interventions are justified because they benefit all consumers (e.g. regulations concerning airline safety or environmental protection) while others have strayed and intervened in matters which are best left to the market to resolve. These interventions which included requiring (private) airlines to deliver ill-defined (public) social justice could either trigger or resolve alleged market inefficiencies and failures. They include:

1. *lack of competition* occurs where there are few suppliers (oligopolists) selling homogeneous products or a single supplier (monopolist) supplying a product with no close substitutes and where there are high barriers to prevent new entrants into the market (as was the case for aviation before it was liberalised). Oligopolists or monopolists could block new entrants into their markets and set their own prices, both of which are detrimental for consumers. Furthermore, lack of competition can lead to a concentration of firms which governments might feel obliged to break up in order to give the consumers more choice and free the market. Where free markets are contestable (i.e. competitive) they encourage the entry of more entrepreneurs with their product and service innovations, lower costs and competitive pricing. This occurred when many governments liberated their airlines from State control. Following liberalisation, airline competition began in earnest and encouraged market innovation evidenced by the arrival of low-cost, low-fare carriers.

2. ***missing markets*** occur where no markets exist, e.g. a market for silence or for landscapes or even for carbon dioxide (CO_2) (see Chapter 6). Often a good or a service is considered so desirable and necessary that governments intervene, either to supply the market or to support it with subsidies to get it started. Accordingly, many governments created airlines and airports because they believed that this was in the national good and government provision was the only means of starting such expensive and innovative enterprises. Alternatively, having identified missing markets, governments can make mandated provision incumbent on (privately owned) organisations. This can be tantamount to confiscation of property and could be exampled by retrospective taxation or where private enterprises are obliged to support services which are not productive to the enterprise. Government-identified missing airline markets include security requirements, aircraft emissions and CSERplus social and environmental report writing. Airline-favourable missing markets could include charging for the carriage of duty-free goods purchased at airport concessions.

3. ***externalities (or 'external costs')*** are not costed into the production decision and occur outside of the market. They are the unintended consequences of an economic activity and arise when consumers' private costs and benefits differ from those of society. No one owns externalities until such time as they are identified. The greater are the externalities, the greater is the likelihood of market failure. Externalities can be positive (when the social benefits exceed the private benefits) or negative (when the social costs (private costs plus external costs) exceed the private costs). The true costs of negative externalities are not charged to the consumers and as a result there can be overproduction (an indication of economic inefficiency). Negative externalities in aviation include airport waste discharges; pollution from aircraft noise, emissions or illuminations; and delays caused by congestion on runways or in airspace. Any of these might eventually trigger government intervention to regulate, issue permits, apply quotas or decree eligible for 'sin' taxes which means that government would be assigning property rights to the externality. This action would support the view that the presence of externalities is not a sign of market failure but rather an indicator of a missing market. This could be solved by assigning well-defined, enforceable, tradeable property rights and ensuring there were low or zero transaction costs (the costs of establishing, maintaining, monitoring and terminating a transaction) (Coase, 1960). In doing so, mankind could purportedly avoid the overexploitation of natural resources but it would raise the costs of consumption, including the prices for travel. In contrast, positive aviation externalities include the speed of international shipping of time-sensitive goods, potential for tourism with all its opportunities to increase employment and national prosperity, and the opportunities for airport shopping when flights are delayed and passengers increase their spending (however, this becomes a negative externality for airlines).

4. ***imperfect knowledge*** is identified where lack of knowledge leads to misallocation of resources (often corrected by government regulation). However, much of the information that influences markets is private, not public. Lack of perfect

knowledge exists in many instances including where single-interest groups conduct biased, advocacy research to sway a population without acknowledging the real purpose of their investigation. They often focus only on the benefits and not the costs – a form of asymmetric (i.e. biased) information. This can sometimes persuade governments to legislate with boondoggles for which no prior economic impact analysis has been undertaken (see Chapter 5 and Chapter 6). In aviation, one airline example is the regulated complimentary provisions for ageing, obese and medical passengers (see Chapter 5) where only the social benefits and not the private costs were considered. Imperfect knowledge also supports cronyism where the system favours an entrenched few who can circumvent democracy, influence government policy and eventually even undermine the operation of free markets.

5. *principal-agent problem* occurs where an agent acts in self-interest rather than the interests of their principal. One example of how this can occur is when a politician (the agent) possesses imperfect or asymmetrical knowledge and has his own interests in mind when he influences legislation for the citizens who elected him (i.e. the principals) (see Chapter 6). Cronyism is also one manifestation of the principal-agent problem.

6. *government provision* occurs if governments believe that the private market would not provide public goods and services that they – the elected or imposed rulers – believe are needed to reduce social inequalities. Markets by their very nature under-provide public goods. Public goods provision cannot be restricted and consumption by one person does not prevent others from consuming. Alternatively, if government does not provide all the goods and services required it can subsidise them to encourage a market or it can provide regulations which will require taxpayers' money to fulfil. UK airline-related examples of government provisions using taxpayers' funds include the services for Immigration, Emigration or Customs. Examples where airlines must make government-required provision include security, passport examinations and visa checks.

7. *inequalities* can lead to some households being able to consume fewer goods and services (such as airline travel) than others because of lack of income and/or higher base expenditure. Governments sometimes believe that individuals are not capable of acting in their own best interests and make provision to ensure universal consumption either by directly providing certain goods and services, or by subsidising the programmes, facilities or consumers. This encourages consumption of items that society judges to be in the interests of the nation and for which consumption should not be based only on the ability to pay. Such provisions include State-provided free education, public vaccination programmes, free ground transport for qualified individuals or in the UK, free health care through the National Health Service (NHS). In the airline industry, liberalisation of the market has led to lower fares so that more lower-income passengers could travel. This democratisation of consumption reduces some social inequalities. However, inequality is often a driver for those who want to better their situation.

8. *free riders* are those who receive the benefit from provision but have no incentive to pay for it and as a result the market underprovides. In fact, individuals can increase their personal welfare by not paying for the goods or services. In airlines this occurs when passengers claim to have a disability in order to access the regulated, complimentary services provided for disabled passengers (see Chapter 5). Free ridership also occurs when individuals rely on others to assume their duties or responsibilities, such as when shareholders do not exercise their voting rights and let others assume their deflected duty or when governments expect airlines to fulfil some of the State's responsibilities without reimbursement.

9. *moral hazards* arise when a party takes a risk because they know that they are unlikely to be affected by the consequences. This means they do not need to change their risky behaviour. An airline example occurs when passengers who cause aircraft diversions through unacceptable behaviour know that they are unlikely to be pursued for damages because litigation costs are (i) disproportionate to the offence or (ii) are far greater than the assets to which the miscreants have access. Airlines often avoid or settle claims because the cost of defending them would be disproportionate and while this is economically justifiable, it actually increases the moral hazard.

10. *moral panic* describes the exaggerated importance of an issue despite a lack of evidence. Such issues are whipped up by the media as presenting a threat to society which justifies a legitimate basis for non-governmental organisation (NGO) creation and influence and ultimately regulation. In turn this leads to a chain reaction with a disproportionate effect on a wider population than anyone directly affected.

The efficiency of markets is reduced by the inefficient allocation of resources including time and/or financial capital. The impact on industries is a loss of revenue and corresponding loss of profits. In the UK, the 1997–2010 Labour Government created a 'very British mess' which was characterised by a 'grotesque mishandling of the economy' (Morgan, 2011: 2). Such mishandling fuelled record levels of personal debt which in turn increased living standards by increasing consumption. Some of that debt was undoubtedly used to purchase air travel but exactly how much is unknown. Too much consumer borrowing increased the vulnerability of the non-scheduled airlines relying on the leisure traveller. Passengers can rein in spending in the short-term but airlines have long-term planning horizons. However, any economically sustainable airline would have had its economic 'radar' scanning the horizon and been mitigating the potential risks. In the UK passenger demand usually recovers quickly from external shocks and generally increases in income tend to lead to more than proportionate increases in demand for air travel (Civil Aviation Authority (CAA), 2008). Income is an important determinant in passenger demand. In 2009, passengers with less than £Stg20,000 ($US29,000 or €26,000) annual income averaged two flights per year and those earning £Stg60,000 ($US86,000 or €77,000) or more flew just under four times per year (Committee on Climate Change (CCC), 2009). In general, the higher the income, the more likely the earner is to fly.

Where governments are airline owners, they almost always intervene by supporting inefficiencies (such as excess seat and freight capacity) all of which lead to insufficient and inefficient competition and higher costs for consumers. As an example, in 2015 State-operated Air Zimbabwe flew just one passenger from Johannesburg to Victoria Falls in a Boeing 737 with capacity of more than 100 seats (Kitching, 2015). Some governments protect their bankrupt carriers ('zombie carriers') which should have closed; others have allocated social welfare to airlines in order to reduce government expenditure (see Chapter 5 and Chapter 6). Some governments have monetised negative aviation externalities without hypothecating the revenue received (e.g. so-called 'aviation' environmental taxes which are not applied to either aviation or the environment (see Chapter 6)). A fundamental conflict is apparent: government policies aimed at income redistribution are often at odds with their desire to increase economic growth. Merely transferring resources (e.g. taxes) between groups distorts resource allocation and does not necessarily increase overall welfare.

Unprofitable passenger markets

Airlines do not compete for unprofitable passenger groups. These passengers include those most likely to be excluded from air travel – i.e. those who do not have the discretionary income and/or who are disabled, ill or elderly (McCabe, 2009). It is this group for whom many governments (including the USA and the nations of the EU) have legislated to shift the extra care and costs onto the air carriers with the intention of reducing social inequality.

Unfunded mandates

Some passengers have limited mobility when accessing aircraft. This grouping is loosely described as 'passengers with reduced mobility' (PRMs) (see Chapter 5) and for the purpose of this text includes anyone who needs airline assistance to board, disembark or while on board. In the EU, PRMs are protected by Regulation EC 1107/2006 'concerning the rights of disabled persons and persons with reduced mobility when travelling by air' (European Union, 2006) (see Chapter 5). In the USA they are protected by the Rehabilitation Act 1973 and the Americans with Disabilities Act 1990. Governments have recognised that there is a missing market for these passengers and consequently responded with regulations in the form of unfunded mandates which require what is tantamount to a transfer payment (i.e. a subsidy) from airlines to passengers. (Transfer payments are a form of income redistribution. However, the term 'subsidy' and its derivatives will be used predominantly throughout this text as it is a term which is more commonly understood.) UK public ground transport has annual government-provided subsidies with rail receiving approximately £Stg5bn ($US7.2bn or €6.4bn), and buses and coaches £Stg2.9bn ($US4.2bn or €3.7bn). Qualified PRMs on these transports have their entitlements to free or reduced-price travel filtered by the issue of disability permits. In contrast, governments provide neither industry subsidies nor passenger filters for the airline industry. Instead they have regulated to ensure that unfiltered and often unqualified PRMs have the same access opportunities as able-bodied passengers (see Chapter 5). (Ferries (like airlines) are exempt from fuel duty but do not have any PRM requirements imposed.) This intervention has created free riders – those who are not entitled but who take advantage of the PRM provisions (see Chapter 5). Consequently this mandated provision has weakened the principles and one of the benefits of deregulation. The EU is supposed to undertake impact analyses before mandating; however, none was undertaken before EC 1107/2006 supporting PRMs was implemented (European Union, 2014a). It is possible that this might have been because the regulators regarded air travel as a 'luxury' at the time and therefore few PRMs would use it or it could also have been because they thought it would be too expensive to implement any of the filtering that applies to ground transport (e.g. government-supplied disability permits). It could even have been an economic decision because they did not want the complexities involved in managing an international system of permits and subsidies (i.e. compassion and politics vs airline economics). The reality is that airline fares are priced for mobile, able-bodied passengers who can be surcharged for any excess weight over the airline's free baggage allowance. However, in effect many PRMs are subsidised by either shareholders' funds, employees' potential rewards and/or charges on other passengers.

1.3 GOVERNMENT MARKET INTERVENTIONS

Politics vs airline economics

Governments perceived flag-carrying airlines as symbols of national pride and a source of much-needed revenue. Politics and economics are often at opposite ends of the sustainable airline industry continuum. What is often good for politicians is frequently bad for airline economics. It is a question of political philosophy. Social welfare is enshrined in politics, and multi-national organisations such as the UN and supranational governments such as the EU frequently attempt to relocate social responsibilities to private enterprises. In the EU, social welfare payments increase with the recipients' declining circumstances. In contrast, other nations such as the USA and Singapore emphasise personal responsibility and welfare payments are based on previous contributions. This philosophy rewards work and enterprise. These contrasting models have had a significant economic impact on airline-focussed regulation. Social welfare is best left to government provision while industry's role is to provide jobs, supply markets and pay taxes on re-investable profits. This improves welfare for nations.

Public and private transport provision

When owned by governments, air transport was considered to be a public good. Public goods are provided because their availability is considered to be in the public interest and private citizens cannot be relied on to supply them. Public goods have two key characteristics: non-rivalry and non-excludability. In other words, one individual's consumption does not deprive another and no individual who is unable to pay can be excluded from consuming. It also means that there is no actual consumer demand to be supplied by a market. Included in this inventory are such items as air, free broadcasting, landscape views and the light from lighthouses. Public transport has two additional features: it has a set of fares and runs on a schedule.

However, in contrast to public provision, consumers can be excluded from private goods and services which have the economic characteristics of excludability, rivalry and the possibility of consumers' rejection. Exclusion can be on the grounds that consumers cannot or will not pay for provision. Rivalry in private goods means that one person's consumption reduces the amount available for others since scarce resources are used to provide the goods. Unlike public provisions, private goods and services are provided for profit.

All of which raises the question: what is 'public' transport? It can be argued historically that in some nations public transport was simultaneously public in ownership, supply and consumption. However, many public transport entities have now been sold to private companies and 'public' transport now most commonly means 'public in consumption' and commonly in connection with land transport. Privately owned airlines fit the definition of 'public' transport because they transport the public with a set of fares and a schedule of flights. However, they also have the characteristics of a private service because they are rivalrous (one person's consumption prevents another from consuming), they are excludable (by virtue of payment) and most aim to operate profitably. Airlines also supply some regulated public consumer services free of charge many of which (in the absence of cost-benefit analysis) are believed to be loss-making (see Chapter 5). When the airlines were publicly owned, these services were originally supplied free of charge to qualified citizens as part of governments' agendas to equalise society. Upon privatisation and instead of treating air travel as the luxury good that it was at the time, many nations placed airlines in the same category as essential services such as public ground transport (see Chapter 5) and utility companies (gas, water, sewerage and electricity).

Air travel taxes

The airline industry is vulnerable to changes in the price of fares (whether competitively induced or government-imposed) as well as other variables which affect the sensitivity of air travel demand. Demand elasticities measure the change in the number of seats required in response to changes in other variables such as population growth, income levels and tax rates. Used in an air travel context, elasticities can give an indication of route sensitivities and they vary according to factors such as the number of competitors and the location of the market. IATA (2008) found that at route level, the elasticity of demand to price changes was high where demand was relatively price sensitive, and that elasticities on short-haul routes were higher than on long-haul because of the availability of transport substitutes (rail, car or coach).

Governments would appear to avoid elasticity calculations which can demonstrate the impact of proposed changes. These include higher prices due to a change in factors such as landing charges or a departure tax. Any airline tax would be ineffective if the price sensitivity of outbound travel was low. However, there will most likely be greater price sensitivity for potential inbound international travellers who could divert to other destinations since their outbound fare will be inflated by any tax. This in turn could reduce the number and spending of tourists in the national economy.

UK air travel tax – Air Passenger Duty (APD)

Having 'democratised' air travel consumption by liberating it from government ownership and allowed low-cost airlines to flourish, the UK government imposed the second highest airline passenger tax in the world. 'Air Passenger Duty' (APD) (HM Revenue and Customs (HMRC), 2014) subverted some of the inequality eliminated as a result of the widening access. This tax was initially proposed as an environmental tax but was ultimately used to fulfil social purposes. It was imposed on all outbound passengers (including children) and collected by the airlines. It was introduced by a free enterprise Conservative Government in 1994 and instead of being hypothecated was actually used by the Treasury for projects to benefit social welfare. Originally APD was in two bands: European and non-European destinations. In 2008 (socialist-leaning Labour Government) it was fractured into four bands (A, B, C and D) based on the distance between London and capital cities and in 2014 (Conservative–Liberal Democrat coalition) it was back to two bands. These distance taxes were not justified by the aircraft emissions (i.e. one of the reasons for any airline environmental tax) and the costs bore no relation to any negative externalities. An example is included in Table 1.3.

For the UK Treasury APD was 'primarily a revenue raising duty which makes an important contribution to the public finances, whilst also giving rise to secondary

Table 1.3 Snapshot of taxes, fees and charges only (NB: no economy airfare included)

FLIGHT: LONDON–LOS ANGELES–LONDON
22 June 2014: economy cabin

Government, authority and airport charges	*Per adult £Stg*
US [inbound processing charge]	10.40
Air Passenger Duty – United Kingdom	69.00
Passenger Service Charge – United Kingdom	39.75
US [outbound processing charge]	10.40
Animal & Plant Health User Fee (Aphus) – USA	3.00
Immigration User Fee – USA	4.20
Customs User Fee – USA	3.30
Passenger Facility Charge	2.70
Total government, authority and airport charges	142.75

environmental benefits' (HM Treasury, 2011: 10). UK airlines argued that the tax damaged their competitiveness and in doing so, restrained growth in the UK. In an attempt at social equality, passengers in the premium cabins (larger seats, more legroom, higher fares) paid enhanced APD since they enjoyed 'a range of comfort aboard flights which should be reflected in the rates of APD charged' (HM Treasury, 2011: 7). APD continues to deliver in excess of £Stg3.2bn ($US4.9bn or €4.4bn) for the Treasury each year, none of which is directly invested in either aviation or any related research. It is a tax on consumption (like VAT).

The government subsequently reduced the rates for travellers on direct long-haul routes for airlines flying from Belfast Airport in Northern Ireland. The British airlines had to compete with those in the Irish Republic (just across the land border) which abolished its departure tax in 2014. It was argued that such a reduction was a political move as much as an economic one: Northern Ireland is a region which receives considerable social funding to increase and maintain employment and civil stability. USA carrier Continental Airlines, flying out of Belfast, protested at the increased tax and in order to ensure the service continued the government eventually granted the carrier a reduced rate. Subsequently the government has also considered devolving APD to the Northern Ireland Assembly (HM Treasury, 2011). At the time of publication, Scotland was considering its abolition which would affect competitiveness among UK home nations.

APD effect on UK travel growth

APD is a restraint on the growth of the travel market. A computer-modelling study by PwC (2013) predicted that removing APD would boost gross domestic product (GDP) by £Stg16bn ($US23bn or €21bn) and create almost 60,000 extra jobs by 2020. The report claimed APD abolition would be self-sustaining since it would be replaced by increased tax receipts from other sources which would benefit. The World Economic Forum (WEF, 2013) ranked the UK as 138th out of 140 countries in terms of the price competitiveness of its tourism and travel 'in large part because it has the 2nd highest tax rate on fares and airport charges worldwide'.

APD impacts

The APD increase plus the world economic downturn of 2008 to 2013 had a considerable effect on sustainable airlines and tourism numbers to some destinations. APD was blamed for route closures including Ryanair (2012) to Italy (Liverpool to Milan, Rome and Rimini), Virgin Atlantic (2012) to Nairobi, Kenya and British Airways (2012) to the Caribbean (Montego Bay closed; Barbados reduced by 30% and Tobago by 50%). The Caribbean closures were particularly hard on the economies and societies of former British colonies – a source of many UK im-migrant workers and their descendants. The Caribbean was described as the 'most tourism dependent region in the world' by the Caribbean Tourism Organisation (2010: 7) with 75% of UK visits to the area involving two or more people travelling together. Because the bands are allocated from capital-city-to-capital-city, the

Caribbean – a nine-hour flight from the UK – was allocated into Band C (an extra £Stg83 per person) so travellers paid more than if they were heading to Los Angeles (11 hours) or Hawaii (16 hours) because the USA's capital city is Washington DC (8 flying hours). A family of four flying to the Caribbean would have paid £Stg332 extra; the same family flying to Hawaii would have paid an additional £Stg268. Any application of the EU Emissions Trading Scheme (EU ETS) for aircraft emissions (see Chapter 6) would only further compound the economic hardship for the islands. The UK government did not appear to consider the full economic, social and environmental impacts on the affected destinations.

1.4 CORPORATE SOCIAL AND ENVIRONMENTAL RESPONSIBILITY (CSER)

CSER evolution

'CSERplus capitalism' was promoted by many social and environmental advocates seeking to involve private enterprise in the pursuit of activities which are incompatible with profit-making and which require companies to accept responsibility for some social welfare provisions. Developed world governments have encouraged and often regulated to ensure that CSERplus policies are embedded in the private sector (see in particular Chapter 5 and Chapter 6). Ultimately this cascade undermines competitive, international markets by pushing costs onto consumers unless the shareholders and employees are prepared to assume any additional burdens. It also becomes a potential trigger for government-induced market failure.

CSERplus capitalism evolved possibly as a response to some of the enormous wealth accumulated by risk-taking venture capitalists during investor capitalism or as a reaction to some of the industrial social and environmental disasters of previous decades when some multi-national enterprises (MNEs) behaved irresponsibly in globalised locations (see Chapter 6). One of the most notably catastrophic of these disasters occurred in 1984 when Union Carbide, a USA-owned pesticide company, had a toxic leak of methyl isocyanate gas and other chemicals near the village of Bhopal, India which killed at least 5,000 people and disabled an estimated 500,000 more (Elliott, 2014). The second influential event was an environmental disaster. In 1989, crude oil tanker Exxon Valdez ran aground in Prince William Sound, Alaska spilling its contents across the pristine wilderness. The pollution radiated through the waters onto the land destroying vegetation and killing wildlife. Before and after these disasters were many examples of bad corporate behaviour where aggressive and sometimes corrupt enterprises pursued profit at the expense of indigenous populations and wildlife. In 1987, the NGO UNWCED produced a report (later titled the 'Brundtland Report' (UNWCED, 1987) after its coordinator, former Norwegian Prime Minister Gro Harlem Brundtland). Its focus was sustainable development – the progress of economic development which preserves the environment while trying to avoid natural resource depletion. The Report meshed social and environmental issues and had two key concepts, the first of which was focussing on the needs of the world's poor, for which it asked for priority; and the second was outlining the limitations imposed by technology and social organisations on the ability of the natural environment to meet present and future needs.

The legacy of the two notable disasters during the investor capitalism period had been an awakening of globalising MNEs to the concerns of social campaigners and environmentalists. The realisation that MNEs (drivers of poverty reduction and therefore social benefit in advancing nations) could also cause harm prompted public outcry and legislation concerning MNEs' responsibilities for damage caused (which ultimately had to be paid by consumers or from shareholders' earnings). It also marked the increasing integration of NGOs into democratic processes as outlined in the Brundtland Report (Drexhage and Murphy, 2010).

> Most governments realize how much NGOs can contribute to issues; and some governments work closely with NGOs and business, and include representatives on their delegations to meetings of various environmental treaties. A particularly positive development over the past 20 years is the increased collaboration and networking among NGOs from developed and developing countries. NGOs have also experienced a cross fertilization of interests in various issues, including environment, development, human rights, women's rights and social issues.
>
> (Drexhage and Murphy, 2010: 12) (NB: these are social and environmental issues with no mention of economics)

This collaboration was also noted by economist Henderson (2001) who observed that businesses were aligning with anti-business NGOs, some of which were violent. He surmised that these relationships meant that businesses had 'gone out of their way to strengthen the position of organisations which are hostile to business and which, in the case of some at any rate of the NGOs, may present a threat to order and due process in political life' (Henderson, 2001: 124). At that time the World Business Council for Sustainable Development (WBCSD) (a global grouping of international commercial organisations concerned with business and sustainable development) was supported by over 200 Chief Executives from some of the biggest international companies. The WBCSD has been credited with:

> moving industry from the periphery to the centre of the sustainable development debate. . . Business has become more proactive by encouraging the CSR [corporate social responsibility] movement and using its investment in sustainable ways. But these initiatives are voluntary and involve relatively few companies
>
> (Drexhage and Murphy, 2010: 12)

Why did industries feel they had to become involved in these activities? Did they feel pressure to conform? More worryingly, was this conformance a type of 'genteel extortion'?

There was a desire to see more of the small and medium-sized enterprises (i.e. the firms which generate jobs and stimulate national economic growth) become involved in the sustainable development movement particularly in the countries which were (at that time) potential economic powerhouses – Brazil, Russia, India and China (Drexhage and Murphy, 2010). Many of these countries are now beneficiaries of international financial aid from taxpayers of developed nations (see Chapter 6). Furthermore, involving the advancing nations' entrepreneurial companies in supplying social and environmental programmes beyond those which are regulated increases their costs, decreases their international competitiveness and in turn reduces their nations' welfare. Besides, as long as their nations are net receivers of international aid there is little incentive for them to vary their practices (an example of moral hazard) which is one of the arguments against subsidies of all types.

Stakeholders

The main actors in aviation markets are airlines, passengers, aviation organisations, owners and national, multi-national and supranational governments; however, with CSERplus the interested parties widen to embrace the concept of stakeholders – those individuals or groups with an interest in the business (see Chapter 7). Any advanced-world industry is now considered responsible for and to its stakeholders (see Table 2.1). Stakeholders can be from inside (such as employees and shareholders) or outside (which could include suppliers, competitors, regulators, partners, communities, NGOs and other public interest groups). They can be further classified as primary (who are essential to the firm – the investors, shareholders, employees, customers and suppliers as well as governments and communities) and secondary (who can influence or affect the firm but do not transact with it and are not essential for its survival) (Clarkson, 1995). This broadened definition makes the commercial organisation responsible to more of society and 'allows each stakeholder – including the managers – to elevate pursuit of his own interests over both the ostensible organisational objective and the interests of other stakeholders' (Sternberg, 2009: 7). It can be argued that the widened stakeholder doctrine undermines accountability (by damaging the principal-agency relationship), is unjustified (suffering from fundamental conceptual and practical defects) and attracts 'the promoters of worthy causes who (unrealistically) believe they would be the beneficiaries if organisational (and particularly business) assets were diverted from their owners' (Sternberg, 2009: 7–8). Furthermore, the supporters of CSERplus believed that stakeholder theory was compatible with value maximisation (howsoever defined and measured) without acknowledging that there are trade-offs to be made (Jensen, 2001).

The concepts of CSERplus and stakeholders are suitable for authoritarian and collectivist political systems 'because their nominal association with unobjectionable doctrines lends them a superficial plausibility; [and] their apparent generosity encourages people to accept them uncritically' (Sternberg, 2009: 4). Because the two concepts are used to justify State intervention, it is unsurprising that they are being used to form the official policies of the USA, UK and EU (Sternberg, 2009) (i.e. left-of-centre governments). Licensing is a means by which governments can protect consumers and in the CSERplus context, the 'licence to operate' is what organisations receive when they become accountable to society through the stakeholders. This undermines free society because in free society, what is not prohibited is permissible (Sternberg, 2009). This implicit licence is awarded by nation states and stakeholders (including customers and suppliers) and retained by virtue of commercial organisations adhering to legislation of all types whether economic (including paying taxes, invoices, employee wages and expenses in a timely manner), social (treating its stakeholders fairly) or environmental (avoiding polluting and reducing resource consumption and wastes). This implicit licence can be perceived as a threat: either business submits to society or it would be prevented from trading, i.e. a form of 'genteel extortion'. Furthermore, it can be argued that conventional CSER and 'its presumed "licence to operate" are essentially inimical to liberty' (Sternberg, 2009: 8).

Airlines have accepted the wider view of CSERplus with its stakeholder concept (see Chapter 7). There are insufficient spare resources to fight it when making a profit has to be fundamental to economic sustainability (see also Chapter 6). What any economically sustainable airline must do is ensure that it works with the stakeholders who are material to its survival. Airline stakeholders have strengths, weaknesses, influences and expectations (see Chapter 3). At root for all of them are airline decisions delivering the best outcomes for economic sustainability, which take account of the social and environmental impacts and which are (as responsible enterprises) in turn cognisant of potential risks (see Chapter 7).

Collaboration with material stakeholders reduces friction and stress and supports the efficient use of time, thereby improving productivity. In particular, collaboration with stakeholder-suppliers allows them to offer their expertise and ultimately the least cost and most efficient solution (see Chapter 7 – performance-based procurement).

Markets as cause for dissent

Henderson (using the narrower term CSR, but which implicitly included the environment) wrote with considerable foresight before the real impact of CSERplus would be evident on the aviation industry. He believed that rather than crediting the free market as a vehicle for innovation, many CSR advocates viewed the market as a 'prime cause of inequality, social exclusion and environmental destruction' (Henderson, 2001: 159). Henderson (in objecting to the CSR doctrine because it relied on a distorted picture of issues and events) argued that putting it into effect would actually reduce national welfare. Eventually this reduction would have a detrimental impact on society as a whole and it could even do harm. He perceived business as part of civil society with a duty to act responsibly but that government policies caused markets to send the wrong signals to businesses and consumers (Henderson, 2002). He challenged the idea that big MNEs should act to improve the 'quality of life' as required by the WBCSD (2000). Although its recommendations initially appeared reasonable, further investigation revealed the potential for unintended consequences. Existing businesses which agreed with its proposals would be committing to social and environmental regulation for which the compliance costs could prevent new entrants coming into the market or lead to the closure of existing organisations. Either outcome would undermine competition (one of the necessary features of a successful market) because if organisations were allocating resources to non-competitive activities they would be performing at less than optimal output and that would reduce shareholders' returns, employees' rewards and overall welfare.

Many MNEs have behaved despicably and should have been punished by the law. But many MNEs were also law-abiding and should not have been intimidated by the CSERplus movement. Henderson (2001) believed that large MNEs have been the architects and advocates of CSR within the business community. CSERplus distorts and undermines the workings of a market. It has costs which must ultimately be passed onto consumers in order to ensure the economic viability of the enterprise. Henderson (2001) wondered how smaller or medium-sized firms whose public profile was lower and concerns are more locally focussed than MNEs could afford to support the CSERplus principles, the adoption of which would eventually reduce national welfare and undermine the markets which contribute to national prosperity.

Airline sustainability issues

Specific airline sustainability issues vary depending on the airline's domicile, available funds and the advocacy groups to which it is subjected. Reputational risk is closely woven into the behaviours exhibited by the airline's interaction with its stakeholders. Examining airline sustainability reports gives an indication of what most bothers them and it would appear that most airlines worry about the same issues (Table 1.4) under the broad headings of economics, society, environment and governance. Apart from perhaps 'community' or 'citizenship', these are all basic 'hygiene' issues which airlines practise to ensure safe and responsible business practices.

Measuring CSERplus

CSERplus' advocates have long campaigned for non-economic activities to have equal ranking in the annual financial reports by showing an organisation's impact on the 'triple bottom line' of people, planet and profit. This would highlight commercial organisations' non-financial achievements, a radical departure from reporting profitability and shareholder value which has been the dominant historic disclosure. However, Henderson's concern was that CSR 'rests on a mistaken view of issues and events' (Henderson, 2001: 18) and he wondered who would set the success criteria and measures which would appear in such reports. His concern was also for the unintended consequences in the advancing-world which is where CSR is supposedly beneficial and yet that is where the socio-economic impacts could be most detrimental. Raising advancing-world labour rates to advanced-world levels could reduce workers' welfare by increasing corporate costs so that employers would

Table 1.4 Commonality in airline sustainability concerns (2013–2014)

Full-service carriers	Summarised sustainability issues
Etihad Airways	employees, community, environment (with emphasis on carbon reduction)
Lufthansa	economic sustainability (including data protection); social; climate and environment and research; citizenship and social commitment
Singapore Airlines Ltd	stakeholder engagement, supporting communities, environment
Low-cost carriers	
easyJet plc	environment, human rights, customers, communities, charities, governance
Ryanair plc	employees and labour relations, environment, code of ethics
Southwest Airlines	environment impacts and conservation, waste management, suppliers, employees, customers, communities

be unable to afford more employees – a trade-off between social impacts and economics.

Similarly, businesses would have increased costs owing to diverting resources to CSERplus monitoring and enforcement. This could involve costs varying from employing 'sustainability experts' who recommend appropriate CSERplus policies through to hiring specialist CSERplus writers and assurers for the social and environmental sections of the annual corporate report (see Chapter 7). Such diversion of funds could mean lowered profits which could have been spent on investing in assets to grow, rewarding shareholders for their risk capital or employees for their efforts, or even improving working conditions for any employees in the advancing-world.

CSERplus and social justice

Firms are urged by CSERplus advocates, governments and often their competitors (who want to ensure the CSERplus costs are shared) to further the cause of ill-defined social justice. This would (the advocates believe) increase the social equality and equity achieved by actions which perversely would narrow markets and increase corporate costs.

> Leading instances are the pursuit of 'diversity' within businesses, and enforcing in poorer countries terms of employment that are based not on local market conditions but on the ideas of foreign governments and [advanced economies'] public opinion as to what is to be viewed as acceptable.
>
> (Henderson, 2001: 159)

The concern is that with management focussing on non-profit-making processes and being distracted by social welfare requirements, businesses will not be economically sustainable. Furthermore, subscribing overzealously to the principles of CSERplus erodes 'the commercial effectiveness of management . . . [and] . . . can make a company less competent in carrying out its primary task of serving the wishes, tastes and interests of its customers' (Henderson, 2001: 60).

Economic case against CSERplus

Henderson also examined CSR/CSERplus and the role of business.

> I believe that companies and those directing them should act responsibly, and that they should be seen to do so. I believe that, now as in the past, there are situations in which managers and directors and sometimes shareholders also, should ask themselves what is right for their company to do, as well as what is legally permitted to it or required of it. However, I do not believe that responsible corporate behaviour today should be identified with endorsing, and giving effect to, the current and now widely accepted doctrine of CSR.
>
> (Henderson, 2009: 11)

The role of business is to pursue profits responsibly in order to be able to deliver goods and services competitively and sustainably. Businesses should consider the impact of their behaviours; however, this does not mean they must assume non-business functions which are more appropriately the responsibility of either the individual or the State. If a State wants its entrepreneurs to thrive, its intervention should not require industry to altruistically undertake public deeds. Economic freedom will increase national welfare and would eventually satisfy the social justice proponents if private production and service provision are permitted, the free movement of labour and goods is allowed and property rights are protected. Protecting property rights gives incentives to entrepreneurs which they do not have with the imposition of taxes and regulations which inherently confiscate property. There is a strong correlation between the number of super-entrepreneurs and countries with low tax rates and low levels of national regulation (Sanandaji and Sanandaji, 2014). In other words, in order to encourage entrepreneurship with its potential to stimulate national economic growth, governments should create the best economic environment for entrepreneurship – low taxes and low regulatory burden – rather than load commercial enterprises with regulation and high taxes to fund socially equalising public welfare programmes. This has been particularly onerous on the airline industry with the implementation of unfunded mandates (see Chapter 5).

Society's expectations

As Henderson (2001) notes, commercial organisations have supported CSR/CSERplus by appeasing and accommodating the arguments and demands of anti-business activist groups and consequently 'show little awareness that the case for private business derives from its links with competition and economic freedom . . . [commercial organisations] mistakenly identify defence of the market economy with making businesses more popular and respected through meeting "society's expectations"' (Henderson, 2001: 18). Society's expectations are often framed by the NGOs or CSERplus community. Their concerns are supported by advocacy research as evidence of the worthiness of their particular strand of social or environmental justice which often requires taxpayers' support to fulfil it. Henderson believed that if businesses adopted CSERplus principles overall welfare would be reduced particularly in the developing world where CSERplus was supposedly of the most benefit. The adoption of enforced uniformity would be particularly damaging to labour markets (Table 1.1). 'Imposing common international standards, despite the fact that circumstances may be widely different across countries, restricts the scope of mutually beneficial trade and investment flows . . . [and] . . . is liable to hold back the development of poor countries through the suppression of employment opportunities within them' (Henderson, 2001: 17). Competition in labour markets occurs in countries and between countries and if a surplus of regulations increases costs then purchasers will move elsewhere denying employment to the local labour force. If Bangladesh labour is too expensive, purchasers could move to the Philippines; if Philippines' labour is too expensive, purchasers could move to Sri Lanka and if Sri Lanka is too expensive purchasers could explore options in China. Applied to the airline industry, the installation of the labour programmes requested by many NGOs and CSERplus' advocates could increase airlines' costs and ultimately fares and freight charges. This could prevent them procuring supplies in countries where costs are increasing. Eventually this would reduce overall economic and social welfare in those nations unless fares (a consumption barrier for lower-income earners) were increased to cover excessive costs. This could actually increase the inequality that CSERplus social justice proponents are keen to reduce through the implementation of various subsidies or mandates.

Concept of 'good corporate citizens'

Airlines want to be considered reliable, responsible, safe and secure which are all human characteristics that fit with CSERplus' supporters' concept of the 'corporate citizen'. Citizens can own property, enter contracts, pay taxes and have human rights. Using this rationale, Henderson (2001) noted that corporate citizenship gave capitalism a 'human face' and that if it had a human face the CSERplus proponents would find it acceptable for business to make profits. CSERplus' advocates believe that only by focussing on performance in the environment and social spheres (rather than focussing on the economics of profitability and shareholder value) will an organisation earn and retain its socially awarded 'licence to operate'. These advocates believe that 'a commitment to corporate citizenship is the key to long-run profitability for individual firms and to ensuring public support for the market economy'

(Henderson, 2001: 15). In any event, airlines did not need intervention from CSERplus' proponents to tell them to behave honestly and responsibly like good citizens should. That is the role of customers and regulators.

Moral panic and environmentalists

The aviation industry – including aeroplane manufacturers, airport operators, airlines and outsourced suppliers – has many stakeholder detractors, particularly among environmentalists, because aviation is accused of creating negative externalities, in particular atmospheric pollution which will purportedly take millennia to disappear (see Chapter 6). Collaboration with environmentalists has been difficult. Environmentalism has successfully blocked airline industry expansion in many democratic nations and any deviation from the expected corporately responsible behaviour could bring an airline into disrepute and jeopardise its implicit 'licence to operate'. The State can levy fiscal sanctions or public interest groups can exert pressure for behavioural change, urge customers to boycott or even pressure the supply chain or trades unions to cease cooperating.

However, airline environmental issues (see Chapter 6) have been used as a 'moral panic'. Henderson (2001: 86) describes this phenomenon as 'a strong and consistent bias towards pessimism, drama and overstatement' accepted by both the businesses pursuing CSERplus and the NGOs pressuring them. Moral panics – based on emotion rather than clear thinking – require stemming before they tip into mass hysteria at which point politicians often indulge in a knee-jerk reaction and pass new legislation. Politicians are often swayed by the advocates and sometimes allow their personal vested interests to override national interests. For example, they can stifle local airport development ahead of an election in order to support their candidate while overriding the potential national benefit from such an addition to national infrastructure. Similarly, they can impose 'green' taxes which are not hypothecated and which could affect international competitiveness.

The aviation industry's effects on the natural environment receive much attention and yet it is economics which underpins aviation's environmental impacts. There is an imbalance of influence from powerful environmental public pressure groups which can have a significant impact on the airlines' licences to operate. These lobby groups frequently produce incomplete, asymmetric data and information – one of the triggers of alleged market inefficiencies or failures – often because there is no cost-benefit analysis to balance their opinions. It is the task of governments to ensure balance in the policies they set but if the data and/or information on which they legislate are skewed in the favour of vested interests then any legislation would be unbalanced from the outset. Legislation without economic appraisal has delivered boondoggles supporting social and environmental causes – which raises the question of who judges what is good for society?

Over the past decades, a sustainability 'industry' has developed and it has also spawned specialist businesses including sustainability auditors, consultancies, report writers, lobbyists, specialist software producers as well as NGOs which police commercial organisations. NGOs became the *de facto* regulators backfilling the space that retreating governments left behind (Brugmann and Prahalad, 2007). In previous years, NGOs had influenced many markets including 'chemical regulation, oil spill liability, air emissions, liquid waste, pharmaceutical and food standards, child labour and employment discrimination. Their influence has created a regulatory framework tougher than the legal requirements corporations face' (Brugmann and Prahalad, 2007: 83). The NGOs with which airlines interact include organisations as diverse as human rights (Amnesty International); disability prevention and assistance (Scope, Age Concern); environmental concerns (Friends of the Earth, Greenpeace, Royal Society for the Protection of Birds and WWF); poverty and children's welfare improvement (Oxfam and Save the Children Fund) and corruption prevention (Transparency International) as well as air industry-focussed groups. They can all have an influence – proportionate or disproportionate – on airlines' reputations and therefore on the retention of their licences to operate.

1.5 SIGNIFICANCE OF AIRLINE ECONOMIC SUSTAINABILITY

Economic sustainability

Airlines have accepted that CSERplus is not going to disappear in the short-term and so have adapted to its requirements with activities they perceive to be appropriate. Airline CSER has always been a 'hygiene' issue – fundamental to airline operations – and it would be wrong to assign credit for it to the CSERplus movement or to NGOs. Many special interest groups with different agendas have an interest in how airlines behave. Today's special interest groups have unprecedented resources, communications capability, influence and commercial sophistication. Similarly, local, national, multi-national and supranational governments and international governing bodies have collective power which increases cumulatively. Airlines cannot afford to ignore them and yet cannot please them all at any one time. Some will never be satisfied. In order to pacify as many of these stakeholders as possible, airlines need a defendable decision-making process (see Chapter 7) which shows they are aware of their stakeholders' concerns. Loosely, these concerns fall into the three dimensions: economic, social and environmental where economics is the knowledge integrator for decision-making. Focussing on economics and stretching corporate thinking allows the decision-makers to consider the benefits of:

(a) future-proof thinking
(b) ensuring compliance
(c) protecting against volatility
(d) capturing reputational risks and
(e) identifying hidden subsidising.

(a) Future-proof thinking

Airline economic sustainability involves scanning the horizon for likely enablers for growth and opportunity as well as for barriers such as the objections of special interest groups. Ultimately future-proofing the airline needs identification of immediate or potential vulnerabilities and searching for short-term fluctuations which might become long-term trends or iceberg issues (see Chapter 7) and which could eventually sink the airline. This information is found in many sources including industry and general news feeds, customer feedback, and academic and commercial research. Future travellers in 2020 would most likely comprise four types of passengers: active seniors (aged between 50 and 75 years), global clans (global migrants including multi-generational participants), cosmopolitan commuters (time-pressured commuters living and working in different regions) and global executives (the most affluent group requiring highly personalised service) (*Amadeus*, 2013). As travellers, they would be part of a burgeoning global population notable for its rising affluence and increasing global migration, travel and tourism (*Amadeus*, 2013). A sustainable airline needs to prepare for them since lead times for assets and facilities such as aeroplanes, hangars and airports can sometimes be considerable. Although passengers profess environmental concerns these will not stop airline growth which is predicted to be 31% by 2017 (i.e. an increase of 930 million passengers over 2012) (IATA, 2013a).

Economic-based sustainability-thinking (see Chapter 7) provides a lens to predict potential government interventions which could oblige airlines to subsidise not only some passenger groups but also, curiously, their competitors (see Chapter 6). By employing economics airlines can horizon-scan to identify, assess, evaluate and eventually monitor potential social and environmental regulatory interventions. These present risks which might be avoided through discussions with regulators early in the process or transferred, shared, reduced or even ignored.

Horizon-scanning can reveal new issues which an airline might need to tackle for future-proofing (Table 1.5).

Future-proof aviation has detractors – and not always those who are obvious. Alfred Kahn, air market deregulation proponent and former Chairman, US Civil Aeronautics Board between 1977 and 1978 (and therefore a government employee) had no foresight for his industry when he declared, 'I don't think it's my highest aspiration to make it possible for people to jet all over the world when the future clearly has to belong to substituting telecommunications for travel' (Hershey, 2010).

(b) Ensuring compliance

The law seeks to guide, deter, punish, control and support enterprises of all types (Veljanovski, 2006) and not just aviation. Among other functions, economists see the law as a means of enforcing market pricing mechanisms, regulating market activity, supporting freedom of choice and securing property.

The economic function of law is not to prevent all harm but to minimise costs or maximise benefits (Veljanovski, 2006). Laws are made by governments which,

Table 1.5 Some social-impact horizon-scanning revelations

Horizon-scan revelation	Economically sustainable airline responses
value for money	advertising zero-cost add-ons for passengers (e.g. it is taken-for-granted that duty-free purchases will always be carried free of charge)
approximately 30% of UK population are economically active at night	offering special fares for night owls (an example of price discrimination)
social media impact	training for employees to avoid mobile phone-filmable displays of unfavourable corporate behaviour, e.g. arguments at the check-in desk
active older consumers (healthier than previous generations) with increased leisure time and disposable income	preparing for the problems of ageing bodies by ensuring retractable armrests (or extra crew would be needed on board to assist elderly travellers) and increasing the quantity of airport mobility aids
changing family balance including UK government agenda for mothers to return to work	examining the potential for families with compacted leisure times to travel together during school holidays at low prices
rise of the single traveller	providing an on-board social space (physical or technologically enabled) to counter possible loneliness
time-poor travellers	maximising their time using mobile technologies for minimising their reporting time at the airport and departure gate
possible passenger guilt with purported environmental damage	promoting guilt-free travel by supporting lowered engine emissions and noises, minimising airport lighting pollution as far as it is possible without compromising safety; promoting the economic benefits that tourism can offer for developing and emerging nations
families travelling together	providing crèche facilities on board (with air crew nannies?) with family areas for children's breakout activities and intergenerational mixing areas
changing expectations of economy cabin passengers	examining the ratcheting effect of each cabin and the occupants' expectations
measure travel in time as well as miles/ kilometres	lengthening the luxurious flight experience for passengers who enjoy longer flights on full-service carriers with sumptuous surroundings (e.g. the personal cabin concept with bathroom, bedroom and lounge); other passengers perceive travel as a functional commodity to be completed as quickly as possible in the economy cabins
growth of Asia Pacific, Middle East and Africa – predicted to become the biggest economic regions by 2020 (Oxford Economics, 2013)	opening new routes; expand capacity; recruiting local staff; training home-base staff (ground and air) to speak the language of the next predicted markets (e.g. African continent and Indian Ocean nations); ensuring culturally appropriate on-board catering; showing language-appropriate films on board; ensuring signage is in comfort language

as noted, also intervene in markets. government intervention in markets gives rise to imperfect working, inflates costs and creates distortions (Coase, 1988). Intervention is only justified in the event that the market is inefficient or failing and not to provoke market failure. A frequent cause of economic inefficiencies is the transaction costs which make markets costly to use. (Hidden transaction costs are also one of the barriers to successful mergers, alliances and takeovers preventing newly enlarged carriers from delivering the required contribution to overheads.) The more information available and communicated during a transaction the lower the transaction costs. Transaction costs have reduced dramatically with the arrival of information technology and communications (ITC); however, in contravention of the idea that governments should only intervene if markets fail (Coase, 1988), governments have intervened with the result that airlines' markets have been undermined. The effect has been to increase the transaction costs by placing more social and environmental costs into airlines' undertakings. This affects airline fares and freight charges, competitiveness and ultimately, aviation economic sustainability.

Once airline deregulation was effected and national airlines and airports liberated from State ownership, governments began intervening in the aviation markets to control, punish and tax whilst ensuring that aviation (although often privately owned) was still integral to national transport strategies and policies. Freedom from State ownership did not mean freedom from State control. Economically sustainable airlines obey the rules for fear of fiscal sanctions for breach of what are often social rather than the 'hygiene' factors of safety or environmental regulations. The ripple effects could eventually include suspension of their operation by regulators. Obeying aviation laws is an absolute necessity for safety, industry consistency and reputation; however, many of the service requirements, regulations and rules legislated by advanced-world governments are not for safety but for relocation of social costs. This can reduce sustainable airlines' profitability and the shareholders' dividends (their rewards under capitalism for providing the risk capital needed to invest for growth).

Airlines know that illegal short-term activities can prove expensive in the long term. From around 1990 onwards, British Airways hacked the computer systems of its much smaller rivals Virgin Atlantic, Dan Air and Air Europe to obtain competitive information. By doing this, British Airways broke the law in a bid to undermine its competitors and obtain customers' names and information on load factors. The intention was to crush the small competitors by increasing flights and offering lower prices. Three years later, British Airways paid damages (£Stg600,000+) and legal costs (£Stg3m) to Virgin Atlantic (Gregory, 1993). In 2014 Virgin Atlantic was the only one of the three targeted carriers still operating.

(c) Protecting against volatility

To paraphrase naturalist and ecologist Charles Darwin (1809–1882) the organisation which survives is not necessarily the strongest: it is the one which responds best to changes in its operating environment. Since 1990 airlines have had to adapt to a turbulent economic, social, environmental and legislative world which included oil price fluctuations; wars in Iraq (2003 to 2011), Libya (2003), the Balkans (1992 to 1995) and Afghanistan (2001 to 2014); terrorism both threatened and real (Lockerbie in Scotland, UK (1988) and World Trade Centre (WTC) in New York, USA (2001)); erupting Icelandic volcano Eyjafjallajökull (2010); health epidemics (bird flu, severe acute respiratory syndrome (SARS) and Ebola); national and world economic crises (several); passenger growth fluctuations and a decline in premium traffic (particularly after the WTC destruction); legacy labour union challenges (e.g. United Airlines, USA) as well as aircraft delays caused by intrusive security measures. These events and others caused the demise of many carriers (e.g. Pan American), the mergers and alliancing of others and laid the foundations for the rise of the new breed of no-frills, low-cost, low-fare carriers. Some of the legacy carriers were not sufficiently flexible and adaptable to compete and in a desperate attempt to remain viable, responded by drip-pricing for services such as carrying an extra bag. Many of the largest carriers merged or went bankrupt (some several times). Some American carriers filed for Chapter 11 protection under the watchful eye of an independent, supervisory judiciary. This is not economically sustainable but it was politically expedient. Airline business cycles are not short-term: they are long-term with many interim fluctuations. However, over ensuing decades, assorted EU and other governments also supported their 'zombie' flag carriers so they could continue flying despite their unhealthy financial state.

The shape of airline competition has changed yet again. No longer are airlines just competing within their industry. They are also competing with tele-presence systems which negate the need for the profitable business passengers to travel. TNT, the Dutch logistics company, predicted that future increases in energy costs would require a larger travel budget so rather than spend more on travel the company installed desktop video-conferencing systems. In doing so it saved the negative emissions externalities, any productive employee time lost through aircraft delays and the business travel costs (*VC Insight*, 2008).

Today private-sector airlines are forced to complete globally with State-owned airlines protected from management inefficiencies, over-manning and uneconomic operations. Many airlines struggle to make a profit – a powerful capitalist incentive and one of the most important means of future-proofing. Its magnitude is often indicative of the level of management skill. Many airlines, however, stumble making profits since their economic health is tied to the frailties of world economies. Profits are necessary for many reasons including the timely payment of taxes in each country (to be spent as governments decide) and to fund corporate growth. The airline aim of achieving profitability is to maximise the gap (the yield) between the breakeven load factor and the actual achieved load factor. Yields increase with more full-fare passengers (i.e. not travelling on discounted fares). Investors must have faith that the airline will be sufficiently sound for investments. Although some airlines have been unprofitable for many years owing to factors including industrial disputes, accidents and the global economic situation, financial institutions which are so critical to airlines' economic sustainability have continued to support them because of the quality of the management.

(d) Capturing reputational risks

Reputational risk is an outcome of perception. If an airline is perceived as untrustworthy then it is regarded as unsafe by potential passengers and they will travel with a rival. Scruffy interiors could intimidate passengers into thinking that the airline is not taking care of the engines (the aircraft power source). This quantum leap in thinking ought to be untrue. However, if resources are limited (such as during the downturn after 2001) the airline might simply have preferred to allocate them to where they have the biggest impact on safety (i.e. the engines) but to a passenger, perception is reality. The association is 'shiny interiors mean safe engines'.

Good reputations are extremely important for airlines and (depending on the research or advocates consulted) can comprise 60% of a listed firm's market value. Different stakeholders have different views of airlines' reputations; however, since reputation is integral to every transaction – and because it is an asset and vulnerable to attack – it must be protected. Reputational risks cover all risks which cumulatively or singly can damage the esteem in which airlines are held (see Chapter 7). There are many advocacy groups which affect airlines' reputations but some have undeclared origins (see Chapters 2, 3, 6, 7 and 8). Their existence relies on their advocates making news headlines because such coverage brings in donations and enhances their credibility and influence. Damaging a corporate reputation can engender a slide in an airline's business and undermine its competitiveness. Airlines face one of the most competitive environments ever and in order to protect their 'licence to operate' they must protect their reputations by abiding by all laws and ensuring the safety of stakeholders. Costs of breaches include fiscal sanctions as well as loss of passenger and freight revenue, debt financing, trust and ultimately economic sustainability.

Increasing quantities of corporate vulnerabilities derive from the growing compliance required with legislation, regulations and policies from multiple sources such as the European Civil Aviation Conference (ECAC), governments' air transport departments, aircraft manufacturers and the international organisations such as ICAO and IATA. Failure to comply will damage reputations (and often profits if fines are incurred as a result). Airlines' reputations are hard won and easily lost – often by something seemingly as trivial as mishandling a difficult customer at the check-in desk which could be simultaneously live streamed on social media by observing passengers. However, there are also pressures from many NGOs in different economic, social and environmental spheres. 'By publicly inflicting harm to a market leader's reputation, which eventually forces the entire industry to change its practices, the civil society is often successful in getting corporations to conform to its norms' (Brugmann and Prahalad, 2007: 83). Many NGOs are trying to implement their view of a fairer society by influencing commercial organisations which react more quickly than governments (see Chapter 5). However, sometimes these minority views work against the economic interests of the aviation industry and its shareholders, and ultimately the optimal welfare of the nation.

Economic risks have many roots and are sometimes not always obvious. Broadly they are internal (e.g. strikes and data theft) or external (e.g. war, economic forces and computer hacking) and all can damage an airline's reputation. Before they become a threat, vulnerabilities need to be mitigated or adaptations provided. Minimising risks involves knowing what is right or wrong (i.e. ethical behaviour) and acting accordingly by obtaining economic intelligence from as many sources as deemed necessary. Wide-ranging sources for reputational risk assessment include customer feedback, news lines and broadcasts as well as aviation industry research (from IATA, ICAO, CAA or USA's Federal Aviation Administration (FAA)), government statistics (such as those from the UK Office of National Statistics (ONS)), networking, commissioned research and subscription services. Various commercial consultancies share their research in the public domain. One of the more comprehensive and airline-appropriate sources is the annual Global Risk report from the WEF (2014). Their coverage includes geopolitical, technological, societal, environmental and economic risks about which airline managements would have to be nimble in order to protect their economic sustainability. Other sources come from investment departments in banks, insurance companies, aircraft equipment manufacturers as well as academic research. In terms of reliability, the sources should always be examined for potential bias such as that from advocacy research. What is really important is that decision-makers have access to impartial, reliable information and data and can join with other key decision-makers to be certain that the risks are responsibly assessed.

Economic, social and environmental sustainability risks (see Table 7.2 in Chapter 7) are interdependent and all have the potential to damage reputations if not appropriately considered. Retaining a positive image is of the utmost importance to dictators and democratic leaders alike since both seek support to enable them to retain power. It is also important to Chief Executives who want to recruit and retain quality personnel, increase sales, maintain access to capital markets and support for the share price. They also want their airline to be respected as a good neighbour, supplier and customer. For individuals it is about personal values (the 'spiritual capital') and self-belief as well as friendships and society membership. Reputation encompasses concepts and core values such as trust, honesty and openness – all necessary for building and cementing strategic relationships and sustainable organisations (see Chapter 3).

Once identified, reputational risks should have owners who are responsible and accountable for them. Risks also have a cost – the higher the risk, the higher the cost of protecting against the risk (see Table 7.2 in Chapter 7). Airlines which are considered well managed have lower risk premiums than those which are considered 'risky'. Economically sustainable airlines are those which manage all their risks and avoid paying fines for breaches or failures in what is a heavily regulated industry. Finally, reputational risk protection is also best served by a culture which allows challenge (see Chapter 3). Promotion of an open culture – where challenge is welcomed and innovation is a core activity – protects the airline against the under-assessed reputational risks (see Chapter 7) by empowering staff. 'Publicity is justly commended as a remedy for social and industrial diseases. Sunlight is said to be the best of disinfectants; electric light the most efficient policeman' (Brandeis, n.d.). If decision-makers believe that their decisions for which they are accountable and responsible could be exposed to challenge (the disinfectant of sunlight and the scrutiny of electric light) they would take much more care when making them. Transparency comes in many forms, the most obvious and public being the annual corporate financial reports to shareholders as required by law. It is almost inconceivable that members of an industry that is so reliant on its reputation would be late submitting annual information and data requirements to the statutory bodies. Late submission could appear that there was something to hide – which could make passengers feel unsafe – and consequently, could impact on the airline's reputation and ultimately its economic survival.

(e) Identifying hidden subsidising

Airlines pay national and local taxes in exchange for the support of civil society and as part of this exchange they receive 'subsidies' because they are not taxed on procurements such as fuel, aircraft supply and maintenance. Furthermore, it can be argued that aviation's negative externalities are borne by society whereas the private benefits are awarded to owners. In exchange for some tax-free concessions airlines have social obligations beyond those of corporate citizenship and unacknowledged and often unrecognised, they subsidise and support many public and private activities stretching from governments through to various passenger groups as well as Acts of God. All of these were (before identification) missing markets. Airlines also cover many public costs (particularly in welfare states) which are not recognised as such and which can create significant unacknowledged private costs. These unidentified subsidies include support for the following:

- passengers who cause a delay
- uninsured passengers
- sick, disabled and obese passengers and medical tourists
- pregnant passengers
- dead passengers
- disruptions and Acts of God
- UK NHS
- government security measures and revenue collection
- airport duty-free shopping concessions.

In exchange airlines receive subsidies including:

- tax-free aviation fuel, aircraft and fares
- negative social and environmental externalities (except for the UK's APD, various waste disposal taxes and similar levies)
- support from national infrastructure.

Subsidies provided by airlines

Passengers who cause a delay

Passengers who cause a delay through not arriving at the aircraft on time for their flight are not charged for the additional costs even if this means time has to be spent unloading their luggage. One overly late passenger can delay a full aircraft and create additional airline expense while the aircraft remains hooked to a jetty and losing its take-off slot. Aircraft delays knock into the airline schedule, affecting more than just the departing airport. The economic effect is therefore magnified exponentially depending on the length of the delay. Not charging the passengers for the inconvenience amounts to a subsidy and another extension of moral hazard.

However, in 2004 the EU passed Regulation EC 261/2004 which established common rules on how airlines were to compensate passengers in the event of denied boarding, flight cancellation or long delays. The rules were to be implemented in the event of circumstances which were not considered 'extraordinary', i.e. external, unavoidable and unpredictable. Factors which could be considered extraordinary (in the view of the EU (European Union, 2013c)) included war or political instability, acts of terrorism or sabotage, security concerns, damage to an aircraft due to bird strikes, crew or passenger illness, unforeseen technical problems, industrial action and bad weather at the airport of departure, arrival, or on the intended flight route. The amendments to EC 261/2004 to be implemented by 2015 included:

(a) if, for any delay over 12 hours the airline cannot provide another flight, then passengers must be re-routed on a rival carrier (assuming these carriers are not similarly stranded)

(b) passengers must be able to disembark if the aircraft cannot take off in less than five hours

(c) delays of more than one hour require airlines to provide drinking water, air conditioning and lavatories

(d) airlines will be responsible for up to three nights' accommodation if the flight is delayed

(e) passengers must be informed of any delays and provided with an explanation not later than 30 minutes after the scheduled departure time

(f) complaints must be acknowledged within one week and a formal reply sent within two months (European Union, 2014b).

The assistance comprises re-routing and/or refunding and provision of refreshments, communication facilities and accommodation. The compensation cash amounts depend on the length of flight and the route. This Regulation can make some flights economically unsustainable. Under this Regulation, a three-and-a-half-hour delay for a Boeing 737 on a short-haul European flight could require more than £Stg35,000 in passenger compensation – possibly 300% more than the airline received in fares which is 'on top of anything it has to pay for hotels and meals if the delay strands passengers overnight' (Trend, 2014). Inevitably, passengers will have to pay for this Regulation through increased fares, i.e. a little extra on everyone could mean that few passengers would feel the loss. In an application of the precautionary principle (see Chapter 6) the first-mover airline to charge these incremental amounts could create a significant insurance fund or alternatively, such a surcharge on top of other social costs could damage their competitiveness.

All passengers travelling on EU airlines will have their rights protected by the airlines irrespective of the value of their paid fare (European Union, 2013a). The European Court of Justice (ECJ) (another arm of the EU) euphemistically recognised that the compensation claims could have 'substantial negative economic consequences' for the airlines involved. The economic adage of 'you get what you pay for' has been overridden by the social needs of passengers who have demanded regulation to alleviate their discomfort rather than taking personal responsibility through travel insurance. Governments recognised that any such intention would require legislation (in the form of an unfunded mandate) since airlines would not normally have volunteered for something which would involve them in higher costs and lower profits and which would subsidise passengers who might be avoiding taking personal responsibility against risk. The reality is that this Regulation is only for airlines and not for other forms of transport and will particularly affect the low-cost and charter carriers with slimmer margins. MNEs from other industries, which have been instigators and supporters of CSERplus, do not appear to be affected by any equivalent regulations. It will be a significant challenge to accommodate thousands of displaced passengers in hotel rooms accessible to the airport. After major disruption, aircraft are out of place and it often takes many movements to realign them with the timetable. If Heathrow Airport (which processed 73.4m passengers in 2014 (Heathrow Airport, 2014)) was closed for 24 hours (as it has been on occasions) that would mean accommodating almost 600,000 passengers in hotel rooms (assuming that many were available) to be paid by airlines. There is a further knock-on into other subsequent flights resulting in airlines paying compensation for more flights than just the original delayed flight. The Regulation was tested in *Jet2.com v Huzar* (2014) (compensation awarded over a technical fault which caused delay) and *James Dawson v Thomson Airways Limited* (2014) (challenging the six-year limitation period under the Limitation Act 1980 for bringing a case which would have been barred under the Montreal Convention's two-year time limit). Both airlines lost (Williams, 2014). (In the case of *Frederique Jager v easyJet*, adverse weather delayed the previous flight but this was not considered sufficiently 'extraordinary' to account for subsequent flight delays. easyJet had to pay compensation (Smith, 2013).)

In an example of the inequality which marks the relationship of the airline industry with its passengers, airlines would not automatically be compensated by any passengers who caused a delay unless the airline pursued a claim (see Chapter 4). The penalties for aircraft delay are disproportionately severe. No other transport industry is similarly impacted, e.g. if there is a major delay on a motorway, ferry or railway no compensation is paid.

Subsequent case law has led to the ECJ ruling that as of 2015 airlines will bear the social costs for delays if they were caused by ill-defined 'extraordinary circumstances'. The definition of 'extraordinary circumstances' is not complete. In an analogous example, funding for cancer drugs in the UK varies from region to region with each doctor making the case for individual patients. The demand for these expensive drugs is extremely high and the award of treatment depends on successfully complying with pre-determined criteria. Where the patient does not fit the criteria a case has to be made on 'extraordinary circumstances'. However, in a paradox, if the same 'extraordinary circumstances' are used too frequently they are no longer considered 'extraordinary' and therefore become reasons to exclude the patient from treatment. Similarly, technical defects which should have been identified in airline maintenance do not constitute 'extraordinary circumstances' (although the affected airline could argue that such an event was 'extraordinary' for it) and therefore the full compensation and accommodation package would be applied. In any event, sustainable airlines take maintenance seriously and would do their utmost to ensure the safety and comfort of their passengers aware that any compensation would only be passed on to future passengers. This would affect the competitiveness of the carrier. Accommodation has been fixed at maximum three nights for mainstream passengers. However, PRMs and their carers, pregnant women, medical passengers and unaccompanied minors (UMs) will have this extended until they are able to be re-flighted. (NB: some airlines now refuse to carry UMs.) These additional costs have to be paid for by the airlines which will have to find a reimbursement mechanism − most likely a surcharge on every seat sold. These are social costs in the CSERplus mould and are also transfer payments to passengers, i.e. subsidies which undermine the working of markets. The costs are also a social justice issue: those passengers who have not suffered any delay will be subsidising those who will be enriched by compensation.

Although the EU was required to undertake impact analyses, none were prepared before Regulation EC 261/2004 was implemented and socially motivated politicians failed to see that aircraft are not like buses or trains and the next one will not 'appear in 15 minutes'. Politicians have given passengers private rights and passed the accompanying social responsibilities to the airlines. The more social responsibilities off-loaded onto airlines, the more costs will have to be transferred to passengers and the less economically sustainable the carriers will become. This could trigger market inefficiencies or even failure. The legislation skews the economics against airline sustainability. With EC 261/2004 'extraordinary circumstances' the airlines have now become insurers of last resort. Protecting passengers' private rights provided by private airlines' social responsibilities is bad economics and bad law.

It would appear that the closure of European airspace in 2010 when Icelandic volcano Eyjafjallajökull erupted did constitute an 'extraordinary circumstance' under the EC 261/2004 for the purpose of caring − but not compensation (*Denise McDonagh v Ryanair Ltd*) (European Union, 2013b). During the emergency, many airlines compensated and accommodated passengers at an estimated loss of revenue of $US1.7bn (IATA, 2010b). Volcanic ash can block the filters for cabin air and aircraft sensor tubes which provide vital information on air speed, outside air pressure and temperature. Depending on the size and composition of the ash, it can also scratch aircraft surfaces particularly damaging windows and impeding cockpit visibility. ICAO's global aviation guidelines showed awareness of the potential danger of contact with ash clouds but at that time the safe levels of airborne ash had not been determined. European civil aviation authorities closed their respective airspaces as the ash cloud moved across Europe but because of the global nature of aviation, closing European airspace impacted on worldwide flights creating massive disruption. Since this event, new tests have been devised and within six hours aviation officials would now know if such eruptions would pose a danger to aircraft. Furthermore, within 24 hours scientists would use computer-modelling to predict the size, density and movement of the ash.

There is an interesting contrast with how governments treated their citizens during this particular natural disaster compared to the Asian tsunami of 2004 (Abeyratne, 2010). With the closure of European airspace at the time of the eruption, the airlines were swamped with passengers' requests for accommodation and assistance and no help was forthcoming from their various consulates. In contrast, during the Asian tsunami of 2004, embassies and consulates worldwide helped their citizens. Why was there a difference in the way the outcomes of these natural events were treated by governments? Was it because the passengers were so dispersed that they could not be gathered at one particular location (e.g. an airport) where the responsibility could be shouldered by a single body and the media responses accumulated? Could the different management of these two natural events help to further shape the definition of 'extraordinary circumstances' for the EU?

Uninsured passengers

Many passengers cannot obtain, or will not pay for, travel insurance which would repatriate them in comfort following accident or illness abroad. The passenger's optimistic expectation is that because they have a valid booking the airline would repatriate them without the extra cost required to meet their changed circumstances. However, the booking would have been issued in the expectation that they would use the return portion in the same physical and mental condition as they were when they departed. European residents can obtain a European Health Insurance Card (EHIC) for access to State-supplied healthcare in the European Economic Area as one of their EU consumer rights which might not cover all their responsibilities while in a non-UK hospital. Their friends or relations might need to supply food and bed coverings and possibly even minor nursing cover. More discouraging still, is the fact that many travellers do not bother to obtain the EHIC in the belief that nothing will happen to them. They are unaware that they might not be able to afford to remain hospitalised whereupon their cheaper option is to return home by air as quickly as possible. Consequently they present themselves at the airport check-in desk with impediments including plaster-encased limbs and braces supporting injured necks or backs. They will often have 'hard luck' stories as to why they need to be upgraded free of charge in order to access extra legroom to contain their recent disability. It is unfortunate but often these passengers cannot be accommodated in the economy section of the aircraft because of the need to elevate and keep the affected limb(s) straight. (Stiffened legs cannot be placed in the aisle.) The dilemma at the check-in desk (with other passengers watching and possibly recording on camera phones for instant transmission on YouTube) is often left to the Check-in Agent to resolve in the short time left to departure when time is pressing. Frequently passengers do not seem to realise that getting medical approval for flight can take more time than is available between the times of check-in desk opening and aircraft departure. Check-in Agents are often the bearer of bad tidings – and the airline's reputation can be damaged if the visibly disabled passenger decides to share what is perceived as unfair treatment with social media.

Even when a passenger does have comprehensive travel insurance, their policy is rarely charged the additional costs of any medical emergency which resulted in a flight diversion. Airlines have preferred diversion airports; however, if an aircraft diverts into an unfamiliar foreign port, there can be problems with emergency visas, languages and obtaining medical treatment even if the passenger does have suitable medical cover. Depending on where the emergency landing occurs, the number of passengers inconvenienced and the location of the diversion airport the costs can be contained as jettisoned fuel, extra landing fees, refuelling and possibly re-catering. However, costs can escalate from these base items to include overnight accommodation for an aircraft full of passengers and a replacement crew. Additionally, if the diversion runway is too short to allow fully laden take-off of the original aircraft then a second aircraft would have to be despatched and the weight dispersed between the two. Further costs can be incurred transporting crew and passengers between accommodation and aircraft. This could happen to up to 800 passengers (the potential passenger capacity of an Airbus A380 super jumbo) with inconvenience for everyone and costs for the airline. Which party bears the diversion costs? Which party compensates all the other passengers if they are late inbound and miss onward connections, rendezvous or business meetings? Subsidising compassion can prove to be extremely expensive and inconvenient for an economically sustainable airline and its passengers.

Sick, disabled, obese passengers and medical tourists

Economists have an interest in the allocation of resources and subsidies. The increasing volume of ageing, obese and medical passengers and longer flights on bigger planes means that there will be more disabled and sick passengers travelling (see Chapter 4 and Chapter 5). From this passenger group there is the increased likelihood of more on-board medical emergencies (particularly strokes and heart attacks). Sick passengers can come from any of the passenger groups but have a higher preponderance from the elderly, disabled and obese. Medical emergencies are only declared in life-limiting situations and the decision to divert rests with the Captain after discussion with qualified medical professionals either via communications with ground control or any doctor who happens to be on board. Cabin crew are trained to use the comprehensive aircraft medical kits and defibrillators (where carried). These are capital expenses which are justified on social and economic grounds. Saving lives and reducing the frequency and cost of diversions (including the aircraft delay and knock-on into the timetable) is a win-win for passengers and airline. The capital and maintenance cost of the life-saving equipment (including replacing date-expired drugs and staff update training) might be socially and economically justified if a diversion is avoided. Further medical safety is provided through a ground link to a medical organisation which provides the aircraft with medical advice (29,903 inflight cases in 2014 (MedAire, 2014)). Passengers who are doctors usually respond to calls for assistance and expect no reward (the Good Samaritan principle). However, one trans-Atlantic carrier tells of the American physician who was asked to assist with a passenger having a heart attack. The physician reluctantly answered the call and queried which party would shoulder any liability if his attempts were unsuccessful because his professional insurance would be activated by treating the patient. Happily, the passenger survived to the diversion airport. On disembarking the physician accepted a bottle of exceptionally fine champagne and one week later sent the carrier an invoice for four hours' consultation.

From time to time lawyers acting for sick or deceased passengers require airlines to document the care delivered as a prelude to litigation. In another incident, a suicidal passenger locked himself in a lavatory pod and slashed his groin artery. He bled to death before the crew realised what had happened. His widow, seeking damages, subsequently attempted to blame the airline for failure to assure his safety. In contrast, the widow was neither asked to compensate the traumatised crew nor reimburse the airline for costs incurred when the aircraft was delayed returning to service.

Where airport facilities fail, airlines have to support their passengers by substituting airport facilities with airline manpower and equipment, i.e. subsidising the airport. In addition to providing passenger support, airlines need to rent airport space to accommodate the supplementary staff and equipment required (e.g. PRM mobility buggies – see Chapter 5). As an example, if there is no moving pavement to take slow-walking passengers to the departure gate, the airline has to supply some form of auxiliary mobility – a manually powered wheelchair or a manned motorised buggy both of which need Mobility Assistants to operate them. This can also involve extra time because the route to the gate for the larger motorised buggy is often not straightforward and might require avoiding crowded areas or using an industrial access route.

Airlines further subsidise entitled and unentitled, self-declared PRMs by transporting their personal mobility scooters and medical equipment free of charge (see Chapter 5). Because this is an unfunded mandated requirement, the manufacturers of these devices have no incentive to reduce either the weight or dimensions of their products all of which require a subsidy from the airline.

Pregnant passengers

Births on board are unusual and when they occur they can create major inflight service disruption while crew attend to the labour (see Chapter 4). Mothers-to-be should not fly after 28 weeks and then only with a doctor's letter confirming a healthy pregnancy. However, the growth of low-cost international travel has created a (formerly missing) market for mothers who wish to have their babies free of charge on the UK NHS. This encourages some mothers to travel late into their pregnancy.

> Hundreds of pregnant foreigners are flying to Britain just days before they give birth to receive free care on the NHS. A government report found that Immigration officials at one airport stopped more than 300 such mothers-to-be over two years. Most of these women had to be admitted and allowed to give birth on the NHS. . . because their pregnancies were too advanced for them to fly home. . . . The problem of 'maternity tourism' has become so acute that staff at Guy's and St Thomas' NHS Trust in London refer to the flow of West African women flying in to give birth as the 'Lagos Shuttle'.
>
> (Gilligan, 2013)

In 2011 in a much-publicised case, one Nigerian woman travelled to the UK to have quintuplets at the expense of the NHS and the reopening of Southend Airport in the UK in 2012 'brought a rush of maternity patients from Portugal' (*The Economist*, 2013). So in addition to births on board, with the possibility of a costly aircraft diversion, airlines have to underwrite the risks and accept the responsibilities for some heavily pregnant women many of whom require subsidised complimentary services such as wheelchair transport to and from the aircraft.

Dead passengers

Deaths on board are a difficult economic and compassionate issue for crew to manage in full view of other cabin occupants and each situation is handled individually (O'Neill, 2014). After an unsuccessful attempt to keep the passenger alive (observed by surrounding passengers who would undoubtedly be upset), the issue of corpse concealment needs to be handled with discretion which is often challenging for the crew working in finite and confined spaces. Options include carrying the shrouded corpse through the cabin to a suitable locker (where rigor mortis might make its later extraction very difficult delaying return of the aircraft into service) or leaving the body in its allocated seat. If the aircraft was full another passenger (such as a staff passenger travelling on a discounted fare) might have to sit next to the deceased until landing. The drama can be escalated if there are shocked, distressed and noisily grieving friends or relatives of the deceased on board. Aircraft diversion after a death would not be a preferred option because of the difficulties of getting the body to burial destination at a later date. In addition, some airport authorities could impound the aircraft as a 'crime scene'. This would delay returning the aircraft to the air and involve the airline in considerable costs none of which are known to have been charged to the deceased passenger's estate. Any loss of the deceased's bodily fluids would require seat replacement (if possible during aircraft turnaround to avoid reducing the number of seats available on the next flight). In any event, these human stories could require internal paperwork, possibly legal documentation, appearance at a Coroner's Court and potential litigation – all of which involves the economically sustainable airline in hidden costs subsidised by the shareholders.

Disruptions and Acts of God

Many airlines have often subsidised the social costs of disruption including the increased costs of compensating passengers and making alternative travel arrangements. Unless passengers pay an additional insurance premium, they are not automatically insured for Acts of God (e.g. floods, tsunamis, volcanic eruptions) which could disrupt their travels. In times past, travellers used to rely on the goodwill of responsible airlines in the event of such disasters and the full-service carriers were generally supportive. However, lower-cost and unscheduled carriers, with thinner margins and increasing passenger numbers, were often less willing to support passengers during disruptions.

In times of major disruption, premium passengers (segregated and hassle-free) on full-service carriers often have access to airline lounges with all facilities. However, non-premium passengers without these facilities would be accommodated with other delayed passengers in what can be overcrowded, cramped and sometimes unsanitary conditions sleeping on airports' floors. Tempers have often erupted in these circumstances threatening the security of the airport. Airline employees are often powerless to do anything to alleviate passengers' distress unless they can offer food and sleeping facilities at the airlines' expense (i.e. subsidising passengers).

UK NHS

Airlines subsidise the UK's free-at-point-of-use NHS in two ways. Firstly, in order to reduce the NHS waiting lists, the organisation pays for sick or disabled people to travel to other countries for their surgical procedures (see Chapter 5). This is fuelling a growing outbound medical tourism industry which is facilitated by the airlines both on the ground and in the air. This can involve the airlines in significant costs. Secondly, many UK passengers expect the same welfare provisions from an airline that they receive from other nationalised services particularly the NHS which supplies medical oxygen. In the past, airlines would charge for the provision of medical oxygen and many passengers objected to having to pay for something they believed they were entitled to receive free (as many do from the NHS). As a result the EU delivered an unfunded and uncosted mandate (Regulation EC 1107/2006) (see Chapter 5) to facilitate PRM travel and then, in an amendment to Regulation EC 261/2004 (flight delay compensation regulation) included the requirement that 'the service providers should ensure that persons with reduced mobility and people with disabilities have the right, at all times, to use safety-approved respiratory devices on aircraft, free of charge' (European Union, 2014b).

Government security measures and revenue collection

Airline Check-in Agents are responsible for checking passengers' passports and deciding whether or not they are valid travel documents. If the passengers are permitted to embark but the destination decides the documents were incorrect, the airline is liable to a fine (see Chapter 4). In the UK, the government has reduced the numbers of immigration and emigration border police so the airlines have had to assume the risk and responsibility for much of the migration documentation. Airlines also act as tax collectors for government taxes and charges. In acting in these regulatory capacities private airlines are supplying a public benefit and subsidising governments.

Airport duty-free shopping concessions

Airport charges to airlines can be calculated on the basis of dual till (where only aeronautical charges are considered) or single till (where aeronautical and commercial revenues are both used to determine prices). The single till acknowledges that the airlines are the providers of the shoppers who enable the development of commercial revenues at airports (IATA, 2007) – however, it does not acknowledge that passengers' shopping is flown free of charges for fuel and emissions (see Chapter 6).

Items sold airside at the duty-free shops generate non-aeronautical revenues for the airport. Every item irrespective of size or weight is intended for free carriage accompanying a passenger aboard an aircraft – and weight has financial costs in both energy consumed and in the payment for negative externalities of emissions expended. It can therefore be argued that airport revenue is achieved at the expense of sustainable airlines' costs. This amounts to a subsidy for the airport and the shops it contains.

Aircraft cabins have a finite amount of space and duty-free purchases can delay boardings since the passengers need time to stow their extra purchases. Passengers can purchase unlimited quantities of shopping once they are airside although it might take them over their allocated hand baggage and duty-free allowances. Items available in duty-free shops have included large (space-hungry) stuffed toys (some almost the size of a small child), boxes of multiple bottles of wine, jeroboams of champagne, heavyweight bronze or fragile plaster statues, sizeable electronic printers and large books. Some routes favour certain purchases (e.g. duty-free liquor to Scandinavia or designer clothing to Japan). In the event that there is insufficient cabin space available, there is often no safe way to send these airside purchases (including fragile items) down to the aircrafts' cargo holds. Sometimes it is not one large or heavy item which is a challenge to squeeze into an overhead locker, but the accumulation of many small dense packages, e.g. one 750ml bottle of wine weighs 1.2kg. In addition, airport offerings often compete with the airlines' on-board shopping goods, the competitive price of which has to include the cost of airborne carriage.

For many airports, concession goods sold airside are the main source of income (Graham, 2009) so the airlines' role in transporting them is critical to the economic sustainability of airport shops. For flight planning and loading purposes, airlines use weight limits which are decided by size of aircraft and sometimes by national regulation. The EU recommends that for aircraft with more than 30 seats, male passengers are assumed to have a 'standard mass' of 94kg and females 75kg – both with 17kg of luggage. On a male/female ratio of 70/30 this averages adult passengers at 88kg plus 17kg of luggage and duty-free purchases (Berdowski *et al.*, 2009). There are variations between summer and winter weights when passengers have heavier garments. If any purchases transacted in the airport could be considered additional weight, airlines could charge for them – or at the very least threaten the airports that they would charge. Depending on the number of passengers per aircraft and the airlines' baggage charging tariffs, this cost will vary: some airlines have a fixed fee per bag; others charge as a percentage of one of the fares. Some flights will have more duty-free purchases than others encumbering these carriers with extra costs and negative externalities. The value of saving 1kg per aircraft is illustrated by Air Canada (2013) which assessed that cutting this weight saved 24,500 litres of fuel annually (approximately $US20,000 at 2013 prices) with a reduction of 63 fewer tonnes of emissions. With 500+ passengers on some flights and the possibility that each could be carrying extra kilogrammes of duty-free purchases, the prospect of charging for the transport of airport concession products is an instrument to include in the airlines' airport negotiating toolkits (and also represents a currently unidentified missing market).

Until recently there has been no mechanism for charging for any excess hand baggage at the departure gate but contactless technology has opened many possibilities. However, charging for airside purchases or excess hand baggage would undoubtedly impact on passengers' perceptions of the airline. Premium passengers could feel it was penny-pinching; mid-price passengers could start to compare the full-service carrier with the no-frills carriers; no-frills passengers would probably pay up because they are used to drip-pricing for additional items. Passengers might, however, refuse to shop at the airport at all if they are charged – or they might prefer to purchase on board to avoid the extra costs of paying separately for carriage of purchases. Currently, those passengers who make airport duty-free purchases are subsidising the flying costs of those who do not. Charging for this additional baggage (and the space required to accommodate it) would therefore be a challenge for the airline. Airports argue that sales from duty-free shops keep landing charges down (the single till principle). Economically sustainable airlines argue that what has no price is not valued – and that the unacknowledged, unpriced carriage of duty-free goods is a subsidy which should be calculated in terms of fuel burned as well as the emissions expended (i.e. negative externality). Such subsidies are not sustainable in the long-term.

The no-frills carriers could be the first to open discussions for charging for the carriage of duty-free goods. It would be expected that such an innovation would come from that sector rather than the full-service carriers. Alternatively, airport shopping concessions could offer collection on arrival or freighting to destination

Table 1.6 Rationale for abolishing complimentary carriage of airport concession purchases

---

In favour:

- passengers' increased awareness of fuel costs and negative externality value of carrying weight possibly paving the way for other potential changes, e.g. charging passengers by their own body weight (see Chapter 5)
- airlines could increase revenue with minimal costs
- airlines might find that reduced quantities of duty-free purchases might speed the boarding process
- airlines could recognise abolition as a powerful airline bargaining tool for landlord-tenant negotiations and for discussions with governments if they should consider introducing different air taxes

---

Against:

- passengers would probably baulk at paying additional charges which could undermine their beliefs that airport airside shopping is lower priced than off-airport shops (however, they might purchase from the selection carried on board the aircraft instead)
- retailers might not want to sell at an airport where passengers are gate-charged for their purchases as this could reduce concession sales (the law of supply and demand)
- airport owners would realise that anything which restricted revenues could affect their share price resulting in reduced investment and dividends
- trade bodies (e.g. IATA/ICAO) might see this 'salami slicing' of revenue as unhelpful towards attaining economic sustainability
- competitors would probably wait to see who blinks first. . . .

---

as options instead of hand carriage by the purchasing passenger. Airports could also consider restricting consumer concession offerings to specified sizes, weights and quantities and ensure that the weight, dimensions and emissions expended are entered onto the packaging for every item available at airport shops. By doing so airlines could calculate the weight/fuel/emissions ratios (dependent upon the aircraft used) and charge for the purchases by using contactless payment technology at the departure gate. It would also be incumbent on the airports to provide a safe means to transfer oversized hand baggage (and passengers' wheelchairs) from the terminal gate-room to the aircraft hold (ideally, using a goods lift beside the aircraft) (Table 1.6).

'Subsidies' received by airlines

Airlines also receive subsidies, some of which are not readily identifiable as such.

Aviation fuel, aircraft and fares

'Aviation fuel for commercial flights is not taxed' (HM Treasury, 2011: 10). This harks back to the 1944 Chicago Convention (also known as Convention on International Civil Aviation (CICA)) when aviation was an infant industry. In Article 24 of the Convention it was promised that aircraft would be free of fuel duty.

Aircraft flying to, from or across, the territory of a state shall be admitted temporarily free of duty. Fuel, oil, spare parts, regular equipment and aircraft stores retained on board are also exempt custom duty, inspection fees or similar charges.

(ICAO, n.d.)

In addition, new aircraft, modifications, repair, maintenance, chartering and hire of aircraft are usually free of value-added tax (VAT) (HM Revenue and Customs, 2011). It would set a dangerous precedent for any nation to upset historic agreements; however, the EU is now the negotiating body for air transport in Europe and is unfettered by history. Airlines are conscious of the current concession and are aware of the EU's ultimate intention to tax aviation. Airlines attempt to conserve fuel because as responsible commercial organisations they do care about their effect on the natural environment. However, aircraft are at the mercy of trans-continental flight routes which are not always direct because of weather or warzones, and the need to go-round while waiting for landing permission at airports which are congested for reasons beyond the airlines' control. If that congestion is a result of lack of capacity due to political intervention in the airport planning process then the extra fuel burnt, costs incurred and emissions expended (i.e. a negative externality) are a direct result of government action or inaction – another example of 'politics vs airline economics'.

In Europe passenger airline fares are currently exempt from VAT. However, the UK government acknowledges that APD is an important revenue-raising means which replaces VAT in the airline sector (HM Treasury, 2011) so effectively airlines and their passengers are not receiving a VAT exemption. Adding 'non-VAT' APD affects the price of fares and dents competition for carriers which have to compete with airlines from other nations without the domestic costs which result from legislated social obligations.

Negative social and environmental externalities

Among the 'subsidies' airlines receive are those for negative externalities. These social and environmental airline costs comprise those items which are not included in the actual price of fares or freight. They are also the costs for which there is no market in the sense that no one owns them so therefore they are not available for sale until they are allocated property rights whereupon they are tradeable in a new marketplace. Negative externalities include aircraft congestion at the airport and traffic jams on the roads around the airports; overcrowded public transport to and from the airport; air and lighting pollution emanating from aircraft, airport and ground vehicles; noise endured by local residents under the flight path and the fuel smells emanating from these activities. Where these social costs are considered greater than private costs, governments could apply taxes to bridge the difference (e.g. so-called 'green' taxes) which would be eventually passed on to passengers.

National infrastructure

Infrastructure has to be cost effective and efficient. Nations often provide the public infrastructure goods necessary to enable airports (and therefore airlines) to function. This includes efficient provision of rail, roads, underground transport systems, emergency vehicles and hospitals, and other supports to which the airlines do not usually contribute directly other than through taxation. For non-domiciled carriers, that is often a minimal contribution. In some nations, these facilities are privately owned but the State can control their location through the national planning system. Where these are inadequate they are inefficient which generates costs for society as well as the aviation industry.

Subsidy summary

In summary, airlines implicitly and unacknowledged subsidise many social functions including health industries, government requirements and airport retailers in exchange for subsidies on negative externalities and tax-free fares, fuel and airport access infrastructure (Table 1.7). Other than the amount contributed by UK APD (£Stg3.2bn p.a.) ($US4.6bn or €4.2bn) the values of these subsidies are as yet uncalculated.

Table 1.7 Summary of airline subsidy offset identification

Airlines subsidise:
• health industry in all its disguises
• passengers with additional needs of all types
• government statutory functions
• airport retail concessions
In exchange, airlines receive:
• range of tax-free supplies
• indirect or minimal charges for negative externalities
• airport access infrastructure

So what?

Airlines have a significant role to play in international economic sustainability, in which they need to compete fairly, enjoy freedom to trade and rely on protected property rights rather than having profits confiscated over and above paying the legally required taxes. National, multi-national and supranational governments and their aviation organisations intervene in airline markets, purportedly to improve citizens' welfare. However, because States often rely on advocacy (rather than economic impact analyses or assessments) they could unintentionally trigger market inefficiency or failure. Furthermore, unacknowledged and unheralded, airlines subsidise many industries, organisations and passenger groups as trade-offs for tax-free fuel and other concessions. The airlines have also been charged with social responsibilities to accommodate passengers' rights. Advanced-world carriers (particularly those in Europe) have heavier social costs imposed than many of their international competitors because of boondoggles and unfunded mandates many of which were the outcomes of CSERplus' advocacy. These requirements could eventually reduce the airlines' international competitiveness, investors' returns, employees' rewards and overall national welfare. The CSERplus' advocates and the politicians who support their ideals have presented many challenges to the airlines the consequences of which have been ignored outside of the industry.

Note

1   © Only European Union legislation printed in the paper edition of the Official Journal of the European Union is deemed authentic European Union, http://eur-lex.europa/eu/

References

Abeyratne, R. (2010), Responsibility and liability aspects of the Icelandic volcanic eruption, *Air Space and Law* available from http://aviationdevelopment.org/eng/sites/default/files/2010090701_publication.pdf accessed 9 August 2014

Air Canada (2013), *Air Canada Issues 2013 Corporate Sustainability Report* available from http://www.aircanada.com/en/about/documents/csr_2013_report_en.pdf?r=Friday,%202 9-Aug-14%2011:30:25 accessed 21 September 2014

Amadeus (2013), *Future traveller tribes 2020 – report for the air travel industry* available from http://www.amadeus.com/amadeus/documents/corporate/travellertribes.pdf accessed 26 June 2014

BBC (2004), *Ronald Regan: in his own words* available from http://news.bbc.co.uk/1/hi/world/americas/3780871.stm accessed 10 June 2016

Berdowski, Z., van den Broek-Serlé, F.N., Jetten, J.T., Kawabata, Y., Schoemaker, J.T. and Versteegh, R. (2009), *Survey on standard weights of passengers and baggage: final report* available from https://www.easa.europa.eu/system/files/dfu/Weight%20Survey%20R200 90095%20Final.pdf accessed 10 June 2016

Brandeis, L.D. (n.d.), *Justice Louis D. Brandeis* available from http://www.brandeis.edu/legacy fund/bio.html accessed 29 March 2015

Brugmann, J. and Prahalad, C.K. (2007), Co-creating business's new social compact, *Harvard Business Review*, February 2007, 80–90 available from https://hbr.org/2007/02/cocreating-businesss-new-social-compact accessed 1 January 2015

Caribbean Tourism Organisation (2010), *The impact of air passenger duty and possible alternatives for the Caribbean* available from http://www.onecaribbean.org/content/files/apdcTORE PORTNov92010.pdf accessed 5 July 2014

Civil Aviation Authority (CAA) (2008), *Recent trends in growth of UK air passenger demand* available from http://www.caa.co.uk/docs/589/erg_recent_trends_final_v2.pdf accessed 6 July 2014

Civil Aviation Authority (2014), *UK Airline Financial Tables*, Table 03 Major UK Airlines Profit and Loss Account Summary 2006–2013.pdf available from http://www.caa.co.uk/default.aspx?catid=80&pagetype=88&pageid=13&sglid=13 accessed 2 November 2015

Clarkson, M.B.E. (1995), A stakeholder framework for analysing and evaluating corporate social performance, *Academy of Management Review* 20(1) 92–117 available from http://www.jstor.org/stable/258888?seq=1#page_scan_tab_contents accessed 1 January 2015

Coase, R.H. (1960), The problem of social cost, *Journal of Law and Economics* 3(1) 1–44

Coase, R.H. (1988), *The Firm, the Market and the Law*, Chicago, University of Chicago Press

Committee on Climate Change (2009), *Meeting the UK Aviation target – options for reducing emissions to 2050* available from http://www.theccc.org.uk/publication/meeting-the-uk-aviation-target-options-for-reducing-emissions-to-2050/ accessed 1 January 2015

Comptroller and Auditor General (2001), *Better Regulation: making good use of regulatory impact assessments* available from http://www.nao.org.uk/wp-content/uploads/2001/11/0102 329.pdf accessed 9 September 2015

Drexhage, J. and Murphy, D. (2010), *Sustainable development: from Brundtland to Rio 2012* available from http://www.un.org/wcm/webdav/site/climatechange/shared/gsp/docs/GSP1–6_Background%20on%20Sustainable%20Devt.pdf accessed 21 February 2015

Economist, The (2013), *Free-for-all: doctors fear that health tourism in the NHS is growing* available from http://www.economist.com/news/britain/21578707-doctors-fear-health-tourism-nhs-growing-free-all accessed 10 April 2014

Economist, The (2014), *Planet plutocrat: the countries where politically connected businessmen are likely to prosper* available from http://www.economist.com/news/international/21599041-countries-where-politically-connected-businessmen-are-most-likely-prosper-planet accessed 20 May 2015

Economist, The (2015), *Airline subsidies in the Gulf: feeling the heat* available from http://www.economist.com/blogs/gulliver/2015/03/airline-subsidies-gulf accessed 2 September 2015

Elliott, J. (2014), *India: after 30 years, Bhopal is still simmering* available from http://www.newsweek.com/india-after-30-years-bhopal-still-simmering-288144 accessed 15 February 2015

European Union (2006), *Rights of people with reduced mobility in air transport* available from http://eur-lex.europa.eu/legal-content/EN/TXT/?qid=1427635031374&uri=URISERV:l24132 accessed 29 March 2015

European Union (2013a), *Air Passenger Rights* available from http://europa.eu/youreurope/citizens/travel/passenger-rights/air/index_en.htm accessed 28 June 2014

European Union (2013b), *Denise McDonagh vs Ryanair Ltd* available from http://eur-lex.europa.eu/LexUriServ/LexUriServ.do?uri=CELEX:62011CJ0012:EN:HTML accessed 29 March 2015

European Union (2013c), *Draft list of extraordinary circumstances following the National Enforcement Bodies (NEB) meeting held on 12 April 2013* available from http://ec.europa.eu/transport/themes/passengers/air/doc/neb-extraordinary-circumstances-list.pdf accessed 7 December 2014

European Union (2014a), *Impact Assessment* available from http://ec.europa.eu/smart-regulation/impact/inded_en.htm accessed 10 March 2015

European Union (2014b), *Compensation and assistance to passengers in the event of denied boarding and of cancellation or long delay of flights* available from http://www.europarl.europa.eu/sides/getDoc.do?pubRef=-//EP//TEXT+TA+P7-TA-2014-0092+0+DOC+XML+V0//EN accessed 4 July 2014

Fenton, S. (2015), *Spanish 'ghost airport' that cost €1bn to build sells at auction for €10,000* available from http://www.independent.co.uk/news/world/europe/spanish-ghost-airport-that-cost-1bn-to-build-sells-at-auction-for-10000-10399433.html accessed 7 September 2015

Gilligan, A. (2013), *The 300 'maternity tourists' – women cheating their way into UK to give birth for free* available from http://www.telegraph.co.uk/news/uknews/immigration/1054 0881/The-300-maternity-tourists.html accessed 7 September 2014

Gordon, S. (2010), *Ryanair confirms it WILL bring in charges for on-board toilets* available from http://www.dailymail.co.uk/travel/article-1263905/Ryanair-toilet-charges-phased-in.html accessed 11 February 2012

Graham, A. (2009), How important are commercial revenues to today's airports? *Journal of Air Transport Management* 15(3) 106–111 available from http://www.sciencedirect.com/science/article/pii/S096969970800152X accessed 2 January 2015

Gregory, M. (1993), *Battle of the Airlines: How the dirty tricks campaign was run* available from http://www.independent.co.uk/news/uk/battle-of-the-airlines-how-the-dirty-tricks-campaign-was-run-martyn-gregory-reports-on-bas-dirty-tricks-campaign-which-he-uncovered-as-producerdirector-of-thames-televisions-this-week-programme-1478010.html accessed 28 June 2014

Haberman, C. (1986), *Protests resume at Japan airport* available from http://www.nytimes.com/1986/10/27/world/protests-resume-at-japan-airport.html accessed 26 August 2014

Heathrow Airport plc (2014), *Facts and figures* available from http://www.heathrowairport.com/about-us/company-news-and-information/company-information/facts-and-figures accessed 31 August 2014

Henderson, D. (2001), *Misguided virtue: false notions of corporate responsibility*, The Institute of Economic Affairs available from http://www.iea.org.uk/publications/research/misguided-virtue-false-notions-of-corporate-social-responsibility accessed 7 October 2014

Henderson, D. (2002), *The debate on CSR: remarks made at the launch of Walking the Talk: The business case for sustainable development by Charles O. Holliday Jr., Stephan Schmidheiny and Philip Watts: 6 November 2002* (source: Henderson's personal notes)

Henderson, D. (2004), *The Role of Business in the Modern World Progress, Pressures and Prospects for the Market Economy*, The Institute of Economic Affairs available from file:///C:/Users/D/Contacts/Documents/RESPONSIBLE%20AIRLINE/Henderson%20-%20Role%20of%20Business%20in%20Modern%20World.pdf accessed 29 May 2015

Henderson, D. (2009), *Misguided corporate virtue: the case against CSR and the true role of business today*, Economic Affairs 29(4) 11–15 available from http://onlinelibrary.wiley.com/doi/10.1111/j.1468-0270.2009.01941.x/full accessed 9 March 2015

Hershey, R. (2010), *Alfred E. Khan does at 93: prime mover of airline deregulation* available from http://www.nytimes.com/2010/12/29/business/29kahn accessed 29 March 2015

HM Revenue and Customs (2011), *VAT notice 744C: ships, aircraft and associated services* available from https://www.gov.uk/government/publications/vat-notice-744c-ships-aircraft-and-associated-services/vat-notice-744c-ships-aircraft-and-associated-services#aircraft-and-qualifying-aircraft accessed 12 April 2015

HM Revenue and Customs (2014), *Air Passenger Duty* available from http://customs.hmrc.gov.uk/channelsPortalWebApp/channelsPortalWebApp.portal?_nfpb=true&_pageabel=pageExcise_ShowContent&id=HMCE_CL_000505&propertyType=document accessed 31 August 2014

HM Treasury (2011), *Reform of Air Passenger Duty Response to Consultation* available from http://www.ukaccs.info/apdconsultresponse.pdf accessed 1 January 2015

Ideaworks (2014), *Global examples of ancillary revenue* available from http://www.ideaworkscompany.com/july-16-2014-press-release/press-release-89-graphic accessed 31 July 2014

Income Data Services (IDS) (2014), *FTSE 100 directors' total earnings jump by 21% in a year* available from http://www.incomesdata.co.uk/wp-content/uploads/2014/10/IDS-FTSE-100-directors-pay-20141.pdf accessed 25 October 2014

International Air Transport Association (IATA) (2007), *Economic Regulation: the case for independent economic regulation of airports and air navigation service providers, IATA economics briefing No 6* available from https://www.iata.org/whatwedo/Documents/economics/EconomicRegulation_web.pdf accessed 10 June 2016

IATA (2008), *Air Travel Demand, IATA economics briefing No 9* available from http://www. iata.org/publications/economics/Documents/air-travel-demand-summary.pdf accessed 24 June 2014

IATA (2010a), *Economic briefing: airline fuel and labour cost share* available from https:// www.iata.org/whatwedo/Documents/economics/Airline_Labour_Cost_Share_Feb2010. pdf accessed 10 January 2015

IATA (2010b), *IATA Economic Briefing May 2010: The impact of Eyjafjallajökull's volcanic ash plume* available from http://www.iata.org/whatwedo/Documents/economics/Volcanic-Ash-Plume-May2010.pdf accessed 4 July 2014

IATA (2012), *Aviation – benefits beyond borders* available from http://www.iata.org/policy/ Pages/benefits.aspx accessed 25 June 2014

IATA (2013a), *Airlines Expect 31% Rise in Passenger Demand by 2017 Press Release No.: 67* (10 December 2013) available from http://www.iata.org/pressroom/pr/Pages/2013-12-10-01.aspx accessed 18 June 2014

IATA (2013b), *Profitability and the air transport value chain, IATA economics briefing No 10* available from http://www.iata.org/whatwedo/Documents/economics/profitability-and-the-air-transport-value%20chain.pdf accessed 1 April 2014

International Civil Aviation Organisation (ICAO) (n.d.), *Convention on International Civil Aviation – Doc 7300* available from http://www.icao.int/publications/Documents/ 7300_orig.pdf accessed 31 August 2014

Jensen, M.C. (2001), Value maximisation, stakeholder theory and the corporate objective function, *European Financial Management*, 7(3) 297–317

Kay, J. and Vickers, J. (2015), *Thirty years of economic policy*, in Wyplosz, C. (ed.), Oxford, Oxford University Press

Kitching, C. (2015), *Upgraded to a 'private' jet! British holidaymaker has ENTIRE Boeing 737 to himself after other passengers failed to show up* available from http://www.dailymail. co.uk/travel/travel_news/article-3202275/British-holidaymaker-ENTIRE-Boeing-737-passengers-failed-addressed-announcements-crew.html accessed 22 August 2015

Lufthansa (2014), *Balance: key data on sustainability with the Lufthansa group* available from http://www.lufthansagroup.com/fileadmin/downloads/en/LH-sustainability-report-2014.pdf accessed 24 February 2015

McCabe, S. (2009), Who needs a holiday? Evaluating social tourism, *Annals of Tourism Research* 36(4) 667–688 available from http://www.sciencedirect.com/science/article/ pii/S0160738309000851 accessed 1 January 2015

MedAire (2014), *Company information* available from http://www.medaire.com/about/ company-information accessed 29 March 2015

Morgan, T. (2011), *Thinking the unthinkable: might there be no way out for Britain? Project Armageddon – the final report* available from http://www.tullettprebon.com/Documents/ strategyinsights/Tim_Morgan_Report_007.pdf accessed 24 March 2013

Morrell, P. (2013), *Airline finance*, 4th edition, Farnham, Ashgate

O'Neill, E. (2014), *What happens when an airplane passenger dies mid-flight? It depends . . .* available from http://www.nj.com/news/index.ssf/2014/12/how_airlines_respond_ when_passengers_dies_onboard.html accessed 1 January 2014

Oxford Economics (2013), *Shaping the Future of Travel: Macro trends driving industry growth over the next decade* available from http://www.amadeus.com/documents/Thought-leadership-reports/Amadeus-Shaping-the-Future-of-Travel-MacroTrends-Report.pdf accessed 1 July 2014

Puller, S. and Taylor, L. (2012), Price discrimination by day-of-week of purchase: Evidence from the US airline industry, *Journal of Economic Behavior & Organisation* 84(3) 801–812 available from http://www.sciencedirect.com/science/article/pii/S016726811200203X accessed 1 January 2015

PwC (2013), *The economic impact of air passenger duty* available from http://corporate.easyjet.com/~/media/Files/E/Easyjet-Plc-V2/pdf/content/APD-study-Abridged.pdf accessed 31 August 2014

Sanandaji, T. and Sanandaji, N. (2014), *Super-entrepreneurs and how your country can get them*, Centre for Policy Studies available from http://www.cps.org.uk/files/reports/original/140429115046-superentrepreneursandhowyourcountrycangetthemupdate.pdf accessed 14 December 2014

Smith, O. (2013), *Air passenger compensated for weather delay* available from http://www.telegraph.co.uk/travel/travelnews/10320318/Air-passenger-compensated-for-weather-delay.html accessed 7 December 2014

Sternberg, E. (2009), *Corporate social responsibility and corporate governance*, The Institute of Economic Affairs, Blackwell, Oxford available from http://www.iea.org.uk/sites/default/files/publications/files/upldeconomicAffairs342pdfSummary.pdf accessed 30 October 2014

Trend, N. (2014), *Why court's flight delay ruling could cost you money* available from http://www.telegraph.co.uk/travel/travel-advice/10898171/Why-courts-flight-delay-ruling-could-cost-you-money.html accessed 6 August 2014

Tretheway, M. and Andriulaitis, R. (2015), *What do we mean by a level playing field in international aviation?* International Transport Forum Discussion Paper No. 2015–06 available from http://www.econstor.eu/handle/10419/109181 accessed 21 November 2015

United Nations World Commission on Environment and Development (UNWCED) (1987), *Our common future* available from http://www.un-documents.net/our-common-future.pdf accessed 13 August 2013

United States Department of Transportation (2015), *Net income (in thousands of dollars $000) – all airlines, all regions* available from http://www.transtats.bts.gov/Data_Elements_Financial.aspx?Data=6 accessed 1 November 2015

VC Insight (2008), *TNT with over 100 sites uses talk and vision managed video conferencing service* available from http://www.vcinsight.com/managed-conferencing-services-case-studies/312/tnt-with-over-sites-uses-talk-and-vision-managed-videoconferencing-service-increasing-useage-by-a-month-initially/ accessed 26 October 2014

Veljanovski, C. (2006), *The economics of law*, The Institute of Economic Affairs available from http://www.iea.org.uk/sites/default/files/publications/files/upldbook391pdf.pdf accessed 1 January 2015

Williams, R. (2014), *Turbulent summer in the courts for airlines*, Chartered Institute of Logistics and Transport, Focus, December 2014 available from http://edc-connection.ebscohost.com/c/articles/99747469/turbulent-summer-courts-airlines accessed 29 March 2015

World Bank, The (2015), *Labour tax and contributions as % of commercial profit* available from http://data.worldbank.org/indicator/IC.TAX.LABR.CP.ZS accessed 11 December 2105

World Business Council for Sustainable Development (WBCSD) (2000), *Corporate social responsibility: making good business sense*, Geneva, Switzerland available from http://www.wbcsd.org/Pages/EDocument/EDocumentDetails.aspx?ID=83&NoSearchContextKey=true accessed 21 February 2015

World Economic Forum (WEF) (2013), *The Travel and Tourism Competitiveness Report, 2013* available from http://www3.weforum.org/docs/WEF_TT_Competitiveness_Report_2013.pdf accessed 27 March 2013

WEF (2014), *Global risks 2014 – 9th edition* available from http://www3.weforum.org/docs/WEF_GlobalRisks_Report_2014.pdf accessed 6 August 2014

Part II
Society

The second of the three intertwined dimensions of airline economic sustainability is **society**, concerning the people with whom airlines interact.

Chapter 2: Society, social responsibility and airline economics examines the context of airlines' interactions with stakeholders and the challenges they present, the use of outsourcing to reduce costs, the trade-offs between manpower and ITC and the impacts of risk management on security and safety. It also examines the social impact of some of the indicators of alleged market inefficiencies or failures – missing markets, externalities, inequalities and free riders. As the industry changes, so too will the roles of the front line employees, with more ITC taking on routine processing and allowing customer service employees to become 'Strategic Corporals' named after soldiers whose roles have changed to simultaneously require them to fight, keep the peace and deliver aid (Krulak, 1999). However, in times of crisis, cost-reducing ITC is often an inadequate substitute for manpower when customers need placating.

Chapter 3: Inside economically sustainable airlines investigates the culture of successful airlines and the need for, and value of, fairness. Airlines and their employees need the pivot of core values for hiring, firing, performance management, succession planning, training and reward. The culture must also allow innovation and creativity to drive competitiveness and to permit challenge as a risk protection measure. A challenge culture is important because it allows dissent and gives employee outliers the opportunity to contribute to problem finding and solutions through divergent thinking. Airlines must be sufficiently flexible and adaptable to enable them to engage with external commercial environments and markets – any of which can be affected by some of the indicators of alleged market inefficiencies or failures, e.g. externalities, principal-agents, inequalities and moral hazards. Philanthropy, if affordable, can involve a significant dispersal of shareholders' funds and/or employees' rewards which might be allocated for management's personal egoism rather than corporate altruism (the intrinsic motivating 'feel good' factor). Moreover, the much-hyped influence of paid celebrity advocates might not necessarily deliver increased seat or freight sales.

Chapter 4: Passenger challenges recognises that although passengers are not homogeneous, they all have the common demand for safety and security when travelling with a responsible airline. Two of the indicators of alleged market inefficiency or failure prevail: filling formerly missing markets and providing free rides for unqualified passengers. Outlier passengers (who do not fit into the mainstream cohort) present many challenges for airlines. They include unaccompanied minors (UMs), abandoned elderly travellers, deviants, stowaways, uncontrolled children as well as dietary restricted, drunk or drugged travellers. Many passengers do not take care of their personal risks and avoid purchasing travel insurance, anticipating that the airlines would supplement their miserliness in the event of illness or accident. This establishes a moral hazard (another trigger for market inefficiency). Airlines also have to make uncomfortable and sometimes expensive decisions when choosing whose baggage must be left behind if the flight is full. Baggage reunification is expensive and the inconvenience caused could impact on the airline's reputation.

Chapter 5: Travelling timebomb uses an economic lens to examine the politically sensitive topic of carrying medically incapacitated, obese, elderly and genuine or self-declared disabled passengers. Airlines are believed to make losses on many of these passengers because of boondoggles and unfunded mandates for which neither preliminary economic analyses nor post-implementation impact assessments were ever conducted. Furthermore, many of the passengers' rights become the airlines' responsibilities and ultimately infringe on airline employees' rights. Timebomb challenges also result from zero additional charges for passengers with excess body weights but surcharging underweight passengers with overweight luggage. These and other outlier challenges provide many tests for fairness of flexibly defined 'social justice'.

2 Society, social responsibility and airline economics

2.1 CSER IN CONTEXT

Challenges

Airlines walk a tightrope strung between being perceived by society as 'mean and hard' (i.e. economically focussed) or by economists as 'soft' (i.e. too compassionately focussed). Governments favour airlines taking the latter compassionate approach since it absorbs some of the nation's social responsibilities and costs; but economically viable airlines need to consider commercial pressures. To be perceived as too 'hard' could frighten customers, suppliers and governments which authorise the 'licence to operate'; to be seen as too 'soft' could frighten investors. Maintaining economic and social sustainability requires airlines to make honest profits by considering as many of the internal and external stakeholders as possible without alienating those who feel aggrieved by its decisions (see Chapter 7).

As 'people' businesses, airlines need to deliver high-value customer service, reliable engineering and 100% safety and security. Their reputations and financial sustainability depend on it. Furthermore, the 'customer promise' must be delivered consistently irrespective of the cabin in which the passenger is seated. This means high performance and high productivity from a competitive cost-base in order to access profitable growth opportunities. These activities must be delivered at home and abroad against a background of volatile economic environments, changing legislation (ranging from human rights, environment, safety and security through to competition, mergers and taxation) and multiple stakeholders with conflicting economic, social and environmental needs. Unlike other businesses with production bases abroad, international airlines are often merely visitors – touchdown, take-off – and any delay to their visit would undermine the profitability of the flights.

Defining social responsibility depends on the definer's viewpoint. The airline industry would argue that it is socially responsible because its commercial interests are enhanced if it provides affordable fares, nurtures and protects passengers and employees and maintains its assets hygienically, safely and securely. However, some special interest groups or individuals would deny that airlines were socially responsible. Their reasons include any dissatisfaction caused through the price of fares, inadequate customer service, lost luggage, delayed flights, allergy-causing

foodstuffs or even insomnia because of late-night flights over airport neighbourhoods. In democracies, societies set social norms and legislators use these as
the basis for legislation. However, the lawmakers are often swayed by NGOs or
lobby groups which claim to speak for society as a whole without having declared
their allegiances (Snowdon, 2014). This is contrary to the spirit of openness and
transparency which legislators urge all industries (including airlines) to follow.

Stakeholders

Economist Friedman believed that businesses should be managed for the benefit
of shareholders who as entrepreneurs risked capital in return for dividends and that
only people – not businesses – can have responsibilities. He derided the discussions
of corporate 'social responsibilities' for their analytical looseness and lack of rigour
believing that 'the social responsibility of business is to increase profits' (Friedman,
2007: 173) which can be invested, taxed and create further employment opportunities. In contrast, and in accordance with the CSERplus view of the corporation
having wider social responsibilities, the alternative view is that:

> the economic and social purpose of the corporation is to create and distribute
> increased wealth and value to all its primary stakeholder groups without favour-
> ing one group at the expense of others . . . Resolving conflicting interests
> fairly requires ethical judgement and choices.
>
> (Clarkson, 1995: 112)

Equality in the broad range of stakeholders as previously defined is not a realistic
economic concept because (among other reasons) stakeholders without a financial
interest in the outcome of an organisation are unequal to those who have their
livelihoods in jeopardy. Focus on the employees will make the airline more
economically sustainable than focussing on any other aspect of the organisation
(see Chapter 3). Shareholders accept risks in exchange for influence over key
decisions since (unlike financial institutions that lend on enforceable contract
terms) they have no contractual right either to receive a dividend or to have their
risk capital returned. Their trust in the management is therefore absolute because
very few of the often vast numbers of smaller shareholders actually exercise their
democratic rights to vote at the annual general meetings (AGMs) (an extension of
the free rider problem mentioned in Chapter 1).

Primary and secondary stakeholders, irrespective of how defined (Table 2.1) –
the investors, employees, customers, governments, lobby groups, suppliers
(including bankers, lawyers, air navigation coordinators and airports) and a plethora
of interested bodies with whom the airline interacts – are rewarded or compensated
(or maybe even ignored) with whatever response is commensurate and appropriate
to their level of accepted risk.

A stakeholder analysis (see Chapter 7) would identify and expose pockets of
internal and external support and resistance and determine legitimacy, urgency and
power (expertise and control) in order to assess the risks posed by various groups.

Table 2.1 Some of the stakeholders of airline economic sustainability

Airline stakeholders include:

shareholders (e.g. individuals, pension funds, charities, sovereign wealth funds)	politicians (e.g. local, national, international)	statutory representatives (e.g. health and safety, local authorities, planning)
employees (past, present, future; outsourced; insourced)	government bodies (Customs, Immigration/ Emigration, Security, Taxation)	administrators (e.g. share registrars, trade bodies, civil aviation)
passengers (e.g. single travellers, families, business, leisure, groups, PRMs, assistance animals, complainants and special needs passengers including diet-specific, religious, UMs and PRMs)	suppliers both insourced and outsourced (e.g. water, aircraft, catering, ground support, engines, facilities management, fuel, specialist security services, risk managers, insurers, bankers)	public transport providers (e.g. local bus, long distance coaches, ferries, overground and underground trains)
other customers (including freight forwarders, exporters)	emergency services (e.g. fire, ambulance, hospitals, police, anti-terrorism support)	criminals (saboteurs, fraudsters, bid-riggers, over-billers, over-payers), illegal migrants (both in the cabin and in the aircraft wheel housing), people traffickers
landlords (e.g. local, national and international; airports, shops, storage, office accommodation, hangars)	advocacy groups (e.g. NGOs, political, government, trades unions, human rights, animal rights etc.)	competitors (other airlines and cruise liners plus ground transport where applicable and tele-presence providers)
trades unions (engineers, pilots, ground staff, cabin crew, suppliers)	press/media/web commentators	animals (can be viewed as live stakeholders as they have very specific requirements and they will have spokespersons lobbying on their behalf, service animals, family pets, zoological exhibits
neighbours (e.g. local residents, schools, councils)	celebrities and Very Important Passengers (VIPs)	service animal representative organisations

Knowing the stakeholders is fundamental to understanding the complex commercial backdrop against which an airline operates. Shareholders are important but in this age of CSERplus capitalism (see Chapter 1), it is now in the airlines' interests that the broader groupings of stakeholders are acknowledged because of their potential to disrupt operations and demand legislation which, instead of supporting markets, is often focussed on smoothing many of society's inequalities.

Stakeholders often form themselves into formal and informal groups representing the interests of society and environment (rarely economics). Formal airline groups can support and protect the industry or they can disrupt either tactically (e.g. protests outside the airport) or strategically (e.g. taking the long-term view and preventing major airport developments). Formal groups with a social focus include the trades unions which protect their airline employee members and the International Air Passenger Association (IAPA) which supports passengers. IAPA provides travelling information including hotels, insurances and a forum for discussion on passenger issues which can enhance or damage an airline's reputation. Formal groups with an economic focus – but which also consider society and the environment – include the airports' ICAO and the airlines' IATA. Informal groups tend to be single-issue focussed on either social issues or environmental factors (rarely economics) and not an integrated combination of the three. The informal groups arise as needs dictate. Employees can form groups to discuss workplace issues; disability groups can focus on access issues; neighbours can focus on airport expansion and charities can focus on social or environmental issues. At some stage these groups might evolve into formally constituted groups with bank accounts, sophisticated communications networks and powerful friends in governments. The IATA (2013) sustainability stance acknowledges that the industry has to negotiate difficult choices and concessions among all its stakeholders.

Employees as stakeholders

Because employees are such significant stakeholders, they are the focus of Chapter 3.

Passengers as stakeholders

Passengers fly for a multitude of reasons, including visiting friends and relations (VFR), business, leisure, study, sport, shopping, joining cruise ships, medical treatment, marriage, holidays and legally assisted suicide. Passengers can categorise flying as luxury (e.g. holidays, VFR) or necessity (e.g. business, medical). Passengers are customers and they come in all shapes, sizes, colours and weights; they speak many different languages and have different fears and aspirations; some are excited, some are tearful, many are afraid and others are disabled by the unfamiliar airport noises and processes. Some will have run out of money – not just to pay for excess luggage but to purchase food while waiting to board their aircraft. Lack of nourishment could make them irritable, and doubly so if they are fuelled by alcohol or drugs. Every take-off has passengers with hope, excitement, despair, anger, exasperation or expectation of what the airline could do to meet their needs at what are often significant portions of their budgets of time and money.

Passengers can fly from small point-to-point airports or large, complicated hub-and-spoke airports. They can choose whether to fly on full-service, low-cost or charter carriers and be direct or transfer with a transit at an intermediate point. Transits can be of considerable duration or merely a matter of hours to 'stretch the legs', change aircraft and patronise the airport shopping concessions.

The departing passenger terminal 'timeline' comprises check-in, baggage drop, transfer to the departure gate via shops or executive lounges, board and depart. Passengers' arrival times at the airport are influenced by the type of flight they are about to take. Some passengers arrive late (sometimes too late to board the flight) while others arrive early because they know the security queues can be difficult and time-consuming to navigate or because they want to shop. Early arrivers tend to be leisure passengers or infrequent flyers. Business passengers or frequent flyers are usually time-sensitive, focussed and efficient and either arrive at the last possible moment or sufficiently early to avail themselves of the executive lounge facilities.

Passengers want to reduce time on the ground unless they control it (e.g. shopping, dining and/or using the lounges); airlines also want to reduce time on the ground (hooked up to the airport is costly) and frequently cannot control it because of multiple factors such as late passengers or airport congestion. Both airlines and passengers dislike unpunctuality and want on-time departures; however, some travellers miscalculate how long it could take them to cover the distance from check-in desk to departure gate. If the distance was a straight line it would take minimal time, but airport designers create a meandering experience to expose the shops' displays so that passengers will dwell and purchase. Shopping travellers need to leave more time to ensure punctual arrival at the departure gate.

Governments as stakeholders

Governments' interference in the democratised air travel market is through legislation and regulation. These interventions include levying departure and environmental taxes, detailing complimentary airline services to fulfil obligations for PRMs as well as stipulating human rights-based compensation for delays or flight disruptions caused by extraordinary circumstances which might have been avoided (Regulation EC 261/2004) (European Union, 2014) (see also Chapter 1). Furthermore, flying (which was once considered a luxury) is now almost considered a necessity, a normal activity and by some activists as a human right (see Chapter 5). At times the legislated individual rights of the passengers overrule the commercial viability of their travel since successive government rulings have reassigned some social responsibilities and costs to the airlines without any compensating subsidy. Furthermore, in the UK the issue is confused. The government perceives privately provided air travel as a human right and a public good, yet it taxes it as a luxury (as well as a negative externality) and places some of the State's social costs and responsibilities onto the airlines. As an integral part of a highly competitive, mostly privately owned, international industry the airline market should work efficiently;

however, governments have intervened using asymmetric information to identify missing markets which have led to inefficiencies. EC 261/2004 intervention is actually an illustration of supranational government (rather than market) failure since it delivers a net welfare loss for the shareholders and employees (whose rewards will be reduced) and passengers (who will pay increased prices). Government intervention of all types has an impact on aviation economic sustainability (see Chapter 5 and Chapter 6) and affects the functioning of the free market in air travel. Airlines are the wrong tool for social engineering.

Social tourism and airline economics

Aviation supports the tourism industry. Governments are keen to ensure that air travel is accessible for as many people as possible because of the benefits tourism is considered to bring to society. Understanding the psychology of passenger motivation gives strength to this ideal and provides the rationale for non-financial government support. Considerable research has been conducted into the psychology of motivations. The work of Murray (1938) measured the strengths of needs to determine motivation and Maslow (1943) with his development of a hierarchy of needs gave rise to the idea that motivations were an inter-connecting, hierarchical pyramid starting with physiological needs at the base, moving up to safety, love, esteem and finally self-actualisation at the pinnacle. Once one level was satisfied, it ceased to be a motivator and the next need became the driver for attainment. From these beginnings came the concept of a travel career ladder (Pearce, 1988). Some travellers ascended the hierarchy while others remained on a particular level. The experience of different cultures and interaction with the natural environment are valuable to the experienced travellers whereas:

> stimulation, personal development, relationship (security), self-actualization, nostalgia, romance and recognition had a higher priority for the less experienced ones. Importantly, a core of travel motivation factors including escape, relaxation, relationship enhancement and self-development seem to comprise the central backbone of motivation for all travellers.
>
> (Pearce and Lee, 2005: 226)

The benefits of tourism include recovery time away from work, the broadening of minds through new experiences and cultural mixing, supporting peace, personal development, VFR, spiritual pilgrimages and improved health (McCabe, 2009). Support for social tourism in Europe for lower-income groups has its origins in the Christian movement in France and Switzerland and in the early youth movements in Germany. (This social focus has spread throughout the EU, with regulations increasing the social and human rights of airline passengers on what are mostly privately owned airlines.) The social benefits are well documented; however, the relevant private costs are often omitted when (and if) cost-benefit analyses are ever undertaken. Effective airline demand is the quantity of products and services for which passengers are willing and able to pay. If potential passengers do not have the means to pay, then economists do not consider that unfulfillable desire to be demand. In the UK social tourism is largely funded by the charities sector with additional support from direct government grants (McCabe, 2009). There are political, cultural and moral dimensions to the role of State provision of holiday services resulting in a diverse provision of access to tourism opportunities. In the UK, affordability is the largest barrier to participation in holidays. The groups most likely to be excluded from tourism include those who are disabled, ill or older (McCabe, 2009), i.e. those who are the most expensive groups for airlines to service. The UN World Travel Organisation (UNWTO) (2001) in its *Global Code of Ethics for Tourism (Article 7: iii) Right to Tourism* states that:

> Social tourism, and in particular associative tourism, which facilitates widespread access to leisure, travel and holidays, should be developed with the support of the public authorities ... senior tourism and tourism for people with disabilities, should be encouraged and facilitated.

Thus tourism, supported by the public authorities is perceived as a social right and a public good. However, if the travel involves privately owned airlines, the accompanying responsibilities and any additional liabilities for the high-cost groups are left to the carriers to accommodate (see Chapter 5). Any failure to accommodate and support these individuals could produce charges of 'discrimination' and provoke fiscal sanctions under assorted equalities legislation including the UK Equalities Act 2010 and the USA Civil Rights Act 1964. Any such breaches could damage the airline's reputation and fiscal sanctions would affect its economic viability.

Airport economics and society interaction

Sometimes the airline cannot control the costs of its commercial environment and in particular, the airport environment. The decision as to the specification for an airport terminal building used for passengers' dwelling and shopping is usually left to the owner in accordance with their business model and in consultation with their potential tenants (i.e. airlines, suppliers and concessions). Itemised airport passenger surveys detail what passengers purportedly want, but surveys never put a price on the options offered. Asking passengers whether they would actually be willing to pay for the services or facilities in the survey might yield different responses. Passengers paying premium fares on scheduled carriers want airport executive lounges (often used as an airline selling tool) which are included in their increased prices and/or repeat purchasing loyalty scheme. However, direct access to such exclusive facilities often means avoiding the shops, for which airports frequently apply a capitation charge to the airlines for these 'absent' passengers.

When constructing an airport, the commissioning owners contract with designers. Architects often want to create signature buildings as a testament to their creativity (lucrative for the shops; delightful for the customers; expensive for the airlines). Airports need to support their primary customers – the airlines – because if it was not for the airlines there would be no shoppers at the airport concessions.

Expensive, glorified testaments to architecture add costs which can only be retrieved by charging more to the airlines, the shopping concessions and ultimately, the passengers. Architects often have more to gain by designing signature buildings than the owners or users (although architectural advocacy research would not agree). This is not always good for airline economics because once the building has been erected the architects have no more 'skin in the game'. Having been paid for their work, they can leave the airport owner to manage the (sometimes exorbitant) operating costs. Simple buildings cost less to erect and maintain and are therefore economically sustainable. After opening in 2008, the architect-designed Terminal 5 at London Heathrow suffered from lack of illumination as various bulbs failed. It was discovered that the high roof made relamping very difficult and it transpired that the possibility of lamp replacement had not been considered during design. This was ultimately solved by employing high-wire artists relamping over several months at an estimated cost of 'several £Stg millions' (Fielding, 2013). In the airports which service the lower-cost airlines and non-scheduled carriers, there is an economic argument for ensuring the airport fit-out matches the budget service these carriers offer. However, if airports used economically and environmentally sustainable methods of total cost of ownership (which includes maintenance) then the building costs could be matched to airlines' economic needs (Hughes *et al.*, 2004).

Airports and stakeholders

The desire to increase airport and runway capacities (with potentially increased negative externalities) can be an emotional issue for the airport neighbours. However, airports must engage with the right stakeholders to avoid being misled by advocates using distorted, partial or partisan information. One illustrative example of this tendency occurred in 2015 at Heathrow Airport, London, which was seeking public approval for a third runway. A large proportion of the complaints against noise in the previous 12 months (which would affect its future 'licence to operate') were sent by automated computer software from a few complainers who, because they forgot to change their computer timers onto daylight saving, actually complained about some flights before they had even flown (*Business Travel News*, 2015).

Some airports are also required to instal retrospective aircraft noise insulation in neighbouring domestic dwellings even though aircraft are up to ten times quieter (*Business Travel News*, 2015) than those of the 1960s when many of the airports (and neighbouring homes) were built. Such noise insulation is not free. Its cost is eventually paid by passengers and other airport users, thereby pushing up the charges for their services and products. Major European airports – including Schiphol, Madrid, Charles de Gaulle and Frankfurt – undertake public consultations to determine the noise-reduction needs of local residents as a means of seeking public approval for continuance of the implicit 'licence to operate'.

Innovative negotiations

Some low-cost carriers take an innovative approach to airports whereby they do not pay the airport for landings rather the airport pays them to come to their region.

This could be perceived as subsidising the airline. Ryanair is expert at these negotiations. It justifies its stance by arguing that the locations to which it flies have enjoyed economic growth (e.g. Charleroi and Strasbourg) and that in effect Ryanair support has enabled the regions to prosper. After a challenge from 54% State-owned (and State-subsidised) Air France against the £Stg1m annual payment received by privately owned Ryanair, the younger carrier threatened to retreat from France completely. Air France successfully argued in the French Courts that the payments were tantamount to a subsidy which distorted competition (Harrison *et al.*, 2003). This ruling was eventually overturned by the European Commission, which upheld that certain discounts were acceptable in support for competition (European Commission, 2004).

Passenger delays and airports

When aircraft are on the ground, they need to be serviced (passengers disembarked, cargo unloaded, interiors cleaned and catered, tanks refuelled, aircraft inspected (and de-iced if necessary), passengers boarded and freight loaded) and returned to the air as quickly as possible. Grounded aircraft are not earning income which undermines their economic viability. However, in a less-than-perfect world, the turnaround is often delayed for multiple reasons and passengers are left airside in the terminals spending time and money in airport shops. In the meantime, the aircraft is waiting and renting a jetty, which is expensive. This is a losing economic situation for sustainable airlines but a definite winner for economically sustainable airports. Airports (like airlines) have government and/or private stakeholders to satisfy in order to maintain their 'licence to operate'. Despite deregulation much of the essential infrastructure on which they rely is still tied to governments either by shareholdings and/or regulation.

Airports are now becoming destinations themselves. Singapore boasts a butterfly garden, Munich has a surfing wave pool facility and Tokyo offers a flavoured oxygen therapy bar. Airports still rely on the revenue from the shopping concessions to keep passenger charges down (the single till charging principle) so reducing airport concession turnover reduces airport revenue and might subsequently result in increased airport passenger charges to compensate. When passengers arrive at the point of checking-in for their flight they have only two resources – time or money: they want an on-time departure while the airport wants their money. Unfortunately, the airline-airport rhythm is frequently disrupted by multiple events including delayed passengers (train or car breakdowns; mistaken recall of reporting time; queues at the check-in desk, bag drop or Security); slow-shuffling elderly passengers (who try to maintain their independence but in reality need mobility assistance); travelling groups arriving piecemeal; incorrect visas or forgotten passports and a multitude of other human failings which upset the perfect workings of an efficient airline operation and which can reduce airport retail concessions' revenues.

Passengers' consumption spending in the dwell time between clearing Security and boarding the aircraft is influenced by their reason for travel. For example, a passenger is more likely to purchase airport concession goods if they are going on vacation and they are likely to spend more than the business passengers (Graham, 2009). It is in the airports' interests to increase the dwell times and exploit airport congestion which in turn drives up concession revenues (D'Alfonso *et al.*, 2013). Airport delays are profitable for the airports' shops but unprofitable for airlines.

2.2 CHALLENGING COSTS AND SOCIETY

Complexity, complication and costs

Reducing complexity saves resources and increases efficiency, and is achieved by standardising products and processes as much as possible. This can be attained by such dispersed decisions as having a single aircraft family fleet or reducing complexity for on-board food choices. However, it must be acknowledged that some people enjoy complexity because it protects their jobs and enhances their self-worth as they negotiate the complications involved. This is not economically sustainable in the long run.

Removing complexity, complication and waste

There are many methods for reducing complexity but in an economically sustainable airline, the question asked of each process and product is 'Would the customer pay for this?'. If the answer is 'No' then a decision is needed as to whether it is worth doing at all. In the premium cabins on full-service carriers there should be sufficient resources to deliver more services and choices; in the economy cabins on full-service carriers or low-cost carriers, costs are often at the margin of profitability so services and choices are restricted. Sustainable economics means that passengers should receive the products and services which are commensurate with the cabin chosen. There are many methods for removing complexity and complication one of which is the 'lean' process pioneered by the Japanese Toyota Motor Corporation. Lean meets customers' demands at maximum efficiency by aiming for a logical flow of resources and eliminating pinch-points where resources are strained. It also eliminates wastes of all types including repeat work, duplication, queuing, complaint handling, supply shortages or abundances and unnecessary transportation. Lean emphasises teams, training, job rotation and reduction of status differences among employees. It also develops an improvement culture throughout an organisation because those involved are empowered to act to reduce inventories, time, space and human effort while still responding to customers' demands. It thrives in an open culture which tolerates challenge and maximises the benefits of new technology (such as 3D printing, which at the time of publication was being trialled for aircraft spares). In short, lean is the integration of economics, society and environment.

Lean has four disciplines (Jacquemont, 2014). First, deliver customer value efficiently through an understanding of what customers truly value. Second, enable employees to lead and contribute to their fullest potential, ensuring they have the

Table 2.2 Application of lean management to airline processes

Lean process	Potential airline applications
Waiting	turn aircraft round rapidly by re-engineering the turnaround process
Overproduction	avoid excess meal waste by reducing meal choices and portions
Rejects and rework	change suppliers if rejects and rework are higher than detailed in the SLAs
Unnecessary **M**otion	minimise transport of aircraft spares from hangar to jetty for minor fixes by having 'travelling spares' which accompany engineers
Unnecessary **P**rocessing	manage each email item immediately rather than defer for another time and handle each document only once; reduce booking errors
Excess **I**nventory	use just-in-time inventory management rather than hold vast stocks or use 3D printing where possible; real-time engine reports can notify maintenance of any performance problems while flying so the spare parts can be sourced and waiting on arrival
Excess **T**ransportation	reduce coaching of passengers between aircraft stands and terminal buildings (necessary when aircraft are off-jetty)

necessary support mechanisms. Third, discover better ways of working. Fourth, connect the strategy and goals with meaningful purpose. Manufacturer Toyota embeds the seven wastes with the nomenclature **WORMPIT**: **W**aiting, **O**verproduction, **R**ejects and rework, unnecessary **M**otion, unnecessary **P**rocessing, excess **I**nventory and excessive **T**ransportation (Table 2.2). (NB: there are other similar lean nomenclatures.)

An example of lean in the aviation industry is the no-frills, low-cost and low-fare airlines – uncomplicated products, competitively priced and efficiently delivered. However, in one of many airline paradoxes, the unbundling of low-fare carriers' products into component and chargeable parts is often counter-intuitive for passengers. When faced with multiple choices for services that they had always believed were integral to their fares many travellers perceive such fracturing as a complication.

Passenger processing complexity, complication and control

The airline industry is one of enormous complexity – especially its fare structures – and it is further complicated when extra processes such as additional security searches on passengers, baggage and freight have to be incorporated. Complexity can be also compounded by restrictive working agreements which are often the comfort zone of inflexible employees unwilling to overcome operating challenges. Outside airlines' controls are issues such as passengers' speeds passing through Security, inadequate airport wayfinding to guide passengers and the activities of

Air Traffic Control (ATC) which decides when and in which order aircraft depart and arrive. However, where passengers have a choice, such choices should be designed to give options at an economic delivery cost. Complexity is sometimes necessary but complications which are unplanned and arise out of ill-thought-through decisions can increase costs. As an example of unnecessary on-board complexity, many airlines do not have a policy for online identification of any seats with fully retracting armrests which are accessible for PRMs. Armrests which do not fully retract to level with the seat back pose difficulties for the Mobility Assistants (who are responsible for lifting immobile passengers to window seats) and for obese passengers who purchase two or more seats. If the default seating specification was fully retractable armrests (apart from bulkhead and exit rows) then passengers would be able to select from the mainstream seating pool. However, many airlines do not have that flexibility and instead of all seats being accessible only some (or maybe none) qualify, which adds an element of complication into seating allocation and possible problems once any PRMs are on board.

Complexity and airline models

Catering is a good example of the complexity required by different airline models. The no-frills, low-cost carriers allow passengers to provide their own food or purchase from a limited selection from an on-board trolley. In contrast, the meal selection in the economy cabin of a full-service carrier can often have as many as 18 choices depending on passengers' religious or health requirements (Table 2.3).

Some passengers require personalised meals which must be distributed correctly. This can delay the meal service for other passengers while these options are delivered. In the extreme case, several meals from each category of these 18 choices could be scattered around the economy cabins, which takes considerable time, planning and cost to deliver – and passengers frequently change seats, adding to the complication. Any failure to deliver the passengers' chosen meals can mean they could endure more than 12 hours without food – a disappointment which would no doubt be communicated when the aircraft lands and the Captain grants permission to switch on communication devices. Furthermore, failure to deliver the correct meal – e.g. gluten-free meal to a person who is gluten intolerant – can make the passenger ill, with the resultant complaint and possibly compensation. Removing catering would eliminate some of the complexity and catering risks (such as price increases and supplier strikes); however, catering is one of the product differentiators for full-service carriers so removal is unlikely. Australia's Qantas Airways used inflight catering as part of its ultimately successful strategy to stem losses and attract more economy passengers. The carrier super-sized its economy meals, doubled the choice and introduced pre-flight selection (*The Guardian*, 2014).

Low-cost carrier simplicity

The simplicity of the low-cost carriers keeps costs and fares lower than full-service carriers. Low-cost carrier booking is almost exclusively online unless passengers are

Table 2.3 Airline meal complexity

Full-service airline	Economy section meal options
Cathay Pacific (Hong Kong) 21 choices	Baby, bland, child, diabetic, fruit platter, gluten-intolerant, Hindu, kosher, low calorie, low fat/low cholesterol, low salt, Moslem, low lactose, vegetarian raw, non-beef, liquid diet, vegetarian vegan, vegetarian Jain/strict Indian vegetarian, vegetarian lacto-ovo, vegetarian Oriental, vegetarian Hindu/Indian vegetarian (Cathay Pacific, 2015)
Lufthansa (Germany) 17 choices	Lactose free, low sodium, low cholesterol, reduction food, gluten-free, diabetic, vegetarian (Western), vegetarian (lacto-ovo), Vegetarian (Oriental), fruit, light whole food, without fish, vegetarian, Asian (Indian), Kosher, Muslim, Hindu (Lufthansa, 2013)
United Airlines (USA) 8 choices	Asian vegetarian, Hindu (Indian) vegetarian, vegan (strict vegetarian), child, gluten-intolerant, Jain, Kosher and Muslim (United Airlines, 2013)

Low-cost airline	Simplified economy section meal options
easyJet (UK)	'. . .passengers can bring their own food and drink on board or purchase from inflight trolley (hot, cold drinks, alcoholic beverages, sandwiches, sweets, confectionery and other snacks)' (easyJet, 2013)
Ryanair (Ireland)	'. . .passengers can bring their own food on-board: food and refreshments available for purchase on board' (Ryanair, 2013)
Southwest Airlines (USA)	'Southwest Airlines serves complimentary coffee, juices, and cold drinks on all flights. If your total flight itinerary includes a series of flights that each are less than two hours in duration, you will be served peanuts/pretzels on each flight segment. If your flight itinerary includes any nonstop flight longer than two hours, you will be served a packaged snack on that flight segment. Southwest Airlines does not serve sandwiches or meals, however, you may bring something to eat on board.' (Southwest Airlines, 2014)

disabled or unable to use the internet, in which case airlines must offer an alternative booking system. However, if passengers do bring their own selections they will be subject to any liquid volume restrictions imposed by Security. Optionally they can often purchase from a simplified range of on-board food and beverages at higher-than-supermarket prices, which boosts ancillary airline revenue. Low-cost carrier meals are generally not included in the fare and where available, choice is very restricted, often to just vegetarian or meat. UK consumer champion organisation *Which?* (2013) compared the price of selected items to show how the consumer was being exploited (socialists' view) or was subsidising low-cost fares (economists' view) (Table 2.4). It was an unfair comparison because the higher-than-supermarket prices might reflect and be justified by the additional transaction costs, plus the extra fuel required and emissions expended transporting the snacks and beverages by air.

Table 2.4 On-board charges for consumer items compared to on-ground suppliers (adapted from *Which?*, 2013: 7)

Product	UK Grocer	Airline £Stg
Volvic water (500ml)	39p (Ocado – online grocer)	2.44 (Ryanair – low-cost)
Kettle Chips (40g)	62p (Ocado)	1.50 (Monarch – charter)
Mini Cheddars (50g)	69p (Ocado)	1.60 (Ryanair – low-cost)
Pringles (40g)	40p (Asda – grocery chain)	1.80 (easyJet – low-cost)

Society and competitive costs

'I don't know one airplane from another; to me they're all just marginal costs with wings,' is attributed to Alfred Kahn in his role as Chairman of the US Civil Aeronautics Board (1977–1978). No discussion on airline economics and society can ignore costs. Differences in aircraft types, interior configurations, numbers of crew and ground staff, turnaround times, procurement and financing arrangements are just some of the elements of airline costs. In the short and medium terms, costs are largely fixed (because of the high capital costs) but in the long-term, all costs are variable. Over time, economies of scale can accrue at varying rates, especially noticeable when processes and products are subject to lean assessment. The USA's Boeing Aircraft Corporation illustrated this principle. It identified that it purchased 200 different kinds of safety glass and 80 different shades of white paper. The corporate aim was simplification, with just two or three types of each product. Similarly, Boeing's Defence and Commercial Airplane divisions had each previously negotiated their own aluminium and titanium sources which meant they did not have sufficient leverage individually, but combined could deliver economies of scale and market power (Holmes, 2006). In another example, the Airbus 380 can take up to 800 passengers and crew in a tight configuration, which offers scope for significant economies of scale for the operating airlines.

Many stakeholders – including employees, bankers, aircraft manufacturers and general suppliers – contribute to keeping airlines' balance sheets strong and cost bases competitive. This is fundamental to survival during times of political and currency uncertainty, fuel price increases (and occasional decreases), expensive technology enablers (and barriers) and a multitude of other factors which make predicting the airlines' economic environment rather like gazing into a crystal ball. There are many routes to economic sustainability all of which could have a direct society impact. They emanate from decisions (see Chapter 7) which should be transparent without undermining competitiveness and which could have a social impact including that of the community multiplier. The multiplier effect is an economic concept that explains how money spent radiates through a community and because of the international nature of aviation some decisions taken in one country can reverberate around many destinations with varying economic and social impacts (Table 2.5).

Table 2.5 Some of the socio-economic impacts of decisions to create a competitive cost-base

Economic decision	Social impacts
improve aircraft usage by increasing the number of flights	• changing employee shift patterns to optimise aircraft flying hours • airport neighbours hear and see more take-offs and landings (potential for flash point) • possibly increased airport smells • potential neighbourhood disruption

reduce employee numbers	• less money into the local economy (reduced multiplier effect) means
	
	  – less money to be spent in local businesses
	  – fewer community taxes collected
	  – possibly increased local unemployment

increase the use of ITC for routine processes	• fewer employees required means a reduction in the community multiplier effect and fewer staff to handle crises when they occur • increased local unemployment • outsourcing of back-room processes to lower-cost regions/nations is socially beneficial for them but possibly detrimental to the home country
instal ITC enablements	• more customer choice from online booking and payment applications • fuel economies and quieter engines from new aircraft (economic, society and environmental win–win)
remove ITC barriers	• less-technologically-agile ageing customers who might be unfamiliar with using online bookings need a booking process which is simple and user-friendly
reduce stocks of inventories such as catering, engineering spares, stationery etc.	• fewer Stores staff needed but more van/truck drivers required to deliver just-in-time inventories therefore increased emissions • reduced cash outflow, but increased environmental considerations since more deliveries would be required to keep supplies sufficient to continue operations
maintain just-in-time inventories	• reduce the need to carry large stocks to support the operation • tighter supply chain needs fewer staff to manage

employ strategic resourcing	• form a purchasing alliance (ensuring no breach of competition regulations) with social consequences including:
	
	  – reduced employee numbers
	  – reduced purchasing, transaction and inventory costs
	  – increased social and environmental impacts (noise, lighting pollution, road congestion, increased emissions) caused by frequent deliveries to compensate for reduced inventories

continued . . .

Table 2.5 Continued

Economic decision	Social impacts
reduce complexity	• simplifying fleet types reduces staff training costs plus economies of scale for aircraft maintenance and substitution
cut routes	• loss of income and increased unemployment in originating and destination communities

Costs and employees

Recruitment and training of employees are expensive activities. One of the measures for assessing an economically and socially sustainable airline can be the level of staff turnover. Lower employee turnover has many benefits including fewer hours lost in training. It also allows sufficient mass to absorb newcomers into embedded routines without disrupting the airline. Conversely, while high employee turnover might indicate low morale, damage organisational memory and be a barrier to innovation it can also refresh and remove outdated irrelevancies (Simon, 1991). Airlines are under pressure to reduce costs and some of the legacy carriers have found it efficient to sweep out older, entrenched-thinking, higher-cost employees and replace them with newer, fresher-thinkers at lower cost. However, this attrition can take many years to accomplish. Changing from full-time employees to the flexibility of using part-time staff is also a major corporate culture change. The airline benefits because it only needs to summon staff as required to meet passenger demand. While some employees relish the flexibility of part-time working, others dislike the uncertainty of such arrangements. This change of employment contracting might be economically desirable but it can be socially divisive.

Society and low-cost carriers

The arrival of low-cost carriers was a seismic shock to the larger legacy carriers with their capital city-focussed routes. Low-cost carriers are characterised by lower overheads and by operating streamlined, modern and efficient fleets often at second-tier airports (see Chapter 1). Unlike the traditional legacy carriers, the low-cost carriers have no interest in serving geographical markets and instead choose locations that maximise their return on assets. However, travelling with a low-fare carrier can sometimes be a false economy for passengers. Many of the low-cost carriers operate from airports which are many miles (and possibly hours) from the major population centres and so incur higher land-transfer costs, wasting time that can negate the airfare savings. Consumers must choose which of their resources they value most – time or money.

The low-cost carriers and the full-service carriers have different cost levels and passenger service fulfilment criteria (Table 2.6). However, a full-service business passenger might choose a low-cost carrier for personal travel and also for reduced-cost business travel if the airports and schedules meet his needs.

Table 2.6 Comparisons of differentiations between low-cost and full-service carriers

Characteristic	Low-cost airlines	Full-service airlines
Seating density	single class cabin (optimising aircraft capacity) is more usual; offering a range of different fares depending on the time available between booking and departure, and other factors (i.e. price discrimination)	multiple cabin classes reduce potential number of seats per aircraft; price discrimination based on departure date, class of cabin, time of day etc.
Baggage allowances	generally lower than full-service carriers (less baggage means quicker turnaround and therefore less time on the ground)	allocated by class of cabin and weights and sizes can be variable
Aircraft types	fewer aircraft types in the fleet; standardisation means lower maintenance and training costs	often mixed fleets as result of mergers and procurement strategies
Turnarounds	faster using smaller airports	can be slower using major congested airport hubs
Flying routes	point-to-point; often no transfers; shorter routes	transfers; hub-to-hub
Airports	smaller airports (cheaper, allow quicker turnarounds); often long distance from town centre with inadequate ground transport links	larger airports, (higher costs, sometimes slower turnarounds); near city centre; usually good ground transport links
Distribution channels	e-booking via internet	multiple channels (travel agents, e-bookings, airport, telephone) incur overheads or commissions
Ancillary revenue streams	anything they can get away with including revenue from sales of snacks, beverages and entertainment items on board to supplement low fares; ancillary charges for reprinting bookings or boarding cards and for using credit cards; charges for sporting equipment; additional baggage charges; inflight advertising etc.	surcharges for credit cards, fuel; charges for extra bags; inflight advertisements etc.
Additional facilities	usually none	fully equipped executive lounges with catering, Wi-Fi, entertainments

Outsourcing for cost reduction

Outsourcing – whether onshore or offshore (i.e. offshoring – see Chapter 7) – can reduce costs and provide an element of resilience for an organisation. Outsourcing is a process which requires social and economic trade-offs and allows the experts to practice what they do best – deliver efficient services at economic prices. However, in the UK (and most EU nations), any employees transferring to the outsourced companies are protected by the Transfer and Undertakings (Protection of Employment) (TUPE) Regulations 2006 which require that transferred employees remain on the same contracted employment conditions as before the transfer. Sometimes the anticipated economies of scale are diminished by these continued overheads in yet another disruption to the working of markets.

Once airlines were liberated from the burden of legacy ownership, many carriers were able to outsource their component functions. Outsourcing could include catering, de-icing, ground handling, facilities maintenance, motor vehicle supply and disabled passenger handling as well as routine tasks such as 'back office' administration functions (e.g. revenue management, customer complaints or employee travel administration) and procurement (e.g. engine servicing) through to wet-leasing a fully equipped aircraft with liveried crews for a fixed period to supplement a peak demand. Great care is necessary to ensure that the lowest price tender does not undermine the best value proposition because at some stage, there could be a customer backlash and the costs of repairing the reputational damage could outweigh the original benefits.

Outsourcing must be strategic with demonstrable alignment with the business objectives and sharing of the risks and revenues (see Chapter 7). It carries reputational and financial risks, among which is the loss of skilled employees and their knowledge. The choice is to decide what, when, how and why outsourcing could be more economic than retaining tasks in-house and to make the decision process transparent as demonstrated by Boeing Aircraft Corporation. Boeing formed an international team of suppliers and engineers for the Boeing 787 Dreamliner components to be assembled in Seattle, USA. The rationale was that 80% of its commercial aeroplane backlog was for international customers. In contrast, European manufacturer Airbus, driven by history and political necessity, created the A380 using large sections made in Britain, France, Germany and Spain. In addition, Airbus intends to assemble the smaller A320 150-seaters in China for their local market and will compete with Boeing on its home turf by establishing a manufacturing plant in Mobile, Alabama. Both Boeing and Airbus ship an increasing quantity of work beyond their traditional borders in order to share the risk and costs of changes aimed at making planes lighter (to save fuel and reduce emissions) and to penetrate emerging markets (Petersen, 2011).

The advent of e-tendering has reduced transaction costs and also given smaller home-based and advancing nations' suppliers a chance to compete with larger, more established commercial organisations. Sending routine tasks to advancing nations with highly educated workforces and comparatively low wage structures (e.g. India) is a tough economic and social decision. The choice is between transferring operations and thereby make a national workforce redundant (at possibly significant social and political cost) or assisting an advancing economy to create new, vibrant and sustainable industries on the back of an economically sustainable airline. The economically focussed airline must take great care not to fall foul of international labour standards which are closely monitored by many special interest groups as well as regulators. It is a reputational risk to employ insourced or outsourced workers offshore at lesser standards of hygiene, health and safety than in the originating nation. Air crews in particular illustrate this issue. 'Crews based in a given country should not have social security systems applied that are to lower standards than that of the country in which the crew is based. However, we should not be dictating to foreign airlines which countries they should choose for crew bases in an attempt to make sure their costs are inflated to the benefit of the home carriers' (Tretheway and Andriulaitis, 2015: 11). Transferring work offshore could mean that the domestic workforce would be made redundant with an impact on reputation. Furthermore, disgruntled, redundant employees who are affiliated to international trades unions could potentially cripple any airline with a worldwide network.

In addition to providing employment in developing and emerging nations, offshoring (see Chapter 7) can also provide a wedge for access rights to potentially lucrative new travel markets. This would be a win–win for the airline and the offshored nations. However, outsourcing can also be a high-risk option because it involves sharing competitive knowledge which requires trust. Furthermore, sometimes the cost of offshoring oversight (another transaction cost) could consume the anticipated benefits and if the quality is lower than agreed, the pursuit of compensation could also undermine the original business case. There is, however, one potential disadvantage to outsourcing efficiency in some advancing nations – their internet capacity can be lacking which can make tendering across the cultures and geographical regions quite problematic and again, could undermine the economies sought.

Core competencies and outsourcing

A company's competitiveness originates from its core products and/or services. The tangible outputs of airline core competencies are derived from skills which can deliver additional value for passengers. Competency-savvy managers and leaders work across organisational boundaries, share resources and think long-term (future-proofing) for the benefit of the organisation as a whole and not just their specific strategic business unit (SBU). Identifying core competencies for airlines is critical in a learning organisation. Organisations which are organised around core competencies are more successful and competitive than those which are not (Prahalad and Hamel, 1990). Practising the core competencies will enable access to a wide variety of potential markets, contribute to customer benefits and above all, be difficult for competitors to imitate because they are part of the uniqueness which exemplifies each airline's culture. However, outsourcing the core competency – in the aviation industry it is customer service in all its guises – is high risk, especially because of the potential for sabotaging future customer relations from disgruntled TUPE'd employees. This was a risk that Finland's loss-making airline Finnair (see Table 1.2 in Chapter 1) considered worth taking. In August 2014 it signed an agreement to outsource its cabin services when they were unable to reach agreement with their own cabin crew unions. Finnair had been trying to negotiate cost savings since 2011; however, the negotiations had ended in spring 2014 with no result (Finnair, 2014), hence the decision to outsource.

Social impacts of mergers, takeovers and acquisitions

The legacy carriers often carried historic overheads which were not the burden of their younger and more nimble competitors. Today's economically sustainable airlines need to be lean, fit, adaptable, agile, flexible and efficient in order to be competitive (see Chapter 3). These characteristics are sometimes achieved by mergers, takeovers or acquisitions.

Mergers, takeovers and acquisitions need to take account of the political and cultural issues of the carriers involved. With airline mergers and takeovers (e.g. Ryanair and buzz in 2003; British Airways and bmi in 2012) there are inevitable consequences for employees and systems. Ryanair's closing of its newly acquired buzz airline meant a loss of 60% of the employees (British Broadcasting Corporation (BBC), 2003). This takeover required increased productivity as measured by the ratio of resources used to outputs produced. The aircraft were changed from BAE146 jets to larger Boeing 737s, pilot hours were increased and uneconomic routes were closed. The impact was felt by passengers, many of whom had purchased holiday homes along routes operated by the low-cost airline in the belief that these routes (particularly to small French airports) would exist in perpetuity. The localities were also hurt by the withdrawal. It was a lose-lose situation for some stakeholders but an eventual win-win for Ryanair.

Alliance formations are beneficial primarily because they increase the traffic but members need to be alert to the possibility of behaving like a cartel. Derived airline benefits can include economies of scale; reduced transaction, staff training and infrastructure costs; and an increased database of target passengers. For passengers, there is usually access to improved rewards schemes such as priority boarding, upgrades and more variety of mileage awards redeemable across the new network partners. The benefit for the airline of reward programmes is that loyal customers are more cost effective to retain rather than seeking new customers (by a ratio of 1:5 up to 1:9, depending on the research selected). Research has shown that company profitability is favourably influenced by the longevity of customer relationships (Zeithaml and Bitner, 1996). Passengers are likely to become complacent until such time as their rewards are altered unfavourably. This loss aversion – where a change often leads to a reversal of consumer preference – will have a much greater impact on perception of loss rather than any potential gains (Tversky and Kahneman, 1991). Sustainable airlines tamper with reward programmes at their peril. There is also the ethical question of who gets to spend the passengers' accumulated rewards if the booking has been paid for by an employer?

To whom do these rewards belong? To the employee who travelled or the employer or (ultimately) the shareholders who paid for the flight (see Chapter 4)?

Supply chain and society

Knowledge of behaviours in the supply chain is of critical importance as it has significant bearing on airlines' reputations. Airlines cannot bury supply chain controversies in the age of open social media, given that airlines are part of many supply chains – some with tangential issues. These include social issues such as child labour (children in advancing nations might be sewing passenger blankets), migrant workers (possibly trafficked for slave labour to work in the food supply chain) or sugar and trans fats (considered unhealthy for use in airline meals and their production could also incur unfavourable environmental impacts). There are also environmental issues such as excessive production noise (hearing damage for factory workers) and the clearing of native forests to grow palm oil (used in some airlines' foods) or biofuels (cultivated as fossil fuel substitutes – see Chapter 6). In addition, there are pollutants or wastes emitted to air or water (from factories producing airline-associated products). Outsourcing a product or service does not mean that the responsible outsourcer has outsourced their responsibilities.

Catering

Inflight catering is a global activity estimated to be worth in excess of €12bn (£Stg9.3bn or $US13.3bn) per year, serving over one billion passengers annually (Jones, 2007). Airline catering is often more than delivering cooked food and liquid refreshments: it can encompass the supply of blankets, newspapers, eyeshades, headphones, viewing guides and a plethora of other items needed on board to service a full complement of passengers. The food, however, is a competitive product for those airlines which serve it and many airlines compete on the luxuriousness of their offering (Jones, 2007).

Airline catering is extremely complicated. Deciding what to feed passengers is just one issue in the complex world of airline management where society, environment, economics and governance coincide. However, economics can override some seemingly ethical considerations when profit margins are extremely thin as is often the situation in the economy cabin on a full-service carrier. Food decisions are fraught with potential ethical pitfalls often emanating from myopic, mono-topic special interest advocates concerned with different aspects of food production or consumption. These issues vary widely from groups against genetically modified (GM) foods (often termed 'franken foods') and advocates supporting animal welfare through to those with religiously based culinary preferences. Among the issues for those people concerned about animal welfare are fois gras (because it involves force feeding geese) and the Islamic halal killing method (regarded as cruel). Many religious groups insist that meat is killed in accordance with strict laws and some airlines are able to leverage economies of scale by using halal as the main method of meat preparation rather than ensuring that just one or two dishes per flight are religiously compliant. To the secular consumer, the end product is the same irrespective of how it was killed. This makes meat supply an issue of competition, economics and ethics, i.e. religion vs animal welfare vs economies of scale and complexity reduction. (Does it affect seat or freight sales?) Should considerations for animal welfare come before religious beliefs in airline catering? Would non-Islamic passengers travel with the airline if they knew the killing method? Should the airline (in the interests of transparency) broadcast its solutions to this conundrum on its website? Other religions also have dietary restrictions including Hindus (avoid beef), Jews (eschew shellfish), Jains (shun root vegetables, meat, eggs and fish) and Yazidis (exclusions include cabbage). Alternatively some of the problems of religious compliance can be avoided as Qantas did in 2013 when they removed all pork products and alcohol used in the preparation of inflight meals from Dubai routes after announcing the partnership with Middle East carrier, Emirates. Pork is considered unholy and forbidden by Islam but it is acceptable in the West. However, there is nothing to stop a passenger taking a ham sandwich on board a Qantas flight to the Middle East (i.e. passenger rights vs airlines' responsibilities).

Other special interest groups are concerned with many different catering issues including unsustainable levels of harvest caused by the over-fishing of cod, tuna or salmon. In addition to these considerations there is also the socially charitable sector which wants to see fairly traded or charity-branded goods on the meal tray (see Chapter 3) as well as allergic passengers who want to be supplied with allergen-free meals (see Chapter 4). Allergy-free foods require special preparation away from allergens and in mass catering anything which is not mainstream food preparation increases costs. It also places huge responsibility on socially responsible airlines to ensure that allergic passengers are not injured. Most carriers have now banned peanuts from their list of catered products to avoid the risk of a nut-allergic passenger being affected (the tyranny of the minority?) despite the fact that new research indicates that peanut dust is too heavy to be transmitted through the air (Spector, 2015) (see Chapter 4). Transparency for these procurement decisions is essential and cost is an economically sustainable reason to refuse compliance with the lobby groups' requests. It is, however, just not possible to please or appease all the supply chain stakeholders all of the time.

At altitude, passengers' sensory abilities – particularly taste and smell – are affected by the low humidity and air pressure. Food does not always taste the same inflight as it would on the ground. Since the meal and cabin service are the most remembered dimensions of travel, airlines compete to make these aspects what the customers remember. This is complicated by expectations and menu descriptions which are not always accurate and recipe names which can be misleading, e.g. the Indian favourite 'butter chicken' and the Caribbean's 'sweet-potato casserole' are actually very spicy, not mild as their names would suggest. In a metal fuselage at 11,000 metres above sea level with no access for resupply and where the economy cabin choice is 'meat or vegetarian' there will inevitably be some disappointed customers and if the taste is not what the passengers expect there will be the environmental and economic issues of disposing of wasted food. Economically sustainable airline catering (particularly in the economy cabin on full-service carriers) has to be supplied according to a very tight budget. If the Catering Department is to attempt to meet the budget, they have to offset the extra costs of being ethically minded with what they can afford to procure and adapt the menu as necessary. The cost of any more expensive, ethically sourced products which comply with lobby groups' religious or welfare standards has to be compensated from another part of the menu either by substituting ingredients or reducing the quantity on each tray. Neither might please the fare-paying passengers – but might please the lobby groups. Such restrictions could also make it difficult for the caterers (possibly outsourced with tightly squeezed margins) to meet the higher specifications required by the airlines' budgets.

Time and society

Time is a critical resource in economically sustainable aviation. It is also one of the biggest assets wasted by people in general. Stressed travellers are often frustrated by delays, which trigger feelings of loss of control. For economically sustainable airlines, punctuality is paramount because time is money and time-poor travellers perceive punctual take-offs as more important than punctual landings. Economically sustainable airlines have spent vast resources pursuing reduced processing time for employees and passengers alike. Time that passengers previously spent queuing at the check-in desks is now reduced by access to airline systems via the internet and fast bag-drop facilities at the airport. This in turn reduces the number of airline staff needed and keeps costs competitive, i.e. economics vs society. But many of the airport functions are neither within the passengers' nor the airlines' control. As a result, airlines can over-promise and under-deliver the customer experience, often because they do not control the airline-airport interface (e.g. Customs, Immigration, Security) which can taint the passengers' experiences. Time-sensitive travellers are often willing to pay extra for their flights in order to be able to travel at peak times; those who are less time-stressed will often pay less. Punctuality also affects economically sustainable airlines because delayed aircraft hooked to a jetty are charged for every minute. There are so many different processes required while the aircraft is on the ground, all of which are on the critical path. Delays can happen as there is very little, if any, buffer time built into the turnaround schedule. Any journey segment with an aircraft delay can have a disproportionately negative impact on the next departure time, especially if the aircraft misses its allocated runway slot.

ITC and society

Minimising airport passenger processing using off-airport ITC (such as internet booking and payment, seat choice and check-in) means fewer passenger-processing employees are needed at the airport for checking-in. In addition to saving employee costs, reducing the number of airport-based employees also reduces the quantity of airport rental space required. ITC as a manpower substitute has many uses in airlines, both in the back office and front-of-house including allocating aircraft, managing the customer database and frequent flyer programme, determining aircraft configurations to match route demand and calculating (among other statistics) labour costs as a prelude to redundancies. ITC departments can, however, exhibit the hegemony sometimes associated with highly specialised expertise and use a language which many stakeholders do not understand. Making decisions using a common language is extremely important given the impact that ITC has on the airline industry. These decisions must also be open and transparent (see Chapter 7). ITC is useful as a tool but it must not be omnipotent in a customer service industry.

The airline customer experience varies from airline to airline, cabin to cabin and crew to crew, much of which is supported by ITC. However, ITC can be a barrier to customer service. There is a conflict between the requirement for passengers to feel welcomed by employees displaying the airline's soft skill set and the need for the airline to use more hard skills such as ITC for efficiency and to keep fares as low as competitively necessary. Self-service and personalised customer service can interact successfully; however, minimal personal service is generally allocated to the lower-cost cabins and more personal service for the premium customers and passengers with disabilities. As more ITC is included in airport processing, customer service employees' roles and responsibilities will be rewritten. They will be required to serve customers through using effective ITC as they evolve into passenger hosts. This is a very different role from today's positions as technical facilitators dispensing boarding cards, baggage tags and customer service. These Strategic Corporals (Krulak, 1999) (named after soldiers whose evolving roles require them simultaneously to fight, keep the peace and deliver aid) will become autonomous masters of their new roles. Sustainable airlines recognise that increasing the use of ITC can be a means of improving worker productivity; however, these airlines are cognisant of research (Aral *et al.*, 2012, and others) which found that increased multi-tasking eventually gives diminishing marginal returns after initially increased outputs.

Occasionally there are gaps between the hard standard service delivery and the soft standards. If the hard standard fails (such as in times of major disruption) then the soft standard of customer service must fill the gaps. The more ITC is in use the fewer will be the available customer service personnel to handle disruptions. In the event of a major disruption (such as those caused by technology outage, inclement weather or engineering failures) airline staff must be available, trained and ready to support customers and enable them to travel as quickly as possible. In times of disruption ITC efficiencies can prove uneconomic and inadequate. There is often insufficient spare labour to provide the human face of customer service needed to pacify, accommodate and cater for what can be very aggrieved passengers whose access to social media could rapidly undermine global confidence in an airline's reputation.

> For a given level of technology, there is an optimal level of service productivity and . . . this level is affected by a set of managerially relevant variables. Either too low or too high a level of productivity damages the firm's profit.
>
> (Rust and Huang, 2012: 62)

Two very different examples of how communication affects customer service illustrate the problem. In 2012 a Virgin Atlantic flight travelling from Orlando, Florida to London Gatwick suffered a repeating malfunction with the aircraft's fire detector circuit. This delayed the aircraft by 24 hours while repairs were made and the passengers were deplaned, fed, accommodated and transported between hotel and airport. However, it was the failure of customer service that led to the airline paying compensation of £Stg47,600 ($US73,000 or €66,000) to the affected passengers. The payment was due under Regulation EC 261/2004 (see Chapter 1) which provided for compensation for delays after mechanical defects. In the age of social media, a Facebook page was established to broadcast the airline's service failing (Nicholson, 2014). The contrast with Air New Zealand could not have been greater. After a lengthy delay during which the passengers were accommodated and kept fully informed, the airline apologised profusely and generously compensated each customer with $1,000 in cash or Airpoints Dollars (*Air Transport News*, 2014). Air New Zealand was voted the Best Airline in the World 2014; Virgin did not appear in the top 10 (*Airline Ratings*, 2014). ITC alone would not have been sufficient in either of these examples. Economically sustainable airlines are aware of the trade-off between passenger needs and ITC, and of the ratio of employees to the number of relevant passengers' complaints.

Airline surcharges

Making surcharges transparent and visible at the commencement of an internet booking is more than just an economic issue. Such openness increases the trust society can place in a product. Action by *Which?* (2013) and the UK Office of Fair Trading (OFT) has pushed airlines to be more open about the composition of ancillary charges and not to include them as a nasty surprise at the end of any internet-based booking transaction. In any event this is a practice which is contrary to the ideal of transparency and fairness to which a sustainable airline should adhere. Using a credit card frequently attracts a surcharge – sometimes a fixed percentage (Jet2.com: 4%) or a fixed fee (Fly Thomas Cook: £Stg4 per person per flight). Some airlines even charge for using a debit card (Wizz Air: £Stg5 per person per travel leg). Other airlines encourage the use of their own credit/debit card (e.g. Ryanair) but levy a smaller charge for that particular option over other credit/debit cards. Using a debit card is the equivalent of using cash – but passengers making internet transactions often have no option but to use a card and so they incur the charge anyway. Airlines using sustainable-thinking behaviours (see Chapter 7) of honesty, transparency and openness will display the charges for using anything other than cash at the commencement of the transaction. Any such charge should not be more than the costs of actually processing the payment. *Which?* (2013) recommends no more than 2% for credit cards and nothing for debit cards. In the UK the government banned excessive charges from April 2013 onwards (the Consumer Protection Payment Surcharges Regulations 2012).

2.3 SECURITY CHALLENGES

Risk, security and economics

'Safety in the air begins on the ground' (IATA, 2012: 7). Airports have airside and landside areas and passengers are regarded as 'clean' (outbound and security screened) or 'dirty' (inbound) and the two must not meet for fear of cross-contamination for such illicit activities as delivering weapons or drugs. Crossing the landside to airside barrier requires security measures including passenger X-ray and/or pat-down, shoe removal, baggage search and a liquids restriction on quantities over 100ml (which has been profitable for airport airside sales). On arrival at the boarding gate, passengers and their hand baggage are often re-screened. Airport security can be as intrusive as a physical search or as unobtrusive as plain-clothes security agents patrolling the terminal and mixing with passengers. Although the landside/airside border is perceived by passengers as where security starts, in reality, flights have been scanned and screened by authorities since they were open for bookings.

Long ago governments and airlines identified security as a missing market and created a new industry. Air security is all encompassing and expensive, with costs recoverable from passengers. Protecting passengers, employees and neighbours is a top priority for every airline. Diplomacy – the cornerstone of foreign relations – has provided insufficient airline protection. Passengers are aware that the world has become a much more dangerous place as a result of the West's forays into regional wars (among other causes) and the military impact has cascaded down to airline security with heightened protection measures. In fulfilling societal obligations, sustainable airlines assess security risks and threats. 'There is no such thing as absolute safety. In aviation it is simply not possible to eliminate all risks. However, risks can be managed to a level "as low as reasonably practicable"' (IATA, 2012: 13).

Security covers many topics: for individuals it embraces health, safety and freedom from criminal attempts; for nation states it includes border control and civil unrest; for international entities it encompasses wars, trade inequalities and (controversially) climate change (see Chapter 6).

Security – a 'necessary boondoggle'

However, one of the peculiarities of airline security is that Check-in Agents (usually chosen for their personalities and customer service orientation) are required to become Security Agents, quizzing passengers at the check-in point on the contents of their bags and packing arrangements. They ask five questions: Are these your bags? Did you pack them yourself? Could anyone else have had access to them? Do they contain any prohibited or dangerous articles? Did anyone give you anything to take on the flight? An economically sustainable airline has to query whether these questions would really intimidate a terrorist who knows their hold luggage will be screened and hand luggage examined. These questions represent another example of boondoggles. While recognising that airport security is a 'hygiene' issue, these questions add complexity, time and costs to airline processes and their effectiveness has to be challenged. Security measures of all types also add extra costs for the airport, which in turn passes them onto the airlines and they recharge the passengers. Check-in Agents are also required to become Immigration and Emigration Agents, checking passports for valid names that match the booked name and visa. (Airlines performing these duties enable governments to take a free ride.) Failure to correctly identify a false passport or fake visa can involve the airline in fiscal sanctions and often includes the repatriation costs of miscreants. This is a huge responsibility for Check-in Agents and a task well above their pay grade but in line with their enhanced role as Strategic Corporals (Krulak, 1999). Economically sustainable airlines follow the processes rigidly in every endeavour to avoid letting security requirements disrupt on-time departures and inflict fines for breach of immigration rules. In a UK CAA survey (2011) most passengers (68%) were satisfied with airport screening processes but the queues, the removal of shoes, restrictions on liquids and slow processing generally were causes for dissatisfaction.

In unforeseen outcomes, manual security searching of some physically disabled passengers can cause them to suffer terrible pain, whereas the use of electronic scanners can be potentially fatal for others wearing internal medical devices such as heart pacemakers (Alexander, 2014).

Changing security needs

Threat combines the enemy's intent and capability (the weapons available); risk is the statistical probability of the likelihood and level of harm that the airline could be targeted either for nationalistic (e.g. freedom fighting) or other specific cause (e.g. passenger upset or animal rights campaigners). Risk mitigation can be measured and balanced against time, cost and the difficulty of taking measures to reduce or eliminate the risk. 'Effective risk management seeks to maximise the benefits of accepting a risk (e.g. a reduction in time and/or cost) while minimising the risk itself' (IATA, 2012: 13). Risks are prioritised and assessed for impact as measured by criteria such as human lives, monetary value and/or disruption time. Governments' anti-terrorist procedures (paid for by the aviation industry and its passengers) are sometimes badly performed by unskilled or inadequately trained personnel and often reflect a misunderstanding between threat and risk. However, airline security is one example of where national, multi-national and even supra-national government interventions are appropriate in the provision of a public good – no one can be excluded from it and there is no rivalry in consumption, i.e. consumption by one person does not reduce its availability to another. Public goods, although legislated, regulated or sometimes outsourced by governments (see Chapter 1), are only provided willingly by the private sector when they can make a profit (as happens with aviation security suppliers). To do otherwise would effectively be donating shareholders' funds or employees' rewards to improve public benefit. If such services are not privately provided, then States will provide them and the payments would come from taxes of varying types.

The nature of terrorism and the counter measures have changed over past decades. The USA, UK and allies entered Afghanistan, Iraq and Libya seeking terrorists who were believed to pose threats which were often directed at aviation. However, since the events of 2001 when terrorists plunged three aircraft into buildings in the USA, threat responses have changed. Cockpits are now locked during flights, preventing access; passengers are more vigilant and likely to intervene in the event of a threat; all airport employees are security screened before employment and now many nations have a form of Advance Passenger Information System (APIS) which requires completion before travel. APIS matches names (sometimes erroneously) with databases of suspects, thereby reducing the threat of terrorists travelling on commercial aircraft. However, these checks can lead to delays, mis-identified passengers and frustration, much of which is vented on the airline Check-in and Customer Service Agents and not the civil servants who create and operate these imperfect processes. (In 2004 the EU wanted to prevent the USA from implementing APIS but the Americans threatened to prevent EU aircraft from landing in the USA unless the passengers were all APIS cleared in advance.)

Many commentators feel that the security costs are now disproportionate to the threat (Kenny, 2012). However, politicians are reluctant to reduce high-profile security prevention measures for fear of being accused of negligence. 'Politicians can often successfully ride out this demand [for short-term action] after the obligatory and essentially cost-free expressions of outrage are prominently issued' (Mueller and Stewart, 2011: 23). However, now that hard-screening systems are in place, dismantling them worldwide will prove problematical. Aviation security is *big* business. The USA Transportation Security Agency (TSA) has 60,000 employees and an annual budget of $7.4bn (TSA, 2016). Risk has a price and the 'political realities supply an understandable excuse for expending money, but not a valid one. In particular, they do not relieve officials of the responsibility of seeking to expend public funds wisely' (Mueller and Stewart, 2011: 22). Despite all these measures, there are always new risks emerging including blinding pilots by directing laser beams into their eyes, unauthorised drones flying near jet engines, interference from computer hackers and complex psychiatric conditions in flight crews. The latter could remain undetected until they cause a catastrophic event such as the 2015 Germanwings' crash. The mentally ill Co-pilot prevented the Captain from re-entering the locked cockpit as the aircraft plunged into the French Alps, killing 150 passengers and crew (Botelho and Smith-Spark, 2015).

The UK's economic and political openness creates both opportunities and vulnerabilities. The UK National Risk Register of Civil Emergencies (2010) incorporates civilian air security measures including passenger, luggage and staff screening plus physical security measures separating inbound and outbound travellers (Cabinet Office, 2010). Similarly, the UK's National Security Strategy (HM Government, 2010) is focussed on the consequences of living in an age of uncertainty and one section was aimed at ensuring safe air travel.

Future-proofing security

National resources were squeezed during the recession of 2008 to 2013. As a result, nations joined together to fight terrorism, and by sharing intelligence and resources they are able to conserve funds. The USA is in a similar economic situation to the EU and is retrenching its global commitments. Neither the USA nor the combined might of the EU nation states are able to regard themselves as guardians of global security. The uncertainty in the Middle East coupled with lack of transparency in China, Russia and other potentially lucrative airline markets is threatening for economically sustainable aviation.

While national and international criminal intelligence has improved, the nature of the threat has changed and the agencies employed to defeat it are often one step behind. Seemingly unrelated events such as the West's economic recession and airline security cannot be overlooked. The European focus on saving the Euro at all costs has meant less government monies for deflecting terrorism in the lawless states from where the terrorists originate. The UK, with its increasing national debt and deficit, has a political will to reduce the armed forces, the first line of physical defence in national crises. Under the 'Armed Forces shake-up', ministers cut the strength of the regular British Army by 20,000 soldiers and had hoped to increase the Army Reserve (the part-time soldiers) by 30,000 as replacements. Despite the £Stg millions spent on an advertising campaign, only 140 recruits actually joined in the first six months of 2014 (Drury, 2014). This is a national vulnerability. During the first Gulf War (1990–1991) there were often more UK troops guarding airports than there were passengers.

Terrorists' activities have had a major impact on aviation for many decades and countering terrorism is tantamount to an act of war outside of national boundaries. By proxy, war can therefore be considered as an airline economic issue, which justifies the concessions that just a few airlines offer to their nation's serving and former servicemen and servicewomen. The threat of participation in war has a major impact on leisure and business air traffic in all destinations. However, airlines can unwittingly support terrorism and illegal activities. Currently 80% of populations live within 50 miles of a coast enabled by all types of connectivity (Kilcullen, 2014) which enables transfers of information, money, energy and legal as well as illegal trades in weapons and drugs (see Chapter 8). Some of these transactions are facilitated by air travel.

Western airlines generally avoid flying to failed or rogue states; however, sometimes a route which had been risk-assessed as 'safe' is actually dangerous or the status changes during flight. In August 1990, a British Airways Boeing 747 was bound for Malaysia. Unfortunately, it landed in Kuwait for refuelling just after the Iraqis invaded, after which the aircraft was impounded and the crew and passengers were taken hostage to be used as human shields. The hostages were finally released in December 1990 and the aircraft destroyed by the Iraqis. In another similar example of under-assessed risk, Malaysian Airlines Flight MH17 overflew Ukraine in July 2014 and was shot down by an anti-aircraft missile believed to be Russian in origin. The route it flew had been risk-assessed as safe (although other airlines had decided that it was not and avoided it). This showed wide variation in regulation and risk assessment throughout the airline industry and prompted calls for one single body to govern these decisions. In response to the threat of European retaliatory economic sanctions, Russia threatened to bar European airlines from flying across Siberia on routes between Europe and Asia. This would have added time and costs to the routes to the Far East and would also have had an environmental impact from increased fuel consumption and negative emissions externalities. This outcome was a mix of political, economic, social and environmental concerns.

Unruly passengers in the air

Only rarely can someone safely escape from an airborne passenger aircraft, no matter how hard they might try (the infamous case of D.B. Cooper being the known exception (Hannaford, 2011)). From time to time, air crew are required to subdue security threats on board ranging from terrorists to unruly passengers. Preserving the safety of the aircraft is paramount and avoiding excessive diversion costs is a secondary consideration in such circumstances. IATA (2012) estimated the diversion cost for several hours for one incident was $US200,000, although one unscheduled landing caused by a row over lack of nuts and crackers on board was estimated to have cost United Airlines $US805,000 (Farmer, 2015). The Tokyo Convention of 1963 (also known as The Convention on Offences and Certain Other Acts Committed on Board Aircraft) makes it unlawful to commit 'acts which, whether or not they are offences [against the penal law of a State], may or do jeopardize the safety of the aircraft or of persons or property therein or which jeopardize good order and discipline on board' (IATA, 2012: 10). The Convention also defined unruly passenger behaviour inflight to be anything which affected the safety and discipline of the aircraft. Crew are trained to deal with such events but depending on circumstances and observers, could be perceived as either heroes, bullies or ineffective. In 2014 Malaysian Airlines' crew impressed passengers and were credited with acting professionally in subduing an aggressive and possibly inebriated passenger (BBC, 2014). Crew actions affect the airline's reputation; however, in this age of social media, any fracas is likely to be found communicated to the world beyond the fuselage even before the aircraft lands.

So what?

One of the challenges for airline economic and social sustainability is ensuring the right stakeholders are involved in key issues and the allocated resources are proportionate. Stakeholders – whether internal or external – hold the key to managing complexity, complication and costs irrespective of whether they lie in outsourcing supplies, lean processing or substituting ITC for frontline customer service. The substitution of employees for technology illustrates one of the socio-economic trade-offs which airlines must make to ensure they remain economically sustainable and protect their reputations as safe and secure carriers in an internationally competitive industry. One of the most challenging future-proofing activities is the transitioning of Check-in Agents to Strategic Corporals, which needs to be strategically integrated into future plans. Governments buttress the aviation industry with international regulations including security protection (a formerly missing market) which is a profitable business for the suppliers with the costs ultimately recoverable from passengers. Unanswered are the questions of how much of this protection is cosmetic and how much is really worthwhile? This is a real challenge for airlines, but it would be politically incorrect to raise this issue in the public domain.

References

Airline Ratings (2014), *Airline Ratings announces its Top Ten airlines for 2015* available from http://www.airlineratings.com/news/402/worlds-top-ten-airlines-#sthash.dLT3whVn.dpuf accessed 4 December 2014

Air Transport News (2014), *Air NZ apologises to and compensates NZ9 passengers for poor customer experience* available from http://www.atn.aero/article.pl?mcateg=&id=51155&member=642E6A2E616E63656C6C40676F6F676C656D61696C2E636F6D7C323537307C323031342D30372D3239 accessed 30 July 2014

Alexander, H. (2014), *Woman dies after airport scanner interferes with her pacemaker* available from http://www.telegraph.co.uk/news/worldnews/europe/russia/11247611/Woman-dies-after-airport-scanner-interferes-with-her-pacemaker.html accessed 23 November 2014

Aral, S., Brynjolfsson, E. and Van Alstyne, M. (2012), Information, technology and information worker productivity, *Information Systems Research*, 23(3) part 2 849–867 available from http://pubsonline.informs.org/doi/abs/10.1287/isre.1110.0408 accessed 1 January 2015

BBC (2003), *Ryanair cuts Buzz routes and jobs* available from http://news.bbc.co.uk/1/hi/business/2800471.stm accessed 5 July 2014

BBC (2014), *Boris Johnson 'calms drunk passenger' on Heathrow flight* available from http://www.bbc.co.uk/news/uk-england-london-30308697 accessed 4 December 2014

Botelho, G. and Smith-Spark L. (2015), *On board Germanwings 9525: An 8-minute descent to death* available from http://edition.cnn.com/2015/03/26/europe/france-germanwings-plane-scene/ accessed 29 August 2015

Business Travel News (2015), *Comment: noise and Heathrow – the truth* available from http://www.btnews.co.uk/article/8355 accessed 27 January 2015

Cabinet Office (2010), *National risk register of civil emergencies (2010)* available from https://www.gov.uk/government/news/national-risk-register-of-civil-emergencies-2010-edition accessed 2 January 2015

Cathay Pacific (2015), *Special Meals* available from http://www.cathaypacific.com/cx/en_GB/travel-information/inflight/food-and-beverages/special-meals.html accessed 8 January 2016

Civil Aviation Authority (CAA) (2011), *Air passenger experience of security screening: Results from CAA survey module (2011)* available from https://www.gov.uk/government/uploads/system/uploads/attachment_data/file/9055/caa-survey-2011.pdf accessed 1 May 2013

Clarkson, M.B.E. (1995), A stakeholder framework for analysing and evaluating corporate social performance, *Academy of Management Review* 20(1) 92–117 available from http://www.jstor.org/stable/258888?seq=1#page_scan_tab_contents accessed 1 January 2015

D'Alfonso, T., Jiang, C. and Wan, Y. (2013), Airport pricing, concession revenues and passenger types, *Journal of Transport Economics and Policy*, 47(1) 71–89 available from http://www.ingentaconnect.com/content/lse/jtep/2013/00000047/00000001/art00005 accessed 30 March 2015

Drury, I. (2014), *Millions spent on advertising campaign to help boost Army Reserve. . .but just 140 recruits join up in six months* available from http://www.dailymail.co.uk/news/article-2739360/Millions-spent-advertising-campaign-help-boost-Army-Reserve-just-140-recruits-join-six-months.html accessed 2 September 2014

easyJet (2013), *On board shop* available from http://support.easyjet.com/case-4173 accessed 23 March 2013

European Commission (2004), *The Commission's decision on Charleroi airport promotes the activities of low-cost airlines and regional development, IP/04/157* available from http://europa.eu/rapid/press-release_IP-04–157_en.htm?locale=en accessed 1 July 2014

European Union (2014), *Compensation and assistance to passengers in the event of denied boarding and of cancellation or long delay of flights* available from http://www.europarl.europa.eu/sides/getDoc.do?pubRef=-//EP//TEXT+TA+P7-TA-2014-0092+0+DOC+XML+V0//EN accessed 30 March 2015

Farmer, B. (2015), *Passenger's demand nuts and crackers cost airline $805,000* available from http://www.nzherald.co.nz/business/news/article.cfm?c_id=3&objectid=11469942 accessed 18 August 2015

Fielding, N. (2013), *Heathrow's troubled T5 calls in specialists to change lightbulbs* available from http://www.exaronews.com/articles/5141/heathrow-s-troubled-t5-calls-in-specialists-to-change-light-bulbs accessed 23 August 2015

Finnair (2014), *Finnair signs an agreement with OSM Aviation on outsourcing of cabin service* available from http://www.finnairgroup.com/mediaen/mediaen_7.html?Id=xml_1684689.html accessed 6 September 2014

Friedman, M. (2007), The social responsibility of business is to increase its profits, *Corporate Ethics and Corporate Governance* 2007 173–178 available from http://link.springer.com/chapter/10.1007%2F978-3-540-70818-6_14 accessed 29 November 2014

Graham, A. (2009), How important are commercial revenues to today's airports? *Journal of Air Transport Management* 15(3) 106–111 available from http://www.sciencedirect.com/science/article/pii/S096969970800152X accessed 2 January 2015

Guardian, The (2014), *Qantas to supersize inflight meals to attract more economy passengers* available from http://www.theguardian.com/business/2014/nov/13/qantas-supersize-inflight-meals-economy-passengers accessed 2 January 2015

Hannaford, A. (2011), *The 40-year mystery of American's greatest hijacking* available from http://www.telegraph.co.uk/culture/8667855/The-40-year-mystery-of-Americas-greatest-skyjacking.html accessed 21 December 2014

Harrison, D., Simpkins, D. and Govan, F. (2003), *We may quit France, says Ryanair, putting at risk cheap flights and second homes* available from http://www.telegraph.co.uk/news/uknews/4189582/We-may-quit-France-says-Ryanair-putting-at-risk-cheap-flights-and-second-homes.html accessed 10 June 2016

HM Government (2010), *A strong Britain in an age of uncertainty: the national security strategy* available from https://www.gov.uk/government/uploads/system/uploads/attachment_data/file/61936/national-security-strategy.pdf accessed 1 January 2015

Holmes, S. (2006), *Cleaning up Boeing* available from http://www.businessweek.com/stories/2006-03-12/cleaning-up-boeing accessed 1 January 2015

Hughes, W., Ancell, D., Gruneberg, S. and Hirst, L. (2004), Exposing the myth of the 1:5:200 ratio relating initial cost, maintenance and staffing costs of office buildings, in *Proceedings 20th ARCOM Conference, 1–3 September 2004*, Khosrowshahi, F. (ed.), Edinburgh, Heriott Watt University 1(2) 373–381 available from http://centaur.reading.ac.uk/12142/ accessed 30 March 2015

IATA (2012), *Unruly passenger prevention and management* available from http://www.iata. org/whatwedo/security/Documents/Guidance-On-Unruly-Passenger-Prevention-And-Management-1st-Edition.pdf accessed 30 March 2013

IATA (2013), *Climate Change: responsibly addressing climate change* available from http://www. iata.org/policy/environment/Pages/climate-change.aspx accessed 17 August 2013

Jacquemont, D. (2014), *The organization that renews itself; lasting value from lean management* available from http://www.mckinsey.com/insights/operations/the_organization_that_renews_itself_lasting_value_from_lean_management accessed 4 August 2014

Jones, P. (2007), Flight-Catering, in *Catering-Management Portrait einer Wachstumsbranche in Theorie und Praxis*, Becker, H. and Grothues, U. (eds), Hamburg, Behr'sVerlag 39–55 available from http://epubs.surrey.ac.uk/2200/2/E66589A3.pdf accessed 2 January 2015

Kenny, C. (2012), *Airport security is killing us* available from http://www.businessweek.com/articles/2012-11-18/how-airport-security-is-killing-us accessed 29 March 2013

Kilcullen, D. (2014), *Out of the mountains: the coming age of the urban guerrilla*, London, C. Hurst & Co. Ltd

Krulak, C. (1999), The Strategic Corporal: Leadership in the Three Block War, *Marines Magazine*, January 1999 available from http://www.au.af.mil/au/awc/awcgate/usmc/strategic_corporal.htm accessed 29 August 2014

Lufthansa (2013), *Special meals* available from http://www.lufthansa.com/uk/en/Special-meals accessed 2 January 2015

Maslow, A.H. (1943), A Theory of Human Motivation, *Psychological Review* 50(4) 370–396 available from http://psycnet.apa.org/journals/rev/50/4/370/ accessed 30 March 2015

McCabe, S. (2009), Who needs a holiday? Evaluating social tourism, *Annals of Tourism Research* 36(4) 667–688 available from http://www.sciencedirect.com/science/article/pii/S0160738309000851 accessed 1 January 2015

Mueller, J. and Stewart M. (2011), *Terror, security and money: balancing the risks, benefits and costs of homeland security* available from http://politicalscience.osu.edu/faculty/jmueller//mid11tsm.pdf accessed 29 March 2013

Murray, H.A. (1938), *Explorations in personality*, Oxford, Oxford University Press available from http://psycnet.apa.org/journals/rev/50/4/370/ accessed 30 March 2015

Nicholson, H. (2014), *Virgin Atlantic pays £47,000 compensation to passengers who set up Facebook group to complain about 26-HOUR flight delay* available from http://www.dailymail.co.uk/travel/article-2683205/Virgin-Atlantic-forced-pay-passengers-47-000-compensation-following-26-HOUR-flight-delay-Florida-UK.html accessed 3 August 2014

Pearce, P.L. (1988), *The Ulysses Factor: evaluating visitors in tourist settings*, New York, Springer-Verlag

Pearce, P.L. and Lee, U.-I. (2005), Developing the travel career approach to tourist motivation, *Journal of Travel Research* 43 226–237 available from http://jtr.sagepub.com/content/43/3/226.short accessed 1 January 2015

Petersen, K. (2011), *A wing and a prayer: outsourcing at Boeing* available from http://uk.reuters. com/article/2011/01/20/us-boeing-dreamliner-idUSTRE70J2UX20110120 accessed 2 January 2014

Prahalad, C.K. and Hamel, G. (1990), The core competence of the corporation, *Harvard Business Review* 68(3) 79–91 available from https://hbr.org/1990/05/the-core-competence-of-the-corporation accessed 2 January 2015

Rust, R.T. and Huang, M.-H. (2012), Optimizing service productivity, *Journal of Marketing* 76(2) 47–66 available from http://journals.ama.org/doi/abs/10.1509/jm.10.0441 accessed 2 January 2015

Ryanair Holdings plc (2013), *Annual Report 2013* available from http://www.ryanair.com/doc/investor/2013/final_annual_report_2013_130731.pdf accessed 5 July 2014

Simon, H.A. (1991), Bounded rationality and organizational learning, *Organization Science* 2(1) 125–134 available from http://pubsonline.informs.org/doi/abs/10.1287/orsc.2.1.125?journalCode=orsc accessed 2 January 2015

Snowdon, C. (2014), *The sock doctrine: what can be done about state-funded political activism? IEA Discussion Paper No. 53* available from http://www.iea.org.uk/sites/default/files/in-the-media/files/The%20sock%20doctrine.pdf accessed 7 February 2014

Southwest Airlines (2014), *Inflight information and services* available from http://www.southwestvacations.com/generalinformation/inflight-services-and-rules accessed 28 July 2014

Spector, T. (2015), '*Airborne peanut allergies on flights are a MYTH': Leading scientist claims it's impossible for a reaction to be triggered this way* available from http://www.dailymail.co.uk/health/article-3222262/Airborne-peanut-allergies-flights-MYTH-Leading-scientist-claims-s-impossible-reaction-triggered-way.html accessed 6 September 2015

Transportation Security Administration (TSA) (2016), *Leadership and organisation* available from https://www.tsa.gov/about/tsa-leadership accessed 12 April 2016

Tretheway, M. and Andriulaitis, R. (2015), *What do we mean by a level playing field in international aviation?* International Transport Forum Discussion Paper No. 2015–06 available from http://www.econstor.eu/handle/10419/109181 accessed 21 November 2015

Tversky, A. and Kahneman, D. (1991), Loss aversion in riskless choice: A reference-dependent model, *The Quarterly Journal of Economics*, 106(4) 1039–1061 available from http://www.jstor.org/discover/10.2307/2937956?uid=2&uid=4&sid=21104255376967 accessed 1 July 2014

United Airlines (2013), *Special meals* available from http://www.united.com/web/en-US/content/travel/inflight/dining/special/default.aspx accessed 23 March 2013

United Nations World Travel Organisation (UNWTO) (2001), *Global Code of Ethics for Tourism* 7 available from http://ethics.unwto.org/en/content/global-code-ethics-tourism-article-7 accessed 16 March 2013

Which? (2013), *Airline surcharges: still too high*, available from www.which.co.uk accessed 16 February 2013

Zeithaml, V.A. and Bitner, M.J. (1996), *Services Marketing*, New York, McGraw Hill

3   Inside economically sustainable airlines

3.1 AIRLINE CULTURE

Cultural focus

Airlines are hubs of conflict as different parts move at different speeds managed by people with different mind-sets. The integration is achieved by the airline culture. Airline culture matters because a strong culture is an asset which can deliver sustainable competitive advantage – or as a weak culture, it is a liability which can undermine an enterprise and act as a predictor of failure. A winning culture is highly prized because of what it offers employees, including opportunities for learning and rewards in exchange for creative thinking and innovative problem-solving. In turn, the employees provide passengers with the service they expect. A 'right first time' culture means fewer accidents, customer complaints and compensation claims. It is simply more economic for a sustainable airline to have the appropriate strategically focussed culture. However, no matter how clever the business strategy, it is wasted if the culture cannot deliver and sustain it. Culture is extremely complex, often resistant to change and continually evolving through contact with both internal and external stakeholders. It cannot be imposed or it could encounter resistance and trigger unintended consequences such as sabotage or strikes.

Employees as guardians of the corporate culture should be focussed and aligned to one goal: to ensure the passengers enjoy their transient encounters and after disembarking will spread the good news around their social network. In the pre-technology age a customer would only tell two to four people of a good experience but would communicate a bad experience to many more. With today's expanse of electronic media, those numbers are now magnified many times and airlines' reputations are under continual scrutiny. In an instant, passengers communicating good and bad experiences can have a significant impact on an airline's reputation and its potential for future revenue.

Airline sustainability-thinking

The culture determines the airline's reputation and one of the means of building and retaining reputation is to implement complete sustainability-thinking throughout (see Figure 7.2 in Chapter 7). Sustainability-thinking warrants a chapter of its own (see Chapter 7). In summary: when a decision is needed, sustainability-thinking requires the airline to take account of the economic, social and environmental impacts of a proposed activity on all its locations. Sustainability-thinking does not need specialist languages. The most technical and complicated topics must be cascaded in language understood by all the stakeholders. If the decision-makers understand each other, the resultant decision is liable to be much better formed and risks will be reduced. (As a salutary lesson to simplicity, this did not happen in the banking crisis of 2008. The Directors of some of the failed banks confessed that their banks' products were too technical and too complicated for them to understand.) A sustainable airline has sustainability-thinking in the veins of every employee since they are the most important stakeholder group. Whether they are Administrators, Managers, Tug Drivers, Cargo Loaders, Customer Service Agents, Call Centre Operators, Catering Assistants or Board members their primary function is to service customers and in order to do so efficiently and effectively they must consider the potential impacts of their decisions before they commit to them. Underpinning the sustainable decision-making process (see Chapter 7) is a thread of decency – 'ethical' behaviour – showing that decision-makers know the difference between right and wrong. Ethical behaviour defined as such means that any decision is made giving due regard for transparency and honesty and impartiality of information and data. This will create a strong reputation for the airline which, after all, is where passengers place their trust while flying, in a metal tube, 11,000 metres above the earth.

Airlines probably need to consider their sustainability factors more than other industries because of their organisational complexity, international profile and contrail visibility as they cross continents. Their behaviour determines whether they will be able to continue operating between and within nations. In theory they have the freedom of the skies; in reality their movements are grounded in a myriad of treaties and contracts many of which have been negotiated by national, multi-national and supranational governments or NGOs rather than the airlines themselves. By slavishly adhering to these agreements the aviation industry will retain a high reputation and be regarded as a safe means of travel. However, legislation and regulations designed for aviation can sometimes stray further than 'hygiene' factors such as health and safety and into those domains which are more appropriate for the State (see Chapter 5).

Any airline using sustainability-thinking will also have the confidence of regulators and suppliers (including airports, banks and insurers) all of whom are so essential to ongoing economic viability. Pursuing high sustainability-thinking and delivering sustainability-support activities minimises risks meaning that airlines can focus on their businesses and will ultimately profit. Low sustainability-thinking airlines run high risks playing 'catch up' by focussing on clean-up mitigations and paying fines. Society sets the social norms upheld by democratically elected legislators. Eventually legislation commits commercial organisations to support governments' aims. Advanced-world governments are now obligating private enterprises to assume responsibilities for social and environmental issues over which airlines have little or no control (see Chapter 5 and Chapter 6). Legislators appear unconcerned that the more regulation is placed upon commercial enterprises the more costs and prices will have to rise which can affect international competitiveness. The increased price of the impacted goods and services is eventually felt hardest by those consumers who have the least disposable income. Unlike other forms of public transport in many democratised nations, airlines receive no State funding for fulfilling the social obligations of governments, an omission which might inadvertently precipitate one of the characteristics of market inefficiency or failure (see Chapter 1 and Chapter 8).

Mission, vision, values, goals and objectives

Culture needs definition through clearly stated and memorable mission, vision and values, understood by all employees, and aligned with, and displayed by, their behaviours. This is the economic sustainability 'scaffolding'. Mission and vision statements are often confused. Mission statements (Table 3.1) are simple outlines of the purpose of the organisation and why it exists; however, it is sometimes impossible to memorise and often muddled with (and indistinguishable from) the vision. Mission statements motivate employees and can entice customers.

Table 3.1 Mission statements – why the airlines exist

Airline	Mission
Ryanair (2015)	'Ryanair's objective is to firmly establish itself as Europe's leading low-fares scheduled passenger airline through continued improvements and expanded offerings of its low-fares service. Ryanair aims to offer low fares that generate increased passenger traffic while maintaining a continuous focus on cost-containment and operating efficiencies.'
Southwest Airlines (2013)	'The mission of Southwest Airlines is dedication to the highest quality of Customer Service delivered with a sense of warmth, friendliness, individual pride, and Company Spirit.'
Virgin Atlantic plc (2013)	'To grow a profitable airline where people love to fly and where people love to work.' (2013)
Virgin Atlantic plc (2014a)	'Our mission statement is simple yet the foundation of everything we do here at Virgin Atlantic Airways . . . to embrace the human spirit and let it fly.' (2014a)
United Airlines Inc. (2014)	'Our mission is to create an inclusive work environment, characterized by dignity and respect that empowers every employee to serve the global marketplace and contribute to our success. Specifically, Diversity and Inclusion is managed purposefully and strategically to enable United to operate more productively and efficiently.'

Creating a mission statement can be the output of a specialised group, the Board of Directors, Human Resources Department, external consultants, employee suggestions (for which employees can vote) or even a team-building exercise. The mission statements are supported by visions ('what' is aspired to be achieved) which can be as diverse as 'the best airline in the world' (implicit emphasis on customer service but undeliverable if the aircraft are shabby, the crew uncooperative and food inedible); 'the greenest airline ever' (environmentally focussed strategy but difficult to achieve with the fossil-based fuels needed); 'the cheapest airline' (focus on lower costs, lower fares – and possibly low-paid employees?) and 'the most efficient airline in the universe' (over-ambitious, unrealistic, open to ridicule and doomed to fail).

The mission and vision statements need to be clear, concise and memorable so that internal and external stakeholders can have confidence in them. They are underpinned by employees exhibiting supporting behaviours through living the core values (the 'how' of delivering the mission and vision) and focussing on delivering their goals which are in turn formed by the objectives (Figure 3.1). Objectives should be Specific, Measurable, Achievable, Realistic and Timely (SMART) and described by the qualitative CSFs and measured by the quantitative KPIs.

The core values need to be authentic. The formerly State-owned British Overseas Airways Corporation (BOAC) was once renowned for its inefficiencies which undermined its mission statement ('To fly to serve'). Its detractors mocked the lack of authenticity, renaming it as 'Better On A Camel'. Once it was privatised it became 'British Airways' (BA) and during the transition phase the initials were

Figure 3.1 The performance pyramid

interpreted as 'Bloody Awful'. This mockery was induced by the lack of passenger service which undermined its mission and vision statements. Similarly, Boeing's reputation was undermined by its nomenclature of 'Bits Of Engines In Neighbourhood Gardens' following aircraft accidents, incidents and near-misses in the 1960s, all of which provided learning points incorporated into making future aircraft safer.

Sustainable airline core values

Supporting the mission and vision are the core values which underpin the airline culture (a social system of behavioural norms). The core values of decision-makers help them prioritise the problems they solve and the solutions they consider. Employees are the greatest advocates for their airline and should embody the airline's values before they are employed because it is too time-consuming and productivity-negating to change attitudes. However, human beings are not identical and there are often insufficient numbers of potential employees with the right attitude and aptitude in the recruitment pool. Furthermore, the legacy of bad industrial relations still hovers over many carriers (especially some of the more established operators). The younger carriers have had the opportunity to hire fresh, enthusiastic employees and begin operations without what is sometimes a negative cultural legacy.

There are four significant categories of values: core, aspirational, permission-to-play or accidental (Table 3.2).

If the core values do not support the aspirational values, there is a gap (a dissonance) revealed when the airline over-promises and under-delivers on passengers' expectations (e.g. punctuality and service consistency). The employees, too, can find a dissonance between what they expected from the organisation and what the organisation delivers as expressed by inconsistent management and unstable industrial relations. So core values which resonate with employees are fundamental to a well-managed organisation of any type.

A value is a core value when it has more control than most of the other values (Pant and Lachman, 1998). The core values of an airline are central to understanding employee attitudes, behaviours, motivations and decision-making. They are expressed in words which are memorable (e.g. 'honest', 'efficient', 'fun', 'fair') and should be lived by every member of the organisation. They are the almost inflexible core of the company (the corporate DNA) and are the guiding principles of

Table 3.2 Types of organisational values (Lencioni, 2002)

Value	Explanation
core	change little over time
aspirational	needed for future development (must not dilute the core values)
permission-to-play	minimum behavioural and social standards
accidental	arise spontaneously

behaviour which, led by the leadership who live and breathe them, must be embedded throughout the organisation. However, core values can also be used to misrepresent an organisation. One of the best examples of this is Enron, the bankrupt American energy conglomerate. In its heyday it formed Enron Air, the private jet company used to ferry corporate executives, families and friends on business and personal trips (unethical behaviour only visible after it failed). Enron was a much-admired company because of its spectacular financial performance until it went bankrupt owing $US13.12bn (£Stg9.3bn or €11.8bn) (*USA Today*, 2002). Enron's core values were: communication ('we have an obligation to communicate'); respect ('we treat others as we would like to be treated'); integrity ('we work with customers and prospects openly, honestly and sincerely') and excellence ('we are satisfied with nothing less than the very best in everything we do') (Burkus, 2011: n.p.). (Its Code of Ethics purportedly ran to over 60 pages.) This example of misrepresentation and dissonant core values accompanied by breathtakingly unethical behaviour illustrated the importance of employing sustainability-thinking (see Chapter 7) with an accompanying challenge culture. The collapse of Enron illustrated the consequences of moral hazard, asymmetric information, imperfect knowledge and the principal-agent problem (where the agent acted in his own self-interest using information to which only he had access). This market failure resulted in suicides, unemployment, bankruptcies and jail time.

Core values are the axis of corporate behaviour and do not change when the world changes around them (Lencioni, 2002). If values are authentic, they will reflect consistent employee behaviour. Values are also cultural enablers, hard to identify and categorise, difficult to change and yet portable within the organisation so they can absorb new experiences to prompt action (Mileti *et al.*, 2002). They are the day-to-day glue for routine interactions, but in turbulent times such as during disruption caused by an industrial strike or natural disaster, they become central to mitigating actions as the 'pivots' around which other (less critical) values can circulate and interact. They are also often repetitions of the same words as competitors ('honesty', 'integrity', 'efficiency', 'trust', 'reliability'), dressed up with a corporate logo and launched with public relations and advertising fanfare. In a no-challenge culture they can lead to a false consensus – a form of groupthink – in which members make poor quality decisions because of a failure to challenge. This in turn encourages overly optimistic risk-taking, ignores warning signs, hides doubts and pressures conformance (Janis, 1997).

Benefits of core values

Core values can deliver competitive advantage. Because they set the behaviours needed, they can also reduce costs by minimising bureaucracy, sick leave, absenteeism, processes and rules. They should be based on performance and allow flexibility in interpretation. They are not prescriptive (i.e. 'Employees must not . . .'), but they are a unifying force to improve corporate morale as evidenced by CSFs such as 'lower employee turnover'. Challenging under the core values (e.g. 'I do not believe that you behaved in accordance with the core value of 'honesty' when you decided to . . .') can give an objective framework for employees to challenge upwards through the hierarchy. In this way, using the values can reduce the intimidation from hierarchical behaviours. This matters because being able to challenge is a risk prevention measure particularly in a safety-conscious industry like aviation.

Core values can be used during business transformations such as changing cultures, creating mergers, forming alliances or completing takeovers. If there is a mismatch between the strategy and the culture, then either a change in strategy or a change in culture is needed – and sometimes changes in both.

An example of successful culture change occurred at the Boeing Aircraft Corporation (Holmes, 2006). The Boeing 787 Dreamliner fleet was plagued with minor technical problems after launch but was finally grounded in 2013 by a problem with the lithium batteries (Boeing, 2013). Critics believed that the problems started in 1997 when military aircraft manufacturer McDonnell Douglas merged with commercial aircraft manufacturer Boeing Aircraft. When McDonnell Douglas' personnel were installed in the leadership the culture changed from engineering dominance to finance focus on profits. They prioritised on outsourcing the innovative and complex systems and materials needed to build the Dreamliner and it was believed that as a consequence, Boeing lost control of the output. There appeared to be no accountability. These matters were compounded by a series of personal scandals which led to senior personnel changes with the appointment of a new Chief Executive Officer. He created a culture which allowed challenge without risk and where employees could speak up if they believed something was wrong. He also broke down the organisational silos (the deep and narrow employee funnels with little communication between them) and encouraged collaboration by linking pay and bonuses to how executives embraced the 'Living Boeing Values' which promoted integrity and avoided abusive behaviour. Financial rewards would reflect the cyclical nature of the aerospace industry rather than the previous system that rewarded for a higher share price. Since the former reward system did not take account of the management's performance it therefore provided few incentives to improve when the industry was on a downturn (Holmes, 2006).

Guardians of the values

In theory, Human Resources (the 'people' department) should be the keeper of the core values using them for hiring, firing, performance management, reward, training and succession planning. What must not be forgotten is that aviation (and airlines as a subset) is a people business. Aviation should be internally led by the Human Resources Department recruiting those employees whose values fit with the corporate core values. In contrast, the aspirational values as uncovered by the Marketing Department are formed from passenger feedback on the expressed behaviours. This is conveyed to the Human Resources Department for training packages which will ultimately deliver the desired customer service to passengers. However, there is sometimes a shortage of the 'right' people available at recruitment time and the aspirational behaviours are sometimes not easily fulfilled.

Determining the core values

Core values can attract ridicule (as illustrated by Enron) because they do not always reflect the cultural core of the company, having been created by the optimistic Marketing Department as the voice of the customer rather than the Human Resources Department as the voice of the employees. Ideally, the core values uncovered by Human Resources would match the Marketing Department's aspirations. Placing the emphasis on employee-oriented culture is more appropriate in customer service organisations than a market-focussed emphasis (Igo and Skitmore, 2006). Successful Southwest Airlines would be the exemplar of this practice since its culture focusses on the employees and they in turn focus on their customers. Determining the core values requires undertaking a full cultural assessment to determine the core 'temperature' of the airline and a cultural change programme developed to bridge any dissonance between the customers' perceptions and the airline's service delivery (Table 3.3).

In the example in Table 3.3, Human Resources' role would be to convert 'snooty' (column 3) to 'welcoming' (column 2) through working with the employees to alter their feelings of being 'miserable' (column 1) with an appropriate training programme. Taking the corporate temperature involves surveying the employees to uncover what they really believe to be the corporate atmosphere, i.e. the exhibited behaviours.

There are many methods available to determine an organisation's actual behaviours and core values, including:

• **recruiting an anthropologist** who could ensure that the core temperature of the airline is accurately recorded through observation of employees interacting with each other (including those at Board level) as well as with customers.

Table 3.3 Dissonance among exhibited values, aspirational values and the expressed behaviours

What the Human Resources Department found when analysing employees' exhibited behaviours (1)	Values as espoused by the Marketing Department and the advertising campaign (aspirational behaviours) (2)	What the customers told the Marketing Department about how they were treated (expressed behaviours) (3)
hierarchical	warm	unsmiling
bullying	democratic	bossy
miserable	welcoming	snooty
stuffy	entrepreneurial	old-fashioned
inflexible	innovative	inflexible
silos	helpful	impolite
selfish	proactive	unhelpful
begrudging	team players	uncooperative
authoritarian	flexible	unsympathetic
disorganised	punctual	unpunctual

From these observations (column 1, Table 3.3), the actual behaviours could be derived and used as a baseline for comparing with the customer-desired, aspirational behaviours (column 2, Table 3.3).

- ***surveying employees' perceptions*** on eight key factors of airline operations to test for (i) cultural stability and (ii) adaptability to uncover the values that drive employees' behaviours (Gordon and DiTomaso, 1992). The key factors for cultural stability are integration and communication, development and promotion from within, and fairness of reward. Testing adaptability requires a combination of action-orientation, innovation and risk-taking, clarity of strategy and shared goals, systematic decision-making and accountability. Cultural strength is measured by all eight factors (Gordon and DiTomaso, 1992). Once the perceptions are uncovered they should be matched to the customers' desired service values (column 2). If a gap is revealed, the necessary culture change programme should be instituted to convert column 3 expressed behaviours to deliver those service qualities desired in column 2 (Table 3.3).
- ***imposing core values*** decided by the Board of Directors. These would be values they believe could be instrumental in future growth. However, these values would be cascaded downwards and imposing the Board's opinions would miss the opportunity to collect the true values of daily corporate life. The values would lack authenticity and could reflect more aspirational than core values (van Rekom *et al.*, 2006). Furthermore, their application would most likely be unsuccessful.
- ***employing cognitive mapping*** to measure the core values of daily corporate life by analysing the behaviour of airline employees. This would show the support the values receive and give an indication of what actions must be taken to serve the values. By questioning employees about what they did, why they did it in that way and why it was important to them it is possible to determine which current values – and employees – are likely to be resistant to change (i.e. the blockers). This can be plotted on an organisational cultural assessment indicator (OCAI) (Cameron and Quinn, 2006). The cultural profile revealed would reflect the 'underlying attributes, including the management style, strategic plans, climate, reward system, means of bonding, leadership, and basic values of the organisation' (Cameron and Quinn, 2006: 83). As multi-faceted entities, airlines are externally focussed, customer-oriented industries which must also maintain an internal focus on employees with core values which reflect both the internal and external dimensions. Airlines must also exhibit the characteristics of stable industries (which rely on routines for operations) as well as those of dynamic industries (Table 3.4).

The emergent cultures are in four broad categories: (a) hierarchy – characterised by efficiency and bureaucratic rules including hierarchy and meritocracy; (b) clan – a friendly workplace rather like a family; (c) adhocracy – characterised by no centralised power or authority but the formation of ad hoc groups and (d) market – a results-oriented workplace led by pursuit of competitiveness (Cameron and

Table 3.4 Suggested values for internally and externally focussed industries (adapted from and based on Cameron and Quinn, 2006)

Industry focus	OCAI values	Possible airline core values (common words for both internally and externally focussed organisations in italics)
Externally focussed		
stable industries	efficiency, timeliness, consistency, uniformity	communication, friendly, loyal, traditional, organised, dependable, secure, dedicated, cooperation, performance, *competitive, teamwork, trust, excellence, fun*
dynamic industries	commitment, communication, development	
Internally focussed		
stable industries	market share, goal achievement, profitability	challenge, anticipating, creative, innovative, openness, invest, performance, winning, pioneering, inspiring, enjoyment, *competitive, teamwork, trust, excellence, fun*
dynamic industries	innovation, transformation, agility	

Quinn, 2006). Each category has a little of the others in it but one type will be dominant at any particular time.

The dynamic, externally focussed airline industry should aim to be dominant in the clan category responding to employee needs and building teams and collaboration. This would then fan outwards into a customer focus (market culture) but with a touch of hierarchy (incorporating the stable industry characteristics of efficiency, timeliness, consistency and uniformity) to ensure operational perform-ance. There will also be a need for a touch of the adhocracy culture (forming teams for special projects, decentralised decision-making and shared risk-taking) to innovate and drive the airline forwards. NASA illustrated how an organisation can respond to a crisis after the 'successful failure of the Apollo 13 space mission' (Cameron and Quinn, 2006: 44) by being flexible, adaptable, creative and dynamic and yet these characteristics might not be apparent at non-crisis times. The airline industry has certainly had many crises to manage – infectious diseases, terrorism, volcanic eruptions, fleet groundings – all of which have given it a chance to show its adaptable and flexible characteristics. These crises were managed against a background of competition, stakeholder and customer pressures, changes in industry structure and regulation, ITC evolution and the opening of new trade routes. Faced with the turmoil, some airlines' cultures were infinitely more flexible, adaptable and sustainable than others.

Appropriate values

Values have to be appropriate and reflect the type of airline and the commercial environment in which it conducts its business. A comparison of airline industry values is illuminating. 'Fun' is an all embracing value implying enjoyment; however, many airlines do not consider fun to be an 'appropriate' value which is short-sighted because where employees are empowered to have fun they also have the freedom to innovate. ('Fun' in the airline context does not imply 'irresponsible'.) Some organisations' values (Table 3.5) can be complicated. Where these are not clearly expressed – or easy to locate on the website – it can be extremely difficult for the employees to live by them. What is also important is that the values are memorable and some of those in Table 3.5 are not easily memorised. Simplicity is best.

Some of the values would be better included in a separate Code of Conduct, i.e. it would be better to simplify the accompanying explanations and have two documents (one for easy-to-remember values and one for conduct) rather than muddle and complicate what should be a very simple concept.

Values must be lived by every employee to give them meaning. As an example: one airline's Engineering Overhaul SBU was working on a Friday afternoon ahead of the Christmas party later that evening. The Trade Union Convener approached the Chief Executive with a request that the employees be allowed to finish one hour earlier to allow sufficient time to prepare for the party. Making the challenge using the 'fun' value, the Convener explained that in the time available between the shift finishing and the party starting, the employees would have insufficient time to return home, shower, change clothes and arrive on time at the party. The Chief Executive understood the significance of the challenge and conceded despite the obvious cost of the loss of one hour's output. This gave real traction to, and confidence in, the values.

Core values cannot be used in isolation. They need the organisation structures and systems to make them effective because on their own they are meaningless: they have to fit within the overall aim of serving the customer. If they are not properly used they can become obstacles to change as happened in the downfall of low-cost, American carrier People Express (1982–1987) (Hackman, 1998). The management wanted to create an innovative, non-bureaucratic organisation structure which would unleash the inherent power of individuals and teams previously locked into traditional structures. The airline's vision was developed and training ensued. While People Express was less than 1,000 employees it was a success with coordinating teams forming naturally. However, with growth it became apparent that the self-managing workforce lacked the supporting structure needed. The founders felt that installing structures and systems would undermine their vision and retreat from their values. Instead of solving the **real** problem (see Chapter 7) and installing the support framework, the management focussed on reiterating the values. 'In a time of trouble, the founders reaffirmed the principles that had been responsible for their early success and behaved more vigorously than ever in accord with them. It did not work' (Hackman, 1998: 259). The airline could not compete with other airlines which had the structures supporting their values and eventually it was merged into Continental Express.

Table 3.5 Examples of aviation industry core values

Aviation organisation	Core values
IATA (n.d.)	'Values are important. We make IATA a great place to work through living and upholding our values every day. They also support our commitment to deliver results for the industry. These values are: People focus, Speed, Innovation, Openness to change, Integrity, Teamwork and cultural intelligence, Results orientation, Leadership.'
Southwest Airlines (USA) (2013)	'Live the Southwest Way **Warrior Spirit:** Work Hard, Desire to be the best, Be courageous, Display urgency, Persevere, Innovate **Servant's Heart:** Follow The Golden Rule, Adhere to the Principles, Treat others with respect, Put others first, Be egalitarian, Demonstrate proactive Customer Service, Embrace the SWA Family **Fun-LUVing Attitude:** Have FUN, Don't take yourself too seriously, Maintain perspective, Celebrate successes, Enjoy your work, Be a passionate Teamplayer **Work the Southwest Way:** Safety and Reliability, Friendly Customer Service, Low Cost.'
The Emirates Group (n.d.)	**'Our Vision & Values:** The principles that propel us forward A strong and stable leadership team, ambitious yet calculated decision-making and ground-breaking ideas all contribute to the creation of great companies. Of course, these have played a major part in our development, but we believe our business ethics are the foundation on which our success has been built. Caring for our employees and stakeholders, as well as the environment and the communities we serve, have played a huge part in our past and will continue to shape our future.'

continued . . .

Table 3.5 Continued

Singapore Airlines (n.d.)	**'Pursuit of Excellence** We strive for the highest professional standards in our work and aim to be the best in everything we do. **Safety** We regard safety as an essential part of all our operations. We maintain our equipment and adopt practices that promote the safety of our customers and staff. **Customer First** Our customers are foremost in our minds all the time. We go the extra mile to exceed their expectations. **Concern for Staff** We value our staff and care for their well-being. We treat them with respect and dignity and seek to provide them with appropriate training and development so that they can lead fulfilling careers. **Integrity** We strive for fairness in all our business and working relationships. **Teamwork** We work with pride as a worldwide team to achieve success together.'

Change and core values

Using the core values as a reference point in the change process means there is a commonality – a behavioural language – which will withstand the cultural chaos that inevitably follows such transitions. Such changes can be particularly difficult when complicated by different languages both national and technical. The leadership must share their vision of where they want the airline to go and make any cultural change easy and mandatory. Employees must sign up to the values and since employees' attitudes dictate their behaviour, the values will initially be practised to varying degrees. If the transition is significant such as in a merger, acquisition, downsizing or takeover and is a result of organisational failure (e.g. the airline selling a loss-making subsidiary) then employees must understand that the previous behaviours which necessitated the transition cannot continue unchecked. How they behave determines the level of trust that passengers will have in the carrier – and how the airline's reputation will be measured.

Performance mechanisms

There are formal and informal mechanisms (Table 3.6) for getting the most out of corporate culture all of which demonstrate planning as well as thoughtfulness and consideration (the characteristics airline employees are asked to communicate to passengers).

Learning organisations vs training organisations

In support of the performance mechanisms, learning organisations embed changes and re-measure their impact at regular intervals. If the learning is not embedded then the airline might only be a 'training organisation' – one that wastes resources without adding any value. All employees should be empowered and encouraged to participate and share knowledge howsoever it is (legally) acquired. Acquisition, internal transmission and storing information all comprise organisational memory and can give an airline an innovative edge stemming from a culture which no competitor can replicate. Sources are everywhere: university links, job swaps or even establishing lunchtime seminars to share knowledge. There are endless possibilities often with minimal cost. Organisations are systems of interrelated roles which guide members as to reasoning about the problems and decisions facing them and recommending where to seek appropriate and legitimate information (Simon, 1991). Each role interacts with others forming a role system which is activated through knowledge. All learning takes place in human heads but an organisation only learns in two ways: either through the learning of its existing members or by the ingestion of new members importing their externally acquired knowledge. The linking and transmission of knowledge in the organisation has a bearing on how the organisation behaves. The transference from member or group of members to others determines whether knowledge is available to decision-makers. It is therefore important to know where knowledge is stored and who has

Table 3.6 Mechanisms for maximising cultural benefits (adapted from Katzenbach et al., 2012: 8)

Formal mechanisms		Informal mechanisms	
reporting structures (e.g. annual reports; organisational hierarchy)	performance management (e.g. annual employee reviews)	behaviour modelling by senior leaders	peer-to-peer interactions (e.g. sharing coffee breaks and knowledge)
decision rules and rights (e.g. policies and procedures)	compensation and rewards	meaningful manager-employee connections (e.g. open door policies, informal gatherings)	communities of interest (e.g. forming improvement circles, sports clubs, dance clubs etc.)
business processes and policies (e.g. organisational mechanisms and structures)	internal communications (e.g. regular corporate news distribution, team meetings)	internal cross-organisational networks (e.g. sharing knowledge across organisational silos)	engagement of exemplars and motivational leaders (e.g. encouraging relevant specialists to share their knowledge with the employees)
training, leadership and organisational development programmes (e.g. continuing professional development which can be internally or externally delivered)	councils and committees (e.g. works councils, trades unions)	ad hoc gatherings (e.g. to celebrate successes such as the end of a major or difficult project)	changes to physical plant, resources and aesthetics

learned it (Simon, 1991). Storing the information or data so that it can be found (especially after an employee has departed) is critical to keeping the information within the organisation. Sometimes this means storing it in ITC: at other times it can mean producing a policy or strategy to carry the learning through once the knowledgeable employee has departed. One example of failure to carry through policy occurred in an airline which had decided ten years previously that all armrests in the economy section (except for the bulkhead and exit row seats) should lift to level with the seat backs (see Chapter 5). This would enable larger passengers to sit across two seats and immobile passengers to be moved across to the window seats without injury. A policy was produced that should have continued into the future but with employee changes and no continuity, the airline 'forgot'. As a result, the armrests in the 2013-onwards aircraft retracted to only 60°. This meant that obese passengers could not use two adjacent economy seats and more damagingly, immobile passengers could not easily be transferred over the aisle and possibly mid-seat to the window seat. This could cause injuries to both the passengers and the Mobility Assistants who lifted them particularly because the aisle armrests did not lift either. It also meant that some elderly passengers could not leave their seats without some crew-provided lifting assistance (which is forbidden – see Chapter 5) especially if the seat in front was in the recline position. The consequence could eventually mean increasing the numbers of crew members to assist less mobile passengers and widening employers' liability insurance to cover any crew injuries – both of which would increase operating costs.

3.2 FAIRNESS

Employees and fairness

The principle of fairness is important in all organisations. Life is sometimes unfair: some people have more luck – both good and bad – than others. Some unfairness is undeserved; some is self-inflicted. Fairness is reflected in three justice principles: distributive (connected to honesty, excellent service and compensation), procedural (consistent procedures free of personal biases) and interactional (which relates to honesty, openness and politeness) (Bowen *et al.*, 1999). These are the fairness principles to which a sustainable airline should adhere.

Fairness needs to underpin sustainable airline behaviour towards employees who, in turn, will show fairness to passengers. Fairness is a virtuous circle and applied through Human Resources processes to employee selection, hiring, performance management, reward, promotion, succession planning and – if necessary – firing. Airlines are labour-intensive service businesses and fairly treated employees will feel sufficiently empowered to treat the passengers in the same manner that they feel treated (distributive, procedural and interactional fairness). Employee satisfaction closely correlates with customer satisfaction and can be undermined by evidence of nepotism or favouritism giving less than equal treatment to everyone regardless of age, disability, gender or gender reassignment, religion or belief, sexual orientation, race, culture, language, marriage or civil partnership, pregnancy, maternity and/or paternity, size, intergenerational obligations, political persuasion or trade union membership.

Fairness can, however, have wider connotations. As part of its community outreach efforts, one airline recognised the difficulties for learning-disabled adults to find employment and attempted to provide suitable career opportunities for them. After examining many departments and many tasks it was decided that the Catering Department had the most potential with a collegiate atmosphere and a range of duties which were not too intellectually taxing. A visit to the catering facility determined that most of the employees were from ethnic minorities and linked by birth, nationality, language and/or community and they did not want to open opportunities for anyone who did not fit their nepotistic criteria. This was a lost opportunity to help a disadvantaged minority – a social-economic-ethical challenge – and was blatantly unfair on the learning-disabled adults. Airline management would not tackle this issue for fear of a catering strike which would disrupt the airline. The learning-disabled people remained unemployed.

Power-distance relationships and fairness

While class structures have been diminishing in society, there are still strains of hierarchical behaviours in many of the legacy carriers. Constructs like the power-distance index (PDIs) (Franke *et al.*, 1991) can be used to examine the level of inequality, tolerance and challenge in an organisation by explaining how less powerful members perceive, accept and expect the unequal distribution of power. The distance between leader and led is perceived as low in cultures that are more consultative or democratic and when people feel more equal they will challenge decision-makers. Where the distance between leader and led is perceived as high, there is less challenge and the autocratic or paternalistic leaders retain their power due to their exalted position in the hierarchy.

Much airline terminology (Captain, Crew, First Officer, Engineer) is hierarchical and was derived from the Navy environment where so many of the employees of legacy carriers began their careers. This gave rise to a military, hierarchical culture which did not prove to be adaptable in a competitive environment such as that which followed liberalisation. Early airline management was rather like war leadership with authority vested in the most senior employee present. Employees were subservient and unchallenging (as in the antecedent armed forces) and this has proved to be a source of unfairness as well as a competitive handicap for many of the older-established carriers. Employee promotion was by steps – not leaps – following the armed forces' procedures. Before deregulation, employees in State-owned airlines would be expected to follow instructions as a means of avoiding any risks with which authoritative managers were not comfortable. However, once airlines were liberated from State control, the rigid internal structures could not operate as before because they were intertwined with external markets and their competitive pressures. Competition for customers and employees changed the airlines' cultures. While the State was effectively underwriting the business much uncertainty (and therefore risk) was eliminated. This was not sustainable after liberalisation when aviation bounded into one of the most uncertain commercial environments ever. Consequently airline leaders have to be adaptable, flexible and efficient to guide their organisations safely and sustainably through the chaos. They can no longer rely on their position in the hierarchy to ensure employee conformance.

Passengers and fairness

Customers' expectations of fairness are that the airline will deliver 'dependably and consistently (reliability), to offer clean, comfortable facilities (tangibles), to give prompt service (responsiveness), to be competent and courteous (assurance) and to extend caring, individualised attention (empathy)' (Bowen *et al.*, 1999: 11). If the airline fails to meet customers' expectations there follows the costly process of service recovery involving letter-writing, compensation payments, complaints broadcast and reputational loss. It can also mean a loss of trust (that intangible on which sustainable airlines depend for passengers' repurchase intentions) and ultimately loss of custom.

Airlines are sensitive to passengers' complaints; however, sifting the genuine from the vexatious is often a challenge particularly with the willingness of no-win-no-fee lawyers to tackle airlines. Passengers of low-cost carriers are less likely to complain about service quality than passengers of networked carriers given the same levels of service (Wittman, 2014). Possible explanations might lie in 'price-based expectations of service quality, lack of information about how to complain ... or qualitative differences in front-line customer service between airlines' (Wittman, 2014: 64).

Determining service quality and customer satisfaction is always challenging in a service industry where so much subjectivity reigns. Essentially there are three components of quality (Torres, 2014). The first, customer-service quality, is influenced by expectations, perceptions and service delivery. The second, expert-driven quality, is a product of service standards and any system of awards or ratings and the third is the internal quality, i.e. the output of quality improvement and standards. In the USA the Department of Transportation (2015) measures quality by collecting customer complaint data under two broad headings: (a) flight problems (over-sales, reservations, ticketing and denied boarding, fares, refunds and mis-handled baggage) and (b) customer service (disabled passengers, advertising, discrimination, animals and 'other').

Human rights and fairness

The international nature of aviation means that fairness also involves political systems and human rights. Many airlines fly on profitable routes to nations with regimes which employees (and their fellow citizens) believe are abhorrent. Trade with such regimes might be repugnant to socially inclined stakeholders but in the commercial world, each airline has to trade-off its economic and competitive needs with any unfairness at some of its destinations. However, trade can do much good as well as inadvertently supporting some corrupt and unacceptable regimes. 'If goods don't cross borders, armies will' has been attributed to Frédéric Bastiat (1801–1850), French economist and champion of free markets and limited government. However, this is almost negated by events of the last decades when the West has traded with regimes such as Saudi Arabia, China, Azerbaijan and Russia which supply products essential for airline operations and which are also lucrative revenue-earning airline destinations. At what point does the economically sustainable airline surrender a lucrative route because of what the developed world perceives as human rights abuses (see Chapter 7)? This situation is a trade-off: airline economics vs society and ethics (and possibly politics).

3.3 LEADERSHIP IN AN ECONOMICALLY SUSTAINABLE AIRLINE

Adaptable, flexible and powerful leadership

Economically sustainable airlines require future-proofing leadership. Different leadership characteristics are required for different situations and the leaders will, in turn, make decisions in different ways depending on the quality of decisions required, the commitment of subordinates and the time available to make them. Leadership has many sources of power which are used to influence subordinates and peers (French and Raven, 1959). Each type of power (Table 3.7) has different uses and the ability to use them all is a skill few leaders possess although most tend to understand at least some of these sources. For example, a leader in autocratic mode would make the decision and inform the stakeholders; in consultative mode the leader using the specialists at his/her disposal would gather information and then make the decision; and using reward power, the leader could decide performance-linked pay increases.

Occasionally groupthink (see Chapter 7) is actually useful for a charismatic and powerful leader who has to work with a large number of people and needs quick decisions to complete projects (Janis, 1997). Leadership is a critical airline management skill because of the increasing complexity and complication which surrounds the industry and through which the leaders must find a sustainable route. Sustainable leaders are differentiated from managers by an unquenchable thirst for new knowledge while constantly horizon-scanning. Unlike management, leadership is focussed on creating goals and relies on relationships and the building of networks to achieve economic sustainability. Leaders broaden their own knowledge by encouraging others to take risks and showcase their talents. Such thinking also builds the recruitment pool from which roles can be filled. Longer term partnering with educational institutions (high schools, technical colleges and universities) can assist with future employee recruitment as well as access to new knowledge which could give individual airlines a competitive edge. This would be a win-win for society and airline economics.

Table 3.7 Types of power (adapted from French and Raven, 1959)

Type of power	Manifestation
autocratic	concentrated in one person
charisma	intangible quality of personal influence which has a positive impact
coercive	ability to punish a subordinate
expert	attained by skills, knowledge or previous experience
information	power belongs with the specialist
legitimate	corresponds to the executive level within the organisation: higher positions have higher power
referent	gained by association such as in the role of deputy or assistant
reward	power to influence rewards as a result of work performance

Crises and leadership

In the event of a crisis, the leadership team must pull together to support their sustainable airline and in the last few decades – with the multiple pressures placed upon the industry – many airlines have not survived. Those that did without government protection (such as USA's Chapter 11 bankruptcy provisions) were a credit to the team spirit of their organisations. There were as many examples of extraordinarily courageous and successful leadership as there were woefully inadequate exhibitions. During the 2001 world airline crisis engendered by the destruction at the USA's WTC and the Pentagon, one airline's director was observed with his head in his hands sobbing, 'We're all doomed! We're all doomed!' (He resigned shortly afterwards, citing 'stress'.)

Change and leadership

Airlines exist in volatile commercial and legislative environments with upward pressure on costs and downward pressure on revenues. The industry's responses are usually focussed around traditional change mechanisms including changing the structure, outsourcing functions, increasing efficiency and reducing costs by using more ITC and employing fewer people. What would be most useful is for airlines, led by their Human Resources Departments, to develop change *leaders* and not change *managers*. These leaders would uplift flagging morale, promote collaboration instead of conflict and encourage dialogue instead of dictating. Simply hiring high-achieving university graduates and placing them on the in-house management training scheme does not guarantee excellent people leaders which is what airlines need. In an example of leadership failure, one airline was recruiting fast-track management trainees from top UK universities for potential management roles. The criteria required a minimum of a 2:1 degree or above. These predicted high achievers were academically intelligent but many of them lacked the necessary emotional intelligence and match with the core values. Most of the new recruits left after completing the in-house training scheme. That left many gaps in succession planning into which these graduates had been leapfrogged over and above many equally able, longer-serving employees. However, the following year, the same airline's renamed 'Graduate Leaders' intake was based on the core values. This intake included graduates with lower level degrees from second-tier universities as well as those from the top institutions. It was also opened to serving employees. Two of the lower level graduates topped the training scheme in every subject – including the essential people management tasks. Both exhibited emotional intelligence and went on to promotion above the higher-achieving academic graduates because they understood people – their colleagues and their passengers.

Motivation, recognition and reward

Motivation can be best illustrated as a pyramid. A person's motivations progress in a loose hierarchical structure from satisfying physiological needs at the base up to the next level of safety, then love and belonging followed by recognition and esteem and ultimately to self-actualisation (Maslow, 1943). Once each need is satisfied it ceases to be a motivating factor as the pyramid is ascended (see Chapter 2).

Non-financial motivators can be more effective than cash as a means of long-term employee engagement. However, what motivates airline employees could be the more intrinsic rewards – a sense of satisfaction or achievement – rather than extrinsic rewards ('carrots and sticks') such as bonus payments (Pink, 2009). The extrinsic motivation approach is no longer considered wholly appropriate. Economically sustainable airlines, linked into academic research streams, would have recognised the importance of this fact and harnessed it. While routine work can be outsourced (or mechanised), the more challenging creative work cannot. Seven deadly flaws of extrinsic motivation have been identified: it can kill intrinsic motivation (altruism), diminish performance, crush creativity, override good behaviour, encourage unethical behaviours, become habit forming and promote short-termism (Pink, 2009).

There is a tendency for some organisations to confuse motivation with incentives. What contented employees want is a sense of achievement, recognition, responsibility and the opportunity to learn and master their roles. Flourishing organisations understand autonomy (over task, time, technique and team), mastery (engagement) and purpose (working for a greater goal than oneself) and allow their willing 'partners' (rather than 'human capital') to excel (Pink, 2009). Employees would still be accountable and responsible; however, their engagement would shift to focus on the intrinsic factors. If the employee-partners are paid adequately, their minds would be focussed on their tasks – not on the extrinsic rewards that follow if the task is successfully completed. This is a deeply motivating factor and important for economically sustainable airlines grasping the links between motivation, effort and pay. Higher level rewards should reflect the higher levels of decision-making. However, high reward levels can often have detrimental effects on performance (Ariely *et al.*, 2005) and (against common belief) paying higher incentives can actually lead to reduced performance. It is worth considering whether those who link motivation and effort and set compensation contingent on performance base their decisions on experience and empirically derived knowledge or merely make assumptions that incentives will enhance performance. Formal NGOs such as trades unions focus on pay, often unaware that this could run counter to performance, i.e. productivity improvements which would be essential to the continuation of employment. Rewards for performance recognition are not always about money (which is just as well in the cash-strapped airline industry). For people with sufficient salary, long-term motivation can be delivered from non-financial rewards. The three highest non-cash motivators are 'praise from immediate managers, leadership attention (for example one-on-one conversations) and a chance to lead projects or task forces' (Dewhurst *et al.*, 2009: n.p.).

Over-reliance on financial rewards can have serious unintended consequences as evidenced by the financial industry failures (and yet many of these 'experts' sit in judgement on the financing viability of airlines). The ultimate rewards in an economically sustainable airline are strategic growth, increased market share and higher profits (all of which contribute to job security) as well as the employee travel benefit. Many airline employees join for the motivation (and incentive) of employee travel concessions the awards of which varies from airline to airline. In full-service carriers, there is the possibility of travelling in all classes; in the one-class, low-cost carriers there is no optional upgrading. Within the industry, employees are also able to travel on selected rival carriers at industry discounts. Being able to travel for free or at a significant industry discount on commercial fares was once a huge incentive to draw new employees into the airline industry. However, for the lower paid employees this no longer provides the same incentive since the advent of taxes on fares (particularly the UK's APD – see Chapter 1) which have disproportionately raised fares when wages have not increased at anything like the same rate.

3.4 CULTURE

Culture, teams and enemies

Culture is the key to raising productivity and morale, providing the resilience to weather economic cycles and the adaptability to meet the pressures of legitimate competition. The culture has to be led by leaders who can understand it, analyse it and finally manipulate it to meet changing markets and competition. Appropriate corporate culture is the most valuable intangible asset an economically sustainable airline possesses. It does not have a direct financial allocation in the balance sheet and yet it is the 'glue' which binds employees' knowledge and behaviours together and makes customers return. Identifying culture means finding the uniqueness which makes the organisation impossible to copy. In 1994, full-service carrier United Airlines decided to emulate successful, no-frills carrier, Southwest Airlines by creating 'Shuttle by United' with separate crews and a fleet of Boeing 737s. In contrast to the United Airlines' main fleet, Shuttle staff wore casual clothes and no food was served. As they tried to map Southwest's rapid turnaround and flight frequency it became apparent that none of these measures reflected the Southwest advantage in its culture, management philosophy and the importance given to supporting employees. The service was eventually closed in 2001 (Pfeffer and Sutton, 2006).

Corporate culture is a competitive issue. Competing airlines can copy products, services, business models, routes, prices and structures but they can never successfully mimic the culture. Culture is unique. Low-cost, high-service Southwest Airlines with its mantra of 'hire for attitude, train for skills' is the exemplar of this practice. Their promise for employees is written as follows:

To Our Employees

We are committed to provide our Employees a stable work environment with equal opportunity for learning and personal growth. Creativity and innovation are encouraged for improving the effectiveness of Southwest Airlines. Above all, Employees will be provided the same concern, respect, and caring attitude within the organization that they are expected to share externally with every Southwest Customer.

(Southwest Airlines, 1988)

In airline sustainability terms: happy employees deliver happy customers. Service quality and customer satisfaction are influenced by employee satisfaction and will ultimately influence profits (Yee *et al.*, 2008). Underpinning airline cultures is the belief that harnessing the energy and synergies from team work is more effective than individuals working alone. Hierarchical behaviours are necessary for decisions which need authority, to determine resource allocations or to ensure accountabilities but they can prevent challenge if they are used inappropriately. In 1999, Korean Air freighter Flight 8509 crashed at Stansted Airport, UK, killing all four crew members. The investigation found entrenched cultural values were based around long standing rules of hierarchy. The Captain was a former Korean Air Force pilot and military hierarchical behaviours dominated his cockpit management. The causes of the crash were low aircraft maintenance and low cockpit resource management coupled with communication difficulties where the Captain never really 'heard' what the First Officer was deferentially trying to tell him. These contributing factors are now much improved with cockpit teams exhibiting team spirit and support behaviours (Halsey, 2013).

As well as being necessary in cockpits and cabins, teams are also required for efficient operations in critical processes including gate-room departures, baggage loading and time-critical engineering. However, teams come with some caveats. Structure and support differentiate teams that are successful from those that crash and burn. Surprisingly, a unit's effectiveness is not driven by stability, right number of team members, well-defined roles and responsibilities with appropriate rewards, recognition and resources, strong leadership, or a clear vision (Hackman, 1998). The most important factor in high-performing teams is help-giving (Grant, 2013), i.e. willingness to help others, share knowledge, offer mentoring and making connections without expecting anything in return. This contrasts with the taker cultures where the opposites prevail. Most organisations fall somewhere in between the two extremes. Giver cultures enable people to reach further than just their immediate team; however, organisations often place barriers in the way. Economically sustainable airline leaders are attuned to such potential obstacles. If they are canny they would be hooking into the latest research to attune them to what could be happening to their own teams.

Team barriers

There are six pernicious mistakes of designers and leaders of work groups (Hackman, 1998). One is a failure to recognise that some work is better done by individuals. Another error is to name a group 'team' but to manage the members individually and skimp on the organisational supports needed. These include an appropriate reward system that recognises the importance of the team and the resources (including tools, space and money) which grease the team's performance. (Too often the reward process recognises individual performance and not that of the team.) An imbalance of authority between managers and teams can be a failure as well as the omission of dismantling existing organisational structures which inhibit team empowerment. Some teams are too large to be effective; others are too small. Finally the underlying assumption is that the team members are already skilled to function as a team – an assumption which could eventually require significant coaching intervention to ensure its veracity (Hackman, 1998).

Airline culture and enemies

There are good and bad cultures. A good culture aligned with employees' core values encourages openness, challenge and creativity. It also fosters loyalty and diligence and ensures employees understand what is expected of them. On the other hand, a bad culture is characterised by bullying, hegemony, silos, no-challenge and hierarchical behaviours. Hierarchies are needed for the purpose of organisation structure – but hierarchical behaviours are not. No-challenge cultures destroy cultural flexibility which is essential to enable response to external triggers and in particular, to potential deviations.

The enemy for a sustainable airline should be its competitors – not internal factions. The most quoted tale of enemies is attributed to former UK Prime Minister Winston Churchill who was talking to a newly elected, enthusiastic Conservative Member of Parliament (MP). The MP pointed to the benches opposite and is reported to have said 'There sits the enemy' to which Churchill is credited with replying: 'No son, that's the Opposition.' Churchill indicated the benches behind, 'That is the enemy.'

Fighting internal factions wastes resources – time, emotional energy, money and goodwill. It can also kill creativity, team spirit, innovation and challenge.

Ego as an enemy

In an open, transparent culture where challenge is welcomed, egos would be just one bias (see Chapter 7) which would be uncovered. The detrimental cost of ego in the workplace is the invisible line item on every company's profit and loss statement (Marcum and Smith, 2007). This is represented by such phenomena as people hearing but not listening, putting oneself ahead of the organisation, believing only the 'right' people have the good ideas, failing to challenge the status quo, creating and tolerating silos, longer meetings than necessary for efficiency, fear of making or admitting mistakes (because there is no feedback loop) and lastly, conducting candid discussions outside of meetings (Marcum and Smith, 2007). These are also indicators of inadequate leadership.

Further enemies abound in the cold-blooded, remorseless egomaniacs in the boardroom who are a hidden threat to organisational sustainability (Whittell, 2002). In many failed commercial organisations (e.g. Enron, WorldCom, Royal Bank of Scotland) the leaders were unchallenged and unchallengeable risk takers.

They might even have been untrustworthy and narcissistic (i.e. arrogant, lacking empathy and possessing inflated self-importance) possibly bordering on the psychopathic spectrum since psychopaths exist in all cultures. Initially, these 'snakes' identify and cultivate those who can help their progress; next they pinpoint those who can harm with a view to outflanking and back-stabbing them and finally they make a 'sycophantic but ultimately devastating beeline towards the source of power' (Whittell, 2002). They seek victims – people over whom they have power. It boosts their ego. However, eventually these egotists damage the corporate culture: they are not team players. They do not encapsulate the core values and their presence undermines the sustainability of any organisation. They are not appropriate for an economically sustainable airline which relies on the teamwork of its employees and the practice of its core values to maintain its reputation.

Challenge, risk-taking and trust

Organisational risk propensity is dictated by the nature of the industry and the people within it. Too much risk aversion can make an organisation moribund; too much risk-taking can make it unsafe. Airlines (and other organisations) need to keep a balance: overprotective risk can add to costs, stifle punctuality and profits whereas minimal risk protection can be dangerous and leave the airline exposed. In making risk assessments the decision-makers must consider the social, environmental and economic factors in order to be sure of having covered all potential risks (see Chapter 7).

Human beings have a propensity for risk. Some are risk averse; some are risk neutral weighing each opportunity on its merits; others are risk takers. Airline cultures are a mixture of all types. Any risk decision should be based on impartial information, data and evidence and consider the full sustainability aspects (economic, social, environmental and governance (see Chapter 7)) before using skill and judgement to deliver the outcome. Human behaviour can be unpredictable so trust is a factor in risk determination. Accepting high risk should equate with high reward for those who are prepared to take the challenge. More trust means less risk and trusting colleagues reduces risk. Trust can also be a substitute for a legal contract. If mankind was trustworthy there would be no need for contracts to enforce employment, outsourcing, building procurement, engine power or the plethora of other airline activities which are governed by contracts. Breaches of contracts damage reputations. However, contracts can never be complete: there will always be unforeseen circumstances which are not covered. As long as the culture is one of openness and challenges are allowed, trust should prevail and decisions will be as reasonable and as sustainable as humanly possible. In a no-challenge culture which is driven by hierarchies and silos, challenges can only be delivered from upper levels in the silos. This impedes any cultural flexibility, undermines trust and most likely negates the core values. It also affects long-term economic sustainability.

Internal sustainability risks can sometimes be ill-considered (Table 3.8). Judgement is affected by propensity to risk and judgement is needed to balance priorities (see also Chapter 7).

Table 3.8 Some internal sustainability risks for an economically sustainable airline

Risks	Impacts
innovation (successful or unsuccessful)	unsuccessful innovations can be perceived as either wasted funds or as a learning opportunity; successful innovations might be exploited by competitors usurping the first-mover advantage and using them more successfully
organisation structure	hierarchies are needed for 'pay-and-rations' but not for behaviours; organisational silos minimise communication, trust and challenge
culture	if the core values are not lived they become 'wallpaper' or 'screensavers' and nothing more since values must be expressed by deeds as well as words; a no-challenge culture inhibits disclosures of wrong doings
recruitment	recruitment on the basis of higher academic qualifications (e.g. First Class degree, MBA, PhD) will not necessarily attract employees with the appropriate core values. Potential employees with lower level degrees might embody the qualities needed as well as, or even better than, those with higher-graded degrees. The recruiter cannot know what a student has endured to obtain any degree and a lower-level degree might represent a triumph over considerable adversity since lower examination grades are not always an indicator of intelligence or lack of diligence. Selection underpinned by the core values would help avoid academic snobbery.
training	not training newly promoted leaders is wasting opportunity because, although some aspects of leadership are instinctive, other aspects have to be taught
internal politics	internal politics are destructive and so are incompetent employees who survive by undermining their teams and the core values; egos are enemies
non-experts	beware the 'expert' who gained his expertise from reading an item in a book and who can bluff his/her way through the organisation
policies	too many policies (which few employees remember anyway) can stifle creative thinking and innovation – besides, a surplus of policies does not mean the airline is protected: core values should suffice for most aspects of corporate life

Every day airlines are faced with risk-based economic decisions ranging from the tactical to the strategic: despatch the aircraft for an on-time departure or hold it pending arrival of late inbound transfer traffic? Delay the aircraft for extra de-icing or just push-and-go before the snow thickens? Purchase a failing competitor or leave the cash in the bank? These choices exercise the risk judgement of those paid to make such decisions.

Safety culture and risk

Economically sustainable airlines have a non-negotiable safety culture which must be **lived** by everyone in the airline industry – role modelled by the Chairman and his Board and followed by all stakeholders. This means that the role-modelling Chairman must follow the law (in the UK this includes behaviours such as not using his hand-held mobile phone while driving a car or smoking cigarettes in the office) as well as airline safety rules (including buckling his seat belt for take-off and landings).

Safety must **never** be compromised despite pressures for on-time departures and arrivals. Safety training is integral to sustainable airline culture. Whistle-blowers (see Chapter 7) are essential and they must be heard – not silenced, fired or paid off. Employees (and particularly flying crews) are encouraged to have a positive attitude to errors in order to make flying safer. The corporate defence that 'safety is our first concern' is hollow when it is not considered at the outset of any new procedure, process or restructuring and assessed against the sustainability dimensions. Safety has to be as fundamental to airline culture as air is to breathing.

Decades of crashed aircraft and lost lives taught many lessons. Safety now runs through airlines' DNA. It must. Safety audits are conducted under the auspices of IATA and ICAO. ICAO, founded during the Chicago Convention 1944, also ensures that any incidents (e.g. catering trucks accidentally damaging aircraft during loading or aircraft landing on the wrong runway) are logged and the resulting recommendations are treated as a learning opportunity and not an ascription of blame. ICAO, IATA and national regulatory agencies monitor airports' and airlines' compliance to ensure safety standards across the industry and penalties are imposed for breaches. The penalties can include excluding high-risk airlines from prescribed airspaces. By stringent self-policing, the industry can avoid the over-regulation which, paradoxically, can lead to increased compliance but has little impact on accident rates. Furthermore, failures need to be seen as contributing to success. Recognising failure and treating it as a learning opportunity is a measure of a mature corporate culture. Airline employees are encouraged to report all accidents, incidents and near-misses in the knowledge that these will be used as learning sources in a no-blame culture (i.e. the Mandatory Occurrence Reporting scheme under EC 376/2014). Such a blame-free culture encourages reporting of errors and since human errors are part of life they will always be with us (Table 3.9). How the industry manages lapses is what really matters.

The passengers must also share in airline safety by fully understanding the often boring, dull and mechanical safety briefings and demonstrations. Crew must make safety briefings understandable giving due weight to language differences and attention spans for what is a 'hygiene' issue (see Chapter 4).

Airlines make rules for safety but do not always enforce them. Hand baggage limits – always a flash point – are rarely enforced and oversized and overweight hand baggage is frequently stowed in overhead lockers. (Stowing hand baggage is often one of the reasons for slowed boardings and delayed departures.) Heavy bags in overhead lockers are a safety hazard not just for the people who have to lift

Table 3.9 Some examples of human error in aviation

Year	Error	Impact	Outcome
2000	Air France 4590, Concorde, Paris runway	debris on the runway punctured a tyre on take-off; tyre debris then penetrated the wing fuel tank; fuel ignited causing catastrophic fire; crew fought valiantly to control the aircraft	109 passengers and crew died
2005	Helios 522, crash near Athens, Greece	cabin compression switch which monitored oxygen was not on automatic; crew misunderstood the alarm warning of a drop in cabin pressure; the same alarm sound also warned of incorrectly set take-off instruments: oxygen supply was exhausted; crew unconscious	121 passengers and crew died
2009	Air France 447, Atlantic Ocean	aircraft hit a violent storm and rolled uncontrollably; airspeed sensors gave false readings; crew mistakenly raised the aircraft nose	228 passengers and crew died
2013	United Airlines, Newark, USA	instead of travelling from Newark (New Jersey, USA) to Phoenix (Arizona, USA) a dog travelled to Shannon, Ireland; extra costs for airline of comforting, feeding, watering and watering; return flight to USA	airline apologised and offered refund to owners; dog returned safely to USA
2015	Germanwings 9525, French Alps, France	locked cockpit door prevented Captain's re-entry while the aircraft, under the control of the Co-pilot, descended at speed into the French Alps	144 passengers and crew died

them up and over their heads but also for the passengers seated underneath. Cabin crew are not usually permitted to lift passengers' hand baggage ('if it doesn't stow, it doesn't go') because they could injure themselves. It is not known how many airlines actually insure their employees to assist passengers in this way. Some employees do lift baggage for elderly or disabled passengers but that places the employees at risk of injury for which the airline does not usually compensate them. From a customer perspective it would be better for fairness and service consistency if all employees refused to lift items and to enforce the hand baggage rules; however, employees (chosen for their customer-friendly approach) are often uncomfortable taking the role of enforcer as would be required by the enhanced Strategic Corporal role (Krulak, 1999) (see also Chapter 2).

Normalisation of deviance

Safety literature is littered with historic failures that were just accidents waiting to be discovered. The acceptance of repeated occurrences of minor errors or wrong doings as normal is known as the 'normalisation of deviance'. The term was coined after the shuttle disasters resulting from the sealant failure on Challenger in 1986 (Roger's Commission, 1986) and insulating foam loss on Columbia in 2003. Airlines can learn much from these well-researched failures which were largely attributed to the NASA history and organisational culture (Table 3.10).

Deviances become normalised when small and frequent failures became part of normal operations. Because the NASA failures were attritional rather than catastrophic they went unnoticed. Extrapolated into airlines, it could be activities which occur regularly (such as an aircraft door left open without safety strap

Table 3.10 The former NASA culture (adapted from Rogers Commission, 1986)

NASA historical factors

- past successes obscured failures
- organisational communication barriers prevented critical safety information being dispersed
- no-challenge culture and imbalances of power between departments
- not being a 'learning' organisation as a result of buyouts and downsizing resulting in loss of skilled resources

NASA organisational factors

- the safety culture became reactive with an unintentional erosion of independent checks and balances in favour of detailed processes producing copious amounts of data which communicated minimal benefit
- centralised structure made it difficult for supporting organisations to push back; the decentralised Debris Assessment Team was unclear on their task
- the programme structure resisted new information evidenced by the decision that Columbia's attritional foam loss was a maintenance problem before any analysis had been conducted (i.e. the organisation failed to recognise the significance of deviations)

protection, ignored fuel spills or absence of a wingman when backing an aircraft out of a cul de sac) where one occasion is not significant but where repetitions become institutionalised and hazardous. Errors are further compounded when powerful hierarchies overrule the specialists. In NASA the challenges from less powerful (specialised) departments were rebuffed in favour of the more powerful (but less knowledgeable) departments (an example of departmental hegemony). The dissenting voices from challengers must be clearly heard against the background organisational efficiency conflicts of time, cost and quality. It is a rare organisation that has sufficient resource in all three. However, avoidance of normalising deviance lies in the corporate culture since some cultures actively prevent it whereas others, by omission, almost encourage it. When an activity is high risk (such as sending space shuttles into orbit or aeroplanes into the sky) any deviation from the norm, or from the models predicting the norm, requires examination and scenario testing. One single deviation from the norm on its own might not be detrimental; but if the context changed (such as when the weather turned cold and caused the Challenger 1986 sealant failure) or was cumulative (such as the attritional loss of foam on Columbia which led to the 2003 catastrophe) then that deviation could prove catastrophic. Flight deck crews practising safety in the cockpit know this as they perfect their routines. Any changes from the norm should be noticed. Deviance detection should also extend to occasions when airline employees are flying as passengers. They should be able to critique (praise and criticise) the end-to-end journey and note any deviations from the norm. For example, if the check-in process was efficient, terminal experience enjoyable, boarding was swift and cabin crew were pleasant, then praise is deserved. On the other hand, if the lavatories were unusable, meal was inedible and inflight entertainment was malfunctioning then employee-passengers should be able to report these shortfalls into a no-blame system. The harshest critics of any system are those whose livelihoods depend on it.

Deviance and crew weights

Deviance occurs in many ways including the thorny issue of crew weights. It might seem frivolous to mention this in the context of safety but it is a very real challenge for some airlines. Body weights can creep up over time to the extent that crew members can become overweight which then becomes the new 'normal'. In an emergency, overweight crews slow evacuation and block exits and aisles. Their weight also contributes to the amount of fuel burned and therefore emissions expended (see Chapter 6). Air India was (at the time of publication) the latest airline to make crew weight an employment issue (*Economic Times*, 2014).

Avoiding normalising deviance

Airlines need to ensure an open, challenge culture so that whistle-blowers are able to speak up and powerful, hierarchical behaviours do not dominate. Team members (including outsourced contractors) should all have an equal voice and be able to challenge without fear. Any challenges should be explored, claimed expertise must be evidenced and risks ought to be assessed and mitigated. Roles, responsibilities and accountabilities must be assigned to clarify goals and objectives.

Outliers and culture

In statistics there are often numbers that lie outside of the norm and often at the extremes of a statistical distribution. These are outliers and they exist because of variations in measurement, chance appearance or experimental error. Outliers can be at either end of the distribution and therefore they can be both good and bad. Their effect is to distort the statistical mean (also known as the 'average'). Similarly, in organisations there are outliers (also known as 'deviants'), i.e. those people whose thinking does not fit with the norm but whose interventions as devil's advocates can stretch the thinking of the group. Some culturally homogeneous airlines outsource the role of outlier to consultants whose ideas might not resonate and who might merely create stress and tension within the airline. Outliers do things differently and often more effectively provided they are given the opportunity. They need to have their talents channelled for the good of the economically sustainable airline. However, in many organisations, the outlier is treated as the 'oddball' and side-lined from the corporate mainstream. The good outlier employees are innovators, challengers, 'pains in the necks' and can have a tough time in the wrong airline culture. Hackman (psychologist and team specialist) understood outlier deviants and in an interview noted that:

> Every team needs a deviant, someone who can help the team by challenging the tendency to want too much homogeneity, which can stifle creativity and learning. Deviants are the ones who stand back and say, "Well, wait a minute, why are we even doing this at all? What if we looked at the thing backwards or turned it inside out?" That's when people say, "Oh, no, no, no, that's ridiculous," and so the discussion about what's ridiculous comes up . . . the deviant opens up more ideas, and that gets you a lot more originality . . . teams with deviants outperformed teams without them. In many cases, deviant thinking is a source of great innovation . . . often the deviant veers from the norm at great personal cost. Deviants are the individuals who are willing to say the thing that nobody else is willing to articulate. The deviant raises people's level of anxiety, which is a brave thing to do. When the boat is floating with the current, it really is extraordinarily courageous for somebody to stand up and say, "We've got to pause and probably change direction." Nobody on the team wants to hear that, which is precisely why many team leaders crack down on deviants and try to get them to stop asking difficult questions, maybe even knock them off the team. And yet it's when you lose the deviant that the team can become mediocre.
>
> (Coutu, 2009: n.p.)

History is littered with people who did not challenge and who claimed to have been following the orders of superiors whose commands have had terrible consequences. No-challenge cultures are the death of an organisation where challenging a long-held view can be a daunting prospect. However, challenging long-term plans at regular intervals to ensure they are on target is essential because commercial environments change in the short-term and sometimes projects need to adapt. If there is no challenge the plans can often run unfettered by reality. Those outliers brave enough to challenge in a no-challenge, silo culture can lose power, influence, rewards and eventually employment. They are often ridiculed even if they are subsequently proved right (as many examples testify). However, if there is a no-challenge culture, the outliers need to be at the right level and in the right silo to issue a challenge or their talents are wasted. This is where recruiting employees on values, aptitudes and attitudes (rather than educational attainment) supports the airline culture.

Good outlier employees are creative and operate in two ways: first they can foresee challenges before they become problems and second, they can be used to solve problems which others cannot. As with all challenges, those commissioning the problem-solving must be certain that the **real** problem is being solved (see Chapter 7). Once the problem is defined, the solvers can seek role models who exemplify best behaviour and understand their uniqueness. These people are the creatives who can design an intervention which could be mainstreamed for appropriate stakeholders – and which would eventually be understood as 'common sense'. The innovative outlier will face many obstacles if the culture is not supportive and outliers will often feel very alone. Since rewards are often for conformity with a hierarchical set of tasks, the innovative outlier might find that their strengths do not necessarily lie within such a tight framework and their contribution can therefore pass unnoticed.

Bad outlier employees are the ones who are not good for any organisation. They thrive in the no-challenge culture which allows bullying and harassment of their targets. They can be characterised by addictions – alcohol, drugs, power, flouting safety – as much as their aggressive, manipulative personalities. Their behaviour can undermine morale and in extreme, jeopardise the airline. It needs to be curtailed before it does significant damage.

Well-meaning but misguided employees

Airlines are (by and large) populated with kind, compassionate employees at the customer front who care for their passengers and who want to deliver the best customer service possible. Sometimes, however, their compassion is misplaced and creates more problems than it solves. Sometimes they misjudge their well-meaning but misguided actions and airline managers do not know how to handle overly kind and caring endeavours without appearing to be mean-spirited. Many employees obtain private (altruistic) benefit from assisting with social problems. (Altruism is the intrinsic motivating 'feel good' factor which one person derives from helping another (Husted and Salazar, 2006).) As an example, elderly relatives are sometimes abandoned at airport check-in desks and if there is no one to take care of them in the event of delay they become the responsibility of the airline. Some of these frail people are incapable of being self-reliant and should not be allowed to fly without a carer (who has often departed long before flight time – see Chapter 5). The responsibility for risk assessment and payment for additional PRM support in the absence of a carer is always with the airline. Furthermore, in the event of flight disruption or delay it is not unknown for caring employees to take the abandoned PRM home overnight and return with them the following day for their resumed journey. This creates a risk which needs to be covered by any airline which has insufficient processes in place to avoid these occurrences. Similarly, UMs are often left at the check-in desk by boarding schools' drivers who leave the airport before the children's flights have departed. UMs need to be supervised, marshalled, fed, toileted and protected – all of which comes at a price (see Chapter 2). Someone has to look after these children until the flight departs and if it is delayed overnight they could require the provision of a nanny since they cannot sleep on the airport floor with other delayed passengers. In the absence of other provisions, well-meaning but misguidedly altruistic employees have been known to take stranded children home with them thus placing both the airline and themselves at risk. Solving one problem sometimes creates another. These well-meaning kindnesses could have had dangerous repercussions for the employee who should not have been placed in that situation by the airline, the abandoning relatives or any boarding school.

Employee stress

Employee stress is often highest at touch-points such as where airlines interact with the airports and statutory authorities and where passengers interact with airlines (by telephone or in person). On one occasion, an ageing British film star arrived with her entourage accompanied by two airport porters each with one large trolley piled high with her luggage (she was known for being high maintenance). The Check-in Agent could not locate the booking and had to request assistance from her Supervisor which caused a minor delay. This displeased the impatient actress and in a scene reminiscent of one of her movies, she wrenched the bundle of paper tickets from the Agent's hand and slapped her hard across her head. Once the transaction was completed, luggage despatched and actress departed to the First Class lounge, the stunned Agent was prematurely relieved from her duties by her supportive Supervisor. When the actress later complained to the airline's Chairman about her 'treatment' he sent her flowers as an apology instead of supporting an assault charge against her. This further demonstrated his inadequate leadership and remoteness from front line employees and the stresses they encounter. He did not even bother with as much as a consoling word for the Agent which later fuelled resentment among the front line employees.

Stress and airline employees

Stress can have a major impact on how employees behave. Telephone contact can be frustrating for airline employees since such communication can be aggravated by passengers with language difficulties, speech defects, fear, weeping, complaints and time wasting. These customer contact employees are meant to react calmly often against the background of call-centre distractions as they try to resolve the customer's challenges and hopefully, sell them a seat (or freight space) at the end of the conversation. Back-room tasks are often delivered from outsourced call centres in lower-cost nations working to SLAs and meeting inevitably tight CSFs and KPIs to ensure they retain the contract.

At the airport, the customer interface can also be extremely stressful due to delayed and overfilled flights, lost luggage, inaccurate information, frustrated and angry passengers and a plethora of other causes which can turn customer-friendly staff into impatient, unsmiling, impolite, begrudging and stressed airline employees. A sustainable airline monitors all its employees to identify their work stress levels as part of workplace health and safety assessments. Individuals have different levels of stress tolerance and coping strategies some of which can undermine the organisation. Pressure on costs has meant fewer airline employees are doing more thereby improving the productivity statistics – but at what cost? If doing more with less is making the employees stressed and they, in turn, are making the customers unhappy, hegemonic accountants have to ask if they are solving the 'right' problem. Away from the frontline, and at the higher levels in the airline, the stress can be even greater but for different reasons. Investment decisions which involve complicated negotiations and often £Stg, $US or € millions can ultimately create stress throughout the airline. Managers with power who overuse it become megalomaniacs; those on whom it is targeted become victims.

Time creates many stresses in airlines. The baggage loaders have time pressures as part of the operations team; the de-icing squad are often thinly stretched in periods of high demand and the catering suppliers have strict delivery schedules. Precision is critical to on-time departures and arrivals. Stress affects employees in different ways and airlines monitor the health of their employees carefully (particularly cockpit crews). However, ground staff can also feel intense pressure. One very stressed senior airline manager with a budget more than £Stg500m ($US770m or €688m) was responsible for the construction of a time-critical building. He was noted for his passion for oranges and ate from the bowl on his desk throughout the day. It transpired that he had injected them with vodka and was keeping his alcohol level topped up before he drove home in his airline-provided, high-performance car. His behaviour was erratic and his decisions were irrational but more importantly he was a danger to innocent road users, his team and the £Stg500m investment. His manager neglected his duty of care for this employee who was eventually medically retired.

Much of the stress occurs where employees and passengers interact and is derived from employees not being empowered to act as their instinct and corporate values would suggest. If, for example, frontline employees could offer instant compensation to an angry passenger (instead of subsequent protracted letter-writing by the Customer Complaints Department) the service recovery could more than justify the food voucher offered by ground-based employees or the extra bottles of complimentary wine proffered by crew on board. Once again, empowering the employees to act in the company's best interest might also 'save' the customer and persuade him/her to return. This empowerment – to react within a pre-agreed selection of pacifying measures – enables employees to manage the situation as they see fit. It also encourages them to future-proof the organisation by alerting managers to the most common challenges they have to face – and in turn the management can take steps to mitigate or avoid these events. Empowering employees also leads to hazard-reduction which is one of the most important outcomes of sustainability-thinking.

But much of the stress is not caused directly by the passengers – rather it is the intermediaries, i.e. systems and processes which delay aircraft, unreliable airport facilities including inadequate terminal wayfinding, inclement weather and people (Security, Customs, Immigration, retail employees and cleaners). In short, stress comes from feeling a lack of control over the workplace and it manifests in many ways. Much of the stress could be eliminated if sustainable airlines, airports and their agencies employed core values and adhered to them.

Intergenerational stresses

Many airline employees are caught in a stressful intergenerational vice trapped between ageing parents requiring care and children needing parenting. This has an impact on their work/life balance. Government interference in employer-provided nursery provision could eventually be stretched to employer-provided intergenerational care. The question is: how far could the developed world governments (particularly in Europe) stray in legislation? Any corporately provided social programmes have to be funded by shareholders, passengers or even by employees so any such imposition would only add to airline costs which have to be recouped from revenues. This would affect international competitiveness. Unfortunately, there is only limited research available on this evolving social issue. Failure of any employing organisation to support both young and old family members equally could eventually bring charges of discrimination.

Similarly, the workforce is ageing and many more workers are staying in the workplace because of insufficient pension provision. The future-proofing airlines will be cognisant of this factor and will be taking steps to understand the implications of ageing on their various SBUs. Ageing employees can become slower and tire more easily. How could this manifest in cabin crew? On the loading ramp? In the offices? On workplace ergonomics? Would a sustainable airline challenge itself and recruit experienced older workers instead of younger graduates into its leadership roles (as other service organisations have done) – or would that not fit with the concept of an agile, adaptable workforce?

Fairness in stress research

Cockpit and cabin crews receive much research with regards to stress. Decades ago, flight attendants were almost exclusively female and pilots were male. Today gender no longer defines employment and flight attendants now include males and the cockpit crews include females (admittedly not many of the latter but the numbers are growing). Where there was once a surplus of pilots, there is now a looming shortage largely the result of the ageing population, lowered wages, lack of career progression, training costs, successive economic recessions requiring layoffs and the slowing supply of ex-military pilots (Higgins *et al.*, 2013). However, there is an endless supply of applicants to become flight attendants. Their tasks are primarily focussed on safety and there is documented evidence that their workplace behaviour can be impacted by job stress (Chen and Kao, 2011) which, combined with family needs, can lead to higher employee turnover and less than optimal cabin crew safety behaviours (Chen and Chen, 2014). There are links too between burnout and reduced performance in cabin crew with high work engagement: those who hold their jobs longest are more resistant to burnout and are able to perform at a consistently high level (Chen and Kao, 2012). In other words, older, longer-serving crews are often higher performers than younger newcomers.

Unfortunately, similar research resources have not been ploughed into studying stresses in the roles of Check-in Agents, Ramp Loaders, Mobility Assistants and the multitude of other tasks undertaken by airlines' workforces and yet these employees are also believed to suffer many of the same stresses as cabin crew. (An economically sustainable airline might consider supporting research into this topic to avoid charges of elitism or unfairness.) Limited research, however, has examined the occupational burnout and work engagement among white-collar workers generally. Where a discrepancy was detected between individual and organisational values there was an increase in occupational burnout and a decrease in work engagement (Dylag *et al.*, 2013) loosely mirroring the research findings on flight attendants' reduced performance.

Stress prevention

Sometimes, however, despite all the best intentions, some employees are uncomfortable with changes focussed towards developing a new culture and become stressed as they try to adapt. This is a cognitive dissonance which can only be changed by the individual either adjusting their attitude or their behaviour to reduce the gap (Festinger, 1957). Efforts have to be made to accommodate them while assessing their suitability. There are three stress prevention options (Cooper and Cartwright, 1997) for individuals who have a 'lack of fit' with their work environment. The primary intervention requires the organisation to adapt to the individual by redesigning tasks; the secondary requires that the individual adapts to the new environment and the third prevention employs assistance programmes including treatment, rehabilitation and recovery. If none of the measures are successful then redundancy is the kindest exit route. However, in the event of redundancies, a sustainable airline must not forget that such change could also affect the remaining employees as well as those departing.

Change and culture

The sustainability ideal of horizon-scanning to determine what future barriers might evolve is essential in a volatile and unstable industry like airlines where paradoxically, the only constant is change. Indicators of trouble ahead such as difficulty in hiring quality employees, hierarchical behaviours preventing teams pulling together or increases in employee turnover and customer complaints are all warning signals. The employees stop trying to please the customers and the customers stop flying. Tackling poor airline morale requires an evaluation of its internal belief systems, core values and practices. Change, like the wine served in the premium cabins, takes time to mature and is also a risk which can be minimised by taking eight key steps (Kotter, 2007). First, increase the urgency; second, build the guiding team of people; third, develop the change vision and strategy; fourth, communicate for understanding and buy-in; fifth, empower action; sixth, create short-term wins; seventh, persevere; and finally, eighth, create the new culture (Kotter, 2007). Displayed in such concise terms, change sounds easy but the reality is that it can be extremely difficult to implement successfully. Changes must have a purpose – such as moving the performance from unpunctual to punctual – and many incumbents will be opposed to change.

Air carriers need to be nimble and agile to be sustainable. Economically sustainable, customer-responsive organisations (as airlines should be) need to be able to react quickly to capitalise on the changes around them and gain competitive advantage. Sometimes this advantage is achieved through mergers, acquisitions and takeovers which could require downsizing and/or outsourcing. Both of these are risky change strategies which can result in a loss of expertise, core knowledge and innovation. Downsizing inevitably means change in all its forms – redundancies, restructuring, working practices and almost inevitably, loss of morale while the change is embedding.

Culture change has to be systemic and spread through the entire airline – from top down – and since organisations can become inefficient over time, the time for considering change is before the inefficiencies become obvious. Changing culture takes time and yet that will be the most significant resource an economically unsustainable airline does not possess. If the culture appears to be a looming problem (determined by CSFs such as employee unrest or customer dissatisfaction) then the time for remedy is immediate. It is best pursued by building a network of change champions supported by training interventions to address and repair identifiable manifestations of unsatisfactory culture. The qualitative CSFs – such as reducing costs or customers' complaints – would have quantitative KPIs to measure the success of the matching programmes.

Change and emotion

Just as the brain has two sides – emotional (impulsive, fear) and intellectual (rational, problem-solving) – so does change. Those leading the change must appeal to both sides of the brain. Employees faced with drastic change (e.g. downsizing or relocation of their workplace) can react with shock, become immobilised and go into denial or sabotage mode – or they could accept that this will be the new 'normal' and adapt. What would make the change acceptable will be determined by how it is communicated and presenting slides or a video will not necessarily harness the hearts and minds. Affected employees need to understand why the change is necessary and the consequences if it is unsuccessful. Employees can be resilient in the face of change but the reality is that loss of employment can often mean loss of self-esteem and a sustainable airline would put in place the measures necessary to support those leaving. Reputation is important and ex-employees can still advocate for their airline.

Change can be threatening to many groups and what is critical to one group might be irrelevant to another. Many older employees are uncomfortable with change and can sabotage their airline as their power bases unravel. One airline which was undergoing organisational upheaval decided to move the Engineering Spares Department to another location many miles from where it had resided for the past ten years. The employee resistance was so severe that they sabotaged the building including the goods lifts, without which the Department could not distribute its raw materials. In a chain reaction, no materials meant no spare parts, which in turn meant grounded aircraft, i.e. no flights. The Trade Union would not allow a camera installation to detect the culprits and without that the management had no evidence for a prosecution. With the looming prospect of airline shutdown the management backed down, changed the strategy and relocated a less challenging department instead. (The resistance could have been uncovered if the original decision had taken account of the social as well as the economic factors (see Chapter 7).)

Change affects stakeholders inside and outside the airline and (like fear) is emotional and is often forced by a crisis which is actually the wrong time to look at strategic change. Ideally, change comes through a strategy which takes the long-term view but which requires short-term action to secure it. The process of change also places the airline's economic sustainability and reputation at risk. Every change decision eventually has an internal impact: loss of profits might mean making employees redundant with the multiplier effect of lost income in their neighbourhoods; changes in aircraft arrival times might impact on local residents by increasing noise and lighting pollution, reducing their sleep and eventually triggering protests at airports (possibly affecting future expansion or the 'licence to operate'); increased departure taxes could mean closure of routes with an impact on tourist revenues in smaller countries and loss of revenue for the carrier; new aircraft might require longer runways absorbing sites of special scientific interest (SSSIs) which could agitate environmental pressure groups who could blockade roads and prevent employees getting to work, freight being shipped and passengers flying. The change impacts can vary from minor tactical through to major strategic (see also Table 2.5 in Chapter 2).

Forward thinking on the need to cut costs and ease employees from entrenched behaviours stimulated several airlines to change their physical surroundings in the 1990s in order to engender culture changes. They constructed intelligent buildings purposefully designed to support the change process and invested heavily in digital technology. Through a series of induction programmes employees were familiarised with their new surroundings and working practices. Initially, the building-induced culture changes were judged to be successful. However, a later post-occupancy evaluation uncovered significant design errors which did not support the operation and some of the learning was lost when occupants reverted to previous 'bad habits' because behaviour changes were not enforced since enforcement was against the corporate culture (other than for safety reasons).

Complacency

Over the last volatile decade, airlines should have become specialists in adapting to change. They cannot be complacent faced with economic, social and environmental turbulence. Complacency is deadly and can manifest itself in many ways including despatching memos instead of brainstorming any barriers with key people, insufficient action to galvanise the majority, mistaking quick wins for strategic fulfilment and relying on a coterie of senior managers who probably helped create the crisis (Kotter, 2008) (see also Chapter 7). In no-challenge cultures, this closed circle would be unable to critique any new proposals which might threaten their comfort zones. It would be far better to have a broader base to provide the challenge to proposals – and to ensure that the economic, social and environmental sustainability dimensions have been covered and any anticipated barriers mitigated. Sustainable airline leaders need to demonstrate the urgency (the first step) rather than playing the role of urbane, paternal figures who reassure the employees that everything is under control. That gives the wrong message and could be inconsistent with living the corporate core values.

3.5 CREATIVITY AND INNOVATION

Importance of creativity and innovation

Creativity is the generation of innovative problem solutions. Among other benefits it can hatch opportunities to add value to the customer experience. One of the strengths of free-market capitalism is that it encourages creative and innovative entrepreneurs to take risks. However, paradoxically, because creativity allows risk-taking, it has a weakness since it permits failure. Failure involves wasted resources but without creativity enterprise would fail. Economically sustainable airlines – whether established or new – must innovate and can do so successfully if the culture is agile, adaptive and receptive to challenge. However, in a trade-off which typifies economics, what is a solution for one organisation can become a problem for another.

Today's airline is effectively a work in progress and it should therefore encourage employees to test programmes and experiment – even if it results in failure. Such enterprise would develop knowledge, create a reservoir of learning and would also confirm that challenge and openness are the preferred cultures. Creativity and innovation are infectious and everyone is capable of creating. The creativity part of human brains is often subdued under pressure from teachers (or later, employers) in favour of what they consider to be the essentials of productivity. And yet, innovators can be extremely productive but in ways which observers might not immediately discern. Pioneering aviators, the Wright Brothers, were problem solvers innovating to enable connectivity between populations. But in solving one problem, they created many more – economic, social and environmental – which were, or are, being solved by other innovators.

Sustainable airlines must make innovation a way of life. Often in the cost-cutting and downsizing which the airline industry has undergone over past decades, innovation has been overlooked or sacrificed with the loss of experienced employees. Airline stakeholders – including employees, passengers, suppliers and even airport neighbours – are all capable of innovating for the benefit of the airline and yet usually only a few ever volunteer for fear of mockery or isolation. Some high-profile departments (such as ITC or Marketing) believe they have a monopoly on innovation and yet others with lower profile (like Engineering and Facilities Management) often have innovation in their core without the airline really being aware.

Innovative outliers and agile cultures

Innovative people are outliers and they need to be persistent and brave because innovation means organisational disruption which can make colleagues uncomfortable. The innovator needs to be disruptive and prepared for criticism, isolation and loneliness when offering contrary views. Some people are uncomfortable with creativity and innovation because they believe there is no spare time for experimenting and others even find the process threatening. Although everyone is capable of innovation, not everyone does it or wants to do it. No idea can be delivered unless the corporate environment nurtures the innovation spirit and it is not just products or services that need innovative thinking but processes.

Competitive organisations like airlines display three characteristics: efficiency (mastery of routines through accumulating operating experience), flexibility (quick and effective response to the unexpected) and adaptability (anticipating problems and mastering the process of changing routines – the most difficult characteristic to gain) (Basadur and Gelade, 2006). Adaptability and flexibility depend on innovative thinking and are critical for success in volatile, highly competitive and elastic-inelastic industries (like airlines). In the short-term, airlines have limited scope to flex aircraft capacity to match increased or decreased demand.

However, efficient organisations mastering their stable routines can deliver high-quality, large quantities of homogeneous products or services at low cost (Basadur and Gelade, 2006) but with a volatile environment, efficiency alone is insufficient. Adaptability is almost the reverse of efficiency and requires looking outside the airline for new technologies, ideas and processes that might improve or completely change its routines. Adaptable airlines are constantly horizon-scanning, seeking the next disruption to their routines and preparing for its arrival because if an airline is adaptable, it can adopt innovations more quickly than it would if it viewed them merely as disruptions to the routines. Adaptability and flexibility depend on innovative thinking and require using knowledge creatively. Airlines must be able to react quickly to unforeseen events while still maintaining their routines. This was demonstrated by many carriers which survived the dramas and traumas of the last decades by continuing their flying schedule while in the background they were downsizing, improving productivity and reducing costs.

Efficiency and adaptability are hallmarks of the most effective and flexible organisations (Basadur and Gelade, 2006) where challenge is allowed without fear of loss of power, influence, employment or reward. Adaptability can also be affected by trades unions' relationships. At one extreme, the union/airline relationship is characterised by commitment and partnering (Southwest Airlines); at the other it is control and avoidance (Ryanair, AirAsia) and in between there are the airlines and trades unions which accommodate each other (USAirways, Qantas) (Gittell and Bamber, 2010).

Although airline pilots have intensive training on procedures, processes and safety, they must still be able to think innovatively when faced with an unforeseen crisis. In an example of extreme experimentation and innovative quick-thinking Captain Sullenberger and First Officer Skiles landed US Airways' Flight 1549 on the Hudson River, New York in 2009. The Airbus A320 lost power following ingestion of a flock of geese. The cockpit team brought the aircraft down for its first-ever water landing so that 155 passengers and crew were safely evacuated from the floating fuselage. In applying their skills, the duo exemplified adaptable, flexible and innovative thinking and in taking an extraordinarily high risk they were rewarded with the survival of all the passengers and crew.

Problem-solving and creativity

Fundamental to sustainability, is the empowerment of airline employees to solve the problems they encounter every day. Equipping employees with the tools needed to problem-solve should filter down through the entire organisation. Profiling job candidates or existing employees is worthwhile to understand an individual's unique problem-solving style (Basadur and Gelade, 2006). An individual's dominant style and preference for acquiring and expressing knowledge can be revealed through one of four profiles: generators (create and start new opportunities), conceptualisers (create options for problems and solutions – divergent thinkers), optimisers (create options for successful implementation) and implementers (create the actions that gain acceptance for a change or a new idea) (Basadur and Gelade, 2006).

There are numerous methods for problem-solving. One of the easiest is Edward de Bono's Thinking Hats (1985). Each of six coloured hats has a function and by changing the hats decision-makers can broaden their thinking and knowledge (Table 3.11).

This process is simple and requires little learning for it to be embedded. It is appropriate for use at all levels and by all employees.

Problems can also be tackled by asking analogous questions to determine how exemplars would solve a similar problem, e.g. how would Twickenham Stadium handle an airline check-in queue? How would technology company Apple manage the airline technology? How would search engine Google manage the information?

Table 3.11 Summary of de Bono's Thinking Hats (adapted from de Bono, 1985)

Hat colour	Activity
blue (thinking and managing)	clarify the goal of the process; this hat also acts as control during the process and if necessary the chairman can redirect the thinkers to back different coloured hats if ideas are running dry
white (knowledge)	focus on the available data and information; find gaps; analyse past trends and historical data
red (emotions)	examine the problems using intuition, gut reaction, opinions and emotion; consider how others could react
black (logical aspects)	find the weaknesses and the barriers in the plan; determine mitigations; play devil's advocate
yellow (positivity)	think positively and optimistically to find the benefits
green (creativity)	creativity – provoke and investigate (there are many additional creativity tools available from many other authors to support this hat) (e.g. Basadur and Gelade, 2006)

How would retailers Amazon manage the airline supply chain? How would hoteliers Travelodge manage a customer loyalty programme? How would a hospital cope with an influx of 500 patients who needed overnight accommodation? How does the local bus company maintain on-time departures when so many elderly passengers are so slow to board? How would the facilities management industry solve the problem of urine damage and smell in an aircraft lavatory? (Answer: building facilities management has shown that by placing the image of a fly (or similar insect) in the lavatory bowl, men will concentrate on the direction of flow. The result would be less spillage, less cleaning, longer lasting lavatory floors and therefore lower costs.)

Why innovate?

Somehow airlines have to compete to overcome regulatory anchors and innovation is one means of differentiating themselves from the competition. The more unconventional the innovation the longer it will take competitors to catch up – all of which contributes to competitiveness and future-proofing. Innovation also allows airlines to reinvent themselves when circumstances change (which they do frequently) and it is also a collaborative force (such as between airline employee and passenger). Airlines need to be looking ahead to their next challenge and if the culture is dominated by routines and checklists (masquerading as risk protection measures) it will be unsustainable. Companies which are bound by checklists are not innovative. Innovation is the risky part of adaptable and flexible cultures and can only happen if the cultures allow. Some airlines (with no-challenge, silo cultures) avoid it while others (with entrepreneurial, challenge cultures) embrace it. Innovation, like economics, often requires choosing between alternatives. Airline culture is underpinned by economic choices of efficient and effective resource allocations as well as the cultural norms and practices which create the structures that affect market behaviours. In that spirit, airline economics encourages internal entrepreneurs and their innovations to work to the lean principles (see Chapter 2), i.e. minimise waste, reduce costs and only provide that for which customers are willing to pay. However, innovations must be kept confidential until revealed so competitors are not forewarned.

Innovation should also be encouraged in airline partners and suppliers including airports. They are the specialists in their own industries. Encouraging innovation in service partners such as outsourced suppliers can reduce costs for both parties and create future opportunities (see performance-based specification (PBS) in Chapter 7).

When innovation is not captured within a formal structure (e.g. a Research and Development Department) employees need to be permitted time to think (time being one of the most precious resources). This is known as 'slack resources' and is critical to successfully embedding innovation in an organisation even though the concept conflicts with the lean principles of removing organisational waste. Taking time out can be misinterpreted as unproductive laziness but without unallocated time it can be increasingly difficult to develop new ideas or undertake reflection. Slack resources can also be redeployed in a different department from that in which they occur thus giving employees a chance to experience another role (even if only on a temporary basis) as a means of stimulating innovation. Slack resources accompanied by adequate power are also needed for champions to drive through innovations. Champions – just like entrepreneurs – need to have the energy to take the risks and to follow them through. The champion's role is at three levels:

(1) the technical champion who carries an idea from initial concept through development to a viable product or process; (2) the business champion who provides a business framework and (3) the executive champion who sponsors the idea at the highest level.

(Tatum, 1987: 650)

Types of innovations

Innovations can create new markets opening new employment and growth opportunities. Innovations can be incremental, radical, modular or systemic and have many drivers including the need for cost savings, product enhancement, operation changes and possibly even organisational structural realignment as the innovation process evolves from input-based to output-focussed (see performance-based procurement in Chapter 7). Most important for innovation to flourish is the need for an open culture which can tolerate challenges. Innovative organisations can develop strategic and tactical innovations. Strategic innovations could identify emerging customer segments, re-examine customer value and reshape the value chain. Tactical innovations support the strategic and could involve developing new products or services.

Airline innovation comes in many forms including product (equipment, materials), market, pricing, routes, organisation, management and processes (such as improvements in services or supply chain). There are three main locations for potential innovation (Franke, 2007): advanced segmentation (based on customers' changed behaviour which could be supported by using more ITC), new business models (such as the no-frills airlines and emergence of intercontinental carriers from advancing countries) and the new technologies (including aircraft and distribution channels). Market driven processes are excellent at generating incremental innovation but they only occasionally produce the radical innovations which underlie the market drivers (Kumar *et al.*, 2000). Market driving companies tend to be new entrants that have delivered a leap in customer value while taking a high risk but with the potential to offer vast rewards, e.g. the no-frills carriers. There are major obstacles in developing and launching radical market driving business ideas largely because such ideas are maverick in nature and therefore high risk. Furthermore, new business development processes tend to be biased against more innovative breakthrough ideas when established firms often perceive they have too much invested in the status quo to take the risk (Kumar *et al.*, 2000).

There are 12 recognised dimensions for innovation: the offerings themselves, the platform from which to build the business, the solutions to customer problems, customers and their experiences, value capture, operating processes, the organisation itself, supply chain sourcing, presence in the market, networking opportunities and brand developments (Sawhney *et al.*, 2006), all of which have applications in the airline industry (Table 3.12).

Innovation process

An entrepreneurial culture gives employees the freedom to employ the core values and norms to solve a problem within the corporate cultural framework. Fear of failure kills innovation. If innovation is not threaded through airline DNA then by setting up an innovations team with support processes, an airline can harness internal expertise to create new products and services which can align more quickly with the external changes (one of the characteristics of an adaptable organisation). Democratising innovation gives people a participating voice and taps the expertise of those who are closest to the customer and who know where the bottlenecks are choking growth.

Innovation is not linear. It is often the by-product of serendipitous conversations and insights involving random events. Serendipity is often thought of as associated with luck; however, luck requires preparation. 'While serendipity might seem like a random process, creative firms also realize that new insights and connections do not happen by accident and that it needs to be encouraged through deliberately structured processes' (Loosemore, 2013: 637). There are barriers to, and enablers of, serendipitous innovation throughout an organisation's leadership, strategy, structure and collaborations. However, to enable serendipitous innovation the entire

Table 3.12 12 dimensions of business innovation (adapted from Sawhney et al., 2006)

Dimension	Definition	Airline Examples
offerings	develop innovative new products or services	low-cost airline developments including charging for the use of every service and product
platform	use common components or building blocks to create derivative offerings	computerised reservations systems which allow add-ons such as seat selection or meal booking
solutions	create integrated and customised offerings that solve end-to-end customer problems	one-stop processing from internet booking through to aircraft boarding gate
customers	discover unmet customer needs or identify underserved customer segments	look at emerging trends (such as the ageing of the population) and decide what they could need to service them
customer experience	redesign customer interactions across all touch-points and all moments of contact	end-to-end processing of customer service involving ITC and human interaction at touch-points without sacrificing the core competency
value capture	create innovative new revenue streams	brand extensions such as selling airline-branded products (e.g. meals and/or suitcases) at the airport or off-site
processes	redesign core operating processes to improve efficiency and effectiveness	restrict the number of aeroplane families to ensure economies for training, operations and maintenance
organisation	change form, function or activity scope of the firm	reduce layers of management; divest SBUs to their markets
supply chain	think differently and sustainably about sourcing, contract conditions and fulfilment	outsource vs in-house; offshore vs onshore; consider performance-based procurement (see Chapter 7)
presence	create new distribution channels or innovative points of presence, including the places where offerings can be bought or used by customers	web-based sales for collection of airline-branded products on board; automated bag drops on terminal concourses
networking	create network-centric intelligent and integrated offerings	using ITC systems to support innovation problem solvers' network
brand	leverage a brand into new domains	healthcare, banking, gymnasia

organisation needs to make opportunities available for randomness and connectivity. This process can be supported in several ways including using ITC, refitting or constructing buildings to encourage serendipitous encounters as well as moving employees to different SBUs either temporarily or permanently (Loosemore, 2013). Once approved, innovations must be delivered, integrated into operational products, services or processes and the innovator recognised with appropriate reward.

Ideas can come from any stakeholder but are more commonly sourced from employees, suppliers and customers. Generating innovation is a process at which some airlines excel giving them that much-sought-after competitive edge.

Singapore Airlines is an exemplar of the sustainability strategy of innovatively delivering superior customer service and profits. It has a '40–30–30' rule. It focusses 40% of resources on training, 30% on review of processes and procedures and 30% on creating new product and service ideas. Innovation is in their culture – their corporate DNA – and it is included as an objective in functional department strategies. They have a Product Development Department the role of which is to take selected product innovations through the development cycle to commercial production. The ideas come from customers, employees, research sources or possibly even competitor benchmarking – but often the best ideas are stumbled upon serendipitously when pursuing other ideas. The culture also allows support for un-learning of legacy behaviours (not just changing to new behaviours). They have six stages in innovation development: any discovery is captured on an e-log (electronic storage space of innovative ideas); 'War Cabinet' meetings are held to explore feasibility and flesh out details; Senior Vice Presidents give preliminary endorsement; frequent flyers are invited to debate the idea and a robust business case is developed. Finally, senior management give their approval followed by any further refinement and ultimately implementation (Heracleous *et al.*, 2004 and 2005).

Convergent and divergent thinking for innovation

The innovative airline understands innovation and knows that the processes to capture it must be uncomplicated and easy to implement. Innovation involves two types of thinking: convergent (bringing ideas together) and divergent (i.e. pushing ideas apart to test them).

There are four stages in the innovation process which are executed by 'thinking organisations', i.e. those organisations which proactively seek problems and which make innovative thinking integral to corporate routines (Basadur, 2001). The first step is to create, followed by conceptualising, optimising and finally implementing (Table 3.13).

Some organisations avoid the divergent thinking stages (particularly in no-challenge cultures) thereby short circuiting the process and making the innovation outcome less effective. (The lack of divergent thinking also occurs in regulators where often only the social and/or environmental sustainability factors are considered.) Two airline examples are memorable: the first is the installation of voluntary emissions offset schemes as a means of pre-empting government legislation, placating

Table 3.13 Creative problem-solving stages (adapted from Basadur, 2001)

Step	Activity
creating	starting the process: proactively gathering information (experience, questioning, imagining, horizon-scanning), divergent thinking, i.e. solving the *real* problem
conceptualising	more divergent thinking: assembling new ideas, discovering insights, creating models
optimising	abstract thinking and convergence: evaluating and converting the chosen idea to practical solutions, open minds needed
implementing	more convergent thinking: actioning the decision which includes gaining acceptance from stakeholders

environmentalists and covering the costs of a negative externality. These schemes have not had wide take-up by passengers. If passengers had wanted these programmes they would have paid for their emission offsets; however, the take-up was very low at about 3% (Kahya, 2009) (see also Chapter 6). These programmes, which lacked sufficient divergent thinking, could not have passed the lean test and did not prevent legislation or regulation. A second example was the Convair XF2Y-1 Sea Dart. This was a waterborne supersonic jet fighter which was mobilised by using water skis. It was originally a 1948 entry into the USA Navy's competition to build a supersonic interceptor aircraft; however, although several prototypes were built, the aircraft never made it into full production after the test pilot was killed. There were design flaws including overlooking the consequences of saltwater-ingestion into the jet engines and corrosion on the metallic frame. Furthermore, the aircraft could only land on calm seas (Dorr, 2011) which were highly unlikely in the locations for its proposed use.

In contrast, an overindulgence of convergent thinking (and a lack of lean thinking) occurred when one airline tried to solve the problem of hand baggage stowage causing departure delays. It appointed a matrix team of four employees who took six months to solve the problem. Their solution was to place flimsy paper labels on one of the two permitted cabin bags which passengers would designate to be the bag stowed under the seat in front. The labels were attached before passengers crossed the landside-airside border and processed through Security. Consequently, with all the process handling, the labels tore before the passengers arrived at the departure gate. This was an extremely inefficient and ineffective solution given that this same airline had many years earlier installed expensive steel cradles at each gate to filter oversized hand baggage. It possibly just needed to enforce the previous hand baggage rules: if bags did not fit into the frames then they had to go into the hold.

Homeless innovation

Innovation is enabled by open and challenge cultures. It can improve competitive advantage and drive growth but its spread can be blocked by bullying, bureaucratic, hierarchical, no-challenge and silo-driven cultures and its success can also be stifled by having no logical 'home' in which to assess it. This is a paradox: with no home, there is nowhere to assess it therefore the innovation goes nowhere (which is why the Singapore Airline's process is laudable). Pioneering and unique innovations without a home must have an owner so pursuing 'homeless' innovations needs to be incorporated into someone's job description – a champion who has the appropriate accountability, responsibility and authority. Some innovations could have several potential 'homes' or an Innovations Department might have to be created to support the proving process. Such a Department could comprise a matrix of key personnel (led by a champion) to pursue an innovation through to delivery and upon completion the team would splinter and return to their originating departments. As an example of an innovation with many potential homes, the advent of contactless technology has opened the possibility that passengers could be charged at the departure gate for what has previously been the free carriage of airport concession goods (see Chapter 1). Pursuing this idea could fall into the departmental ownership of ITC (for the installation of the technology), Customer Services (for implementation), Human Resources (employee training), Estates Department (for landlord negotiations regarding the trade-off with airport concessionaires and discussions on the single till principle), Environment Department (to calculate emissions charges), Finance Department (for funding) and any other departments which might need to be involved.

Active innovation

There are many examples of worthwhile innovation but also some that can be described as 'vanity projects' which give no discernible benefit and which can waste shareholders' funds.

Examples of successful innovative airline-thinking occurred in the 2013 American Airlines' hackathon.

This was a collaboration between American Airlines and 60 ITC developers which resulted in the first-ever travel hackathon tasked to create and deliver mobile apps to help global travellers. In less than 30 hours (and with the spur of a $US10,000 prize) three winners were selected from 15 apps. First place winner provided customers with live updates for flight changes or delays plus estimated travel times to the airport. Simultaneously it also provided the airline with real-time information on passengers' locations to indicate how many seats would be available for standby passengers (useful for yield management and employees' travel redemption). Second place winner gamified air travel whereby passengers received points (redeemable for American Airlines' miles and other incentives) for completing prescribed travel activities such as checking-in by a certain time or for visiting American Airlines' merchants' and retailers' websites. Third place winner helped travellers from origin to destination by (among other tasks) planning the best route to the airport and obtaining weather updates (Donovan, 2013).

In another example of innovative thinking, Air New Zealand created last-minute bookings 'grabaseat' which optimised its web sales. Since fares fluctuate (sometimes hourly depending on the bookings profile) Air New Zealand also offered potential passengers the option of paying a nominal deposit to reserve the fare for three days while the passenger decided whether to confirm or cancel the booking (Air New Zealand, 2014). Similarly, Lufthansa created 'MySkyStatus' service which would update registered users' Facebook and Twitter accounts with their live flight position and actual arrival time. This innovation enabled passenger decision-making as to the most efficient use of their time (Lufthansa, 2014).

In 2013, and in contrast to airline-focussed, customer-driven innovations, another airline tried to use creative thinking to solve global social challenges by arranging a private flight from San Francisco to London for specially selected passengers. Their monumental task was to create solutions for the UN to employ in developing and emerging nations. At the time of publication it was not obvious what the identified problems and their solutions added to shareholders' value by way of increased sales and nor was it possible to determine the success of the flight in terms of the UN's objectives and achievements.

ITC and innovation

Creativity, innovation and knowledge management (the apprehension and use of knowledge) are intertwined and need delivery. Possessing knowledge is not sufficient. To avoid it being useless, it must be integrated with other knowledge (including that contained in other departments) (Basadur and Gelade, 2006) for which ITC can be an integrator. However, one common error in corporate thinking is that innovation can only be delivered through ITC. ITC is useful in knowledge capture and management but it is not the only delivery route. Knowledge only becomes valuable when it is used 'to improve efficiency, flexibility or adaptability' (Basadur and Gelade, 2006: 48). However, even ITC has its limitations. In order for ITC to be used as intended, it must be useful and easy. If it does not fulfil these two criteria then it will not be used successfully (Davis, 1989). As well as considering the employee-users, ITC departments in sustainable airlines need to consider the customer-user – many of whom are ageing and are not comfortable with much of the specialist ITC language and operation.

Employees' empowerment for innovation

Innovating as part of future-proofing should be part of every employee's corporate DNA. Those employees working directly with customers are closer to the action than those at the top of the airline and are therefore more likely to want to innovate based on customer-focussed activity. However, those at the top must support the innovation culture so that the process works from top down as well as bottom up. Innovative employees identify and fix gaps and then use their intelligence to prevent future problems. Unfortunately, some airlines hire employees for their problem-solving and innovative abilities and then place them in a creative straightjacket which makes them afraid to use their initiative. Economically sustainable airline employees need to feel empowered and able to perform their roles because they are trusted. One airline hired happy, smiling, creative, innovative people with a can-do attitude for their new cabin crew intake. It then placed them in a creative straightjacket by micro-managing the crew announcements.

> Good morning ladies and gentlemen: welcome aboard Flight . . . today your Captain is . . . and he is assisted by . . . in the front cabin we have Michelle assisted by . . . and in the rear cabin we have Helmut who is assisted by . . .

Predictable and dull. This almost became unpatriotic when the National Junior Gymnastics Squad was flown to the International Youth Games. The youngsters received no special welcome because the crew was not permitted to go outside of the Marketing Department's standardised, printed and laminated card containing the on-board announcements. Routines and rules were paramount instead of flexibility and adaptability which would have surprised and delighted the team and their fellow passengers.

Allocating research and development funding

Allocating innovation funds (often titled 'research and development') to the same departments each year does not harness the innovation talent available in an airline. A sustainable airline would investigate dispersing these funds to SBUs beyond the usual recipients. The Customer Service Teams who interact with passengers will have ideas on how their workload could be reduced at no extra cost, or how resources (time and money) could be conserved by more efficient workload allocation or even how the units with which they interact could waste fewer resources at the interface. The Aircraft Cleaning teams will have ideas as to how to make their tasks more efficient; the Facilities Management teams would know how to cut costs and the most innovative products to help them succeed. These challengers need an outlet for their ideas. Suggestions to develop an innovations culture include:

- maintaining an in-house suggestion scheme
- inviting external groups to contribute via open source
- brainstorming sessions with stimuli to kick start the thinking
- wondering . . . 'I've always wondered if. . .' or 'what if we. . .'
- including innovation as an item on meeting agendas (and on the reputational risk register (RRR) (see Table 7.2 in Chapter 7))
- finding gaps in services, products and processes
- 'conducting' serendipitous meetings
- remixing teams and individuals
- visiting customers and suppliers
- sponsoring competitions for problem solutions
- inviting representatives from specific passenger groups for discussions (e.g. learning-disabled passengers).

Innovation does not always require a big budget to get it started. What it does require is a challenge culture where any member – however junior – feels sufficiently empowered to contribute to any project in which they have a stake whether through formal means such as a corporate questionnaire or informal such as a personal letter to the Chief Executive (which might first have to pass his gatekeeper – a difficult task in a no-challenge culture).

Risk and innovation

Innovation involves risk. Applying full sustainability-thinking to decision-making is both a risk and a challenge to established order. Innovation is not for those who are risk averse – and yet airlines by their nature are both risk averse (with safety and training) and risk takers (with new aircraft, products, markets and ITC applications). (Understandably, no passenger would want to fly with a risky airline.) Engineering is one department that is both risk averse and yet risk-taking. Engineers, innovators to the core, will punish an innovation until all known risks are eliminated and only then would it be considered safe for use. The risks of new innovations can also be reduced by using national and international codes and standards (where they exist).

Sustainable airlines need to innovate endlessly. Innovation has to be in their DNA but its success and acceptance as a process is dependent on the carrier's risk profile. Leading organisations need to be risk-taking innovators; however, in aviation, innovators should proceed with caution because the first-mover advantage is often a myth. The real advantage often lies with the first organisation to use the innovation successfully having waited for it to be de-bugged by others. This was illustrated by the Boeing 787 Dreamliner which was expected to go into service in 2008. It was delayed by production difficulties and finally entered service three years late. After the first deliveries, a battery problem occurred which eventually grounded the operating aircraft causing a real problem for the airlines which were relying on them to fulfil flying schedules. The airlines which had waited until the first deliveries were fully operational reaped the benefits of their rivals' original enthusiasm and ultimate misfortune when their new fleets were grounded.

Power of academic research

Employee education is another potential, innovative category for research and development spending. Encouraging employees into further and higher education fosters an innovation and challenge culture; however, their learning needs to find a 'space' when they return. Employees' development must have a focus. If there is nowhere for their learning to be implemented then the organisation would have over-developed the employee. An organisation of PhDs with no proper roles and responsibilities is wasting a potentially valuable employee resource. The process of education (particularly the acquisition of research skills) changes the student and the economically sustainable airline should harness their learning into on-the-job benefits.

Table 3.14 Comparison of academic and industry research outcomes (Haimes, 2013)

Academics want . . .	Industry wants . . .
creation of new models	use of knowledge to create value
peer-reviewed group study	competitive advantage
source of income	improved financial performance

Encouraging links with research establishments such as universities gives access to impartial and objective new knowledge. It should be clearly distinguished from advocacy research (see Chapters 1, 2, 5, 6, 7 and 8). Using academics from many intellectual spheres (including economics, change management, social sciences, mathematics and environment) can help with airline sustainability-thinking provided the airline is ready to consider the output of these academic outliers. Many established organisations are ill-prepared for externally generated challenges. Furthermore, some organisations are not learning organisations and simply prefer to perpetuate the mistakes of the past (Simon, 1991).

When academic institutions partner with commercial organisations, the corporates gain access to cutting-edge research. However, in contrast to corporate research, academic research is unlikely to be supported by a business case and yet it could deliver significant competitive advantage. The relationship between the parties will determine the success of the partnership whether it is transitional, long-term, purely transactional, 'master and servant' or even a 'marriage' with both parties having equal voice.

There can be a conflict between academics and commercial organisations with regard to output. For academics, output is a published research paper and academic prizes: for commercial organisations output is a timely delivered and profitable innovation. Sometimes these two aims are incompatible (Table 3.14).

Accompanying cutting-edge research are uncertainties over timing and dates for output delivery and anticipated benefit accrual, as well as the time between collaboration commencement and the delivery date of any output to market. Commercial organisations need to keep pace with their fast-moving environment and in contrast, academic output tends to move more slowly. The business case for academic research is also a challenge for industry since research needs to be owned and budgeted by an SBU which will be focussed on meeting targets while academic research does not always deliver to a timetable. Such a venture would need recognisable benchmarks to be sure it is progressing, and with the tenuous nature of research the timescales of the contracting parties could be incompatible. There is also the problem of which organisation would own any subsequent intellectual property – the academic institution or the sponsoring organisation?

Diffusion of innovation

Innovations are not always adopted by everyone simultaneously. There is a frequently appearing pattern of rolling acceptance approximating the normal statistical distribution (Rogers and Shoemaker, 1971). The outliers comprise the enthusiastic innovators at the opposite end of the distribution from the laggards who might never, ever, support the innovation. This might mean they no longer have a cultural fit with the emerging, economically sustainable airline. Sandwiched between them are the early adopters, early majority and the late majority who all adopt the innovation at different speeds.

Innovation and competitors

The best innovations will eventually be emulated by competitors. (Online check-in was an innovation when Alaska Airlines first used it in 1999. It was eventually copied by almost every airline worldwide.) While urging transparency and disclosure for materiality in sustainable airline decision-making, there is also a need for discretion. Sometimes the desire for openness combined with pressure from external lobby groups can inadvertently undermine competitive advantage. However, reading other airlines' sustainability reports gives an indication of what bothers them and is often a guide to their overall innovation strategy.

Innovation barriers

Stifling innovation can happen in many ways including the nature of innovation itself. If it is 'new' it could be perceived as disruptive and threatening to the existing order. As a result, existing departments might not want to spend resources on it (but competitors might).

Cross-functional SBU collaboration on innovation can be complex and focussing on convergent thinking (resulting in groupthink – see Chapter 7) does not encourage divergent thinking and challenge. Challenges from the 'wrong' departmental silo can lead to the feared loss of power, influence, rewards and on occasion, employment. What is needed is a balance of divergent and convergent thinking skills. Without these the airline behaves like a risk-averse firm in a stable industry (Table 3.4) retaining the bureaucracy and hierarchy of the past instead of the entrepreneurial qualities needed to galvanise it into 'future-proofing'.

Barriers also materialise from the hierarchical and silo cultures. Employees who are too lowly in the hierarchy or from the 'wrong' department can have their innovation suggestions blocked, ignored or worse – stolen by others who obtain the recognition and reward. The hierarchical, silo organisation is therefore often unable to take advantage of innovations because it lacks the 'completeness of thinking' and open-mindedness which incubates creativity and innovation, i.e. sustainability-thinking.

Finding the 'golden nugget'

Finally, the corporate golden nuggets of innovation are rare but when found, are a source of wonder, excitement and pride. Finding those nuggets can be a long and frustrating process which involves preparation, perspiration, disappointment, failures and opportunity costs. However, the more innovation is practised, the greater are the chances of reaping success.

3.6 AIRLINE PHILANTHROPY

Context

Historically, great philanthropists accumulated wealth from selling products or services. Great wealth gave them great power and influence. However, if the historical philanthropists – the entrepreneurs of their age – had charged less for their products or services (thereby reducing their profits) their customers could have retained more of their personal earnings and could have donated to causes for which they had strong feelings rather than those preferred by their supplier. This would have meant that generous philanthropists such as the Rockefellers (finance) or the Hewletts (computers) would have had less wealth for the philanthropic causes about which they cared but which might not have been of concern for their customers. Markets ruled: consumers paid the prices that the supplier asked or they went without the products.

There is a strong correlation between the number of super-entrepreneurs (such as today's Gateses, Zuckerbergs and Musks) and donations to charity as a share of GDP (Sanandaji and Sanandaji, 2014). By purchasing products and services offered by the philanthropist producers and suppliers consumers enable the profits some of which are later donated. However, generous personal or corporate philanthropy (on which some governments occasionally rely for provision of unaffordable public goods and services) can skew politics and public opinion. It can also undermine democracy and markets. Some philanthropists or their charitable foundations are using their influence to persuade governments to provide the services that they believe citizens want or need. In a democracy, this could undermine the electorate's wishes and be perceived as an example of CSERplus advocacy and the principal-agent problem (see Table 8.1 in Chapter 8) (especially as some of today's philanthropists stand to gain from the supply of their products into the (formerly missing) markets they are persuading governments need expanding).

Purposeful philanthropy

Competitive advantage is determined by how the airline allocates resources to support the sale of space in the cargo hold and in the aircraft cabin. If the carriers chose to donate any quantity then there would be reduced inventory available for sale. Airline philanthropy is an economic and social issue which alternately unites and divides stakeholders on whether a firm should donate and if so, to which individuals or organisations? Airlines can choose whether or not to embed philanthropy; however, it is somehow expected that all airlines would have a philanthropic thread in their corporate DNA. Airlines, like nation states, can only afford philanthropy if there is an economic surplus and then only after they have rewarded the shareholders and employees. Corporate philanthropy is, after all, the removal of shareholders' funds (Lawson, 2012) and employees' rewards. Redistributing their monies without having received their approval for this disbursement might not add to their welfare. Besides, some shareholders and employees might feel that they contribute sufficiently to charities through their taxes or personal donations so that further contributions through their diverted rewards are unnecessary. Furthermore, the managers might donate to a cause which could have no resonance with shareholders, employees, customers or other stakeholders. Donations of corporate resources could be regarded as 'passive' philanthropy because the people who decide to donate and gain the 'feel-good glow' are not donating their own time or money. Passive donating is also an activity of governments when they donate taxpayers' funds. 'Active' philanthropy involves donors committing their own resources whether time (as volunteers), money or goods.

The economists' view is that corporate philanthropy (another form of transfer payment) does not fit with the lean principles of minimising waste, reducing costs and only providing those goods and services for which customers are willing to pay. The socialists' view is that philanthropy supports the fundamental CSERplus principle of equalising societies. If an airline has difficulties with its stakeholders, wishes to enhance its neighbourly reputation or to enjoy a 'feel-good glow', it can indulge in some tactical corporate philanthropy. However, corporate philanthropy should not be used to repair historic errors, cover regulated shortfalls or as a trade-off to avoid bad publicity. Such tactical repairs should either be funded elsewhere or not funded at all. If philanthropy is part of the airlines' business strategy – it is, after all, the ultimate overhead – it should be approached strategically and not used to provide a bandage for a reputational haemorrhage. Such largesse could, however, open an airline to charges of 'buying' off opposition, unduly influencing support, wasting shareholders' money or succumbing to 'genteel extortion' whereby the organisation submits to the will of the CSERplus' advocates to protect its trading. There is an argument that 'strategic philanthropy' is a myth in itself because most corporate philanthropic programmes are actually tactical aimed at 'generating goodwill and positive publicity and boosting employee morale' (Porter and Kramer, 2002: 58).

Charity glow

Airline employees' charitable support can be perceived as an expression of the corporate culture. Social investment is usually motivated by egoism (utility derived from consumption) or altruism (utility derived from the consumption of others as well as one's own) (Husted and Salazar, 2006). However, 'giving is motivated by many things other than altruism. Guilt, sympathy, an ethic for duty, a taste for fairness, or a desire for recognition may all influence an individual's contribution to charity' (Andreoni, 1988: 57). It is acknowledged that doing good makes people feel good (altruism) and since airline employees by their nature are often charitably inclined, they like their employer to support charities. 'Firms . . . typically have a portfolio of [CSERplus] projects, some of which may be coerced [i.e. genteel extortion], others altruistic, and still others strategic in nature' (Husted and Salazar, 2006: 87). There are three circumstances under which firms (such as airlines) might engage in strategic philanthropic activities which benefit the environment and/or society: first, where it is possible that government intervention looms (such as proposing an emissions tax), second where there is the opportunity to differentiate products (perhaps through alignment with a charity with the prospect of increasing seat or freight sales) or third where internal cost reductions are possible (Husted and Salazar, 2006). However, despite charitable donations, airlines did not succeed in preventing environmental taxes (see Chapter 6) and furthermore, airline alignment with charities is not known to have increased seat or freight sales. If involvement in charities is strategic – designed to reduce costs, prevent legislation, enhance reputation or mitigate genteel extortion – then it might be more successful. Moreover, where corporates are slow to voluntarily support national social programmes, governments in many countries legislate to obligate them into the role by creating more boondoggles (see Chapter 5 and Chapter 6).

Volunteering

Supporting both the egoism and altruism concepts, employer-sponsored volunteering with charities is purported to offer employees opportunities to raise their corporate profile as well as giving them the chance to acquire new skills and responsibilities. It is claimed that volunteering can provide serendipitous opportunities for innovation as well as providing some slack resource for employees to contemplate extrapolating their learning back into their original workplace (another means of disseminating innovation).

Some employees form charities under the airline's philanthropic umbrella thereby mixing passive and active volunteering, i.e. company's resources plus employee's own time. However, volunteering during company time removes productive time from the enterprise and can reduce overall welfare because if the volunteers are not working in the airline then their roles are either unnecessary or being filled by another employee.

Some advocacy research claims that volunteering is good for employees' morale, could reduce the organisation's training costs and might even provide the opportunity for volunteers to develop new skills. Volunteering activities can be as diverse as reading to children in local schools through to travelling to a poverty-relief project in an advancing country. Some advocates suggest that such volunteering could also form part of the employee's performance evaluation as a prelude to promotion while others believe that promotions or pay rises should go to employees who have completed the most volunteering hours (Birdwell and Wybron, 2014). This is a social viewpoint which could be challenged by non-advocacy, economic research. Volunteering in corporate time is low risk for the employee who can shift the costs of his/her altruism onto the commercial enterprise's shareholders. Some external airline consultancies proudly advertise their commitment to volunteering during working hours. (Does this attract more airline clients or is it to entice potential employees?) Such altruism is ultimately paid for by their clients – the airlines – and that means that eventually passengers would pay for the consultancies' altruism. These costs become yet another charge to be embedded in passengers' fares (unless the airlines cease using boastful consultants).

Corporate philanthropic models

The challenge for airlines which decide to be philanthropic is to devise a set of criteria and perhaps a central theme around which to objectively evaluate suitable charities for strategic and tactical support. Any subsequent decision to donate or decline would then have an objective basis. This is in keeping with the ideal of decision-making transparency. If the request fits then it should be considered (subject to there being sufficient budget to fulfil it). Any charity selected must also resonate with the airline's culture and take account of the numerous stakeholders' sensitivities including religion, politics, race and envy. Leadership sensitivity in awarding corporate charitable support is important because inappropriate choices can reverberate.

There are no rules for corporate philanthropy but the justification and its links to the business strategy should be transparent. There are many models including (but not limited to):

- structured, strategic, long-term relationship building which provides a framework for supporting approved and vetted charities and activities which fit with the business strategy
- a core of several large charities for longer term, strategic community investment with a number of smaller, satellite charities for shorter term support
- formation of in-house charities managed by employees (these are usually long-term, open-ended commitments)
- development of a hybrid philanthropic strategy which incorporates some structured and unstructured elements
- unstructured philanthropy or one-off tactical support such as the 'Chairman's whim' which can support particular specific groups or individuals for a short time.

'Chairman's whim'

Contrary to strategic philanthropy is the 'Chairman's whim' as an analogy for donations which do not have a strategic fit but which are meaningful to the airline's executives who exercise autocratic power (Table 3.7) to support personal interests (e.g. football, horse racing, polo, Formula 1 motor racing). These donations can override the corporate philanthropic strategy and can be made without acknowledging any influence. This lack of transparency can place the airline's reputation at risk and if disclosed, could undermine much of the good work completed in the airline's name. News headlines work best on scandals. The Chairman's whim must be wielded carefully or cynics might ask 'What does the Chairman stand to gain?' to which the response could be 'His name on a horse race', 'A seat in the Royal Box for the Wimbledon tennis final' or (more cynically in the UK) 'A knighthood or a seat in the House of Lords'. While such philanthropy can provide senior executives with networking opportunities which could otherwise be denied to them, the Chairman's whim might only engender resentment among employees who could see his choice as elite and of no benefit to the economic sustainability of the airline. It might not resonate at all with lower paid employees because their ideas of philanthropy are generally more tuned to vulnerable populations or crisis relief in foreign destinations. Furthermore, the insensitivity of sponsoring elite events if employees' wages are being suppressed (such as during an economic recession or passenger downturn) or when dividends remain unpaid would show that management is out of touch with some of its key stakeholders. Philanthropy is not an economically sustainable proposition for airlines in such circumstances unless it can be shown to sell more seats or freight space, reduce costs or prevent legislation.

Philanthropy's darker side

While it is acknowledged that strategic philanthropy might have a useful role in reputation building, it can also lead to accusations of 'buying favours', not just with legislators but with CSERplus' advocates who are industry detractors. The ulterior motive of donating can be to prevent a consumer boycott or disruption to operations, i.e. a form of commercial 'protection'. One airline tells the tale of a welfare organisation which threatened to blockade the main arterial road route and prevent its commercial vehicles accessing the engineering base. This was in protest against the airline's conveyance of deportees on commercial flights. In the subsequent negotiations, the charity was able to secure donations (complimentary seats and overhead funding) as well as airline representations on their behalf with the government. This generosity could have been perceived as 'protection payments' or 'genteel extortion'. In accordance with the negotiated outcome, the airline refused to carry repatriations, the engineering base stayed open and flying operations continued uninterrupted. Another airline recounted the tale of the Chief Executive of a major charity with Royal connections who claimed to speak for the Royal Patron. She was extremely influential with government ministers and would only conduct discussions at airline Board level. She influenced the Board to support her charity in exchange for promises (which she fulfilled) of meetings with Royalty in their London accommodation and attendances at exclusive, prestigious gatherings. Such powerful and influential networking is rarely ignored by decision-makers even if it deviates from the carefully assembled philanthropic strategy.

Tangible airline philanthropic support

Airline philanthropy requires employees to administer and resources to fulfil its mandate, all of which take potential dividends away from the shareholders and rewards from employees. Airline philanthropy can take many forms ranging from tactically donating one seat to a worthy cause through to strategically donating many seats (or freight) over a period of time to multiple worthy causes. It could also encompass donations of cash or goods or even flying disabled or life-limited children to their dream holiday. Some airlines donate an entire aircraft to deliver disaster relief supplies as Norwegian Air Shuttle ASA did in 2014 as part of its relief for the UN International Children's Emergency Fund (UNICEF). Norwegian provided an aircraft and crew to carry emergency aid and life-saving equipment to the war-torn Central African Republic (CAR). The 'fill a plane' campaign began in August 2014 and culminated in raising three million kroner (£Stg233,000 or $US366,000) among passengers and employees for the October flight (Norwegian, 2014). (The cost of this gesture to the airline's shareholders is unknown. The French-speaking CAR is not on any known current Norwegian network. Why did they choose the CAR when there were so many other desperately poor and deprived nations on that continent? Was this a tactical, altruistic gesture or a strategic signal portending a future route perhaps?)

Support can also comprise donations of standby or firm bookings, cargo space, auction proceeds from passengers' lost property, unused complimentary airline gifts and cash. Donating out-of-date uniforms is an innovative but possibly misguided recycling gesture since there are security issues with this option. (Terrorists could use the uniforms to access secure areas and aircraft.) However, creative philanthropic thinking can deliver some very innovative economic solutions to some difficult social problems. After a large-scale redesign of its cabins, Southwest Airlines was left with 43 acres of used leather seat coverings. Although a USA domestic carrier, they partnered with social enterprises in Kenya, Malawi and the USA to turn these discards into new products which will benefit communities by providing employment, skills training and livelihoods (Southwest Airlines, 2014). Another airline donated spare places on its training courses in order for their partner charities to enhance their skills.

Complimentary airline bookings for passengers and freight are much valued by cash-strapped charities. However, with the imposition of increasing amounts of travel taxes the value of these donations diminishes since, in an unintended consequence, the charities (often with many tax exemptions) are frequently required to pay the travel taxes themselves.

Philanthropic overheads

Corporate philanthropic activities can receive widespread and favourable reportage and generate a halo effect. The location of philanthropic disbursements is often an indicator of the airline's intentions since philanthropy might have a department of its own or be subsumed under another of the social responsibility departmental titles (such as CSR, CSER, CCI or even Corporate Responsibility) (see Chapter 7). Often philanthropy dwells in the Public Relations Department; however, 'as long as companies remain focussed on the public relations benefit of their contributions, they will sacrifice opportunities to create social value' (Porter and Kramer, 2002: 67) (but who decides the 'social value'?).

NGO or charity selection challenges

Because of the fragility of the 'licence to operate', airlines are more vulnerable to some stakeholder groups than others. Risk assessment before involvement is essential to determine whether such a link would be harmful or beneficial. Weaving external groups' preferences into a strategy can be challenging as often there is no obvious (or strategic) link. Some would argue that animal welfare is appropriate for airline philanthropic support because of the airlines' links with food or leather products; others might recommend health charities that support lung disease because of the pollution around airports; and yet others might recommend social programmes such as those affecting disabled or elderly people or impoverished children. Airlines need to be wary of just what politics lurk behind some of the requests for support and to be aware of any hidden allegiances. Airlines' philanthropic involvement cannot afford to be tainted by scandal. Due diligence is key to ensuring airline support is appropriate and would enhance rather than damage donor airlines' reputations. Strategic alignment is possible by partnering with specialist NGOs which could give credibility to the airline's efforts to increase profits or reduce costs. In doing so, the NGO can often assist with future-proofing the organisation. One small, well-run NGO specialising in preventing disability helped assess the impact of ageing on future passengers and were rewarded with complimentary bookings for passengers and freight to support their programmes. As a strategic economic planning tool, this particular relationship meant the airline had sufficient lead time to instal retractable armrests on new aircraft so that ageing passengers could move in and out of the rows without cabin crew assistance. This installation negated the need for extra cabin crew who might have been required to manage increasing numbers of elderly travellers (see Chapter 5). It was a fruitful airline-NGO partnering and it was a win-win for society and economics even though there is an ongoing weight penalty of approximately 1kg for each modified armrest (see Table 5.2 in Chapter 5). It was also directly focussed on reducing future airline costs (i.e. one of the targets for strategic philanthropy).

If an airline was trying to promote a route then a strategic link with a charity working in the target country could be useful for opening the air corridor – but great care must be taken to ensure that the charity is working in the best interests of its recipients and not in the vested interests of its executives (i.e. principal-agent problem and possibly even cronyism – see Chapter 1). Charity assessment decisions must be transparent and able to withstand challenge. The halo effect can very quickly evaporate and impact on the airline's reputational risk profile.

The final selection for tactical or strategic philanthropic support from a short list could be achieved by the departmental team, employee voting or even selection by the Board of Directors. Howsoever the choice is made it must be made transparently and in accordance with the airline's philanthropic strategy and governance procedures (see Chapter 7).

Funding risks

Independent and impartial scrutiny is a critical factor during assessment for philanthropic support and donors have a duty to monitor these relationships carefully until the exit date arrives and support is terminated or reduced. Since airlines are so reliant on passenger trust to retain their reputations they must be very wary when selecting organisations for partnering. Careful analysis of annual accounts, discussions with the NGO itself, understanding their long-term strategy and examining other organisations with which it has been involved are actions which help to reduce any risk. Virgin Atlantic (2015) (along with many other commercial organisations) was an enthusiastic donor and corporate partner of the high-profiled, celebrity-supported, formerly popular, scandal-ridden London (UK) charity, Kids Company. When a charity fails through mis-management, those who have supported it feel betrayed. Its demise could also hurt the reputations of the supporting corporate organisations since it could demonstrate a lack of due diligence and monitoring on their part.

Airlines must also ensure that any influential stakeholders have declared their vested interests because hidden lobbying can distort charities – especially when governments might be one of the charity funders as happens particularly in the UK and EU. These offices often use taxpayers' funds to support charities which are selected by politicians (Snowdon, 2012 and 2014). Donations are not charitable if they are made by the State from taxpayers' compulsorily acquired funds as exampled by the UK's Department for International Development (DfID) which matches public donations for selected charitable appeals. In 2014, the UK appealed for funds to fight Ebola in West Africa. The appeal was fronted by the Disasters Emergency Committee (DEC) a compilation of 13 leading aid charities. DfID offered matching funding. 'DEC says it has been overwhelmed by the "extraordinary generosity" of the British public after £4m [$US6.15m or €5.5m] was donated in just two days to a campaign to help people affected by the Ebola crisis in West Africa. The UK government had pledged to match the first £5m given by the public and its £4m contribution so far brings the fund total to £8m since the campaign was launched' (Press Association, 2014). However, money was the wrong measure. Had the government counted the number of individuals donating, there would have been a more accurate indication of the level of popular support. The donating minority swayed an elected government and in doing so undermined democratic process. (NB: this is not to say that the cause was unworthy – rather that the process of measurement of public support was flawed.)

The UK (along with many other nations) has channelled £Stg billions into overseas aid, working with organisations many of which have been started by consortiums of church groups (Birrell, 2013). Their programmes were socially based, often made only minimal improvements and in many countries benefitted only the despots and warlords. The UK government has donated 0.7% of the debt-ridden UK's GDP (i.e. borrowed funds) to be sent to international development projects for which there is only limited oversight. Fixed-proportion donating cannot be considered a universal success because there is less incentive for self-improvement when funds are to be gifted in perpetuity. This creates a moral hazard. Aid fosters dependency, encourages corruption, hinders economic growth, perpetuates poverty and turns a blind eye to inadequate governance (Moyo, 2011). It also creates a moral hazard where the recipients do not to have to change the behaviour which led to poverty because aid will allow life to continue unchanged. The focus should be on education and reducing deficits (Moyo, 2011). In other words, such philanthropy is well-meaning but often misguided. Ultimately, airline philanthropy results in the distribution of shareholders' funds and employees' rewards often into short-term programmes managed by NGOs which might or might not be favoured by the shareholders or employees. Furthermore, many of these programmes might not provide long-term benefit to the recipients. The impacts would need to be measured other than by feelings of altruism in the few employees who participate.

As another example, the European Community favours organisations which support closer European ties and which 'enhance tolerance and mutual under-standing' (Snowdon, 2013: 9). The outcome is the situation where campaigning groups funded by governments in turn lobby the same governments (see Chapter 6). In this way, politics is less open and transparent in contrast to the behaviours politicians expect from sustainable commercial airlines. While politicians urge airlines to make transparent decisions, their own decisions are often anything but transparent. In an extension of the principal-agent problem, 11 of 25 Special Advisers (SPADs) to former UK Labour Prime Minister Gordon Brown went to work for 'supposedly neutral think tanks or charities many of which speak out against the [Conservative/Liberal Democrat Coalition] government or lobby ministers to change laws' (Hope, 2014). In other words, from under the cover of their charities they lobby behind the scenes to bring about social changes which were rejected by the electorate. This undermines the democratic process. There is a danger that without careful preliminary checks, an airline could become a donor to such organisations.

British Airways has a long-term, strategic partnership with political campaigner Comic Relief to distribute passengers' loose change to help children. There is a £Stg2.5m ($US3.9m or €3.4m) goal with monthly targets to raise the funds – a business-focussed concept which contrasts with the original idea of charity being for altruistic amateurs rattling collection tins on the High Street. The collecting envelope placed in the seat back states that '£1 could provide a hot meal for a child in the UK living in extreme poverty'. This message has political overtones as the UK Coalition Government (2010 to 2015) attempted to reduce the welfare budget. Comic Relief is also one of the charities calling for a finance industry transaction tax to:

> raise hundreds of billions of pounds to fight poverty, protect public services and tackle climate change . . . the campaign is calling on the leaders of the UK's political parties to support a global tax on the banks to help protect public services at home, fight poverty at home and abroad and help foot the bill for climate change.
>
> (Comic Relief, 2010)

This is not a politically neutral stance. The charity has the support of the State-owned broadcaster, the BBC, which is supposed to be an impartial organisation. In the interests of openness and transparency, it is worth querying whether a privately owned airline's philanthropic support is appropriate for a politically campaigning organisation – especially one with an aim to reduce social inequality and to 'foot the bill for climate change' when climate change is not confirmed to be either man-made or controllable (see Chapter 6). The social and environmental causes have been merged in this appeal supported by a national broadcaster with a pro-climate change stance (see Chapter 6). Whether this fundraising has encouraged increased seat or freight sales is not noted in the annual report.

Politics and religion vs airline philanthropy

Hidden lobbying can further distort charitable giving especially when government might be one of the NGO funders. If charities (or indeed airlines) are State-funded their independence is compromised and they are therefore less likely to criticise government policies (Snowdon, 2014; Birrell, 2013). This has implications for sustainable airlines which cannot afford to be enmeshed in political manoeuvrings. It is complicated in the UK because 'State-funded activists tend to be on the political left [and] . . . left-wingers have taken ownership of issues such as climate change, overseas aid and public health' (Snowdon, 2014: 16, 19). Eight of the biggest environmental NGOs receive at least a third of their income from the EU (Mackonis and Silenas, 2013). Coincidentally the environment is one of the topics that features prominently in many airlines' sustainability programmes (see Chapter 6). Religious citizens are more likely to be 'civically engaged', volunteer in their communities and 'more likely to hold progressive political values' (Birdwell and Littler, 2012: 15) and (importantly for airport development) more likely to feel they have an influence over local and national decisions. Again, any potential bias or advocacy in research must be considered by those who come to use it. It is ironic that private shareholders in economically sustainable airlines might inadvertently enable the funding of left-wing environmental causes which could halt aviation industry expansion.

Religion – another example of groupthink (see also Chapter 7 and Chapter 8) – can also skew philanthropic donations and a sustainable airline needs to be aware of just how such bodies could influence CSERplus programmes. Research into the role of religion in the voting and values of Britain for Theos, a religion and society think tank, found that there were clear alignments between religion and politics. Catholics were the most left-wing of Christian groups and more pro-welfare than Anglicans. Although it was harder to analyse smaller samples of non-Christian groups it was identified that Muslims, Hindus and Sikhs tended to vote Labour; Jews voted for the Conservative Party and Buddhists tended to vote Liberal Democrats (Clements and Spencer, 2014). Any of these backgrounds could provide bias in decision-making (see Chapter 7) if the philanthropy-administering depart-ment was disproportionately populated with members of one particular religion or political party.

Appropriate philanthropy

Not every NGO or charity is appropriate for airline support; however, the greater the charity's persistence the more likely it is to get an audience with the department handling philanthropic disbursements. Some commercial organisations hire consultants who specialise in the NGO sector and dispense advice on strategic and tactical philanthropy. Airlines have to be very wary of being deflected into supporting a cause which (a) might not resonate with its employees, owners and customers and (b) might not fit with its economic or philanthropic strategies. One example in particular illustrates the problem. A sportswoman who founded an animal charity which she supported by running fundraising marathons was stranded in Antarctica at the end of a 25-mile race in $-20°$ blizzards. She missed her connecting flights with Air France. The airline refused to change her booking unless she paid a penalty fare which would mean that the charitable funds she raised would have to be spent on her repatriation. She protested to the media and threatened to close her animal sanctuary (another example of 'genteel extortion'). The airline insisted it acted correctly (Arkell, 2014). Had she used full sustainability-thinking (see Chapter 7) she would have realised the Antarctic weather could alter the risk profile of the venture. Should the airline's shareholders have been forced to donate complimentary commercial seats for this lady (and her companion) in order to save her charity and the rescued animals? Her egoism and altruism presented an economic and social dilemma for the airline and ultimately for her charity.

Every month, UK newspapers have reports of travellers stranded abroad who have been uninsured and are appealing for funds for repatriation now that they are injured or ill and cannot afford their medical costs (see Chapter 4). (UK nationals prefer to return home to avail themselves of free NHS care.) If these passengers had taken personal responsibility for the potential risks of their travels they could have subscribed to travel insurance at a similar price to a manicure, tattoo or a bottle of vodka. They cannot rely on airline charitable funding for repatriation because in most nations airlines are no longer an extension of a welfare state. Airlines must make a profit and repatriation costs can sometimes be very expensive. One stretcher case can require the requisitioning of a minimum of nine economy cabin seats. The aircraft would need to be taken out of service to fit the stretcher before departure and would have to return to the hangar for its removal and seat reinstatement after the journey. This is extremely costly and many airlines now refuse to do this because the schedule disruption cost is greater than the fares charged for the passenger and any medical support team. The alternative for the passenger is to charter a medi-vac aircraft. The airline's refusal to donate space or seats is a tough letter for the Charities Department to write in the face of what is usually a real tragedy. This is a no-win situation for the airline – and sadly, a no-win for the uninsured passenger.

In another example, various fair trading organisations urge commercial organisations to support their aims of helping the poor in the advancing-world. Fairtrade supplies Virgin Atlantic airlines with selected products (Virgin Atlantic, 2014b). Fairtrade believes that the poor are harmed by free trade because it supports 'the absence of the price-fixing arrangements and tariff barriers that restrict international trade' (Sidwell, 2008: 5). Fairtrade's view is contrary to airlines which benefit from free trade, absence of price fixing and reduced regulatory barriers. Fairtrade prefers to 'manage production and restricts the marketplace' (Sidwell, 2008: 5) and is not a good fit as supplier to airlines which advocate free-market principles. Supermarket support for Fairtrade is widespread and is a lazy means for grocers to claim their compassionate credentials which are actually reimbursed by the shoppers. Shoppers, however, might not agree with the organisation and its origins but are captive to purchasing its products where the products enjoy a monopoly position (i.e. an imperfect market). Monopolies (indicators of market inefficiencies and alleged failure (see Chapter 1)) restrict consumer choice since they rely on zero competition and asymmetric knowledge. Further investigation reveals that:

> Fairtrade does not aid economic development [and] is unfair. It offers only a very small number of farmers a higher, fixed price for their goods. These higher prices come at the expense of the great majority of farmers, who – unable to qualify for Fairtrade certification – are left even worse off. Most of the farmers helped by Fairtrade are in Mexico, a relatively developed country, and not in places like Ethiopia.
>
> (Sidwell, 2008: 4)

These factors are not broadcast to airline passengers or supermarket shoppers who pay a premium for Fairtrade goods, and yet just 10% of that premium actually goes to the producers. A more recent study focussing on Ethiopia and Uganda (Cramer *et al.*, 2014) showed that wages were actually higher on many non-Fairtrade farms and that social projects were found not to provide equal benefit to all. This information is not displayed to consumers who are led to believe that they are supporting poverty reduction regimes in developing and emerging nations.

Overheads or project funding?

Charities pose many challenges for commercial organisations – and not just for airlines. One of these dilemmas is whether to donate to support charity overheads or to enable a specific project which can be branded in the donor's colours and logo. Charities need overheads but philanthropists rarely find overheads sufficiently glamorous or noteworthy to attract their name as much as a specific project could. Donors like to see their names on a building, a garden, a scholarship or similar endowment with longevity (all variations on vanity projects). They do not like to donate anonymously by contributing to overheads and yet without overheads charities cannot survive.

A related issue is that concerning the size of charity overheads as measured by the effectiveness of projects undertaken. Large charities attract expensive fundraisers and Chief Executives (some earning more than double what the UK Prime Minister earns) who should be sufficiently effective to increase revenue and expand the charity. The justification is that these are businesses that need commercially savvy managers to be responsible for the stewardship of significant assets – just as their commercial equivalents are responsible for the assets they control. There is something ironic about charities fighting poverty which pay their executives at commercial rates. Oxfam's USA President receives £Stg277,500 ($US399,000 or €366,000); Save the Children's International Chief Executive receives £Stg234,000 ($US337,000 or €308,000) (Birrell, 2014). However, it can be argued that these Chief Executives deserve appropriately commensurate, commercially equivalent rewards since they are managing significant enterprises which need to make a profit to survive. Charities are now commercial enterprises, the concept of which almost runs counter to the idea of 'charity' except that many of these charitable-businesses get tax advantages which purely commercial enterprises do not. The concept of volunteers rattling collecting tins in the High Street has long been superseded by established shops with national price lists and other profitable enterprises. In the UK their Chief Executives or founders (like their commercial equivalents) are recognised for national honours. Many charities are now big businesses wielding considerable influence and political power. However, charities with such high-paid executives require significant inward capital flows to maintain their activities – and governments or altruistically motivated philanthropists are important sources for such large sums rather than small donations from individual supporters. Consequently, charity survival is often dependent on successful lobbying of governments but if governments are funding charities this can compromise charitable independence (Snowdon, 2012 and 2014). Furthermore, government donating reduces charitable fundraising efforts (Andreoni and Payne, 2003). The significant size of some donations given by altruistic donors (e.g. William and Flora Hewlett Foundation's $US549m (£Stg387m or €494m)) to support environmental causes (Osuri, 2010) (see also Chapter 6) can wield considerable political influence (Snowdon, 2014) and could undermine voters' wishes. Airlines need to be wary.

Charity pitches

Airlines' philanthropy budgets are usually modest in comparison to those of large MNEs. Should airlines focus on larger, well-known recipients or smaller charities where their donations could have a bigger impact? Small charities working with the support of volunteers and paying their employees minimum wages have difficulty attracting the large sponsors needed to expand their activities, especially as their presentations are less likely to be as professional as those from large, well-known, well-funded charities. Where small charities have been able to attract a main sponsor they have often been able to leverage the sponsor's public relations and advertising resources to boost their public profile – something the larger charities take for granted. However, when airlines (or other supporting funders) request that a small charity makes a presentation to pitch for corporate support, it is essential that the charity receives some acknowledgement of the opportunity costs involved for doing so. Preparing presentation pitches involves resources – time and money – which could have been used for other opportunities (particularly in resource-strapped charities). Businesses receive many presentations from people who get paid to do so but in general, commercial organisations do not consider charities in the same way and expect them to present at no cost. Many charities are happy to give presentations free of charge such is their desperation to obtain commercial support. However, a corporate gesture to acknowledge the costs of presenting would be appropriate. If philanthropy is part of the airline's strategy the airline should also realise that it is the bedrock of the receiving charity. That means the airline must honour promises made and ensure that both parties agree on an exit strategy before the commencement of any support. One airline suggested that for every donated seat or freight space, the receiving charity placed an equivalent commercial amount in a bank account as a buffer for when the support was ended.

One of the other charity challenges is the need to make applications to grant-making bodies. These bodies often have lengthy and convoluted application processes (duplicate, triplicate, soft and hard copies) written as if the potential donors were oblivious to the strains such applications make on small charities. Completing such forms for what could actually be a lottery is a drain on resources and represents an opportunity cost – time and effort which might have been better directed. The winning applicants would do well while the losers would have wasted valuable resources. Because economically sustainable airlines understand resource allocation they should ensure that their application processes are simple and robust.

Awards, ceremonies and titles

NGOs create awards to publicise their views of best CSERplus practices and to honour corporate philanthropists. An award can communicate corporate credentials for something other than profitability (the one element that CSERplus campaigners forget keeps an economically sustainable airline afloat). Awards such as 'Best supply chain engagement', 'Best corporate and charity partnership', 'Best employee enrichment scheme' and 'Best consumer engagement' can often also engage a third body in the relationship, i.e. the professional CSERplus organisation or social enterprise which would be able to make a profit from running such awards schemes. Their funds come from selling their services and seat sales for their awards events. These 'social' enterprises might style themselves as 'charities'; however, they are profit-making ventures just the same as the corporates they advise, i.e. they are free-market capitalists at heart. They are often well-meaning but misguided and their expertise is founded on their view of 'ethical' principles. It could therefore be argued that attending awards ceremonies (egos vs altruism) and hiring awards consultants are inappropriate uses of shareholders' funds or employees' rewards. However, if sustainable airlines behave appropriately (i.e. focus on their core competency) there will be no need to be part of the awards circuit because the world would know why they are successful (see also Chapter 7).

Cause-related marketing

Philanthropy can also be perceived as a form of sponsorship (and possibly therefore more appropriately supported from the Marketing or Public Relations' budget).

Measuring its success can be difficult because methods of measuring such impacts are currently inadequate. (It is estimated that about 30–50% of US companies do not have a system to measure sponsorship return on investment.) Such measures include 'cost per reach', 'sales related to sponsorship spend' and 'sales as a result of activating the sponsorship with support activities' (Jacobs *et al.*, 2014). There is no known research which links increased airline seat or freight sales with the airline industries' philanthropic gestures.

In cause-related marketing a commercial organisation seeks to gain a 'halo' effect from alliancing with a charity. In the consumers' minds the charitable aims spill over onto the supporting corporate; however, it is consumers' continued purchasing which determines the sustainability of the relationship. Cause-related marketing differentiates one corporation from another, supposedly enhances corporate reputation and can be a competitive tool provided it is compatible with the brand. It should fit with the overall image of a sustainable airline and be free from politics. The most usual manifestation is the support for sports, entertainment or social causes such as education or health. It can be perceived as opportunistic by cynics since there is usually a welter of publicity available for such affinities. It is the element of publicity which differentiates cause-related marketing from pure philanthropy ('doing good' without expecting public acclaim) although airline shareholders should know where their funds are spent. It would be anticipated that the outcomes would include greater brand awareness, customer loyalty and increased market share measured by pre-determined CSFs and KPIs. Furthermore, depending on the cause selected, philanthropic support might enhance the airline's reputation with stakeholders (including regulators) which could be perceived as a risk-reduction activity. Cause-related marketing is usually part of a strategic approach by the Marketing Department and would be budgeted accordingly. Continued vigilance is necessary to ensure that any ongoing relationship is appropriate, that the original basis on which the spend was justified remains valid and that it has a positive influence on revenue.

Philanthropic reality

It is an economic matter of affordability and resource allocation as to what and how much an airline can realistically donate. However, if shareholders (the providers of risk capital) are not receiving dividends and employees are not receiving uplifts in rewards, is it fair to make any donations at all?

3.7 CELEBRITY ADVOCACY

Fame and celebrity

How to define a 'celebrity'? An American Senator? A UK Member of Parliament (who might or might not have participated in the UK Parliamentary expenses scandal)? A successful industrialist/film star/television personality/rock star/

diplomat/member of the Royal household? What quality or activity comprises 'celebrity' sufficient to warrant their endorsement of an airline in exchange for free flights or cash donation to support their altruism? Airline charity departments have anecdotes of Very-Very Important Passengers (V-VIPs) who wrote to the Chairman (who possibly cascaded the request downwards) and demanded charitable support for their favourite charity. Major charities frequently employ celebrity liaison managers to provide a link between corporates, celebrities and charities. Many of these celebrities are from show business or from politics and they attempt to influence airline philanthropy in support of their own aims. They are well-meaning but often misguided. Furthermore, their myopic altruism has often had disproportionate influence on governments. The campaign by musicians Bono and Sir Bob Geldof to influence governments to commit an annual fixed percentage of 0.7% of GDP for development aid has been embedded in the UK. In 2014 it cost approximately £Stg12bn ($US17bn or €16bn) annually. What qualification did these musicians acquire in order to advocate as economic development advisers and influence so many governments to their beliefs? Were the negotiating ministers simply star struck? Eventually Bono came to believe that trade instead of aid was a more successful means of lifting nations out of poverty (Olson, 2012) – a practice which had been supported by many airlines (and other industries) which outsource various commercial activities offshore to developing nations (see Chapter 7). Would the government reconsider its policy now that one of the CSERplus' advocates has changed his mind?

Some medical charities are very high profile, led by celebrities with vested interests because their relatives or friends have endured or died from a specific illness. However, their focus on one particular medical or social problem can obscure other problems which affect far greater numbers of people and which do not have high-profile celebrity support (Table 3.15).

Furthermore, research into celebrity advocacy in achieving social and political change suggests that, in contrast to popular belief, such influences are not a particularly worthwhile phenomenon particularly if they are measured by the CSF

Table 3.15 Top ten diseases in low-income countries, most of which have no celebrity supporters (World Health Organisation (WHO), 2011)

Position	Low-income countries: causes of death	% of deaths
1st	Lower respiratory infections	11.3
2nd	Diarrhoeal diseases	8.2
3rd	HIV/AIDS	7.8
4th	Ischaemic heart disease	6.1
5th	Malaria	5.2
6th	Stroke and other cerebrovascular disease	4.9
7th	Tuberculosis	4.3
8th	Prematurity and low birth weight	3.2
9th	Birth asphyxia and birth trauma	2.9
10th	Neonatal infections	2.6

of 'increases in donations'. The celebrities would appear to benefit more than the charities they support. Celebrity advocacy 'is an extension of media power but not a reflection of popular endorsement' (Brockington and Henson, 2014: 15) and is 'firmly entrenched in post-democratic politics and part of the public alienation from politics that the term describes. Nevertheless, because celebrity advocacy also works well with political and business elites it might still be a good vehicle for pursuing some of the goals of development advocates' (Brockington and Henson, 2014: 1) – a sentiment which fits the CSERplus celebrity agenda. The UN is expert in attaching celebrities to humanitarian causes but the link between celebrity and heightened charitable fundraising is yet to be made. Savvy economically sustainable airlines would be cognisant that associating with a celebrity might not produce the desired effect as far as influencing the public to purchase more revenue-earning seats or freight space.

Celebrities as airline philanthropy stakeholders

The thorny issue of celebrity endorsement is a challenge for high-profile industries like airlines. Airline employees like to see celebrity backing for their charities and it is not unknown for them to ask the celebrity for endorsement at the check-in point or during flight. Celebrity support is believed to boost employee morale and usually gains media attention. Besides, airline employees interact with these V-VIPs and find such contact the norm. Some celebrities are unpretentious, pleasant passengers who make journeys memorable for their generosity (one is known to give economy cabin passengers an unscheduled concert) and kindness (changing seats and downgrading to assist a fellow passenger). Others are attention-seeking prima donnas who make the journey miserable for crew and fellow passengers alike. It is also not unknown for some V-VIPs to use their celebrity as genteel extortion to support their favoured charitable causes. Others purchase economy seats for themselves and their entourage secure in the knowledge that they would probably be upgraded free of charge to ensure privacy. Sustainable airline employees treat all passengers as appropriate and in accordance with the company's core values. This was taken to extreme when one very petite, 30-year-old, successful female singer boarded the premium cabin and was asked by crew where her parents were seated? She was very good-natured about it but nevertheless, it was a gaffe.

Gratitude and ingratitude

The problem with some V-VIPs is they expect support from the carrier as a reward for their custom – and they have the power to irritate public opinion through social media if the carrier refuses the request. However, when celebrity V-VIPs fly in the premium cabins and use tax havens to avoid (and sometimes evade) paying taxes their requests for the airlines to donate in support of their altruism or egoism would appear to conflict with their personal core values. Not all airline stake-holders (who might not be able to avoid taxes) would necessarily agree with the chosen V-VIP priorities. They might have causes they consider more worthwhile which had been rejected for support – something V–VIPs tend to forget when they broadcast their grievance.

Two case studies illustrate the contrast in V–VIP expectations. Celebrity A (actor and singer) wanted a pair of seats to offer as a prize in a golf tournament he was holding to raise money for deaf students – a cause which was integral to the airline's strategic support. In exchange, he offered to appear at a fundraiser to help raise money for the airline's in-house charity. Offer accepted; tickets issued. Celebrity B (a magician) wanted ten seats for the charity he founded and which bore his name. His request was to fly his executives to an international conference on a very popular tourist route to save spending his charity's funds. The aims of the charity did not fit with the airline's charitable support strategy and the travel required was during the summer peak when the route was always fully booked with fare-paying passengers. When the request was rejected he appealed to the Chairman as a 'loyal customer'. Fearing a Twitter backlash, the Chairman exercised his power and whim and overruled the Charities Office. This meant that the Charities Office had ten fewer return seats to donate to strategically appropriate causes. It also meant that the airline's shareholders were directly supporting the egotistical celebrity's charity. In yet another example, the Chief Executive of an international human-itarian organisation used his complimentary return ticket on an oversold flight from London to New York. Upon checking-in, he was allocated a seat in the economy section. He complained to the Check-in Agent because he felt that, as the Chief Executive of such a high-profile organisation, he should be in the first class cabin. The Agent politely told him that his (free) booking did not entitle him to an upgrade. His response was that the airline's Chairman had approved it but had not put it in writing. She said she could easily check with the Chairman as he was standing in the queue two passengers behind. The Chief Executive took his boarding card and left without further discussion.

So what?

Successful airlines are dependent on their culture, the practising of authentic core values and their successful management of outliers, internal enemies, stress, fairness, innovative problem-solving and philanthropic requests (some of which could be almost classed as 'genteel extortion'). There are many challenges to be resolved on the journey towards future-proofing and maintaining competitive-ness. These include trading with unscrupulous nations irrespective of how highly profitable the routes might become and inadvertently supporting advocacy groups masquerading as charities and led by altruistic egotists with hidden allegiances. Many airline-charity relationships are one-sided, with no CSFs or KPIs to measure. If the same investment criteria were applied to charities as to corporate investment decisions, these would be reasons not to invest. Under the influence of many diverse and often conflicting stakeholders (who include CSERplus' advocates, celebrities and philanthropists), airlines are often expected to implement many social programmes irrespective of the appropriateness of fit with their business models. However, in summary: *happy employees lead to happy customers and successful, economically sustainable airlines which might make charitable donations from economic surpluses.* Culture matters.

References

Air New Zealand (2014), *Grab a seat* available from http://grabaseat.co.nz/ accessed 2 September 2014

Andreoni, J. (1988), Privately provided public goods in a large economy: the limits of altruism, *Journal of Public Economics* 35(1) 57–73 available from http://econweb.ucsd.edu/~jandreon/Publications/JPubE88Limits.pdf accessed 1 January 2015

Andreoni, J. and Payne, A. (2003), Do government grants to private charities crowd out giving or fund-raising? *American Economic Review* 93(3) 792–812 available from http://econweb.ucsd.edu/~jandreon/Publications/AER03-A&P.pdf accessed 30 March 2015

Ariely, D., Gneezy, U., Lowenstein, G. and Mazar, N. (2005), *Large stakes and big mistakes*, Research Centre for Behavioral Economics and Decision-making, Federal Reserve Bank of Boston Working Paper No. 05–11 available from https://www.bostonfed.org/economic/wp/wp2005/wp0511.pdf accessed 4 September 2014

Arkell, H. (2014), *Air France charges £6,400 for an extreme marathon runner to change her flights after she was trapped in Antarctica by blizzards* available from http://www.dailymail.co.uk/news/article-2548000/Air-France-no-heart-Marathon-runner-raising-funds-animal-sanctuary-close-6-500-bill.html accessed 1 August 2014

Basadur, M. (2001), *The Power of Innovation – how to make innovation a way of life and put creative solutions to work*, Toronto, Canada, Applied Creativity Press

Basadur, M. and Gelade, G.A. (2006), The role of knowledge management in the innovation process, *Creativity and Innovation Management* 15(1) 45–62 available from http://onlinelibrary.wiley.com/doi/10.1111/j.1467-8691.2006.00368.x/abstract accessed 2 January 2015

Birdwell, J. and Littler, M. (2012), *Why those who do God do good: faithful citizens* available from http://www.demos.co.uk/publications/faithfulcitizens accessed 10 April 2012

Birdwell, J. and Wybron, I. (2014), *Scouting for skills* available from http://www.demos.co.uk/publications/scoutingforskills accessed 4 August 2014

Birrell, I. (2013), *This isn't ending world hunger. It's just a sham. Ministers and their mates in the swollen aid industry came up with something cynical* available from http://www.independent.co.uk/voices/comment/this-isnt-ending-world-hunger-its-just-a-sham-8663821.html accessed 1 August 2014

Birrell, I. (2014), *A nauseating award for Blair and a bloated aid industry sucking up to its political paymasters* available from http://www.dailymail.co.uk/debate/article-2851200/A-nauseating-award-Blair-bloated-aid-industry-sucking-political-paymasters.html accessed 6 December 2014

Boeing (2013), *Boeing Statement on Federal Aviation Administration 787 Action* available from http://boeing.mediaroom.com/2013-01-16-Boeing-Statement-on-Federal-Aviation-Administration-787-Action accessed 24 June 2014

Bowen, D., Gilliland, S. and Folger, R. (1999), HRM and service fairness: how being fair with employees spills over to customers, *Organisational Dynamics* 27(3) 7–23 available from http://www.sciencedirect.com/science/article/pii/S0090261699900189 accessed 1 January 2015

Brockington, D. and Henson, S. (2014), Signifying the public: celebrity advocacy and post-democratic politics, *International Journal of Cultural Studies* 1–18 available from http://

danielbrockington.files.wordpress.com/2013/11/international-journal-of-cultural-studies-2014-brockington-henson.pdf accessed 9 August 2014

Burkus, D. (2011), A tale of two cultures: why culture trumps core values in building ethical organisations, *The Journal of Values Based Leadership* 4(1) n.p. available from http://www.valuesbasedleadershipjournal.com/issues/vol4issue1/tale_2culture.php accessed 2 January 2015

Cameron, K. and Quinn, R. (2006), *Diagnosing and changing organisational culture*, San Francisco, Jossey-Bass, John Wiley & Sons

Chen, C.-F. and Chen, S.-C. (2014), Investigating the effects of job demands and job resources on cabin crew safety behaviors, *Tourism Management* 41 45–52 available from http://www.sciencedirect.com/science/article/pii/S0261517713001556 accessed 1 January 2015

Chen, C.-F. and Kao, Y.-L. (2011), The antecedents and consequences of job stress of flight attendants – evidence from Taiwan, *Journal of Air Transport Management* 17(4) 253–255 available from http://www.sciencedirect.com/science/article/pii/S09696997 11000135 accessed 30 March 2015

Chen, C.-F. and Kao, Y.-L. (2012), Moderating effects of work engagement and job tenure on burnout-performance among flight attendants, *Journal of Air Transport Management* 25 61–63 available from http://www.sciencedirect.com/science/article/pii/S096969971200 1135 accessed 2 January 2015

Clements, B. and Spencer, N. (2014), *Voting and values in Britain: does religion count?* available from http://www.theosthinktank.co.uk/files/files/Reports/Voting%20and%20Values%20 in%20Britain%2012.pdf accessed 1 August 2013

Comic Relief (2010), *Comic Relief supports Robin Hood Tax* available from http://www.comicrelief.com/news/comic-relief-supports-robin-hood-tax accessed 17 September 2014

Cooper, C.L. and Cartwright, S. (1997), An intervention strategy for workplace stress, *Journal of Psychosomatic Research* 43(1) 7–16 available from file:///C:/Users/D/Contacts/Docu ments/RESPONSIBLE%20AIRLINE/CooperCartwright1997.pdf accessed 30 March 2015

Coutu, D. (2009), *Why Teams Don't Work* available from http://hbr.org/2009/05/why-teams-dont-work/ar/1 accessed 16 July 2014

Cramer, C., Johnston, D., Oya, C. and Sender, J. (2014), *Fairtrade, employment and poverty reduction in Uganda and Ethiopia* available from http://ftepr.org/wp-content/uploads/FTEPR-Final-Report-19-May-2014-FINAL.pdf accessed 28 September 2014

Davis, F.D. (1989), Perceived usefulness, perceived ease of use, and user acceptance of information technology, *MIS Quarterly* 13(3) 319–340 available from file:///C:/Users/D/Contacts/Documents/RESPONSIBLE%20AIRLINE/Perceived%20Usefulness%20ease% 20of%20use.pdf accessed 2 January 2015

de Bono, E. (1985), *Six thinking hats*, USA, Little, Brown and Company

Department of Transportation (2015), *File a Consumer Complaint* available from http://www.dot.gov/airconsumer/file-consumer-complaint accessed 30 March 2015

Dewhurst, M., Guthridge, M. and Mohr, E. (2009), *Motivating people, getting beyond money* available from http://www.mckinsey.com/insights/organization/motivating_people_getting_beyond_money accessed 21 June 2012

Donovan, J. (2013), *Hacking the Skies: Taking Innovation to New Heights at SXSW* available from http://www.attinnovationspace.com/innovation/story/a7788204 accessed 2 September 2014

Dorr, R.F. (2011), *XF2Y-1 Sea Dart: A Jet Fighter on Water Skis: Convair's Sea Dart waterborne jet fighter was a brilliant mistake whose time never came* available from http://www.defense

medianetwork.com/stories/xf2y-1yf2y-1-sea-dart-a-jet-fighter-on-water-skis/ accessed 26 August 2014

Dylag, A., Jaworek, M., Karwowski, W., Kozusznik, M. and Tadeusz, M. (2013), Discrepancy between individual and organizational values: occupational burnout and worker engagement among white-collar workers, *International Journal of Industrial Ergonomics* 43(3) 225–231 available from http://www.sciencedirect.com/science/article/pii/S0169 814113000036 accessed 2 January 2015

Economic Times, India (2014), *Air India's cabin crew fight back over weight loss rules* available from http://economictimes.indiatimes.com/industry/transportation/airlines-/-aviation/ air-indias-cabin-crew-fight-back-over-weight-loss-rules/articleshow/35074429.cms accessed 4 September 2014

Emirates Group, The (n.d.), *Our vision & values: the principles that propel us forward* available from http://www.theemiratesgroup.com/english/our-vision-values/our-vision-values. aspx accessed 2 January 2015

Festinger, L. (1957), *A theory of cognitive dissonance*, Stanford, CA, Stanford University Press

Franke, M. (2007), Innovation: the winning formula to regain profitability in aviation? *Journal of Air Transport Management* 13(1) 23–30 available from http://www.sciencedirect. com/science/article/pii/S0969699706000998 accessed 2 January 2015

Franke, R.H., Hofstede, G. and Bond, M.H. (1991), Cultural roots of economic performance, *Strategic Management Journal*, Special Issue 12 (S1) 165–173 available from http://onlinelibrary.wiley.com/doi/10.1002/smj.4250120912/abstract accessed 30 March 2015

French, J. and Raven, B. (1959), The Bases of Social Power, in *Studies in Social Power*, Cartwright, D. (ed.), Ann Arbor, MI, Institute for Social Research 150–167 available from http://web.mit.edu/curhan/www/docs/Articles/15341_Readings/Power/French_ &_Raven_Studies_Social_Power_ch9_pp150–167.pdf accessed 30 March 2015

Gittell, J.H. and Bamber, G.J. (2010), High- and low-road strategies for competing on costs and their implications for employment relations: international studies in the airline industry, *The International Journal of Human Resource Management* 21(2) 165–179 available from http://www.tandfonline.com/doi/abs/10.1080/09585190903509464#.VKevHius VqU accessed 2 January 2015

Gordon, G. and DiTomaso, N. (1992), Predicting corporate performance from organizational culture, *Journal of Management Studies*, 29(6) 783–798 available from http://onlinelibrary. wiley.com/doi/10.1111/j.1467-6486.1992.tb00689.x/abstract accessed 2 January 2015

Grant, A. (2013), *Givers take all: the hidden dimension of corporate culture* available from http://www.mckinsey.com/insights/organization/givers_take_all_the_hidden_dimension _of_corporate_culture accessed 4 August 2014

Hackman, J. R. (1998), Why teams don't work, in *Theory and research on small groups*, Scott Tindale, R. *et al.* (eds), New York, Plenum Press 245–267 chapter available from http:// econ.au.dk/fileadmin/Economics_Business/Currently/Events/PhDFinance/Kauttu_Why -Teams-Dont-Work-by-J.-Richard-Hackman.pdf accessed 1 January 2015

Haimes D. (2013), *Do we understand each other? Connecting Academia and Industry in Innovation and Research*, CIOB/ARCOM Joint Workshop, Reading, UK, 4 September 2013

Halsey, A. (2013), *Lack of cockpit communication recalls 1999 Korean Airlines crash near London* available from http://www.washingtonpost.com/local/trafficandcommuting/lack-of- cockpit-communication-recalls-1999-korean-airlines-crash-near-london/2013/07/08/ 0e61b3ca-e7f5-11e2-a301-ea5a8116d211_story.html accessed 17 August 2014

Heracleous, L., Wirtz, J. and Johnston, R. (2004), Cost-effective service excellence: lessons from Singapore Airlines, *Business Strategy Review*, Spring 2004 15(1) 33–38 available from http://onlinelibrary.wiley.com/doi/10.1111/j.0955-6419.2004.00298.x/full   accessed 2 January 2015

Heracleous, L., Wirtz, J. and Johnston, R. (2005), Kung-fu service development at Singapore Airlines, *Business Strategy Review*, Winter 2005 16(4) 26–31 available from http://online library.wiley.com/doi/10.1111/j.0955-6419.2005.00376.x/abstract accessed 2 January 2015

Higgins, J., Lovelace, K., Bjerke, E., Lounsberry, N., Lutte, R., Friedenzohn, D., Pavel, S. and Chase, B. (2013), *An Investigation of the United States Airline Pilot Labor Supply* available from http://www.aabi.aero/AirlinePilotLaborSupply1.pdf accessed 11 August 2014

Holmes, S. (2006), *Cleaning up Boeing* available from http://www.businessweek.com/stories/2006-03-12/cleaning-up-boeing accessed 1 April 2013

Hope, C. (2014), *Half of Gordon Brown's 'spads' work for charities lobbying Coalition, as Tories condemn 'revolving door'* available from http://www.telegraph.co.uk/news/politics/1103 7088/Half-of-Gordon-Browns-spads-work-for-charities-lobbying-Coalition-as-Tories-condemn-revolving-door.html accessed 6 September 2014

Husted, B. and Salazar, J.J. (2006), Taking Friedman seriously: maximizing profits and social performance, *Journal of Management Studies* 43(1) 75–91 available from http://online library.wiley.com/doi/10.1111/j.1467-6486.2006.00583.x/abstract accessed 1 January 2015

IATA (n.d.), *IATA values* available from http://www.iata.org/about/pages/mission.aspx accessed 12 August 2014

Igo, T. and Skitmore, M. (2006), Diagnosing the organisational culture of an Australian engineering consultancy using the competing values framework, *Construction Innovation* 6(2) 121–139 available from http://eprints.qut.edu.au/4227/1/4227_1.pdf?origin=publica tion_detail accessed 1 January 2015

Jacobs, J., Jain, P. and Surana, K. (2014), *Is sports sponsorship worth it?* McKinsey & Company available from http://www.mckinsey.com/insights/marketing_sales/is_sports_sponsor ship_worth_it accessed 6 August 2014

Janis, I. (1997) Groupthink, in *Leadership: Understanding the dynamics of power and influence in organizations*, Vecchio, Robert P. (ed.), Notre Dame, IN, University of Notre Dame Press 163–176 available from http://psycnet.apa.org/psycinfo/1997-36918-010 accessed 10 September 2015

Kahya, D. (2009), *Who pays and who gains from carbon offsetting?* available from http://news. bbc.co.uk/1/hi/business/8378592.stm accessed 20 July 2011

Katzenbach, J., Steffen, I. and Kronley, C. (2012), Cultural change that sticks: start with what's already working, *Harvard Business Review* July–August 1–9 available from http://strategyand-dev01.atlasworks.com/media/file/HBR_Cultural-Change-That-Sticks.pdf accessed 2 January 2015

Kotter, J.P. (2007), Leading change: why transformation efforts fail, *Harvard Business Review* available from https://hbr.org/2007/01/leading-change-why-transformation-efforts-fail/ ar/1 accessed 2 January 2015

Kotter, J. (2008), Shared Urgency, *Leadership Excellence* 25(9) 3–4

Krulak, C. (1999), The Strategic Corporal: Leadership in the Three Block War, *Marines Magazine*, January 1999 available from http://www.au.af.mil/au/awc/awcgate/usmc/strategic_corporal.htm accessed 29 August 2014

Kumar, N., Scheer, L. and Kotler, P. (2000), From market driven to market driving, *European Management Journal* 18(2) 129–142 available from http://www.sciencedirect.com/science/article/pii/S0263237399000845 accessed 2 January 2015

Lawson, D. (2012), 'Responsible' firms are really just stealing, *The Sunday Times* available from http://www.thesundaytimes.co.uk/sto/comment/columns/dominiclawson/article 877984.ece accessed 2 January 2015

Lencioni, P. (2002), Make your values mean something, *Harvard Business Review* July 3–8 available from https://hbr.org/2002/07/make-your-values-mean-something accessed 2 January 2015

Loosemore, M. (2013), Serendipitous innovation: enablers and barriers in the construction industry, in *Procs 29th Annual ARCOM Conference*, Smith, S.D. and Ahiaga-Dagbui, D.D. (eds), 2–4 September 2013, Reading, UK, Association of Researchers in Construction Management 635–644 available from http://www.arcom.ac.uk/-docs/proceedings/ar2013-0635-0644_Loosemore.pdf accessed 2 January 2015

Lufthansa (2014), *MySkyStatus* available from http://www.generationfly.com/offers/landing/9 accessed 2 September 2014

Mackonis, A. and Silenas, Z. (2013), *Helping themselves: six ways to reform EU funding of NGOs* available from http://newdirectionfoundation.org/content/call-reform-eus-75bn-eur-ngo-budget accessed 1 August 2014

Marcum, D. and Smith, S. (2007), *Egonomics: what makes ego our greatest asset (or most expensive liability)*, New York, Fireside, Simon & Schuster

Maslow, A.H. (1943), A Theory of Human Motivation, *Psychological Review* 50(4) 370–396 available from http://psycnet.apa.org/journals/rev/50/4/370/ accessed 30 March 2015

Mileti, D., Cress, D. and Darlington, J. (2002), Earthquake culture and corporate action, *Sociological Forum* 17(1) 161–180 available from http://link.springer.com/article/10.1023/A:1014549708645 accessed 2 January 2015

Moyo, D. (2011), *How the West was Lost*, London, Allen Lane

Norwegian (2014), *Today, Norwegian will fly a fully loaded aircraft with emergency aid to Africa* available from http://www.atn.aero/print_article.pl?id=52337 accessed 2 November 2014

Olson, P. (2012), *Bono's humbling realizations about aid, capitalism and nerds* available from http://www.forbes.com/sites/parmyolson/2012/10/22/bonos-humbling-realizations-about-aid-capitalism-and-nerds/#42898d38495f accessed 10 December 2014

Osuri, L. (2010), Charities warm to climate: Philanthropic support for climate-change issues tripled in 2008, *Nature* 464 821 available from http://www.nature.com/news/2010/100406/full/464821a.html accessed 12 December 2014

Pant, P.N. and Lachman, R. (1998), Value incongruity and strategic choice, *Journal of Management Studies* 35(2) 195–212 available from http://onlinelibrary.wiley.com/doi/10.1111/1467-6486.00090/abstract;jsessionid=83C346A8EE4E1A10A4C7295C403DCF10.f04t03?deniedAccessCustomisedMessage=&userIsAuthenticated=false accessed 1 January 2015

Pfeffer, J. and Sutton, R.I. (2006), Evidence-based management, *Harvard Business Review*, January 2006 available from https://hbr.org/2006/01/evidence-based-management accessed 1 January 2015

Pink, D.H. (2009), *Drive: the surprising truth about what motivates us*, New York, Riverhead Books, Penguin Group (USA) Inc.

Porter, M. and Kramer, M. (2002), The competitive advantage of corporate philanthropy, *Harvard Business Review*, December 2002 80(12) 56–68 available from http://www.ncbi.nlm.nih.gov/pubmed/12510538 accessed 2 January 2015

Press Association (2014), *DEC praises 'overwhelming' British response to Ebola appeal* available from http://www.theguardian.com/world/2014/nov/01/dec-overwhelming-british-response-ebola-appeal accessed 2 November 2014

Rogers Commission (1986), *Report of the Presidential Commission on the Space Shuttle Challenger Accident* available from http://history.nasa.gov/rogersrep/genindex.htm accessed 4 April 2013

Rogers, E.M. and Shoemaker, F.F. (1971), *Communication of Innovation*, New York, The Free Press

Ryanair (2015), *Mission statement* available from http://www.vryr.eu/airline accessed 18 September 2015

Sanandaji, T. and Sanandaji, N. (2014), *Super-entrepreneurs and how your country can get them*, Centre for Policy Studies available from http://www.cps.org.uk/files/reports/original/140429115046-superentrepreneursandhowyourcountrycangetthemupdate.pdf accessed 14 December 2014

Sawhney, M., Wolcott, R. and Arroniz, I. (2006), The 12 different ways for companies to innovate, *MIT Sloan Management Review* available from http://sloanreview.mit.edu/article/the-different-ways-for-companies-to-innovate/ accessed 2 January 2015

Sidwell, M. (2008), *Unfair Trade*, London, Adam Smith Institute available from http://www.adamsmith.org/sites/default/files/images/pdf/unfair_trade.pdf accessed 2 January 2015

Simon, H.A. (1991), Bounded rationality and organizational learning, *Organization Science* 2(1) 125–134 available from http://pubsonline.informs.org/doi/abs/10.1287/orsc.2.1.125?journalCode=orsc accessed 2 January 2015

Singapore Airlines (n.d.), *Core values of Singapore Airlines* available from http://www.siasu.org.sg/about_corevalues.asp accessed 11 July 2014

Snowdon, C. (2012), *Sock puppets: how the government lobbies itself and why, IEA Discussion Paper No. 39* available from http://www.iea.org.uk/publications/research/sock-puppets-how-the-government-lobbies-itself-and-why accessed 15 May 2013

Snowdon, C. (2013), *Euro Puppets: the European Commission's remaking of civil society: IEA Discussion Paper No. 45* available from http://www.iea.org.uk/publications/research/euro-puppets-the-european-commission%E2%80%99s-remaking-of-civil-society accessed 31 July 2014

Snowdon, C. (2014), *The sock doctrine: what can be done about state-funded political activism? IEA Discussion Paper No. 53* available from http://www.iea.org.uk/sites/default/files/in-the-media/files/The%20sock%20doctrine.pdf accessed 7 February 2014

Southwest Airlines (1988), *To our employees* available from http://www.southwest.com/html/about-southwest/index.html?int=GFOOTER-ABOUT-CUSTOMER-COMMITMENTS&tab=5#about_southwest_index_vertical_menu accessed 18 September 2013

Southwest Airlines (2013), *Mission statement* available from http://www.southwest.com/html/about-southwest/index.html?int=GFOOTER-ABOUT-CUSTOMER-COMMITMENTS&tab=5#about_southwest_index_vertical_menu accessed 18 September 2013

Southwest Airlines (2014), *Project Luvseat* press release available from www.swamedia.com/luvseat accessed 15 July 2014

Tatum, C.B. (1987), Process of innovation in construction firm, *Journal of Construction Engineering and Management* 113(4) 648–663 available from http://ascelibrary.org/doi/abs/10.1061/(ASCE)0733-9364(1987)113:4(648) accessed 19 August 2015

Torres, E.N. (2014), Deconstructing service quality and customer satisfaction: challenges and directions for future research, *Journal of Hospitality Marketing & Management* 23(6) 652–677 available from http://www.tandfonline.com/doi/abs/10.1080/19368623.2014.846839?journalCode=whmm20#.VRlv7fnF9qU accessed 1 January 2015

United Airlines Inc. (2014), *Diversity and inclusion* available from http://www.united.com/web/en-US/content/company/globalcitizenship/diversity.aspx accessed 30 March 2015

USA Today (2002), *The Enron scandal by the numbers* available from http://usatoday30. usatoday.com/money/energy/2002-01-22-enron-numbers.htm accessed 2 January 2015

van Rekom, J., van Riel, C. and Wierenga, B. (2006), A methodology for assessing organisational core values, *Journal of Management Studies* 43(2) 175–202 available from http://onlinelibrary.wiley.com/doi/10.1111/j.1467–6486.2006.00587.x/abstract;jsession id=BA7AB549F33C6EF286B53C26A930E5AA.f01t01?userIsAuthenticated=false& deniedAccessCustomisedMessage accessed 10 June 2016

Virgin Atlantic plc (2013), *Mission statement* available from available from http://www.virgin-atlantic.com/gb/en.html accessed 16 September 2013

Virgin Atlantic plc (2014a), *Mission statement* available from http://www.virgin-atlantic.com/ gb/en/footer/about-us.html accessed 2 January 2015

Virgin Atlantic plc (2014b), *Virgin Atlantic launches Fairtrade tea and coffee on board all flights* available from http://www.virgin-atlantic.com/en/gb/allaboutus/pressoffice/pressreleases/ news/pr240907.jsp accessed 2 January 2015

Virgin Atlantic plc (2015), *Sustainability Report 2015* available from http://www.virgin-atlantic.com/content/dam/VAA/Documents/sustainabilitypdf/Virgin%20Atlantic%20 Sustainability%20Report%202015%20Full.pdf accessed 19 August 2015

Whittell, G. (2002), Snakes in suits and how to spot them, *The Times* 11 November T2(4) available from http://www.thetimes.co.uk/tto/life/article1727238.ece accessed 2 January 2015

Wittman, M.D. (2014), Are low-cost carrier passengers less likely to complain about service quality? *Journal of Air Transport Management* March 2014 35 64–71 available from http:// www.sciencedirect.com/science/article/pii/S0969699713001385 accessed 2 January 2015

World Health Organisation (WHO) (2011), *The top 10 causes of death* available from http://www.who.int/mediacentre/factsheets/fs310/en/ accessed 11 April 2013

Yee, R.W.Y., Yeung, A.C.L. and Cheng, T.C.E. (2008), The impact of employee satisfaction on quality and profitability in high-contact service industries, *Journal of Operations Management* 26 651–668 available from http://www.sciencedirect.com/science/ article/pii/S0272696308000028 accessed 1 January 2015

4   Passenger challenges

4.1 CONTEXT

Challenges

Airline passengers are varied in shapes, colours, sizes and languages with different levels of mobility, preparedness and stress. They fly in different cabins on different airlines according to their budgets of time and/or money. Passengers are just one group of sustainable airlines' stakeholders but they are the force which drives the airline towards economic sustainability. However, it must not be forgotten that, in economic terms, effective demand is the quantity of airline products and services for which customers are willing and able to pay. If customers are neither willing nor able to pay for a service or a product, then it should no longer be offered (the lean principle – see Chapter 2) and it ceases to be effective demand. Airlines want to keep customers happy because, as already noted, it is more cost effective to retain a customer than to seek a new one.

However, whether called 'passengers', 'customers', 'consumers' or even the disparaging 'self-loading freight' (SLF), airline travellers' flight choices are motivated by time (their own and airlines' schedules), space (aircraft seat, airline lounge) and money (premium or economy seats) and all are underpinned by the knowledge that the airline is safe, responsible, reliable and willing to service them. They chose the airline: it has their trust and is responsible for their welfare.

Passengers' markets

Fundamental to any marketing strategy is the need to understand the customers. Airline markets can be segmented in several ways including the traditional bases – geographic, demographic (age, occupation, working status), benefits sought (punctual, environmentally favourable aircraft, safe, secure, value for money), geographical (location of departure and arrival airports), behavioural (passenger brand loyalty, frequency of flying) and product characteristics (such as full catering, online check-in and self-selecting seat allocation). In order for a market segment to be worthwhile for pursuit, it must rate favourably on five key criteria: measurable, substantial, accessible, differentiable and actionable (Table 4.1).

Table 4.1 Effective segmentation criteria (Kotler and Keller, 2012: 231)

Segmentation criteria	Segment characteristic
measurable	size, purchasing power and characteristic of the segments can be measured
substantial	large and profitable enough to serve
accessible	effectively reached and served
differentiable	conceptually distinguishable and respond differently to different marketing-mix elements and programmes
actionable	effective programmes can be formulated for attracting and serving the segments

Examining UMs under the segmentation criteria shows that as a potential market they do not rank strongly in four of the five categories (measurable, substantial, accessible and differentiable). It is arguable that programmes could be devised under the 'actionable' criteria to attract these passengers if airlines considered it would be worthwhile. The belief was that if child passengers had a good experience with an airline they would become loyal customers when they flew as adults. That might have been appropriate when legacy carriers were dominant, competition was minimal and airlines were part of the national social infrastructure. However, many airlines eventually realised that UMs were an expensive market to service. They required much more care, attention, corporate responsibility and cost, all of which took them out of the passenger mainstream. Furthermore, standard, reduced-price children's fares were possibly not covering their additional costs. If the costs are not covered, flying UMs becomes a social service rather than a profit generator. An economic assessment recognised that UMs were high-risk passengers so consequently many airlines began to charge for their additional requirements with a range of fees (*Business Travel News*, 2014). As a result, because of the foregoing segmentation assessment, UMs are not currently a market that airlines are actively pursuing. Some airlines have adult-free zones for the UMs on board, others provide a nanny service to accompany UM groups (particularly at school term closing times) and yet others now refuse to take them.

Airline products

Airlines sell space and weight and should make a profit on both. Price is the number-one determinant of airline passenger selection (43%) followed by schedule and convenient flight time (21%) and frequent flyer programme (13%) (IATA, 2015). On these and other seemingly less important criteria (food, drink, historic experience), airlines implicitly compete for lightweight, able-bodied passengers with briefcases, i.e. no impediments or encumbrances. There are, however, some unprofitable markets for which airlines do not compete. These are the missing markets which include intending travellers with low incomes and elderly, disabled or sick passengers (see Chapter 5). The most profitable passengers for a full-service carrier are those in the premium cabins. They are more driven by their emotions rather than the functional features of travel. In acknowledgement of their status, they want high staff-service ratios throughout their journey as well as the perks of travel including loyalty reward points many of which are often owned by the organisation which paid for the travel (possibly their employer). These loyalty rewards become a perk of the job to be redeemed by the travelling employee. (Ethical question: is this tax avoidance, tax evasion or theft of their shareholders' funds? – see Chapter 2, Chapter 7 and Chapter 8.)

4.2 CUSTOMER SERVICE

Seating and boarding

There are some passenger issues which are almost inflammatory for passenger servicing and about which some passengers care deeply.

Seat allocation

One of the most emotionally charged issues is seating, irrespective of whether it is allocated by the airline, selected by the passengers online or allocated on the first-one-onto-the-aircraft-gets-the-best-seat basis. Aeroplane manufacturers and seating designers are innovative in their attempts to make economy aeroplane seating comfortable and safe for passengers, and economic for the airline operators. However, seating is a competitive issue and seat allocation is a major cause of complaints, something cost-conscious airlines try to avoid. Even though passengers might have pre-selected their seats they could find they have been downgraded at the airport, off-loaded (with compensation where required), separated from their group or had the extra legroom or window seat they had reserved reallocated. A last-minute aircraft substitution could also wreak havoc with pre-arranged seating plans. Legroom is one of the most important issues for passengers on flights of more than four hours' duration.

Seating is such an emotional issue that in various guises it is often a cause of air rage, along with drunk and rowdy passengers, bad hygiene, seat kicking and crying babies. Lack of legroom, overweight passengers or those who invade personal space are also ranked highly (*Travelmail Reporter*, 2014). Passengers seated by the window inconvenience their neighbours as they access the lavatories or stretch their legs, and seat recline can annoy the passengers behind. Passengers occupying the mid-seats of a middle row have to decide who they want to inconvenience least and sometimes that means considering the reclining passengers in front as well as the passengers either side. Passengers purchasing premium air travel buy more space and improved seating comfort. Those in the non-premium cabins could have their seating compromised by neighbouring passengers who could be implementing knee defenders, a two-piece gadget which prevents the seat in front from reclining. Its growing popularity has led to air rage incidents sufficiently severe to warrant aircraft diversions. Public opinion would appear to be divided between those who favour them and attach them to the seat in front to prevent recline and those who object to them since it means they would have to sit upright for the journey. Sustainable airlines need to take stakeholders' concerns into account (perhaps also consulting IAPA, FAA and CAA) and develop a policy which allows passengers to know in advance whether the knee defenders would be permitted (Wright, 2014). Ultimately, all economy seats might be non-reclining as consumer preferences change. Some low-cost airlines are already installing them on short-haul routes.

Aircraft boarding – science or art?

Boarding passengers can resemble a rugby scrum, especially in the economy section. Passengers feel frustrated when they are called to join boarding but then find themselves in a long queue either at gate security or on the aircraft jetty, delayed by other passengers already on board stowing their jackets, handbags and duty-free purchases. There are various sequential boarding processes used by different airlines. The options include:

- window-seated passengers called forward first, middle-seated passengers summoned next and aisle passengers last (however, this can inevitably lead to problems with splitting groups, especially families with children)
- board back rows first, then the next rows, moving towards the front of the aircraft
- free seating where the first passengers into the aircraft obtain their preferred seat (this method resembles a pack of hungry lions pursuing prey)
- Titanic approach: mothers, children and PRMs are boarded first (but deplaned last)
- discriminatory pricing by charging a fee for early boarding in preferred seats.

Marshalling passengers efficiently (and economically) is a challenge but it is important. Delayed passenger boardings mean increased airline costs. Time costs money. However, research (Steffen, 2008) showed that loading passengers in groups of ten starting from the back in alternating rows eliminated the gridlock of passengers lifting hand baggage into overhead lockers. Further research modelled passengers with the most hand baggage being allocated seats by the windows because it took them longest to stow their possessions; next to be seated would be those passengers with less hand baggage on the middle seats as they would take less time than the first group; and finally those passengers with the least hand baggage would be seated on the aisle seats (Milne and Kelly, 2014). Whilst appreciating that this might save airlines £Stg, $US or € millions (Milne and Kelly, 2014) it is questionable as to whether passengers would conform and allow their seat locations to be dictated by increasing quantities of hand baggage (however, it could be an incentive for passengers to shop at the airside concessions). Computer-modelling is useful; however, such models are not always sensitive to passenger experience. Behavioural science sometimes ignores practicalities and it is the Customer Service Agents in the departure gate-rooms who will ultimately have to manage this contentious issue. Economically sustainable airlines would be horizon-scanning, identifying boarding efficiencies as research becomes available.

Upgrade economics

Passengers love upgrades – especially if they are unexpected and free. The economically sustainable airline would not be sustainable for long if it upgraded travellers as often as they would like. Excessive complimentary upgrading actually dilutes the airline's brand. When passengers realise they do not need to pay for extra services and increased legroom because they could be given for free, they do not bother to book them. Skyscanner (2016), a website for canny travellers, has some tongue-in-cheek advice for those who wish to hook an upgrade, including travelling at quiet times, displaying loyalty and/or politeness, purchasing full-fare tickets and getting a diplomatic passport. However, these optimistic suggestions take no account of the fact that upgrading is not always a chance opportunity. It is very often controlled by ITC using the criteria of fare level, possession of airline loyalty card and frequent flying patterns. If the technology concludes that all eligible passengers have been upgraded, it then seeks the next most eligible passengers down the scale in order to give them a taste of the premium cabins. Some airlines (including Virgin Atlantic and Air New Zealand) offer economy passengers the opportunity to upgrade in an online blind bidding process. It gives the airlines a chance to generate extra revenue for what would otherwise be empty and expensive inventory.

Passenger stress

Passengers like to feel in control, which is something they have to surrender once they become part of the process of public air transportation. They often arrive at the airport in stressed conditions derived from multiple causes including fear of flying, lost passports (and sometimes lost relatives or friends) and/or arriving too late for their flight on a non-refundable, non-exchangeable, reduced-price fare. For them the overall experience can be one of great trauma and drama, often compounded by high levels of noise from baggage belts, loud speakers, fellow travellers, fire alarms and the other distractions which mark airports. Passenger stress manifests itself in many ways: tears, shouting, swearing, disbelief and denial – emotions which are either visible while a queue accumulates in front of the check-in desk or heard in the telephone call centre.

The complex airport processes can cause considerable stress and anxiety to those who are used to controlling their businesses, families and lives. Sustainable airlines decide what services and products could allow passengers to feel in control of their travel. For those passengers with privileges, this can translate to the ability to self-check-in, extra baggage allowance, choice of seat and relaxation in the airline lounge where they would probably have access to complimentary food, beverages, wireless connections and even loyalty rewards (see Chapter 2 and Chapter 7). However, concerns over personal space, legroom, catering, mishandled bags, malfunctioning inflight entertainment and poor punctuality are all factors which can influence the passengers' stress. This can be compounded by feelings of loss of control irrespective of the cause which could range from late fellow passengers through to insufficient staff. Every delay factor can affect an airline's reputation. Stress is also often high at touch-points where passengers interact with the airport and airline and it will be magnified if the passengers are denied permission to smoke tobacco (particularly if they are about to undertake a long-haul flight). But stress can also emanate from statutory authorities (e.g. Customs, Security, Immigration, ATC), airport facilities (which are occasionally unreliable), inadequate airport wayfinding, airline processes ('computer says "no"'), long distances to the gate-rooms and general passenger angst.

Passengers do not perceive arrivals punctuality as a problem as much as delayed departures (which do not always portend late arrivals). A sustainable airline understands the economics of time and stress. During disruptions and delays the feeling of powerlessness can be overwhelming. It can start with failures of airport facilities such as indicator boards not showing departures or luggage conveyors failing to deliver bags to the aircraft. On the aircraft, if the passenger's personal light and inflight entertainment system were faulty, their meal choice unavailable and a lavatory blocked, it could be considered as the worst trip ever. They would forget that the engines functioned faultlessly, there was no turbulence and they managed six hours' sleep. They would have also forgotten the sympathetic crew who countered their frustration with kindness and the other criteria by which they could have assessed the service such as cabin cleanliness, comfort, catering, lounges and boarding services (Skytrax, 2014). Passengers' lasting memories are usually only of what went wrong.

Trade-off: ITC and customer service

Additional stresses come from the installation of more ITC into the processes. ITC is frequently a substitute for personal service, which means the airline needs fewer employees who, outside of Asia (see Table 1.1 and Table 1.2 in Chapter 1), are one of the biggest overhead costs. Not so long ago, passengers came to the airport, queued for paper boarding cards and seat allocation, checked luggage into the baggage system and went airside through Security. Now they can use ITC to check-in at home – and yet when they arrive at the airport they often have to queue to answer the security questions before surrendering their luggage. The time saving is sometimes not as great as the ITC manufacturers would have passengers believe, often because the organisation and processes have not been changed to support the new technology. Furthermore, employing state-of-the-art ITC systems in place of customer service staff (and hiring celebrities to endorse the airline – see Chapter 3) might not encourage passenger loyalty and trust – whereas helpful, enthusiastic, knowledgeable and available staff members might be the best advocates for the carrier and its ultimate economic sustainability.

Just how far can ITC assist with passenger servicing before it becomes a deterrent rather than a competitive advantage? The traditional buyer-seller relationship is changing. Passengers want lower priced fares which can only be delivered with more ITC – but they also want their touch-points to be human, especially if there is a problem with their journey. Talking with an automated service will not placate an angry passenger whose flight is delayed and who could miss onwards connections. Another irritation often overlooked is the issue of false intimacy where a computer-generated document speaks to the customer as if he/she is a long lost friend, even to the extent of using their first name. (This is an interesting use of the PDI; see Chapter 3.) If the Check-in Agents never use customers' first names, why should a machine? It is actually just bad manners and it undermines the airlines' reputation for professionalism.

Keeping costs low without compromising quality is a competitive challenge for the industry, while the use of the internet with its flexible fare offerings grows unabated, although its potential is not considered to be fully developed (Harcar and Yucelt, 2012). Consumers tended to use the internet 'for research of airlines and airfares not for purchase of tickets' (Harcar and Yucelt, 2012: 60). Passengers' willingness to make a booking online has many aspects according to their familiarity with online processes and their views of security, privacy, fares, prices, times, dates, trust and perceived risks (Harcar and Yucelt, 2012). Booking an airline ticket online is taking a risk (as with all other internet transactions) and customers rely on their trust in the airline's reputation to reduce their purchasing risks (Table 4.2).

However, some passengers want a more personal service and prefer to use a travel agent or to phone if those options are available (both of which add costs to transactions). Price-sensitive passengers are attracted to the online travel agencies' offers of lower prices and faster service, which could persuade them to switch from offline agencies (Kim *et al.*, 2009). Customer satisfaction research did not show any significant difference between online and offline travel agencies. However, (at the time of publication) the UK CAA was investigating the transaction and other costs involved with some of the comparison websites because they advertised flights at prices comparable or cheaper than the airlines' own websites only to add in extra charges which were already included in the airlines' original prices (Linning,

Table 4.2 Perceived risks when purchasing online (adapted from Harcar and Yucelt, 2012; Kim et al., 2009)

Risk	Impact
performance	consumers fear that products and services acquired might not meet their expectations
psychological	risk of loss of self-esteem due to wrong choice of product and/or service
time	time wasting associated with online bookings
social	making an unacceptable choice that it is considered embarrassing
price	might purchase at the wrong time leading to financial loss
privacy	personal information that might be shared with others without the person's knowledge
security	most important predictor of overall risk

2014). Such deception undermines trust but could actually favour the airlines by deflecting purchasers directly to the carriers' sites for better value.

Unfortunately, using online processing can also create problems at the airport. Passengers using online check-in can avoid human contact with airline employees who might be in a position to assess that the traveller is too ill to fly. Many uninsured passengers fly with potentially infectious diseases rather than lose the cost of their booking. In doing so, they are breaking the implicit contract between passenger and airline. They are a hazard for the crew and their fellow passengers and might even require an aircraft diversion for emergency treatment (see Chapter 5 and Chapter 7).

4.3 PASSENGERS' SECURITY AND SAFETY

Safety of passengers

Passenger safety and security are paramount and cover all aspects of the travel journey. A safe and secure airline is what every passenger expects and retaining reputation is the most significant risk. The crew are present first and foremost for safety. The safety briefings matter. A Taiwan survey of 300 international and domestic passengers to determine the effect of airline safety briefings on cabin safety awareness concluded that safety education positively affected safety knowledge, attitude and behaviour (Chang and Liao, 2009).

However, sometimes communicating health and safety in the air (see Chapter 3) relies on videos which are often dull, boring and do not inspire passengers to look up from their entertainment devices and pay attention. A sustainable airline is always looking for a fresh approach to safety and finding means of engaging passengers with their hearts and minds rather than mere compliance. In an attempt not to frighten passengers, airlines sometimes soften what is often a hard message; and yet practising the evacuation tasks would embed the safety message and increase evacuation knowledge (particularly for nervous passengers).

Air New Zealand has recognised the importance of passenger attentiveness to safety briefings and has innovative and thought-provoking safety videos which actually encourage passengers to look online before flight to see what the airline wants them to know. The airline also innovates by providing competitions for observant passengers and uses well-known media faces to attract interest. The briefing itself is regularly changed and updated to keep the passengers alert. In 2012 the airline showed body-painted crew members narrating the safety instructions and the first of several of Tolkien's *Lord of the Rings* safety videos (12 million YouTube hits) (Griggs, 2014). During 2013 they used the analogy of safety in the bush with a well-known adventurer. In 2014 they invoked the ire of feminists when they used scantily clad women to hone their message, and in 2015 they merged the movie *Men in Black* with the nation's successful 'All Blacks' rugby team, acquiring millions of viewings within two weeks of release. The company's innovative safety videos have been viewed online 53 million times (O'Hare, 2015).

Table 4.3 On-board safety actions and reasons

Action	Reason
check life vests are in place	if they were ever needed, they might not be where they should be (however, in the last few sea landings, including the Hudson River (see Chapter 3), no one used a life vest)
do not inflate life jacket before leaving the aircraft	in the panic passengers could be trapped by the inflated vest between the seat back and the ceiling which could also block the exit for other evacuees
place own oxygen mask before helping others	oxygen deprivation puts the brain onto a 'high' (hypoxia) which can render the passenger unable to help themselves let alone others
brace position with the least used hand placed over the most used hand covering the skull	covering the passenger's most used hand (usually the right) with the other hand as protection should something injure their most used hand (which would be needed to open the seat belt)
follow the red lights on the floor when the cabin is full of smoke	red lights are more detectable than other colours in conditions of smoke (or fog)
seat upright on take-off and landing	in the event of an emergency valuable seconds can be lost while the passenger scrambles up from a reclining position and could block other passengers' escape
count seatbacks between passenger's seat and the nearest exit	if the cabin is filled with smoke passengers might have to rely on their ability to touch the seat backs to count their way to the exit

Learning is better ingrained if it is followed by action. Repetitive actions such as opening and closing the safety belt two or three times to prepare the brain for emergency evacuation (just as a car driver repeatedly activates and remembers how to open a seat belt) would assist some nervous passengers. Alternatively, airlines could issue a safety quiz during the flight (with a prize for the winner) or test passengers on their knowledge of safety measures to see if the processes are embedded in their thinking (e.g. which passengers recall how many seats are between them and the exit?). Perhaps they could have passengers compete for who could fasten the (dummy) life jacket the quickest? Some of the reasons for certain safety requirements are often not obvious to inexperienced passengers (Table 4.3). Furthermore, making the safety video available throughout the journey (and online before travel as Air New Zealand does) would also give nervous flyers more confidence that they could evacuate if necessary.

Hygiene on board

Hygiene on board is an essential component of health for protecting the passengers and crew. It involves crew being scrupulously clean when handling food (which is why they cannot help disabled people into the lavatory). Airline catering is prepared to the strictest of hygiene measures and that includes the washing of re-usable cutlery and plates as well as disposal of unwanted foodstuffs. However, sometimes standards slip and the result is very expensive for the insurers. It is also damaging for the airlines' reputations and undermines trust in the industry. In 1975 one of Japan Airlines' flights from Tokyo to Copenhagen experienced an outbreak of food poisoning. The cause was traced back to the transit catering station at Anchorage where a service cook had two fingers infected with staphylococcal bacteria. Similarly, in 1984, passengers on 100 British Airways flights (including the Concorde, which carried some V-VIPs) became ill with suspected salmonella. Their symptoms (fever, cramps, vomiting and diarrhoea, which are also manifestations of other highly infectious diseases) were eventually attributed to the hors d'oeuvres (Nordheimer, 1984). Examples are fewer as hygiene knowledge and standards have improved.

Keeping lavatories clean is also the crews' responsibility but unfortunately, some passengers are not as lavatory-trained as others and certain routes are renowned for their lack of hygiene. The ratio of lavatories in the economy section is approximately one for every 50 passengers (although it does not feel like that at landing time when everyone needs to use them). In premium cabins on full-service carriers the ratio is much lower. Unfortunately, hygienic habits are no respecters of cabin class. The problem of passengers staying too long in the lavatories is also a challenge for crews. The dilemma is deciding the purpose of the lengthy stay and whether the occupant could be (a) ill, (b) applying make-up, (c) puffing on an illicit cigarette, (d) attempting suicide (see Chapter 1) or any of the other excuses which have been offered in the past.

On-board hygiene is also important in the prevention of transmission of infectious diseases. The world has been concerned with swine flu, Spanish flu, Ebola, tuberculosis and other pandemics all of which could be spread by airline passengers.

Passengers' personal risk management

Travel insurance is just one form of risk protection. In a welfare state, the perception of risk is different from those countries where the State does not underwrite illness or injury (e.g. the USA). Risk in a welfare state like the UK is shared between public and private sector with the balance shifting in response to changes in legislation, economics and demographics. Changes in the balance between public risks, private insurance and social welfare spills onto airlines. Public welfare provision cushions citizens against the true cost of their personal responsibilities and many travellers insure their homes, cars, employment and perhaps health but avoid the add-on cost of travel insurance (see Chapter 3 and Chapter 5). This might be a welfare-state phenomenon, but it exposes the traveller (and the airline) to avoidable risk. However, governments such as the UK often tax insurance premiums, and for those who cannot afford travel insurance a further tax (on top of any environmental and passenger taxes) acts as yet another deterrent to UK passengers taking personal responsibility for any mishap which might occur while away from the security of the NHS.

The pace of technological and scientific progress has increased living standards and enabled people to live longer and healthier lives. This often means enjoying early retirement when one of the pleasures is to have leisure time for travel. Unfortunately, an ageing population runs a high risk of medical bills abroad and great expense if they do not have medical cover (see Chapter 3 and Chapter 5). Income is a major influence on the level of private insurance cover and those who are ageing (a demographic group which frequently requires medical support) often have lower incomes but can still afford to travel. They optimistically anticipate that nothing will go wrong (because 'it never has before') or that the airline would repatriate them with no extra cost. This initiates an ethical, economic and social challenge: should airlines make travel insurance compulsory? Should people who choose not to purchase travel insurance be allowed to travel? If passengers can afford holidays – with alcohol, leisure parks, car hire and hotels – then surely they can afford to purchase travel insurance? Is it simply the fact that passengers resent purchasing something that is 'invisible' – or are they risk-accepting because they believe that nothing untoward will happen?

After injury or illness abroad a passenger might need to return to their home base and there is a frequent expectation that the airline will accommodate their changed physical, mental or medical incapacity (see Chapter 3 and Chapter 5). As an example, a passenger with a leg encased in plaster and a doctor's letter confirming the he/she is fit to fly can check-in off-airport. On arrival at the airport a wheelchair could be needed to transport them to the aircraft. The gate-room staff (usually compassionately motivated) often permit the passenger to board, thereby creating a problem for the cabin crew. Yet the reality is that stiff-legged passengers with insufficient legroom can become a hindrance to all other passengers and obstruct the on-board service. Any expectation to have the broken leg resting on the seat in front is not possible because seats no longer collapse frontwards; sitting in an exit row (with its provision for extra legroom) is an evacuation risk and banned; and jamming the broken leg into the aisle would make it impossible for others to move around the aircraft. Such an injury could require moving to an upgraded seat which has more space (possibly without additional payment) or in extreme cases, offloading the passenger (incurring a delay for other passengers). Passengers who have severe medical conditions can also check-in off-airport and arrive at the aircraft with the prospect of causing an inflight diversion because of a health emergency. Had they contracted for travel insurance, the insurers might have advised them not to fly.

Litigation

In an age of increasing litigation there are many no-win-no-fee lawyers willing to pursue any claim against airlines. Often the airlines settle the claims because the costs of contesting them are disproportionate to the value of the claims (an example of a moral hazard (see Table 8.1 in Chapter 8)). Economically that is a wise decision but socially it is perhaps unjust and unfair on the shareholders because it encourages spurious claims which absorb their funds. The EU (European Union, 2014) has regulated (EC 261/2004) (see Chapter 1) that complaints against airlines must be acknowledged within one week and a formal reply sent within two months. Handling complaints requires the establishment of a department (more costs which could be outsourced to lower-cost nations) and complaint resolution which might or might not result in some form of compensation. Preventing future litigation for non-safety matters requires full sustainability-thinking (see Chapter 7) at the time when any new product or service idea is discussed. Had Southwest Airlines done so, it might have prevented the drink voucher lawsuit which was settled for approximately $US29m (£Stg20m or €26m). This represented 5.8 million unredeemed alcoholic beverage vouchers which had no expiry date when sold. Subsequently, Southwest added an expiry date which invalidated all pre-sold vouchers. The lawsuit ensured and was settled in favour of the passengers holding the unexpired vouchers (*Huffington Post*, 2012). If Southwest had used systems such as de Bono's Thinking Hats or divergent thinking (see Chapter 3) when deciding to instal the promotion, it might have uncovered the error and the potential consequences.

Outlier passengers

Just as there are employees who are outside the mainstream of thinking and behaviour (see Chapter 3), so too there are passengers who have special requirements which sometimes create safety and service difficulties for economically sustainable airlines. They can also trigger economic challenges if their needs or behaviours require expensive aircraft diversion, subsequent litigation or customer complaints. Passenger outliers – ranging from uncontrolled children through to terrorists – can inconvenience just one or two passengers and crew members or (at the extreme) the entire aircraft with consequences for the airline schedule. Diversion costs cover the unscheduled airport's ability to handle the aircraft, jettisoned and replacement fuel, overnight accommodation and airport transfers for crew and passengers, caring for any PRMs who need individual attention as well as the subsequent customer letters and passenger compensation claims. Outlier passengers include those who are:

(a) allergy sufferers
(b) birthing mothers
(c) uncontrolled children and crying babies
(d) dietary restricted
(e) drunk or drugged
(f) refused
(g) stowaways
(h) suicidal
(i) tall and stiff-kneed
(j) deviants.

(a) Allergy-suffering passengers

In terms of economic and social risks, allergic passengers are very worrying for an airline. Some passengers have allergies to a wide variety of products ranging from animal hair through to nuts. If an allergic passenger is known to be travelling, airlines often request all passengers to surrender their nuts before boarding. Allergies have been known to trigger anaphylactic shocks which can cause passengers great distress (and possibly death) and force an aircraft into a diversion airport. In the USA allergic passengers are even protected by law (Rehabilitation Act, 1973; Americans with Disabilities Act, 1990).

However, some passengers' expectations for airlines' responsibilities are extremely high. Innocent errors such as peanut dust on a seat or dust from a service animal can trigger an asthma attack. In 2014, a four-year-old girl had an anaphylactic shock and became unconscious on a Ryanair flight. She was revived with an EpiPen injection. The cause of her reaction was the nuts eaten by a fellow passenger who had been warned that he was jeopardising the child's health. When the aircraft landed at Stansted, UK, he was escorted off the aircraft and banned from Ryanair flights for two years. He was described as 'selfish' (Allen and Awford, 2014). Did the man have the right to eat peanuts? Was the airline responsible for sanitising the cabin? Should the parents have expected the airline to have accommodated their daughter's allergy? Was it correct to describe the passenger as 'selfish' – or was it the family who were selfish? Whose rights had priority? Was this another example of the tyranny of the minority? There are no easy answers to such customer service challenges. Economically sustainable airlines are alert to these challenges and do their best to mitigate the problems with the cooperation of fellow passengers (which is not always forthcoming).

It is almost impossible to provide an allergy-free aircraft. Some airlines have disclaimers for allergic passengers, while in contrast, the Switzerland-based airline Swiss embraces them and has become the world's first certified 'allergy-minded' airline, presenting a breakthrough for a minority of passengers. Swiss has committed to minimising the presence of allergens within its cabin and lounge environment:

> particularly in upholstery materials, air conditioning or certain food items. Our high-efficiency air conditioning system, for example, filters out pollens from outdoors and animal hair from pets on board. We also make sure no air freshening substances with the potential to irritate the respiratory tract are released on board, and our lavatories are equipped with hypoallergenic soap for sensitive skin. . . Swiss cabin crew members are trained to respond to an allergic emergency, and histamine tablets are available if needed.
>
> (Swiss, 2014)

However, it remains to be seen whether Swiss has an economically sustainable product. What was the size of the anticipated market that encouraged this investment? Did it fulfil Kotler and Keller's (2012) segmentation criteria (Table 4.1)? Has Swiss' offering changed since the revelation that peanut dust might not be considered the dangerous airborne allergen as was previously cited by advocates (Spector, 2015)?

Pressure groups have been vocal in their requirements, and in the USA there was a campaign to prevent anyone with even so much as miniscule amounts of peanut dust from flying when a known allergy sufferer was due to travel. Campaigners also sought peanut-free flights (without considering whether airlines and fellow passengers would want to accede to this demand). Airlines which no longer serve nuts have given into the tyranny of a minority while the rights of the majority of other passengers who might like nuts have been overridden. In an extremely litigious age, it is a question of balancing passengers' risks with airlines' responsibilities.

Eventually, however, the responsibility for allergy avoidance rests with the allergic passenger, who needs to take all precautions including carrying an EpiPen, in the same way that diabetic passengers carry insulin for their emergencies. Most airlines now carry anti-allergy medication and a list of the food ingredients is available should there be any doubt. However, it is sometimes impossible for sustainable airlines to transport all types of passengers where the risks and responsibilities are not sensibly allocated and mitigated.

(b) Passengers giving birth on board

Mothers-to-be should be certified as fit to fly (no longer than 28 weeks pregnant) especially if their due date is close (see Chapter 1). However, even with the precaution of a medical certificate, births on board, although rare, do happen; and on one occasion, twins were safely delivered on a Russian aircraft. (They were reportedly given free lifetime flights (*Parentdish*, 2014).) The impact of one birthing mother in a painful and noisy labour can affect all other passengers. It could also have an impact on cabin service as the crew are diverted from their normal duties to assist the woman. This creates a recognised hazard: one passenger can inconvenience all other passengers and ultimately this distraction could have an impact on cabin safety. Giving birth on board is a high-profile activity which, as well as risking the health of the mother and baby, carries significant reputational airline risk and loss of customer service to other passengers while the birth is in progress. It could result in an expensive aircraft diversion leaving mother and baby in a foreign land with subsequent confusion for the child's nationality and possible medical costs. (NB: it could also be argued that this baby would be the ultimate free rider (see Chapter 1 and Table 8.1 in Chapter 8).)

(c) Uncontrolled children and crying babies

Uncontrolled children and crying babies are a minority among mainstream passengers and are not always to other passengers' tastes. In fact, 'other people's children' can be a real annoyance on aircraft. The following newspaper headline is an example:

Parents escorted off Frontier Airlines' plane and met by police after two-year-old son's tantrum. . . Incident occurred as plane flew from Dominican Republic to St Louis. . . Flight attendant wouldn't allow boy to sit in his father's lap during take-off. . . Couple claims cabin crew threatened to kick them off plane . . . Airline claims couple was verbally and physically abusive to staff. . .

(Kitching, 2014)

Crew requests often go unheeded, making them appear ineffective, and fellow passengers sometimes vow never to fly with that particular airline again. This is unfair on the airline and is yet another means by which reputations are made and lost. An American woman on an Australian carrier Qantas flight brought legal proceedings, claiming that the airline had been negligent because the crew had not prevented a child's screaming from bursting her ear drum. In another example of moral hazard, the matter was settled confidentially 12 months later (Malkin, 2010). The parental responsibilities for this child did not appear to feature in reports of resulting litigation. If children are flying with their parents, fellow passengers could expect that the adults would keep control; however, this is beyond some parents' ability and their inactivity can ruin other passengers' travel experience. Again, it is a question of whose rights vs whose responsibilities? In 2013, recognising that children were posing a problem for some passengers on certain routes, Malaysia Airlines introduced segregated seating between Kuala Lumpur and London with a child-free area in the A380 upper deck and a family- and child-friendly zone on the main deck. Other airlines ban children from specific sections of the aircraft.

(d) Dietary restricted passengers

On-board meals for passengers with dietary needs take additional processing time as well as being more expensive for airlines to manage. Dietary restricted passengers are generally pragmatic about providing their own food; however, depending on the quantity, it might not be possible to take it through Security with the restrictions on volumes. Diabetics, coeliacs, vegans, vegetarians and others are often accommodated on full-service carriers without being surcharged (see Table 2.3 in Chapter 2). Generally, no-frills airlines do not cater for non-mainstream foods at all in order to retain their economies of scale. However, the EU's definition of disability under Regulation EC 1107/2006 on the rights of PRMs (see Chapter 5) is so wide that if the disability has a nutritional aspect, the person would appear to be entitled to the 'appropriate attention and the adaptation to his or her particular needs of the service made available to all passengers' (European Union, 2006). In an anomaly, any airline employees with disabling dietary conditions and who travel on a standby basis are not catered for, owing to there being insufficient time between loading standby passengers and flight departure. Although this is operationally understandable, it is actually discriminatory and is possibly even covered by EC 1107/2006. It is doubtful, however, whether employees would pursue a claim. In contrast, if an employee waiting for a standby seat needed a wheelchair, this would be provided irrespective of the time available; but dietary restrictions as a result of allergies or illnesses are not viewed in the same way as mobility impairments. Is this the limit of 'reasonable effort' as required by EC 1107/2006 (see Chapter 5)?

(e) Drunk or drugged passengers

Alcohol is a challenging issue for all carriers and even for those which do not serve it on board. It is freely available in most airport terminals and many passengers imbibe at the airport bars before boarding. It is usual for full-service carriers to serve complimentary wines, spirits and beers with meals except on some routes to and from the Arabian Gulf. Crews and passengers are often challenged by drunk and/or drugged passengers who can become aggressive, which in turn can lead to delay or diversion, inconvenience for other passengers and possibly a displaced aircraft, incurring costs and disruption. In 2013, three hours into a flight from Cancun, a drunken passenger began fighting with the British Airways' cabin crew and passengers, which forced the aircraft to divert into Orlando. During his arrest by the Orlando police, he made the fundamental error of trying to fight them as well. He was charged with assaulting a police officer and bailed pending trial (Zennie, 2013). (Although the airline reserved the right to pursue the passenger for costs (reducing the future risk of moral hazard), the outcome is unknown.) In 2014 a drunken passenger on a Virgin Australia flight caused sufficient concern to require the flight to return to Perth, Western Australia where he was arrested. His fellow passengers were either placed on the next available flight later that night or were accommodated overnight (ABC, 2014). His threatening and abusive behaviour inconvenienced other passengers and incurred additional carrier costs (i.e. passengers' rights vs airlines' responsibilities).

(f) Refused passengers

Passengers can be refused travel for a number of reasons including lack of appropriate visa. Some countries insist on visas before departure; others allow them to be purchased on arrival. This is a really important part of the Check-in Agent's role because the airline that incorrectly checks-in passengers for the UK can be fined up to £Stg4,000 ($US6,500 or €5,500) for incorrect entry documentation under The Carriers' Liability Regulations 2002. This places the airline in the role of government policeman with no offsetting rewards for all the correct visas that airlines approve. Should nations expect Check-in Agents to act as Immigration Agents or should the State take responsibility for its processes and approve all passengers' visas at check-in? Privately owned airlines acting in the capacity of governments' agents are absorbing another social cost without any government-awarded financial offset.

(g) Stowaways

Stowaways are a problem for airlines, particularly in locations where airport perimeter security might not be fully secure while the aircraft is on the ground. Stowaways have many motivations for attempting something which is often very dangerous (such as stowing in the wheel housing or the cargo hold). The conditions at high altitude are freezing cold and lacking in air pressure and oxygen. Asylum-seeking, thrill-seeking, homesickness or other causes drive them to risk their lives in an inhospitable space. Whatever their motivation, their presence in or under the aircraft exposes a major security vulnerability as well as huge personal risk which can result in death or incarceration when caught. It can also indicate the presence of people-smuggling rackets and other criminal involvement. Whatever the cause, it creates significant problems for airlines and can delay aircraft, triggering increased airline costs and passenger inconvenience.

(h) Suicidal passengers

There are three acknowledged types of suicidal passengers on aircraft – those who intend to die in another country, those who intend to die alone on the aircraft and those who intend to kill all the other passengers as well as themselves.

- In some countries it is legal to commit suicide and facilities are established to help those who wish to end their lives while they still have the ability to do so. This trade is facilitated by airlines. These passengers are in poor physical, medical and sometimes mental condition and their travel is one-way, sometimes accompanied by relatives, friends or carers. It is a distressing trip for the passengers and airline employees who become aware of the intent. It also leaves the airline with a dilemma if the passenger becomes ill during flight. Should it divert to enable relief of the passenger's distress or continue to the destination so the passenger can die as intended?
- The second group of suicidal passengers are those who intend to take their own lives on board the aircraft through ingesting or injecting drugs or by other means (such as slashing an artery – see Chapter 1). Usually the only harm is to themselves although the crew and other passengers could be traumatised by the suicidal person's actions. If discovered in time, many of these passengers can be saved by medically trained crew and/or aircraft diversion for further treatment.
- The third group are those who intend to destroy themselves and their fellow passengers in order to promote their political or criminal cause. This category includes terrorists who use commercial aircraft as weapons. Examples include the unsuccessful attempts in 2001 of the 'shoe bomber' on American Airlines Flight 63 and the 2009 'underwear bomber' on Northwest Airlines Flight 253. Successful attacks include the 2001 destruction when four hijacked aircraft were crashed into buildings in New York and Arlington, USA.

(i) Tall and stiff-kneed passengers

Tall passengers with long legs and those with stiff knees (which are often difficult and painful to flex when seated in an economy seat) want additional legroom and often it is only available in the exit row which is for occupation by able-bodied passengers only. Some airlines are now charging extra for this space. Passengers who are mobility restricted in any way whatsoever should not be seated in the exit row in case it is needed during an emergency. This means economy passengers with stiff knees must be seated in what are usually the space-restricted seats, which is often painful for them, particularly on long journeys. Their use of knee defenders might be justified as self-protection at the expense of the passenger in the row in front, whose ability to lean backwards would be compromised, forcing them to endure a painful and uncomfortable journey. How are crew on board supposed to manage these inflammatory situations? Whose human rights have priority?

(j) Deviant passenger outliers

Identifying a potential deviant is problematic, but it is worse to mis-identify them and accuse an innocent passenger. This is a reputational risk which could prove alarmingly expensive for the airline if the embarrassed passenger is litigious. An economically sustainable airline will have appropriate processes which must not breach legislation such as the UK Human Rights Act 1998. Deviants' motives are unknown until revealed, which could result in a seat change, removal from the aircraft and aircraft delay, or at extremes, unscheduled aircraft diversion. A Catholic priest who groped and traumatised a woman passenger on a US Airways flight to Philadelphia in 2014 was finally sentenced to six months in prison and ordered to register as a sex offender (Reuters, 2015). The aircraft was not diverted and the situation was managed by the crew until landing, whereupon the priest was arrested. (There were no diversion costs involved in this incident and it is not known if the female passenger sought any damages (unlike the woman affected by the screaming child on the Qantas flight).)

The sensitive issue of paedophiles on aeroplanes is rarely reported, but for airlines it is a reputational threat. UMs, trusted to the airlines' care, are sometimes seated next to strangers. Some airlines have a protected seating area for UMs, but if there is only one UM on board and the aircraft is full, finding appropriate seating can pose problems. Once all the passengers are seated, the crew have to judge whether the person sitting next to the child could pose any danger. On one occasion, an innocent, lone, male passenger was asked to change his seat simply because he was male and travelling alone. This caused him embarrassment and unwanted attention from other passengers. Ideally, pre-flight editing would solve this problem, but with self-check-in systems and online seat choice, this is not always feasible. Instead, most airlines opt for a blanket policy, seating UMs together in one area or avoiding seating single adults near these vulnerable youngsters. The solution is not perfect, but a policy needs to be in place to give authority to the crew if faced with such challenges.

Deviant outliers can present economic, social and possibly also environmental challenges if extra fuel is burned taking the aircraft to a diversion airport. Such diversion is allowed under the 'extraordinary circumstances' of EC 261/2004, but if the airline does not take steps to recover any damages, it would be creating a moral hazard.

Passenger expectations

Should economically sustainable airlines accede to requests to accommodate any of these minority outlier passengers especially if accepting them could delay or impede the travel of the majority? What does a culturally sensitive, economically sustainable airline do when confronted on board with these complexities while trying to close the aircraft door for a punctual departure? The most sustainable airlines publish their rules; however, they are not always read or followed by passengers and not all situations can be predicted.

A sustainable airline's relationship with its passengers is symbiotic. However, some passengers need educating in what the airline expects from them. There is in effect an implicit contract in operation. Passengers must comply with the processes to ensure airline efficiency and this includes compliance with check-in times, luggage contents and visa and health requirements. Passengers should not fly knowing they have an infectious disease or would be liable to need medical treatment on board with the prospect of diverting the aircraft (and fellow passengers). However, passenger expectations are constantly being raised. The President of Argentina decreed that the State-run carrier would permit small pets (like her own toy poodle) in the passenger cabin (Gadd, 2015). Similarly, American musicians are allowed (by permission of the Department of Transportation (2014)) to bring their instruments as carry-on luggage to place in the overhead bin, locker or under the seat. Unfortunately the necessary space is not always available if other passengers have loaded their carry-on luggage earlier in the boarding process. Furthermore, accommodating a guitar case (or a cello) can be extremely difficult in a fully occupied aircraft.

Airlines train their crews to be culturally sensitive. However, in some cultures, women are inferiors, homosexuals are abnormal, alcohol is evil, prawns are unclean, debate is silenced and criminals are mutilated without a fair trial. There are limits to what an airline can do to accommodate outlier behaviours due to faiths, sex, colour and general preferences. Examples abound. Saudi Arabian Airlines is reported to be introducing gender segregation for those who are not close relatives. Other airlines are concerned with Orthodox Jewish men and women who are not allowed to mix in public. (One woman reportedly sued an airline after being moved to the back of the plane when an ultra-Orthodox male objected to being seated next to her.) Another passenger, believed to be a religious descendant of the priests of ancient Israel, covered himself in a plastic bag to protect his purity as the aircraft flew over cemeteries. He believed that the bag provided a potential barrier from the impurities of the dead but there were concerns that he could neither breathe properly inside the plastic tent nor safely unbuckle his seat belt (Golgowski and Yaqoob, 2013). In the final days of apartheid in South Africa, the last passenger who boarded was a white woman arriving just as the aircraft door was closed. She was led to her seat whereupon she saw her neighbouring companion was a black man. She demanded to be moved (clearly angling for an upgrade) and protested loudly stating that she should not have had to sit next to him. The crew agreed. They moved the gentleman to first class.

Discrimination

Sustainable airlines must not discriminate but flight refusals can be for many reasons. The situation often becomes a question of passengers' human rights vs airlines' responsibilities as illustrated by the two UK cases of *Hook v British Airways* and *Stott v Thomas Cook Tour Operators Ltd*. Both cases claimed discrimination in their seating under Regulation 9 of the Civil Aviation (Access to Air Travel for Disabled Persons and Persons with Reduced Mobility) Regulations 2007 (Office of Public Sector Information, 2007).

Although discrimination was proved, the Court of Appeal decided neither passenger was entitled to damages for hurt feelings because the Montreal Convention 1999, which specifically covers injury, death and loss of baggage, takes precedence over EU law. The judgement reinforced the principle that mental suffering without any physical injury is not recoverable under the Montreal Convention.

Able-bodied people apparently have a difficult time saying 'no' to disabled individuals (Norton *et al.*, 2012). Ground-based agents (selected because of their customer service focus) want to make transactions go smoothly, and having to refuse a traveller can be against their personal values, especially if the passenger has a visible handicap. In all probability the Check-in Agent will do their best to accommodate the passenger – but this might be misguided and result in disappointment once the passenger is actually on the aircraft, when the crew might not be able to accommodate the particular handicap.

Excess baggage vs human rights and airlines' responsibilities

In the days when airline travel was only for the rich, wealth was reflected in the contents of their luggage (silk, leather, cashmere) whereas with the democratisation of consumption (see Chapter 1), today's popular suitcase contents (t-shirts, sandals and jeans) are replaceable at minimal cost. Economics challenges the wisdom and environmental costs of taking suitcases filled with low-priced goods when they are more than likely available at disposable prices at the destination. The socially minded eco-flyers know that taking zero luggage cuts weight, reducing fuel burn and emissions expended. It also offers the prospect of assisting a developing nation by purchasing the holiday wardrobe in the country where it was more than likely produced (a social and environmental win–win).

However, reducing luggage also reduces airline handling costs and the potential injury to baggage handlers from lifting heavy bags. In the UK, baggage handlers are often limited to a maximum luggage weight of 35kg (with a label marked 'HEAVY'). This is to minimise the likelihood of back injuries among the manual workers on whose muscle the safe stowage of baggage depends. In 2011–2012, musculoskeletal injuries of the back and upper body affected 438,000 people in the UK (Health and Safety Executive (HSE), 2012). Manual handling is one of the most frequent causes of injury in the workplace (HSE, 2012) and affects baggage loaders. Their health and safety and human rights are sometimes compromised by overly heavy loads. In the UK, such injuries incurred during the course of employment in a private airline become a social cost for the NHS and could eventually trigger payment of disability benefits.

Luggage and opportunities lost

What can be carried in the aircraft accompanying the passengers depends on the size of the aircraft and capacity of the cargo space. This creates opportunity costs for the airline and sometimes choices have to be made as to what luggage will be

Table 4.4 Loading dilemmas: choosing what to leave behind when the freight hold is full

Passengers' luggage	Impact if left behind
PRM's 175kg personal motorised wheelchair (or electric mobility scooter) which also needs to be stowed in a separate baggage container to prevent damage	without the mobility device the immobile passenger's journey will be wasted; however, its space requirements have implications for other passengers' luggage, which might have to be left behind to accommodate it
fishing equipment for world angling tournament	the fisherman is representing his country, so if his equipment cannot accompany him, the trip will be wasted
soldier's 90kg backpack	this soldier has served his country overseas for the past year: everything he needs for his next deployment is in that pack and he could face disciplinary action if he arrives late and unprepared for his new assignment
two wind sail boards for windsurfing honeymooners	the honeymoon will be ruined if both sail boards are not loaded
Formula 1 replacement racing engine (an expensive cargo which needs fragile handling and protected space)	if the engine is not loaded then the entire racing team (and £Stg/$US and € millions) will be wasted as the race is within hours of the aircraft arriving
time-sensitive freight, e.g. fruit, vegetables, fish and medical supplies	perishable goods *must* be loaded or the entire shipment could be spoiled with insurance claims to follow
delayed luggage from a previous flight	passengers' holidays have already been ruined with no luggage on arrival; they will demand compensation as well as the bags delivered to their home which is 400 miles from the airport (an expensive reunion for the airline)
two large suitcases belonging to a couple celebrating their 60th wedding anniversary	they are joining a two-week cruise to Antarctica which leaves shortly after the aircraft arrives, so without their luggage they will have no clothes for the trip and certainly no cold-weather clothing

left behind – and the costs of reuniting passengers and baggage can sometimes be more than the passengers' fares. (Airline employees travelling on discounted fares can be left behind in favour of profitable freight.) The greater the aircraft capacity, the more freight and passenger luggage can be accommodated – or alternatively short-shipped (i.e. on the manifest but not delivered), short-landed (i.e. when it was on the aircraft but not unloaded at the destination) or even lost. Accompanied luggage comprises many varied items including suitcases, sports equipment (snow skis, surfboards, snowboards, windsurfing boards, golf clubs, bicycles, hang gliders, diving gear and even fishing tackle) as well as mobility equipment. Sometimes, however, passenger baggage has to be prioritised, which can upset many passengers whose luggage might not have been loaded. The question is: whose luggage has priority if the aircraft is too heavy or freight space is limited (Table 4.4)?

Sometimes it is not the fault of the airlines, but the airport baggage system which causes the luggage chaos. However, ultimately the cost of reuniting passengers with their bags is more than just the repatriation expenses: it creates havoc with passengers' plans and damages the airlines' reputations.

So what?

Passengers are the reasons airlines thrive. A safe, efficient and pleasant transaction – from booking through to arrival at destination – fulfils expectations and relies on the behaviour of both employees and passengers. The journey is underpinned by an implicit contract based on trust – that intangible item which supports the airline's reputation. Outlier or deviant passenger behaviour can be extremely challenging for public transport carriers to manage safely because sometimes travellers' requirements are unreasonable and at other times they are extremely expensive to fulfil. However, passengers sometimes take unjustified risks and avoid taking personal responsibility in the expectation that airlines would repatriate them after misfortune. Just as passengers claim compensation from airlines, so too the airlines should claim compensation from deviant passengers. The airlines' omissions to initiate claims against individuals who cause economic harm undermines social justice (equality, equity and fairness) for other passengers, creates moral hazards and damages sustainable airlines' economics.

References

ABC (2014), '*Drunken' passenger allegedly abuses crew and passengers, forces Virgin flight to turn back to Perth* available from http://www.abc.net.au/news/2014–07–10/man-who-caused-virgin-flight-to-be-turned-back-to-perth-arreste/5588162 accessed 2 January 2015

Allen, V. and Awford, J. (2014), *Girl, 4, went into anaphylactic shock and lost consciousness on a plane after selfish passenger ignored three warnings not to eat nuts on board* available from http://www.dailymail.co.uk/news/article-2724684/Nut-allergy-girl-went-anaphylactic-shock-plane-passenger-ignored-three-warnings-not-eat-nuts-board.html accessed 2 November 2014

Business Travel News (2014), *Unaccompanied minors* available from http://www.btnews.co.uk/article/7824 accessed 1 September 2014

Chang Y.-H. and Liao, M.-Y. (2009), The effect of aviation safety education on passenger cabin safety awareness, *Safety Science* 47(10) 1,337–1,345 available from http://www.sciencedirect.com/science/article/pii/S0925753509000186 accessed 2 January 2015

Department of Transportation (2014), *U.S. Department of Transportation Issues Final Rule Regarding Air Travel with Musical Instruments* available from http://www.dot.gov/briefing-room/us-department-transportation-issues-final-rule-regarding-air-travel-musical accessed 4 April 2015

European Union (2006), *Regulation (EC) No 1107/2006 of the European Parliament and of the Council* available from http://eur-lex.europa.eu/legal-content/EN/ALL/?uri=CELEX:32006R1107 accessed 29 March 2015

European Union (2014), *Compensation and assistance to passengers in the event of denied boarding and of cancellation or long delay of flights* available from http://www.europarl.europa.eu/sides/getDoc.do?pubRef=-//EP//TEXT+TA+P7-TA-2014-0092+0+DOC+XML+V0//EN accessed 4 July 2014

Gadd, M. (2015), *Pet-loving President of Argentina announces state-run airline will allow lapdogs on flights with passenger* available from http://www.dailymail.co.uk/travel/travel_news/article-2894365/Pet-loving-president-Argentina-announces-state-run-airline-allow-lapdogs-flights.html accessed 10 March 2015

Golgowski, N. and Yaqoob, J. (2013), *Orthodox Jewish man photographed covering himself in plastic bag during flight because faith forbids him to fly over cemeteries* available from http://www.dailymail.co.uk/news/article-2307713/Pictured-Orthodox-Jewish-man-covers-PLASTIC-BAG-flight.html accessed 25 December 2014

Griggs, B. (2014), *Air New Zealand posts new Hobbit Safety Video* available from http://edition.cnn.com/2014/10/22/travel/air-new-zealand-safety-video/ accessed 1 November 2014

Harcar, T. and Yucelt, U. (2012), American consumer's attitudes towards different airline companies channels: a comparison of transaction methods, *Pasos* 10(2) 59–68 available from http://www.pasosonline.org/Publicados/10212special/PS0212_07.pdf accessed 2 January 2015

Health and Safety Executive (HSE) (2012), *At a glance: Health and Safety Statistics 2011/12* available from http://www.hse.gov.uk/statistics/at-a-glance.pdf accessed 4 May 2012

Huffington Post (2012), *Southwest Airlines Settles Lawsuit For 5.8 Million Drink Vouchers* available from http://www.huffingtonpost.com/2012/12/14/southwest-airlines-drink-voucher-settlement_n_2301140.html accessed 13 August 2014

IATA (2015), *2015 IATA Global Passenger Survey* available from https://www.iata.org/publications/Pages/global-passenger-survey.aspx accessed 6 March 2016

Kim, L., Qu, H. and Kim, D. (2009), A study of perceived risk and risk prediction of purchasing air tickets online, *Journal of Travel and Tourism Marketing* 26(3) 203–224 available from http://www.tandfonline.com/doi/abs/10.1080/10548400902925031#.VKf4oiusVqU accessed 2 January 2015

Kitching, C. (2014), *Parents escorted off Frontier Airlines plane and met by police after two-year-old son's tantrum* available from http://www.dailymail.co.uk/travel/travel_news/article-2806747/Frontier-Airlines-passengers-escorted-plane-son-s-crying-led-argument-cabin-crew.html accessed 2 November 2014

Kotler, P. and Keller, K.L. (2012), *Marketing management*, 14th ed., Upper Saddle River, New Jersey, Pearson Education

Linning, S. (2014), *Revealed: How 'discount' travel websites end up costing you MORE than buying tickets direct from budget airlines* available from http://www.dailymail.co.uk/travel/travel_news/article-2721135/Revealed-How-discount-travel-websites-end-costing-MORE-buying-tickets-direct-budget-airlines.html accessed 5 April 2015

Malkin, B. (2010), *Air passenger says child in neighbouring seat burst her ear drum* available from http://www.telegraph.co.uk/news/worldnews/australiaandthepacific/australia/7900185/Air-passenger-says-child-in-neighbouring-seat-burst-her-eardrums.html accessed 20 May 2014

Milne, R.J. and Kelly, A.R. (2014), A new method for boarding passengers onto an airplane, *Journal of Air Transport Management* 34(C) 93–100 available from http://www.sciencedirect.com/science/article/pii/S0969699713001166 accessed 2 January 2015

Nordheimer, J. (1984), *British airline links poisoning cases to powder in hors d'oeuvres* available from http://www.nytimes.com/1984/03/23/world/british-airline-links-poisoning-cases-to-powder-in-hors-d-oeuvres.html accessed 12 August 2014

Norton, M., Dunn, E., Carney, D. and Ariely, D. (2012), The persuasive 'power' of stigma, *Organizational Behavior and Human Decision Processes* 117(2) 261–268 available from http://www.sciencedirect.com/science/article/pii/S0749597811001087 accessed 2 January 2015

Office of Public Sector Information (2007), *The Civil Aviation (Access to Air Travel for Disabled Persons and Persons with Reduced Mobility) Regulations 2007* available from http://webarchive.nationalarchives.gov.uk/20071001175136/opsi.gov.uk/si/si2007/uksi_2007 1895_en_1 accessed 10 January 2015

O'Hare, M. (2015), *All Blacks rugby stars rap in new Air New Zealand safety video* available from http://edition.cnn.com/2015/08/14/travel/air-nz-all-blacks-video/ accessed 19 August 2015

Parentdish (2014), *Giving birth: Russian woman welcomes twins on plane* available from http://www.parentdish.ca/2014/05/09/woman-births-twins-on-plane/ accessed 7 September 2014

Reuters (2015), *Priest gets six months in prison for groping woman on a plane* available from http://nypost.com/2015/08/24/priest-gets-six-months-in-prison-for-groping-woman-on-plane/ accessed 28 August 2015

Skyscanner (2016), *How to get a flight upgrade: 15 ways to get bumped up to business* available from http://www.skyscanner.net/news/how-get-flight-upgrade-15-ways-get-bumped-business?utm_source=facebook_uk&utm_medium=social&utm_content=business_upgrade accessed 10 June 2016

Skytrax (2014), *What is evaluated in the Rating of Airport/Ground service?* available from http://www.airlinequality.com/StarRanking/star_system.htm accessed 4 April 2015

Spector, T. (2015), *'Airborne peanut allergies on flights are a MYTH': Leading scientist claims it's impossible for a reaction to be triggered this way* available from http://www.dailymail.co.uk/health/article-3222262/Airborne-peanut-allergies-flights-MYTH-Leading-scientist-claims-s-impossible-reaction-triggered-way.html accessed 6 September 2015

Steffen, J. (2008), Optimal boarding method for airline passengers, *Journal of Air Transport Management* 14(3) 146–150 available from http://www.sciencedirect.com/science/article/pii/S0969699708000239 accessed 2 January 2015

Swiss (2014), *Allergy-friendly airline: Allergy sufferers in good hands with SWISS* available from http://www.swiss.com/gb/en/various/allergy-friendly-airline accessed 6 December 2014

Travelmail Reporter (2014), *Air rage: the most annoying passengers or other irritants encountered on a flight* available from http://www.dailymail.co.uk/travel/article-2621402/Babies-planes-70-cent-Britons-want-child-free-zones-aircraft.html accessed 4 April 2015

Wright, B. (2014), *Why knee defenders are good for air passengers* available from http://www.telegraph.co.uk/finance/newsbysector/transport/11066589/Knee-defenders-why-they-are-good-for-the-airline-industry.html accessed 1 September 2014

Zennie, M. (2013), *'Let's have a go!' The drunken British man who forced a flight to divert its course after he 'spat on flight attendants and picked fights with everyone aboard'* available from http://www.dailymail.co.uk/news/article-2306358/Sean-Jude-Kelly-British-Airways-flight-Cancun-diverted-Orlando-Briton-picks-fight-plane.html accessed 3 January 2015

5 Travelling timebomb

5.1 CONTEXT

Scale of the challenge

Occasionally there is an issue which is so sensitive that public discussion is considered amoral, heartless or even unjust. In the spirit of openness and challenge which sustainability-thinking encourages, it is appropriate that the legal, social, human rights, safety and economic dimensions of disabled, sick, elderly, obese or other passengers with reduced mobility (the term 'PRM' in this text includes all groups) are discussed with the same frankness as other economic airline issues. PRMs are outlier airline customers who need to be managed separately from the passenger mainstream since they comprise many different disabilities, each of which could require individualised airline and/or airport assistance in order to enable travel.

Disability has many causes including genetic inheritance, mental illness, sports and auto accidents, ageing, war, obesity and medical conditions, all of which could give rise to physical, sensory, intellectual and/or hidden disabilities as varied as inability to walk, blindness, post-traumatic stress disorder or speech impediments. Some disabilities are temporary; some are permanent and stable; others, unfortunately, are permanent, unstable and increase cumulatively. Passengers who are not classified as disabled in their home environment become disabled in the context of an airport with unfamiliar surroundings, distances, noises and processes. This temporary disorientation requires assistance from the airline and/or airport to overcome it, therefore the generic terms 'disabled' or 'PRM' can have very different definitions and requirements depending on the disability.

By 2017, global air passenger numbers are predicted to rise to 3.91 billion (IATA, 2013a) of whom approximately 1% could have some form of reduced mobility mostly due to ageing, obesity or medical needs. Although estimates vary approximately 10% could require barrier-free travel (IPK, 2012) which means they would possibly require airline support for which the additional costs (by the authority of many laws in many jurisdictions) cannot be recharged to the PRMs themselves. PRMs represent a missing market identified by national, multi-national and supranational governments, NGOs and CSERplus' advocates. This market has been fulfilled through various unfunded mandates even though in many countries economic impact analyses were not completed and no compensating State subsidies were awarded to cover the extra services and facilities PRMs need.

History of disabled passengers' access

Disability in the passenger population is now a social and economic issue rather than a medical matter. When physically disabled, wheelchair-using airline passengers were few in number, they were considered to be medical passengers and were processed outside of the passenger mainstream. They were usually lifted on and off the aircraft by the airport fire service, airline baggage handlers or other physically strong and able-bodied personnel operating on an ad hoc basis. Their labour was paid for by the airlines directly (if their staff were involved) or costs absorbed by miscellaneous contracted services (e.g. catering supply trucks with tail lifts) as part of airport goodwill. The ad hoc PRM servicing arrangements sometimes led to aircraft delay owing to lack of available personnel and lifting equipment and as PRM numbers grew, it was apparent that disabled passenger handling needed to become an SBU in its own right. This missing market was filled by either specially trained in-house personnel with customised equipment, or by specialist, outsourced contractors. Sometimes, however, the costs of the extra services required were greater than the passengers' fares. One severely physically disabled passenger was tracked on a return trip from London to Rome. Her needs were for an ambulift vehicle on departure and arrival at both airports, complimentary wheelchair service through both airports to and from departure and arrival gates, carriage of her heavyweight electric wheelchair, bath board and other disability accessories plus oxygen on the journey. The estimated cost of her travel was approximately ten times her £Stg140 fare.

Legislation and PRMs

During the 1970s and onwards, many governments realised that they could no longer afford the investment needs of their national utility and transport providers. As a result, many of these parastatals were privatised with the condition that following liberalisation these enterprises would subsidise the most economically deprived citizens to enable their access to essential services. The correct pricing of any goods or services is a powerful means of achieving competitive efficiency. However, airlines are different from the utility and domestic transport suppliers because (a) they have international competitors to consider; (b) flying is not normally regarded as an essential social service like water, gas, sewerage, electricity or local transport and (c) they cannot make extra charges for additional costs. Doganis (2001) in his text on aviation evolution noted that privatisation preparations should have included identification of any social subsidies because the airlines would no longer receive any government support. Lack of future subsidies (either to the consumers or the industry) should have negated any social obligations on behalf of privatised airlines; however, formerly nationalised airlines are now privately owned, and without the social subsidies as identified by Doganis. Consequently, these airlines are obliged by regulation to undertake some unprofitable social activities – including the complimentary carriage of PRMs' heavyweight mobility aids – as a condition of their implicit 'licence to operate' enforced by regulations. Some mobility aids are lightweight and portable; some are space consuming and extremely heavy (175kg or more), posing a hazard to the baggage loaders charged with on-loading them. When governments legislated to develop missing markets, subsidies should have been awarded to cover the social costs but policy makers took the view 'that airlines operating in a competitive market would not make adequate provision' for PRMs (Cambridge Economic Policy Associates, 2010: 24). Without conducting adequate (or sometimes any) economic impact analyses, legislators in many jurisdictions (including the UK, EU and USA) decided that unfunded mandates would ensure that competitive airlines provided services for PRMs in support of policies to reduce social inequalities. The ruling was to ensure that having disabilities would not prevent people from participating in mainstream life. In the UK, and in much of the EU, the privatisation legislation for ground-based public transport provided support for disabled and elderly people, either through subsidising the transport company and/or giving discounted or free fares to entitled passengers filtered by the award of concessions matched to personal identity cards. No equivalent subsidies or filtering permits were available for air transport for either the carriers or the passengers and yet air travel, with its multiple transactions transporting PRMs and their equipment, is more complicated and expensive than ground transport when providing equality of access. This is largely because the design of airports means that there is a distance between the check-in point and the aircraft which has to be bridged by a paid-for service. This can comprise airline Customer Service Agent, Mobility Assistant with motorised buggy or manually powered wheelchair, and/or a high-lift/ambulift vehicle with up to four Assistants to lift a highly immobile passenger. These service provisions could be multiplied fourfold on a return journey (Table 5.1). There are also additional costs for services and facilities provided on board.

The International Transport Forum (ITF) report on mobility rights, obligations and equity in an ageing society (ITF, 2011) wondered if it would be feasible for ground subsidies for land transport providers to continue since the annual cost in England alone was estimated at £Stg870m ($US1.3bn or €1.2bn). The ITF noted that 'the "right" to accessible public transport . . . cannot be achieved without imposing obligations on those responsible for transport delivery' (ITF, 2011: 5). Obligations for airlines are far greater than those for ground transport providers and extend from complimentary services and freight through to physical lifting. The higher the level of immobility, the more the airline spends in assisting a PRM. While it was politically expedient at the time of legislating for public ground transport – perceived as an essential element in equality of social opportunity – it is doubtful whether their subsidies are economically sustainable in the longer term. Withdrawal of these subsidies could have a significant effect on ground transport companies and affect the human rights of the disabled passengers themselves. Withdrawal could also precipitate increased fares for all passengers.

Table 5.1 Some of the differences PRMs sustain between accessing public ground
transport and air travel

Public ground transport (buses, trams, trains, coaches and taxis)	Air travel
immediate access to travel vehicle (rail and local buses and most coaches)	long distances to and from aircraft have to be covered by intermediate transport
luggage loaded into carriage with the travelling PRM	luggage is separated from PRM, sent on a separate route and either loaded directly into the freight hold or placed in its own container and then loaded
passengers can remain in their own mobility equipment on local buses and trains: usually a separation of passenger and mobility equipment is necessary on long distance coaches	• PRMs are separated from their personal mobility equipment and transferred into an airport mobility vehicle (manually operated wheelchair or motorised buggy) • some PRM mobility aids require dismantling, battery detached and packaged, and placed into a special baggage container to ensure safe transport • PRMs and their mobility aids arrive at the aircraft by separate routes • immobile PRMs need to be transferred from the airport wheelchair to aisle wheelchairs to be moved along the aircraft
no need for interim transfer	PRMs have to be transferred to their aircraft seats possibly being lifted over other seats to access the window seat
passenger plus luggage and mobility equipment disembark together	PRMs and luggage to be disembarked separately and taken to the Arrivals Hall where PRMs are reunited with their luggage and mobility equipment; mobility equipment is reassembled (and in UK PRM is delivered to next transport interchange, e.g. car, coach, bus, train)
repeat in reverse on return journey	repeat in reverse on return journey (including detaching/reattaching and packaging/unpackaging battery of passenger's own mobility device and device's reassembly if necessary)
permit scheme for discounted or free travel administered by either government or local authority to restrict benefits to qualified users only	no permit scheme

European regulation

In 1986 the USA passed the Air Carrier Access Act (ACAA) which prevents airlines from discriminating against disabled passengers. It was written to support the many young men who were disabled by the Vietnam War. When the EU was formulating PRM regulations (through the ECAC) the early drafts relied on the ACAA provisions without acknowledging that few of the disabled people in Europe were actually disabled through fighting for their country, i.e. this was a very different PRM population. Furthermore, at the ECAC meetings some of the airline representatives had mobility impairments themselves and this compromised any impartiality in the preparation of eventual legislation and regulations. Airlines' economists, outnumbered by government and disabled representatives, argued unsuccessfully that the provisions for PRMs would eventually become economically onerous with increasing numbers of ageing and obese passengers. Consequently, the provisions which were originally established to assist a minority of wheelchair users have become the umbrella for increasing numbers of more broadly defined and often self-declared PRMs. As often happens, no economic impact analysis was completed before the Regulations were passed. The ECAC preparations eventually became Article 2(a) of EU Regulation (EC) No 1107/2006 which states that:

> 'Disabled person' or 'person with reduced mobility' means any person whose mobility when using transport is reduced due to any physical disability (sensory or locomotor, permanent or temporary), intellectual disability or impairment, or any other cause of disability, or age, and whose situation needs appropriate attention and the adaptation to his or her particular needs of the service made available to all passengers.
>
> (European Union, 2006)

Regulation EC 1107/2006 also provided for PRMs to be accompanied by medical equipment and up to two pieces of mobility equipment in the aircraft cargo hold subject to a recommended minimum of 48 hours' notice. However, the pre-notification requirement is neither mandatory nor enforceable. Failure of PRMs to pre-notify their needs at the time of booking leads to airport inefficiencies in allocations of assistance personnel (Mobility Assistants) who operate the airport wheelchairs or motorised buggies. The result is that sometimes pre-notified PRMs unfairly have to wait for their mobility assistance longer than they would have expected. This can also mean that aircraft might have to wait for them, which in turn could increase the airline's costs. Anecdotes abound of groups of disabled passengers arriving at the check-in desk accompanied by multiple un-notified personal mobility scooters or motorised wheelchairs. Because of their bulk and shape many motorised aids cannot be placed in the hold without leaving other passengers' luggage behind, which could cause them considerable inconvenience (see Table 4.4 in Chapter 4). Their rights would have been subsumed to those of PRMs, and reacquainting passengers with their delayed luggage is always at the airline's expense. Furthermore, accommodating a group of six PRMs' un-notified electric mobility scooters is known on at least one occasion to have caused a last-minute aircraft substitution to avoid disappointing passengers who did not realise the importance of pre-notification. This would have considerably increased the sympathetic charter carrier's costs.

Some of the mobility aids (e.g. motorised mobility scooters) are bulky, requiring significant cargo space and often airline-supplied protective packaging. Many are also heavy, and weight generates a fuel requirement which (when burned) generates increased emissions (see Chapter 6). The lean principle (see Chapter 2) is that customers should only receive those services for which they are willing to pay, and using resources for any service which is not reimbursed by a passenger would normally be considered wasteful. However, the economic reality is that there are PRMs with high dependency on complimentary value-added services and products for which there is no airline gain, and if the passengers had to pay for these services, many would not be able to afford to fly.

Regulation EC 1107/2006 requires airlines to make 'reasonable efforts' for PRMs. However, the limits for this requirement are not specified – nor who decides what is 'reasonable effort'. As an example: it is unlikely that a PRM with Parkinson's disease would be able to manage the meal cutlery in the economy cabin because of the inherent tremors which accompany the condition. However, entrepreneurs have devised a new eating utensil which neutralises much of the shaking (Prigg, 2014). When this is commercially available, would airlines be required to provide the utensil 'as reasonable effort' to ensure that PRMs with Parkinson's disease do not suffer discrimination when trying to eat an airline meal? Failure to provide this tool could mean that any passenger with such a disabling condition would be treated unequally with other disabled passengers whose needs are more easily accommodated in mainstream disability provisions (e.g. those passengers who cannot walk long distances, for whom a wheelchair is provided). Are some disabled passengers to be treated more 'equally' than others? This situation is yet another example where solving one problem creates another to be solved by someone else.

Building on Regulation EC 1107/2006 the EU (again without any airline economic impact analysis) proposed changes for compensation arrangements for PRMs under Regulation EC 261/2004 to be implemented by 2015. These include the following amendments:

> (13b) Disabled passengers or passengers with reduced mobility who miss a connecting flight due to a delay caused by airport assistance services should be adequately cared for while they are waiting for re-routing. Such passengers should be able to claim compensation from the airport managing body on a similar basis to passengers whose flights are delayed or cancelled by the air carrier . . .

> (18) For disabled persons, persons with reduced mobility and other persons with special needs such as unaccompanied children, pregnant women and

persons in need of specific medical attention, it may be more difficult to arrange accommodation when flight disruptions occur. Therefore, any limitations on the right for accommodation in cases of extraordinary circumstances should on no account apply to these categories of passenger.

(18a) Where the Community air carrier requires disabled persons or persons with reduced mobility to be accompanied by a carer, carers should not be subject to the payment of the relevant airport departure tax . . .

(18b) The service providers should ensure that persons with reduced mobility and people with disabilities have the right, at all times, to use safety-approved respiratory devices on aircraft, free of charge. The Commission should draw up a list of approved medical oxygen equipment in co-operation with the industry and organisations representing people with disabilities and PRMs, taking due account of safety requirements . . .

(27) In order to ensure that the damage to or loss of mobility equipment is compensated to its full value, air carriers and airport assistance services shall inform disabled passengers or passengers with reduced mobility at the time of booking and again at check-in of the opportunity to make a special declaration of interest, which pursuant to the Montreal Convention, allows them to seek full compensation for loss or damage. Air carriers should inform passengers of this declaration and the rights attaching to it whenever they make a ticket booking.

(© European Union, 2014)[1]

Given that there is no disability filtering system in place (at the time of publication), how clause 18a would be administered is an unresolved issue; it is also uncertain which of the taxes in Table 1.3 in Chapter 1 would be exempt. Airlines will bear all of these additional costs – unfunded, mandated, privately provided, social benefits – to enable equality and ill-defined social justice in the consumption of air travel.

EC 1107/2006 costs

The airlines were unprepared for the ECAC discussions because they were working from a compassionate, altruistic stance and had not prepared a comprehensive economically based estimate of their future costs (Table 5.2). There was therefore no basis on which to argue that these costs could be recovered from either the PRMs directly or the European governments which provide land transport mobility allowances for disabled and elderly people.

Free riders and PRM service provisions

It is unlawful for an airline to discriminate against a disabled person by refusing to provide them with the service offered to members of the public on the same

Table 5.2 Uncalculated PRM costs (adapted from Ancell and Graham, 2016)

PRM's direct costs
- services required by PRMs in each SSR category carried each flight
- staff training, frequency and time spent at departure and destination of (a) dismantling of mobility scooters or electric wheelchairs; (b) detaching, packaging and reattaching batteries and (c) reassembly of device plus battery

---

Mobility aids
- quantity, weight and dimensions of PRM mobility aids and medical equipment which accompanies each PRM per flight
- supply of battery packaging
- additional fuel needed and emissions generated carrying heavier mobility aids

---

Opportunity costs
- opportunity cost of carriage of PRM's mobility aids (i.e. the freight and/or luggage left behind) (see Table 4.4 in Chapter 4)
- weight penalty for on-board PRM fittings (e.g. retractable armrests, on-board wheelchair)
- loss of any seating to enable wider lavatory compartments

Discounts
- value of any discounted seats for accompanying carer/s
- value of any discounted additional seats for PRMs requiring more than one seat for personal occupation

---

Aircraft delays/diversions costs for MEDAs or other PRMs
- numbers, frequency and causes of diversions
- departure delays incurred on aircraft turnaround by the loading and unloading of mobility aids
- aircraft delays owing to late-notified or late-delivered PRMs

---

Airline employee training costs
- cabin crew training to assist PRMs
- ground crew training to assist PRMs
- third-party training for PRM assistance at airports and for handling dangerous goods (i.e. packaging of batteries)

Airline and airport employee health, safety and welfare including number, frequency and cost of:
- injuries to PRMs and airport or airline Mobility Assistants
- compensation payments to airport or airline Mobility Assistants for injuries sustained during fulfilment of their duties

---

Equipment costs
- capital, maintenance, procurement, fuel and ground equipment costs for additional aircraft fixtures and fittings to enable PRM travel (including the aisle-width wheelchair)
- seat belt extensions and bariatric life jackets for obese passengers
- ground-based mobility equipment

Airline and airport operating costs
- Mobility Assistants' wages
- space rental for desking, equipment stowage and staff rest areas for PRM ground teams and passenger waiting areas
- administration costs (including any outsourced supplier contract transaction costs)

---

terms (Department for Transport, 2008). It is also unlawful for airlines to challenge passengers on their needs for assistance or charge them for the additional services or carriage of mobility equipment. In this sense, the privately owned airlines are providing a public service, but because of the mandated regulations they are not being compensated for any additional costs. Before the mandating, airlines provided these services altruistically, willingly and free of charge. Now, with growing numbers of PRMs requiring assistance and no filtering permitted, some unentitled airline passengers are taking advantage of the regulated provisions. These free riders (see Chapter 1) consider only their personal benefit and it is documented that self-declaration of need has led to abuse of the service provisions (Airport Operators Association (AOA), 2009). The free riders include those who cannot carry their own hand baggage ('too heavy') or be bothered to walk the distance to the gate ('too far'). An anecdote from one inbound flight to London's Heathrow recounts the tale of the Cabin Service Director who announced over the public address system that because 100+ wheelchairs were needed to clear the aircraft there would be at least a one hour wait for the PRMs before they could disembark. After the able-bodied passengers had all left the aircraft, only five wheelchair passengers remained – the other 95+ had suddenly found their mobility.

In the airline service-value chain, the PRM service and equipment providers are permitted to make a profit but airlines are not. UK ground transport has in-built filters with genuinely disabled people granted passes to obtain reduced fares and complimentary assistance. Any equivalent filter system for airlines would be extremely difficult and expensive to manage, particularly for international flights. Furthermore, any such permit system would signal yet another missing market, i.e. that of creating and maintaining a PRM database. Consequently, unqualified, able-bodied passengers can request wheelchairs and customer support simply to gain priority Security clearance on departure and rapid clearance of Customs and Immigration on arrival. A service which has no filters or price is neither valued nor used as intended and consequently costs could escalate beyond anything the airlines could ever have anticipated (presenting yet more unexpected consequences). Governments have filters for social welfare recipients to ensure only those citizens who are entitled receive payments and that these disbursements remain affordable for the nation. Airlines are not permitted to do the same. (This particular free rider problem should be contrasted with the UK government's determination to crack down on welfare cheats who pretend to be disabled.)

At the time of the ECAC meetings, some airlines invested in disability charities to understand their PRMs' needs, because in some circumstances corporate philanthropy can be effective if it is strategic and it could contribute to preventing government legislation (Husted and Salazar, 2006) (see also Chapter 3). While the charities were grateful, the philanthropy so invested (and which delivered PRM service and facilities improvements) failed to make any impact on the regulators whose focus was purely on public (social) benefit. However, airlines would be justified in future if they claimed that all unrecoverable PRM carriage costs (Table 5.2) were included in the annual totals of corporate philanthropic donations.

Airport and airline PRM services

The majority of PRMs are those who are disabled by ageing, obesity or medical challenges. PRMs' needs are noted by a series of IATA special service request (SSRs) codes (IATA, 2013c) which detail the services the passengers need but which do not necessarily describe the disability or illness (Table 5.3). The codes decide the airline or airport assistance to be offered so the airline is often unaware of the root cause. WCHC, for example, could apply to a stable physical disability that prevents the passenger having any independent movement or it could apply to someone who is very ill and might be travelling to die elsewhere (they could also be a MEDA).

Table 5.3 Some IATA SSR assistance codes and appropriate support (adapted from IATA, 2013c)

SSR code	Disability	Airline and airport assistance
BLND	passenger has limited or nil vision	escort through the airport to the departure gate; crew assistance on board includes personal explanations for safety, lavatory location, menu and meal tray outlay
DEAF	passenger who is deaf or deaf without speech	passenger needs to be met and escorted (possibly with sign language speaker)
DEAF/ BLND	deaf and blind passenger	passenger and companion need to be met and escorted
MAAS	meet and assist	passenger needs to be met and escorted (could be because of inability to read or lack of local language)
MEDA	passenger has medical condition	medical condition is detailed if it is relevant to travel: passenger possibly needs mobility assistance to and from the aircraft as well as care on board
PETC	an assistance animal accompanies the passenger	passenger accompanied by a service animal needs to be met and escorted
PHOH	passenger has a hearing impairment	as for BLND plus on-screen captions for inflight entertainment
WCHC	passenger is immobile (PRM must travel with an escort who can take responsibility for their needs)	the PRM will need to be transported to and from the aircraft and lifted into and out of their seat
WCHR	cannot walk long distances	supply of airport wheelchair and Mobility Assistant to push it to the departure or arrival gate
WCHS	cannot climb stairs	if the aircraft is off-jetty the PRM will need to be provided with mechanical hoist (such as ambulift or scissor lift) to enter the aircraft

Non-ambulant orthopaedic and mobility-impaired passengers with heavy electric personal mobility equipment are the most challenging and expensive for an airline to service. The higher the level of immobility – regardless of cause – the more the airline has to do to ensure the PRM's pain-free access and safe flight. Airline margins are often thinner in the economy cabin (where most of the PRMs are seated) and the additional costs of servicing passengers outside of the mainstream can impact heavily on the marginal profitability of some flights.

Airport assistance

The arrival of a visibly disabled passenger (wheelchair, crutches, white cane and/or service animal) is an opportunity for the airline to showcase its compassion watched by other passengers in the vicinity. Provided the airline is pre-notified of the level and type of disability, it should be able to process these passengers without delay (Table 5.4).

When check-in scenarios deteriorate in full view of the public, they can quickly undermine an airline's reputation for caring customer service, especially if the scene is shared on social media. Where passengers do not declare their disability before check-in, the airline – represented by the Check-in Agent – can be faced with the decision as to whether or not to let them fly. Sometimes, only a trained medic can make that decision – and that advice is not always available in the short time between checking-in and aircraft departure. In the meantime, the passenger would possibly become visibly distressed. Any aircraft delay or subsequent diversion (with inconvenience to fellow passengers) due to one passenger's failure to pre-notify their needs is not claimable on any insurance policy. Such omissions can increase PRM costs for an economically sustainable airline.

Table 5.4 PRM airport assistance inventory

Airport mobility assistance	Function
Customer Service Agent	accompanies ambulant passengers who need confidence to navigate the airport
manually powered wheelchair	wheelchairs are supplied at the airport and are pushed by trained Mobility Assistants
motorised buggy	a mobility device (usually manned by one or two Mobility Assistants) which can simultaneously transport several passengers and their hand luggage
ambulift, scissorlift or high-lift vehicle	a vehicle with a passenger lift which can elevate an immobile passenger up to the aircraft door for loading if the aircraft is not on a jetty. Up to four personnel can be required to lift obese, immobile PRMs into their seats.

Airport facilities vs airlines' reputations

The EU requires that airport buildings are made accessible for passengers with all disabilities but legislates without acknowledging that where airport buildings fail, airline customer service will bear the costs. Airport facilities are a one-off cost and a tax deductible investment; airline customer service is an ongoing operating cost and therefore not tax deductible. For example, airport failure to instal a means of vertical transfer at the heads of aircraft stands (a capital cost which adds to the airport's asset base) means that passengers must surrender their wheelchairs at the check-in desk so that they can be taken through an alternative route to the aircraft. This will incur an airline operating cost which usually involves one or more employees in the process. This additional transfer can also increase the possibility that the mobility aids could be damaged during transit (another airline cost). Insufficient vertical transfer facilities can also lead to injuries to the baggage handlers charged with loading the mobility devices into the aircraft hold.

Consequences of inadequate airport facilities

The longer some passengers spend out of their customised wheelchairs and the more lifting transfers they have to undergo, the more they are liable to injury. If passengers are wheelchair dependent they should ideally remain in their personal wheelchair for as long as possible. Sitting in a standard airport wheelchair can mean that passengers could sustain injury or skin damage, particularly during transfers onto aircraft seats. Damaged skin heals very slowly in persons with spinal injuries and often requires a long period of hospitalisation for painful and debilitating pressure sores. On arrival at destination, wheelchair-dependent passengers (WCHCs) need their wheelchairs immediately and often for the lack of airport facilities this cannot be achieved. The passenger's best hope is that the chair arrives undamaged and ready in the Arrivals Hall. This did not happen to one quadriplegic passenger who, seated at the aircraft window on his outbound journey, watched his high-tech, customised wheelchair being crushed by heavy baggage during loading onto the luggage conveyor. His two-week trip was wrecked because he did not have his personalised wheelchair and, as a result of using a temporary replacement which did not fit him, his skin broke down into pressure sores that took months to heal. The airline eventually replaced his chair but it took many weeks of wrangling. The baggage loaders had no idea how much harm their carelessness caused. It was just that type of thoughtless activity which contributed to the pressure for regulation.

Airports' failures to instal moving pavements to transfer passengers across and around the airport mean that the airlines must provide supplementary assistance for PRMs who cannot walk long distances (the WCHR PRMs). Many PRMs can often manage to traverse a large airport independently if there are sufficient vertical and horizontal mobility facilities provided. Moving pavements can be designed to enable PRMs to manage gradients; vertical transfers (for the WCHS PRMs) can be assisted by elevators or escalators. Wheelchairs and a Mobility

Assistant are a lower-cost option for European airports because, as operating costs, they are reimbursed by the airlines.

If a passenger can maintain independent mobility then the costs to the airline are merely those of a mainstream passenger. In addition to vertical and horizontal mobility provisions, airports should help passengers maintain their independence by including tactile signage for visually impaired PRMs and induction loops for hearing impaired passengers. In silent terminals (with no boarding announcements) it is very difficult for the increasing numbers of ageing, deaf and visually impaired passengers to move independently – another facilities failure which adds to airlines' costs since they must supply the assistants to guide these passengers to their next transfer point.

Airports should also be able to accommodate the increasing number of travelling service animals by providing them with spaces to rest, water and toilet.

5.2 PRMs' RIGHTS AND AIRLINES' RESPONSIBILITIES

Logistical challenges

A distinction must be made between disabled and medical passengers (SSR code MEDA) who are also treated as 'disabled' for the purposes of airline services. Medical passengers should have a doctor's letter certifying that they are fit to fly and outlining their needs which might involve inflight attention. (It is often a requirement that the airline's own doctor also certifies some passengers as fit to fly.) If medical attention is known to be needed inflight, the passenger needs to supply someone – a friend, relative, nurse or carer – to assist them. This involves an extra cost for the passenger and can become an incentive to hide their medical needs from the airline. It is also possible that a passenger who checks-in as disabled becomes a mid-air medical emergency with any costs borne by the airline. Irrespective of type of disability, PRMs who can be self-reliant in the cabin can fly without a doctor's letter and without an attendant. Many medical passengers often need the services which are also provided to disabled passengers. MEDA passengers are more likely to cause an aircraft diversion due to medical emergencies such as heart attack or deep vein thrombosis (DVT), one of the causes of which is immobility on a long flight. The EU requires:

> The making of all reasonable efforts to arrange seating to meet the needs of individuals with disability or reduced mobility on request and subject to safety requirements and availability . . . Where a disabled person or person with reduced mobility is assisted by an accompanying person, the air carrier will make all reasonable efforts to give such person a seat next to the disabled person or person with reduced mobility (ANNEX II of Regulation (EC) No 1107/2006).

> (© European Union, 2006)[2] (see also Chapter 4)

Whilst understanding the sentiment, this is often impossible because other customers are able to check-in online in advance of travel. Currently the CRS cannot allocate seats far in advance for practical as well as technical reasons. In the event of an aircraft substitution, for example, the seating arrangements could also change. As another example, an obese person who purchases an extra seat might not always get what they believe has been contracted. Sometimes the CRS cannot allocate two adjacent seats at selection time. On one occasion, a 200kg passenger who had purchased two seats checked in late and was allocated two mid-seats in consecutive rows (29E and 30E). To add to his frustration, the new aircraft did not have fully retractable armrests in the economy cabin so that even two neighbouring seats would not have fulfilled his requirements. The airline eventually upgraded him to a wider seat in the business cabin by downgrading a staff passenger.

Human rights and PRMs

Travelling by air is perceived as an issue of equality of opportunity and social justice (Abeyratne, 2001; Shaw and Thomas, 2006) and therefore of positive social benefit. It enables PRMs to maximise their participation in mainstream economic activity. By participating in air travel, disabled people can exercise their independence and choice, making their own decisions about what suits them best. However, the rights of PRMs can sometimes impact on the human rights of other passengers and sometimes the human rights of the staff employed to assist them. Solving one passenger problem can create a problem for other passengers and employees. Advanced-world governments aim for ill-defined social justice, which is why safeguards are often placed into many privatising government enterprises. 'The future cost of air transport . . . has important implications for social and spatial equity . . . [and] highlights the transformation of many people's desire for air travel into a consumer expectation, a norm, or even a "right"' (Shaw and Thomas, 2006: 209). There are many advocacy groups with the aim of enabling disabled people to access the skies as a right; however, the corresponding social and economic responsibilities frequently fall to the airlines. There are also challenges for equality of treatment as illustrated by an incident in 2013. An Auckland to Wellington (New Zealand) flight was delayed when a passenger who had checked in ahead of a wheelchair user did not want to surrender her front-row seat (1A) to accommodate the disabled passenger who had been allocated a seat three rows behind. Seat 1A had additional legroom which the premium passenger felt better suited her requirements. The crew tried to persuade her to move but she would not relent. The disabled passenger went to the press claiming 'I felt humiliated. For anybody with a disability to be humiliated . . . it destroyed my faith in humanity for the day' (Deane, 2013). The passenger in 1A also had her rights and she might even have had an undisclosed disability. Whose rights were superior and judged by what criteria? Legislation cannot cover every eventuality when one person's human rights become another person's responsibilities.

Airline employees' rights and PRMs' rights

There is often conflict between the rights of PRMs and those of airline employees. Airlines, as employers, have a duty of care to their employees to avoid injuring them in the course of their employment. Airlines have generally restricted the maximum weight of luggage to avoid injury to the baggage handlers; however, in contrast the UK Mobility Assistants are not restricted by law to the weights they can carry. They are often placed in unenviable situations where their human rights are compromised because of their duty to a PRM. As an example, an immobile and obese passenger has the 'right' to fly but the airline (or Mobility Assistants on its behalf) has the responsibility to lift him/her safely into the aircraft seat. Manoeuvring a very obese passenger from the bariatric airport wheelchair to the narrower aisle-wide, on-board wheelchair and finally into a (usually economy) seat can cause back injuries to the manual lifters. The provision of the wider bariatric chair as far as the aircraft door does not act as a filter for either the aircraft's transfer wheelchair or the narrower aircraft seat. If the allocated seat is a window seat and the passenger is immobile, it is often very challenging for the Mobility Assistants to lift the PRMs over the armrests and onto the seat. However, if it is an aisle seat which has been allocated, the passenger can impede access and egress for neighbouring passengers particularly in an emergency (another challenge for rights vs responsibilities).

Many PRMs use motorised mobility scooters and wheelchairs, which did not exist when the original pioneering manual wheelchair users originally supported regulating their air travel. The invention and democratisation of personal motorised mobility scooters has helped many PRMs (both those with age and non-age-related physical disabilities) to retain or regain their independence. Some of this equipment is not only heavy (and weight takes fuel to move it) but also takes a significant amount of space in the aircraft hold. Furthermore, motorised mobility equipment has batteries which must be safely disconnected, packaged (the responsibility of the airline or its contractor) and then reconnected at destination (Table 5.2). Batteries contain liquids or gels which could be extremely dangerous to the aircraft if spilt (and expensive to remedy). These packaging requirements are a particularly onerous burden on a carrier but it is more efficient than cleaning up after a spill. There are also other hazards with transporting this equipment. In 2008, at Manchester Airport, UK, the aircraft loaders saw blue sparks emanating from a motorised mobility aid:

> The device was removed from the aircraft and placed on a baggage belt vehicle where it immediately burst into flames and was destroyed. From subsequent investigations, it appeared that the device's electrical circuit had not been protected from inadvertent operation prior to loading. It was probable that, during flight, baggage moved the control joystick causing the motor to be engaged thus causing friction or an electrical load causing ignition. Since the 2008 incident, the CAA has received over 70 further reports concerning electric mobility aids where the requirements of the . . . ICAO Technical Instructions had not been complied with.
>
> (CAA, 2012: 1)

The responsibility for safe handling of such mobility aids lies with the airline and requires dangerous goods training for relevant staff.

Heavy motorised mobility aids also pose a challenge to the human rights of aircraft loaders. The UK CAA (2012: 5) recognises that the 'manual handling of heavy electric mobility aids during the loading process can pose a risk of musculoskeletal disorder to the staff involved.' However, 'manual handling concerns are not a legally permissible reason for failing to comply with the PRM Regulations so loading of a mobility aid cannot be refused because of such concerns' (CAA, 2012: 5). The rights of airline employees are therefore overridden by the rights of PRMs. By solving one challenge, the legislation has created another. This is equality and social justice – but for whom? What happens if the aircraft loaders are disabled by lifting heavy PRM equipment? What rights and remedies are available for them?

Cabin crew are not permitted either to lift passengers or to assist with toileting, which often causes much frustration for PRMs. The EU agrees: 'for the safety of crew and passengers cabin crew must not lift passengers . . . passengers requiring lifting must travel with personal assistant(s) capable of providing this assistance' (Department for Transport, 2008: 73). However, the EU in ANNEX II of Regulation (EC) No 1107/2006 (Department for Transport, 2008: 70) has decreed that crew will offer 'assistance in moving to toilet facilities if required'. This involves transfer onto the aircraft's aisle-width wheelchair and pushing it to the lavatory (the most common need for PRMs for flight attendant assistance (Wang and Cole, 2013)) and precisely what the crew should not do. Scheduling physically stronger crews can be a challenge for some of the carriers which are renowned for their petite cabin attendants (and female employees are more amenable to assisting PRMs than males (Chang and Chen, 2012b)).

5.3 PASSENGER SPECIFICS

Ageing passengers

The population is ageing. Older able-bodied passengers are a potentially profitable airline market as they are able to use off-peak travel when there is spare aircraft capacity, are price sensitive and often book close to departure date. Increasing numbers of elderly people are travelling to more and further destinations than ever before. It is predicted that between 2000 and 2050, the proportion of the world's population who are over 60 could double from about 11% to 22%, increasing from 605 million to 2 billion (WHO, 2012), with the fastest growth in the proportion of people older than 85.

There are few analyses. A survey of 203 Taiwanese travellers over 65 years of age outlined the characteristics of elderly airline passengers, which included problems with vision, hearing, cognitive capabilities, physical strength and inability to walk long distances (Chang and Chen, 2012a). In air travel these characteristics manifest as stiff joints, reduced flexibility, slower walking and reduced mental processing, all of which could require individualised passenger support. The management of growing numbers of ageing passengers' health in flight could also require new skills to enable crew to respond to increasing numbers of medical emergencies (Stefanacci, 2012). Upcoming seniors (born between 1946 and 1964) are over-represented in the overweight and obese categories of chronic disease and risk factors compared to the rest of the population (Hugo *et al.*, 2008). The increased incidents of chronic illness, mental incapacity and disability could destabilise national health systems with the extra costs to be incurred (Hugo *et al.*, 2008) and would also place a burden on airlines. There is also a link between obesity, disability and dementia, and elderly passengers with psychiatric disorders can pose particular challenges for cabin crew.

> Many of the very old lose their ability to live independently because of limited mobility, frailty or other physical or mental health problems. Worldwide, there will be a dramatic increase in the number of people with dementias such as Alzheimer's disease, [and] as people live longer. . . the risk of dementia rises sharply with age with an estimated 25–30% of people aged 85 or older having some degree of cognitive decline.
>
> (WHO, 2012)

Such passengers can experience 'sundowning syndrome', where abnormal behaviours increase at certain times of the day, and the disorientation of long-haul travel can affect them disproportionately. In one incident, an 84-year-old Canadian dementia sufferer arrived alone at Gatwick Airport (UK) whereupon he was hand-cuffed and taken to an immigration detention centre to await deportation. Unfortunately his condition deteriorated and he died (Gander, 2014). He should never have been accepted for travel and certainly should not have been travelling without a carer. Whoever arranged his travel was culpable. Such elderly passengers should always be accompanied by a flight companion who can attend to their needs, otherwise the crew would have to assume the additional responsibility (Stefanacci, 2012). However, the crew's responsibility is primarily for safety, with customer service as a secondary feature. If they are attending to high-needs passengers then the remainder of the passenger cohort could receive a lower standard of service.

Increased affluence and cheaper airfares encourage increasing numbers of older people to travel (Low and Chan, 2002; Stefanacci, 2012). The aircraft cabin with its low oxygen, humidity and pressure can be unfavourable to elderly travellers. Older flyers can present multiple symptoms which alter their normal behaviour. 'Anxiety-provoking situations include flight delays, customs and baggage reclaim and aeroplane take-off and landing' (Low and Chan, 2002: 18). Other elderly passenger challenges present as medical hazards (including hypoxia, deep vein thrombosis, leg oedema, expansion of body gases and syncope) as well as physical challenges induced by frailty, requiring a longer time to prepare for a journey and more assistance with reading signs, listening for announcements and mobility (Table 5.5).

Table 5.5 represents challenges for economically sustainable airlines because ageing PRMs have the potential to become an economic burden – not just in terms of attention during flight – but also the additional services and facilities needed to assist them on departure and arrival.

Table 5.5 Some challenges of carrying ageing airline passengers

Ageing PRM problem and possible SSR codes	Manifestation	Passengers' needs
passengers with stiff joints (could be WCHS, WCHR or WCHC)	slower boarding and disembarking which can lead to slower aircraft turnaround times	• manually powered wheelchair push or motorised buggy to departure gate • ambulift for an aircraft off-jetty • on-board assistance • special meals • retractable armrests • more legroom
more elderly women travelling alone (MAAS)	ageing women lose their upper body strength more quickly than other strengths: this means that they cannot always lift hand luggage overhead or sometimes lift themselves out of their seats	• ground-based assistance with transfers between flights • possibly supplementary mobility assistance • cabin crew assistance to stow hand luggage and possibly to lift passengers out of their seats (conflicting with industry practice that crew must not lift either passengers or luggage and are uninsured if they are injured in doing so)
medical emergency in flight (e.g. stroke, heart attack) (MEDA)	disruption to aircraft routine as crew work with (and often around) a recumbent passenger	• urgent treatment either in the air and/or on the ground • supplementary mobility assistance • possible aircraft diversion
mental health (e.g. dementia) (MAAS or possibly even WCHC)	confusion and forgetfulness; possibly inappropriate behaviour	• travel companion or carer • mobility assistance to access the boarding gate (and also on disembarking) • cabin crew comfort and support

Exporting the fragile elderly

When the cost of care for elderly relatives becomes excessive, some families decide to send them on a one-way fare to other countries (e.g. the Philippines) where they are nurtured in low-cost, compassionate environments (Lacey and Foulkes, 2014). This is a new missing market which evolved from people living longer and to the age when they tend to become chronically ill. WHO (2012) noted that the need for long-term care is rising as many elderly people cannot look after themselves. It is not uncommon for some long-haul flights between UK and India or Australia to carry 100+ elderly PRMs (WCHRs, WCHSs and WCHCs) most of whom require wheelchair assistance before and after the flight and who might have required additional inflight attention. However, once PRMs are presented to the Check-in Agent they become the responsibility of the airline and can take advantage of the PRM provisions. Anecdotally, it is not unknown for families to arrive at the airport with their fragile, frightened relative and abandon them rather than wait to ensure successful check-in and departure. Some of these passengers are incapable of being self-reliant in the aircraft and therefore crew (in addition to their regular cabin duties) would be required to care for them. In the event that the flight is delayed or cancelled, the airline has the responsibility for someone who might not even be able to take care of their own needs or even communicate (because of language barriers, deafness or other communication disabilities). Furthermore, airline employees are not always trained to manage these difficulties. The responsibilities and costs of caring falls to the airline – before, during and after the flight – until the passengers are collected at destination. Similarly, if the flight is delayed for any significant period of time, the airline is responsible for accommodating the vulnerable passenger including providing a carer to ensure safety (see Chapter 3). Such welfare is expensive and can absorb more than one staff member before it is resolved. It could also prove to be very distressing for the passenger and it is irresponsible of the PRM's carers to expect the airline to carry such a risk. Furthermore, it is likely that because of the nature of the illness the passenger would not have been able to obtain travel insurance.

Obese passengers and social justice

Over many decades, many populations have become heavier and yet airline seats in the economy section (where most passengers sit) have mostly been reduced in size to fit more travellers into a fixed cabin space. 'One size fits all' seating enables airlines to access economies of scale and to reduce fares; however, passengers are not all one size.

The standard passenger weight including luggage is 105kg (Berdowski *et al.*, 2009) which is approximately 10kg heavier than 70 years ago. The 105kg averaged weight represents the passenger, their baggage and hand baggage allowances and illustrates the equality principle, whereby all passengers' weights are averaged and no one is penalised for excessive body weight – but it is not fair on those who are significantly under the weight (Bhatta, 2013). Once again, the concepts of social justice and fairness (see Chapter 3), the principle of 'user pays' and the workings of markets are challenged. The costs of transporting one passenger vary from airline to airline and depend on many factors which are airline specific (such as type of aircraft and seat configuration) and are covered by the fixed and variable costs (including fuel, maintenance, landing and parking fees, crew expenses and catering). Obesity is not always caused by overconsumption of foods and is not always a disability issue, although in the UK some obese people are able to obtain welfare benefits. However, branding 'obesity' as a disability places the passengers' additional travel costs onto the airline. Many larger people are disabled when travelling by air and claim airline assistance accordingly. There are no statistics on what proportion of PRMs is disabled by obesity (although it is estimated at one in four UK people

(Coleman, 2014)). Another consideration is the increased emissions per seat and the point loading on a single seat. Furthermore, extra weight requires extra fuel and burning extra fuel produces increased emissions. In 2013, Samoa Air (a small aircraft operator servicing islands around the Pacific Ocean rim) became the first airline to implement the weighing of passengers and charging them accordingly (an economic, social and environmental solution). This enabled accurate calculation of aircraft weight, economically efficient fuel loading and increased safety by allowing more even weight distribution. Their passengers disclose their weight at the time of internet booking and this is confirmed at the airport (Stuff, 2013). Equality legislation in other jurisdictions would probably veto weighing passengers, although charging for extra seats as required by larger passengers is acceptable.

Irrespective of what has caused the obesity, once the obese person has become a passenger they present the airline with customer service, economic and environmental challenges. Obese passengers claim they have a right to fly, but they also have a responsibility to ensure that they are accommodated in the space purchased, or they should acquire an extra or an upgraded seat. Some obese passengers need three economy seats (with additional seat belt extensions) for which some airlines allow a discount or a free seat if they purchase one seat. Most airlines have a policy regarding these passengers. United Airlines' policy is very clear:

> A customer is required to purchase an additional seat or upgrade if they do not meet one of the following criteria:
>
> The customer must be able to properly attach, buckle and wear the seat belt, with one extension if necessary, whenever the seatbelt sign is illuminated or as instructed by a crew member.
>
> The customer must be able to remain seated with the seat armrest(s) down for the entirety of the flight. The customer must not significantly encroach upon the adjacent seating space.
>
> (United Airlines, 2015)

In 2002, a Virgin Atlantic holidaymaker won £Stg13,000 compensation for severe internal bleeding, bruising and torn leg muscles after being squashed by an obese woman on an 11-hour flight. The claimant was seated next to a passenger who was so large that she could neither fit into her economy seat without the armrest raised nor use the lavatory during flight because of the narrow width of the door. Virgin recommended that particularly obese passengers book two seats; however, this was difficult to enforce because the airline rarely saw passengers before they turned up at the airport (Clark, 2002). Which passenger had rights that trumped the other's rights? Where did the corresponding responsibilities lie?

On the other hand, airlines might actually be able to help obese passengers as illustrated by the headline: 'A slimmer who vowed to lose weight after suffering the humiliation of needing a seat-belt extension on a plane has shed a sensational 10st. (140lbs)' (Winter, 2014). (In a piece of innovative thinking – would it help or humiliate if seat belts had waist measurement markings on them? What if the calorie content was written on the meal tray contents? What if the sweets and cakes available as meal tray desserts were replaced with a piece of fruit? What if passengers on long-haul flights were advised how much walking they would need to do at the transit airport to burn off the calorie content of their meal?)

Slim passengers complain on airline blogs that they are being charged for excess luggage weights when obese passengers are not charged for their extra body weight. This tips the issue of social justice in favour of the obese passengers. Slim passengers also complain about obese passengers encroaching on their seat space and it is indeed unfortunate that some obese passengers do not always disclose their need for additional seating at booking time. Furthermore, with internet booking it is often not until the passenger is at the check-in desk or even on the aircraft that the airline realises there might be a problem. This can make the journey extremely uncomfortable for neighbouring travellers if the flight is full and if there are no spare seats into which the heavier passenger can be decanted. Arguments for making seats wider would mean that airlines would have to charge more or lose revenue. Variations on a widened seat are available from aircraft manufacturers. Airbus, for example, has proposed one wider aisle seat by sacrificing space in the middle and window seats. This can lead to airline dilemmas such as whether to charge more for the larger seat (without contravening equalities legislation); whether they could charge less for the smaller seats; and how to handle the challenge posed by a passenger purchasing the smaller seat at lower cost and then discovering they were too large for it. Visual contact with the passenger would be essential, adding more complexity and costs into passenger processing. Technological progress means that a solution might eventually be available to charge fairly (i.e. social justice for underweight passengers) by using the Samoa Air weighing process.

Some airlines have not fully grasped the implications of ageing and obese passengers with regard to seat design and many have removed the option of fully retractable middle armrests. If the aircraft is empty, full retraction gives other passengers the opportunity to stretch and sleep across several seats as well as enabling access to the inner seats by those who are physically disabled. Department for Transport guidance recommends:

> that at least 50% of all aisle seats should have moveable armrests in aircraft with 30 or more seats. There might be less need to provide lifting armrests in cabins where the seat spacing allows for ease of movement in front of the seats.
>
> (Department for Transport, 2008: 64)

Is this perhaps an opening for official sanctioning of knee defenders (see Chapter 4)?

Medical emergencies and diversions

Over five years, some 10,000 inflight emergencies were identified in a European survey (Mattison and Zeidel, 2011) and now the chances of an inflight medical emergency are increasing with the advent of larger aircraft and more PRMs (an Airbus A380 can take over 800 passengers, although usually configured at around 500+). Coinciding with an ageing population, it is anticipated that aircraft capacities will increase and fares reduce, accompanied by the possibility that more elderly and sick passengers could be flying further more frequently, increasing the risk of medical incident (Tonks, 2008). Inflight emergencies are not recorded consistently from airline to airline. In 2008, for example, British Airways recorded 375 emergencies out of 36 million passengers (Tonks, 2008), which is obviously a very low proportion. However, that means 375 flights each carrying up to potentially 500 other passengers (i.e. in the worst case, potentially 187,500 people) who could have been inconvenienced by a diversion or delay, which magnifies the impact significantly. Fellow passengers might have missed cruise ship connections, business meetings, saying goodbye to dying relatives and a multitude of other events. The impact could also have had a multiplier effect on the people waiting to meet and greet these 187,500 passengers and the next cohorts waiting to embark. Is this social justice?

Dealing with an inflight emergency can be extremely difficult in a confined space without any real privacy for the patient. One study found that the most common diversion cause was suspected strokes, followed by chest pains from heart problems and deaths (Hung *et al.*, 2013) which are all conditions common to ageing, obese or medical passengers. Mid-air heart attacks are now survivable because many airlines carry defibrillators on board. However, sometimes, no matter how hard the crew try, passengers die. Many examples abound, including that of the passenger whose survival from a heart attack was compromised because his chest was too hairy to allow the immediate attachment of the defibrillator. By the time his chest was hair-free and the device in use, it was too late to save him (Laist.com, 2014).

The rate of inflight deaths and medical emergencies in older adults doubled between 2002 and 2005 (Stefanacci, 2012). There were 35 emergencies per one million passengers, of which cardiac issues accounted for the majority of inflight deaths. The decision to divert is humane, but there are economic consequences since landings can involve blowing tyres (if the aircraft is heavier than the recommended landing weight), jettisoning fuel (to obtain a safe landing weight), refuelling and re-catering or possibly even accommodating passengers and crew overnight. In extreme cases (as well as the costs already mentioned) the unrecoverable medical diversion costs can include despatch of replacement crew if the original crew are 'out of hours'. If the passenger load includes UMs and high-needs PRMs then they have to be specially accommodated in addition to the costs of the mainstream passenger group. This makes an aircraft diversion economically, socially and environmentally undesirable and another unrecoverable airline cost. Furthermore, if the flight schedule recovery is sufficiently delayed, it could have a knock-on effect onto future flights which could even trigger compensation for affected passengers under EC 261/2004.

In view of the foregoing, it was surprising to find that Alitalia has signed agreements with six specialised Italian health clinics to offer discounted rates to transport patients. The hospital provides a dedicated booking service for passengers and companions to obtain the 50% reduction on domestic return fares to selected medical destinations. The services provided would be outside of mainstream passenger costs but according to loss-making Alitalia these provisions will contribute to the airline's social responsibility programme (Alitalia, 2014) (a further justification for including the PRM costs in CSERplus-philanthropy totals). Can a loss-making airline afford such a social responsibility programme? Did Alitalia assess the economic impact? Was this the product of an incomplete internal decision-making (see Chapter 7) or was it implemented because majority-State-owned Alitalia was obligated to support national social policies? There was no mention of any State subsidy for this additional service, the provision of which supports Henderson's (2001) argument that increased CSERplus could do more harm than good. Subsequent to this programme commencement, Etihad Airways took a 49% stake in Alitalia. At the time of publication, the impact of this change of ownership on Alitalia's social programmes was unknown. When airlines work at the margins of profitability, such CSERplus gestures are economically challengeable (see Chapter 3).

Medical tourists

People who are already ill often travel to long-haul destinations for treatment for unstable medical or mental health conditions. Healthcare in developed nations is expensive and its spinoff industry, medical tourism (a previously missing market), is growing (Lunt *et al.*, 2013) facilitated and unheralded by airlines. The market value for medical tourism is estimated at around \$US40bn to \$US60bn annually and growing at around 20% p.a. (Lunt *et al.*, 2013). An estimated '3–4% of the world population already travels to foreign countries for medical treatment while the pent-up demand could be much larger with as many as 53% of Europeans saying they would travel abroad for treatment.' (IPK, 2012: 23). Medical- or health-related travel in 2011 accounted for approximately 9.4 million journeys (which was 2.4% of the total of European outward trips (IPK, 2012: 23). These visits were facilitated by agencies that specialised in all aspects of medical treatment including travel bookings, particularly from the ageing population in developed countries.

This clearly has an impact on airline economics. If it was a profitable market, airlines would chase it (see Table 4.1 in Chapter 4 and Table 5.6 in this chapter) but it is another example of a missing market based on asymmetric knowledge, fuelled by PRM regulations and underpinned by a profitable non-airline supply chain.

UK National Health Service (NHS)

The UK has the NHS, which is free at the point of use, and if sick people can afford a fare to the UK they can take advantage of the NHS. Since these people are ill, they are usually in need of airline assistance in order to travel so are classed as 'PRMs'. When patients can pay for their NHS treatment it can be profitable for the NHS. In 2010–2011, private income from international tourists at 18 NHS foundation trust hospitals was £Stg42m, which was 25% of the hospitals' total private income (Wise, 2013). Almost all of these patients would have travelled by air.

UK citizens are entitled to assorted surgical procedures delivered by the NHS, many of which are the result of ageing. Because of the population bulge, there are waiting lists for surgical repair of age-related procedures such as hip and knee replacements. To reduce the waiting lists, the UK NHS pays for many treatments abroad, whereupon the patients are often able to enjoy a holiday as well as excellent medical care. International air travel has become affordable and easy, and in 2010 more than 63,000 UK individuals chose to go abroad for treatment (Hanefeld *et al.*, 2013). Surgeries also include cardio, cosmetic, dental, orthopaedic and bariatric as well as in vitro fertilisation, and transplant of organs and tissues (Lunt *et al.*, 2013). Many ex-UK long-haul destinations are favoured: e.g. India for cardiology, bariatric surgery, knee and hip replacement; Pakistan, India and Turkey for organ transplantation; and Poland, Hungary, Turkey and Thailand for breast, face and liposuction cosmetic surgery (Lunt *et al.*, 2013; Gan and Frederick, 2013). In Europe, the leading surgical-import nations are Hungary, Germany and the Czech Republic (IPK, 2012). It will be of no consolation to airlines, but the medical tourism market is expected to rise, particularly to long-haul destinations (IPK, 2012), making these the most hazardous journeys for people who are already ill.

The NHS 'export payments' are an extension of the social justice principle. Rather than wait for the NHS to find a surgical operating slot for non-urgent treatments, UK residents who cannot afford the immediacy of private medical treatment can now have care abroad if the waiting period breaches the government's guidelines. It is predicted that increasing the UK outbound medical tourism trade with India alone would save the UK NHS from £Stg120m to £Stg200m ($US173m to $US286m or €155m to €256m) annually and reduce the UK waiting lists (Lunt *et al.*, 2013). Once again, airlines would be the enabler of this trade and an example of a missing market for which, because of government intervention, they will not be reimbursed for any additional costs. The 63,000 UK residents who opted for NHS-paid treatment abroad placed huge responsibilities and risks on the transferring carriers. Additional medical treatment either during or after travelling to developing or emerging countries is required by 8% of travellers, largely because of their inadequate understanding of the risks. This can involve flying in pain or discomfort, which has to be managed by the airline. These occurrences are statistically elusive as central records are not maintained. However, what is relevant in the context of economic airline sustainability is that one returning patient can require the attention of many of the cabin crew and this might involve lower levels of service to other passengers. It will also require significant complimentary service support at the airports on departure and arrival.

Tour operators sense the medical tourism business opportunity and advertise priority treatment at the airport and on board as a selling feature. They make the experience easy for patients by offering medical packages comprising consultation, surgery, recuperation, holiday/sightseeing, post-operative check-up and return fares to origin with complimentary airline PRM services. However, in an unintended consequence, an influx of medical tourists into advancing nations could force up the treatment prices for local patients. Medical tourism is lucrative for the receiving nations since many patients also become leisure tourists, with the resultant benefits to the local economy (a positive externality), but none of this would be possible without airlines enabling this often life-saving trade. South Africa provides many examples of this industry. Their international hospitals attract medical tourists, often with promises which are not always in their gift. One hospital in Cape Town promises its patients that after hip replacement, 'We will assist you in making sure that you receive the very best care from the airline on your flight home' (*Surgical Bliss*, 2015). This is a promise which will clearly be the airlines' to fulfil (without reimbursement).

Inbound medical tourists to UK

During 2010, some 52,000 overseas visitors travelled to the UK for medical treatment (Lunt *et al.*, 2013), which confirmed NHS doctors' fears that inbound health tourism to the UK was increasing (*The Economist*, 2013). The availability of cheap travel was considered to be one of the factors. In particular, passengers from Eastern Europe (short-haul) and West Africa (long-haul) were arriving for expensive treatments such as multiple births, complex maternity, cancer, kidney failure and HIV-AIDS treatment. Airlines are thus unwittingly complicit in undermining the NHS. Each of these passengers presents the risk of airborne medical emergency as well as additional servicing costs, which were originally established for a small number of wheelchair users. These sick passengers and their additional care represent extra airline risks and magnify the free rider principle.

Transplant tourism

Fulfilling another previously missing market is an industry of brokers who help potential transplant patients plan their medical trips for which air transport is an integral part (Lunt *et al.*, 2013). Broker assistance covers flights, hotels, treatment and recuperation, with some brokers extending into the organ supply market and paying cash to live donors for their unneeded organ or part organ. The donors are usually impoverished people from the advancing nations for whom the chance to earn some life-sustaining cash is not to be ignored. This is another example of an imperfect market where information is often asymmetric and the product not always homogeneous (see Chapter 1). Organs can also be obtained from 'presumed consent' which means that transplantable organs or tissues can be taken from a brain-dead person unless they have registered their disagreement before dying. Countries where there is presumed consent (e.g. Spain, Singapore) have shorter transplant waiting lists than countries where consent must be sought from the deceased's relatives. These countries can attract cash-rich but extremely sick patients who expect to fly to obtain life-saving treatments – and the airlines are expected to carry them (subject to medical disclosure) with the additional complimentary costs of service provision and mobility equipment carriage, as well as the risk of aircraft diversion. If the airline knew how sick some of the passengers were, they might refuse carriage, so the patient's better option is often not to disclose. As long as passengers' illnesses are not visible, they would be able to check-in as normal (with perhaps just buggy assistance to access the aircraft). The airline would be unaware until something went wrong. These passengers are unlikely to have medical insurance which covers their particular health problem, so diverting the aircraft and leaving them in a foreign land could create financial crises for the passenger and inconvenience for fellow passengers. This also raises the issue of passengers' rights and airlines' responsibilities.

PRM travel barriers

Studies have found that there are physical, communication and cost challenges to disabled people's intention to travel. Travel barriers for PRMs fall into three categories: economic (Can I afford to travel?), physical (Can I get to and through the airport?) and attitudinal (How will the staff treat me?) (Chang and Chen, 2012b). The top complaints regarding airline facilities and services in 2012 were: wheelchair services, on-board lavatory (not user-friendly, insufficient space and distance from passenger's seat), emergency evacuation information and consignment and retrieval of PRM's own wheelchair (Chang and Chen, 2012b). These complaints have service implications for carriers. Furthermore, PRMs did not like waiting in line for passport and security inspection and missing the chance to shop at the duty-free concessions due to time pressures on the ground staff assisting them (Chang and Chen, 2012b). If the Mobility Assistants take PRMs airport shopping, the airlines would in effect be subsidising the airports and the shopping concessions (another item for the airline-airport negotiation toolkit). Shopping in the duty-free concessions takes time and supports the airport; however, Mobility Assistants are either paid by the airline directly (USA) or by airlines to the contracting airport (e.g. UK and Europe) and not the retailers.

In 2004, UK wheelchair-user passenger Ross successfully claimed against low-cost carrier Ryanair for being charged to use an airport wheelchair from check-in desk to departure gate. As a result of *Ross v Ryanair Limited* (2004), disabled passenger services from car park or transport interchange are now supplied by the UK airport landlord through a service contractor. Consequently, carriers in Europe share an airport pool of motorised buggies and manually pushed wheelchairs managed by either the airport itself or outsourced providers on its behalf. All costs are recovered from a surcharge on passengers' fares. (Scandinavian carrier SAS vigorously defended and lost the demand for 20 million kroner (approximately £Stg1.7m, $US2.6m or €2.3m) for wheelchair services at Copenhagen Airport (Weaver, 2014).)

PRMs want more comfortable and spacious seats, and in particular many prefer the bulkhead seats where the infant cots are located (Wang and Cole, 2013). Which group – PRMs or parents – has the 'right' to those seats? PRMs also want lifting armrests on aisle seats for ease of access; however, what aircraft seating manufacturers can provide is not always what the airlines would order. Similarly, PRMs need to have their service expectations managed carefully because with more than one PRM on board, cabin crew might not be able to provide the personalised care each expects resulting in a perception of inadequate service (Wang and Cole, 2013).

Travel insurance and PRMs

The cost and/or availability of travel insurance can also be a barrier for PRMs. All passengers should carry travel insurance, but according to the Association of British Travel Agents (ABTA) (2013), the reality is that one in four people do not; and yet a conservative estimate is that 'between 30–50% of travellers become ill or injured whilst travelling' (Leggat *et al.*, 1999: 243). During travel, older men were more liable to have cardiovascular incidents and women were more likely to have accidents to their extremities possibly because of osteoporosis (Somer Kniestedt and Steffen, 2003). According to the Association of British Insurers (ABI), older travellers are more likely to have changing medical conditions so it can be difficult for insurers to provide a quotation for annual trip policies when the customer's health can change significantly during the life of the policy (ABI, 2014). However, this means that passengers' insurance options are reduced because purchasing single trip insurance can be very expensive. Since all pre-existing conditions must be declared, some elderly, obese and medical travellers might not be able to obtain medical insurance. Travellers need to know which destinations are safe for them if they have a chronic or acute medical condition because international aeromedi-cal evacuations cost upwards of \$US100,000 (€93,000 or £Stg70,000) irrespective of whether evacuation is on a commercial flight or a specially adapted aircraft (Leggat *et al.*, 1999; Stefanacci, 2012). However, when an illness or disability occurs during travel uninsured passengers might not be physically able to travel in the seat they have booked. This might invalidate their conditions of carriage, especially if they need extra space for such misfortunes as a broken leg. This leaves the economically sustainable airline with a problem – to honour the booking if the passenger needs more accommodation, or dishonour it and require the passenger to travel with a medical air carrier? Uninsured passengers deflect part of their financial risks onto their airlines.

For the UK, this means that the carrying airline subsidises risk-avoiding passengers, risk-averse travel insurers and risk-accepting UK NHS. This particular private airline social subsidy is also unheralded and if acknowledged, is actually increasing the number of UK State services privatised by stealth – an aspect of government policy opposed by many political parties (i.e. health politics vs airline economics). The UK and EU do not acknowledge that most airlines are privately owned and do not receive the subsidies awarded to ground transport providers. Increasing numbers of flying PRMs can only mean increased costs, making some carriers' fares more expensive. Increasing developed nations' privately owned airlines' fares can make them internationally uncompetitive with lower-cost nations' carriers, and yet if the fares do not increase, the shareholders' returns are further reduced and these airlines could become uneconomic 'zombie' carriers.

5.4 PRMs' MARKETS AND MYTHS

PRM markets

Estimates of the market size of this new generation of PRM travellers vary from country to country. In the UK, users of PRM airport services were approximately 1.75 million between July 2008 and March 2010 (CAA, 2010) with 80% travelling through one of the top five UK airports. In the USA, wheelchair assists from 2002 to 2011 increased over 13% each year, with just one airline alone at Newark averaging 35,000 assists per month. Most of these requests were from elderly travellers who could not queue to check-in, walk the long distances to the gate or navigate the airport without assistance. Furthermore, the use of mobility aids such as motorised scooters is rising faster than wheelchair use (Lipp and van Horn, 2013).

The obese PRM market is also growing. In 2013, WHO estimated that 'more than 1.4 billion adults were overweight in 2008 and more than half a billion obese', these figures having doubled between 1980 and 2008. The airline industry, unlike fellow passengers, is silent on obesity as it is regarded as a sensitive issue (Small and Harris, 2012). However, obese passengers were formerly another unidentified missing market:

> A former 50-stone man who was refused NHS bariatric surgery because he was not classed as sufficiently obese paid £Stg9,000 for a gastric sleeve procedure in India. At his heaviest [he] was three times heavier than the weight considered safe for his height. After losing 27 stone he returned to India to have his excess skin removed.
>
> (BBC News Wales, 2014)

Admittedly this PRM paid for four long-haul flights, but he was a risk for the carrier and any Mobility Assistants who might have had to lift him. Did carrying his risks and responsibilities outweigh the value of his custom to the airline (i.e. passenger rights vs airline social responsibilities and economic risks)?

PRM market value

The basis of the relevant regulations is that all PRMs are impoverished, cannot afford to pay for the full cost of their air services and are entitled to equalising complimentary airline services to fulfil the social justice requirements for air travel. CSERplus advocacy researchers are quick to indicate the potential size of the 'disability market' which is lucrative for most suppliers of sick or disabled people's products and services. In terms of value, the estimated spending power of UK disabled people is around £Stg80bn ($US123bn or €110bn) per year (Papworth Trust, 2014; Office for Disability Issues (ODI), 2012a). Similarly, the spending power of USA PRMs on airline travel alone was estimated at $US2.9bn (€2.7bn or £Stg1.9bn) annually (Lipp and van Horn, 2007). In the USA there are now estimated to be 54 million Americans with disabilities with an estimated spending power on all goods and services of $US220bn (€204bn or £Stg154bn) (Business Disability Forum, 2014). However, these optimistic assessments of spending power conflict with the often stated facts that people with disabilities are twice as likely to be in poverty as non-disabled adults and more likely to live in low-income households (Papworth Trust, 2014). In any event, additional air service provisions derived from an unfunded mandate cannot be charged to the users, meaning that airlines are unique among the privatised providers of products and services for disabled, sick or high-risk consumers. Passengers are price sensitive and increased fares have a social cost which can prevent travel for those who have lower incomes, especially since household income is the strongest determinant of whether people will fly. Therefore, when it is recognised that everybody benefits from travel, one wonders why governments (and the UK in particular) choose only to tax airfares while subsidising other forms of public transport. In short, government intervention in the market increases fares which might prohibit lower-earning consumers from enjoying the benefits of air travel. This is contrary to assorted governments' aims of increasing equality of opportunity and achieving social justice (i.e. political-social aims vs private-airline economic aims).

Impoverishment might have been the situation in the past; however, today's PRMs also include an ageing population which is prepared to spend money on leisure such as air travel. Many are newly retired and often have considerable pension spending power, although those over 65 are more price sensitive (Gan and Frederick, 2013). The 65+ age group could be a potentially lucrative market for airlines if they did not require any additional assistance to compensate for body weaknesses (ODI, 2012b). During the recession of 2008 to 2013 (precipitating many market failures) when the tourism industry was hard hit, the 65+ age group showed an increased participation rate of more than 10% over those five years. Their expenditure increased to account for 20% of all tourism spending by Europeans (vs 15% in 2006) totalling more than €53bn (£Stg40bn or $US57bn) on holidays (20% of the total spending of EU residents) (Demunter, 2012). Today's elderly travellers are possibly living on capital rather than their income since savings are not currently rewarded (0.5% Bank of England rate at time of publication). This means that their discretionary spend is also likely to be reduced and they could be flying on lower fares at a time when they would probably need extra airline services. Of concern to airlines is that by 2060 nearly 30% of the European population will be 65 or older. This group could possibly expand quickly and it is predicted they will spend generously on tourism.

Servicing the PRM market

The increasing numbers of disabled travellers, plus the development of legislation, has changed the airline focus from compassionate to regulated, with inherent costs (Table 5.2). PRMs who have to wait for airline assistance need seating areas, for which most airports apply rental charges to the airlines (another missing market). Consequently, since it is another cost, many airlines do not rent additional space, preferring to rely on prompt assistance from the mobility service operators to move the PRMs with minimal delay (which is also what travelling PRMs would prefer). However, Mobility Assistants are finite and cannot always appear when summoned (and if the passengers' needs have not been pre-notified then there is almost inevitably a delay). What was a complimentary service 20 years ago delivered with compassion for a few disabled people has become a substantial service for many more passengers than was ever envisaged.

Economies of scale

Handling PRMs with additional needs is a non-reimbursable activity for airlines that does not offer opportunities for economies of scale other than the airport buggy carrying several PRMs at once. The only economic means of handling increasing numbers of PRMs is to mainstream them – and that is impracticable because PRMs have a wide variety of individual and different requirements compared to non-PRMs. However, if each PRM has the standard economy luggage allowance of approximately 23kg plus motorised wheelchair weighing anything between 25–175kg (plus one other mobility aid as permissible by the Regulations), then the airline must absorb the costs of handling each passenger individually, including additional freight and fuel as well as funding any negative externality emissions.

Aircraft lavatory facilities

If passengers are unable to be self-reliant in the cabin, they must have a companion who can help with eating, drinking, emergency evacuation and using the lavatory. Toileting often requires access by means of an aisle-width wheelchair (if carried) and adaptations in the lavatory pod. However, what many PRMs really require are accessible lavatories to allow their companion to assist. Any space in an aircraft fuselage represents an opportunity to increase revenue and maintain competitive fares; however, accessible lavatories can often only be installed at the sacrifice of revenue-earning seats. Airbus Industries offer the option of a bi-fold door (operable by crew with a special key) between two lavatories to accommodate wider passengers and those needing assistance. This is a practicable and economic solution.

PRM service animal requirements

Changes in legislation in the USA, Canada and the EU ensure that assistance or therapeutic animals (including dogs, monkeys, pigs and even turkeys) are eligible to fly free of charge in the passenger cabin provided they have the correct documentation. However, it is believed that some passengers claim their pig, turkey or handbag dog are service animals to avoid paying for their carriage in the aircraft hold. Genuine working animals should only be handled by their owners and should be accommodated in sufficient space for the journey, especially if it is a long-haul flight. These animals could eventually travel for up to 15 hours in a cabin with insufficient space since few aircraft are configured to allow them to stretch in comfort. It is, however, possible to reconfigure wardrobe walls with a recess to allow a sleeping area for service animals, many of which are deprived of food and water to enable them to make a long journey without toileting. This is a stressful practice which is not endorsed by animal charities. Some service animals wear disposable diapers to help them survive the longer journeys in comfort. In a complication, some neighbouring passengers can be allergic to animals, which can pose a challenge for the crew and socially and economically sustainable airlines (see Chapter 4). Whose rights should triumph – those of the pet-owning PRM or the allergic passenger? Furthermore, it is also not unknown for animals to become part of the free rider problem. In 2000 a woman boarded an American Airways flight with a fully grown 127kg pig and claimed it was her 'therapeutic companion pet' using the rationale that the need was equivalent to a blind person having a guide dog (Davis, 2000). As it ran around the cabin it created mayhem. Similarly in 2014, US Airways disembarked a 36kg 'emotional support' pig and its owner before flight departure after the porcine passenger had been squealing uncontrollably and defecating on the cabin floor (Robinson, 2014). What is needed is an international permit system which certifies that the animal is service-trained and recognised as a qualified support animal.

Competition for PRMs

In the UK, suppliers of disability services and products are permitted to make a profit, and many of these enablements are sold at reduced rate (or are exempt from) VAT. Such exceptions establish a strong and profitable (formerly) missing market and in effect are a government-supported subsidy for the customers. In some countries, governments have recognised that a subsidy is required to fulfil a market for assorted products and services – and yet no similar financial assistance is given to the PRMs when purchasing airfares, or to the privately owned airlines which are providing the PRMs with complimentary public services. Vendors of disability products and services would not survive if they continuously made a loss. However, provision of airline services is not perceived in the same way as provision of other services or tangible products. Private hospitals, care homes, airport PRM service suppliers, crematoria and home care services make a profit from servicing the changing demographics. If airlines were allowed to increase PRMs' fares to cover their additional costs, the increases could push PRMs to fly with the lowest-cost carriers, i.e. the budget carriers or those from the advancing-world with their lower national social costs. This then would increase their operating costs and ultimately lead to an increase in their fares, possibly disproportionately and non-competitively in relation to developed world carriers. If any airline flies a disproportionate number of PRMs because of its reputation as a caring airline then its costs would be expected to be higher and unless it can cover these costs, its economic sustainability could be jeopardised and the returns to shareholders and rewards to employees would be lower.

Table 5.6 Porter's five forces in the PRM market (adapted from Porter (1979); see also IATA (2013b))

Porter's five forces of competitive intensity	Airline competition assessment for pursuit of PRM market	Threat summary
power of customers	PRMs have regulatory support and therefore have high customer power	high
power of suppliers	suppliers of PRM services such as the Mobility Assistants who push wheelchairs, drive the electric mobility buggies and lift PRMs also have regulatory support, therefore supplier bargaining power is high	high
rivalry among existing competitors	rivalry among carriers competing for PRMs is low	low
availability of substitutes	some PRM journeys are time critical so there is no substitute for air travel: threat from substitutes is low	low
threat of new entrants	no airline would supply solely for PRMs: the threat of new entrants disrupting the market is low	low

In another example of imperfect market operation – incorporating both missing markets and asymmetric knowledge – airlines neither compete for (nor pursue the market in) PRMs because the additional costs necessary for some PRMs could be disproportionate to the fare paid. There are many models under which the PRM market could be scrutinised including the previously discussed Kotler and Keller (2012) segmentation criteria (see Table 4.1 in Chapter 4) and Porter's (1979) five forces (Table 5.6), which is a framework for analysing the level of competition. This can be used to assess an industry's profitability and shape its firms' competitive strategies. Where customers have the power to demand more services at no extra charge (as the PRMs can because they are backed by regulations) then provision could lead to losses. Where there are near-monopoly suppliers (such as PRM Mobility Assistants at airports who are also backed by regulations) then suppliers have high bargaining power. In contrast, there is low competition for PRMs from rivals, few product substitutes and minimal threat from new entrants. However, the reality is that since the airlines cannot cover the higher costs as required by high-needs PRMs, the market has low prospects for profits. The conclusion is that there would be no active airline competition for this particular missing market because the power that lies with the customers and suppliers distorts its functioning.

Chasing the PRM market would be an economically unstable and unsustainable model. Paradoxically, delivering excellent customer service (the core competence – see Chapter 3) and attracting more PRMs could lose money for the best-servicing airline and thus creating a 'disabled airline'.

5.5 UNSPOKEN ISSUES

Safety and PRM evacuation

Airlines are faced with the paradox of wanting to establish a pleasant relaxed image of flying and yet ensuring that passengers are aware that there could be a frightening emergency.

One of the most sensitive issues to discuss when considering PRMs in the airline sustainability context is evacuation. There are no satisfactory answers. Evacuation of PRMs is an emotive social issue which goes unresolved because legislators avoid the topic. It is in the 'too politically sensitive' category and not available for sustainability-thinking (see Chapter 3 and Chapter 7). Disabled people are not included in aircraft manufacturers' evacuation tests. In a real evacuation, able-bodied passengers scramble over seats, pushing and shoving to evacuate, avoiding flames, fumes, smoke and/or water as well as other passengers. It is a frightening situation – but no matter how well trained the crew, panicking passengers' survival instincts can disrupt the most careful evacuation planning. Some airlines limit the number of severely disabled passengers they carry because of evacuation issues; however, flights of sick and disabled pilgrims (e.g. to Lourdes, France) can have 50% or more PRMs with their able-bodied carers making the balance. In the event of an accident, clearing the aircraft quickly would be extremely challenging.

A successful test evacuation has an aircraft emptied in 90 seconds with the 'passengers' often paid a bonus for successful exit. However, these tests do not reflect the more likely demographics of the aircraft cabin. There are no allowances for children, disabilities, language differences or behavioural challenges such as panic should an exit be blocked. Real evacuations can also be complicated by any service animals and their reaction in a very stressful situation. While the passengers have rights and the airline has their corresponding responsibilities, the location of rights and responsibilities for these valuable animals is not discussed.

Computer simulations have been used to model aircraft evacuations. In one simulation, two scenarios were tested: all exits available and only one side of exits operable. The simulations also took account of passengers' physical characteristics (able-bodied and a randomly generated selection of disabled passengers) and found that passengers with disabilities (ranging from hearing, vision, ambulatory and cognitive difficulties through to self-care and independent living challenges) had a significant impact on the evacuation process in both scenarios (Liu *et al.*, 2014). Furthermore, in an aircraft emergency, passengers can be immobilised by fear, inaction or panic or alternatively, could seek lost friends and family or altruistically support the evacuation of others (Chang, 2012). The role of trained, calm and willing cabin crew is critical to swift, safe evacuation and survivability. However, PRMs pose a safety risk for a complete evacuation (Chang, 2012) because their slower moving speed would most likely delay other passengers. Passengers' physical characteristics such as girth, sex, age and mobility also have an impact on egress time whereas group density, passenger height and location of the open exit have minimal influence. However, disabled and ill passengers cannot be seated next to an emergency exit despite the understandable desire for them to have a fast evacuation (Chang and Yang, 2011). PRMs could prevent safe exit for the majority of passengers in the scramble to evacuate as quickly as possible and in real emergency situations, PRMs have slowed evacuation speeds. In 1968, BOAC Flight 712 departed London Heathrow bound for Sydney when an engine failed during take-off. The aircraft landed and emergency chutes were deployed. One of the five people who died was a stewardess who sacrificed her life attempting to rescue a PRM. Similarly, in 2007, one of the engines on China Airways' Flight 120 began smoking on landing in Japan. All 157 passengers and 8 crew were safely evacuated through emergency slides, although it was subsequently found that a PRM in the middle section was not given prompt attention by the crew, leaving him fearful that he would not escape. Furthermore, one exit was blocked by carry-on baggage, and a disabled passenger and an 80-year-old man caused an obstruction for approximately 60 seconds (Chang and Yang, 2011). In 2012, Air Berlin refused to carry six disabled passengers and their five carers flying from Moscow to Dusseldorf because the Captain invoked the airline's restriction of four PRMs per flight. This is reduced to two per flight if the PRMs are unable to move around the cabin, although it is reportedly unclear if this applies to accompanied PRMs. The airline offered alternatives and noted the issue as one of communication failure (Castiglioni, 2012). Similarly, in 2013, Thomson Holidays refused travel to two self-reliant blind passengers who were planning to travel without a carer. The Regulation did not require them to travel with a companion unless they were unable to fulfil safety-related actions such as being able to use the life jacket unaided. On this basis, Thomson correctly adhered to the requirements of the UKs Department of Transport's Code of Practice (Cooper, 2013).

Disability discrimination challenges

Airlines cannot by law discriminate against passengers except where carrying them poses a danger or where PRMs cannot physically access the aircraft. All passengers must be able to sit upright for take-off and landing as required by Regulations. Unfortunately, some PRMs cannot be accommodated because of such disabilities as stiff limbs (which are not allowed to block the aisles) or some back injuries. However, this is changing. At the time of publication, Qantas was seeking regulatory approval for a Business Class seat which can recline during take-off and landing, which could be useful for these particular PRMs (Kollau, 2015).

Disability discrimination challenges are frequent and often unresolvable. Many have been created by the unfunded mandates and others by human rights legislation or lack of common sense. Passengers who are less than average height (such as those with dwarfism) have been known to ask for discounted fares because they are the same size and have the same needs as travelling children (who often pay 50% fare or less). This is a reasonable request. Similarly, there is no logic for charging a child's fare for a youth who is taller than average when he occupies the same space as an adult. Charging by age might not be socially just, whereas charging by weight might be fairer and could include any additional emissions discharged by increased fuel needed (see Chapter 6). These are unresolved economic and social equalities issues.

Escorts are needed if passengers cannot be self-reliant in the confines of the aircraft cabin. Campaigners complain that since disabled passengers have lower incomes, their escorts or assistants should receive lower fares (a suggestion which contradicts the proponents who emphasise the potential market for PRMs' spending). There is some sympathy for this argument and many airlines do allow a lower fare for PRMs' companions; however, the Check-in Agent is not in a position to argue this case at the airport, especially if bookings were made online. In competitive markets, discounts are offered as a means to attract more business, but in the case of PRMs, offering discounted companion fares would be one means of ensuring that the passenger has the necessary on-board assistance, thereby reducing potential demands on the crew.

5.6 SOLUTIONS?

Controversial approaches

The challenges posed to airlines by PRMs cannot be underestimated, either in terms of economics (costs including facilities and services such as boarding, deplaning, freight and diversions), society (human rights and safety of PRMs and the airline employees charged with lifting them) or environment (the emissions expended carrying extra weights). The situation cannot continue as it is because the open-ended costs and anticipated growth in PRM numbers will reduce overall welfare. Airlines, airports, medical and mobility equipment suppliers as well as national, multi-national and supranational governments and the PRMs themselves all have a role to play. Possible solutions for some of the challenges from the key stakeholders include the following:

Airlines

Airlines could consider:

- calculating the costs of carrying PRMs (Table 5.2) so they have a basis for future regulatory discussions
- requiring mandatory pre-notification of passenger needs and mobility aids (including weights and packaging needs)
- applying filters at booking time to eliminate free riders (people and animals)
- lobbying regulators to limit the number of PRMs per aircraft because of (a) needing more crew for safety, thereby increasing operating costs and (b) ensuring a higher probability of safe evacuation. (This would also distribute PRM costs around more airlines and could deter unentitled users from availing themselves of the benefits of disability entitlements.)
- including PRMs' supplementary costs in the philanthropic totals at financial year end
- developing appropriate spaces for service animals in the cabins

- investigating a permit system which certifies service animals as trained and genuinely required by the handler's specific disability
- investigating the legality of any regulations for which no economic analysis was ever undertaken
- examining the implications of increasing the 105kg passenger limit to reflect the changes in society.

Airport mobility enablers

Airports could be permitted to sell their services to buggy-riding passengers just the same as other airport concessionaires, e.g. £Stg10 per transfer (genuinely disabled people can reclaim it from their welfare-oriented States).

PRM equipment suppliers

Equipment suppliers could consider innovating to devise airline-friendly mobility equipment (collapsible, lightweight with a battery which neither spontaneously combusts nor requires special packaging, disconnection and reconnection).

Governments

Governments could consider:

- consulting with the commercial airline stakeholders as well as the PRMs and their advocates before any future regulating
- calculating the retrospective economic impacts for existing regulations using Table 5.2
- developing a PRM filter system as happens with disability concessions in the UK with qualifying identification presented at check-in before any extra equipment can be carried or complimentary buggy service provided. (It would need some innovative problem-solving with regards to PRMs from non-compliant nations and it would also be needed for legitimate exemptions under EC 1107/2006 paragraph 18a.)
- authorising mandatory, pre-notification of PRMs' needs and mobility aids (including notification of weights and packaging needs)
- providing for entitled PRMs to hire heavy equipment (e.g. electric mobility scooters) at destination airports so airlines avoid the costs of freighting, dismantling and reassembly of the mobility device including battery packaging, disconnection and reconnection. It would also reduce emissions because it would be saving weight (see Chapter 6).
- developing human rights for those who have to handle extreme weights in a confined working space (to prevent their injuries) and assign the appropriate responsibilities to those who use the services
- allowing tax deductions for any on-board PRM fixtures and fittings (as happens with some airport PRM installations in various jurisdictions) and tax rebates for any PRM services provided

- subsidising PRM services provided by airlines flying out of any jurisdiction which is impacted by PRM regulations ahead of considering the removal of any national ground transport subsidies (i.e. equality of opportunity)
- relieving registered PRMs of air taxes (e.g. APD) so the qualifying passengers could then apply this relief to paying for any airport services and by doing so, the State would be taking a stake in the process. This would be over and above the provisions in clause 18a of EC 1107/2006 (i.e. 'carers should not be subject to the payment of the relevant airport departure tax').

Passengers

PRMs must consider the responsibilities which are commensurate with their rights in order to ensure that Mobility Assistants will not be injured in the course of their employment.

So what?

This sensitive topic needs to be aired using openness and transparency (i.e. sustainability-thinking – see Chapter 7) in the context of how a caring society really looks after its less able citizens. It is an economic, social, environmental and governance issue. Without any economic impact analysis, national, multi-national and supranational governments intervened in the market, requiring airlines to support social justice (equality and equity). The challenges of political-social pursuit and private economic airline delivery of equality, human rights and responsibilities for entitled and unentitled PRMs are unresolved. The airline industry appears reluctant to discuss these issues because it fears a backlash. Governments use statistics to plan resource allocations for society and yet, in contrast, the airlines cannot plan for PRMs because the projected need for support is unquantifiable and unconstrained. Any future national, multi-national or supranational government and industry negotiations of public benefits should include the private costs of the unfunded PRM mandates (i.e. the economic, social and environmental dimensions) as a trade-off for any concessions granted under any of the other dimensions.

Privately owned organisations usually make profits from selling the products and services which support disabled people, but private airlines are obliged to provide disability services without charging the users (whether entitled or unentitled) for either their costs or negative externalities. This makes airlines unique among commercial organisations. Furthermore, legislation and regulations cannot cover every eventuality when one person's human rights become another person's responsibilities. If the fares increase to cover PRMs' costs then fewer economically deprived PRMs might be able to afford to travel. Alternatively, PRMs might travel with lower-cost airlines, which in the worst case would disproportionately increase their handling costs. These would have to be recovered by increasing fares, which would affect their competitiveness. If the fares did not increase, the airlines could even become uneconomic 'zombie' carriers, returning less to the shareholders and employees. Airline profitability has been weakened by the boondoggles and unfunded mandates which could eventually make airlines in the developed world uncompetitive and economically unsustainable. Flying would once again be the preserve of the rich travelling on advancing-world airlines. The problem is manageable for now but with the increase in ageing and obese populations it could escalate beyond what is reasonable. There are no easy or politically acceptable answers to the air travel challenges posed by this new generation of PRMs. What is regretful is that the altruistic support given willingly (but sometimes, mistakenly) to a small number of manual wheelchair users has become regulated by politicians and abused by unentitled users. Bureaucratic, mandated, universal welfare has usurped kindness. A society built on kindness is more compassionate than one built on regulation. Eventually, these particular unfunded mandates might have the reverse effect to their intention.

Notes

1   © Only European Union legislation printed in the paper edition of the Official Journal of the European Union is deemed authentic European Union, http://eur-lex.europa/eu/
2   © Only European Union legislation printed in the paper edition of the Official Journal of the European Union is deemed authentic European Union, http://eur-lex.europa/eu/

References

Abeyratne, R. (2001), Ethical and moral considerations of airline management, *Journal of Air Transport Management* 7(6) 339–348 available from http://www.sciencedirect.com/science/article/pii/S0969699701000199 accessed 3 January 2015

Airport Operators Association (AOA) (2009), *Airport Operators response to CAA Review of PRM Regulation Implementation* available from http://www.caa.co.uk/docs/5/ergdocs/PRMAOA.pdf accessed 4 May 2013

Alitalia (2014), *Alitalia special rates to reach excellent specialized health clinic* available from http://corporate.alitalia.it/en/media/press-releases/09-09-2014.html accessed 18 September 2014

Ancell, D. and Graham, A. (2016), A framework for evaluating the European airline costs of disabled persons and persons with reduced mobility, *Journal of Air Transport Management* 50 41–44 available from http://www.sciencedirect.com/science/article/pii/S0969699715001179 accessed 10 March 2016

Association of British Insurers (ABI) (2014), *Age and travel insurance* available from https://www.abi.org.uk/Insurance-and-savings/Topics-and-issues/How-insurance-is-priced/Risk-pricing-characteristics/Risk-pricing-and-age/Age-and-travel-insurance accessed 9 April 2014

Association of British Travel Agents (ABTA) (2013), *ABTA updates travel insurance guidance following survey* available from http://travelbulletin.co.uk/news-mainmenu/abta-updates-travel-insurance-guidance-following-survey accessed 24 April 2013

BBC News Wales (2014), *Former 50 stone man frustrated at NHS surgery rules*, 5 August available from http://www.bbc.co.uk/news/uk-wales-28642696 accessed 4 September 2014

Berdowski, Z., van den Broek-Serlé, F.N., Jetten, J.T., Kawabata, Y., Schoemaker, J.T. and Versteegh, R. (2009), *Survey on standard weights of passengers and baggage: final report* available from http://www.easa.europa.eu/system/files/dfu/Weight%20Survey%20R20090095%20Final.pdf accessed 10 March 2015

Bhatta, B.P. (2013), Pay-as-you-weigh pricing of an air ticket: economics and major issues for discussion and investigations, *Journal of Revenue & Pricing Management* 12 103–119 available from http://www.palgrave-journals.com/rpm/journal/v12/n2/abs/rpm201247a.html accessed 1 January 2015

Business Disability Forum (2014), *A market you can't ignore* available from http://business disabilityforum.org.uk/customer-experience/the-evidence accessed 4 April 2015

Cambridge Economic Policy Associates (2010), *The extent to which airlines' interests are aligned with those of passengers* available from https://www.gov.uk/government/uploads/system/uploads/attachment_data/file/3196/airline-and-passenger-interests.pdf accessed 5 May 2014

Castiglioni, R. (2012), *Air Berlin throws group of disabled passengers off flight* available from http://www.reducedmobility.eu/20121008256/The-News/air-berlin-throws-group-of-disabled-passengers-off-flight.html accessed 2 January 2015

Chang, Y.-C. (2012), Cabin safety behavioural intentions of passengers with reduced mobility, *Journal of Air Transport Management* 25 64–66 available from http://www.science direct.com/science/article/pii/S0969699712001147 accessed 2 January 2015

Chang, Y.-C. and Chen, C.-F. (2012a), Service needs of elderly air passengers, *Journal of Air Transport Management* 18(1) 26–29 available from http://www.sciencedirect.com/science/article/pii/S0969699711000834 accessed 3 January 2015

Chang, Y.-C. and Chen, C.-F. (2012b), Meeting the needs of disabled air passengers: factors that facilitate help from airlines and airports, *Tourism Management* 33(3) 529–536 available from http://www.sciencedirect.com/science/article/pii/S0261517711001130 accessed 3 January 2015

Chang, Y.-H. and Yang, H.-H. (2011), Cabin safety and emergency evacuation: passenger experience of flight CI-12 accident, *Accident Analysis and Prevention* 43(3) 1,049–1,055 available from http://www.sciencedirect.com/science/article/pii/S0001457510003866 accessed 3 January 2015

Civil Aviation Authority (CAA) (2010), *Accessible Air Travel* available from www.caa.co.uk/accessibleairtravel accessed 10 April 2013

Civil Aviation Authority (CAA) (2012), *Civil Aviation Safety Notice number: SN-2012–13 – Safety Requirements Applicable to the Carriage of Electric Mobility Aids* available from http://www.caa.co.uk/docs/33/SafetyNotice2012003.pdf accessed 27 January 2014

Clark, A. (2002), *Woman squashed on long flight gets £13,000* available from http://www.the guardian.com/business/2002/oct/22/theairlineindustry.travelnews accessed 24 April 2014

Coleman, C. (2014), *Obesity 'could be a disability' EU Courts rule* available from http://www.bbc.co.uk/news/health-30529791 accessed 19 December 2014

Cooper, R. (2013), *Blind friends told by Thomson Holidays they can't fly to Majorca because they won't be able to see the safety demonstration* available from http://www.dailymail.co.uk/news/article-2317564/Blind-friends-told-Thomson-Holidays-fly-Majorca-wont-able-safety-demonstration.html#ixzz305EbLim4 accessed 27 April 2014

Davis, S. (2000), *Pigs might fly but never again on American Airlines* available from http://www.telegraph.co.uk/news/worldnews/asia/1372494/Pigs-might-fly-.-.-.-but-never-again-on-American-airline.html accessed 7 December 2014

Deane, S. (2013), 'Elite' flyer refuses to give up her seat, *New Zealand Herald*, 16 May available from http://www.nzherald.co.nz/nz/news/article.cfm?c_id=1&objectid=10883942 accessed 24 April 2014

Demunter, C. (2012), *Europeans aged 65+ spent a third more on tourism in 2011 compared with 2006: ageing and tourism in the European Union*, Eurostat Statistics in Focus 43.2012 available from http://ec.europa.eu/eurostat/en/web/products-statistics-in-focus/-/KS-SF-12–043 accessed 3 January 2015

Department for Transport (2008), *Access to air travel for disabled persons and persons with reduced mobility – Code of Practice* available from http://www.ukaccs.info/accesstoairtravelfor disabled.pdf accessed 25 April 2013

Department of Transportation (2014), *U.S. Department of Transportation issues final rule regarding air travel with musical instruments* available from http://www.dot.gov/briefing-room/us-department-transportation-issues-final-rule-regarding-air-travel-musical accessed 7 January 2015

Doganis, R. (2001), *The airline business in the 21st century*, London, Routledge

Economist, The (2013), *Free-for-all: doctors fear that health tourism in the NHS is growing* available from http://www.economist.com/news/britain/21578707-doctors-fear-health-tourism-nhs-growing-free-all accessed 10 April 2014

European Union (2006), *Regulation (EC) No 1107/2006 of the European Parliament and of the Council* available from http://eur-lex.europa.eu/legal-content/EN/ALL/?uri=CELEX: 32006R1107 accessed 4 January 2015

European Union (2014), *Compensation and assistance to passengers in the event of denied boarding and of cancellation or long delay of flight* available from http://www.europarl.europa.eu/sides/getDoc.do?pubRef=-//EP//TEXT+TA+P7-TA-2014-0092+0+DOC+XML+V0//EN accessed 5 July 2014

Gan, L.L. and Frederick, J.R. (2013), Medical Tourists: who goes and what motivates them? *Health Marketing Quarterly* 30(2) 177–194 available from http://www.ncbi.nlm.nih.gov/pubmed/23697856 accessed 2 January 2015

Gander, K. (2014), *84 year old dementia patient died in handcuffs at immigration detention centre* available from http://www.independent.co.uk/news/uk/home-news/84yearold-dementia-patient-died-in-handcuffs-at-immigration-detention-centre-9063548.html accessed 5 September 2014

Hanefeld, J., Horsfall, D., Lunt, N. and Smith, R. (2013), Medical tourism: a cost or benefit to the NHS? *PLOS ONE* 8(10) available from http://www.plosone.org/article/info%3Adoi%2F10.1371%2Fjournal.pone.0070406 accessed 25 October 2014

Henderson, D. (2001), *Misguided virtue: false notions of corporate responsibility*, The Institute of Economic Affairs available from http://www.iea.org.uk/publications/research/misguided-virtue-false-notions-of-corporate-social-responsibility accessed 7 October 2014

Hugo, G., Taylor, A. and Dal Grande, E. (2008), Are baby boomers booming too much? An epidemiological description of overweight and obese baby boomers, *Obesity Research & Clinical Practice* 2(3) 203–214 available from http://www.sciencedirect.com/science/article/pii/S1871403X08000379 accessed 3 January2015

Hung, K., Cocks, R., Poon, W., Chan, E., Rainer, T. and Graham, C. (2013), Medical volunteers in commercial flight medical diversions, *Aviation Space Environmental Medicine* 84(5) 491–497 available from http://www.ncbi.nlm.nih.gov/pubmed/23713215 accessed 3 January 2015

Husted, B. and Salazar, J.J. (2006), Taking Friedman seriously: maximizing profits and social performance, *Journal of Management Studies* 43(1) 75–91 available from http://onlinelibrary.wiley.com/doi/10.1111/j.1467–6486.2006.00583.x/abstract accessed 1 January 2015

International Air Transport Association (IATA) (2013a), *Airlines Expect 31% Rise in Passenger Demand by 2017 Press Release No. 67 Date: 10 December 2013* available from http://www.iata.org/pressroom/pr/Pages/2013–12–10–01.aspx accessed 18 June 2014

International Air Transport Association (IATA) (2013b), *Profitability and the air transport value chain, IATA economics briefing No 10* available from http://www.iata.org/whatwedo/Documents/economics/profitability-and-the-air-transport-value%20chain.pdf accessed 1 April 2014

International Air Transport Association (IATA) (2013c), *IATA Interline Reservations Messages Procedures – Passenger (AIRIMP)* available from http://www.iata.org/publications/Pages/airimp.aspx accessed 16 January 2016

International Transport Forum (ITF) (2011), *Mobility: rights obligations and equity in and [sic] ageing society: discussion paper 2011 05* available from http://www.internationaltransportforum.org/jtrc/DiscussionPapers/DP201105.pdf accessed 21 April 2014

IPK (2012), *ITB World Travel Trends Report 2012–13* available from http://www.itb-berlin.de/media/itbk/itbk_dl_all/itbk_dl_all_itbkongress/itbk_dl_all_itbkongress_itbkongress365/itbk_dl_all_itbkongress_itbkongress365_itblibrary/itbk_dl_all_itbkongress_itbkongres s365_itblibrary_studien/ITB_World_Travel_Trends_Report_2012_2013.pdf accessed 3 March 2015

Kotler, P. and Keller, K.L. (2012), *Marketing management*, 14th ed., Upper Saddle River, New Jersey, Pearson Education

Kollau, R. (2015), *Qantas new A330 business suite to offer 'gate-to-gate' recline* available from http://www.airlinetrends.com/2014/12/09/qantas-new-a330-business-suite-to-offer-gate-to-gate-recline/ accessed 21 August 2015

Lacey, A. and Foulkes, I. (2014), *Exporting Grandma to care homes abroad* available from http://www.bbc.co.uk/news/health-25438325 accessed 26 May 2014

Laist.com (2014), *Man Dies Of Heart Attack On Southwest Flight, Chest Was 'Too Hairy' For Defibrillator* available from http://laist.com/2014/08/30/man_dies_of_heart_attack_on_southwe.php accessed 31 August 2014

Leggat, P.A., Carne, J. and Kedjarune, U. (1999), Travel insurance and health, *Journal of Travel Medicine* 6(4) 243–248 available from http://www.ncbi.nlm.nih.gov/pubmed/10575173 accessed 3 January 2015

Lipp, E. and van Horn, L. (2007), Disability travel in the United States: recent research and findings, *11th International Conference on Mobility and Transport for Elderly and Disabled Persons (TRANSED)*, Montreal available from http://www.rollingrains.com/archives/001743.html accessed 12 April 2014

Lipp, E. and van Horn, L. (2013), *Marketing Outlook Forum 2013 – Open Doors Organization (ODO) Forecast: The disability travel market – diverse, growing and increasingly mainstream* available from http://opendoorsnfp.org/market-studies/research-papers/ accessed 23 May 2014

Liu, Y., Wang, W., Huang, H.-Z., Li, Y. and Yang, Y. (2014), A new simulation model for assessing aircraft emergency evacuation considering passenger physical characteristics, *Reliability Engineering & System Safety* 121 187–197 available from http://www.sciencedirect.com/science/article/pii/S0951832013002585 accessed 3 January 2015

Low, J.A. and Chan, D.K.Y. (2002), Air travel in older people, *Age and Ageing* 31(1) 17–22 available from http://ageing.oxfordjournals.org/content/31/1/17.short accessed 3 January 2015

Lunt, N., Mannion, R. and Exworthy, M. (2013), A framework for exploring the policy implications of UK medical tourism and international patient flows, *Social Policy & Administration* 47(1) 1–25 available from http://www.birmingham.ac.uk/Documents/college-social-sciences/social-policy/HSMC/publications/2012/medical-tourism-spa-article.pdf accessed 13 April 2014

Mattison, M.L.P. and Zeidel, M. (2011), Navigating the challenge of in-flight emergencies, *Journal of American Medical Assn* 305(19) available from http://www.semae.es/wp-content/uploads/2011/05/jama-in-fkight-emergencies-2011.pdf accessed 26 May 2014

Office for Disability Issues (ODI) (2012a), *Growing your customer base to include disabled people – a guide for businesses* available from http://webarchive.nationalarchives.gov.uk/20130812104657/http://odi.dwp.gov.uk/docs/idp/Growing-your-customer-base-to-include-disabled-people.pdf accessed 19 April 2014

Office for Disability Issues (ODI) (2012b), *Disability prevalence estimates 2010/11* available from https://www.gov.uk/government/publications/disability-facts-and-figures/disability-facts-and-figures accessed 3 January 2015

Papworth Trust (2014), *Disability in the United Kingdom 2014: facts and figures* available from http://www.papworthtrust.org.uk/sites/default/files/UK%20Disability%20facts%20and%20figures%20report%202014.pdf accessed 4 April 2015

Porter, M. (1979), How competitive forces shape strategy, *Harvard Business Review* March/April available from https://hbr.orghttp://businessdisabilityforum.org.uk/customer-experience/the-evidence/1979/03/how-competitive-forces-shape-strategy/ar/1 accessed 1 January 2015

Prigg, M. (2014), *From search to spoons: Google unveils its latest product – smart cutlery that steadies tremors* available from http://www.dailymail.co.uk/sciencetech/article-2851098/From-search-spoons-Google-unveils-latest-product-smart-cutlery-steadies-tremors.html accessed 7 December 2014

Robinson, W. (2014), *It's official Pigs CANNOT fly! Woman's 'emotional support' pet defecated in the aisle and was squealing wildly before it was escorted off US Airways flight* available from http://www.dailymail.co.uk/news/article-2853779/EXCLUSIVE-little-piggy-plane-Woman-s-emotional-support-pig-defecated-aisles-squealing-uncontrollably-escorted-Airways-flight-passenger-reveals.html accessed 7 December 2014

Shaw, S. and Thomas, C. (2006), Discussion note: social and cultural dimensions of air travel demand: hyper-mobility in the UK? *Journal of Sustainable Tourism* 14(2) 209–215 available from http://www.tandfonline.com/doi/abs/10.1080/09669580608669053#.VSFuW_nF9qU accessed 4 April 2015

Small, J. and Harris, C. (2012), Obesity and tourism: rights and responsibilities, *Annals of Tourism Research* 39(2) 686–707 available from http://www.sciencedirect.com/science/article/pii/S0160738311001502 accessed 3 January 2015

Somer Kniestedt, R.A. and Steffen, R. (2003), Travel Health Insurance: indicator of serious travel health risks, *Journal of Travel Medicine* 10(3) 185–188 available from http://www.ncbi.nlm.nih.gov/pubmed/12757694 accessed 3 January 2015

Stefanacci, R.G. (2012), Caring for older adults at 30,000 feet, *Clinical Geriatrics* 20(5) 24–28 available from http://www.consultant360.com/articles/caring-older-adults-30000-feet accessed 2 January 2015

Stuff.co.nz (2013), *Pay as you weigh airfare a success* available from http://www.stuff.co.nz/travel/news/9509629/Pay-as-you-weigh-airfare-a-success accessed 27 April 2014

Surgical Bliss (2015), *Hip surgery – orthopaedics* available from http://www.surgicalbliss.com/surgery/orthopeadics/hip.php accessed 3 January 2015

Tonks, A. (2008), Cabin fever, *British Medical Journal* 336(7644) 584–586 available from http://www.bmj.com/content/336/7644/584 accessed 3 January 2015

United Airlines (2015), *Customers requiring extra seating* available from http://www.united.com/web/en-US/content/travel/specialneeds/customersize/default.aspx accessed 26 October 2015

Wang, W. and Cole, S. (2013), Perceived on board service needs of passengers with mobility limitations: an investigation among flight attendants, *Asia Pacific Journal of Tourism Research* 19(11) 1239–1259 available from http://www.tandfonline.com/doi/abs/10.1080/10941665.2013.852116#.VKkflyusVqU accessed 3 January 2015

Weaver, R. (2014), *SAS required to pay for disabled costs* available from http://cphpost.dk/sas-required-to-pay-for-disabled-costs/ accessed 4 April 2015

Winter, K. (2014), *Former secret eater lost 10 STONE after suffering the embarrassment of being too large for an aeroplane seatbelt* available from http://www.dailymail.co.uk/femail/article-2749015/Former-secret-eater-lost-10-STONE-suffering-embarrassment-large-aeroplane-seatbelt.html accessed 10 September 2014

Wise, J. (2013), Medical tourism is a profitable source of income for the NHS, study finds, *British Medical Journal* 347 available from http://www.bmj.com/content/347/bmj.f6456 accessed 8 September 2014

World Health Organisation (WHO) (2012), *Interesting facts about ageing* available from http://www.who.int/ageing/about/facts/en/ accessed 24 April 2014

Part III

Environment

The **environment** is the third dimension of sustainability.

Chapter 6: Environment, science and politics illustrates some of the worst excesses of alleged market inefficiencies and failure. It outlines the confluence of the environmental and social movements which morphed into CSERplus with the ultimate aim of reducing global social inequalities and 'global warming'. Many industries capitulated to the CSERplus' advocates' environmental demands despite the lack of confirmatory science. In aviation's environmental challenges, there is a proliferation of vested interests, all of which inadvertently support some of the inefficiencies inherent in alleged market failure. These include incomplete or asymmetric information as well as the presence of principal-agents and cronies, missing markets, free riders and moral panic. Aviation environmental concerns have two significant drivers: (1) evidence-based environmental protection regulations and (2) unevidenced claims concerning the warming of the planet. The national and supranational solution for the latter was to ascribe property rights and monetise negative externalities (filling a formerly missing market). However, frequently absent in any discussion of 'global warming' is impartial and objective information and replicable, observable science with reliable data because many influential researchers and campaigners are funded either by vested interests or by national, multi-national or supranational governments. Almost all rely on computer models for 'evidence' to endorse their predictions although that is not the function of computer-modelling. The international dimensions of treaties which only some nations have adopted add costs and affect international aviation markets by undermining competitiveness – interventions which are supported by the proceeds of non-hypothecated environmental taxes imposed on the advanced-world. These are despatched to the advancing-world to equalise global social inequalities. However, the advancing nations have their own airlines with lower overheads. Such subsidies effectively give these airlines a free ride which could affect the competitive capability of advanced nations' carriers. As responsible organisations, airports and their tenant airlines comply with environmental law to protect their stakeholders and destinations. This includes taking account of any negative externalities such as those caused by combustion of fossil fuels or biofuels, and noise and lighting emanating from buildings, vehicles and aircraft.

Part II

Environment

6 Environment, science and politics

6.1 CONTEXT

Challenges

The environment is the airline industry's Achilles' Heel. Its negative externalities include noise and lighting pollution, traffic congestion near airports and in the skies, engine emissions and wastes of all types. Every airline which has any form of annual sustainability report has an environment section and indeed, some might have only produced an environment report. This overlooks the fact that economics is at the root of airline environmental sustainability. There is a tension between aviation economists and environmentalists about the allocation of scarce environmental resources. Aeroplanes need engines to generate lift and stay aloft; however, aircraft engines burn aviation kerosene, a fossil fuel derivative for which there are currently insufficient quantities of sustainable, economically priced, alternative energy sources. Environmentally sensitive decisions – as diverse as engine procurement or waste disposal policy – will actually be decided by economic, performance-based criteria and regulatory compliances in all destinations. Aviation economic-environmental sustainability is dependent on the market forces of supply and demand: airport neighbours demanded quieter aircraft and manufacturers supplied; airlines demanded improved fuel efficiency with fewer emissions and manufacturers complied.

Aviation has its detractors, including environmental extremists who want to eliminate all unnecessary uses of fossil fuels including air travel. However, although the airline industry also has its strong advocates, not all are as extreme as the Chief Executive of no-frills, low-cost, low-fare carrier Ryanair who said that:

> The best thing we can do with environmentalists is shoot them. These head bangers want to make air travel the preserve of the rich. They are Luddites marching us back to the 18th century. If preserving the environment means stopping poor people flying so the rich can fly, then screw it.
>
> (*Sunday Telegraph*, 2014)

Light, medium and dark green environmentalists

Not everyone concerned with the environment is against aviation. Despite the environmental pressures, demand for air services is still high and environmental guilt has not stopped people flying (Dickinson *et al.*, 2010; Gossling and Peeters, 2007). As justification, passengers express their green credentials in other areas of life as a common defence mechanism (Dickinson *et al.*, 2010). The environmental special interest groups appear in various shades of green depending on how deeply they hold their views. 'Light' greens might regularly reuse plastic shopping bags, drive hybrid SUVs, unplug mobile telephone chargers when not in use and fly when they can afford it. The 'dark' greens shun public transport in favour of bicycles, drink tap water rather than bottled, use wind-up radios and wear recycled clothes. They would probably keep their elderly television (not scrapping it in favour of an energy-hungry plasma screen) and would holiday locally rather than fly anywhere. In between light and dark there are the 'medium' greens who practise a little of both dark and light green behaviours, such as using online grocery shopping to reduce their personal emissions footprint, taking showers instead of baths and switching on the dishwasher only when it is full – but flying long-haul for holidays.

Social and environmental trade-offs

Airlines link transport systems, trading mechanisms and people. These interactions create positive and negative social and environmental externalities (see Chapter 1). The negative environmental externalities are derived from pollutants such as noise, lighting and smells, all of which are important when considering efficient resource allocation and costs of all types. Life comprises many trade-offs, e.g. reducing flight frequency and increasing aircraft size could produce social and environmental benefits including less noise and reduced local air pollution from fewer take-offs and landings. However, if a passenger wanted to cover a long distance in minimal time, it would most likely be achieved by flying and spending money to obtain a private benefit (the economic trade-off of time for money). Using large, wide-bodied aircraft for short distances would be neither economic nor efficient, and fewer flights would not necessarily fit with passengers' schedule requirements (Givoni and Rietveld, 2008). This social-environmental trade-off would not necessarily prove economically beneficial. There are, however, social-environmental costs (i.e. negative externalities – see Chapter 1) such as congestion on the roads around the airport, aircraft emissions from the flight itself and a share of the airport terminal buildings' discharges (e.g. from the lighting, lavatories and packaging wastes).

Climate science

Earth's atmosphere comprises many gases in varying proportions at different levels away from the surface. Nitrogen (N_2) is approximately 78% and two other gases

– oxygen (O_2) at 21% and carbon dioxide (CO_2) at 0.03% – are critical: without them, living organisms would die. Mankind cannot survive without plants. During photosynthesis, plants convert sunlight, water vapour and CO_2 into sugars and O_2 to grow leaves, roots, branches and fruits. CO_2 is necessary for life: it is not a pollutant. Indeed if CO_2 levels fall too low, plants cannot photosynthesise and produce the O_2 mankind needs. Life would freeze. CO_2 prevents the earth returning to another Ice Age. The origins of CO_2 are traced back to outgassing from volcanic eruptions, after which some remained in the atmosphere while the rest was absorbed by plants, oceans and marine species. They combined it with calcium to form calcium carbonate exoskeletons which ultimately became carbonaceous rocks such as chalk and limestone. After it has been liberated into the atmosphere (often as a by-product of consumption of energy-producing fossil fuels), CO_2 becomes an airborne fertiliser. (In inaccurate scientific short form, plants are often referred to as 'carbon sinks' because they absorb atmospheric CO_2 during photosynthesis. Confusingly the term 'carbon' is often used in place of 'CO_2' which actually implies that there is no 'dioxide' element. This abbreviated terminology gives rise to inaccurately described measures such as 'carbon reduction' or 'carbon sequestration'. This lack of specificity is not scientific.)

The importance of CO_2 for plants was apparent when the USA Water Conservation Laboratory conducted a 27-year controlled experiment with trees. Half were grown in natural conditions and half in concentrated atmospheric CO_2. The trees, which grew in enhanced CO_2, contained in excess of 2.8 times more sequestered CO_2 than the control trees. When the experiment ended in 2005, these trees showed 85% more wood and fruit mass than those grown in natural conditions (Ballonoff, 2014). This knowledge has long been harnessed by gardeners who leak-proof their greenhouses (to ensure maximum gas take-up) and then pump in concentrated CO_2 to enrich the atmosphere and encourage growth.

Earth's atmosphere comprises gases other than N_2, O_2 and CO_2, including (in various proportions) oxides of nitrogen (NO_x) (nitric oxide (N_2O) and nitrogen dioxide (NO_2) from industrial processes), hydrofluorocarbons (HFCs), perfluorocarbons (PFCs), sulphur hexafluoride (SF_6), ozone (O_3), methane (CH_4) (an agricultural by-product), carbon monoxide (CO) and soot (sulphate and black carbon) as well as water vapour (H_2O) at approximately 1% to 3%. Over many geological ages, the proportions of atmospheric elements have varied considerably. Of the gases mentioned, six (CO_2, CH_4, N_2O, HFCs, PFCs and SF_6) are described metaphorically as 'greenhouse gases' (GHGs) because they are believed by CSERplus' advocates to behave like the glass that traps air in a greenhouse. However, 'so-called greenhouse gases have absolutely nothing to do with greenhouses' (Essex and McKitrick, 2007: 129). In reality they are 'infrared-absorbing gases' (Essex and McKitrick, 2007: 129), the most important of which is water vapour – a fact which further illustrates some of the inaccurate and confused language which permeates this topic. (Infrared-absorbing gases absorb light with a longer wavelength and lower frequency than visible light.) The metaphor of the greenhouse is, however, easier for the public to understand rather than the science of physics with its precise formulae and language.

Excess water eventually falls as rain only to be evaporated, and in doing so raises the atmospheric water content – a process which is believed to stimulate atmospheric warming mirroring that which occurs in a sealed container (like a greenhouse). Equatorial regions receive the most energy from the sun and lift the greatest amounts of water vapour. However, unlike water, excess CO_2 accumulates in the atmosphere and absorbs radiation (heat) emanating from the earth. This 'radiative forcing' is the difference between sunlight absorbed by the earth and energy radiated back to space. Incoming energy from the sun warms the earth (positive radiative forcing) and as the energy passes out to space earth cools (negative radiative forcing). (This passing-out of energy in random directions is believed by some researchers to impede the natural circulation of atmospheric gases disrupting Earth's energy balance.) As the earth revolves, the northern hemisphere winds and tides move clockwise and in the southern hemisphere they move anti-clockwise with each seeking an unattainable equilibrium. In reality, there is no global energy balance during seasonal rotations because the earth absorbs energy in different proportions in different locations during the day and emits it at night.

Mankind's burning of fossil fuels adds to the natural flows of CO_2 which, for millennia, were believed to have cancelled themselves out, leaving constant concentrations in the atmosphere and oceans (MacKay, 2009; Carter *et al.*, 2006). Releasing stored carbon adds energy to the earth's surface but there is no evidence as to whether it will have a major effect on climate (de Freitas, 2007). (Increasing concentrations of CO_2 are believed to create a positive feedback loop fuelling atmospheric warming while reducing CO_2 (negative feedback) is believed to slow it down. Feedback is also influenced by the presence of clouds (water vapour) and oceans (in their role as carbon sinks).)

Most of the GHGs emitted by human activities are destroyed by atmospheric chemical reactions or are reabsorbed by the biosphere (Carter *et al.*, 2006). Mankind's contribution is termed 'anthropogenic' and when it is applied to temperature increases on a global scale it is known as 'anthropogenic global warming' (AGW). Environmentalists and their lobby groups have convinced national, multi-national and supranational legislators that mankind's contribution is damaging because they believe it has the potential to overheat the planet (i.e. AGW is harmful): 'On climate change, *everything* is [considered to be] "global", even things like temperature which are intrinsically local' (Essex and McKitrick, 2007: 41).

However:

> for significant global warming to occur, increased concentrations of carbon dioxide must set in motion positive (or destabilising) feedback processes . . . [which]. . . would cause temperatures to rise by some other mechanism (such as increased absorption of solar energy) or cause increases in the concentration of other greenhouse gases, the most important of which is, by far, water vapour.
>
> (de Freitas, 2007)

Scientific evidence points to the opposite occurring and 'negative (or stabilising) feedback processes prevail which might explain why over hundreds of millions of years Earth's climate has never experienced runaway warming' (de Freitas, 2007).

6.2 COMPUTER MODELS

Climate computer models

Scepticism drives scientists to prove or disprove hypotheses. Science relies on first-hand experience such as that derived from testing theories in experiments followed by repetition and objective peer review to preserve scientific integrity. 'The peer review system was developed . . . by editors of publications to maintain the quality of their journals' (Carter *et al.*, 2006: 27). However, 'It was never intended to provide a guarantee that hypotheses or recommendations advanced in papers were correct or unchallengeable' (Carter *et al.*, 2006: 27). Peer reviewing should challenge the research – an activity which accords with sustainability-thinking (see Chapter 3 and Chapter 7) and should provide 'a guarantee of quality and objectivity . . . [however, in climate change studies] . . . This is not so' (Carter *et al.*, 2006: 4). The process when applied to climate science 'has tolerated gross failures in due disclosure and archiving, and . . . is both too inbred and insufficiently thorough to serve any audit purpose which we believe is now essential for science studies that are to be used to drive trillion-dollar policies' (Carter *et al.*, 2006: 4).

Peer review and expertise are often linked. In the context of current environmental issues, expertise is considered to be 'something different in the culture of the wider world. There, it means authority in the sense of being authoritarian' (Essex and McKitrick, 2007: 35). When 'experts' make pronouncements any challenges are not seen as truth-seeking – rather they are perceived as affronts to power and a test of strength. 'Shrewd politicians know that political power can be enhanced with an air of scientific authority, while scientists know that political power can give science the recognition and resources it needs. . .' (Essex and McKitrick, 2007: 36). Many of the most influential advocates for the AGW-is-harmful theory are 'experts' in the political mould but claim to speak for science. Consequently many of the scientists are overruled by 'experts' (as similarly happened with the Challenger and Columbia disasters – see Chapter 3). They exert their authority and claim the backing of a consensus which supports their opinions. 'This is the age of the populist, where truth matters less than sentiment and where sanity is shouted down by the roar of a credulous crowd' (CityAM, 2016). That is not how either science or peer review should perform.

Computer models are constructed to explain observed behaviour, but in climate change, modelling is now being used to predict changes. It must be remembered that 'all models are wrong but some are useful' (Box and Draper, 1987: 424). Models are not evidence. Furthermore, 'Models, forecasts and predictions are only valuable or worthwhile if they actually work. Models alone are not science and they are wildly deceptive foundations on which to base energy policy' (National Centre for Policy Analysis (NCPA), 2014) which is, unfortunately, exactly what has occurred. Climate simulations from computer-modelling are proving unreliable forecasters because that is not what they were designed to do (Macilwain, 2014). Since 'the models have not been verified . . . their output is merely conjecture and not capable of being the mainstay of policy' (de Freitas, 2007). It has been suggested that climate modellers might be better to mirror the models of weather forecasting or economics since they are more attuned to probabilities rather than the physics models which seem to dominate the climate debate (Macilwain, 2014).

Models are highly sensitive to the inputs, and work on the principle that the data fed into them decides the output. They should be tested against observations when, and if, they ever occur. The climate models 'start by dividing the atmosphere into a huge 3D grid of boxlike elements with horizontal edges typically 100 kilometers long and up to 1 kilometer high' (Macilwain, 2014: 1222). The smaller the grid, the more accurate will be the local measurement (but not necessarily the resultant prediction).

> Equations based on physical laws describe how variables in each box – mainly pressure, temperature, humidity and wind speed – influence matching variables in adjacent ones. For processes that operate at scales much smaller than the grid, such as cloud formation, scientists represent typical behaviour across the grid element with deterministic formulas that they have refined over many years. The equations are then solved by crunching the whole grid in a super-computer.
>
> (Macilwain, 2014: 1222)

There are, however, many more variables which could be used in computer-modelled environmental measurement, including dryness, wetness and relative humidity (Essex and McKitrick, 2008).

From the outputs of computer-modelling, some researchers have predicted that the climate would be out of control if there was a rise of more than 2°C over global average temperatures (IPCC, 1995) which is regarded as the tipping point for irrevocably damaging the earth (MacKay, 2009). Earth has never experienced the 'runaway warming' (de Freitas, 2007) as portrayed by the alarmists who attempt to prove that CO_2 is the main cause of climate change. However, 'average temperature is meaningless. . . temperature only means something locally, because the thermodynamic conditions vary from point to point' (Essex and McKitrick, 2007: 112). Despite this and based on the output of multiple computer models, it has been concluded that by-products from man-made industrial processes will be responsible for any damaging global warming, i.e. AGW is global and it is harmful. There is, however, no way to distinguish between man-made or natural increases in either temperature or CO_2, or to measure a 'global' temperature.

Throughout the centuries, CO_2 has been much higher and lower than today. Using computer-modelling, many scientists, non-scientists and vested interests have tried to make the link between rises in global temperatures and movements in CO_2. Historically, average temperatures have oscillated:

> between 54° F and 72°F [12°C and 22°C] while CO_2 concentrations dropped from about 5,000 [parts per million (ppm)] to under 300 ppm. . . [but] the Earth's temperature however varied independently of the CO_2 . . . [it] was an average of 72°F [22°C] – far higher than today – when CO_2 was both 5,000 ppm and under 750 ppm. . . . Today's average temperature is about 59°F [15°C] and CO_2 is about 350–380 [ppm].
>
> (Lewis, 2009: 236; 235)

In the past 150 years, Earth has warmed by 0.8°C and CO_2 levels have risen (Happer, 2011), so the less than 1°C by which the planet warmed last century is within the range of natural temperature variations. Currently CO_2 and other GHGs are estimated at around 430 ppm (Stern, 2006: iii). This, however, does not take account of the amount of CO_2 which was already in the atmosphere before industrialisation (Carter *et al.*, 2006: 32). This reduces the current 'human-induced' CO_2 to 150ppm (Carter *et al.*, 2006). (How can man-made GHGs be distinguished from those which occur naturally when quantities are so small?)

Despite this, a target of 350 ppm for CO_2 has been recommended (Hansen *et al.*, 2008) even though there is no evidence that adding more CO_2 to the atmosphere is actually dangerous or harmful. In fact, many stakeholders acknowledge that it would be beneficial because it increases plant growth and also prevents another Ice Age occurring prematurely. Some even talk of a CO_2 shortage arguing that 'since current levels of carbon dioxide are well below optimum levels for plant growth' (de Freitas, 2007) more of the gas will actually be beneficial.

The computer models predict that AGW will cause harm but they assume that the earth is a leak-proof container where trapped gases can be uniformly mixed as would happen in a sealed greenhouse. 'We hear about "greenhouses" even though greenhouses don't work by the greenhouse effect. We hear about "holes" in the atmosphere. There are no holes' (Essex and McKitrick, 2007: 41). Responsibility for Earth's purported 'greenhouse effect' is claimed to be shared by water vapour at 50%, clouds (another form of water) at 25% and CO_2 at 20%, with other gases accounting for the remainder (Chandler, 2007). CO_2 is accused of letting the light energy through to the earth but preventing all of the heat energy from returning to the atmosphere (i.e. similar to the role of glass in a greenhouse). 'However, too often water vapour will not be on the list of "greenhouse gases", even within some professional discussions. Moreover, its obvious link to the fluid motions, clouds, and aerosols, will often be omitted when it is mentioned' (Essex and McKitrick, 2007: 129). Clouds are the wild cards in climate modelling – impossible to predict – and furthermore, there is no evidence of a blanket of CO_2 (and other gases) covering the earth retaining the heat (Essex, 2015a). In addition, the concept of the greenhouse as applied to Earth's atmosphere does not appear in any fundamental work of thermodynamics, physical kinetics or radiation theory (Gerlich and Tscheuschner, 2009), all of which are relevant to proving the concept.

Computer-modelling and challenges

There is no proof that 'increasing atmospheric concentrations of greenhouse gases, notably carbon dioxide, will have disastrous consequences for mankind and for the planet . . . carbon is the stuff of life. Our bodies are made of carbon' (Happer, 2011: 2). Human beings exhale around 1kg of CO_2 per day and therefore, based on the AGW-is-harmful rationale, people are rendering the air 'unclean, defiling or desecrating it' simply by breathing (Happer, 2011: 3). Just because the earth has warmed by 0.8°C in the past 150 years as CO_2 levels have risen, it cannot be said that correlation is definitely causation, especially since 'there have been many warmings and coolings in the past when the CO_2 levels did not change' (Happer, 2011: 5). Furthermore, climate changes could be geological as well as meteorological in origin (Carter, 2007).

The computer-modelled GHG theory has been disputed by many dissenting scientists who believe that actual atmospheric conditions are not represented by comparison with a greenhouse. 'It is not the "trapped" infrared radiation, which explains the warming phenomenon in a real greenhouse, but it is the suppression of air cooling' (Gerlich and Tscheuschner, 2009: 34). In a real greenhouse, the pre-existing flow of warmer air away from the ground is stopped by glass, leading to a build-up of energy that would otherwise have escaped. However, on Earth, as additional gases active in the infrared region of the spectrum are added, more infrared light is returned to the surface which will require additional cooling to restore balance.

> When you add up the net amount of energy flow away from the surface by pure (infrared) radiation, it turns out to be roughly the same as that carried away by wind, air movements and evaporation. These are the two basic mechanisms for carrying away the energy: infrared radiation and fluid dynamics.
>
> (Essex and McKitrick, 2008: 114)

Atmospheric balance can be restored by additional movement of the air (like air conditioning); however, this is not a consequence of increased temperature, but increased differences in temperatures or pressures, i.e. the temperature at the surface does not have to rise. The uncertainty in the greenhouse effect comes from the unpredictability and turbulence of the fluid dynamics (i.e. the turbulence of air and water which also carries 'dust and aerosols into the atmosphere' (Essex and McKitrick, 2008: 115)).

The 'greenhouse effect' as a metaphor for the warming of the planet has an uncertain and therefore unpredictable outcome (Essex and McKitrick, 2008) which is impossible to fully capture because no one can solve the Navier–Stokes equation for fluid movements. (Solving the equation is considered to be so challenging that there is a \$US1m prize available for its solution (Essex, 2015b).) The layers of atmosphere outward from the earth comprise troposphere, tropopause, stratosphere and mesosphere. In the real world the adiabatic lapse rate (the observed rate of decrease in temperature with height) is actually measured globally many times daily by weather balloons. The data collected reveals the troposphere's convective heat transport and does not fit the concept of simple radiative heat transport. Furthermore, 'there is no blanket of CO_2 "holding the heat in"' (Essex, 2015a). Furthermore:

> by showing that (a) there are no common physical laws between the warming phenomenon in glass houses and the fictitious atmospheric greenhouse effects, (b) there are no calculations to determine an average surface temperature of a planet, (c) the frequently mentioned difference of 33 degrees Celsius [by which climatologists claim GHGs keep the earth warmer] is a meaningless number calculated wrongly, (d) the formulas of cavity radiation are used inappropriately, (e) the assumption of a radiative balance is unphysical, [and] (f) thermal conductivity and friction must not be set to zero, [it can be concluded that] the atmospheric greenhouse conjecture is falsified.
>
> (Gerlich and Tscheuschner, 2009: 1)

Many scientists, physicists, mathematicians, economists and others have challenged the computer-modelled connection between increased water vapour and the predicted amplification of the CO_2 effects when this has not happened in the past (Ridley, 2013). In the past 'atmospheric CO_2 was ~16 times higher than today. However, this enhanced level of atmospheric CO_2 does not seem to have been accompanied by unusually warm temperatures in the tropics and in fact may have been contemporaneous with high-latitude continental glaciation on Gondwanaland' (Yapp and Poths, 1992: 342). (NB: Gondwanaland comprised most of today's southern hemisphere land masses.) Clouds and water vapour together can, however, increase or reduce temperature and any clouds which include soot might lead to amplification of warming and a rise in temperature.

So, 'Actual climate sensitivity is [still] a matter of vigorous scientific debate' (Peiser, 2013: 1) and any predictions are just guesses. Although computer-modelling might be suitable for investigating the mechanics of the earth's weather, it is not appropriate for the future climate predictions which are what is needed by policy makers. Computer predictions are not evidence.

6.3 UN INTERGOVERNMENTAL PANEL ON CLIMATE CHANGE (IPCC)

UN intervention

A social-environmental coalition evolved from anti-poverty campaigners and the remnants of the anti-nuclear movement of the 1960s. They engaged with governments and created a niche in many sympathetic nations advising politicians of all political hues of the worthiness of their causes. Again their success was due to their doctrines with 'superficial plausibility' and 'apparent generosity' (Sternberg, 2009) (see Chapter 1). The critics of man-made environmental disasters such as those which occurred at Bhopal and in Prince William Sound (see Chapter 1) found a common purpose fuelled by the fact that most of the responsible executives escaped any personal penalties. Eventually, environmentalism and development economics (i.e. sustainable development) were merged into an alliance between advancing-world aspirations and advanced-world social and environmental causes under 'sustainable development'. This was supported by national, multi-national and supranational government bodies including NGOs such as the UNWCED (1987; see also Chapter 1) (reminder: sustainable development is not the same as economic sustainability). Advocates believed that the capitalist economic system exploited human as well as natural resources particularly in the advancing-world and furthermore, that this system increased inequality by enabling wealth transfers from the many to just a few capitalists (some of whom happen to live in the advancing nations). Eventually the UN, in its capacity as a supranational organisation, became involved.

The UN's Environment Programme (UNEP) was founded by socialist, oil entrepreneur and multimillionaire Maurice Strong. Strong was much lauded for his UN work but was eventually stripped of many of his titles after accusations of bribery and corruption, whereupon he retired to China (a major emitter of atmospheric pollutants). Strong, a co-author of the Brundtland Report and promoter of CO_2 as a cause of environmental damage, profoundly believed that the UN had the potential to be the world government (i.e. the ultimate supranational organisation), an aspiration which (if implemented) could eventually undermine democracies (Bell, 2013; Booker, 2015). The UNEP joined forces with the World Meterological Organisation to form the UN Intergovernmental Panel on Climate Change (IPCC). Their mandate from the UN is to focus on 'a change of climate which is attributed directly or indirectly to human activity that alters the composition of the atmosphere, and which is in addition to natural climate variability' (IPCC, 2013: 1,450). The underlying assumption is that man has to be responsible for the changes in climate. This is not a neutral stance but without it, the IPCC has no role. The IPCC opinion, based on numerous documents – only some of which are scientifically peer reviewed (Bell, 2013) – is that man-made GHGs are responsible for whatever global warming is occurring and that this is unnaturally changing the climate. Even the IPCC has acknowledged the existence of natural climate warming:

> Global-mean surface air temperature has increased by 0.3°C to 0.6°C over the last 100 years, with the five global-average warmest years being in the 1980s . . . [while] . . . global sea level has increased by 10–20cm. These increases have not been smooth with time, nor uniform over the globe. The size of this warming is broadly consistent with predictions of climate models, but it is also of the same magnitude as natural climate variability. Thus the observed increase could be largely due to this natural variability, alternatively this variability and other human factors could have offset a still larger human-induced greenhouse warming.
>
> (IPCC, 1990: *xii*)

In fact, as already noted, there have been many warmings and coolings throughout many centuries, for which the causes are unclear (de Freitas, 2007).

The IPCC has produced many reports in support of claims of damaging (and not beneficial) effects of AGW. Its 1995 report (IPCC, 1995) relying on computer models predicted 'an increase in global mean surface air temperature relative to 1990 of about 2°C by 2100' (IPCC, 1995: 6). However, eventually even the IPCC recognised the difficulty with measuring climate changes globally, and in its *Third Assessment Report* stated that:

> In climate research and modelling, we should recognise that we are dealing with a coupled non-linear chaotic system, and therefore that *the long-term prediction of future climate states is not possible* [author's emphasis]. The most that we can expect to achieve is the prediction of the probability distribution of the system's future possible states by the generation of ensembles of model solutions.
>
> (IPCC, 2001: 774)

That is, in the absence of evidence, the IPCC will rely on computer-modelling. Subsequent reports overlooked this admission and instead the Committee predicted rises in global temperatures of up to 3.5°C (again with no evidence other than computer models). (NB: average 'global' temperatures have almost stood still (Whitehouse, 2013) while CO_2 continues to rise implying that other factors might have an influence.) In 1999 the IPCC produced one of the more alarming predictions from the apocalyptic scenarios that 'In all cases the average rate of warming would probably be greater than any seen in the last 10,000 years' (IPCC, 1999a). This has not been fulfilled. In fact, the temperature rise has been negligible for the years since the IPCC's 1999 report was written, during which time the so-called GHGs have increased. Any observed rises are minimal, inconsequential and within natural variations (de Freitas, 2007; Essex, 2015b; Tollefson, 2014). In the 40 years before 1979, global temperatures did rise, but according to the IPCC this was not caused by mankind; therefore 'why should the recent 1979–1998 warming be notable when the trend is statistically indistinguishable from the pre-1940 rise? Neither trend caused "damaging" climate change' (de Freitas, 2007).

> If past is prologue to the future, how much more CO_2 induced warming is likely to occur? Very little it would appear; for the most warming that is claimed for the globe over the course of the Industrial Revolution is about 0.5°C; and it can be effectively argued that only a portion of that warming might be attributed to CO_2 and other trace gas increases.
>
> (Idso, 1991: 964)

In 2005, the IPCC's predictions were for a doubling of the CO_2 concentration with a corresponding temperature rise; however, they omitted six scenarios that yielded a *global cooling* (Gerlich and Tscheuschner, 2009) which would still have fitted within their mandate. This lack of transparency has contributed to an imbalance in the knowledge supplied to policy makers (one of the factors which trigger imperfect market functioning (see Chapter 1)). Natural climate variations (both warming and cooling) are a hazard for the societies affected. It is this that the IPCC is attempting to mitigate by recommending reductions in CO_2 emissions, believing that CO_2 is retaining warmth over the earth like a quilt.

Many scientific members of the IPCC dissociated themselves from the predictions which are actually merely 'speculation' (de Freitas, 2007). These sceptics have been criticised by the IPCC's scientists and others who will not tolerate challenges to their modelling despite the contrary observational evidence. Moreover, 'the official expert advisory process, and the IPCC process as its leading element, have been revealed as professionally not up to the mark' (Henderson, 2014: 623–624). 'The question is not about warming *per se*, but about how much warming there will be compared to natural variability. The available evidence is entirely consistent with the answer "not much"' (Global Warming Policy Foundation (GWPF), 2015: 8). Furthermore, accurate measurement is extremely difficult because the changes being studied are minute (reliant on thermometers often located thousands of miles apart) and occur over many centuries at many locations which can change throughout the measuring period. The 'social, economic and political factors have also distorted the global temperature record; when the Soviet Union collapsed, for instance, thousands of [measuring] stations in Siberia were lost, which caused an upward shift in global temperature averages' (Lewis, 2009: 243).

Mankind's contribution to the changing climate is uncertain and whether it is damaging rather than beneficial remains to be ascertained.

6.4 'EXPERTS', 97% CONSENSUS AND PRECAUTIONARY PRINCIPLE

The 97% consensus

Unfortunately, the scepticism which should seek scientific confirmation of any anthropogenic climate impacts is missing replaced instead by a dominant 'consensus' of scientists aligned to the IPCC. The claim (derived from a few surveys and abstract-counting exercises that have since been contradicted) is that up to 97% of peer-reviewed scientific articles agree that the climate is changing dangerously, that it is caused by human activity and that the number of peer-reviewed articles which rejected the AGW-is-harmful proposition 'is a vanishingly small proportion of the published research' (Cook *et al.*, 2013: 1). These claims have been evidenced as misleading as are many more by other authors which have been robustly rejected as a distorted reading of the literature, misrepresentation of the findings and bias in the methods used (see Taylor (2013), Bell (2015), Bast and Spencer (2014) and Montford (2014) among others).

The AGW-is-harmful consensus scientists believe the world must move to a 'low carbon' economy to avoid filling the atmosphere with pollutants; however, 'carbon dioxide is not one of these pollutants' (Happer, 2011: 2). Many sceptical researchers believe that the actual evidence does not support the computer-modelling showing that rises in CO_2 are damaging the planet. 'We have only begun to understand the Earth's climate system and our computer models do not account for its complexity. . . [and consequently] the science of climate change is far from settled' (Lewis, 2009: 231–232). This includes the science of 'catastrophic' AGW which suggests that since the Industrial Revolution the levels of CO_2 and other GHGs have been rising and are going to cause a dangerous increase in global temperatures (far greater than the approximately 0.8° measured in the past 150 years (Happer, 2011)).

'"Scientific consensus" is not related whatsoever to scientific truth as countless examples in history have shown. "Consensus" is a political term, not a scientific term' (Gerlich and Tscheuschner, 2009: 11–12). Science is not built on consensus but is determined by experiments for which data is available for observation, repetition, challenge and peer review. The so-called consensus' conclusions have engendered scepticism among scientists and non-scientists alike who were unconvinced by the lack of observations, availability of historical evidence, credence given to computer-modelling, uncertainty over the role of CO_2 and predicted negative effects of any warming. There was also some concern about the accuracy of some of the consensus' data because even actual measurements have been wrong. 'Predictions of increasing humidity and temperature in the tropical troposphere, a key prediction of rapid greenhouse warming, have been falsified by experimental data casting doubt on whether the [minimal] warming of 1980–2000 was man-made' (Peiser, 2013: 2). Trend measurement is also affected by the chosen start point because data can produce supporting trends merely by choosing a particular starting point that suits the needs of the interpreter (Huff, 1954). However, despite these misgivings, the '97% consensus' has been accepted as accurate by many regulators, policy makers and politicians including the USA's President Obama and his Secretary of State Kerry.

'Global warming' or 'climate change'?

'Global warming' was renamed 'climate change' when the earth did not warm as models predicted. This opened the prospect that the earth might not always warm and gave room for some uncertainty. The dearth of scientific debate has only served to fuel the moral panic (see Chapter 1). The apocalyptic scenarios predicted floods, storms, super-droughts, crop failures, extinctions, melting ice caps, rising sea levels and drowning vulnerable islands in the advancing-world. AGW, it is claimed, would affect the security of food supplies (and therefore the corporations that run them), drown the Maldives (a false claim: see sea-level specialist Morner (2009)), submerge buildings near water (including the UK Houses of Parliament), decimate Caribbean and Australian coral reefs, destroy Amazon forests and kill Arctic polar bears, as well as many other purported effects.

The climate has always changed – heated and cooled – and has been influenced by many factors other than CO_2 and temperature. These include natural processes (which have no human link) such as animal-produced methane, clouds, tides, volcanoes or even solar-planetary interaction. Mankind's contribution ranges 'from land use and urbanisation to puffing fossil-fuel particulate emissions' (Korhola, 2013: 395). However, sometimes man-made pollutants are blamed for effects such as any melting of Arctic (summer) sea ice, since any loss could have been caused by black carbon (soot) originating from dirty diesel engines and coal-fired power stations. Soot is blamed for an amplification of warming and a rise in temperature because it absorbs sunlight. (The soot from diesel and coal needs to be captured at the point of emission before it enters the atmosphere and as 'a short-lived pollutant, [it is] easily dealt with by local rather than global action' (Ridley, 2013: 4).)

Two degrees of warming?

There are still many open questions about the science, and claims that the science is settled are premature. The 2°C limit (IPCC, 1995) which has predicated so much legislation, regulation and policy is regarded by sceptical scientists and other challengers as ambiguous, unachievable and of questionable legitimacy (Knopf *et al.*, 2012). The relationship between 'the input (human forcing) and output (global temperature) is deeply uncertain [therefore] agreeing a target of "two degrees" helps little in specifying what the various input factors should be' (Knopf *et al.*, 2012: 123). The 2°C target (adopted by the EU, USA, other nations and NGOs) was:

> supported by rather thin arguments, based on inadequate methods, sloppy reasoning, and selective citation. In the scientific literature on 'dangerous interference with the climate system', most studies discuss either methodological issues, or carefully lay out the arguments for or against a particular target. These studies do not make specific recommendations, with the exception of cost-benefit analyses which argue for less stringent policy targets . . . Overall, the 2°C target of the EU [European Union] seems unfounded.
>
> (Tol, 2007: 424)

Furthermore, computer-modelling has informed us that emissions need to be stabilised in the next 20 years and fall between 1% and 3% after that. Forcing this stabilisation (implying that it might be possible to control nature) would cost an estimated 1% of UK GDP (Stern, 2006). However:

> given that we know that the warming so far has increased global vegetation cover, increased precipitation, lengthened growing seasons, caused minimal ecological change and had no impact on extreme weather events, I need persuading that future warming will be fast enough and large enough to do net harm rather than net good. Unless water-vapour-supercharged, the models suggest a high probability of temperatures changing less than 2°C, which almost everybody agrees will do net good . . .
>
> (Ridley, 2013: 5)

This view is at odds with the computer-modelled predictions and opinions which have led to regulations, but it fits with the evidence including increased crop yields and extended growing seasons.

Temperature measurements and predictions

Climate changes are now monitored by different computer models measuring different elements which would appear not to account for natural variability. However, 'one thing remains clear: overall temperature and CO_2 have not correlated as the AGW hypothesis requires. This strongly suggests that other natural factors, not atmospheric CO_2 concentrations, were controlling the temperature changes' (Lewis, 2009: 236). Furthermore, 'we now know there is nothing unprecedented about the level and rate of change of temperature today compared with Medieval, Roman, Holocene Optimum and other post-glacial periods when CO_2 levels did not change significantly but temperatures did' (Ridley, 2013: 4). In fact, 'the ice core data clearly shows carbon dioxide responding to temperature changes rather than preceding them during glaciations and deglaciation episodes' (Peiser, 2013: 2), i.e. the reverse of what the AGW-is-harmful campaigners advocate. In fact, 'temperature rise precedes a rise in carbon dioxide by about 500 to 800 years' (de Freitas, 2007) because CO_2 outgases slowly from warming oceans which in reverse, absorb CO_2 from the atmosphere as they cool (de Freitas, 2007). The climate is not warming nearly as quickly as the IPCC's (and other) computer models predicted. In fact CO_2 concentration is higher than it has been in the past 600,000 years and 'yet mean global temperature was much higher during all the major interglacial periods' (de Freitas, 2007).

It was even predicted that between 2004 and 2014 increased warming would occur 'with the year 2014 predicted to be $0.30° \pm 0.21°C$ . . . warmer than the observed value for 2004 . . . at least half of the years after 2009 are predicted to be warmer than 1998, the warmest year currently on record' (Smith *et al.*, 2007: 799). However, by 2014 measured evidence did not support these predictions – in fact, since 1900 average surface temperatures have only increased by about 0.8°C (GWPF, 2015) and the temperature has hardly risen since 1997 (Ferrara, 2014). Furthermore:

> Average growth in atmospheric carbon dioxide has slowed since early last decade, at a time when reported emissions increased at an unprecedented rate . . . the discrepancy [is attributed] to an early underestimate in reported global emissions. The findings, based on over 20 years of observations . . . suggest a reported 'surge' in emissions between 2000 and 2008 [and] reflect a bias in the early emissions.
>
> (Ross, 2013)

This is also supported by the loss of Siberian measuring stations and other evidenced examples (Lewis, 2009).

However, many of the changes in so-called 'global' temperature measurement depend on where the thermometers are placed, and the locations are not always consistent so as to be directly comparable. There are many more thermometers in, for example, the USA than there are in the Arctic or Antarctic.

> Three of the four methods of measuring global temperature show no signs of global warming:
>
> 1. proxy measurements (tree rings, sediments etc.) for the past 1000 years
> 2. weather balloons (radiosondes) for the past 44 years
> 3. satellites . . . for the past 21 years
>
> The fourth method, surface measurement at weather stations, gives an averaged mean global rise of a mere 0.6°C over 140 years, but is intermittent and irregular.
>
> (Gray, 2001: 613)

There is variability and regional nature in individual records and in particularly remote areas there is no change and sometimes even a temperature fall. Furthermore:

> temperature measurements carried out away from human influence show no evidence of global warming. The small and irregular rise shown by many surface stations must therefore be caused by changes in their thermal environment over long periods of time, such as better heating, larger buildings, darkening of surfaces, sealing of roads, increases in vehicles and aircraft, increased shielding from the atmosphere and deterioration of painted surfaces.
>
> (Gray, 2001: 613)

These are termed the 'heat island' effects, where an urban area is warmer than its surroundings due to human activities such as buildings, roads and other surfaces which retain heat.

> In summary, the last 500 million years of data reveal an energetic and immensely complex set of factors that constitute the Earth's climate. We do not understand it well enough either to posit a single cause of climate change or to create software programs to replicate it. But we do know that we did not cause such changes a million years ago . . .
>
> (Lewis, 2009: 245)

Aviation, precautionary principle and moral panic

It cannot be denied that aircraft do something to the atmosphere because the impact is observable when, in certain conditions, the water vapour from aircraft engines forms visible contrails and cirrus clouds. 'Is flying extra-bad for climate change in some way? Yes, that's the experts' view though uncertainty remains about this topic' (MacKay, 2009: 36). (It is possible that the often-quoted 'experts' are from the 97% 'consensus'.) The truth is that the aviation industry, scientists and campaigners just do not know the exact impact of aircraft on weather or climate. Despite this, national, multi-national and supranational governments and NGOs (such as the IPCC) rely on the 'experts' for 'impartial' information and data and as a result have taken action justified by the 'precautionary principle'. This has resulted in the creation of many new (formerly missing) markets among other inefficiencies.

The principle of taking precautions to prevent adverse circumstances has been supported by many regulatory bodies and has also been incorporated into the 1992 UN-sponsored Rio Declaration on Environment and Development which melded poverty reduction and environmental protection (United Nations, 1992). The European Union summarises the precautionary intent of many international groupings:

> when there are reasonable grounds for concern that potential hazards may affect the environment or human, animal or plant health, and when at the same time the available data preclude a detailed risk evaluation, the precautionary basis has been politically accepted as a risk management strategy.
> (Commission of the European Communities, 2000: 8)

Note the terminology: 'politically accepted' not 'economically accepted'. The document continues that the measures taken to manage any consequent risks must be continued for as long as the scientific data is inconclusive and the risks remain unacceptable. Since the climate predictions rely on computer-produced data which can be manipulated to suit the researchers' needs, this provides an unrestricted economic opportunity for the AGW-is-harmful proponents – not so much a 'licence to operate' but more a 'licence to print money'. (Insurers work on the precautionary basis and perceive insurance as an investment as well as risk protection. They are very enthusiastic about precautionary principles which provide justification for increased insurance premiums.) The absence of conclusive scientific environmental evidence (and therefore any proof of future harm) has not stopped the proliferation of environmental and social regulations which absorb significant commercial resources. These provisions have been justified on moral and/or ethical grounds to bolster support for investment in environmental precautions to prevent the climate changing despite lacking evidence that mankind has any control.

Stern Review

In 2006 economist Sir Nicholas (now Lord) Stern, Head of the UK's Economic Service, was charged with a review of the economics of climate change (Stern, 2006) with the contents provided by impartial civil servants who should have presented at least four scenarios before recommendation. These would have included the 'upsides and downsides of doing nothing and of doing something [however] those who give only the upside of doing something and the downside of doing nothing are in fact lobbying' (Kelly, 2015). The Stern Review influenced the application of the precautionary basis to offset the purported negative effects of AGW. Lord Stern was aware of the possibility of accepting false positive or false negative errors from the computer-modelling on which he placed such reliance. He conflated computer-modelling with scientific evidence.

> Remember that the science predicts outcomes with risk and uncertainty Type I error (false alarm) – if we accept the science as giving us a strong signal to act, and the science turns out to have over-estimated the risk, then we will have incurred possibly unnecessary costs of action.
>
> (Stern, 2012: 18)

The benefits of accepting Type I would mean that there would be cleaner, more efficient and secure energy technologies available to support the natural environment. However, if the Type II error (false negative) was accepted and nations failed to act, this would be rejecting the outcome of the computer models on the grounds that they were misleading by which time concentrations of CO_2 could have built to very dangerous levels and 'it will be extremely difficult to back out because CO_2 is so long lasting. Basic common-sense, in this case, points strongly to action' (Stern, 2012: 18). Lord Stern appears to have accepted both the Type I and Type II errors. His description of the climate science has been described as an uncritical acceptance of the worst case put by the IPCC and is 'one from which many in the climate science community are now distancing themselves' (Kelly, 2015). Lord Stern further noted that the (computer-modelled) science should not be undermined by those who challenge it by confusing

> risk/uncertainty with assumption that best guess of impacts may be taken as zero, fail to distinguish oscillations and trends, find a handful of erroneous papers and imply that all the other many thousands can be disregarded, . . . [and those who] fail to recognise compelling refutations of (often crucial) counter-arguments [including] urban heat islands . . .
>
> (Stern, 2012)

In other words, in contrast to the open, challenge culture delivered by sustainability-thinking (see Chapter 3 and Chapter 7), there is to be no challenge to the computer-modelling contained in his report. This tendency to promote groupthink (see Chapter 7) rather than debate undermines the challenge culture so visible in genuine scientific endeavour. Furthermore, the report is based on the belief that CO_2 is responsible for the minimal rise in temperature rather than the possibility that there might be no causal link. Many of the Stern Review's CO_2 findings are not supported by observations and in fact, 'water is more important to the radiative transfer of energy than all of the other infrared gases combined' (Essex and McKitrick, 2007: 129). Lord Stern would appear to have accepted that (a) CO_2 (at approximately 0.03% of atmosphere) is harmful because he believes it triggers increases in temperature and (b) unlimited spending on the precautionary basis is justified to reverse what could actually be natural changes in climate.

An alternative solution to the expense of the precautionary principle is to implement mitigations.

> As for other major natural disasters, the appropriate preparation for extreme climate events is to mitigate and manage the negative effects when they occur, and especially so for dangerous coolings. Attempting instead to 'stop climate change' by reducing human carbon dioxide emissions is a costly exercise of utter futility. Rational climate policies must be based on adaptation to dangerous change as and when it occurs, and irrespective of its sign or causation.
>
> (Carter, 2007: 4)

This proposal is contrary to the Stern Review and the IPCC recommendations.

6.5 ENVIRONMENTAL TRIGGERS FOR MARKET INEFFICIENCY OR FAILURE

Market inefficiency or failure and scientific consensus

Perversely, environmental regulations can trigger, and be triggered by, some of the recognised features of alleged market inefficiencies or failures (see Chapter 1) including:

- incomplete or asymmetric information
- presence of principal-agents and cronies
- missing markets and negative externalities
- free riders and
- moral panic.

(a) Incomplete or asymmetric information

Aside from the fact that any warming might be natural in origin (Carter, 2007; Lewis, 2009) or localised (e.g. the result of the heat island effect (Gray, 2001)), research has found that deserts (just like plants and oceans) might also be CO_2 sinks (Evans *et al.*, 2014). Furthermore, there might be a connection between CO_2 and infrared energy (Feldman *et al.*, 2014), solar activity (Adolphi *et al.*, 2014), cosmic rays (Friis-Christensen and Svensmark, 1997), halocarbons (Lu, 2013), soot (Ridley, 2013), cloud cover (Svensmark and Friis-Christensen, 1997) and/or chlorofluorocarbons (CFCs) among other links. Developed nations have phased out CFCs through the 1987 UNEP Montreal Protocol on Substances that Deplete the Ozone [O_3] Layer (UNEP, 1987) but at that time there were readily substitutable products available. CO_2 is different: it is part of daily living, occurs naturally, has no substitutes and is unlikely to be reduced significantly by decreasing aircraft flights. Despite this, the IPCC is taking the same approach used to eliminate CFCs to reduce anthropogenic CO_2. 'Much remains unknown about the pathways [CO_2] takes from emission source to the atmosphere or carbon reservoirs such as oceans and forests' (NASA, 2014). Any statements to the contrary are merely speculation.

Policy makers are failing to consider any challenges to the computer-modelled theories of the AGW–is-harmful advocates that CO_2 is damaging the planet. IPCC data is supplied by scientists who are, by and large, funded by national and supranational governments and philanthropic donors with high power and high influence (e.g. the Hewlett Foundation's \$US500m to the Climate Works Foundation (Osuri, 2010)). The alarmists have found a missing market (see Chapter 1) largely funded by national or supranational governments. This is an example of asymmetric influencing – one of the triggers for alleged market inefficiency and failure (see Chapter 1 and Chapter 8). Of Europe's top ten environmental groups (the 'Green 10'), nine rely on the European Union for substantial funding (Snowdon, 2013). 'The Green 10 campaigns for 25 per cent of the European Union budget to be spent on climate change projects' (Snowdon, 2013: 19):

> there has been a bias towards centre-left organisations, with a particular emphasis on issues about which the public is often indifferent, such as climate change, overseas development and public health . . . [by using] . . . government consultations, media briefings, quasi-grassroots campaigning and face-to-face lobbying to bring about controversial legislation.
>
> (Snowdon, 2013: 18)

Unless this legislation is what voters have chosen, such campaigning even undermines democracy.

Having decided that climate change is a threat, a key priority for the European Union is climate action to be integrated into all spending categories. It has agreed that at least 20% of its budget for 2014 to 2020 – 'as much as €180bn [£Stg127bn or \$US196bn] – should be spent on climate change-related action' (European Union, n.d.). To support their cause they intend to integrate mitigation and adaptations into 'all major EU spending programmes, in particular cohesion policy, regional development, energy, transport, research and innovation and the Common Agricultural Policy' (European Union, n.d.). This takes the precautionary principle to extremes. Policies will be focussed on supporting 'public authorities, NGOs and private actors, especially small and medium-sized enterprises, in implementing small-scale low-carbon and adaptation technologies and new approaches and methodologies [*sic*]' (European Union, n.d.) (NB: 'methodology' is the study of methods). Furthermore, the EU will also contribute to climate change measures in developing countries spending by €1.7bn (£Stg1.24bn or \$US1.92bn) between 2014 and 2015, and €14bn (£Stg10.25bn or \$US15.84bn) between 2014 and 2020. There appears to be no equivalent funding allocated to support research into contrary views – an omission which ignores the importance of providing impartial, balanced, full information and data to policy makers and which actually undermines the democratic process.

The USA has similar aspirations to the EU. In addition to the $US millions that AGW-is-harmful advocates and environmental researchers have received from private philanthropists:

> Government agencies . . . have poured billions into academic research aligned with the environmental movement's agenda. The EPA [Environmental Protection Agency] alone has spent more than $333 million in the last 15 years sponsoring sustainability fellowships . . . in addition to another $60 million in research grants. The National Oceanic and Atmospheric Administration (NOAA) records show more than $3bn in grants for climate science research since 1998 . . . while the National Institutes of Health has granted in the last four years alone $28 million for research on climate change and another $580 million on Climate-Related Exposures and Conditions.
>
> (Peterson and Wood, 2015: 15)

The average is calculated at '$465 million in federal funding for sustainability and climate change research each year – though in recent years government funding for climate research has increased substantially' (Peterson and Wood, 2015: 15). Others calculate that the USA Government spent over $US185bn (£Stg130bn or €162bn) between 2003 and 2010 on climate change items (Bell, 2015). Climate change is *big* business (Table 6.1).

Industry also funds climate change research and is often accused of acting with bias. 'People making this argument should attend to the fact that government-funded research has become the real problem in climate-change science' (Essex and McKitrick, 2007: 61). Such disproportionate national and supranational governments' spending – concentrating only on the detrimental effects of climate changing – pits the resources of the State against those of private industry. It has not been possible to accurately calculate the value of spending by the groups opposed to the AGW-is-harmful theory, therefore comparisons with the billions of £Stg, $US and € awarded by multiple governments and their agencies are not possible. In any event, because privately owned businesses (including airlines) have to make a profit to ensure their economic viability, they just do not have the resources (time or money) to match the huge scale of national- or supranational-funded advocacy and research. State-funded bureaucrats or researchers do not have commercial pressures. Shareholders would rightly be alarmed if private industry even attempted to match the volumes of global, taxpayer-funded spending. There are a few privately funded sceptical think tanks, such as the UK's GWPF and the USA's Committee for a Constructive Tomorrow, but their income is miniscule in comparison with that given to the AGW-is-harmful advocates. This dispro-portionate allocation of resources leads to asymmetric information, imperfect knowledge, inequality, moral hazards and possibly even the activation of the principal-agent problem. These are all triggers for the imperfect functioning of markets (see Chapter 1). In contrast to the ideal of a sustainable, open and challenge culture (see Chapter 3), the outliers who dared to challenge the negative AGW theories have been threatened by the proponents who will not tolerate any dissent.

Table 6.1 Examples of national and supranational spend on climate change investigations

Year bands	Source of funds	Value	Source
1998 to 2015	The National Oceanic and Atmospheric Administration (USA)	$US3bn	Peterson and Wood (2015)
1998 to 2015	National Science Foundation (USA)	$US1.7bn	Peterson and Wood (2015)
2001–2015	Environmental Protection Agency (USA)	$US393m	Peterson and Wood (2015)
2003–2010	• US Government • climate change technology research • green energy subsidies • provisions in 2009 Stimulus Bill for climate change programmes	$US107bn $US79bn $US16.1bn $US26bn	Bell (2015)
2011	National Institute of Health (USA)	$US608m	Peterson and Wood (2015)
2014–2020	EU to spend 20% of its total budget on climate projects	€180bn	European Union (n.d.)
2014–2015	EU (to spend in developing countries – included in €180 billion above)	€1.7bn	European Union (n.d.)
2015–2020	EU (to spend in developing countries)	€14bn	European Union (n.d.)

Indeed, some of the USA's AGW advocates for harmful warming want 'deniers' of 'global warming' to be arrested, prosecuted and criminalised under the USA's Racketeer Influenced and Corrupt Organizations Act (RICO) (Olsen, 2015; Bastasch, 2015) (i.e. contrary to the sustainability-thinking behaviours which encourage openness and challenge, and the American Constitution which guarantees freedom of speech). In France, the chief weatherman for television station France 2 has been taken off air as punishment for publishing a book on the positive consequences of climate change which disagrees with the national view and is considered politically incorrect by his employers. He argued that climate change was beneficial because the warmer weather would attract more tourists, improve wines and lower death rates and energy costs (Samuel, 2015). The funding imbalance, combined with biases (see Table 7.1 in Chapter 7), absence of cost-benefit analysis, misrepresentation and fear allows asymmetric information and data to flourish. Furthermore, such inefficient allocation of resources (which could be better spent on health, education or other social needs) ultimately reduces national welfare.

The GWPF noted that the alarmism is not secure because 'all sides of scientific debates have vested interests and display confirmation bias' (i.e. where new evidence is taken to be confirmation of existing beliefs or theories – see Chapter 7). 'Science keeps itself honest by encouraging challenge and diverse interpretations of data, rather than trying to enforce a single "consensus"' (Peiser, 2013). And yet once democratic governments committed taxpayers' funds to the AGW-is-harmful advocates, NGOs and vested interests, they avoided the divergent thinking (see Chapter 3) which is so critical in debate. In so doing they have undermined the freedom of speech on which democracy depends.

(b) Presence of principal-agents and cronyism

The influence of the principal-agent problem and cronyism in the 'green' industries could undermine democratic processes and the fair operation of markets. And because of these two indicators of alleged market inefficiency or failure the decisions of policy-making politicians on behalf of their electorates are possibly neither impartial nor fully informed (see Chapter 7). In a further illustration of the possibility of market failure caused by asymmetric information, environmental decision-makers often exhibit an imbalance of information, data and opinions some of which is derived from computer predictions which cannot always be guaranteed as accurate until the events predicted have occurred. Furthermore, it would appear that sometimes green politics are pitted against national economics. In the UK:

> Four of the nine-person Climate Change Committee [CCC], the official watchdog that dictates green energy policy, are, or were until very recently, being paid by firms that benefit from Committee decisions. A new breed of lucrative green investment funds, which were set up to expand windfarm energy, are in practice a means of taking green levies paid by hard-pressed consumers and handing them to City investors and financiers.
>
> (Rose, 2013)

In other words, captive consumers provide the guaranteed revenue streams for 'green' investment. Furthermore, 'firms lobbying for renewables can virtually guarantee access to key Government policy makers, because they are staffed by former very senior [Government, ex-Government or quasi-Government] officials – a striking example of Whitehall's "revolving door"' (Rose, 2013). In an excess of UK cronyism, vested influencers include government and ex-government ministers (one of whom was convicted of perverting the course of justice) who are paid advisers to energy suppliers and special interest groups as well as financiers of alternative energy sources. The Chairman of the cross-party Energy and Climate Change Commons Select Committee (who held multiple shareholdings and chairmanships of various energy companies) proposed an amendment to the UK's Energy Bill that would have set a binding target in 2030 for CO_2 emitted by power generation. Effectively this proposal was for a cut of 90% in national CO_2 levels to be covered by a tax on consumers' electricity bills (*The Week*, 2013). It would benefit the renewable sector in which the Chairman had commercial interests. The UK government also placed £Stg3.8bn ($US5.9bn or €5.2bn) into a new Green Investment Bank. One of its largest deals involved an energy company selling its windfarms to one of the Bank's funds. The Chairman of that company was also the Chairman of the Green Investment Bank (Rose, 2013). In terms of economic theory, these Chairmen were the agents in positions to influence decisions which could have maximised their private welfare and which might or might not have maximised the welfare of their principals (i.e. the electorate and/or consumers respectively). It is possible to surmise that rather than making policy on evidence, some governments could be influenced by advocacy comprising asymmetric, incomplete and possibly inaccurate information and data.

(c) Missing markets and negative externalities

Despite the rhetoric from vested interests, there are only three ways to cut CO_2 emissions:

> and renewable energy is not one of them: the collapse of Communism in Europe (the biggest single factor); recession; and the dash-for-gas (replacing coal-fired electricity generation with natural gas). The first is unrepeatable, and the second and third are the reasons why the US has been reducing emissions. To avoid the lights going out, the Germans are being forced back onto reliance on carbon-intensive coal.
>
> (Darwall, 2013)

National, multi-national and supranational governments have been persuaded that emissions will be reduced if they create a new marketplace in which to trade them, and yet reductions will not be achieved by governments wasting billions of £Stg, $US or € on inappropriate policies. So far '90% of the measures adopted in Britain and elsewhere . . . to cut global emissions are a waste of time and money – including windfarms in Scotland, carbon taxes and Byzantine carbon trading systems' (Allen, 2013).

There are many vested interests in promoting climate change and the measures to mitigate (e.g. decarbonisation strategies including wind farms) or adapt (e.g. increasing flood defences). One of these measures is the identification and fulfilment of a previously missing market for CO_2 and to endow it with property rights. The origins for this strategy would appear to lie in the 1990s with Enron – the failed USA energy conglomerate (see Chapter 1) – which was a major influence in establishing the market for trading sulphur dioxide (SO_2), the antecedent of today's CO_2 trading. At that time, USA Vice President Gore was enthused by the idea of an international environmental regulatory regime. His belief that CO_2 emissions reductions were desirable coincided with Enron's desire to expand their pollutant trading credits business. Enron persuaded President Clinton and Congress that the Environmental Protection Act (EPA) should include CO_2 and the Enron Foundation donated generously to various environmental NGOs and projects which supported the concept of global warming. Enron also commissioned climate scientists to report on global warming, only to discredit the findings because they did not suit Enron's agenda (Bell, 2010). It then changed tactics to undermine any scientists who were sufficiently bold to challenge the concept of global warming and many scientists reportedly backed down under pressure. Enron then lobbied to create a CO_2 market for which it needed the USA to sign the IPCC's international emissions reduction agreement. However, the Senate decided against the idea and would not be signatory to any agreement which would harm the USA's energy-hungry industries.

Vice President Gore wanted to use global warming as the focal point for his own 2000 presidential campaign and was a supporter of legislation enabling cap-and-trade (where emissions are capped and any surplus sold or deficit purchased) as a tool for emissions reductions. After his failure to succeed the presidency, he became an evangelist for the AGW-is-harmful movement. In 2004 he founded Generation Investment Management LLP to manage carbon trading credits. It was estimated to have $US7.3bn under management as at December 2014 (Stockpickr. com, 2014). He also produced a book and drama-documentary to support his ventures – both titled *An Inconvenient Truth*. He is reported to have earned more than $US50m for the book and reportedly 'earns $US100,000 to $US150,000 for every lecture he gives on global warming' (Jeffrey, 2011: 90). However, the drama-documentary which promoted the book 'incorporated Hollywood special effects, including footage from the cli-fi movie *The Day After Tomorrow*. The haunting images of glaciers falling into the sea in Gore's film were actually computer-generated imagery from the movie, passed off as the real thing' (Peterson and Wood, 2015: 113). Credibility for the Gore production also relied heavily on a 'hockey stick' graph (named after its upward slope) produced in a peer-reviewed paper by Mann *et al.* (1998) which showed a rise in CO_2 and a rise in temperature over 650,000 years. Although Mr Gore claimed these were an exact fit, this also was misleading because 'Mann's "trick" was to substitute thermometer data for proxy data and vice versa as necessary [in order] to produce the hockey stick-shaped graph, without noting these substitutions' (Peterson and Wood, 2015: 111). The graph also ignored the Medieval Warm Period (about AD 800–1300) and the Little Ice Age (AD 1300–1850) when CO_2 levels barely changed but temperature increased. Subsequently the graph was also misinterpreted as 'definitive evidence of anthropogenic causes of recent climate change' (National Research Council, 2006: ix). Further criticism has been levelled because the graph

> does not accommodate the earlier CO_2 levels of up to 5,000 ppm, or sixteen times of those today . . . it omits values on the temperature axis [making] it impossible to quantify the scale of temperature variations . . . conflates correlation with causation . . . [therefore we] . . . may properly conclude that Gore's CO_2/temperature graph is a distortion of the historical record designed to elicit an emotional response for a political purpose.
>
> (Lewis, 2009: 238)

Although the hockey stick has been discredited many times, this did not stop many governments (advised by their experts) defending it as they made policies. Furthermore, despite these challenges, the graph was given prominence and credibility in the IPCC's 2001 report as well as within the broader science community and the media. In essence, the graph was presented as evidence for apocalyptic levels of global warming even though its validity was questioned. Therefore that should give 'reason to doubt the conclusions inferred from it' (Lewis, 2009: 244).

A British parent, alarmed by the contents of the film *An Inconvenient Truth*, challenged it in the British Courts as a violation of the UK Education Act 1996 which forbids the promotion of partisan political views in the classroom. While the Judge described the film as 'powerful, dramatically presented and highly professionally produced' (*National Post*, 2007), he also determined that it was a political film based on research and opinion which blurred the line between science, politics and environmental advocacy. The Judge found nine key scientific errors in the film (although other reviewers claimed there were more), that its alarmist and apocalyptic vision exaggerated the likely effects of any change in climate and it did not represent an impartial scientific analysis (Peck, 2007). Furthermore, the two graphs (one showing a rise in temperature and the other a rise in CO_2) which were a cornerstone of the production, did not justify the assertions made and there were later claims of manipulated data. The film can only be shown in UK schools if the teachers are prepared to discuss the scientific errors.

Despite the foregoing, in 2007 the USA Supreme Court ruled that GHGs exist as such and are 'air pollutants' although the science regarding impacts on public health or welfare endangerment were inconclusive (Bell, 2010; Lewis, 2009). That ruling gave credibility to the idea that CO_2 – essential for life – was an undesirable externality and required the allocating of property rights, regulating, pricing and taxing thereby creating and fulfilling a formerly unidentified, missing market. The graph in which the IPCC had previously vested so much authority was subsequently omitted from their 2007 report and yet 'despite the loss of this evidence, the political agenda of the IPCC has not changed and . . . Gore still relies on this graph to support his political agenda' (Lewis, 2009: 244). Subsequently, the USA (the driver behind environmental emissions trading but which would not initially sign up to international emissions restraint agreements) has experienced a significant drop in emissions because of the shale gas revolution which produces only half the emissions of coal and oil. This fortuitous discovery has transformed the USA's energy production and US citizens are therefore minimally impacted by any restrictions on CO_2 (or CO_2e, an expression which converts other gases to CO_2 equivalents for the purpose of measuring their impact on warming). CO_2e is another formerly missing-now-discovered market. 'CO_2e levels are concentrations and concentrations do not simply increase by the amount of emissions from human activities' (Carter *et al.*, 2006: 32). Concentrations and emissions are different. The concentration of CO_2 warms the atmosphere on a logarithmic scale rather than linearly so that 'while the first CO_2 molecules matter a lot, successive ones have less and less effect' (Bell, 2015: 35). 'In fact, [radiative] forcing declines with concentration increments' (Carter *et al.*, 2006: 34). The effect of CO_2 'on global temperature is already close to its maximum so adding more has an ever decreasing effect' (de Freitas, 2007). In other words, the law of diminishing marginal returns applies and higher concentrations of CO_2 are unlikely to have a significant influence on the climate.

(d) Free riders

Many environmental taxes imposed on citizens of developed nations are used to offset social and environmental programmes in advancing nations enabling them a free ride (as well as creating a moral hazard). Eventually, the industries and citizens from the countries benefitting from the capital inflows enjoy their free ride at the expense of advanced nations. The problem is compounded by increasingly vocal demands from the developing nations for compensation for adverse weather events which they blame on climate change caused by historic emissions of carbon [dioxide] from developed nations. The process by which they will claim is the 'Warsaw Mechanism' (McGrath, 2015). This was named after the 2013 Climate Change conference in that city held under the auspices of the UN Framework Convention on Climate Change (UNFCCC). (The UNFCCC is an international treaty which was formed 'to cooperatively consider what [the joining countries] could do to limit average global temperature increases and the resulting climate change and to cope with whatever impacts were, by then, inevitable' (UNFCCC, n.d.a).) The 'Warsaw International Mechanism for Loss and Damage associated with Climate Change Impacts' will

> address loss and damage associated with impacts of climate change, including extreme events and slow onset events in developing countries that are particularly vulnerable to the adverse effects of climate change. The implementation of the functions of the Loss and Damage Mechanism will be guided by the Executive Committee under the guidance of the COP [Conference of the Parties].
>
> (UNFCCC, n.d.b)

In other words, when there is a hurricane, drought or flood which can be claimed to have been caused by historic emissions from advanced nations, the advancing nations can ask for compensation for 'loss and damage' a term which is usually used in the insurance industry. (How can it be distinguished whether the cause was natural or man-made?) This premise could become an 'endless liability running into billions of dollars' (McGrath, 2015) which is actually based on the output of computer-modelling and unconfirmed science and which stretches the precautionary principle to financial infinity. In the Pacific Islands, for example, the Pacific Islands Development Forum (PIDF) is asking for the 'worlds' biggest emitters of GHGs to compensate all Pacific Islands that are affected by climate change' for resultant loss and damage (Qounadovu, 2015). The rationale is that those advanced nations which are believed historically responsible for the largest quantities of GHGs should endlessly compensate the advancing nations of the PIDF as agreed under the Warsaw Mechanism. However, China and India (among others), whose emissions have been increasing, will not have to compensate because they are categorised as 'advancing nations'.

From the Warsaw Mechanism, a new genre of refugees has evolved – 'climate change refugees' – which was tested in New Zealand (Moir, 2015) when a Pacific Islands' resident overstayed his New Zealand visa. He unsuccessfully claimed he had no future back in his homeland because of the impact of climate change and sought to remain in New Zealand. If it had been successful, this test case could have had far-reaching implications for the millions of ocean island inhabitants worldwide. All of this ignores the fact that 'recent extreme weather events, including hurricanes, droughts, floods, and tornadoes, have not increased in recent decades due to human-caused climate change' (Pielke, 2014).

Advancing nations (such as those in the Asia Pacific region) which do not have to make national welfare provisions from their own resources can supply their customers at lower cost (a competitively advantageous economic impact) (see Table 1.1 in Chapter 1) and do not have to change their behaviours (a social impact and another application of the market failure indicator of 'moral hazard'). They can therefore price their products more competitively in international markets to the detriment of competing industries in the donor nations. The economic implications of such wealth redistribution should not be underestimated – and not just for airlines.

(e) Moral panic

The AGW-is-harmful mantra has parallels with the Millennium Bug of 1999/2000 which was also tackled on a precautionary basis. 'It was a confluence of politics, commercial money, journalists who had a story too good to check and local interest' (Jones, 2014). The Millennium Bug was a moral panic in the same way that the AGW-is-harmful consensus is a moral panic caused by 'unevidenced assertions not based on empirical analysis' (Jones, 2014, n.p.). The AGW moral panic could have deleterious economic consequences for countries which have signed up as 'believers' and for the airline industry in particular. 'Exaggerated alarmism is not harmless and is not scientific' (Peiser, 2013: 2).

6.6 AVIATION IMPACTS

Challenges

Different countries produce different quantities and proportions of mixed emissions per head of population with the largest measures occurring in the established industrialised nations of North America, Oceania and Europe. The lesser developed countries such as India and China with their growing, aspirant middle class are catching up because they manufacture and then export goods by air and sea to developed nations. In short, the industrialised world has 'exported' many of its negative atmospheric externalities to the industrialising world. However, many technologies perfected during developed world industrialisation are available to the developing and emerging nations. This enables them to leapfrog onto many of these innovations without enduring the costs, the often slow pace of research and development or the cumulative emissions which accompany growth. Ironically, they were spared these historic emissions for which the developed world is now being asked to compensate them.

In 2013 the UK was recovering from the recession and GDP grew at less than 1%. During the recession jobs were lost and many were outsourced to advancing nations with lower wage levels and less stringent social and environmental legislation. This led to more CO_2-intensive production in those countries which would have also incurred additional emissions from freighting by sea or air. The UK might have cut the domestic negative externality, but because it was reliant on imports the total emissions attributable to British economic activity actually increased by 19% between 1990 and 2005 (Helm, 2013).

The atmospheric quantities and toxins attributed to aviation vary depending on the source of the research which is often conflicting or produced incomparably. 'Aviation contributes about 1.6 to 2.2% of the global anthropogenic CO_2 emissions, 10 to 13% of all traffic CO_2 and 2% of all NO_x sources' (Schumann, 2000: 30). However, aircraft CO_2 emissions are indistinguishable from CO_2 emitted simultaneously from any other sources (Schumann, 2000) including natural sources and shipping or ITC (each of which also purportedly emits approximately 2% of global CO_2). Aviation contributes 2% of whatever proportion of the 0.03% of atmospheric computer-modelled CO_2 which is attributable to man-made causes. These percentage contributions are not statistically significant. In an economic-environment trade-off, airlines are cutting costs by substituting employees with 'green' ITC and passenger self-servicing. This could improve productivity and reduce employee costs but could increase emissions through the increased quantity of energy required to power more devices.

Aircraft and emissions

Aircraft engines emit particulates and gases (including CO_2) from burning kerosene (a fossil fuel derivative) in a fixed ratio to fuel burned (Lee, 2009). Other emissions are apparently miniscule in comparison to CO_2 and not measurable in aircraft cruise conditions. Emissions differ throughout the operating cycle with CO_2 engine emissions higher per passenger for take-off and landing (when more fuel is consumed) than in cruise conditions. Wide-bodied aircraft on long distance flights reportedly burn about 30% of their fuel above the tropopause (the boundary between the upper troposphere and the lower stratosphere) (Schumann, 2000). During cruise and take-off, aircraft mostly emit CO_2 and NO_x. When they are idling, they emit CO_2, other hydrocarbons plus NO_x and carbon (i.e. black soot) in the form of smoke (European Aviation Safety Agency (EASA), n.d.). The largest quantity of subsonic aircraft emissions is believed derived from CO_2 and from water vapour. Releasing emissions into the troposphere is believed to increase O_3 formation and although O_3 at those levels becomes a greenhouse gas 'CO_2 is [considered to be] the main greenhouse gas' (Pearce and Pearce, 2000: 16). However, water vapour is regarded as the most potent GHG and remains in the colder, higher atmosphere where it forms artificial cirrus ice-clouds. They are sometimes visible as aircraft condensation trails when sunlight passes through them. (Some observers believe this prevents the ground heat from returning to atmosphere and fuels the apocalyptic global warming theory by 'capping' the atmosphere.) Aircraft gases and particulates are exhausted

> directly into the upper troposphere and lower stratosphere, mainly at northern mid-latitudes, where they have an impact on atmospheric compositions. These gases and particulates alter the concentration of atmospheric GHGs, including CO_2, ozone (O_3) and methane (CH_4); provoke formation of condensation trails (contrails) and may increase cirrus cover and change other cloud properties all of which may contribute to climate change at the regional and global scale.
>
> (Schumann, 2000: 29)

(Evidence of these claims is awaited.) O_3 is necessary because it filters out the destructive short-wave ultraviolet radiation (Egli, 1991) but it was believed to increase temperature above the troposphere (where it absorbs sunlight), the level closest to Earth and where most of the weather phenomena occur. According to the IPCC aircraft trigger formation of contrails 'and may increase cirrus cloudiness – all of which contribute to climate change' (IPCC, 1999a: 13) (note the confirmatory language). Furthermore, 'Aircraft jet engines directly emit solid soot particles. Soot encompasses all primary, carbon-containing products from incomplete combustion processes in the engine' (IPCC, 1999b). NO_x at ground level can be washed out by rain but above 10,000 metres (the approximate aircraft cruise height) they linger for about 12 months (Egli, 1991). Above 12,000 metres they contribute to the breakdown of O_3 in the stratosphere by reacting with water vapour to form nitric acid. 'Air travel is energy intensive, so that carbon-per-passenger kilometre in passenger air travel is comparable to that for cars and light trucks, short-haul being more carbon intensive than long-haul' (Pearce and Pearce, 2000:3). The conclusion is that the emissions might have more effect at higher levels than on the ground because at high altitude where the air is thinner and colder, modern aircraft encounter less resistance (Air Transport Advisory Group (ATAG), 2010).

The IPCC (1999a: n.p.) postulated that the climate impacts of aviation emissions were more difficult to quantify than the emissions themselves and compared their effects to the (computer-modelled) results of 'other sectors'. The accuracy of this method of assessment and selection is open to debate as is the method of comparing aviation with different industrial sectors. There are a wide range of estimates as to how long CO_2 could stay in the atmosphere and climate alarmists tend to take the worst case scenario as justification for their precautionary actions.

> Because carbon dioxide has a long atmospheric residence time ($=100$ years) and so becomes well mixed throughout the atmosphere, the effects of its emissions from aircraft are indistinguishable from the same quantity of carbon dioxide emitted by any other source [e.g. shipping and ITC]. The other gases (e.g., NOx, SOxO, water vapour) and particles have shorter atmospheric residence times and remain concentrated near flight routes, mainly in the northern mid-latitudes. These emissions can lead to radiative forcing that is regionally located near the flight routes for some components (e.g. O_3 and contrails) in contrast to emissions that are globally mixed (e.g. carbon dioxide and methane).
>
> (IPCC, 1999a: n.p.)

While a contrail lasts a day, the CO_2 released from a plane lingers in the atmosphere for hundreds of years. For example, while contrails – and their warming potential – disappeared from European skies last April [2010] when an Icelandic volcanic ash cloud grounded flights, atmospheric CO_2 continued to warm the world.

(Marshall, 2011)

(Could any warming have been enhanced by the volcanic ash (which kept aircraft grounded) and outgassing from the volcano?) Irrespective of the claims about the impacts of aircraft atmospheric exhausts, aviation emissions are the output of fossil-fuelled energy and that is what keeps aircraft aloft.

Predicted airline market growth

The airline industry wants to grow but its constraints include the environmental considerations of land (for airports and runways), infrastructure (including transport access to airports) and emissions. Aircraft manufacturer Boeing (2012) predicted that between 2012 and 2032 world GDP could grow by 3.2% with a 5% increase in revenue passenger kilometres (RPKs) (i.e. the revenue per passenger per seat flown and occupied). Boeing also predicted similar increases in cargo traffic. The aircraft market predictions include replacements for older, less efficient and less environmentally friendly aircraft with new aircraft with lower CO_2 emissions. Overall, this growth would increase aircraft emissions over the 2012 levels – but by what quantity is unknown although many computer models have attempted to predict. While the current level of aviation CO_2 emissions is not believed to be a major concern, it is the predicted growth of the industry in the pursuit of democratised social mobility that bothers environmentalists.

However, by 2050 'the share of all aviation (international, domestic, military and other) as a source of CO_2 emissions might rise to above 15% of all CO_2 emissions' (Olsthoorn, 2001: 87) (i.e. 15% of 0.03% of atmosphere, which is an extremely small quantity to accurately measure). Some of this increase is explained in the assumptions that the travel aspirations of the advancing-world would eventually catch up to the developed world and result in an increase in the number of flights (one of the equalising consequences of the quest for social justice). With advancing countries increasing their own aviation capacities, this growth is projected to continue – and with it the corresponding emissions. However, there is no way of knowing by what percentage aircraft-produced negative environmental externalities (including soot) could decrease owing to improvements in engine technology in the decades to follow. Engine manufacturer Rolls Royce is working towards performance improvement targets set by the Advisory Council for Aeronautics Research in Europe (ACARE) where, by 2020, 'emissions are to be reduced by 50% per passenger kilometre, noise by 50% and NOx by 80%' (Rolls Royce, n.d.). The required reductions depend on significant improvements in engines, air frames, ATC management and operations.

6.7 SOCIETY AND AVIATION ENVIRONMENTAL CHALLENGES

Social justice

Airline travel exemplifies the merging of the social and environment dimensions of CSERplus; however, in the search for social justice neither the criteria nor who judges and determines 'social justice' is clear. As an example, weight takes fuel to move it; burning fuel creates emissions. All passengers, regardless of body weight, pay additional charges for overweight luggage. However, overweight passengers (with or without heavy, motorised scooters or wheelchairs) do not pay for either any extra fuel required or the emissions produced transporting them and any accompanying mobility or medical equipment (see Chapter 5). Similarly, underweight passengers do not receive a corresponding credit for their reduced weight (remembering that Air Canada valued the annual saving of 1kg of weight per aircraft at approximately $US20,000 at 2013 prices and 63 tonnes of emissions (see Chapter 1)). Where is the social justice in an underweight passenger subsi- dising a heavier passenger (see Chapter 5)? Charging by weight would be socially responsible, economically efficient, environmentally and socially just and unarguably, equality-based; but it would be politically unacceptable. Obesity in the developed world tends to occur in those with lower incomes – thus the poor might have to pay more for air travel, undermining one of the dimensions of the social justice proponents. The principle of payment by body weight would support the social dimension of 'justice' for the lighter-weight passengers, who could be identified as another missing market. Unfortunately, levying weight-related fares would be tactically difficult to manage at the present time. Economically based social justice currently occurs when passengers in the premium cabins pay higher fares and increased UK APD as an equalising 'penalty' for the greater space, services and comfort acquired.

Believers and alarmists vs sceptics, deniers, outliers and challengers

Many authors disagree with the principles of the social-environmental movement and the equalised societies sought. As predictions of global over-heating become more entrenched, the few scientific outliers, economists, environmentalists and others of many disciplines who were willing to engage with the partisan AGW- is-harmful groups found themselves branded as 'sceptics'. Those dissenters who were completely against the consensus view were branded as 'deniers' which is a pejorative term with unhappy echoes. As non-conformists and therefore outliers (see Chapter 3) they face ridicule, *ad hominem* attacks and threats to their liberty (e.g. such as the previously mentioned threat of prosecution under the USA's RICO Act or loss of employment in the case of the French weatherman). Many of these dissenting voices are retired because they recognised that it was too career- limiting to speak out against the AGW-is-harmful alarmists while in employment.

Furthermore, the resources of the dissenters cannot match the funding available to the AGW-is-harmful proponents who are heavily supported by many vested interests as well as national and supranational governments using taxpayers' money. When democratic nations have legal systems which require equal presentation of evidence from the prosecution and the defence, it is reasonable to wonder why this equivalence is not afforded to the climate change debate when only one side is so generously funded. Many of the results are not replicable which makes them unscientific and yet many State funders have spent vast amounts mitigating the impacts of 'climate change'. This includes installing expensive and unreliable wind turbines, importing fossil fuel substitute biofuels which are grown on food acreages (which in turn affect food prices) and establishing wood-fuelled power stations that can actually create as much supposedly harmful CO_2 emissions as burning coal (Harrabin, 2014).

> The AGW premise has merged into a broader political, economic, educational and even psychological program of enormous ambitions. AGW is used as the rationalization for various initiatives, including the subordination of property rights to political control, government takeover of industry, redistribution of wealth on national and global levels, and a melange of laws to compel people to act in 'environmentally friendly' patterns (e.g. bans on incandescent light bulbs, showerhead flow restrictors, and garbage sorting laws).
>
> (Lewis, 2009: 267)

Furthermore, 'subordination of property rights' removes incentives for entre-preneurs to invest (Coyne, 2013; Sanandaji and Sanandaji, 2014).

Global warming is seen as a confluence of ideas into one BIG idea (Darwall, 2013). Climate science with its adherence to 'climate change derangement syndrome' is now considered too big to fail (Darwall, 2013) (as were the banks before the financial crisis of 2008). The government of the USA's annual spend on believers' and alarmists' research has been focussing on CO_2 and ignoring powerful natural forces which have always influenced climate change. This has led to 'claims that are erroneous and deceitful . . . [and which are] consistently contradicted by actual climate and weather records and so alarmists increasingly emphasize computer models that reinvent and substitute for reality' (Driessen, 2015). Furthermore, any objectivity (i.e. evidence-based critical analysis) has been ignored through the peer review process of scientific journals which shun contrary climate change views (Darwall, 2013; Happer, 2011 and others) in favour of the claims of the erroneously named '97% consensus'. The voices of the few challengers receive neither the inflated publicity nor the volume of funding of the AGW lobby.

'Green' passengers

Passengers would appear to be fairly relaxed in their approach to the environmental impacts of flying but if they were really bothered they have two choices: not to fly or to fly as little as possible. An individual's carbon footprint (i.e. their GHG contribution to AGW) might not have been top of their worries during the economic recession of 2008 to 2013. (NB: the concept of a carbon footprint represents another missing market which has now been identified and associated with property rights.) Visualising a tonne of CO_2 is difficult and if it is not damaging the environment, passengers might not need to picture it. Furthermore, it is easier to be 'green' on the ground than in the air because there is more scope for individual improvement. However, decisions regarding airborne 'green' are actually made on the ground by the airlines' procurement departments and passengers. Each passenger on a return intercontinental flight emits two tonnes of CO_2 which equates to more than 30% of an individual's average carbon emissions (MacKay, 2009). Flying to Cape Town and back once per year is the approximate energy equivalent of 'slightly bigger than leaving a 1kW electric fire on, nonstop, 24 hours a day, all year' (MacKay, 2009: 35). This reflects some of the economic-environmental-social trade-offs which have to be made if CO_2 is a problem and people still want to fly.

Do passengers care about their impact on the environment? Depending on the type of aircraft, seating configuration and the cabin in which a passenger is seated, the individual carbon footprint can be varied considerably. For example, the carbon footprint of a seat in the premium cabins on a full-service carrier is greater than that of an economy seat because premium seats are wider, are allocated more space and therefore require more fuel to keep them airborne. It can also be argued that premium cabin passengers take more luggage than the economy cabin because they have a higher luggage weight allowance which consumes more fuel. In theory, if the size of carbon footprint was used as a performance measure then corporate airline customers could reduce their firm's carbon footprint and travel costs by restricting employees to the economy cabin. This would be economically efficient and could also represent an application of an equality-envy-social justice principle. However, as already noted, the calculation of personal carbon emissions is not thought to have much influence on personal transport choice 'which could be seen as being dominated by issues of cost (both in time and money), comfort and convenience' (Chatterton *et al.*, 2009: 45).

Tourists in their 'away' environments appear to 'reduce, suppress or abandon' their environmental concerns in contrast to their concerns when at 'home' (Cohen *et al.*, 2013). As a result policy makers have been asked to exercise more intervention to reduce aviation's impact on the climate. There is apparently only limited scope for voluntary public behaviour changes with regards to discretionary air travel unless governments intervene, which raises the issue of conflict between social justice (i.e. air travel accessible for all regardless of income) and the environment. Governments' intervention inevitably means more transactions which trigger higher costs for which prices would have to rise. Tourists might not consider climate impacts when planning holidays and share a common belief that politicians should lead by example. As 'citizens' representatives' politicians were expected to role model appropriate behaviours including not driving cars, flying frequently or owning second homes (Hare *et al.*, 2010). Once again the social justice argument features but this time in the guise of envy. Air travellers might not want to make changes in their own travel behaviour because they value their holidays and they also do not want to adapt their arrangements for climate change especially as they feel that environmental responsibility lies elsewhere (Hare *et al.*, 2010).

A UK ONS (2010) survey, using pre-determined criteria, tried to assess passengers' thoughts on the environment and air travel given their state of knowledge. Those who agreed that 'air travel harms the environment' (the underlying bias in this questionnaire would appear to be that air travel *does* damage the environment) confirmed the criteria of 'pollution/poor air quality' (82%), 'climate change/global warming/ozone damage' (45%), 'noise' (36%) and 'uses up/wastes a lot of fuel' (24%). The survey found that the proportion of respondents who agreed that 'air travel harms the environment' fell from 70% in 2006 to 62% in 2010 with the older adults showing the largest fall. However, the proportion of respondents who agreed that people should be able to travel by plane as much as they wanted – irrespective of environmental harm – increased to 29% (from 17% in 2006). Interestingly, among those who believed that air travel harmed the environment 59% agreed the price of air travel should reflect the environmental damage (i.e. the negative externality) but the proportion willing to pay extra fell from 69% in 2006 to 60% in 2010. This finding is at odds with the reality that approximately only 3% of passengers currently purchase carbon [dioxide] offsets (Kahya, 2009) but it might reflect the fact that (a) more people who are taking early retirement and living on reduced incomes are now flying; (b) the growth of no-frills, low-cost carriers making flying more affordable and/or (c) airfares are now more expensive (especially out of the UK) because of non-hypothecated environmental taxes. On the other hand, passengers are willing to pay extra for flights at times that suit them and for additional services and facilities which they can enjoy and for which they can benefit – but not for invisible environmental externalities. Would purchasing offsets encourage feelings of altruism (see Chapter 3)? The same survey indicated that 47% of respondents agreed that new terminals and runways should be built to boost the economy. However, 57% believed that airport expansion should be limited to protect the local environment and 51% to limit it to reduce the impact of climate change. These statistics reveal economic, social and environmental challenges.

Passengers have been accused of having a 'psychology of denial' (Gossling and Peeters, 2007) when it comes to air travel. When in apparent denial they believe that air travel is energy efficient, accounts for only marginal emissions of CO_2 and is too socially and economically important to be restricted (i.e. the argument for access to a public good (see Chapter 1)). They also believed that fuel use is being minimised and that its unfavourable impacts were being solved by the advent of new technology; that air travel is treated unfairly compared to other means of transport; and that aviation created jobs and economic growth (but at a high environmental cost, i.e. the trade-off: economics vs environment). Low-cost airlines were not considered to be more or less environmentally friendly than full-service network airlines; however, passengers did perceive differences in environmental images of individual airlines (rather than the industry as a whole) (Mayer *et al.*, 2012). Of the proposed measures to improve airlines' environmental performance (which included increasing the number of seats per aircraft, reducing on-board waste, offering carbon offsetting and testing biofuels) using newer aircraft was perceived to be the most effective means to address passengers' environmental concerns (Mayer *et al.*, 2012). Although investing in new aircraft has significant capital cost they should bring operating economies since newer aircraft are credited with fuel efficiencies and reduced emissions.

'Green' messages

There are five key variables which determine a flight's carbon [dioxide] efficiency per passenger per mile: aircraft model, seating density, load factor, freight share and distance (Kling and Hough, 2011). In theory, passengers could choose their flights according to the CO_2 (or CO_2e) sensitivity of their journey enabling them to be 'environmentally friendly'. This is only appropriate if passengers believe that CO_2 is the cause of the harm that some researchers claim even though the science is inconclusive.

It has been suggested by the AGW-is-harmful advocates that sustainable airlines could promote green marketing messages as a quicker marketing win than procuring newer, environmentally sustainable aircraft. One example given was that of British Airways whose provision of carbon offset schemes was suggested to be a potential marketing tool – 'carbon branding' – as a means of neutralising the purported consequences of flying. There were claims that providing this offsetting facility meant that British Airways could

> present its climate-conscious passengers with the option of flying free from concern over the impact of their emissions. This shift to what is essentially an unregulated and disputed form of eco-taxation away from the company and onto the consumer has gained British Airways an enormous amount of favourable publicity.
>
> (Smith, 2007: 10)

(The author, Smith, wrote for the Transnational Institute – an international research and advocacy organisation which at that time was aiming to work towards economic, social and environmental justice.) It was not possible either to quantify or to verify the author's assertions, to know whether this 'favourable publicity' increased seat or freight sales or to validate how many passengers actually paid to offset their emissions – possibly few if other airlines' experiences are typical. 'Easyjet and Virgin both estimate that some 3% of their passengers offset the carbon from their flight, though numbers have come down during the recession [2008 to 2013]' (Kahya, 2009), i.e. passengers are price sensitive. Furthermore, it is not known how many or whether these offsets were paid by individuals or organisations (such as governments, charities, NGOs, or even firms) on behalf of their employees. The proportion of passengers who use offsetting indicates that few flyers connect their behaviour with any environmental impact. In another study, it was found that passengers regarded the airlines' positive attitude towards the environment as effective in reducing the environmental impact of air travel and thus contributing to a 'green' image. The authors believed that this could give airlines a chance to differentiate themselves from their competitors by discussing their green credentials and might offer the opportunity to encourage passengers to pay for a 'green product' (Mayer *et al.*, 2012) (i.e. another missing market perhaps?). However, this willingness would appear unlikely if current voluntary offset purchasing behaviour is a guide.

In a case study of airline Swiss it was found that passengers were interested in an airline's environmental responsibility but that price played an important role in choosing an airline (Wittmer, 2010) (reconfirming that airline passengers are price sensitive). Passengers were favourably supportive of Swiss' environmental protection measures (operating with a modern fleet and making an effort to reduce noise emissions) because they did not have to be proactive. However, when given an opportunity to make a contribution towards climate protection (i.e. pay for their carbon taxes), there was minimal support which conflicted with many AGW-is-harmful advocates' assertions. Further into the research, 44% (of 325 respondents) agreed that the State or the airline should carry the environmental costs – and not the passengers themselves. This is naive economic thinking. If the State carries the environmental costs they would be recovered from taxation. If the airline covers them they would be reflected in fares. The conclusion is that price is a barrier for passengers to proactively protect the environment (Wittmer, 2010). Whilst accepting that this was indeed a small sample of the total passenger population, it nevertheless provided an interesting insight into passengers' relationships with guilt, economics and environmental awareness.

Socially responsible investments (SRIs)

No matter how hard airlines try, there will always be stakeholders who do not accept that the industry is doing its best to preserve the environment. Some corporates even go so far as to avoid aviation as an investment opportunity despite the benefits that the industry brings to both advanced and advancing nations. An example of this would be Scottish Widows and Standard Life Investments which eliminated airlines from their lists of socially responsible investments (SRIs) because 13% of all carbon emissions in the UK are purported to emanate from aviation (in other words, 13% of the UK's share of 0.03% of the world's CO_2). In the case of Standard Life Investments, the boycott was a response to a survey in which 30% of 3,000 respondents from a potential population of 39,000 holders of Standard Life Investment's ethical funds wanted a boycott, i.e. approximately 2.5% of those entitled to vote (Jamieson, 2008), enabling 36,000 holders to be free riders (see Chapter 1). (NB: what did the remaining 70% of free rider fund holders want?) However, the finance and investment industry uses airlines and there is neither a note of a flying boycott by SRI executives nor whether they flew in premium or economy cabins with the varying emissions footprints.

6.8 MORE INTERVENTIONS

Biofuels, poverty and politics

Aside from funding the AGW-is-harmful advocates and relying on them for policy recommendations, politicians have many ideas for resolving their view of aviation-induced atmospheric problems. Solutions range from emissions trading, allocating an annual personal green air mile allowance through to imposing air taxes. One of the propositions was to increase the use of biofuels as aviation fuel substitutes. As biofuels (such as Brazil's sugar cane-based farnesane) are burnt, they release the CO_2 previously absorbed photosynthesising during their growth.

However, there are political roots to biofuels (Bailey, 2013). They began as transfers to agriculture, i.e. subsidies – one of the triggers for imperfect market operation (see Chapter 1). In the late 1970s the USA subsidised ethanol to support corn farmers. In 2003 the EU saw similar transfers as a way of increasing farm-gate prices and supporting the rural sectors of poorer incoming member states. In both examples it was hoped that using agricultural surpluses would support farm prices and reduce direct rural support payments – actions which undermine the competitiveness of markets and restrict allocative resource efficiency. Using farm surpluses for biofuels is different from purposefully growing specific fuel crops and since these policies have now become expensively embedded, unravelling them would be politically unpalatable but economically desirable (i.e. environmental politics vs airline economics). Biodiesel made from vegetable oil is reportedly worse for the climate than fossil fuels – and yet under EU law, biofuels were set to make up 5% of the UK's transport fuel from 2013 onwards. Growing crops such as rapeseed for biofuels is not considered to be an efficient use of either land or resources (Bailey, 2013). Similarly, computer-modelling showed that changing land use from forests and grasslands to grow potential fuel crops (such as corn-based ethanol) has nearly doubled GHGs over 30 years, an increase which would last for 167 years and growing biofuels from switchgrass on cornlands would increase emissions by 50% (Searchinger *et al.*, 2008). (However, since 'GHG' is actually a metaphorical collective noun for an accumulation of possibly naturally occurring atmospheric (infrared-absorbing) gases rather than a description of harmful emissions, does this change the expression of the biofuels problem?)

Green groups have advanced biofuels as a GHG-emissions-reducing weapon against the effects of AGW but their views can conflict with those of the social justice proponents. According to UK poverty-reduction charity Oxfam, targets for European biofuel (to be used as a fossil fuel substitute) are contributing to global hunger by creating spikes in food prices. In 2012 Oxfam called for the EU to scrap the mandates that committed States to obtaining 10% of transport energy from renewable sources by 2020 because the land required to meet the mandate could feed 127 million people for one year (Lawrence, 2012). Social and environmental concerns were mixed in Oxfam's call to reduce the impact of the biofuel policies on the poorest people because it was worsening their hunger and increasing the effects of what the charity perceived to be man-made climate change.

Demand for biofuels in Europe is also putting pressure on land and water resources globally . . . [it is] estimated that around two-thirds of all large-scale land deals around the world in the past 10 years have been acquisitions made to grow biofuel crops, including soya, sugar, palm oil and jatropha. Many of these deals have displaced local communities with claims on the land or have involved laying claim to water rights.

(Lawrence, 2012)

There is an environmental-economic trade-off between agricultural food production and biofuels for energy with concerns that projected demand for food would drive agricultural expansion at the expense of emissions (Bajželj *et al.*, 2014). Nutritional demand puts pressure on land use for biofuel production. Where should any priority be placed? Any crop growing for biofuel production should not require sacrificing agricultural land, absorbing drinking water or destroying native forests (the habitats of many diverse and threatened species as well as providing CO_2 sinks). Growing biofuels can also lead to increased costs for animal feed (which would have been grown on that same soil) and therefore escalating consumer food prices. Reducing food production would result in decreased food supply (an unintended consequence of saving emissions). Crop-based fuels are not CO_2 neutral because the sources of other emissions encountered in the process must also be considered including any chemical production, farm machinery or refineries (Bailey, 2013). Furthermore, land use changes to support biofuel growing (such as peat drainage or deforestation) generate the largest potential emission sources.

Alternative strategies

Despite the foregoing, and under pressure from environmentalists and governments, the airline industry continues to seek alternatives to fossil fuels. In a 2008 trial, a Virgin Atlantic Boeing 747 flew from Amsterdam to Heathrow (BBC, 2008a) with one of its four engines connected to a tank of 20% fuel derived from a mixture of Brazilian babassu nuts and coconuts (cellulosic ethanol) and the remainder from aviation kerosene. This test required the equivalent of 150,000 coconuts but to run the entire flight on this mix would have required three million (Strahan, 2008). To grow sufficient jet-fuel substitute to supply the industry for one day would require the equivalent of double the landmass of France (Strahan, 2008). Similarly, Boeing Aircraft Corporation and South African Airways have trialled growing energy-rich tobacco to produce sustainable biofuels (Boeing, 2014). There is hope for algae which grows quickly, could take up less land and deliver higher yields than oil crops (Strahan, 2008) but its progress is not without challenges. Producing biodiesel from waste products (such as cooking oil or latterly, plastic refuse) currently offers the most environmentally sustainable route but the risk of indirect emissions which occur elsewhere in the process escalates as use increases. Through further improvements in aircraft efficiency and development of alternative fuels, aviation emissions are supposed to return to 50% of 2005 levels by 2050. Improvements in engine and airframe technologies over the last 40 years have halved the quantity of fuel used to fly one tonne one kilometre (IATA, 2013) – a move which was largely stimulated by the market during volatile and rising fuel prices. There have also been quantum leaps in engine technology. The Airbus A350 and A380 are credited with 20% fuel improvement as well as reductions in emissions and noise. Environmentally sustainable airlines are renewing their fleets with aircraft and engines which are quieter and more fuel efficient than previous generations. However, caps on emissions (or alternatively, taxing aircraft fuels) will ultimately require increased fares which would make flying more expensive. This could endorse Ryanair's Chief Executive's comments about ultimately allowing only the rich to fly which would severely dent the social benefit and social justice arguments (i.e. politics vs environment vs airline economics). At the extreme, it could even return air travel back to being a luxury product.

6.9 LEGISLATION, REGULATION AND POLICIES

Political moral panic

AGW-is-harmful can be considered the 21st-century cause célèbre, championed by proponents including the UN, most Western governments and major churches, the supposedly free press, many MNEs (including the now-defunct Enron) and the public (Carter, 2007). There is a contrast between the AGW-is-harmful science and the volume of public concern. Too few dissenting voices are heard against the vested commercial and scientific interests occupying the warming alarmist community. 'Public opinion will soon demand an explanation as to why experienced editors and hardened investigative journalists, worldwide, have melted before the blowtorch of self-induced guilt, political correctness and special interest expediency that marks the sophisms of global warming alarmists' (Carter, 2007: 4). (Once again, there are echoes of the media response to the fears of the Millennium Bug.)

Politicians have reacted to warming concerns with national, multi-national and supranational legislation (some of which can be categorised as boondoggles) without considering just how their aims would be achieved especially since much of the technology required has yet to be invented. Environmental economics has been given thrust by assorted national and supranational legislation, regulation, policies and agreements forged to reduce global warming/climate change. These long-term laws encumber future generations with the present uncertainties and negative externalities which have been determined by many 'expert' advisers. They use imperfect knowledge as a basis for their asymmetric influencing (one of the triggers for alleged market inefficiency and failure). However, 'The political proposals to alleviate this alleged problem – especially plans by the U.S. Environmental Protection Agency – are shown to offer no alternative to fossil fuels [unlike CFC replacement], and to portend a major economic decline and permanent losses of liberty' (Lewis, 2009: 31), particularly in advanced, democratic nations.

Kyoto Protocol 1997 and Clean Development Mechanisms (CDMs)

The UNFCCC engineered a legally binding agreement (the Kyoto Protocol) to reduce global emissions of all so-called 'GHGs' by 5.4% by 2012 relative to 1990 levels. The UK's target was 12.5%. The means was to be an environmental 'cap-and-trade' programme under which nations were awarded a quantity of free allowance amount units (AAUs) which they could expend or trade with one AAU equal to one tonne of CO_2 equivalent. (National AAUs were based on emissions for the first five-year commitment period.) The advancing industrial nations took part in discussions and as nations with high emissions, they were expected to agree to limit their emissions but without targets. Of the 192 countries involved in the negotiations only 34 ratified the original agreement including eventually, Russia in 2004. The USA originally refused to sign but when it did, it did not submit it to the Senate for ratification. The main output of the protocol, reviewed annually, is to give incentives to polluters through procuring monetised CO_2 offsets as a trade-off for negative externalities. Trade in CO_2 and CO_2e monetises the negative externalities, fills a formerly missing market and provides funds to support pollution-reducing projects in developing and emerging nations. These funds are known as 'clean development mechanisms' (CDMs). If the polluting organisation exceeds its emissions savings targets it can buy the necessary credits from an under-emitting producer in another market and conversely, can sell any surplus credits. The credits can be certified by the UN as guaranteeing an offset emission reduction elsewhere or certified by other standards boards in the 'voluntary market'. (The spawning of UN and non-UN CDM standards has uncovered another new (missing) industry, i.e. that of certification.) The CDM funds procure non-pollutant energy sources such as solar panels, water turbines or other projects which could reduce negative emissions externalities in advancing nations. The funds are channelled through middle-men (the carbon offset brokers) who charge between 15% and 25% of the value of the transaction (Kahya, 2009). (NB: in 2008 the annual trade in CDM credits was \$US8.2bn (Broderick, 2009).) However, the CDM is also a market, a subsidy and a political mechanism and its political goals were actually achieved early (Wara, 2007). It is also a concept which evidences Henderson's (2001) concern about global-salvationism-environmental-alarmism which combines over-alarming pessimism about the damage business has inflicted on the environment with predictions of future effects for which there are 'collectivist solutions'. Initially, the advancing nations had more immediate priorities than climate change but once they recognised the net inward financial benefits they became supporters.

> The anthropogenic global warming claims are largely motivated not by science, but by a desire for socialist intervention on a national and a global scale. Neither the claims to an impending climate catastrophe nor the political proposals attached to those claims should be accepted.
>
> (Lewis, 2009: 231)

It is possible to conclude that the environmental externality-compensating market in advanced nations has been established to support social welfare in developing and emerging nations. Furthermore, it is difficult to definitively draw a scientific conclusion that there is a correlation between atmospheric CO_2, CO_2e and Earth's temperature rises when the underpinning science and lack of economic analysis appear politically motivated.

CDM Policy Dialogue

Contrary to the wishes of the CDM instigators and due largely to the falling price of CO_2 (a by-product of an overhang of the original free allowances, reduced emissions and the economic recession), some of the offset projects have not been economically successful and have actually provided little long-term benefit. CDM Policy Dialogue (2012a) (established under the auspices of the UN) examined what was considered to be a failing CDM market and urged governments to do more to increase the take-up of CDMs to make the programme fit for the future. According to this panel, if nations permitted the CDM mechanism to disintegrate, the political consensus for truly global carbon markets might evaporate. This was unacceptable so it asked 'nations to increase their mitigation ambition . . . to investigate the establishment of a new fund to purchase and cancel part of the current overhang of emission allowances [i.e. AAUs] held by countries under the Kyoto Protocol' (CDM Policy Dialogue, 2012b). The report made recommendations to cover 'the crisis of demand, mitigation impact, linking of carbon markets, sustainable development, regional distribution, governance structure, additionality, stakeholder and public engagement, as well as mechanisms for appeals and grievances' (CDM Policy Dialogue, 2012c). The Dialogue continues:

> the international community *must* [author's emphasis] take four essential and mutually reinforcing actions as a matter of great urgency: First, nations *must* intervene forcefully to address the immediate crisis [of the failing emissions market]. . . Second, the international community *must* adapt the CDM to new political and market conditions by enhancing its role. . . Third, the CDM *must* substantially reform its operating procedures and greatly expand its assistance to participating countries to maximise its impact. . . Fourth, the CDM *must* strengthen and restructure its governance to become a more accountable and efficient organization.
>
> (CDM Policy Dialogue, 2012a: 3)

If implemented, these 'musts' emanating from an unelected body would undermine democracy in democratic nations. While noble in its aims, the CDM has a democratic deficit, lacks external challenge and sustainability-thinking and howsoever it is promoted, it still amounts to a tax taken from developed nations to support projects in advancing nations which could ultimately give their industries an international competitive advantage. It also extends the concept of advancing-world public (social) benefits onto advanced-world private industries with costs ultimately paid by their customers. Recommendations of this nature are not economically sustainable and could damage the competitiveness of privately owned international industries. Furthermore, the valuation of CO_2 as an externality bears no relationship to any actual monetised negative impact. It is merely a tax on energy in the developed world to be traded (in a market through commission-earning brokers) and donated (minus the commissions or brokerage fees) to advancing nations to offset the unquantifiable and possibly natural effects of climate changing.

CDM dissent

The trade in GHGs has been considered as a form of 'climate fraud' because of the inadequate way that the projects are monitored. It is also seen as a form of 'carbon colonialism' because it is supporting a new form of imperialism which uses 'climate policies to bring about a variation on the traditional means by which the global South is dominated' (Bachram, 2004: 10). Even the 2°C temperature target has been derided as colonialism because Europe has decided it is to be 'a global target' (Tol, 2005). Indeed, environmental movement Greenpeace had its bank accounts frozen and its licence suspended in India because of fears that the 'green' influence of Britain (the former colonial power) was becoming detrimental to Indian development (Pandey, 2015).

Seeking society's approval for some offset projects might be easier with some generations than others. One research paper claimed that young adults would willingly pay for CO_2 offsets which (among other benefits touted) could support poverty reduction, human development and biodiversity preservation (MacKerron *et al.*, 2009). However, one of the five authors came from a carbon finance company and three from climate research institutes. Another of their findings was that airline passengers would voluntarily offset any emissions from their travel if only the advantages of investments in projects with environmental benefits could be communicated to them. The questionnaire included the premise that 'extra CO_2 in the atmosphere is causing climate change which could have serious and damaging effects worldwide, on people and the environment' (MacKerron *et al.*, 2009: 1,375). This could influence the respondents and undermine the expected impartiality and reliability of peer-reviewed research.

Mark-to-market

The carbon offset companies are using present value accounting for estimating future growth, i.e. future savings are brought back to present day prices which is the same technique bankrupt Enron used with its 'mark-to-market' accounting. When an asset is market valued at a certain date, the value at that date is what is included in the accounts, i.e. its value to the market. However, if the value of the asset is undefined – as at some point in the future – then capitalising on its fantasised future value at the present day is inaccurate, misleading and could even be dishonest. Mark-to-market is a highly risky strategy which gives distorted current valuations. In terms of emissions, capitalising now on future (increased) quantities could lead to a deficit in CO_2 sinks at a later date unless technology can deliver the extra savings required. By the time the deficit is realised, those who have profited today could be long dead. CO_2 sequestration agreements for forests (in their role as CO_2 sinks) provide a good example. They have a mixed reputation. Some of the 'carbon [dioxide] offset' companies simply take over an existing forest and buy up the emissions permits rather than planting whole new forests to absorb the CO_2 for which they have sold the credits to polluters. In the case of air travel, that effectively means that there could actually be no neutralisation of passengers' emissions. There is also a challenge as to how much CO_2 a particular forest can absorb, the number of trees required to offset any quantities of CO_2 and how long the absorption could take (remembering that CO_2 is purported to reside for approximately 100 years (IPCC, 1999a)). 'Jet aircraft emit tons of fossil carbon [dioxide] every hour whereas trees planted as offsets absorb it slowly, erratically and impermanently' (Garrard, 2013: 178). In other words, equating the buyers' need with the sellers' offering is not an exact calculation and using mark-to-market could even be fraudulent. It is, however, extremely profitable for the traders in the middle and the countries which are net receivers of any monetised offsets which would have been marked-to-market.

UK's Climate Change Act 2008

In the UK, the government-commissioned Stern Review (Stern, 2006) is regarded as the benchmark even though science is updating climate knowledge and perhaps changing the basis on which its recommendations were made. This review was to have a significant impact on the UK economy; however, once it was completed it was not subjected to a complete scientific or economic peer review. Without this balancing critique, the Stern Review predicted unstable economies unless emissions of CO_2 (to which the author referred as 'carbon') were reduced, and yet it did not acknowledge that the 20th-century observations were formed from hundreds or thousands of years rather than just the time since observations began and that the majority of emissions are from natural sources (reminder: only 150ppm of the approximate 350ppm (Lewis, 2009) to 430ppm (Stern, 2006) of CO_2 and other GHGs in the atmosphere are attributable to human sources (Carter *et al.*, 2006)).

From this review came the UK Climate Change Act 2008 with its three aspirations: to deliver carbon [dioxide] reduction targets (80% by 2050), to set carbon [dioxide] budgets (excluding aviation and shipping) and to create a national climate adaptation plan. The Act devolved its responsibilities to an independent body – the Committee on Climate Change (CCC) – to advise it on managing climate change (but it did not create a body to examine whether climate change is (a) man-made and therefore (b) can be prevented or controlled). The CCC's report – *Building a Low Carbon Economy* – suggested that the aviation industry should be included in the UK's commitment to reducing CO_2 emissions by 80% by 2050 (CCC, 2008) without acknowledging the intricate mechanics of achieving this target. The UK had the most stringent targets among the nations which had committed to the Kyoto Agreement.

Shipping, aviation and taxes

In the mid-2000s shipping and aviation represented around 3.2% and 2.1% respectively of total global CO_2 emissions (Vidal, 2007) but aviation has had more political and advocate pressure because of the growing popularity of travel due to the arrival of the low-cost, low-fare carriers. Over the past 20 years, shipping (responsible for 90% of world trade) has been excused by governments and environmental groups for the purpose of emissions reductions. It is expected that shipping emissions will increase dramatically in ensuing decades with increasing globalisation and consumer demand (Vidal, 2007). Shipping was also ignored by the Kyoto Protocol (Vidal, 2007) and a decision on whether to include GHGs emitted by shipping and aviation into the UK's carbon targets was postponed until 2016 (after the UK's 2015 General Election) which will coincide with the fifth carbon [dioxide] budget detailing the UK's permitted emissions from 2028 to 2032. However, the Climate Change Act 2008 recognised that there were difficulties with including shipping and aviation in carbon [dioxide] budgets because of lack of international agreement about measurement and allocation of inter-national emissions to individual countries. Concern was also expressed that without international commitment to emissions reductions there would be perverse incentives for mobile industries (including aviation) to move away from the UK. Consequently, international aviation and shipping emissions are not currently included within the 2050 target as defined by the Act (UK Department for Energy and Climate Change (DECC), 2012). However, if aviation was not to be included in carbon [dioxide] budgets, other industries would have to compensate. This could mean less heat in homes or reductions in other means of transport (such as the trucks that transport food). This creates a mind-set that food and shelter are more important than business trips and holidays and therefore flying could be perceived as a guilty pleasure and a luxury. It was acknowledged that there were difficulties with aviation being included in the emissions budgets because of the impossibility of allocation at the national level and also because of the environmental trade-offs with growing biofuels as an alternative fuel source. Its concerns for aviation emissions noted that burning aviation fuel created water vapour mixed with sulphate aerosol and soot visible as contrails which might increase the frequency of cirrus cloud formation. Contrails were also believed to contribute to the radiative effects while considerable uncertainly also surrounded the consequences of other aviation emissions such as NO_x (believed to contribute to O_3) and clouds. However, the dispersion and radiative effects do not affect everyone equally simultaneously. 'The effect of aviation particles on clouds (with and without contrails) may give rise to either a positive forcing or a negative forcing: the modelling and the under-lying processes are highly uncertain' (Lee *et al.*, 2010: 4,678). In other words, scientists are not sure. In summary, 'The level of current scientific understanding of these two processes [contrail formation and aircraft activity] are thus classed as 'Fair' and 'Poor' respectively' (CCC, 2008: 310).

However, according to the CCC (2008) UK aviation is dominated by international travel for which few alternatives exist. Aircraft emissions do not affect everyone to the same extent but emissions taxes would affect passengers disproportionately. Government policies on emissions taxes represent yet more conflict between economics and the environment since governments are not always transparent to the real reason that non-hypothecated taxes are necessary (another example of asymmetric and incomplete information). Such taxes could have the greatest effect on the private economic benefit felt by passengers with lower disposable incomes, i.e. a regressive tax. However, measuring the social costs of any externality is very difficult because many of the costs are private and possibly even psychological (Baumol, 1972). Even collecting such data from individuals can be problematic and furthermore, it is often not possible to find the optimal output level at which such a tax could be applied to achieve maximum social benefit. Alarmingly for the airline industry, the establishment of an emissions tax could have a detrimental impact on the UK tourist industry (in which airlines play a vital part) if an Australian study (Dwyer *et al.*, 2012) is any guide. Among the predictions are reductions in GDP, growth, consumption and employment and 'since tourism is an industry that depends substantially on the natural environment, stakeholders have a particular interest and concern in how the policies that are being developed to mitigate the impacts of climate change will impact on their operations' (Dwyer *et al.*, 2012: 143–144).

European Union Emissions Trading Scheme (EU ETS)

By applying property rights to emissions and creating a new market, the EU intended that its emissions trading scheme (ETS) would reduce annual GHG (i.e. infrared-absorbing gas) emissions in Europe. Airlines were originally required to enter into EU ETS in 2012

> with a specific allocation, some of which will be allocated to airlines and some auctioned [i.e. cap-and-trade]. The total allocation for airlines administered by a Member State will be calculated and a percentage (15% in 2012, then 15% in 2013–2020 unless changed by the 2020 package negotiation) top-sliced for auction. However, the Committee [on Climate Change] agrees with the European Commission's desire for a move towards 100% auctioning of allowances for aviation by 2020. The aviation cap will be based on an average of the emissions in the years 2004 to 2006, with 97% of that baseline in the first year 2012 and 95% post, unless the percentage reduction is changed as part of the general review of the ETS. Including aviation effectively adds to the total emissions cap within EU ETS, and results in a percentage rate of reduction in the total which is slightly less than for all covered sectors excluding aviation. The total EU ETS cap, including aviation, has however been set so as to be broadly compatible with the EU's 20%–30% GHG targets.
>
> (CCC, 2008: 320)

In other words, all this is confusion and obfuscation for an industry which it is estimated contributes around 2% of international GHGs – which themselves comprise approximately 1% of total atmosphere – and which are misnamed because the greenhouse metaphor is inaccurate.

The cap was to be applied only to flights within Europe while governments worked towards a global climate change solution. Polluters had their free allowance over which they either had to procure credits or pay for their excess thereby neutralising any negative externalities. The cap-and-trade scheme monetises emissions which can be traded in an emissions marketplace and offset by three means: (1) if the polluter under-uses the allowance they can save or sell the credits to another polluter on the open market; (2) the polluter uses their entire allowance and has to purchase more to remain in compliance; (3) the polluter offsets emissions by investing in pollution reduction schemes (i.e. CDMs) in economically advancing regions. Cap-and-trade transactions are conducted by a central authority (e.g. the EU) which allocates (or auctions) permits for participants to trade within their marketplace. There are a finite number of permits for any given industry and outside of those permits the polluters need to enter the marketplace of another industry to purchase their surplus permits. In all cases, there is an intermediary (financial institution, NGO or other organisation) acting as broker and taking an arrangement fee or commission (of perhaps 15% to 25%) (Kahya, 2009). Carbon [dioxide] trading is *big* business.

The 2008 EU Directive 208/101 (European Union, 2008) which included 'aviation activities in the scheme for greenhouse gas emission allowance trading within the Community' included aviation from 2012 onwards whereby all carriers to the EU ETS countries (at that time comprising the 28 EU nations plus Iceland, Lichtenstein and Norway) should have secured allowances for CO_2 emissions. Many air carriers argued that this contravened international treaties (in particular the Chicago Convention 1944 – Annex 16 Environmental Protection regarding noise and engine emissions (ICAO, 2006)). The formula for allocating EU allowances was complicated involving free allowances and auctionable allowances based around the carrier's 2010 market share which ultimately favoured the incumbent airlines. Processing this complication would add transactions costs. However, airlines have been accused of profiteering from the free allowances. According to a report commissioned by the European Federation for Transport and the Environment (which derives approximately 20% of its funding from EU sources) windfall gains from the free allowances were estimated at that time to be £Stg1.2bn ($US1.7bn or €1.5bn) (Goldenberg, 2013). This claim was dismissed by IATA as 'ludicrous'. (Had it been true, and comprehensive sustainability-thinking been used, the 'windfall' could have offset the PRM costs (see Chapter 5) if they were known. Society vs environment vs economics?)

Aviation could expand the amount of allowable emissions (over the cap) by purchasing emissions permits from non-aviation industries. 'Traffic growth drives increases in CO_2 emissions, but emissions increases are smaller than traffic increases as the fleet becomes more efficient over time. The lowest annual growth in emissions occurs when airlines pass on all costs associated with CO_2 allowances' (Malina *et al.*, 2012: 39), i.e. when the costs are passed onto customers they should trigger seat and freight price increases. In the law of supply and demand, if prices increase the quantity of products sold will reduce *(ceteris paribus)*. In the extreme, higher costs would lead to higher fares or freight charges so that fewer customers will purchase from fewer flights thereby reducing emissions. This could work against the social justice agenda in the developed world unless their governments were prepared to subsidise low-income passengers because fewer seats on fewer flights could trigger fare rises making them unaffordable for less well-off citizens, i.e. politics and environment vs society and economics.

CDM offset schemes 'can be broadly categorised as being forestry and land use, fuel switching, renewable energy, energy efficiency, methane capture or fugitive industrial gas destruction. Projects do not solely reduce CO_2 emissions from fossil fuel consumption as other GHGs are made equivalent by defining their global warming potential [i.e. CO_2e]' (Broderick, 2009: 335). However, the biggest national polluters – including China, India and Russia – do not tax their polluting industries and so their businesses have a competitive advantage in international markets – and their goods are exported (often by air) to the EU and to other nations which have signed up to the Kyoto Protocol and are paying for permits. It is therefore not surprising that 'developing nations that were initially sceptical of the CDM – notably China and India – have entered the market with great enthusiasm and now sell the most credits' (Wara, 2007: 595). Advanced-world airlines procuring these monetised carbon [dioxide] credits could become increasingly uncompetitive compared to advancing-world carriers with their generally lower overhead costs and labour taxes (see Table 1.1 and Table 1.2 in Chapter 1). The airlines of advancing nations would be receiving the benefit from reduced national energy emissions costs. However, in effect, the passengers and shareholders of airlines in the advanced-world are going to be subsidising international rivals and supporting social projects in countries with regimes with which they might not agree and where oversight and governance might be inadequate. Should privately owned, developed world airlines be used for political and social purposes in this way?

EU ETS dissent

The USA was one of many non-EU countries which protested at the inclusion of aviation in the EU ETS. The USA claimed that the EU ETS breached the Chicago Convention (1944) (which regulates air travel) and furthermore, such issues should be solved by ICAO. Unsurprisingly the ECJ (as an arm of the EU) decided that including aviation in the EU ETS was valid. In 2011 the USA prohibited its airlines from complying with the EU legislation. The EU subsequently suspended the EU ETS pending a global resolution through ICAO in 2013. It will now be implemented post-2016 after which passengers will pay an extra £Stg4 (rising to £Stg10 by 2020) on intra-EU flights and £Stg16 (rising to £Stg60 by 2020) on flights outside of the EU. Outbound UK passengers will pay this in addition to any distance-related APD or its successor. However, canny UK outbound passengers could fly to local European destinations (Paris, Frankfurt, Amsterdam, Stockholm) and start their long-haul journey from there to avoid paying APD – a move which would affect UK airlines and restrict their economic sustainability and competitiveness. Ironically truncating the journey from the UK (and thereby increasing the number of flights taken) could increase the demand for short-haul flights which would, in turn, increase aviation's CO_2 emissions – the negative externality that such taxes were originally intended to reduce. In computer-modelling, 'doubling APD had the perverse effect of increasing carbon dioxide emissions, albeit only slightly, because it reduced the relative price difference between near and far holidays' (Mayor and Tol, 2007: 507). Taxing emissions directly gives more strength to the argument for taxing passengers by the weight of their body and luggage (i.e. society vs political correctness vs airline economics).

UK CCC and EU ETS

The expansion of the EU ETS fits with the Stern Review (Stern, 2006) which recommended that UK government actions required to prevent climate meltdown included the creation of a market for CO_2, and pricing and extending the EU ETS globally. This would bring into line diverse countries such as the USA, India and China. In the case of developing and emerging nations there is no incentive to join such a scheme when they are net beneficiaries of offsets. The UK CCC advocated setting a new target for EU ETS to reduce CO_2 emissions by 30% by 2020 and 80% by 2050, passing legislation to enshrine CO_2 reduction targets and creating a new independent body to monitor progress (another new industry to fill a missing market). It also proposed a new Commission to spearhead British company investment in green technology with the aim of creating 100,000 new jobs, hiring former USA Vice President Gore to advise the government, partnering with Brazil, Papua New Guinea and Costa Rica to promote sustainable forestry and prevent deforestation, and working with The World Bank and other financial institutions to help poor countries adjust to climate change challenges by the creation of a fund of $US20bn (£Stg1.2bn or €18.4bn) (on which it is possible that 15% to 25% brokerage fees could be paid) (Kahya, 2009). Virgin Airlines pays 15% 'administration fee' whereas easyJet buys the credits itself and claims no charges for administration (Kahya, 2009). 'The offsets they buy may already have been traded several times by banks, with the price going up and down with the market' (Kahya, 2009). It was hoped that 'decisions made now on . . . EU ETS [would] provide an opportunity for the scheme to influence and become the nucleus of future global carbon [dioxide] markets' (Stern, 2006: xxiii). 'Broadening par-ticipation to other major industrial sectors, and to sectors such as aviation, would help deepen the market, and increased use of auctioning would promote [economic] efficiency' (Stern, 2006: xxiv). This widening meshes aviation even more tightly into global emissions trading and increases costs and prices both of which could ultimately work against the principles of free markets eventually eroding many governments' aims of social equality and equity. Inevitably flying in advanced nations' carriers would become more expensive to support advancing nations' economies and undermine the competitiveness of a global industry.

Political influences, environmentalists and questionable behaviour

UK's DECC admitted it spent £Stg3.3m on flights in the three years to 2013 but they claim to always offset the carbon [dioxide] on their flights (Watts, 2013). These offsets were ultimately paid by the UK taxpayers. In other words, the UK government (which preaches reducing wastes of all types) is paying for carbon offsets with taxpayers' money to donate to a charity of the Government's choosing (which is an inappropriate use of taxpayers' money especially if the chosen charity has political connections (see Chapter 3) and/or does not have the support of the electorate). Charitable donations should be voluntary and not paid from compulsory taxation.

It is notable that so many environmentalists and legislators fly to annual climate conferences in luxury venues many of which are supposedly threatened by global warming, e.g. Bali, Indonesia (2007); Bangkok, Thailand (2008); Copenhagen, Denmark (2009); Cancun, Mexico (2010); Durban, South Africa (2011); Rio de Janeiro, Brazil (2012); Port Louis, Mauritius (2013). These meetings can involve upwards of 10,000 attendees. They could perhaps have arranged their meetings using tele-conferencing instead of travel. Furthermore, not all delegates fly in the economy cabins with their lower emissions' footprints. Additional examples of questionable behaviour abound. Environmental activists Greenpeace's International Programme Director commuted 250 miles by air twice a month to work. This was despite the organisation's avowed intent to curb aviation growth which it claimed was 'ruining our chances of stopping dangerous climate change' (Gosden, 2014). In another headline example a 'green activist who stopped Heathrow's third runway heads to U.S. to explain how he did it . . . by aeroplane of course' (Massey, 2011). Actor and AGW-is-harmful advocate, Leonardo di Caprio, has been branded a hypocrite for taking six private jet flights in six weeks (Radaronline, 2015). He is not alone. More tellingly, given the power of asymmetric information (see Chapter 1) to sway legislators, former UK Deputy Prime Minister Lord Prescott reportedly flew '40,000 miles – that's nearly twice around the world – in five months . . . to lecture on climate change . . . the ex-Deputy PM has attended all-expenses paid summits in Europe, North America, India and China. He has discussed new legislation which could restrict the ability of others to fly or drive cars in future' (Goslett, 2014). Arnold Schwarzenegger, climate change campaigner and former Governor of eco-friendly California, USA, flies in a 'highly-polluting private jet' (*Metro*, 2016).

Irrespective of their personal behaviours, anti-aviation CSERplus' advocates continue to have significant influence over governments and democratically elected politicians who wield the power to decide major issues such as airport development, air capacity restrictions and aviation taxes.

6.10 AVIATION INDUSTRY RESPONSES

IATA promises

Full aircraft with paying passengers make profitable flights. If aeroplanes are full then their emissions per passenger are minimised. Perversely, full aeroplanes on a particular route mean demand is high and can support more flights which could lead to increased flying frequency with accompanying emissions. This is a challenge for airlines. At the 2013 IATA AGM members endorsed a resolution on 'Implementation of the Aviation Carbon-Neutral Growth (CNG2020)' (IATA, 2013) which applies from 2020 onwards. This provided governments with a set of principles as to how they could support the aviation industry – primarily by establishing procedures for a single global market-based measure (MBM) as part of an overall package of measures to achieve CNG2020. The hope was that the supply industry (including aircraft, engines, fuels and biofuels) would deliver the promise. But the technological improvements are now incremental rather than radical so delivering on these promises could prove challenging. According to the consensus the solutions lie in eliminating GHG emissions or discovering a means of affordably capturing them. Irrespective, the perfect technology is a long way off leaving IATA with its challenging targets. (Horizon-scanning, economically sustainable airlines contemplating their futures should start considering the punitive monetised measures which could result from failure to achieve the industry promise.)

There are four pillars of the IATA industry strategy; firstly, improved technology (including the deployment of sustainable low-carbon [dioxide] fuels). IATA has had to accept the idea of CO_2 as a detrimental climate changing emission and is aiming to cap emissions from 2020 onwards (i.e. CNG2020) and to reduce them by 50% by 2050 relative to 2005 levels (IATA, 2013). It is also aiming for fuel efficiencies of an average of 1.5% per year from 2009 to 2020. Secondly, IATA is aiming for more efficient aircraft operations such as straighter flying routes. Thirdly, IATA is targeting infrastructure improvements such as increasing aviation industry capacity, avoiding stacking while waiting to land and modernising air traffic management systems (including ensuring that ATC maintains minimal flying distances while still leaving sufficient buffer spaces between aircraft for safety). Fourthly, it is pursuing MBMs (to fill the remaining emissions gap). The latter two tasks cannot be achieved without support from governments around the world – the same governments which are using the airline industry to generate non-hypothecated environmental taxes.

Environmentally responsible airlines

So, where does this uncertain science, asymmetric influencing, political lobbying and legislating leave the environmentally responsible airline? Creativity and inno-vation (see Chapter 3) combined with willingness and technology improvements have done much to improve the environmental credentials of the industry but there is still a long way to go before it can truly call itself 'green' and 'socially just' howsoever they are defined and indeed, whether the industry even needs to do so.

A study of airline sustainability/corporate responsibility reports indicates that airlines are concerned about the environment and of the seven major environmental themes, emissions reduction programmes were dominant (Cowper-Smith and de Grosbois, 2011). Other common programmes include reducing wastes, energy and water consumption, and pollutions from noise and air (Table 6.2).

Some of the environment measures are low cost to mitigate, others are expensive; some are enforceable by law and others represent common sense and best practice. Internal and external stakeholders have written many reports about damaging aviation environmental impacts and many trees were presumably culled to produce them. Such reports are felt to be necessary so that society can judge airlines' environmental impacts (Table 6.3).

Airlines try hard but sometimes they could do better. On-board beverage services can illustrate a mismatch between well-intentioned but misguided attempts at pleasing the flying environmentalists and the socially conscious. Using waxed recycled-paper beverage cups is environmentally preferable to plastic vessels. Filling the cups with 'ethically'-grown beverages (tea, coffee) satisfies CSER plus' advocates; however, supplying a plastic (non-biodegradable) stirrer instead of a wooden implement is not environmentally defensible unless it is made from recyclable materials. Some airlines also supply a plastic (non-biodegradable) bag for each passenger to collect their own trash. This enables faster aircraft turnaround which is economically desirable but the plastic bag is environmentally undesirable. Airline environmental sustainability has many facets – and many challenges (i.e. environment vs ethics vs economics).

Table 6.2 Some airlines and their environment-focussed actions

Airline	Year	Environment concern highlights	Voluntary carbon offset scheme?
American Airlines	2013	noise, carbon emissions, waste, fuel consumption and support for recycling	yes
Japan Airlines	2013	biofuels, CO_2 emissions, fuel, energy and water	yes
Qantas Airways	2013	electricity, water, waste to landfill, fuel, carbon [dioxide], emissions	yes
Virgin Atlantic Airways	2013	wastes (water, energy, fuel), carbon [dioxide], ground transport, procurement	yes

Table 6.3 Aviation environmental impacts

On the ground	In the air
airport construction effects on land use, flora and fauna; requires cavernous buildings (like hangars) which are generally considered responsible for 8% of CO_2 emissions (Stern, 2006) and in winter often need heating (energy intensive and expensive)	bio-mimicry (aircraft imitating nature to obtain efficiencies which could reduce fuel consumption, e.g. the honeycomb structures manufactured from composite materials that are strong but lightweight)
runoff around the airport (e.g. from de-icing, refuelling or jettisoning fuel which could affect the water table if not captured)	hygienic environmental conditions for all travellers including crew (e.g. incorporating ultra-hygienic food handling; smoking ban on board; regular cleaning of vulnerable surfaces such as tray tables or overhead air vents)
ground wastes (and ensuring safe and appropriate disposal)	formation of solid and liquid wastes from aircraft (e.g. wastes from food, packaging and lavatories)
energy consumption (including use of renewable fuels and electrically powered vehicles to reduce emissions)	extra fuel required to transport extra weight produces increased emissions
noise from many sources (e.g. take-offs and landings, ground vehicles, or aircraft engine start-ups and testing which can affect local residents)	occasional damage on buildings near the airport from aircraft vortices (rotating air resulting from a wing as it generates lift)
conservation of natural resources to reduce consumption	natural resource consumption (e.g. metals for air frame, aircraft skin and instruments)
procurement (using of life cycle costing methods for 'cradle to grave and beyond')	noise footprint over urban areas (can be distressing if it is at anti-social hours)
transport to and from airport (affects land used for runways, terminal buildings and car parking)	engine emissions
lighting pollution (negative externality) from airport buildings	contribution to lighting pollution (a negative externality)
congestion at airports (can cause delays) because demands exceeds supply (a sign of inefficient market operation)	congestion in the skies which causes delays because demand exceeds supply (a sign of inefficient market operation)
accidents (on the airport roads; air accidents)	air accidents

Practicable steps

Aside from the legislated mechanisms, sustainable airlines have many programmes to voluntarily deliver as much cost saving and environmentally focussed economic sustainability as possible. Many of these are minor and designed to convert employees from wasteful habits or to take ownership of the green issues which are within their control. Environmentalism has to be made easy for them and environmental NGOs such as Global Action Plan (GAP) (2014) can advise. GAP has common-sense suggestions for gently nudging employees to 'do the right thing' by placing green footprints leading walkers to the stairs and red footprints leading to the elevators (reducing the use of mechanical movement saves energy which ultimately reduces airline costs). However, some environmental programmes are significant and require an environmental/economic trade-off, and if they disrupt the operation of the airline could possibly even trigger payment of passenger compensation under Regulation EC 261/2004 (i.e. economics vs society vs environment). Since the flying operation must not be compromised, a full economic impact analysis (which would automatically include environmental and social impacts) should always be undertaken before any new national or international regulations or airline environmental programmes are introduced.

Noise and airports

Airlines, in conjunction with the airports they use, try to ameliorate noise. Aircraft noise can engender health problems in people on the ground due to associated stress and sleeplessness. The fact that many of the airports have probably existed longer than the communities that have grown around them does not seem to influence the neighbours' views. New aircraft reportedly produce 75% less noise than previous generations (exceeding ICAO standards) and steeper descents cut jet noise by passing higher over urban areas. The airports too try to ameliorate the problems of noise by changing runways, alternating flight routes and flexing the hours of operations all of which can make a difference to local residents.

Aircraft procurement

Overall, aircraft are becoming more efficient. The largest passenger plane (at the time of publication) is the Airbus 380 – nearly 73 metres long, almost 24 metres high, and with a wingspan of more than 80 metres. This double-decker aircraft has a seating capacity in excess of 800 depending on the configuration but is frequently configured at around 500+ passengers and crew. One of the means of achieving CNG in aviation is to replace older aircraft with a newer, more fuel efficient fleet for which the prices of kerosene, CO_2 and CO_2e are influential. Assessing these prices for short-haul and long-haul aircraft purchase options shows the importance of ensuring that the discounted future values are included during procurement calculations. The present value lifetime CO_2 costs (which amount to almost 10% of kerosene costs for one long-haul aircraft) would be on average €1.1m

(£Stg840,000 or \$US1.2m) for a short-haul aircraft and €4.1m (£Stg3.1m or \$US4.6m) for long-haul (Girardet and Spinler, 2013) which would ultimately be charged to passengers.

On-board broadcasts

Inflight entertainment presents an ideal opportunity to begin a dialogue with passengers on aviation environmental issues. However, some expectedly impartial sources should be carefully scanned before on-board screening to avoid prejudices such as those associated with the inadvertent showing of biased, AGW-is-harmful news bulletins. As an example, the UK national broadcaster, the BBC, appears to have a stance which supports AGW-is-harmful advocacy rather than the impartiality expected. BBC broadcasting is a public good (see Chapter 1) (i.e. non-rivalrous and non-excludable) and part of the free press. Its news broadcasts are shown on many inflight entertainment systems. It should present impartial assessment and not asymmetric information otherwise the result is ultimately a loss of welfare through inefficient resource allocations. The following anecdotes illustrate the concerns:

'The row between former Chancellor Lord Lawson and the BBC has escalated . . . the Head of BBC Editorial Complaints Unit . . . has reportedly apologised for Lawson's appearance on the BBC Today Programme to discuss climate change . . . responding to complaints that Lawson was "not a scientist" [he] wrote that Lawson's views on this issue were not supported by "the evidence from computer-modelling"' (Bourne, 2014). (NB: computer-modelling is not evidence, and economist Lord Stern (on whose advice the UK's climate change policy has been formulated) is not a scientist either.)

'BBC spends £500k to ask 33,000 Asians 5,000 miles from UK what they think of climate change . . . farmers and villagers in India, China, Vietnam, Nepal, Pakistan and Indonesia were asked how climate change was "affecting their lives already" and about their future concerns . . . They described less predictable rainfall, droughts, declining harvests and an increase in respiratory diseases caused by dustier soil and blamed them on global warming' (Rose, 2014). (It is reasonable to wonder how the questions were phrased, the observations that formed the baseline measures, the derivations of questionnaire criteria, the sampling method employed, the data gathering techniques and the motives which justified such expense. It is also reasonable to ponder just how such distant communities knew about climate change as a threat to their existence before the BBC arrived. It is also reasonable to wonder whether the BBC informed them that they could lay claim to being potential 'climate change refugees'.)

Since airlines' Inflight Entertainment Departments usually act independently from the Environment Departments, it is possible that neither SBU would communicate over the appropriateness of on-board screenings. However, a sustainable airline is interested in fostering balanced environmental debate since passengers do not always have a clear understanding of the economic-environment challenges.

On-board viewing gives the airlines opportunities to promote environmental messages to counter the partial and partisan communications which appear to dominate aviation and the environment.

Company vehicles for private use

Aside from the vehicles provided for business purposes (including ground tugs, mobility buggies, delivery trucks and passenger transfer coaches) airlines often supply vehicles for personal use for their more senior employees. These vehicles should be as environmentally friendly as technology (and budget) will allow. One airline admitted that its Head of Environment selected a fuel-hungry sports vehicle with high emission levels for his personal use. This was procured three days before changes in the environmental vehicle procurement criteria (which he had approved) took effect. These changes were to ensure that future airline-supplied employee vehicles complied with criteria including minimal fuel consumption and emissions which his vehicle exceeded significantly.

Jettisoning fuel

In the event of a premature landing (such as an emergency with a sick passenger or an airborne threat) aircraft have to jettison fuel to reach the maximum structural landing weight. Jettisoning is acknowledged as neither economically nor environmentally friendly and is a decision which is only taken rarely and not made lightly. For example, in 2010 Cathay Pacific had 16 occasions which necessitated such action (Cathay Pacific, 2010) and Qantas had only four episodes in 2008 (Qantas, 2008). Airlines are aware of the environmental impact of showering fuel across a wide area particularly if it is over an urban location even though it is usually vaporised before it contacts the ground. There are many safety reasons why jettisoning is chosen to lighten the load. If an aircraft has to land at a higher than maximum landing weight, it is possible that the brakes could overheat and fail under the strain. Airlines do their best to ensure that such fuel dispersal happens only rarely because it is expensive and environmentally undesirable. Airlines are not usually fined for this environmental impact because the authorities recognise that this jettisoning is the environmental-social trade-off necessary to ensure aircraft safety.

Ghost flights

Sometimes aircraft fly with no passengers because airlines have to reposition empty aircraft to maintain the flying schedule. These are the 'ghost flights' which can be the result of mechanical failures at an outstation, crew unable to fly due to illness or having worked too many hours away from base, lack of available crew or even the need to preserve slots at airports during negotiations regarding route expansions or alterations. The result is often an empty aircraft on a one-way journey. This irritates environmentalists and gives impetus to the idea of calculating the emissions per plane rather than per customer. However, while an aircraft might be devoid of passengers it could still carry time-critical freight, which can assuage some of the objectors' concerns.

Saving fuel, saving weight

Economically sustainable airlines need to save on fuel costs by keeping weights low. The ultimate environmentally friendly airline passenger is a naked, light-weight, able-bodied vegan (because livestock reared for meat or leather produce methane) with neither luggage nor hand baggage so that weight-caused fuel emissions would be minimal. Some airlines are opting to reduce weights by cutting passenger hold baggage free-weights and others are limiting passenger luggage to weight-restricted hand baggage only. Not only does this speed turnaround times but it also saves airport handling charges (including loading and unloading baggage) and frees space in the aircraft hold to allow for chargeable cargo. Other airlines are restricting the weight of cabin crews and (in defiance of the equalities agenda) are recruiting women because they are generally lighter weights (Durston, 2013). Frequently ignored is the airlines' complimentary carriage of duty-free goods many of which are encased in wasteful protective packaging and in heavy (but possibly recyclable) glass bottles. However, lighter-weight plastic bottles might not be of biodegradable materials, i.e. environment vs economics (vs environment – there are no perfect answers).

Innovation is needed to find ways of operating aircraft saving weight and carrying only those supplies that are needed for the journey without jeopardising the safety or comfort of passengers. Innovatively, Qantas decided that instead of upgrading the inflight entertainment system and rewiring the aircraft, it would use iPads for every passenger as an alternative to the seat back system. Once the obsolete wiring was stripped out of the aircraft, the airline found a measurable reduction in fuel consumption (*The Australian*, 2011). Qantas also considered removing life-rafts on flights over land (an economic and environmental decision).

Aircraft manufacturers are encouraged to reduce weight by using lighter composite materials and innovating in any way possible. However, health campaigners are keen to see more life-saving equipment such as defibrillators loaded for passenger health irrespective of airline costs for weight and emissions penalties (see Chapter 1 and Chapter 5). Similarly, the manufacturers of PRMs' motorised mobility devices have no incentive to reduce the weight or volume because neither is chargeable. Now that engine emissions are to be costed, these too should form one of the measures on which airlines can calculate costs. These issues and many others can undermine the airlines' efforts to reduce their fuel burn. Flying more people and their luggage more economically (in both fuel and emissions terms) is still an economic and environmental aim worth pursuing.

Reducing waste of all types saves money and is good business practice. (CSERplus' advocates should not claim the credit for waste reduction measures.) There are many potential functions which could be targeted both on the ground and in the air for waste reduction of all types (Table 6.4).

Table 6.4 Some environmentally sensible functions for airlines

On the ground	In the air
minimising wastes in procurement of all types (including contractors and consultants)	compacting trash to reduce inflight waste volumes thereby reducing subsequent quantities for disposal and transport to landfill
constructing and maintaining energy efficient buildings including installing renewable sources of energy and natural ventilation	reducing fuel consumption by flying direct routes and using renewable energy when technically possible
reducing wastes of all types, i.e. solid, liquid and emissions from catering, engineering, maintenance, offices and terminal activities; reducing waste quantities to landfill/incineration; clear runways of debris; recycling where possible	using only environmentally sustainable products, e.g. printed menus and disposable paper cups produced from sustainable sources; sustainable sources for food stuffs such as farmed fish rather than overfished ocean stocks
ensuring a safe, healthy environment: avoid human toxicology, e.g. eliminating cigarette smoke from all working areas	flying energy efficient aircraft which are lighter weight due to the use of new materials such as carbon fibre reinforced plastics and other composites
conserving resources to avoid the depletion of minerals and fossil fuels	ensuring safe, healthy environment by monitoring of airborne human toxicology (e.g. cabin gases)
avoiding/reducing wingtip vortices that can cause turbulence which is sometimes sufficiently powerful to remove tiles from the roof of houses near an airport	ensuring direct monitoring of engine emissions

6.11 AIRPORT–AIRLINE ENVIRONMENTAL INTERACTIONS

Adaptation and mitigation

Economically sustainable airports and airlines collaborate to adapt and mitigate their environmental impacts of all types. It is a symbiotic relationship and relies on the action of both parties to ensure that the 'licence to operate' is unsullied by anti-social, anti-environmental behaviours which could result in economically damaging fiscal sanctions. Sustainable airlines need sustainable airports. Environmental management systems (EMS) are an established means for organisations to gain the metrics to benchmark themselves against internationally recognised standards (e.g. International Standards Organisation's ISO 14001 and the EU's Eco-Management Audit System (EMAS)). In doing so, enterprises are able to plan compliance with legislation and develop policies with accompanying CSFs and KPIs. Just as airlines set environmental standards for their aircraft based on industry CSFs and KPIs, so too do airports and they expect compliance from all their tenants (including airlines, retail concessions, cleaning suppliers and PRM servicing companies). (This requirement targets two of the Stern Review's (2006) significant emissions sectors: transport at 14% and buildings at 8%.) Sustainable buildings now incorporate building management systems which monitor the consumption of water and energy and expulsion of emissions to air. The UK Department of Environment, Transport and the Regions (DETR) (subsequently renamed several times) developed ten performance criteria which help designers, consultants, contractors and sub-contractors to benchmark their performance against their peers in the construction industry. They enable construction clients (such as airlines) to evaluate their service providers against parameters other than price. The criteria are: construction cost and time, predictability of cost and time, defects, client satisfaction for product and service and company performance through safety, profitability and productivity (DETR, 2000). Giving designers a wider, performance-based brief (see Chapter 7) (i.e. working towards output measures such as volume of permitted emissions) allows them to innovate to reduce energy consumption. There are many products and activities which can assist with buildings' environmental sustainability including installing pervious paving, insulating materials, waterless urinals and combined cooling heat and power plants (CHPs) for renewable energy. Collecting storm water and using recyclable materials also assist with environmental (and often economic) sustainability. Targets are also set for reducing wastes to landfill, e.g. zero waste by reducing packaging or ensuring that manufacturers retrieve their packaging for recycling/reuse.

Natural environment neighbours – wildlife vs humans

Airline and airport stakeholders include local residents of all types – humans, fauna and flora. Mankind has expanded and thrived at the expense of wildlife habitats and each major development in the UK has to be the subject of an environmental impact assessment ('the process of identifying, predicting, evaluating and mitigating the biophysical, social, and other relevant effects of development proposals prior to major decisions being taken and commitments made' (International Association for Impact Assessment (IAIA), 1999)).

Sadly, it is almost inevitable that building a new airport will cover the habitats of many species some of which could inhabit designated international SSSIs. Any attempts to overrun these areas with airport facilities will almost always be fiercely fought by environmentalists active in democracies. Mitigation measures such as rehoming the affected fauna and flora could be prohibitively expensive or alternatively, could slow or halt construction. Lighting and noise from the airport can upset flora growth and fauna breeding but near an airport birds are a danger for aircraft which can ingest them into an engine. However, despite significant engine testing to rigorous safety standards, no fool-proof means of protecting aircraft engines from bird strike has yet been devised. On impact they damage the finely tuned fan blades effectively disabling the power source. Airports have a duty to keep flying birds away from the runways and flight paths. Various techniques are used: fake and real hawks, flapping flags, relocation of avian habitat – anything to eliminate injury to the birds and avoid a health and safety hazard for aircraft. If bird strike happens on both engines (as it did for Captain Sullenberger and First Officer Skiles (see Chapter 3)), then the aircraft would lose power and be completely reliant on the flight crew's skill for safe landing.

Human stakeholders, when they are airport neighbours, have a legitimate interest in the operation of the facility and its peripheral buildings. Depending on whether the airport is located in a democracy with public consultation and planning requirements or an authoritarian regime which operates without negotiation, local airport residents have a deep involvement in any new aviation scheme. With ITC and globalisation integrating the cross-border flows of capital, jobs and goods, international activists can be drawn into the fray creating a ripple effect which could gradually increase as an airport expansion project progresses (see Chapter 1).

Airport access and environmental trade-offs

Many airports in urban areas are keen to encourage the use of public ground transport to take the congestion off the local roads and reduce the vehicle emissions (both are negative externalities). This is considered preferable to using private cars (with higher per capita emissions). A UK survey (ONS, 2010) indicated that 87% of adults who had flown from a UK airport in the previous 12 months had travelled by private transport (car/van or taxi/minicab), with 45% leaving a car/van at or near the airport. Travel by taxi increased with age, with 25% of those aged 55 and over using this method. The respondents felt that using private transport was easiest (74%) but not always the quickest (36%). Overall 93% were 'very satisfied' or 'fairly satisfied' with their journey to the airport. However, the costs of providing privately owned airports with road or rail links are often funded by governments (supplying public goods) and so can be perceived as a subsidy (see Chapter 1) from public infrastructure to private transport. This can be recovered through various means including congestion charges on vehicles or local taxes on the aviation industry.

Where airports are landlords they charge tenants for all occupied space whether it is for check-in desks, baggage chutes, staff accommodation or storage. If airlines do not want to incur the costs of storage space it would be incumbent on them to make more frequent deliveries to maintain efficient levels of stocks (e.g. baggage labels, cleaning equipment etc.). More deliveries will, however, create more emissions. Just-in-time lean processes (see Chapter 2) require the retention of minimal inventory particularly of high-value items (e.g. engineering spare parts) or essential operating products (e.g. lavatory paper and soap). Bulk deliveries would save environmental emissions but would increase the costs of carrying inventory and storage space. This is an economic-environmental trade-off. Similarly, moving passengers by coaches around the airport when there is a shortage of aircraft stands creates another source of emissions. Environmentally preferable but more expensive electric-powered track transits would be better for the atmosphere than diesel coaches (diesel having been the preferred fuel for many decades). However, diesel is no longer considered the environmentally preferable fuel that politicians (advised by experts) had previously assured users was desirable. Similarly, for decades nations have advised citizens to avoid saturated fats because they were believed to contribute to disease. These findings and others (at the time of publication) are very much in doubt. Could these scientific reversals also occur with 'political' CO_2?

Airport vs aircraft efficiency

The limit on the size of current airports has an impact on environmental features and efficiency of aircraft. The wingspan of the Airbus A380 super jumbo is limited by the maximum length that can be accommodated at airports, which means that the fuel efficiency is not optimised. If the wingspan could have been 10 metres longer at 90m (Dalhuijsen and Slingerland, 2004) then the estimate is that fuel efficiency could be improved by 11% with 2.4% lower operating costs. Without incorporating folding wingtips, current airports cannot accommodate larger wingspans (a factor recognised by the designers of the forthcoming Boeing 777X). The A380 burns just 12% less fuel per passenger than the rival Boeing 747. The rate of progress of aircraft fuel efficiency is now incremental rather than radical. To that extent aircraft efficiency could be considered optimised and there is little possibility of dramatic improvements. This is another challenge to the feasibility of the IATA promise to reduce net airline CO_2 emissions by 50% by 2050 (IATA, 2013).

6.12 ETHICS AND ENVIRONMENTAL ISSUES

'Ethical' aviation

Detractors could argue that 'ethical' aviation is an oxymoron. Advanced nations are purchasing goods from advancing nations at lower prices because the manufacturing and polluting nations which are absorbing the negative externalities (and in future, CDM payments) also have lower overhead costs, making the goods competitively priced even allowing for the costs of transport by air. Monetising CO_2 emissions in advanced nations is supposed to neutralise the negative externalities in the advancing nations. In the case of economically advancing China, it has been estimated that 40% of its energy goes into producing exports. In terms of social justice, there are billionaires and paupers in China and the developed nations could be supporting them all with CDM payments. Is this what the developed world's social justice campaigners envisaged? Is it an appropriate use of any environmental offset funds?

Water is an ethical issue. Conserving water is extremely important globally and not just in the aviation context. It can be argued that air-exported, water-reliant luxury items from developing and emerging nations to the developed world (such as flowers from water-distressed Kenya) is environmentally unsound but econo-mically desirable since those flowers add valuable foreign earnings. This particular ethical-environmental-economic challenge is unresolved.

Water carried on board the aircraft is essential for the health of the crew and the passengers. However, the greater the volume of water that has to be carried, the more fuel is needed to transport it and at the end of the journey what remains is drained (and impounded if it has bio-security implications). To avoid conta-minating ground water, airport surface water needs to be cleaned (especially if it contains de-icing fluids or spilled fuel) and retained in holding tanks for safe processing. Once cleaned this 'grey' water can be used around airports (e.g. watering grasses or flushing lavatories) while enhancing airport environmental credentials. It is absolutely crucial that no water contaminates aircraft kerosene. If water freezes it can block the engine fuel feed and lead to catastrophic loss of power. This was the cause of the 2008 accident at London's Heathrow Airport when British Airways' Boeing 777 travelling from Beijing landed just short of the runway. Ice crystals had formed in the engine heat exchangers during the cruise and deprived the engines of thrust when it was needed. (All passengers and crew survived this incident but the aircraft was written off (BBC, 2008b).)

Fuel and ethics

When aircraft are delayed (for example, with inclement weather) they often have to run their engines on the ground to maintain power or circle airborne in a holding pattern until they can land. Either event requires using additional fuel and producing increased emissions. Improving the efficiency of operations by reducing delays can reduce fuel consumption and the resultant emissions and affect air quality around airports. However, there is little buffer time allowed in the schedule leaving minimal leeway for recovering from interruptions. Thus one disrupted aircraft can have a knock-on effect in many congested airports with further consequences on worldwide schedules and increased fuel consumption. (It could also trigger compensation payments under EC 261/2004 (see Chapter 1 and Chapter 5).)

Airlines and 'ethical' food

Eco-warriors have devised the construct 'food miles' to measure the distance from grower to diner in order to assess the environmental impact and therefore the contribution to emissions and AGW. (Food miles could become another missing market if they become monetised.) Much of the imported perishable foodstuff travels by air freight which turns the food producers into airline customers. As an example, food is imported to the UK from advanced nations (e.g. New Zealand) and advancing nations (e.g. Ivory Coast). A New Zealand study (Saunders *et al.*, 2006) argued that it is not the distance that should be assessed but rather the total energy consumed throughout the entire production process through to consumption. The study concluded that New Zealand meat and dairy production was more efficient than that of the UK. Exporting the New Zealand products to the UK compared favourably with UK domestic production. Many producers are based in advancing nations which are grateful to have access to air transport for freighting fresh and profitable foodstuffs to worldwide supermarkets. However, including negative externalities in the price could have a detrimental impact on product marketability. Export-import emissions from fresh produce would stop if worldwide trades ceased under CSERplus pressure to include any negative environmental externalities in prices. What would be the economic and social impact on the developing and emerging exporting economies? Would they need more CDM monies to compensate? (i.e. society vs economics vs environment).

Interestingly it is claimed that one bottle of carbonated soft drink (such as Coca Cola) emits 2gms of CO_2 when opened. Overall carbonated drinks release four million tonnes of CO_2 per year (Essex and McKitrick, 2008) and many are carried in aircraft. Should airlines discontinue supplying such refreshments? (Should the beverage manufacturers (which often have CSERplus programmes to offset their CO_2 emissions) refrain from infusing the gas? Would consumers be happy if their cola was bubble-free in order to reduce their carbon footprint?)

Meals on board

In what would at first glance appear to be a simple economic-environment-ethical challenge, the food on board should be obtained from environmentally favourable sources and can often qualify to display the logo of the appropriate sustainable farming organisation. However, this desirability is actually highly complicated. In order to keep meal prices as low as possible, full-service airlines source from the lowest-cost suppliers and purchase in bulk to a tight budget. It is not always possible to economically procure the most ethically sourced products as desired by animal rights campaigners and environmentalists. Furthermore, if on-board food has been imported before processing and serving, the caterers could be guilty of creating many environmental-ethical transgressions measured by duplicated food miles. Serving overfished varieties such as deep sea cod, ocean tuna or salmon is just one of the environmental-ethical food traps for airlines. Meat also poses a particular ethical problem and not just in the killing method (see Chapter 2). Livestock create 18% of annual worldwide GHGs according to the UN Food and Agricultural Organisation (UNFAO) (2006). They claimed that meat contributed more to GHGs than the entire transportation sector; however, this statement was subsequently contradicted and considered misleading due to differences in the methods, scope and geography used to assess the impacts (Pitesky *et al.*, 2009). If a reputable organisation such as the UNFAO could be contradicted in such a critical piece of work then what about all the other reports (e.g. from the IPCC or UK's CCC) on which governments have placed such emphasis, and taxpayers' and passengers' money?

So what?

It is premature to claim settlement in the debate as to whether or not AGW is harmful. The science is inconclusive and frequently distorted by asymmetric, cherry-picked data, funding inequality and market manipulation – all of which are triggers for alleged market inefficiency or failure. What often passes for free-market capitalism in environmental markets can obscure the presence of the principal-agent problem and cronyism, favouring just a few stakeholders at the expense of the many. These factors leave many questions unanswered. Are climate variations problematic and apocalyptic? Are they anthropogenic or natural in origin? What, if any, is the scientific rationale for the 2°C tipping point and would such a rise really be damaging? What, if any, are the links between the earth's temperature and CO_2? How much of the atmosphere's 0.03% of CO_2 is attributable to nature or to mankind, and what proportion of the man-made contribution is attributable to airlines? How can mankind with fixations on time (decadal, annual, monthly) control nature with its own forces and timetables? How can there be a *global* temperature, and what are the timelines and baselines on which to measure changes? Does the slight warming within natural levels justify the expensive applications of the precautionary principle? Which form of social justice is satisfied if developed world airlines and their passengers subsidise their advancing-world competitors through the payment of 'environmental' taxes?

Challenges to the reliance on opinions derived from the output of computer models have been largely dismissed by the AGW-is-harmful advocates. Computer-modelling might be suitable for investigating the mechanics of the earth's weather, but it is not good at future climate predictions which are what policymakers need. More worryingly: what if the IPCC is correct? If anthropogenic CO_2 is harmful its solution has to be decided at global level rather than imposed unilaterally in policies which burden only selected advanced countries. Inflicting high-risk, AGW-is-harmful policies on single nations or regions will make no difference to climate changing but could damage the competitiveness of their industries including aviation. That would reduce their welfare. The developed world airline industry is therefore at risk because of highly contentious science; extravagant, dispro-portionate, national- and supranational-funded partisan research; precautionary mitigations and CDM inflows to advancing nations which could trigger unfair competition in imperfect markets. Developing and emerging nations are now demanding compensation for extreme weather events which they claim are linked to historic carbon [dioxide] emissions from already developed nations. As well as equalising global societies these payments could become a source of opportunism and corruption. Where will the demands from the advancing nations and CSERplus' advocates end? Given the uncertainties, it is too early in the process of scientific discovery to decide definitively that the assumptions of the 'consensus' are correct. All the stakeholders have some valid points; however, the many AGW-is-harmful advocates have closed debate, prevented sustainability-thinking (see Chapters 1, 3, 5 and 7) and overridden the concerns of the challengers who have been silenced or ridiculed by the 'experts'. Science should be open and welcome challenge by exhibiting the characteristics of the sustainability culture (see Chapter 3 and Chapter 7) including fairness (see Chapter 3) in market interventions and in the allocation of national or supranational government-funded climate research.

One of the unintended consequences of the CSERplus movement could be that in future the only economically sustainable airlines would be flying from the advancing-world which would not have had environmental taxes imposed and which would be in receipt of benefits from advanced-world CDM capital inflows. Their airlines would be the most competitive with the lowest fares because they would not be obligated to offset their emissions with national social programmes which would (in effect) be funded by their advanced-world competitors. Advancing nations would be enjoying a free ride – one of the characteristics of market inefficiency or failure. Unilaterally imposing environmental boondoggles on advanced-world carriers could lead to an imperfect international market. Economic-environmental sustainability has many facets and many challenges (environment vs society vs airline economics).

References

Adolphi, F., Muscheler, R., Svensson, A., Aldahan, A., Possnert, G., Beer, J., Sjolte, J., Björck, S., Matthes, K. and Thiéblemont, R. (2014), Persistent link between solar activity and Greenland climate during the Last Glacial Maximum, *Nature Geoscience* 7 662–666 available from http://www.nature.com/ngeo/journal/v7/n9/full/ngeo2225.html accessed 14 December 2015

Air Transport Action Group (ATAG) (2010), *Beginner's guide to aviation efficiency* available from www.atag.org/component/downloads/downloads/59.html accessed 15 July 2014

Allen, M. (2013), *Why I think we're wasting billions on global warming by top British climate scientist* available from http://www.dailymail.co.uk/news/article-2331057/Why-I-think-wasting-billions-global-warming-British-climate-scientist.html accessed 8 February 2014

Australian, The (2011), *Qantas to trial i-Pads for sky-high entertainment* available from http://www.theaustralian.com.au/travel/news/in-flight-entertainment-to-take-off-with-qantas-ipad-trial/story-e6frg8ro-1226137881574?nk=4f4dbeb9cd4bf50c5d8d8f8c9faadedc accessed 28 September 2014

Bachram, H. (2004), Climate fraud and carbon colonialism: the new trade in greenhouse gases, *Capitalism Nature Socialism* 15(4) 5–20 available from http://www.tandfonline.com/doi/abs/10.1080/1045575042000287299#.VSkE9fnF9qU accessed 12 January 2015

Bailey, R. (2013), *The trouble with biofuels: costs and consequences of expanding biofuel use in the United Kingdom*, Chatham House available from http://www.chathamhouse.org/publications/papers/view/190783 accessed 10 May 2013

Bajželj, B., Richards, K.S., Allwood, J.M., Smith, P., Dennis, J.S., Curmi, E., and Gilligan, C.A. (2014), Importance of food-demand management for climate mitigation, *Nature Climate Change* 4 924–929 available from http://www.nature.com/nclimate/journal/vaop/ncurrent/full/nclimate2353.html accessed 2 September 2014

Ballonoff, P. (2014), *A fresh look at climate change*, Cato Institute, Winter 2014 available from http://object.cato.org/sites/cato.org/files/serials/files/cato-journal/2014/2/v34n1–6.pdf accessed 6 January 2015

Bast, J. and Spencer, R. (2014), *The myth of the climate change '97%'* available from http://www.wsj.com/articles/SB10001424052702303480304579578462813553136 accessed 11 September 2015

Bastasch, M. (2015), *Congress investigates scientists wanting to prosecute global warming sceptics* available from http://dailycaller.com/2015/10/02/congress-investigates-scientists-wanting-to-prosecute-global-warming-skeptics/ accessed 1 October 2015

Baumol, W.J. (1972), On taxation and the control of externalities, *The American Economic Review* 62(3) 307–322 available from http://www.jstor.org/stable/1803378 accessed 11 January 2015

BBC (2008a), *Airline in first biofuel flight* available from http://news.bbc.co.uk/1/hi/7261214.stm accessed 13 August 2013

BBC (2008b), *Airline crash-lands at Heathrow* available from http://news.bbc.co.uk/1/hi/england/london/7194086.stm accessed 10 January 2015

Bell, L. (2010), *The EPA's And Enron's End-Runs of Congress* available from http://www.forbes.com/2010/11/29/epa-enron-greenhouse-gases-opinions-contributors-larry-bell.html accessed 7 February 2014

Bell, L. (2013), *The U.N.'s Global Warming War On Capitalism: An Important History Lesson* available from http://www.forbes.com/sites/larrybell/2013/01/22/the-u-n-s-global-warming-war-on-capitalism-an-important-history-lesson-2/3/#2e5f2212112b accessed 22 December 2015

Bell, L. (2015), *Scared witless: prophets and profits of climate doom*, Seattle, Stairway Press

Boeing (2012), *Long term market: current market outlook 2012–2032* available from http://www.boeing.com/boeing/commercial/cmo/ accessed 17 August 2013

Boeing (2014), *Boeing, South African Airways look to first harvest of energy-rich tobacco to make sustainable aviation biofuel* available from http://www.boeing.com/features/2015/02/bca-tobacco-energy-02-03-15.page accessed 8 January 2015

Booker, C. (2015), *Farewell to the man who invented 'climate change' – to this day, global climate policy is still shaped by the agenda of Maurice Strong, a Canadian multimillionaire* available from http://www.telegraph.co.uk/news/earth/paris-climate-change-conference/12035401/Farewell-to-the-man-who-invented-climate-change.html accessed 5 December 2015

Bourne, R. (2014), *Don't silence Lord Lawson: we can't leave climate change policy to the scientists*, CityAM, 21 July available from http://www.cityam.com/1405359599/don-t-silence-lord-lawson-we-can-t-leave-climate-change-policy-scientists accessed 11 January 2015

Box, G.E.P., and Draper, N.R. (1987), *Empirical Model Building and Response Surfaces*, New York, John Wiley & Sons

Broderick, J. (2009), Voluntary carbon offsetting for air travel, in *Climate change and aviation: issues, challenges and solutions*, Gossling, S. and Upham, P. (eds), London, Earthscan

Carter, R.M. (2007), *The myth of dangerous human-caused climate change*, Proceedings of the AusIMM New Leaders' Conference, 2–3 May 2007, Brisbane, Australia 61–74 available from http://scienceandpublicpolicy.org/images/stories/papers/reprint/Carter Myth/carter_myth.pdf accessed 10 January 2015

Carter, R.M., de Freitas, C.R., Goklany, I.M., Holland D. and Lindzen, R.S. (2006), The Stern review: a dual critique, *World Economics* 7(4) 1–68

Cathay Pacific (2010), *The Environment* available from http://downloads.cathaypacific.com/cx/aboutus/sd/2010/environment/climateChange_air.html accessed 10 November 2013

CDM Policy Dialogue (2012a), *Climate change, carbon markets and the CDM: A call to action: report on the CDM Policy Dialogue* available from http://www.cdmpolicydialogue.org/report/rpt110912.pdf accessed 18 September 2014

CDM Policy Dialogue (2012b), *High-level Panel on the CDM Policy Dialogue* available from http://www.cdmpolicydialogue.org/ accessed 18 September 2014

CDM Policy Dialogue (2012c), *High-level panel calls on nations to safeguard future of CDM and carbon market* available from https://cdm.unfccc.int/press/newsroom/latestnews/releases/2012/19_index.html accessed 11 January 2015

Chandler, D. (2007), *Climate myths: CO₂ isn't the most important greenhouse gas* available from http://www.newscientist.com/article/dn11652-climate-myths-co2-isnt-the-most-important-greenhouse-gas.html accessed 1 March 2014

Chatterton, T.J., Coulter, A., Musselwhite, C., Lyons, G. and Clegg, S. (2009), Understanding how transport choices are affected by the environment and health: views expressed in a study on the use of carbon calculators, *Public Health* 123(1) e45–e49 available from http://www.sciencedirect.com/science/article/pii/S0033350608002771 accessed 11 January 2015

CityAM (2016), *New rankings show US democracy on the edge*, CityAM, 21 January available from http://www.cityam.com/232842/new-rankings-show-us-democracy-on-the-edge accessed 21 January 2016

Cohen, S., Higham, J. and Reis, A. (2013), Sociological barriers to developing sustainable discretionary air travel behaviour, *Journal of Sustainable Tourism* 21(7) 982–998 available from http://www.tandfonline.com/doi/abs/10.1080/09669582.2013.809092#.VSjcxPnF9qU accessed 10 January 2015

Commission of the European Communities (2000), *Communication from the Commission on the precautionary principle* available from http://ec.europa.eu/dgs/health_consumer/library/pub/pub07_en.pdf accessed 30 March 2015

Committee on Climate Change (CCC) (2008), *Building a low carbon economy: the UK's contribution to tackling climate change* available from http://archive.theccc.org.uk/aws3/TSO-ClimateChange.pdf accessed 20 August 2013

Cook, J., Nuccitelli, D., Green, S., Richardson, M., Winkler, B., Painting, R., Way, R., Jacobs, P. and Skuce, A. (2013), Quantifying the consensus on anthropogenic global warming in the scientific literature, *Environmental Research Letters* 8(2) available from http://iopscience.iop.org/1748–9326/8/2/024024/article accessed 10 January 2015

Cowper-Smith, A. and de Grosbois, D. (2011), The adoption of corporate social responsibility practices in the airline industry, *Journal of Sustainable Tourism* 19(1) 59–77 available from http://www.tandfonline.com/doi/abs/10.1080/09669582.2010.498918#.VLKjJiusVqU accessed 11 July 2015

Coyne, C.J. (2013), *Doing bad by doing good: why humanitarian action fails*, Stanford, CA, Stanford University Press

Dalhuijsen J. and Slingerland, R. (2004), *Preliminary wing optimisation for very large transport aircraft with wingspan constraints*, 42nd AIAA Aerospace Sciences meeting and Exhibition, Reno, AIAA available from http://arc.aiaa.org/doi/pdf/10.2514/6.2004–699 accessed 11 January 2015

Darwall, R. (2013), *Reality is intruding on the extreme claims of climate change alarmists* available from http://www.cityam.com/article/reality-intruding-extreme-claims-climate-change-alarmists accessed 4 January 2015

de Freitas, C.R. (2007), *Perspectives on global warming science*, AEF Conference, Melbourne, 8–9 September 2007 (updated February, 2011), original available from http://aefweb.info/data/DeFreitas.pdf accessed 19 February 2016

Department of Energy and Climate Change (DECC) (2012), *International aviation and shipping emissions and the UK's carbon budgets and 2050 target* available from https://www.gov.uk/government/uploads/system/uploads/attachment_data/file/65686/7334-int-aviation-shipping-emissions-carb-budg.pdf accessed 14 August 2014

Department of the Environment, Transport and the Regions (DETR) (2000), *Building a Better Quality of Life – a Strategy for More Sustainable Construction* available from http://www.etn-presco.net/library/Sus_cons.pdf accessed 11 January 2015

Dickinson, J., Robbins, D. and Lumsdon, L. (2010), Holiday travel discourses and climate change, *Journal of Transport Geography* 18(3) 482–489 available from http://www.sciencedirect.com/science/journal/09666923/18/3 accessed 10 January 2015

Driessen, P. (2015), *The tip of the climate spending iceberg* available from http://www.cfact.org/2015/03/31/the-tip-of-the-climate-spending-iceberg/ accessed 10 April 2015

Durston, J. (2013), *Airline recruits women to save fuel* available from http://edition.cnn.com/2013/06/29/travel/airline-recruits-women-to-save-fuel/index.html?iref=allsearch accessed 12 August 2013

Dwyer, L., Forsyth, P., Spurr, R. and Hoque, S. (2012), Economic impacts of a carbon tax on the Australian tourism industry, *Journal of Travel Research* 52(2) 143–155 available from http://jtr.sagepub.com/content/52/2/143.short accessed 11 January 2015

Egli, R.A. (1991), Air Traffic and Changing Climate, *Environmental Conservation* 18(1) 73–74 available from http://journals.cambridge.org/action/displayAbstract?fromPage=online&aid=5942928 accessed 19 March 2014

Essex, C. (2015a), personal correspondence

Essex, C. (2015b), *Believing in six impossible things before breakfast, and climate change* available from https://www.youtube.com/watch?v=19q1i-wAUpY accessed 18 March 2015

Essex, C. and McKitrick, R. (2007), *Taken by Storm*, 1st edition, Toronto, Canada, Key Porter Books

Essex, C. and McKitrick, R. (2008), *Taken by Storm*, 2nd edition, Toronto, Canada, Key Porter Books

European Aviation Safety Agency (EASA) (n.d.), *ICAO Aircraft Engine Emissions Databank* available from http://easa.europa.eu/document-library/icao-aircraft-engine-emissions-databank accessed 14 August 2014

European Union (n.d.), *Supporting climate action through the EU budget* available from http://ec.europa.eu/clima/policies/budget/index_en.htm accessed 18 August 2015

European Union (2008), *Directive 2008/101/EC of the European Parliament and of the Council of 19 November 2008* available from http://eur-lex.europa.eu/legal-content/EN/TXT/?uri=CELEX:32008L0101 accessed 10 April 2015

Evans, R.D., Koyama, A., Sonderegger, D.L., Charlet, T.N., Newingham, B.A., Fenstermaker, L.F., Harlow, B., Jin, V.L., Ogle, K., Smith, S.D. and Nowak, R.S. (2014), Greater ecosystem carbon in the Mojave Desert after 10 years exposure to elevated CO_2, *Nature Climate Change* 4 394–397 available from http://www.nature.com/nclimate/journal/v4/n5/full/nclimate2184.html accessed 14 August 2014

Feldman, D., Collins, W., Pincus, R., Huang, X. and Chen, X. (2014), Far-infrared surface emissivity and climate, *Proceedings of the National Academy of Sciences* 111(46) 16,297–16,302 available from http://www.pnas.org/content/111/46/16297.abstract accessed 12 December 2014

Ferrara, P. (2014), The period of no global warming will soon be longer than the period of actual global warming, *Forbes* available from http://www.forbes.com/sites/peterferrara/2014/02/24/the-period-of-no-global-warming-will-soon-be-longer-than-the-period-of-actual-global-warming/ accessed 13 January 2015

Friis-Christensen, E. and Svensmark, H. (1997), What do we really know about the sun-climate connection? *Advanced Space Research* 20(4/5) 913–921 available from http://www-ssc.igpp.ucla.edu/IASTP/43/ accessed 10 January 2015

Garrard, G. (2013), The unbearable lightness of green: air travel, climate change and literature, *Green Letters: Studies in Ecocriticism* 17(2) 175–188 available from http://www.academia.edu/3125102/The_Unbearable_Lightness_of_Green_Air_Travel_Climate_Change_and_Literature accessed 12 January 2015

Gerlich, G. and Tscheuschner, R.D. (2009), Falsification Of The Atmospheric CO_2 Greenhouse Effects Within The Frame Of Physics, *International Journal of Modern Physics B* 23(3) 275–364 available from http://front.math.ucdavis.edu/0707.1161 accessed 4 September 2015

Girardet, D. and Spinler, S. (2013), Does the aviation Emission Trading System influence the financial evaluation of new airplanes? An assessment of present values and purchase options, *Transportation Research Part D* 20 30–39 available from http://www.sciencedirect.com/science/article/pii/S1361920913000060 accessed 10 January 2015

Givoni, M. and Rietveld, P. (2008), *Comparing the environmental impact from using large and small passenger aircraft on short-haul routes*, Transport Studies Unit, Oxford University Centre for the Environment available from http://www.tsu.ox.ac.uk/pubs/1033-givoni-rietveld.pdf accessed 10 January 2015

Global Action Plan (2014), http://www.globalactionplan.org.uk/ accessed 17 December 2014

Global Warming Policy Foundation (GWPF) (2015), *The Small Print: What the Royal Society Left Out: GWPF Briefing 15* available from http://www.thegwpf.org/content/uploads/2015/03/Shortguide.pdf accessed 14 June 2015

Goldenberg, S. (2013), *Airlines 'made billions in windfall profits' from EU carbon tax* available from http://www.theguardian.com/environment/2013/jan/24/airline-windfall-profits-carbon-tax accessed 17 January 2015

Gosden, E. (2014), *Environmental group campaigns to curb growth in air travel but defends paying a senior executive to commute 250 miles to work by plane* available from http://www.telegraph.co.uk/earth/earthnews/10920198/Greenpeace-executive-flies-250-miles-to-work.html accessed 22 June 2014

Goslett, M. (2014), *Prescott flies 40,000 miles – that's nearly twice around the world – in five months . . . to lecture on climate change* available from http://www.dailymail.co.uk/news/article-2720903/Prescott-flies-40–000-miles-s-nearly-twice-world-five-months-lecture-climate-change.html accessed 16 August 2014

Gossling, S. and Peeters, P. (2007), It does not harm the environment! – an analysis of industry discourses on tourism, air travel and the environment, *Journal of Sustainable Tourism* 15(4) 402–417 available from http://www.tandfonline.com/doi/abs/10.2167/jost672.0?journalCode=rsus20#.VLItnyusVqU accessed 10 January 2015

Gray, V.R. (2001), The Cause of Global Warming, *Environment, Climate Change, Energy Economics and Energy Policy* 11(6) 613–629 available from https://clareswinney.wordpress.com/2010/01/14/the-cause-of-global-warming-by-dr-vincent-gray/ accessed 11 April 2015

Hansen, J., Sato, M., Kharecha, P., Beerling, D., Berner, R., Masson-Delmotte, V., Pagani, M., Raymo, M., Royer, D.L. and Zachos, J.C. (2008), Target atmospheric CO_2: where should humanity aim? *The Open Atmospheric Science Journal* 2 217–231 available from http://arxiv.org/abs/0804.1126 accessed 1 July 2015

Happer, W. (2011), *The truth about greenhouse gases – the Global Warming Policy Foundation Briefing Paper No 3*, The Global Warming Policy Foundation available from http://www.thegwpf.org/images/stories/gwpf-reports/happer-the_truth_about_greenhouse_gases.pdf accessed 14 August 2013

Hare, A., Dickinson, J. and Wilkes, K. (2010), Climate change and the air travel decisions of UK tourists, *Journal of Transport Geography* 18(3) 466–473 available from http://www.sciencedirect.com/science/article/pii/S096669230900101X accessed 10 January 2015

Harrabin, R. (2014), *Concerns over carbon emissions from burning wood* available from http://www.bbc.co.uk/news/uk-28457104 accessed 16 August 2014

Helm, D. (2013), *The carbon crunch – how we are getting climate change wrong and how to fix it*, New Haven, CT, Yale University Press

Henderson, D. (2001), *Misguided virtue: false notions of corporate responsibility*, The Institute of Economic Affairs available from http://www.iea.org.uk/publications/research/misguided-virtue-false-notions-of-corporate-social-responsibility accessed 7 October 2014

Henderson, D. (2014), Climate change and related issues: Ian Castles' contributions in perspective, in *Measuring and Promoting Wellbeing*, Podger, A. and Trewin, D. (eds), Canberra, Australian National University Press

Huff, D. (1954), *How to Lie with Statistics*, New York, W.W. Norton & Company Limited

Idso, S.B. (1991), The aerial fertilisation effect of CO2 and its implications for global carbon cycling and greenhouse warming, *Bulletin of the American Meteorological Society* 72(7) 962–965 available from http://journals.ametsoc.org/doi/pdf/10.1175/1520-0477%281991%29072%3C0962%3ATAFEOC%3E2.0.CO%3B2 accessed 10 January 2015

Intergovernmental Panel on Climate Change (IPCC) (1990), *Climate change – the IPCC scientific assessment* available from http://www.ipcc.ch/ipccreports/far/wg_I/ipcc_far_wg_I_full_report.pdf accessed 19 February 1016

Intergovernmental Panel on Climate Change (IPCC) (1995), *Climate Change 1995 – the science of climate change* available from https://www.ipcc.ch/ipccreports/sar/wg_I/ipcc_sar_wg_I_full_report.pdf accessed 4 August 2015

Intergovernmental Panel on Climate Change (IPCC) (1999a), *IPCC special report: aviation and the global atmosphere* available from http://www.ipcc.ch/ipccreports/sres/aviation/004.htm accessed 3 September 2014

Intergovernmental Panel on Climate Change (IPCC) (1999b) *IPCC special report: aviation and the global atmosphere* available from http://www.ipcc.ch/ipccreports/sres/aviation/index.php?idp=35 accessed 12 January 2015

Intergovernmental Panel on Climate Change (IPCC) (2001), *Climate change 2001 – IPCC 3rd assessment report* available from http://www.ipcc.ch/ipccreports/tar/ accessed 12 February 2015

Intergovernmental Panel on Climate Change (IPCC) (2013), Annex III: Glossary [Planton, S. (ed.)], in *Climate Change 2013: The Physical Science Basis. Contribution of Working Group I to the Fifth Assessment Report of the Intergovernmental Panel on Climate Change*, Stocker, T.F., Qin, D., Plattner, G.-K., Tignor, M., Allen, S.K., Boschung, J., Nauels, A., Xia, Y., Bex, V. and Midgley, P.M. (eds), Cambridge and New York, Cambridge University Press available from http://www.ipcc.ch/pdf/assessment-report/ar5/wg1/WG1AR5_AnnexIII_FINAL.pdf accessed 10 January 2015

International Air Transport Association (IATA) (2013), *Climate Change: responsibly addressing climate change* available from http://www.iata.org/policy/environment/Pages/climate-change.aspx accessed 17 August 2013

International Association for Impact Assessment (IAIA) (1999), *Principles of environmental impact assessment best practice* available from http://www.iaia.org/publicdocuments/special-publications/Principles%20of%20IA_web.pdf?AspxAutoDetectCookieSupport=1 accessed 14 August 2014

International Civil Aviation Organisation (ICAO) (2006), *The Convention on International Civil Aviation Annexes 1 to 18* available from http://www.icao.int/safety/airnavigation/NationalityMarks/annexes_booklet_en.pdf accessed 14 August 2014

Jamieson, A. (2008), *Airlines are akin to arms dealers in ethics stakes* available from http://www.scotsman.com/news/scotland/top-stories/airlines-are-akin-to-arms-dealers-in-ethics-stakes-1-1077010 accessed 14 August 2013

Jeffrey, G. (2011), *The Global-Warming Deception: How a Secret Elite Plans to Bankrupt America and Steal Your Freedom*, Colorado Springs, CO, Waterbrook Press

Jones, L. (2014), *How the UK coped with the millennium bug 15 years ago* available from http://www.bbc.co.uk/news/magazine-30576670# accessed 30 December 2014

Kahya, D. (2009), *Who pays and who gains from carbon offsetting?* available from http://news.bbc.co.uk/1/hi/business/8378592.stm accessed 20 July 2011

Kelly, M. (2015), *For climate alarmism, the poor pay the price* available from http://www.standpointmag.co.uk/node/6232/full accessed 27 September 2015

Kling, M. and Hough, I. (2011), *Air travel carbon and energy efficiency*, Brighter Planet available from file:///C:/Users/D/Contacts/Documents/RESPONSIBLE%20AIRLINE/Brighter%20Planet.pdf accessed 11 April 2015

Knopf, B., Kowarsch, M., Flachsland, C. and Edenhofer, O. (2012), *Climate change, justice and sustainability: linking climate and development policy*, Heidelberg, New York, London, Springer Dordrecht available from https://www.pik-potsdam.de/members/knopf/publications/Two%20degree%20reconsidered_Knopf2012.pdf accessed 18 March 2015

Korhola, E.-R. (2013), *The rise and fall of the Kyoto protocol: climate change as a political process* available from https://www.yumpu.com/en/document/view/36214273/nnmwor/9 accessed 11 January 2016

Lawrence, F. (2012), *European biofuel targets contributing to global hunger says Oxfam* available from http://www.greenwisebusiness.co.uk/news/european-biofuel-targets-contributing-to-global-hunger-says-oxfam-3553.aspx#.VLJxrSusVqU accessed 14 August 2014

Lee, D. (2009), Aviation and climate change: the science, in *Climate change and aviation: issues challenges and solutions*, Gossling, S. and Upham, P. (eds), London, Earthscan available from http://www.gci.org.uk/Documents/Aviation-and-Climate-Change_.pdf accessed 10 April 2015

Lee, D.S., Pitari, G., Grewe, V., Gierens, K., Penner, J.E., Petzold, A., Prather, M.J., Schumann, U., Bais, A., Berntsen, T., Iachetti, D., Lim, L.L. and Sausen, R. (2010), Transport impacts on atmosphere and climate: Aviation, *Atmospheric Environment* 44(37) 4,678–4,734 available from http://www.sciencedirect.com/science/article/pii/S1352231009004956 accessed 11 January 2015

Lewis, J. (2009), History, politics and claims of man-made global warming, *Social Philosophy and Policy* 26(2) 231–271 available from http://dx.doi.org/10.1017/S0265052509090232 accessed 10 January 2015

Lu, Q.-B., (2013), Cosmic-ray-driven reaction and greenhouse effect of halogenated molecules: culprits for atmospheric ozone depletion and climate change, *International Journal of Modern Physics B* 27(17) available from http://www.worldscientific.com/doi/abs/10.1142/s0217979213500732 accessed 14 August 2013

Macilwain, C. (2014), A touch of the random, *Science* 344(6,189) 1,221–1,223 available from http://www.sciencemag.org/content/344/6189/1221.full accessed 14 July 2014

MacKay, D. (2009), *Sustainable Energy – without the Hot Air*, Cambridge, UIT Cambridge Limited

MacKerron, G.J., Egerton, C., Gaskell, C., Parpia, A. and Mourato, S. (2009), Willingness to pay for carbon offset certification and co-benefits among (high-) flying young adults in the UK, *Energy Policy* 37(4) 1,372–1,381 available from http://www.sciencedirect.com/science/article/pii/S0301421508007179 accessed 12 January 2015

Malina, R., McConnachie, D., Winchester, N., Wollersheim, C., Paltsev, S. and Waitz, I. (2012), The impact of European Union Emissions Trading Scheme on US aviation, *Journal of Air Transport Management* 19 36–41 available from http://www.sciencedirect.com/science/article/pii/S0969699711001268 accessed 11 January 2015

Mann, M., Bradley, R. and Hughes, M. (1998), Global-scale temperature patterns and climate forcing over the past six centuries, *Nature* 392 779–787 available from http://www.nature.com/nature/journal/v392/n6678/abs/392779a0.html accessed 15 January 2015

Marshall, M. (2011), Contrails warm the world more than aviation emissions, *Nature Climate Change* 2806 available from http://www.newscientist.com/article/dn20304-contrails-warm-the-world-more-than-aviation-emissions.html accessed 10 January 2015

Massey, R. (2011), *Green activist who stopped Heathrow third runway heads to U.S. to explain how he did it. . . by aeroplane of course* available from http://www.dailymail.co.uk/news/article-2040182/Green-activist-John-Stewart-stopped-Heathrow-3rd-runway-flies-US-explain-.html accessed 16 August 2014

Mayer, R., Ryley, T. and Gillingwater, D. (2012), Passenger perceptions of the green image associated with airlines, *Journal of Transport Geography* 22 179–186 available from http://www.sciencedirect.com/science/article/pii/S0966692312000117 accessed 11 January 2015

Mayor, K. and Tol, R.S.J. (2007), The impact of the UK aviation tax on carbon dioxide emissions and visitor numbers, *Transport Policy* 14(6) 507–513 available from http://www.sciencedirect.com/science/article/pii/S0967070X0700056X accessed 11 January 2015

McGrath, M. (2015), *UN climate talks: hints of a compromise on key issue* available from http://www.bbc.co.uk/news/science-environment-34147192 accessed 4 September 2015

Metro (2016), *Terminated your green ideal, Arnie?* Thursday, 21 January 2016

Moir, J. (2015), *Kiribati man Ioane Teitoa loses bid to stay in New Zealand* available from http://www.stuff.co.nz/national/72291170/kiribati-man-ioane-teitoa-loses-bid-to-stay-in-new-zealand accessed 23 September 2015

Montford, A. (2014), *Fraud, bias and public relations: the 97% 'consensus' and its critics* available from http://www.thegwpf.org/content/uploads/2014/09/Warming-consensus-and-it-critics1.pdf accessed 10 January 2015

Morner, N.-A. (2009), *Why the Maldives aren't sinking* available from http://www.spectator.co.uk/features/5592873/why-the-maldives-arent-sinking/ accessed 10 January 2015

NASA (2014), *NASA Computer Model Provides a New Portrait of Carbon Dioxide* available from http://www.nasa.gov/press/goddard/2014/november/nasa-computer-model-provides-a-new-portrait-of-carbon-dioxide/#.VhUvhPlViko accessed 7 October 2015

National Centre for Policy Analysis (NCPA) (2014), *Stop basing climate policy on invalid models* available from http://www.ncpa.org/sub/dpd/index.php?Article_ID=24190 accessed 3 January 2015

National Post (2007), *U.K. judge rules Gore film 'exaggerated'* available from http://www.nationalpost.com/news/story.html?id=44943ea6-410e-4285-afaf-508f9b606867 accessed 12 February 2015

National Research Council (2006), *Surface temperature reconstructions for the last 2,000 years* available from http://oceanservice.noaa.gov/education/pd/climate/teachingclimate/surftemps2000yrs.pdf accessed 10 January 2015

Office of National Statistics (ONS) (2010), *Public experiences of and attitudes towards air travel* available from https://www.gov.uk/government/publications/public-experiences-of-and-attitudes-towards-air-travel accessed 15 August 2013

Olsen, W. (2015), *More buzz about RICO-ing climate skeptics* available from http://www.cato.org/blog/more-buzz-about-rico-ing-climate-skeptics accessed 30 September 2015

Olsthoorn, X. (2001), Carbon dioxide emissions from international aviation: 1950–2001, *Journal of Air Transport Management* 7(87–93) available from https://www.deepdyve.com/

lp/elsevier/carbon-dioxide-emissions-from-international-aviation-1950-2050,YmCLn CIqME accessed 9 April 2015

Osuri, L. (2010), Charities warm to climate: Philanthropic support for climate-change issues tripled in 2008, *Nature* 464 821 available from http://www.nature.com/news/2010/100406/full/464821a.html accessed 12 December 2014

Pandey, D. (2015), *Govt. freezes Greenpeace accounts* available from http://www.thehindu.com/sci-tech/energy-and-environment/mha-suspends-greenpeace-indias-registration/article7084953.ece accessed 13 April 2015

Pearce, B. and Pearce, D. (2000), *Setting environmental taxes for aircraft: a case study of the UK*, Centre for Social and Economic Research on the Global Environment, London, GEC 2000–26 available from http://www.cserge.ac.uk/sites/default/files/gec_2000_26.pdf accessed 13 March 2014

Peck, S. (2007), *Al Gore's 'nine inconvenient Untruths'* available from http://www.telegraph.co.uk/news/earth/earthnews/3310137/Al-Gores-nine-Inconvenient-Untruths.html accessed 14 February 2015

Peiser, B. (2013), *GWPF background paper*, Global Warming Policy Foundation available from http://www.thegwpf.org/content/uploads/2013/05/GWPF-Background-Paper.pdf accessed 18 December 2014

Peterson, R. and Wood, P. (2015), *Sustainability – higher education's new fundamentalism* available from https://www.nas.org/projects/sustainability_report accessed 12 April 2016

Pielke, R. (2014), *An Obama advisor is attacking me for testifying that climate change hasn't increased extreme weather* available from http://www.newrepublic.com/article/116887/does-climate-change-cause-extreme-weather-i-said-no-and-was-attacked accessed 10 October 2015

Pitesky, M., Stackhouse, K. and Mitloehner, F. (2009), Chapter 1 – clearing the air: livestock's contribution to climate change, *Advances in Agronomy* 103 1–40

Qantas (2008), *Sustaining the spirit: sustainability report 2008* available from https://www.qantas.com.au/infodetail/about/investors/sustainability2008.pdf accessed 10 December 2012

Qounadovu, S. (2015) *'Pay up'* available from http://www.fijitimes.com/story.aspx?id=320367&utm_source=CFACT+Updates&utm_campaign=029195b712-Pay_up_9_4_2015&utm_medium=email&utm_term=0_a28eaedb56-029195b712-270095993 accessed 9 September 2015

Radaronline (2015), *'Hypocrite!' Leonardo DiCaprio Took 6 Private Jet Flights In 6 Weeks Sony Emails Reveal – Despite Climate Change Advocacy Work* available from http://radaronline.com/exclusives/2015/04/leonardo-dicaprio-climate-change-hypocrite-sony-emails-wikileaks/ accessed 18 April 2015

Ridley, M. (2013), *A lukewarmer's ten tests* available from http://www.thegwpf.org/content/uploads/2013/02/Ridley-Lukewarmer%20Ten%20Tests.pdf accessed 14 August 2013

Rolls Royce (n.d.), *Rolls Royce and the environment* available from http://www.rolls-royce.com/sustainability/targets-dashboard/better-power/flightpath-2050.aspx accessed 11 April 2015

Rose, D. (2013), *The fatcat ecocrats exposed: Web of 'green' politicians, tycoons and power brokers who help each other benefit from billions raised on your bills* available from http://www.dailymail.co.uk/news/article-2523726/Web-green-politicians-tycoons-power-brokers-help-benefit-billions-raised-bills.html#ixzz2skiMYYyN accessed 7 February 2014

Rose, D. (2014), *BBC spends £500k to ask 33,000 Asians 5,000 miles from UK what they think of climate change* available from http://www.dailymail.co.uk/news/article-2673654/BBC-spends-500k-ask-33–000-Asians-5–000-miles-UK-think-climate-change-Corporation-savaged-astonishing-campaign-survey-global-warming.html accessed 11 January 2015

Ross, J. (2013), Slowing CO$_2$ growth contradicts 'surge', *The Australian*, 11 February available from http://www.theaustralian.com.au/higher-education/slowing-co2-gowth-contradicts-surge/story-e6frgcjx-1226574765914#mm-premium accessed 16 March 2014

Samuel, H. (2015), TV weatherman sacked after he highlights merits of climate change, *The Telegraph*, 15 October

Sanandaji, T. and Sanandaji, N. (2014), *Super-entrepreneurs and how your country can get them*, Centre for Policy Studies available from http://www.cps.org.uk/files/reports/original/140429115046-superentrepreneursandhowyourcountrycangetthemupdate.pdf accessed 14 December 2014

Saunders C., Barber, A. and Taylor, G. (2006), *Food Miles – Comparative Energy/Emissions Performance of New Zealand's Agriculture Industry*, Lincoln University, New Zealand available from http://researcharchive.lincoln.ac.nz/handle/10182/125 accessed 11 January 2015

Schumann, U. (2000), Effects of aircraft emissions on ozone, cirrus clouds and global climate, *Air & Space Europe* 2(3) 29–33 available from http://www.sciencedirect.com/science/article/pii/S1290095800800593 accessed 10 January 2015

Searchinger, T., Heimlich, R., Houghton, R., Dong, F., Elobeid, A., Fabiosa, J., Tokgoz, S., Hayes, D. and Yu, T.-H. (2008), Use of US croplands for biofuels increases greenhouse gases through emissions from land-use change, *Sciencexpress* available from http://www.bio-nica.info/biblioteca/Searchinger2008CroplandsIncreaseGreenhouse.pdf accessed 11 April 2015

Smith, D.M., Cusack, S., Colman, A.W., Folland, C.K., Harris, G.R. and Murphy, J.M. (2007), Improved Surface Temperature Prediction for the Coming Decade from a Global Climate Model, *Science* 317 (5,839) 796–799 available from http://www.sciencemag.org/content/317/5839/796.short accessed 25 July 2014

Smith, K. (2007), *The Carbon Neutral Myth: offset indulgences for your carbon sins*, Carbon Trade Watch, Transnational Institute available from http://www.tni.org/sites/www.tni.org/archives/reports/ctw/carbon_neutral_myth.pdf accessed 16 August 2013

Snowdon, C. (2013), *Euro puppets: the European Commission's remaking of civil society*, The Institute of Economic Affairs available from http://www.iea.org.uk/in-the-media/press-release/european-commission-spending-millions-on-pro-eu-lobby-groups accessed 14 August 2013

Stern, N. (2006), *Stern review: the economics of climate change* summary available from file:///C:/Users/D/Contacts/Documents/RESPONSIBLE%20AIRLINE/Stern%20Review%20-%20summary.pdf accessed 30 August 2015

Stern, N. (2012), *What we risk and how we should cast the economics and ethics*, Lionel Robbins Memorial Lectures Climate Change and the New Industrial Revolution available from http://www.slideshare.net/Calion/climate-change-and-the-new-industrial-revolution-11767855 accessed 12 September 2015

Sternberg, E. (2009), *Corporate social responsibility and corporate governance*, The Institute of Economic Affairs, Oxford, Blackwell available from http://www.iea.org.uk/sites/default/files/publications/files/upldeconomicAffairs342pdfSummary.pdf accessed 30 October 2014

Stockpickr.com (2014), *Al Gore – Generation Investment Management* available from http://www.stockpickr.com/pro/portfolio/al-gore-generation-investment-management/ accessed 24 May 2015

Strahan, D. (2008), Green fuel for the airline industry, *New Scientist* 199 (2,669) 34–37 available from http://www.sciencedirect.com/science/article/pii/S0262407908620679 accessed 17 February 2016

Sunday Telegraph (2014), *Michael O'Leary's most memorable quotes* available from http://www.telegraph.co.uk/travel/travelnews/9522319/Michael-OLearys-most-memorable-quotes.html accessed 27 July 2014

Svensmark, H. and Friis-Christensen, E. (1997), Variation of cosmic ray flux and global cloud coverage – a missing link in solar-climate relationships, *Journal of Atmospheric and Solar-Terrestrial Physics* 59(11) 1,225–1,232 available from http://kbar.sitecore.dtu.dk/upload/institutter/space/forskning/05_afdelinger/sun-climate/full_text_publications/svensmark_96_variations%20of.pdf accessed 11 January 2015

Taylor, J. (2013), *Global warming alarmists caught doctoring '97 per cent consensus' claims* available from http://www.forbes.com/sites/jamestaylor/2013/05/30/global-warming-alarmists-caught-doctoring-97-percent-consensus-claims/ accessed 8 September 2015

Tol, R.S.J. (2005), *Europe's long term climate target: a critical evaluation: working paper FNJ-92* available from http://core.ac.uk/download/pdf/7079907.pdf accessed 15 April 2015

Tol, R.S.J. (2007), Europe's long-term policy goal: A critical evaluation, *Energy Policy* 35(1) 424–432

Tollefson, J. (2014), *Climate change: the case of the missing heat* available from http://www.nature.com/news/climate-change-the-case-of-the-missing-heat-1.14525 accessed 13 December 2014

United Nations (UN) (1992), *UN Conference on Environment and Development (1992)* available from http://www.un.org/geninfo/bp/enviro.html accessed 11 April 2015

United Nations Environment Programme (UNEP) (1987), *The Vienna Convention for the protection of the Ozone Layer and its Montreal Protocol on substances that deplete the Ozone Layer* available from http://montreal-protocol.org/new_site/en/index.php accessed 20 August 2013

United Nations Food and Agricultural Organisation (UNFAO) (2006), *Livestock's Long Shadow* available from ftp://ftp.fao.org/docrep/fao/010/a0701e/a0701e00.pdf accessed 14 August 2013

United Nations Framework Convention on Climate Change (UNFCCC) (n.d.a), *Background on the UNFCCC* available from http://unfccc.int/essential_background/items/6031.php accessed 10 April 2015

United Nations Framework Convention on Climate Change (UNFCCC) (n.d.b), *Warsaw International Mechanism for Loss and Damage associated with Climate Change Impacts* available from http://unfccc.int/adaptation/workstreams/loss_and_damage/items/8134.php accessed 1 January 2016

United Nations World Commission on Environment and Development (UNWCED) (1987), *Our common future* available from http://www.un-documents.net/our-common-future.pdf accessed 13 August 2013

Vidal, J. (2007), CO_2 output from shipping twice as much as airlines, *The Guardian* available from http://www.theguardian.com/environment/2007/mar/03/travelsenvironmentalimpact.transportintheuk accessed 14 March 2014

Wara, M. (2007), Is the global carbon market working? *Nature* 445 595–596 available from http://www.nature.com/nature/journal/v445/n7128/full/445595a.html accessed 11 January 2015

Watts, J. (2013), *Government's anti-global warming department and its £3.3m air travel bill* available from http://www.standard.co.uk/news/politics/governments-antiglobal-warming-department-and-its-33m-air-travel-bill-8599102.html accessed 13 August 2013

Week, The (2013) *Tim Yeo steps aside as energy chair – but the stink remains* available from http://www.theweek.co.uk/politics/53526/tim-yeo-steps-aside-energy-chair-%E2%80%93-stink-remains accessed 10 October 2014

Whitehouse, D. (2013), *The global warming standstill*, Global Warming Policy Foundation available from http://www.thegwpf.org/content/uploads/2013/03/Whitehouse-GT_ Standstill.pdf accessed 14 August 2013

Wittmer, A. (2010), *Passengers' attitude towards environmental activities by airlines*, 12th WCTR, Lisbon, Portugal available from https://www.alexandria.unisg.ch/publications/77029/ L-en accessed 18 December 2014

Yapps, C. and Poths, H. (1992), Ancient atmospheric CO2 pressures inferred from natural geothites, *Nature* 355 342–344 available from http://www.nature.com/nature/journal/ v355/n6358/abs/355342a0.html accessed 1 March 2014

Part IV

Governance, ethics and economics

The fourth aspect of sustainability is **governance** – how decisions are made.

Chapter 7: Getting it right examines the reputation-protection challenges and management of stakeholders, sustainable decision-making (governance), ethics (knowing the difference between right and wrong) and CSERplus standards and indices as well as noting the questionable behaviour with which some law-making institutions ignore the openness and trust which they require from commercial organisations. Such behaviour is indefensible in lawmakers who should be role-modelling the behaviours they require. Asymmetric influencing and resultant bias has enabled CSERplus' advocates to spawn new industries and fill missing markets of dubious commercial value to airlines and their passengers. These markets include CSERplus report writing, auditing, recruitment and consultancy.

Chapter 8: Challenges for sustainability is a summary of the book, bringing together the knowledge, opinions and ideas from the previous chapters and highlighting the role of economics as integrator for the CSER and CSERplus dimensions. Table 8.1 is a re-examination of Chapter 1's indicators of alleged airline market inefficiencies or failure and aligns them to the responses of governments and reactions of the airline industry. In Table 8.2 are suggestions for future-proofing with strategic, tactical and some fanciful innovations. Finally, the book ponders why regulators allowed CSERplus' advocates to ignore economics in their pursuit of ill-defined 'social justice' and what market inefficiencies or failures might originate from this omission.

Appendix: lists potential airline research topics and unresolved issues which would be suitable for academic investigation.

7 Getting it right

7.1 CONTEXT

Challenges

The fundamental principles of airline sustainability lie in economics and in the corporate decisions concerning how resources are used to supply travellers' demands. Applying the principles of full sustainability to a decision ensures that the airline is surrounded by an aura – its reputation – transmitted in the corporate behaviours at stakeholder touch-points and beyond. Corporate behaviours emanate from strategic and tactical decisions made somewhere in the airline: decisions on resource allocation, customer service style, supply chain security, engine procurement, philanthropic strategy, asset ownership and a multitude of other issues of varying magnitude which concern the internal and external stakeholders. Decisions are pivotal to economically sustainable airlines' success and must take account of comprehensive cost-benefit analyses, time frames and opinions. Much has been written about decision-making and governance and every airline has the opportunity to hook into that research. However, in the interests of objectivity, economically sustainable airlines must challenge the origins of any research, always wary of vested interests and their tendency towards advocacy.

Board of Directors

The Board of Directors, selected for their experience and wisdom, comprises executives and non-executive directors (NEDs). NEDs should be independent and able to challenge. At least one should be capable of playing the role of devil's advocate (de Bono's black hat – see Chapter 3) to avoid the groupthink which occurs in homogeneous cliques. NEDs should not be appointed from the network of cronies (see Chapter 1) who might (for example) be friends of Board members. Such asymmetric selection would only perpetuate any groupthink. Cronyism threatens the prosperity of any airline by reducing the scope for challenge and has the potential to engender market inefficiency or failure caused by lack of impartial information and other triggers. NEDs are responsible and accountable for their actions which will be cascaded down through the employee ranks to deliver the safe, secure and friendly service passengers expect. The officers of the airline are responsible for 'doing the right thing' and ensuring that the reputation for which they are the guardians is strengthened by their actions. They will be driven by legality and the desire to role model the core values (see Chapter 3) and in doing so, will protect the airline's assets. Such good governance – timely, well-formed decisions made by appropriate decision-makers who know right from wrong and operate in a challenge culture – protects the airline's reputation. However, because Boards comprise human beings there are bound to be frailties, errors, misjudgements and biases (see Section 2 in this chapter).

Governance

Boards are responsible for corporate governance which sounds like 'government' and implies control. Governance is covered by a proliferation of laws in multiple jurisdictions. With so many different rules under which to operate, there is a danger that best-practice governance could sanitise proceedings and the Board of Directors (with whom the ultimate responsibility for decision-making resides) becomes afraid to take risks as they strive to make objective decisions on behalf of relevant stakeholders. In formal terms: 'Corporate governance is the system by which companies are directed and controlled. Boards of Directors are responsible for the governance of their companies' (Cadbury, 1992). Management by the day-to-day managers is ensuring their purpose becomes action while governance as practised by the Board of Directors is about purpose, culture and succession (Cadbury, 2012).

> The shareholders' role in governance is to appoint the directors and the auditors and to satisfy themselves that an appropriate governance structure is in place. The responsibilities of the board include setting the company's strategic aims, providing the leadership to put them into effect, supervising the management of the business and reporting to shareholders on their stewardship. The independent board's actions are subject to laws, regulations and the shareholders in general meeting.
>
> (Cadbury, 1992)

However, in the economic sustainability context, governance is simply the oversight of decisions and requires clear lines of responsibility and accountability accompanied by role modelling behaviours. (The collapse of Swissair was blamed on a failure of corporate governance (Nwabueze and Mileski, 2008).) Board membership is a position which carries significant responsibility for the economic, social and environmental welfare of all the stakeholders and in particular for shareholders, employees, customers and the general public with whom the airline is in contact. In many countries, failure of commercial oversight could send Board members to jail for many years if caught and convicted.

Informal decision-making is sometimes the most efficient process when time is pressing. A group can be assembled to deal with one specific issue, the outcome of which could support formal decisions. Formal decisions are usually made in the boardroom at scheduled meetings following an agenda and established processes. Outcomes are recorded in minutes showing responsibilities and accountabilities for any approved motions.

Economically sustainable airlines must avoid moribund governance marked by procrastination. They must make speedy, timely decisions in an age when information and data are transmitted swiftly. ITC has a crucial role in decision-making to provide accurate, timely, impartial information and statistical analysis; however, it is also the link to intelligence from sources as diverse as evolving customer research, changing atmospheric information and the success or otherwise of competitors.

If strategic economic sustainability-thinking (incorporating the economic, social and environmental impacts) is integrated into corporate decision-making there would be no need for separate sustainability-focussed business cases or for independent sustainability-only projects. Economic sustainability-thinking is mainstream business and in an open culture where challenge is welcomed, it empowers internal stakeholders to act by default.

Under managerial capitalism (see Chapter 1) airline management was responsible to the shareholders and responsible for employees and customers. With increasing access to knowledge through the internet and the focus changing to place more of society's costs onto commercial organisations, subsequent investor capitalism morphed into CSERplus capitalism. However, its wider net of stakeholders (often derived from self-selecting special interest groups) frequently exhibits a very narrow focus and yet is able to wield significant power and influence over legislators and company management. This asymmetric approach often culminates in a misallocation of resources caused by legislative boondoggles (see Chapter 5 and Chapter 6).

Stakeholder analysis

Airlines serve their customers and in doing so, should also enrich their shareholders (as suppliers of the risk capital) and employees (as providers of the services). They are the primary stakeholders. The identification of stakeholders is through conducting a stakeholder audit. A simple tool to identify stakeholders uses the acronym PESTLE (political, economic, social, technological, legal and environmental). By using SWOT (strengths, weaknesses, opportunities and threats) each stakeholder can be evaluated for their influence and importance with a 'responsible person' allocated to 'own' each relationship. Equally as important during the audit is determining the health of each relationship, the inherent risks and the location of the greatest stakeholder opportunities and threats. Furthermore, understanding the proportion of time to be spent managing these relationships, developing monitoring mechanisms and ensuring the effectiveness of two-way communication between stakeholders and the airline would give an indication of the supporters and resistors and of the esteem in which the airline is held. An audit is always incomplete because stakeholder groups can multiply, expand or contract their memberships and widen their reach especially if the topic is a long-term project such as a new airport. The Board of Directors and the independent NEDs, as guardians of the airline's reputation, need regular strategic stakeholder audits as a tool for reputational risk management.

Following the stakeholder audit, action plans are required formulated at both strategic and tactical levels. In the virtuous circle this becomes a risk-reduction tool by increasing awareness of the stakeholder risks, developing more effective internal controls, being alert to potential hazards and improving stakeholder management. However, different stakeholder groups mean divergent and often conflicting interests at which point any decision taken will almost always displease one or other of them.

Stakeholder management

Once the stakeholders for a particular decision are identified, their stance on an issue needs confirming. Inviting divergent opinions (see Chapter 3) brings balance into the decision and also opens the prospect of assessing the counter-arguments which could deflect successful decision implementation. Fundamental to decision-making is ensuring that any influences are balanced and that power and responsibility are matched in those being consulted. The resources dedicated to stakeholder management must be appropriate and proportionate. Ongoing stakeholder management is a communications issue – explaining the activities, importance and benefits of any activity. The evolving strategic communications should be handled by the communications specialists supported by line management taking responsibility for, and ownership of, any activities.

A simple analytical tool is useful in deciding which stakeholders require influencing to move from their original position (at x) to a position where they are supportive (position y). In the skeletal illustration in Figure 7.1 is an analysis of stakeholder support for the extension of a runway into a wetlands area (an SSSI).

Stakeholder analysis date								
Stakeholder name	Strongly against resistors	Moderately against	Neutral	Moderately supportive	Strongly supportive advocates	Issues/ concerns	Influencing strategy/ tactics	
							Which dept responsible for stakeholder?	Progress?
Field				x ⟶	y	Increased traffic	Environment?	Favour public transport?
Jones			x/y			Wildlife	Environment	Relocate habitat?
Potter		x ——————⟶			y	Water table impact	Environment	Show test results
Sheridan	x ——————————⟶			y		Aircraft noise	Engineering?	Inform of noise reduction in aircraft
Wadham junior school		x ——————⟶		y		Noise in classrooms/ playground	Community/ HR dept for employee volunteering?	Noise proof classroom: new play equipment
Wicks					x/y	Employment increases	Community	Meeting 7 December

Figure 7.1 Stakeholder analysis

Identifying the resistor, neutral or advocate stakeholders and their concerns gives an indication of the size of the task ahead. Stakeholders can be groups or individuals. Field could be moved from 'moderately' to 'strongly supportive' after which he/she could become an advocate and therefore a promoter. Jones is a neutral but could go either way if influenced. Potter (a resistor who is only moderately against the proposal) could be moved as far as 'strongly supportive'. Moving Sheridan (resistor) from 'strongly against' to 'moderately supportive' is probably realistic rather than believing he/she could be moved to 'strongly supportive'. Wadham Junior School has concerns about the potential noise effects on its students but is unlikely to relocate so adaptations must be found to ameliorate their concerns and move them to some point on the supportive continuum. Finally, stakeholder Wicks is an advocate for the decision and could be used to influence others. The reverse movements are also possibilities. One Department (possibly Public Relations or similar) would have strategic oversight of the influencing process and would need the support of tactical project delivery departments.

A four-box power-interest grid with increasing levels of power and interest on the axis can categorise where the main influencers are grouped and indicate where to place the most efficient use of scarce resources to influence the desired outcome (Mendelow, 1991). Those stakeholders with low power but high interest could become resistors in their frustration and if they achieve sufficient critical mass could join other resistors. Influencers (supporters and resistors) with high power and high interest are to be courted because they represent either the greatest opportunity and/or the greatest threat. Those stakeholders with low power and low interest are the least threat. They are possibly non-flying citizens or residents who do not live under the noisy flight path but they do present an opportunity to influence toward building consensus. They need to be monitored for signs of shift. Those with high power but low interest require tolerating in the hope that they might be persuaded to support the decision. Over time, there would be movement around the grid. Advocates can become disillusioned and move to another quadrant; resistors can become advocates; neutral stakeholders could take a stance. Alternatively, influencers could become unfavourably entrenched and immobile. Detailed stakeholder knowledge allows strategic communication planning which should ensure a widened, transparent, impartial and fair debate of any major decision. This is especially important if the decision is airline-strategic, political-governmental and of national significance (such as building a new airport). Such decisions involve significant stakeholder interaction as well as financial and political capital.

There are multiple ways to manage transient and fixed stakeholders depending on the decision under consideration. It could be by donating to their causes through strategic philanthropy (Chapter 3), wining and dining them to reassure them (but always disclosing this activity in the interest of openness) or conversely, threatening legal action. However, sustainable organisations must be very certain to avoid claims of malpractice, bribery, opportunism or corruption (the latter defined as 'the abuse of entrusted power for private gain' (Transparency International, 2010)).

7.2 MINIMISING ERRORS IN DECISION-MAKING

Governance and making sustainable decisions

Decisions can be of many types and range from strategic (such as budgets or organisational structure) to tactical ('Should we hold the flight for transfer passengers or let it go?'). How decisions are made reflect the airlines' cultures. Overall the process of decision-making should be transparent and those making the decisions should be accountable for them and be prepared to be challenged. Airline executives are paid proportionate to the impact of their decisions: high impact means high salary; low impact means lesser earnings. In any organisation, there are executives in positions of high power earning high pay who make bad decisions (most notably in no-challenge cultures). They become megalomaniac in their zeal to pursue their vision at the expense of the sanity of others. In one airline a deeply religious Senior Manager in the Environment Department would not tolerate any dissent. With his face puce, lower lip quivering and jabbing his forefinger in the face of any outlier, he would scream, 'Don't challenge! This is the way it is!' He was not acting in accordance with the airline's core values but he was acting in accordance with his no-challenge, religious-based, groupthink. Unfortunately his bullying intimidated his team and closed down any discussion or divergent thinking. As a result, his decisions were unfiltered and the consequences lived long after he resigned and went to work for the government (i.e. a predominantly no-challenge culture).

Airlines cannot afford to have a no-challenge culture which prevents bad news from moving upwards. Challenges come from every aspect of the commercial environment. In the event of any accident – whether an aircraft disaster or a public relations gaffe – airlines need a store of goodwill in their corporate reputation tank. And if there are many threads of continuing bad press then staff morale might tumble, shareholders could divest and passengers might cease flying. Conversely, cultural failings can be hidden behind various disguises including an upwards movement in the share price which could be precipitated by a one-off announcement such as the purchase of new aircraft or the opening of new routes.

Timely decision-making is important but 'how business *really* gets done has little connection to the strategy developed at corporate headquarters' (Bower and Gilbert, 2007: 74). Strategic commitments fall into two categories: organisational structure and decision-making processes (Bower and Gilbert, 2007):

(a) organisational structure involves the dispersal of knowledge and power and an understanding of how people fulfil their roles with the resources at their disposal. The processes span multiple levels and are iterative activities which proceed on parallel, independent tracks.
(b) decision-making processes are critical to economic sustainability and concern how airlines make their decisions on allocations of resources in the context of competitiveness, legislation, natural phenomena, bio- and security-hazards and the plethora of other challenges which could derail any strategy.

So much of the stakeholders' perceptions of an airline is influenced by decisions made in the boardroom (all of which should protect the airline's reputation). However, strategic Board-level decisions to protect revenue in tough economic times (such as reducing maintenance of cabin interiors but not engines) can have unintended consequences. They can give the wrong impression to the customers who experience the tactical effects which might include failed cabin reading lights, malfunctioning entertainment systems, rattling arm rests and dirty aircraft – none of which might have been the outcomes envisaged by the Board's strategic decisions to conserve cash.

Leadership, formal and informal decision-making

No single leadership style or decision-making process fits all situations. Situations are affected by the speed of decision needed, the commitment of the required stakeholders and the quality of decision required (see Chapter 3). By analysing the situation and evaluating the problem the leader can decide which leadership style is most appropriate and whether it requires a formal (boardroom) or informal (coffee-shop) meeting process. The Jago-Vroom (1978) model of leader behaviour defines a very logical approach towards choosing the style. It is useful for leaders who are trying to balance the need to make decisions effectively and efficiently with the benefits of either autocratic or participative management. When time is pressing and the leader is confident of having sufficient specialist knowledge and the backing of the team then autocratic style is the most efficient. However, participative decision-making (consultative or collaborative) is appropriate where the problem needs definition, wider expertise and buy-in and there is sufficient time available to gather the resources of both people and knowledge (Jago and Vroom, 1978).

Decision processes

A simple sustainability decision-making process is described in Figure 7.2.

Step 1: Define challenges

The first step is to prioritise the decisions which deserve the greatest effort. What are the **real** problems and what are the options available for evaluation? It is critical to the process to ask the **right** questions which must be clearly articulated to ensure the real problems are resolved otherwise there is danger that the decisions could merely treat the symptoms.

Step 2: Select decision-makers

Strategic decisions require a different outlook from tactical decisions. Strategic thinking often requires a specialist team of the **right** people, i.e. those who possess the skills, knowledge, experience, opinions and willingness to challenge and be

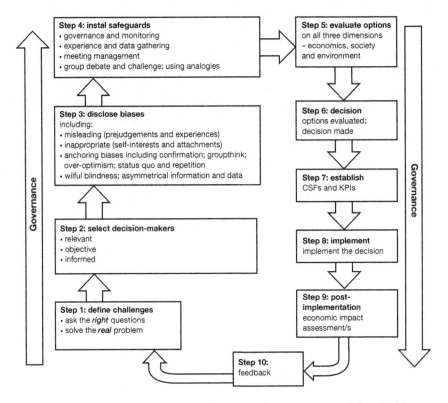

Figure 7.2 The full sustainability route to decision-making using sustainability-thinking (compiled from Lovallo and Sibony, 2010; Finkelstein et al., 2008)

challenged. Strategic decisions include deciding the growth strategy whether it be product development, diversification, market development or penetration (Ansoff, 1965). It could even involve constructing new or maintaining existing infrastructures, or deciding on a merger, takeover or acquisition.

Step 3: Disclose decision-making biases

The discussion needs to contain both convergent and divergent thinking (see Chapter 3) and to avoid groupthink as a form of bias. At boardroom level, any tendency to groupthink should be countered by the independent NEDs doing what they are supposed to do, i.e. challenging the Board. Differences of opinion are acceptable and those who differ (possibly the outliers – see Chapter 3) will understand the rationale for the outcome because it would have been made transparently.

Decision-makers might also have many other cognitive biases formed by their past experiences, interests, influence and power. These include misleading pre-judgements and experiences and inappropriate self-interests and attachments (Finkelstein *et al.*, 2008). These are anchoring biases which give credence to one piece of information over others or allow experiences of the past to upset the balance of a decision.

They also include groupthink, repetition (from believing what one has been told many times by the largest number of sources) and confirmation (ignoring evidence which is counter to beliefs). One of the most poignant examples of confirmation bias in the airline industry occurred in 2010 when Varig Flight 254 crashed in the Amazon jungle. The crew mistakenly entered the wrong compass heading and the flight headed at 270° instead of 27°. Consequently as they deviated from the flight path, further errors compounded their disbelief that they were off course and they did not believe their predicament until the overwhelming evidence was irrefutable. There were 54 survivors and 13 fatalities in this incident (*AviationKnowledge*, n.d.).

Another anchoring bias is status quo (i.e. retaining what already exists rather than gaining something more). Status quo is usually one of the most frequently preferred options (Samuelson and Zeckhauser, 1988) because of the need to feel in control and to avoid risk.

There are many other biases including wishful thinking (over-optimism) and wilful blindness (where the biggest threats are the ones that people just do not want to see). Asymmetric information is also a form of bias (as well as an acknowledged cause of imperfect market operation) (see Chapter 1). As an example, the environmental lobby is powerful when it comes to aviation and substantial EU funds are used to support organisations that share the European Commission's environmentalist agenda 'to support policy development' (Snowdon, 2013: 4) (see also Chapter 6). Since the EU does not fund groups which do not share its agenda there will be an oversupply of asymmetric information and a dearth of impartial or divergent information, data and opinions on which to base balanced decisions (see Chapter 6). This particular decision-making process short-circuits the active divergence required (see Chapter 3) and provides one of the best examples of confirmation bias and wilful blindness. Furthermore, environmentalists' interests rarely coincide with those of the aviation industry and these self-styled experts are often guilty of questionable behaviour in defiance of their expressed biases. Examples abound. One of the worst examples was the gathering of CSERplus' lobbies at the UN's 2009 Copenhagen Climate Change Conference. It had 1,200 private limousines and 140 private jets in attendance (Gilligan, 2009). Other advocacy organisations approve aeroplane use when it suits them such as Green-peace's shuttle to and from their relocated offices (Gosden, 2014). Flying while preaching anti-aviation rhetoric is another manifestation of questionable beha-viour as exemplified by a Heathrow protestor (Massey, 2011) or the former UK Deputy Prime Minister who covered 40,000 miles by air (Goslett, 2014). Influential media figures fly in emissions-concentrating private aircraft (Leonardo di Caprio and Arnold Schwarzenegger) (*Radaronline*, 2015; *Metro*, 2016) which undermines their messages (see Chapter 6). Unfortunately by the time their activities are disclosed, their asymmetric influence is often already embedded in government policy (see Chapter 6). All these biases (and others) need to be aired as a part of the decision-making process (Finkelstein *et al.*, 2008).

However, when faced with choices the anchoring biases can have many effects as diverse as losing opportunities, preventing innovation or change or specifying equipment without considering the changing context in which it might be used. They can also hinder the future-proofing which is the ultimate outcome of Board-level decisions. Decision-makers' biases need to be identified to determine which are most likely to affect critical decisions. Biases can prevent good information in the hands of good managers from yielding a good decision (Lovallo and Sibony, 2010). Biases can also include corporate politics or silo-thinking (where the decision-makers cannot see their role in the context of the airline as a whole). Life has a way of translating past experiences into misleading pre-judgements which can colour a situation unless the decision-maker is aware.

Sometimes, biases can slip in unobserved. When a deadline for cabin refurbishment was looming, the Chief Executive (who was renowned for interfering in matters he should have left to his specialists) ventured an opinion on the new upholstery colours. None of the displayed samples pleased him. He finally invited his wife (a textile supplier) to advise him. It transpired that he was colour-blind and coincidentally she had the 'perfect material' for the new seats in her warehouse. This could never have been regarded as an open and transparent decision which would have withstood either scrutiny of sunlight or policing under the visibility of electric light (Brandeis, n.d.).

At this point there is a slight divergence from the lean principles (see Chapter 2): lean works on facts; however, at higher levels in the hierarchy opinions matter more because they should also be weighted by experience. Leaders and their management must seek new knowledge and insights from inside and outside their organisations and 'keep updating their assumptions, knowledge and skills' (Pfeffer and Sutton, 2006: 64) rather than make excuses for inadequate evidence. However, instead of best evidence, some leaders and managers tend to substitute other sources including 'obsolete knowledge, personal experience, specialist skills, hype, dogma and mindless mimicry of top performers' (Pfeffer and Sutton, 2006: 67).

Step 4: Instal safeguards

Biases need to be challenged or diluted using safeguards (Finkelstein *et al.*, 2008) including meeting management, data gathering, presenting analogies and stimulating debate. These techniques can uncover the inadequate data and information behind which biases often hide (Lovallo and Sibony, 2010).

The safeguards require that sufficient and relevant information and data are available always remembering the principle of bounded rationality – an economic concept which explains that it is not possible for everyone to use the same knowledge in the same way. People are not always as rational as classical economists would like to believe. They are often emotional and irrational (Simon, 1991) which can also trigger biases. It is this tendency to irrationality which can also lead to

Table 7.1 More biases and appropriate counter-actions (adapted from Lovallo and Sibony, 2010)

Type of bias	Counter-action safeguards
1. pattern recognition (including confirmation biases)	change the 'angle of vision' and test different hypotheses with the facts
2. action-orientation (unconsidered risks before acting)	recognise uncertainty (rather than be swayed by over-confidence or over-optimism)
3. interest (motivated by personal interests)	avoid misalignment of interests and accompanying silo-thinking; formulate the criteria for the debate
4. social (conforming to the known position of the leader)	depersonalise the debate; encourage group debate
5. stability (status quo prevails)	set stretch targets to 'shake' the stability

extremes of risk-taking or risk avoidance in decision-making. Counter-action safeguards (Table 7.1) such as depersonalising the debate or setting 'stretch' targets can eliminate much of the emotion and irrationality.

Steps 5, 6, 7, 8, 9 and 10

In addition to the four steps of defining the challenge and the options, selecting decision-makers, disclosing biases and installing safeguards, economically sustainable airlines need to evaluate the options while filtering them through the three sustainability dimensions *(Step 5)*. Recognised assessment techniques such as SWOT and PESTTLE (the second 'T' is for *time*) can inform the knowledge-gathering which in turn supports the SWOT analysis. At this stage a pre-mortem could be undertaken whereby the decision is assessed from the perspective of the future looking back on the decision as a fiasco and failure (Klein, 2007). Steps can then be taken to eliminate or mitigate the risks uncovered. *Step 6* is decision-time when the filtered options have to be narrowed down to the one decision. The outcome is an economically sustainable decision which is defendable, as free from bias as far as humanly possible and which could stand scrutiny in an open culture. *Step 7* establishes the CSFs and KPIs for analysis and for post-implementation assessment. These will enable an understanding of what went right and conversely, what might have gone wrong. *Step 8* is time to implement the decision and *Step 9* is the time to evaluate the post-implementation economic, social and environmental impacts. *Step 10* is feedback which, in a challenge culture, is given willingly and received gracefully. Collecting feedback needs to involve the appropriate stakeholders who will provide the information needed to build knowledge, avoid future mistakes and strengthen the governance process.

Decision-making and risks

Risks categorised by their perceived impact to the airline will arise from the decision-making process and will be resolved at different levels (international, national, corporate and possibly even family and personal) and in all sustainability dimensions. At each stage in the decision process the potential risks of all types are being further reduced and, using this governance process, reputational risk awareness would become an integral and a natural by-product of decision-making. This is ultimately corporate governance in action.

Importance of opinions

Leaders and their managers need opinions rather than rely only on the facts as uncovered in a comprehensive cost-benefit analysis. From opinions competing options can be assessed. Without opinions, there would be only confirmatory facts whereas with an opinion there is a hypothesis which can be tested and those who voice an opinion can accept responsibility for it (Drucker, 1974). However, one feature of testing a hypothesis is to have alternatives – and in decision-making that means divergence and assessment of advantages and disadvantages (Steps 1 to 7). Much of the debate could relate to historical facts even though the decision could take the airline into new realms. But airlines cannot live in the past – they need to be constantly horizon-scanning and watching for what is predicted and forming an opinion on which to base a decision. Unfortunately, economic opinions have been neither voiced nor heard during many of the CSERplus decision-making discussions.

The opinions of consultants are also to be challenged. Consultants 'are *always* rewarded for getting work, only *sometimes* rewarded for doing good work, and *hardly ever* rewarded for evaluating whether they have actually improved things. Worst of all if a client's problems are only partly solved that leads to more work for the consulting firm' (Pfeffer and Sutton, 2006: 66). Often consultant involvement means additional complexity, complication and costs.

Computers and biases

Computer models, on which so many decisions rely, can also exhibit confirmation bias – their output depends on their input – so the importance of information gathering and opinion assessment cannot be underestimated (see Chapter 6). Historically, computer-modelling has not always led to either economically efficient or accurately predicted outcomes. In 2009 the UK government spent £Stg1bn ($US1.54bn or €1.4bn) (Alleyne, 2010) to protect the population against a computer-predicted swine flu epidemic which some computer estimates had predicted would infect two billion people (CBS, 2009). In reality anticipated deaths were computer-modelled at between 151,700 and 575,400 and even this was 15 times higher than the actual, laboratory confirmed deaths (Centres for Disease Control and Prevention, 2012) (i.e. between 10,000 and 38,000 actual deaths).

(This example illustrates some of the inadequacies of computer-modelling on which the climate change moral panic is based (see Chapter 6).)

7.3 REPUTATION PROTECTION

Preventing loss of reputation

The consequences of reputational loss can affect all the stakeholders particularly shareholders, employees, customers, regulators, media and pensioners. (Pension company investments play a critical role in national investments and are not merely a source of retirement funding.) In some industrial sectors – such as tobacco, alcohol and even aviation – good reputations are hard to obtain and then even harder to maintain. In other industries, good reputations are assumed to stem from their origins such as religion or ethics although sometimes these honourable, historical roots can be very misleading (e.g. the UK's almost bankrupted, religiously led, politically aligned, economically flawed but socially conscious Co-Operative Group) (Moore, 2013)). Others rely on their superior stakeholder servicing to maintain their high reputations.

Organisation theory divides a company's actions into operations (e.g. product quality, range and price) and support functions (e.g. philanthropic and other social gestures) all of which should support the reputation. Airline reputations can be levers for continued success by retaining consumer confidence and lifting staff morale. A high reputation can also give confidence to financiers (who lend money for asset acquisitions), employees (who advocate for the airline), shareholders (who trade and boost the share price), suppliers (who need to be sure of being paid all amounts owing on time) and other stakeholders with high interest. Recommendations to enhance corporate reputation include: maintaining programmes that please customers, keeping employees updated, showing concern for the natural environment, recruiting communications staff to safeguard media feeds and maintaining community relationships (Omar and Williams, 2006). When customers have multiple choices, they choose the airline with the most admired reputation as a differentiating factor. 'More than ever, the sales, profitability and growth of a large international corporation appear now to depend on its reputation' (Henderson, 2001: 31). Airlines' employees (as well as other stakeholders) judge a carrier by its record in health and safety, impact on the environment and local communities and its preservation of human rights and behaviours when interacting with commercial partners and sometimes less-than-honourable governments. 'In all these respects companies are now under permanent and often hostile scrutiny and what are seen as failures or acts of misconduct on their part can be given immediate worldwide exposure' (Henderson, 2001: 31). Reputation is determined 'by a firm's social performance, financial performance, market risk, the extent of long-term institutional ownership and the nature of its business activities' (Brammer and Pavelin, 2006: 435). It is communicated by behavioural 'signals' in the market, community and workplace and in the environment. High reputations attract good employees 'who produce new and innovative products and service customers well' (Dortok, 2006: 323), i.e. factors which are fundamental to airline economic sustainability.

Communication in an age of instant reviewers (such as Twitter or Trip Advisor) is challenging for an airline. Controversies cannot be hidden in the digital age and reputations can be unfairly sullied (or unjustifiably enhanced) in quicker time than it takes to have unbalanced reviews removed from a website. In the intervening period the airline's business could be severely dented. Reputations can be lost either incrementally over time or by crisis events. Triggers for business crises include competition creating market shifts, financial crises, inadequacies in top-management succession planning, hostile mergers or takeovers, unstable industrial relations, crises in public perception, product failure, adverse international events such as terrorism, and governments in their roles as regulators or deregulators (Ray, 1999). (The airline industry has had more than its share of all of these events.) Crises have five dimensions: are highly visible, contain surprise, are outside of the organisation's complete control and need immediate attention and action (Pearson and Mitroff, 1993).

Strong financial performance generally signals a successful corporate strategy, professional management and efficient, effective resource allocations. It helps a firm establish and maintain a positive reputation (Brammer and Pavelin, 2006) particularly among financial stakeholders (including debtors, creditors, investors and external analysts). It also signals that the firm offers less risk. However, there are instances when a seemingly strong financial performance misleads such as when assets are over-valued or supplier discounts are recognised ahead of being earned. Financial performance is one tangible measure but intangible assets – intellectual capital and reputational capital – are believed to contribute around 55% of the company value (Dortok, 2006).

Employees and reputation

The most important stakeholders in determining corporate reputation are perceived to be employees and customers, followed by the media and the community (Dortok, 2006). The support of employees is crucial to retaining reputation since they can act as ambassadors for the company and are able to influence other stakeholders. The accumulation of corporate legends and stories which become the corporate history can engender real emotions in employees. The buccaneer aviator who created an airline giant; the heroic crew who saved the pilot when he was sucked out of the aircraft; the Customer Service Agent who foiled a smuggling plot; the security agent who thwarted a potential terrorist – all add to the excitement, pride and reputation that employees try to embody as they follow their daily routines. Claims that employees are committed to the company can only be substantiated by the messages they send with their behaviour (see Chapter 3). Employees need to embrace the company culture and in particular the intangible values (such as happiness and pride) as well as the functional, core values (Dortok, 2006). In contrast to low-reputation companies, high-reputation companies have strong internal communications with regular measurement of effectiveness. Communicating aligns corporate strategies, business objectives and future plans with the employees' expectations. This underlines the fact that 'the employee is the leading stakeholder carrying the corporate reputation, be it good or bad, and influencing it. Similarly, corporate reputation influences employees as well' (Dortok, 2006: 337). Employee involvement is important in reputation building and maintenance. Employees will support the management through reputational threats if the communications are honest, sincere, open and factual. Airline reputation can be underpinned by means of including employees in the brand-building process and the Human Resources Department in any brands team (Omar and Williams, 2006). For airlines which place importance on their core values and customer service, involving Human Resources is vital. However, in many airlines, Marketing Departments (in their role as the passengers' voice) tend to have more budget and power (hegemony) than Human Resources and yet the latter is pivotal to servicing the passengers and fulfilling Marketing's aspirations. Conflicts between the two departments are often visible in poor labour relations and inefficient customer processing. In one airline, the Marketing Department installed a new passenger rewards programme and broadcast it to the premium loyalty card members. Unfortunately, Marketing forgot to notify Human Resources to train the frontline employees so they were unprepared and unable to help irritated flyers collect their mileage points.

Reputational risk protection

Risk management systems are almost always created by statisticians or other quantitative brains and their accuracy depends on people behaving (or events unfolding) as the computer models predict. However, most risk problems are behavioural and occur away from the Risk Manager's carefully prepared spread sheet. An analysis of 41 corporate crises found they were almost all caused in the boardroom (Fitzsimmons and Haslam, 2013). Boards lacked the skills to call executives to account or were blind to the risks which threatened the firm's reputation or 'licence to operate'. Sometimes the working assumptions on which the business was based provided defective information, or there were flaws in leadership which ignored the risks associated with complexity. Most tellingly, the lower level employees could not communicate 'bad news' upwards, i.e. the challenge culture was missing (see Chapter 3).

Many of the scandals which galvanised the CSERplus movement had common failures of senior management. These damaged international corporations including Union Carbide (chemical disaster) and Exxon (oil spill) (see Chapter 1). The derelictions included:

- failure to create a culture which tolerated dissent by not listening to feedback from stakeholders (including employees, customers, shareholders and the media)
- total commitment to a specific project which overwhelmed all other considerations (e.g. financial, ethical or social)

- focus on financial measures of performance and not taking non-financial risks seriously (i.e. social, environmental and reputational risks)
- a closed circle using the same people and information sources rather than seeking people and organisations which disagreed with them or criticised them
- delegation of ethical and social issues to somebody else to resolve (Schwartz and Gibb, 1999; Taylor, 2006).

These same weaknesses were also apparent in many of the commercial failings which occurred in more recent decades.

Risk-aware, innovative organisations have certain characteristics, including the following (a description of organisational cultural perfection):

> a culture where people are open-minded, willing to accept change, flexible and free from dogma; flexibility in the lines of communication, structures that allow top-down, bottom-up and lateral communication within the organisation; a risk-tolerant climate where it is accepted that lessons can be learned through mistakes [and a] knowledge-friendly culture where people are not inhibited about sharing knowledge and do not fear that sharing knowledge [will] cost them 'power and influence' or even their jobs.
>
> (Eaton *et al.*, 2006: 69)

Reputational risk register (RRR)

The top three corporate risks of 1,400 organisations surveyed in 2013 were dictated by the external environment (economic slowdown or slow recovery, regulatory and legislative changes and increasing competition) but the next three (damage to reputation/brand, failure to attract or retain top talent and failure to innovate/meet customer needs) were all within the organisation's control (Aon Risk Management, 2013). One of the most efficient ways of mitigating reputational risks is to examine risks which do not usually appear on the main corporate risk radar. These reputational risks need to be recorded in the reputational risk register (RRR) which is complementary to the main risk register. In all likelihood, the RRR (Table 7.2) would be an assortment of minor risks – 'iceberg' risks – that have the potential to 'melt' and undermine the airline's reputation. (The RRR in Table 7.2 is skeletal: it should be adapted and expanded as required. More columns are needed to cover the contact addresses of the influencers, any updates as events move forward, outcomes and other relevant issues as they become noticed.) Some of these risks require specific actions; others would stretch thinking (e.g. impact of Human Rights legislation) and some will merely require communication to alert the relevant stakeholders to watch carefully. Some issues and actions are risk reducing (the so-called 'hygiene' factors including waste disposal, diversity and PRM compliance); others influence behaviour, drive reputation enhancement or differentiate airlines. These include issues such as animal welfare, passenger allergies or controversies over biofuels. The Customer Relations Department should be alert to the existence of the RRR as its employees can scan customer complaints for any potential issues.

Table 7.2 Skeleton of prototype, simplified Reputational Risk Register (RRR)

Reputational Risk Register

Version number: 1 Date _____

Stakeholder/s and reputational iceberg	Probability of occurrence (i.e. risk)	Economic implications	Social implications	Environment implications	Impact/s	Resources needed (time, £, manpower)	Action/ responsible Department	CSFs	KPIs and dates
Environment Dept. What would happen if GHGs/ infrared-absorbing gases are no longer considered the cause of environmental degradation?	25%... notice increasing appearance in press	Costs: what has been spent to date? What will need to be spent?	Internal and external stakeholders? Who to involve? HR/Comms to advise	Science is evolving: monthly updates needed	Science vs economics: PR issue? Recalculation of emissions; rewrite of regulations and policies?	Significant! Tbd (await matrix group output)	Environment Dept owner: prepare matrix team for scenario planning	CO_2 emissions plus other emissions as appropriate?	Tba (as circumstances evolve)
Charities Dept: what if supported charity becomes insolvent due to bad governance?	10%: already one charity under scrutiny	Finance implications? Reallocate budget? Cancel all unused tickets/ free freight? Any funds lost?	Avoid PR backlash; Legal Dept to advise; reputational impact?	n/a	Significant sponsorship = high risk; heavy press coverage – reputational risk potential	Finance Dept calculating impact	PR Dept owning: local Police involved; cause-related advertising pulled	Amount of unfavourable press; any impact on sales?	Tbd

continued . . .

Table 7.2 Continued

Reputational Risk Register

Version number: 1 Date

Stakeholder/s and reputational iceberg	Probability of occurrence (i.e. risk)	Economic implications	Social implications	Environment implications	Impact/s	Resources needed (time, £, manpower)	Action/ responsible Department	CSFs	KPIs and dates
Customer Service/ Legal: Passenger with dog allergy vs passenger with an assistance dog on board – whose rights trump whose responsibilities?	One passenger per 100 flights?	Offer booking change free of charge to both allergic passenger and passenger with dog and hope one is prepared to change flights; tell passenger to fly with competitor?	Perhaps offer complimentary tickets to encourage flight switch? Allergy medications on board; Legal Dept to advise liability	Additional aircraft clean to ensure cabin is free from dog hair; what are 'reasonable' adjustments under EC 1107/2006?	Conflict with dog owner; medical alert for allergic passenger; inconvenience for other passengers	• At departure gate: Tbd: conflict resolution; deep clean aircraft pre-take-off • On board: Tbd	Reservations Dept to phone customers; make sure ITC will prevent these bookings in future; instal allergy tick-box on booking form for future risk minimisation	Monitor occurrences via feedback; ITC systems change required; budget costs and feasibility	Legal advice a.s.a.p.; feedback monitoring by 3 July; ITC data by 3 July

continued . . .

Table 7.2 Continued

Reputational Risk Register

Version number: 1 Date _____

Stakeholder/s and reputational iceberg	Probability of occurrence (i.e. risk)	Economic implications	Social implications	Environment implications	Impact/s	Resources needed (time, £, manpower)	Action/ responsible Department	CSFs	KPIs and dates
Legal Dept/Anti-corruption organisations: morality of flying to destinations where corruption is acknowledged	100% – on routes to Saudi Arabia, China, Azerbaijan, Russia	Must fly: good revenue-earning routes; competitors will take advantage; no benefit in NOT flying	Don't fly, i.e. flying perceived as giving succour to unsavoury dictators; Transparency International views?	Do lesser environmental standards apply?	Flying boycott? Unfavourable press coverage? Local bribery?	Tbd	Legal Dept to involve anti-corruption NGO to advise/deflect	Avoid human rights-inspired flying boycott	Tbd; monitor monthly
Legal/Catering/Sales: ethical issues: halal meats? GM foods? fois gras? palm oil? effect on sales?	50%: regular press notices	Which stakeholders? Passenger impact of any options? Sales effect?	n/a	Catering Dept investigate; Communications Dept	Tbd: religious, health, welfare and/or economic impact?	Alternatives? costs?	Catering Dept to examine economies of scale for meals	Passenger impact CSFs; financial CSFs	£ financial impact of CSFs and options by 3 June
Legal/Market Depts: normalisation of diplomatic relations with Cuba	100%: if the US is doing it UK will follow	Opening new market; any alliance partner implications?	Headwind with charity involvement to 'influence' airport slots?	Are alliance aircraft compliant? Regulations for airport?	Huge potential for 'soft' skills via charitable involvement (assure due diligence)	Language training; philanthropic allocation; synchronise with Marketing	HR; Marketing; Philanthropy/ (Sustainability Dept?)	Tbd	Tbd

Similarly, those charged with compiling and updating the RRR should have their commercial radar finely tuned by watching/reading/listening to news bulletins, scanning competitors' and suppliers' information and monitoring government thinking as well as research from academic and commercial sources. All issues on the RRR should have a CSF with an allocated KPI measure so they can be monitored for mitigations and/or activity. Sometimes determining the KPIs can be challenging and they can be left open and undated until there is sufficient information and data to decide the appropriate actions and measures which might require moving them to the main risk register. The RRR should be reviewed at regular intervals (monthly, quarterly, annually) with the frequency dependent on the events under scrutiny. Formal minutes must be taken and responsibilities and actions noted.

After a crisis – restoring reputation

Uncertainty during a crisis can do much damage and revolves around questions of cause, blame, response, public perception, resolution, and consequences (Ray, 1999). Any damage to reputation can be repaired provided the responses are adequate and not led by the same team which caused the crisis. People tend to adhere to their initial beliefs (i.e. an anchoring bias) whether or not they are correct, or contradicted by new information (Hoeken and Renkema, 1998). However, it is possible to change beliefs and improve a corporate reputation by reading a correction or an objective version of events. Any changed perspective is, however, possibly dependent on the subject's involvement with the topic and the frequency with which they read such articles. Alternatively, readers might ignore an article or stop reading it before the end. There are also concerns surrounding the time lapse between reading the original article, and the publishing and nature of the corrections which should be directed to counter the most important aspects of the incorrect report (Hoeken and Renkema, 1998).

There is no single best way to organise a response to a reputational crisis since each response will depend on the developing situation. However, restoring reputation after a crisis, irrespective of whether it occurred suddenly or incrementally, can involve many strategies each being contingent on the organisation itself. Stakeholder identification is critical in times of crisis when reputations are often irrevocably damaged. Equally necessary is leadership which is decisive and honest having considered any options under the sustainability dimensions. Irrespective of whether the origin of the crisis was dramatic or incremental the damage can be limited by prompt, honest and objective communications which can improve corporate reputation even after a time lapse between the event and its outcome. The airline can identify the biggest risks and opportunities by conducting regular stakeholder audits to identify the players, allocate internal stakeholder 'owners' and decide the proportional resources needed to manage and monitor them. Charitable giving (see Chapter 3) can also partially restore a company's reputation provided it links the company's social performance and the business itself (Williams and Barrett, 2000) (always remembering that some thoroughly disreputable organisations (e.g. Enron) have made significant donations to a variety of charities). However, association with failing charities could undermine the airline's halo and signal bad judgement, lack of monitoring and inappropriate risk-taking.

A response to a crisis might require a cultural change to prevent any reoccurrence of the cause. This would ensure that the company which emerges from the crisis is not the same company which went into it. The employees should be in a position to support any such change (see Chapter 3) by demonstrating appropriate behaviours since they are the leading stakeholders for the airline's reputation. They will be most affected by any necessary cultural change and in particular by flexing new systems designed to prevent reoccurrence of the original behaviours.

Steps to be taken to manage and recover from corporate crises include the following (adapted from Mitroff *et al.*, 1996):

- recognise the crisis
- respond to the crisis and the media
- activate the Crisis Management Team
- treat the injuries (humans, animals, environment or less tangible 'injuries')
- determine the *real* nature of the crisis
- contain and recover (by fixing the problem and reversing the damage)
- communicate to update as events unfold (better to say 'don't know' than mis-inform).

Once the crisis has passed, the corporate reputation requires restoration to limit damage (Schwartz and Gibb, 1999). Stakeholders need to be audited to identify needs and plan the appropriate strategic and tactical actions. Internal owners need to be identified for the stakeholders who represent the biggest risks and the biggest opportunities and the time allocated to each must be proportionate to any potential impact. The culture needs to change so failings can be identified early and passed up the chain. This task would fall to the Human Resources Department. (The culture change must not be led by those from the former failing culture.) The NEDs need to ensure they are guardians of the reputation and facilitate dissent by inviting outsiders to challenge the 'closed circle'. Damage limitation actions need to be embedded in new systems to prevent a reoccurrence. The time-test will be whether the new systems detect the human failings before they infect the entire airline.

7.4 DEFINING ETHICAL BEHAVIOUR

Embedding ethical behaviour

All economic decisions should have an ethical basis; however, defining ethics is never exact. Sometimes it is 'about how many women, ethnic minorities and lesbian, gay, bisexual and transgender people there are on boards, and how to avoid investing in companies involved in "blood sports", the arms trade, GM crops and tobacco' (Moore, 2013). Different religions have different views; different professions exhibit different behaviours; different politicians espouse different ideologies. Commonality would appear to be around words such as 'behaviour', 'a collection of morals' or 'instructions on how to behave' and the fact that they apply to individuals as well as groups. 'Unethical' or 'immoral' behaviour describes that which is detrimental and outside the normal behavioural expectation. For the economically sustainable airline ethical behaviour is simply ensuring that all stakeholders recognise the difference between right and wrong. Sometimes this is determined by the law; sometimes it is determined by what is held in an individual's conscience. Economically sustainable businesses employ people whom they believe understand how to behave in accordance with the organisation's expectations as defined by its core values. Ethical behaviour should not need plans, compliance systems or a whole department. It just needs hiring the right people with the appropriate core values (see Chapter 3) to work with common sense, openness, transparency and symmetrical, impartial information and data in a culture which permits and enables challenge. Simple (*if only* . . .)!

Ethical risks

Airlines face many ethical risks which, because of the international nature of the business, are not faced by other industries to the same extent (or if at all). Airlines often interact with other less scrupulous industries and nations. Aside from the 'ethical-technical' issue of using fossil fuels (see Chapter 6), airlines have many other ethical challenges which can create reputational risks under stakeholder pressure. They are frequently pressured by socially oriented stakeholders to seek only those suppliers who can prove the ethical lineage of their products. Monitoring supply chains is a transaction cost which can be bureaucratic, complex and expensive especially since there are many suppliers in airline supply chains. As an example, the supply chain for the sale of goods on board covers a wide variety of products and is fraught with potential ethical risks and which, if not managed, could affect reputations. Some of the ethical supply traps include products possibly made by child labour (wash bags), mined by slaves ('blood' diamonds), created from endangered species (ivory) or are harmful to users (tobacco). The economic argument runs that if there is no market for these unethical goods then the unsavoury trades will cease. However, the reality is that child labour often supports whole families; slave-wrought jewellery and electronic devices would still be purchased by less discerning buyers in lesser concerned cultures; impoverished peasant farmers will slaughter endangered rhinoceroses and elephants to trade their horns and tusks for family food and low-paid cultivators of unhealthy flora will supply a growing market particularly in the advancing nations. Who is the judge of what is 'ethical'? What is unethical to developed nations is often ethical in advancing nations. Tactically, airlines can take steps to ensure the reputability of their supply chains by engaging with relevant NGOs (e.g. Transparency International). The challenge is to decide the trade-offs needed to support 'ethical' stances. Should airlines continue to fly to destinations which have recorded abuses of human rights (e.g. Saudi Arabia or China (Amnesty International UK, 2015)) in the belief that free trade will liberate the inhabitants and possibly even prevent further wars? Or should they pull off the route knowing that their unscrupulous competitors will continue to fly and probably enjoy a profitable monopoly?

Legislation and regulation enforce supply chain ethics as determined desirable by the developed world. In the USA one minor clause in the Dodd–Frank Wall Street Reform Consumer Protection Act of 2010 (US Government, 2010) links the impact of the mining and sales of rare minerals with human rights and the funding for terrorism. It requires disclosure of origin of any products containing conflict minerals such as coltan, tantalum, tin, tungsten, gold or their derivatives mined in or near the Democratic Republic of the Congo (DRC). Some of these minerals are essential elements in the world's electronic infrastructure. They could possibly already be included in aircraft instruments, air navigation systems and the multitude of other devices that keep aircraft flying safely. Refusing to procure sources from the DRC means that some formerly well-paid miners have turned to hunting endangered animals for food (Delawala, 2016) – a terrible outcome for the DRC. Australia with its similar mineral deposits was the ultimate beneficiary of this Act. Was sustainability-thinking used when this clause was proposed, i.e. were the potential economic and environmental impacts considered along with the social consequences? Airlines should not be assessed by the same criteria as, for example, miscreant mining or agribusiness companies which plough virgin lands, abuse human rights, support corruption and sacrifice endangered species. One-size-fits-all CSERplus is not appropriate.

Supporting ethical airline procurement and supply decisions are assorted product certifications under international codes such as the Convention on International Trade in Endangered Species (CITES), which is designed to eliminate the trade in rare and endangered animals or plants. Further ethical risks and pressures come from animal welfare groups concerned about the killing of animals for meat, leather or fur and the carriage of animals for medical experiments. These groups can garner much social media support for their causes and can sometimes disrupt flying operations with the threat of protest. Animal welfare campaigners, People for the Ethical Treatment of Animals (PETA), have been campaigning to prevent the airborne shipments of live animals for laboratory experiments. 'Air France is the only major airline in the world that still ships thousands of monkeys a year to laboratories, where they're caged, poisoned, cut into and killed' (PETA, 2015). Their message for Air France is as follows:

Stop Air France From Shipping Monkeys to Their Deaths!

Air France claims to be 'making the sky the best place on Earth'. But in reality, the airline is making the sky a dangerous and scary place, as it is one of the largest traffickers of primates in the world. Air France continues to ship monkeys to laboratories, despite the fact that every other major airline in the world has ceased sending primates on these horrific one-way flights! . . . Almost every other airline in the world – including United, Aer Lingus, Air China,

American, British Airways, Cathay Pacific, Delta, Lufthansa, China Southern, and Qantas – have shown great compassion by refusing to transport monkeys to laboratories. Air France even cancelled an individual shipment of primates after a public outcry by PETA and its supporters. Now we must convince the airline to end this barbarism once and for all. Tell Air France officials that you won't be flying with the airline until it stops this cruel practice.

(PETA, n.d.)

Similarly and in response to public outcry, many airlines including USA's Delta, American and United refused to carry big-game hunting trophies. This prohibition followed public outrage after American trophy hunters shot and killed 'Cecil' the much revered South African lion (Cummings, 2015).

Ethics and health tourists

Health tourists (see Chapter 1, Chapter 4 and Chapter 5) provide many challenges for the airlines some of which are ethical in origin. The responsibility placed on airlines is, at times, onerous especially if the health tourists are travelling for life-saving surgery or with an undeclared communicable disease (i.e. a negative externality), such as tuberculosis, bacterial pneumonia or Ebola, which could infect air crew and fellow passengers. (This is another example of asymmetric information and moral hazard (see Chapter 1).) These passengers are also unlikely to have travel insurance because insurers would probably consider the risks to be excessive. The airline implicitly asks all passengers to be honest – to travel only when healthy – and it trusts them to be truthful. But desperate passengers are not always truthful especially if disclosure means they could be either denied travel or have the added expense of an extra seat for an attendant (see Chapter 4 and Chapter 5). There are significant ethical, litigation and compensation implications of denying travel to a sick passenger. This was the case with an obese woman who died shortly after being denied a seat on a return flight to New York from Hungary in 2012. Her husband eventually settled his $US6m lawsuit with the airlines involved. He filed the wrongful death suit against Delta, KLM and Lufthansa airlines because his wife – who weighed over 400lbs (182kg) and had an amputated leg – had been removed from several New York-bound flights. This might have caused her stress which contributed to her deteriorating condition (NBC News, 2014). The ethical challenges for the airlines also included the problem of physically lifting the woman onto the aircraft without injuring the Mobility Assistants who had to lift her. This is an example of passenger's rights vs airline's responsibilities vs economics (in the form of compensation for any injured employees and ultimately for the passenger's widower). Should this passenger ever have been accepted for the outbound journey?

Supply chain payment

Airlines have undergone some economically challenging years and some even relied on the goodwill of their supply chains to keep them afloat. It is therefore only ethical and fair that when the cash flow improves, airlines comply with payment terms for suppliers – especially smaller suppliers with limited access to financial resources. The Prompt Payment Code, introduced by UK Department for Business Information and Skills (BIS) in 2009 should have reduced the problem of slow payments in the supply chain. Under the Code responsible customers promised to pay promptly but in practice the Code was actually toothless: companies could sign up as long as they adhered to their stated payment terms whatever the duration. Some terms were 90 days or longer which is too long for small companies. Suppliers like to set their own terms and if they wanted money sooner they could have been asked to renegotiate and sacrifice a mandatory discount. The party requesting any renegotiation is usually the weaker party and the one that has the most to lose. Similarly, the Late Payment Directive (an EU initiative in force from March 2013) required that invoices be settled within 60 days (30 days for public sector) with penalties applied to those organisations which did not meet the deadlines. However, vulnerable small suppliers are often reluctant to enforce the Directive for fear of losing future work. Any abuse of the supply chain demonstrates unethical behaviour and airlines, as responsible corporate organisations, should be aware that this behaviour could lead to the demise of a reliable and trustworthy supplier – a failure which could ultimately damage the airline's reputation.

Airlines have enormous buying power. With the growth of alliances, joint ventures and purchase of equity stakes in partners for procurement economies and route sharing purposes their market power can be almost monopolistic. Such power carries responsibilities. However, conversely, pushing down prices (by online tendering or other means) can skew markets – and with lowered prices comes the need for timely, contractually agreed and punctual payments. In an example of industry-generated potential market inefficiency, some alliances behave like cartels driving down prices and compelling sellers to agree to their terms.

Squeezing suppliers too hard can trigger strikes as the suppliers struggle to contain costs (*The Economist*, 2005) or can encourage fraud by acting as an incentive to subvert carefully designed systems. What is missing from the check list is *trust*. Instilling trust into a tick-box system is not easy especially if negotiations are not conducted face-to-face in this internet age. It does, however, provide an incentive for the procurement team members to leave their desks and keep contact with suppliers. This assists with ensuring supply chain security, integrity and ultimately continuity. Face-to-face contact can also reduce some biases.

Corporate citizenship and taxation

Among the characteristics of ethical behaviour and good corporate citizenship (see Chapter 1) is the timely payment of taxes and airlines pay tax where they consider it to be the most efficient for the economic sustainability of the company. Between 2014 and 2015, UK businesses were urged by CSERplus' advocates to pay any avoided tax. This lobbying was a form of mob rule rather than rule by law. Avoiding tax is legal; evading tax is illegal. Paying additional taxes which are not owed is economically irresponsible, unjustified and unsustainable. Governments' first duty is to ensure that tax rates are competitive and the rules simple in order to attract entrepreneurs to create employment and make profits on which they pay tax. However, international chains of MNEs can shift profits to more tax-friendly regimes which penalises the national small and medium-sized enterprises on which an economy relies for growth. So the MNEs which initially advocated and supported CSERplus are not necessarily those which would feel the effects of their actions. The first duty of the airline and its Board of Directors is to obey the law and in this way preserve the value of the assets to which the shareholders and employees have contributed. In doing so, they would avoid wasting resources by paying fines for illegal behaviour. That is economically and ethically sustainable behaviour. Economically sustainable airlines pay only the taxes which are owed. To do any more would be to reduce the welfare of shareholders and employees.

Ethics and investor–customers

There is no mention of whether members of the SRI industry (see Chapter 6) who are boycotting investing in airlines' shares (as well as tobacco, alcohol and pornography (Jamieson, 2008)) decided they would avoid flying around their global businesses – only that some would not invest their clients' money in aviation because of the industry's environmental impact. Any decision which has no personal impact removes the decision-maker from having 'skin in the game'. Different aircraft operated by different airlines have different environmental impacts. Private charter aircraft have different emissions levels from larger commercial aircraft and the emissions per seat also differ. It was a voting minority (just 2.5% of those entitled to vote) which swayed the leaders and managers of Standard Life (see Chapter 6) to boycott investment in aviation. This is another example of when free-riding shareholders' lack of participation might have delivered an uneconomic outcome for the SRI investors.

Similarly, the issue of loyalty awards for regular airline travellers raises the question of the ethics of ownership. If a businessman/woman (or Member of Parliament – particularly those on the CCC (see Chapter 6)) gains mileage loyalty points from business flights (paid for by his/her company's shareholders or constituents) they can redeem them for personal travel. Do these commercially earned loyalty points belong to the passenger or the employing organisation? Are they just another example of unethical behaviour, potential tax avoidance or evasion or just an acceptable tax-free benefit?

Whistle-blowing

Every discussion of governance and ethics must consider the failure of systems and the potential for those who discover the failure to be heard without fear. Whistle-blowing must be accommodated within corporate processes. Because airlines work in some countries where corruption is endemic, they must be particularly alert to potentially damaging situations and have processes in place to support employees who are trying to behave ethically, true to the core values and within the law.

In order to pre-empt reputational crises, outlier whistle-blowers need courage to speak against groupthink and convince the Chief Executive (often many organisational levels above) of any trouble brewing. Among legislation which affects businesses in the UK there are the Proceeds of Crime Act 2002, Money Laundering Regulations 2007 and the Bribery Act 2010 (which supports the Organisation of Economic Cooperation and Development (OECD) Anti-bribery Convention) (OECD, 2014)). The latter covers the giving of bribes, receiving of bribes, bribing of foreign public officials and failure of commercial organisations to prevent bribery. However, there are some 'grey areas' including corporate hospitality: at what point does corporate hospitality tip into bribery and veer into corruption? The safest way to resolve allegations of wrongdoing is to ensure that there is documentary evidence to the contrary. Airlines need processes and policies for employees accepting gifts (they could be donated to the SBU which handles philanthropy), reimbursing expenses (receipts only – unlike the processes in the UK government or EU), offering sponsorships or donations (in accordance with the pre-determined strategy only), enjoying hospitality (with limits specified for giving and receiving to avoid that which is unreasonable and disproportionate), outsourcing selection (tendering processes must be watertight and transparent) and avoiding facilitation payments (such as bribing a Customs official to expedite clearing a shipment).

In order to protect sources within the airline, internal whistle-blowing can be outsourced to external independent specialist organisations which process anonymous tip-offs. This is important because many employees do not reveal corrupt behaviours for fear of jeopardising their jobs. However, it is not always necessary to use an external source for all misdemeanours. Honest behaviours should permeate the economically sustainable airline; inappropriate behaviours, however minor, should be an alert to potential normalising of deviance (see Chapter 3) which can sometimes manifest in unexpected ways. On one occasion a graduate management trainee plagiarised the work of another creative employee and presented it to the Board of Directors as her own. Ironically, the presentation concerned the development of sustainability behaviours core to the airline's culture. By acting dishonestly, she enfeebled the corporate core values (which might not have been her personal core values). Had the airline recruited on core values (see Chapter 3), she might never have been employed.

7.5 OUTSOURCING CHALLENGES

Outsourcing risks

In a sustainable airline, outsourcing procurement can be a commercial minefield unless proper processes are established. Outsourcing decisions can be high risk and need to take account of intangibles such as the business continuity risks and whether the intellectual property and operation should be retained at the home base. Is the outsourced partner in a flood prone area or an earthquake zone? Is the area prone to social unrest? Can the contract be enforced by law if necessary? The decision could be to establish a joint venture (JV) in partnership with a local organisation. By retaining a shareholding the outsourcing airline retains some control, leverage and influence over which other contracts the partner can accept. The outsourced supplier must be able to deliver to the standard the airline considers acceptable because it will be servicing customers who rely heavily on the airline's reputation.

Spreading the risk could also involve setting up a second JV in a third country to reduce reliance on one organisation. Taking the process outside of the home nation means training third parties and providing them with guidelines – a significant risk which requires trust to ensure confidentiality.

Supply chain governance

Examining the supply chain for sustainability risks is critical to ensuring the smooth functioning of airlines' operations. Some airlines perform an annual economic audit of a sample of their suppliers examining any social and environmental risks as they do so. Similarly, as suppliers themselves, airlines are often subjected to multiple annual audits from different corporate buyers working to a wide range of assorted industries' and NGOs' standards. Irrespective of which standard prevails, the airline could be involved in considerable costs often imposed by customers who sometimes seem to have unlimited resources to pursue higher CSERplus ideals. In this way, the demands constitute a form of 'genteel extortion' or 'economic protection' (see Chapter 3). Valuable corporate airline supply contracts could be contingent upon compliance with the client's ethically based supply chain requirements. Such requirements impose external procurement standards upon the airline – sometimes duplicating the airline's own processes and sometimes adding extra cost to servicing a particularly valuable customer. These additional requirements might not fit with an airline's culture and processes and in order to secure a particular customer an airline might have to adopt a parallel CSERplus strategy. However, while subjecting some airlines to expensive, politically correct interrogation these 'arbiters of goodness' sometimes behave unscrupulously themselves (as exhibited in particular by some financial institutions) which raises the question: 'Can self-selected private individuals decide what the social interest is?' (Friedman, 1982: 133). One large bank had a corporate HIV-AIDS policy in its philanthropic strategies. At that time HIV-AIDS was the *third* biggest killer (following respiratory infections and diarrhoeal diseases (see Table 3.15 in Chapter 3)). In addition to negotiating significant travel discounts for their executives to fly in the higher class cabins, this bank also wanted its travel supplier to instal an HIV-AIDS programme in its CSERplus work-stream and threatened to take its business elsewhere if the airline's social policies did not include aspects of the bank's priorities. Was this professional behaviour actually genteel extortion? Did the employee making this demand have the authority of his bank to do so? The proposed interference in the strategic business undermined the prioritised elements in the airline's social sustainability programme. HIV-AIDS might have been an appropriate cause for the bank – but the airline could have decided that supporting other higher ranked diseases (see Table 3.15 in Chapter 3) – or none – might have been more appropriate. Furthermore, if the bank changed

Table 7.3 Supply chain sustainability flash points

Sustainability dimension	Airline issue	Potential impact
Economics	monopolist supplier (e.g. fuel, software etc.)	vulnerability of supply chain to a catastrophic event (e.g. fire at the supply depot could disrupt the operation)
	banking with a financial institution which becomes insolvent	inability to access funds; unable to meet debt obligations; seizure of assets; worst case means closure of airline (i.e. failure)
Society	outsourcing of Customer Complaints Department to an advancing nation with lower costs	labour disruption at home base in response to the outsourcing with consequential impact on operations; trades unions' pickets at operating base; involvement of international trades unions which could scupper the airline's international operation
	change of supplier for uniform manufacture	if supplier is using child labour or factories which were breaching human rights including health and safety conditions, there could be a deflected impact on the airline's reputation resulting in picketing, bad press and lost sales
Environment	diesel engines on ground support vehicles inadequately maintained by outsourced equipment engineering	failure to implement airports' emissions standards as specified in contracts and regulations could lead to subsequent (and expensive) contract amendments and fines
	computer server rooms inadvertently kept at wrong temperature by outsourced facilities management company	this facilities failure could lead to major ITC outages; in any event, back up servers are required as part of risk management (or the entire flying operation could fail)

travel supplier the airline would have been left supporting a programme which neither fitted with their strategy nor delivered a commercial trade-off.

A sustainable airline has many links in its supply chain any of which could cause a disruption to its operation through an ill-considered procurement decision (Table 7.3).

Service-level agreements (SLAs)

Each outsourced contract has SLAs to ensure performance quality. The SLAs must be realistic, easy to monitor and have easily enforceable exit strategies. As an example, if the service level for an airport contract is set with a CSF and KPI of 'no aircraft delay', then finding ownership of any delays could be problematic since no single individual or department would want to own up to having caused it. Finding someone to accept the blame wastes time and is an inefficient use of resources. Similarly, the SLA for outsourced customer complaints processing could incorporate simple measures which could include ensuring that all correspondence is free from spelling errors. There could be escalating penalties payable for minor errors such as one spelling error per ten items of correspondence through to major errors including breaches of confidentiality. Outsourcing decisions are not to be taken lightly and are an example of social risk vs economic risk.

Performance-based procurement

In performance-based specification (PBS) the procurement is specified on the function or output of the contract rather than the more usual contracting on prescriptive inputs or the process of provision. PBS can more closely align the economic objectives of both parties. The client's rewards for the contractor are paid when the output is achieved. Conversely, penalties are paid by the contractor to the client if the output is not achieved. With PBS only the profit margin is in play because the cost-base has been agreed and the profit is the discretionary award. As an example, aircraft engines are often tied to the concept of 'power by the hour' payment where airlines pay for the engine's output. The risks in the performance-based contract (PBC) are allocated to the party most able to handle them. PBS relies on using original manufacturers for innovation and cost savings – not consultants who are regarded as 'middle-men'. The PBS records the client's requirements and matches them to the actual performance the supplier can deliver. It puts the supplier directly in contact with the client with no consultants in between and in doing so, maximises the supplier's specialist knowledge and skills thereby reducing the transaction costs.

In reality, all contracts are incomplete because they cannot contain clauses and remedies for every unforeseeable event therefore trust has real value in commercial relationships. Under a prescriptive contract where the inputs are specified, the SLA monitoring could require spot checks or audits and the matching of invoices to SLAs with continual vigilance for over-billing, bid-rigging and over-payment (Dorée, 2004). These activities are symptoms of breaches of trust as well as corruption – a trigger for market inefficiency and possible failure. These activities all increase the transaction costs. In contrast, PBC transaction costs are kept to a minimum because with specified outputs, all negotiating is completed at contract time. The contract should include SLAs, CSFs and KPIs which meet the airline's prioritised economic sustainability targets such as zero aircraft delays, correct invoicing, hygiene audits and any other CSFs which might be appropriate and specific to the contract.

The benefits of PBS lie in reductions in costs, documentation, claims, communication, decision-making, waste and risks because it allows the supplier (the specialist) the freedom to innovate to produce the output the client requires. In many ways it is an extension of the lean principle (see Chapter 2). Prescriptive contracts can be easier to monitor but their requirements capture can be overly complicated and can become a means of deflecting blame. Sometimes the client and supplier do not communicate sufficiently because of asymmetric knowledge on both sides. Initially, the establishment of PBS SLAs requires criteria and performance data which might not be available in which case the creation of a PBC can be incomplete – an omission which could carry significant risk. After commencement and if the contract is operating successfully it can be extended with further savings because over time economies of scale should occur. Furthermore, if the costs can be reduced through efficiencies, the outsourced organisation could be incentivised with a share of the profits. In the event that the contract is truly successful it can be converted to an 'evergreen' contract and eventually, the JV shareholdings could even be spun off into a separate entity and sold.

Insourcing, outsourcing and offshoring

Outsourcing offshore (offshoring – see Chapter 2) is embedded in economics. Any social benefit is usually felt in the receiving nation while the disbenefits are in the outsourcing nation with redundant employees and local community impacts. If the airline is in the private sector, then government should not be involved in this decision – unless a home-nation politician decides to intervene in the market and persuade the outsourcer not to increase unemployment in his electorate. This would be tantamount to political interference in a market decision, reducing private benefits and ultimately diminishing overall shareholder welfare. Outsourcing, however, is not always successful because it can mean redistribution of the risks with a loss of control and internal knowledge. Furthermore, losing trained and skilled employees and the facilities in which they worked means that the outsourcer becomes more dependent on the outsourced suppliers. They could raise their prices or the foreign exchange rate could change which might even make the project uneconomic and over time, the initial savings could disappear. During outsourcing a business continuity plan is needed to minimise risks of an adverse event in the contracting period. Should this occur, the airline must be able to activate a backup plan to avoid any loss of either service or reputation.

Older, established carriers could have an insourcing problem which does not occur for new start-ups. Legacy carriers tend to have internal mini-industries (often encapsulated as SBUs), e.g. catering, fuelling, accounting, physiotherapy, facilities management. Each of those is incorporated onto the airline's pay scales instead of matching the external markets. The airline employees' terms and conditions could have been negotiated by the trades unions in the belief that all members of the company performing what they perceived as similar roles should be paid similar rates rather than benchmarking using external markets. However, that practice can eventually make internal activities too expensive and uncompetitive when the effects are ultimately felt in the competitive external market for airline services and products. While these mini-industries remain part of the airline's cost structure competitive costs are unattainable without comparative, external market testing.

Subsequent outsourcing of these functions and TUPEing the employees (see Chapter 2) requires the appropriate pay scales to find their levels in competitive marketplaces.

Outsourcing goes to the specialists, i.e. those organisations which innovate, keep their knowledge current and maintain their competitive edge in their industry niche. However, clients sometimes forget that they are using specialists and therefore outsourcing can under-perform if the supplier is restricted by the client. Clients (in all industries and not just aviation) are often nervous about surrendering control of their processes and/or production and require reassurance from a surplus of SLAs and an army of process checkers to supervise the contract as justification for the original decision. Outsourcing organisations need to have confidence in their sustainable, transparent decision (which would have been thoroughly scenario tested) and let the real specialists decide how to run the contract. In exchange, the outsourcing airline must pay the contractor on time on the contracted dates. That is their economic, social and ethical obligation as high-reputation clients.

Non-performance and exit strategy

In the event that outsourcing is not performing, the contract might need termination. These terms, including penalties and notice periods, must be decided at the point of contracting and be included in the initial risk assessment. Exit terms have to be made easy to enforce and attempts made to retain as much goodwill as possible to protect the airline's reputation. Residual resentment must be avoided (particularly with offshoring suppliers) because airlines are vulnerable especially if, for example, access to a new route is in any way tied with its outsourcing behaviour.

7.6 MISSING MARKETS: CSERplus INDUSTRIES

CSERplus standards and indices

CSERplus has spawned many new (formerly missing) industries (see Chapter 1). These range from reputational risk protectors (such as specialist public relations and NGOs advising on a multitude of potential CSERplus risks) through to report writers and KPI assurers. What has never been determined is what these new bureaucrats add to commercial airline value and whether their involvement actually sells more airline seats or freight space (i.e. CSERplus vs airline economics).

MNE support for commercial CSERplus evolved from historic failures of management and not just the moral panics of recent decades. The fear that began with the humanitarian and environmental disaster of the chemical spill in Bhopal India in 1984 and the environmentally disastrous oil spill from tanker Exxon Valdez in Prince William Sound, Alaska in 1989 (see Chapter 1) now permeates most boardrooms. Many organisations were subsequently formed to advise corporates on how best to protect their reputations. Some had their origins in religious orders or were charities for humanitarian or environmental purposes; others were CSERplus advisors, public relations companies or corporate behavioural specialists. Eventually these organisations became fully fledged, profit-making services with the development of standards, indices, ratings, guidance documents, awards for best practice (for which some corporates compete in an extension of the moral panic) and even formation of practitioner guilds to provide a pool of self-proclaimed experts from which commercial organisations could obtain their sustainability-specialist employees. NGOs too became involved focussing on bringing human rights, ethics and environmental concerns into commercial board rooms. The international nature of aviation means that fairness (see Chapter 3) and implementing CSERplus principles in the supply chain also involve political systems and human rights in destinations other than the home nation.

Standards

Airlines in the developed world are encouraged to support NGOs such as the International Labour Organisation (ILO) with its Declaration on Fundamental Principles and Rights at Work (ILO, 1998). This Declaration has four fundamental principles: freedom of association and the right to collective bargaining, abolition of child labour and elimination of all forms of forced labour, and employment discrimination. Similarly, the UN also protects broader human rights with the 30 Articles forming the Universal Declaration on Human Rights (United Nations, 1948). Articles 23 and 24 protect the rights of employees.

Article 23 states that everyone has rights to work, choose employment in favourable conditions and to be protected against unemployment. It also promotes the rights to equal pay for equal work and to join a trades union for workplace protection. Article 24 promotes the right to limitations on working hours, paid holidays and the right to rest. (These have all been accepted by advanced nations.) However, economist Henderson observed that regulating through the imposition of uniform international standards would restrict mutually beneficial trade and investment and could even restrain development by suppressing employment opportunities (Henderson, 2001).

Developed world airlines' suppliers are expected to comply with the UN's international standards irrespective of their national culture and customs and to be held to account if breaches were to be uncovered. Compliance becomes a matter of risk protection. For consistency of standards there are many organisations with guidance. The UN has the UN Global Compact (UNGC) (a network of private-sector companies, international labour organisations and NGOs) which seeks to influence labour unions, governments and businesses regarding their behaviour. However, Henderson (2001: 121) was concerned that 'the Compact is a one-sided affair: within it, only corporations are seen as having obligations'. Furthermore, the UN agencies with which many businesses have chosen to align themselves exaggerate the flaws of the market economy and some even misrepresent the conduct of MNEs to suit their purposes (Henderson, 2001).

The UNGC principles (Table 7.4) should be placed into context. For example, the elimination of child labour is undoubtedly desirable by developed world standards – but if no child working means the children's families would be unable to afford food the aspiration needs to be reconsidered. Advanced-world standards and advancing-world practices are sometimes incompatible. Increasing wages in the developing world (in alignment with CSERplus social justice principles) means that local companies might not be able to compete for local labour and their withdrawal from the market could mean fewer opportunities. Solving one problem creates another. There are no easy decisions to be made in some circumstances.

In addition, the UN also developed the UN Global Principles on Business and Human Rights (UNGP) (United Nations, 2011) which link business activity to human rights. They have three overriding principles: (1) the State duty to protect human rights; (2) the corporate responsibility to respect human rights and (3) access to remedy for victims of business-related abuses.

Table 7.4 Ten Principles of the UN Global Compact (United Nations, n.d.)

Human rights	
PRINCIPLE 1	Businesses should support and respect the protection of internationally proclaimed human rights; and
PRINCIPLE 2	Make sure that they are not complicit in human rights abuses.
Labour	
PRINCIPLE 3	Businesses should uphold the freedom of association and the effective recognition of the right to collective bargaining;
PRINCIPLE 4	The elimination of all forms of forced and compulsory labour;
PRINCIPLE 5	The effective abolition of child labour; and
PRINCIPLE 6	The elimination of discrimination in respect of employment and occupation.
Environment	
PRINCIPLE 7	Businesses should support a precautionary approach to environmental challenges;
PRINCIPLE 8	Undertake initiatives to promote greater environmental responsibility; and
PRINCIPLE 9	Encourage the development and diffusion of environmentally friendly technologies.
Anti-corruption	
PRINCIPLE 10	Businesses should work against corruption in all its forms, including extortion and bribery.

Indices

The complexity of global supply chains means that there is a proliferation of NGOs and their sustainability indices which attempt to equalise and measure social and environmental performance by using common CSFs and KPIs. Airlines can have real difficulties choosing which index (if any) is appropriate for their business. Index membership (the one-size-fits-all concept) is another unproductive overhead. Henderson (2001: 17) noted that 'CSR embodies the notion that progress in relation to environmental and social issues lies in making norms and standards more stringent and more uniform' and that this approach took inadequate consideration of costs and benefits at the margin and the different circumstances which would affect them.

CSERplus index developers set themselves as arbiters of morals, ethics and commercial behaviour. Some industries have even developed their own ethical compliance initiatives and titled them as 'standards' with appropriate CSFs and KPIs for monitoring. The finance industry has its Equator Principles to determine, assess and manage the environmental and social project risks; the garment industry supply chain has the Business Social Compliance Initiative (BSCI, 2014) and works towards better labour conditions in the global garment industry. There are many other organisations, including Sedex (2014) and the Global Social Compliance Programme (GSCP, 2014), which share supply-based information; and the Ethical Trading Initiative (ETI, 2015) which comprises commercial suppliers, trades unions and charities representing labour rights and development. Indices also include the Financial Times' FTSE4Good to which businesses are admitted on their CSER and CSERplus criteria and the Dow Jones Sustainability Index (DJSI) based on market capitalisation. Membership of the DJSI confers a sustainability and risk management status. Some NGOs and their indices are in competition with each other (another fulfilled, formerly missing market). Brazil even has its own corporate sustainability index (the ISE) which is 'based on economic efficiency, environmental balance, social justice and corporate governance' (*Embraer*, 2014). There are many other advisory groups with their own supporting standards including Social Accountability International's (SAI) SA 8000, billed as 'one of the world's first auditable social certification standards for decent workplaces across all industrial sectors' (SAI, 2014). It has nine elements and is based on the UN Declaration of Human Rights and the conventions of the ILO, UN and national laws. What is unknown is whether airline membership of a CSER index persuades travellers to purchase seats or shippers to procure space for air freight – both economic enablers for all airline-supported CSERplus programmes. At the time of publication, there was no index specifically for airlines which have been swept into multiple indices and generic reporting frameworks. It might be timely for the airline industry to develop its own index (i.e. an Airline Industry Sustainability Index (AISI)) as a defence to pre-empt the bureaucrats or sustainability industry and before implementation, to determine whether its existence would encourage seat or freight sales.

Airlines can belong to several indices simultaneously each of which has different criteria with a different (labour-intensive) annual monitoring questionnaire to be completed. Furthermore, not all memberships of sustainability indices are free. In the UK, for example, Business in the Community (BiTC) is a charity which ranks member companies according to their responses to a questionnaire concerning behaviour in the marketplace, community, workplace and environment. It has a charging regime for membership after which members can enter its sustainability index. The organisation is 'open to all companies and organisations, regardless of size, location or experience in managing their business in a responsible and sustainable way' (BiTC, 2014).

The implication is that if organisations do not belong to an index, or do not have awards for their good practices, they are not reputable. Instead of letting the regulators enforce (evidenced by issuing fines) and the marketplace decide (apparent when consumers avoid irresponsible entities), NGOs have found a niche advising corporations on their behaviours. Their advisory costs are another airline transaction cost and expense which might not contribute to increased sales. Ironically, NGOs and CSERplus' advocates have become entrepreneurs and free-market capitalists profit-taking in the new markets.

CSERplus industries in formerly missing markets

Reputational risk management has spawned industries which include sustainability specialists, auditors, report writers, consultants, certifiers and index managers. Their verifications are designed to reassure consumers and other stakeholders that the reputational risks are managed and mitigated as documented and reported. In reality these practitioners add complexity, bureaucracy and cost. Some financial analysts believe that corporate reputation as identifiable through the sustainability report is a precursor to other aspects of corporate performance which financial analysts use to grade, rate and invest in commercial enterprises. (Are these financial analysts – who now rely on CSER reports to assess the strength and ethicality of their investments – the same industry analysts who ranked the USA's Enron and the UK's Co-operative Bank and Royal Bank of Scotland as 'investable grade' stocks based on their reported CSER and CSERplus activities?)

The sustainability indices appear worthy aspirations – 'unobjectionable doctrines' lending 'superficial plausibility' (Sternberg, 2009) – and almost no business could oppose them because exclusion on grounds of economics (i.e. cost) is no longer seen as acceptable by some sections of society. However, there is no proof or otherwise that belonging to such indices actually enhances corporate reputations and the indices are often expensive and labour-intensive to pursue (and they would never pass the lean test (see Chapter 2)). In the case of those indices which require input from the airline in order to complete their monitoring documentation, considerable manpower and resources are consumed after which there are the additional costs of assurance. Sustainability assurance is a growing business particularly within the large accounting, audit and management consultancies which perceive CSER audits as an integral and expanding part of their financial audit functions. (NB: Some of these auditors (maintaining their own elaborate CSERplus programmes which are ultimately paid for by their clients) have been caught in dubious professional practices. Before the financial crisis (2008 to 2013) their audits assured the public and the shareholders that some of the now-bankrupt institutions were producing 'true and fair' financial records. These examples of incompetence and potential negligence which ultimately led to a loss of national welfare were not neutralised by their generous CSERplus programmes.)

Reporting challenges

Sustainability reporting is now complex as different national and international frameworks evolve and the reports themselves become mainstream and integrated with finance reporting. There are many standards designed to encourage transparent sustainability reporting across all industries including the Global Reporting Initiative (GRI), AccountAbility (AA) which has its AA1000 standards ('principles based standards to help organisations become accountable, responsible and sustainable') and the International Standards Organisation (ISO) which has ISO 26000 criteria for sustainability reporting ('Guidance on how businesses can operate in a socially responsible way'). From 2017 onwards, after yielding to CSERplus pressure, the EU will require larger commercial European entities to file an integrated financial and sustainability report detailing their impact on the environment and society (including human rights). This is a regulation targeted at a very small readership designed by an organisation which is operating without being accountable for its own finances and behaviours. Reporting will add to the expense of producing and auditing annual corporate reports. There are also proposals by self-appointed sustainability experts to standardise sustainability reporting and to make report verification compulsory for companies of all sizes. However, standardised CSERplus reporting formats, while they make comparisons easy for the few who read them, do not suit all industries. Furthermore, contrary to the open and challenge-able, sustainability-thinking culture, it would be seen as politically incorrect to even raise concerns about the costs. There are many self-appointed CSERplus stake-holders speaking for NGOs, charities, assurers and political groups claiming high interest and inveigling high power covering these missing markets. Such asymmetric influencing which overlooks economics does not give balance to legislative or regulatory decisions (i.e. society vs airline economics vs politicians).

Awards

The sustainability industry has created multiple awards recognising their view of 'best practice'. The aims of any sponsoring NGOs appear 'reasonable' (Sternberg, 2009); however, many of these well-intentioned organisations are not clear in their language and many even muddle the use of the word 'method' with 'methodology' (i.e. the study of method) which undermines the gravitas they hoped to attain. This year's award winner could be next year's loser as other firms catch up which in theory sets in train the process of striving for betterment. However, emulating last year's winner does not necessarily guarantee success. It can lead to the homogenisation (groupthink) of an industry producing higher costs and lower profits and where competitors and legislators want unregenerate rivals to follow as a means of ensuring that they too sustain the same unproductive overheads (Henderson, 2001). Furthermore, many awards are primarily created to heighten awareness of the organising NGO. If the NGO can attract a commercial sponsor they could make a profit (i.e. embracing free-market capitalism) which many could use to further their activities towards influencing policies which could ultimately restrict commercial enterprise. Airlines are rightly sceptical of some of these awards which do not necessarily compare like-with-like and might place airlines in the same categories as airports, shipping ports, general transport or miscreant MNEs.

7.7 MANAGING SUSTAINABILITY

Fulfilling sustainability challenges

If an airline does not use integrated economic sustainability-thinking it could be vulnerable to the capriciousness of legislators, regulators, CSERplus' advocates and NGOs. Sustainability-thinking needs to determine and rank material sustainability issues. Materiality is determined by risk assessment supported by:

- evaluating the current economic, social and environmental activities within the airline and the industry and determining the dimension-specific activities and paybacks
- discovering (and maybe uncovering), prioritising and engaging the key stakeholders for future material issues
- understanding the trade-offs involved in any reputational risk protection measures
- identifying any dissonance between the current activities and future plans
- exciting the competitive spirit (but not in an anti-competitive way)
- embedding creativity, innovation and challenge in the airline culture for competitive advantage
- finding the gaps in competitiveness which are relevant to the airline and deciding the SBU 'owners' who would be responsible and accountable for their fulfilment
- developing an RRR (Table 7.2) with appropriate CSFs and KPIs and eventually incorporating individual items within the master risk register
- building the supporting processes to identify drivers of reputational risk vulnerabilities.

This is a prelude to the time when employee roles and responsibilities might change as part of future-proofing the airline. It includes the critical transformation of Customer Service Agents into Strategic Corporals (see Chapter 2 and Chapter 3) whereupon they would be expected to act autonomously. Preparing the RRR (Table 7.2) should assist but it will not cover all the challenges. Materiality ranking of the RRR issues should be based on the airline's perception and take account of the anticipated pressures from influencers including governments, special interest groups, CSERplus' advocates, NGOs and charities but always being wary of the source and biases contained in the information and data. Again, properly costed impact analyses which consider the long-term reputational risks and effects are needed to support sustainability-thinking.

A Sustainability Department?

Depending on the size of the airline and where it is on the values-embedding continuum, economic sustainability might not need a specialist department. Sustainability-thinking should be a mainstream activity; however, there will almost inevitably be a hiatus while the process becomes embedded. Sustainability-thinking will not be achieved if it is merely an add-on in the outward-facing Public Relations or Communications Departments. They should be sustainability-support departments communicating on reputational issues and although practising sustainability-thinking, should not be the focus of corporate sustainability activities. First, as part of integrating sustainability-thinking, the core values need to be embedded and lived (the task of the Human Resources Department) in preparation for (among other future events) the evolution of Strategic Corporals (see Chapter 2). Second, there is the issue of ongoing management of sustainability concerns. These could be devolved to various departments and the oversight of the RRR given to the Risk Department. However, if it is decided to establish a Sustainability Department either temporarily or permanently under a sustainability-thinking leader, it could adopt the innovation and philanthropy roles if there are no other logical locations. The members of the Department could be either dedicated employees or a small core team supplemented by seconded employees to complete projects matrix-style. There is a need for overall co-ordination of the evolving sustainability strategy and activities and in particular, a need to alert other SBUs to any sustainability icebergs which could threaten their viability. The latter is a hugely responsible task and would require an outlier with vision who understands the airline, the aviation industry and the wider operating environment.

While there is no one best way to organise any resulting sustainability functions, airlines must give due weight to the quantity of environmental legislation. It needs a focus somewhere in the airline always remembering that some environmental regulation is science-based, reasonable, sensible and necessary. However, these issues must not be confused with the unevidenced claims of the AGW-is-harmful proponents (see Chapter 6).

Departmental naming

Where sustainability-thinking is not incorporated into existing departments and a separate department or SBU has been established, there are many potential departmental names used by many different commercial organisations including 'Corporate Social Responsibility', 'Corporate Responsibility', 'Environment',

'Charities', 'Responsible Business' and 'Sustainability'. (Rarely used is 'Economic Sustainability Department'.) Emphasising 'social' in the title indicates bias and imbalance whereas using 'environment' might emphasise the airline's most immediate and possibly its greatest vulnerability. By incorporating 'economics' in the title, the origins of the resources for the social and environmental spheres are acknowledged.

Job titles

There are also many job titles which encompass the sustainability dimensions but often indicate lack of economic focus while emphasising political correctness. The following titles have been taken from multiple non-aviation sources and include: Ethics Director (a bureaucrat who should be unnecessary if core values are integral); Community Sustainability and Ethical Sourcing Manager (does this title actually fit onto one line of a business card?); Project Manager Ethical Reporting (can this really be a full-time job and if it is, what challenge prompted its creation?); Community Investment Manager; Corporate Social Responsibility Officer/ Manager/Analyst/Director; Socially Responsible Investment Analyst; Environ- mental, Social and Governance Analyst; Sustainability Asset Manager; Social Compliance Unit Leader; Environmental Compliance Manager; Environmental Communications Manager; Social Responsibility Manager; Head of Environmental Efficiency; Sustainability Reporting Manager; Head – Environmental Affairs; Head of CSR; Head of CSER (or CSERplus); Regional Gender Advisor; and Ethics and Competence Practitioner. Any sustainability role irrespective of title needs to 'look both ways' into both the past and the future and *must* incorporate economics.

If the department is to be an SBU it should have a focus on sustainable eco- nomic profitability; however, it might be difficult for some sustainability functions to show a direct contribution to profits. Unfortunately, preventing iceberg events (Table 7.2) will often not show as a success because they did not happen (a paradox). Such activities are justified on the precautionary basis (the same principle on which the AGW alarmism justifies its existence (see Chapter 6)).

Sustainability guilds

In centuries past, guilds were formed to ensure high standards of care especially where lives could be directly affected by negligence (e.g. electricians, plumbers, doctors, airline pilots). However, sustainability is not of that ilk. Forming guilds implies that the 'sustainability skills' can only be practised by those who have served apprenticeships and passed examinations. Integral economic sustainability is the application of common sense in an open, trusting and honest culture. Economic sustainability – with its emphasis on resource allocation, innovation and challenge – would not be best served by the establishment of guilds with the tendency to clone their activities and their focus on social and environmental issues. By their very nature, guilds encourage groupthink and a homogeneous skill set – which, in contrast to sustainability-thinking, would not necessarily challenge the social, environmental or philanthropic status quo. Guilds adopt the role of monopoly supplier which, paradoxically, is exactly the opposite of the openness, transparency and competition which economically sustainable organisations in free-market capitalist economies require (see Chapter 3). Drawing from a small pool of 'sustain-ability specialists' would not necessarily place economic sustainability in the mainstream business. Instead, sustainability could become separate and independent from commercial progress with unbalanced emphasis on social and/or environ-mental 'forces for good'. It would not embody the one-ness that is entailed by using complete sustainability-thinking with its economic origins. Sustainability does not need a separate profession: it is a way of thinking, and of integrating common sense, innovation and good behaviour into commercial life. The creation of guilds as a recruitment source could artificially restrict the pool of sustainability-thinkers. Furthermore, it would appear that recruiters for CSER/CSERplus vacancies prefer to advertise in the more socially or environmentally oriented publications (e.g. the UK's left-wing newspaper *The Guardian*) rather than those focussed on economics. This restrictive, self-perpetuating supply could undermine the functioning of a competitive labour market and fuel the groupthink which hinders innovative sustainability-thinking.

As Henderson (2001) noted CSR obliges practitioners to do their best to ensure that other firms of all sizes conform (i.e. groupthink) which can be damaging for the economy as a whole.

> In so far as 'socially responsible' businesses find that their new role is bringing with it higher costs and lower profits, they have a strong interest in having their unregenerate rivals compelled to follow suit, whether through public pressure or government regulation. The effect of such enforced uniformity is to limit competition and hence to worsen the performance of the economy as a whole. The system effects of CSR, as well as the enterprise effects, will tend to make people in general poorer.
>
> (Henderson, 2001: 18)

The genteel extortion from the bank and the establishment of sustainability guilds are just two realisations of his many concerns.

7.8 POLITICAL CORRECTNESS

Diversity – minorities in management

Diversity in employees should not just be a politically correct tool. It can add real value especially when it comes to avoiding the bias of groupthink and promoting creativity and innovation. The diversity special interest groups begin from the stance that the world is ruled by able-bodied, white men. They might be correct – but to promote a candidate simply because he/she is a member of a minority and a quota needs fulfilment creates a bias which could hinder decision-making rather than support it. In accordance with sustainability-thinking, opinions which differ from any consensus should be aired and welcomed rather than discouraged or silenced (see Chapter 6). Such challenges would come naturally and routinely from diverse participants in an open and challenge culture. Furthermore, a variety of viewpoints would also provide more opportunities to reduce risks.

The presence of women in the boardroom can neutralise some of the testosterone which can dominate rooms of men of power. However, they must only be appointed because of their potential contribution, not because of politically correct quotas or 'eye candy' appeal. To do otherwise is to ignore the achievement that they and so many other minorities have worked so hard to achieve. Pursuit of diversity, along with other 'non-economic' policies 'have the air of virtue; but in every case there are issues of definition, of degree, and of weighing costs and benefits at the margin, and these are typically glossed over . . . and it is possible that [these] actions . . . will do more harm than good' (Henderson, 2001: 50). More women in the boardroom can actually have a negative effect on financial performance. While companies with more women on their boards tend to have better corporate governance, 'on average, firms perform worse the greater is the gender diversity of the board' (Adams and Ferreira, 2009). This finding undermines another of the unevidenced requirements advocated by CSERplus groups seeking the attainment of their view of social justice. The economically sustainable airline knows that recruitment and promotion must be on merit (and adherence to the core values) – not on age, time served, sexual identity, colour, disability, race, creed or nepotism. Only then would the airline achieve the divergent opinions and balance needed for successful sustainability-thinking. However, there is a tendency for governments to pursue affirmative-action employment CSFs and KPIs highlighting their diverse employee mix in pursuit of multi-culturalism. They claim it is 'good for business'. Is this another example of CSERplus-driven interference in the marketplace or merely politicians seeking to widen the populations from which to seek voters? It is worth contemplating that undiversified workforces such as the Japanese managed 'to sell everything from cars to cameras, in countries around the world, without having that mystic "diversity"' (Sowell, 2003). When the Japanese had the edge on innovation, this might have been true but it might also explain Japan's subsequent economic woes and serve as a warning from which commercial ventures could take heed. Sustainable airlines recruit the best staff irrespective of origins or orientations and train them to ensure that the future leadership succession pool will reflect real diversity with well-qualified candidates.

Discrimination and passengers

Passengers should be treated equally within the service levels prescribed for their cabin. Failure to do so could bring charges of discrimination. This was illustrated by a Ryanair passenger who calculated that he had overpaid for his family's trip to Croatia by £Stg444.73. Passengers purchasing Ryanair seats outside of the UK are able to use a more realistic exchange rate than Ryanair's own where, at the time of booking, £Stg1=€1 rather than the actual forex rate of £Stg1=€1.23.

The passenger threatened to pursue a race discrimination case against Ryanair until it refunded the difference and requested that he kept the settlement confidential (Poulter, 2013).

Dubious behaviour, politicians, celebrities and responsible airlines

There is an internet joke that politicians should dress as racing car drivers so the constituents know who their sponsors are. By doing so, they would exhibit the transparency and openness they encourage in commercial organisations, to have high moral and ethical standards and to set the example for those corrupt regimes with which they sometimes trade. This is often perplexing. One example is the supranational government, the EU, which makes so many of the regulations with which good corporate and individual citizens of Europe must comply. It is staffed with unelected officials, fires whistle-blowers, rarely requires supporting documentation for expense claims and its auditors have not signed off its accounts worth €bns ($USbns, £Stgbns) as a 'true and fair record' for over 17 years. If such unethical behaviour occurred in the UK the Board would be punished. Ironically, the EU has legislated to make commercial organisations more socially responsible and their financial and sustainability reporting transparent.

In 2012, some UK Members of Parliament were caught with falsified and unsubstantiated expense claims, an activity which undermined any attempt at role modelling the behaviour expected from law-abiding citizens, commercial organisations and NGOs. Similarly, some members of the UK's most senior legislating body, the House of Lords, were involved in falsified expense claims as well as 'cash for peerages' (i.e. 'bribery' in corporate language). Many who fraudulently claimed expenses were not prosecuted and indeed, in at least one case, the miscreant was able to continue legitimately claiming her daily allowance to pay the fine the House of Lords imposed for theft of taxpayers' money. UK Members of Parliament or the House of Lords do not have formally recognised core values. The appointment (and reappointment) to high public office of those who have lied, cheated or stolen only highlights the questionable behaviour of many law-making-and-breaking organisations and individuals who should be role modelling the behaviours which they regulate for others. (Maybe politicians should be selected on their personal core values rather than political alignment?)

Even some of the CSERplus proponents are tainted including the UN which was tarnished by the 2004 'oil for food' scandal while promulgating the ten desirable behaviours of the UNGC. The IPCC (see Chapter 6), which has influenced so much legislation, regulation, policy and taxation, has credibility issues for its interpretation and obfuscation of information and data. Similarly, environmentalists fly to their 'save the planet' conferences (presumably using responsible airlines) in far-off lands such as Brazil, Mauritius and other areas of purported environmental endangerment and exotic delight. In the same mode are the celebrities who indulge in tax avoidance schemes (see Chapter 3) and who urge their respective governments to support philanthropy, social equality (as defined by who?) and carbon [dioxide] reduction to save the planet while giving scant regard to their means of transport between their various homes in multiple destinations. They fuel the envy culture creating yet more demands for social justice (this time in the form of democratised consumption) which in turn could require more wealth transfers through the imposition of higher taxes (which these same celebrities are avoiding). Such questionable economic, social and environmental behaviours deserve challenging by regulators, politicians, policy makers and all the stakeholders who are ultimately impacted by their influences.

Any credibility that these national and supranational government organisations (and others) might aspire to take the moral high ground is lost because of their unacceptable practices in the corporate world. Furthermore, their subsequent behaviour often fulfilled the criteria of what not to do after a crisis (Schwartz and Gibb, 1999). With the internet 'right to be forgotten' (which is not quite as portrayed, i.e. it is merely the removal of one link when a search is made on a specific name) the misdemeanours of EU officials, UK Members of Parliament, Peers of the Realm and other transgressors could become hidden and therefore difficult to subject to public scrutiny for the disinfectant of sunlight or scrutiny of electric light (Brandeis, n.d.). Is this really the role-modelling transparent and open culture that these organisations aspire for the corporate bodies in their bailiwicks?

So what?

'Getting it right' is not easy for an airline when it works within a framework laid down by legislators who do not always 'get it right' either because they are behaving dishonestly, relying on advocacy rather than balanced information and accurate data or failing to understand marketplace economics. No matter how hard airlines try, they will struggle to keep pace with CSERplus pressures which usually lack preliminary economic evaluation. Airlines need to have the culture which supports internal and external challenges and to become fluent in the process of governance while keeping economics, society and environmental considerations at the root of their decisions. If economics had been more prominent, there is a possibility that internal and external decision-makers might have pushed against some of the market-skewing social and environmental legislation, regulations, policies, boondoggles and unfunded mandates which have delivered so many challenges. Ultimately this lack of foresight and abundance of bureaucratic encumbrance could undermine the international competitiveness of developed world airlines. Sustainability-thinking is not complicated: it does not need specialists, its own language or even single-focussed departments. It just needs common sense, understanding economic, social and environmental issues, knowing the difference between right and wrong and following a recognised decision-making process all of which will protect the airline's reputation. This 'governance scaffolding' needs to be dispersed throughout the airline to all its employees wherever they are located. It should also be role modelled by national, multi-national and supranational governments.

References

Adams, R.B. and Ferreira, D. (2009), Women in the boardroom and their impact on governance and performance, *Journal of Financial Economics* 94(2) 291–309 available from http://personal.lse.ac.uk/FERREIRD/gender.pdf accessed 3 January 2015

Alleyne, R. (2010), *Swine flu killed 457 people and cost £1.24 billion, official figures show* available from http://www.telegraph.co.uk/health/swine-flu/7865796/Swine-flu-killed-457-people-and-cost-1.24-billion-official-figures-show.html accessed 12 October 2010

Amnesty International UK (2015) available from http://www.amnesty.org.uk/ accessed 1 November 2015

Ansoff, H.I. (1965), *Corporate Strategy*, New York, McGraw Hill

Aon Risk Management (2013), *Global Risk Management Survey 2013: the top 10 corporate risks* available from http://www.aon.com/attachments/risk-services/2013-GRMS-Executive-Summary.pdf accessed 30 July 2013

AviationKnowledge (n.d.), *Varig Flight 254: Downed by a decimal point* available from http://aviationknowledge.wikidot.com/asi:varig-flight-254:downed-by-a-decimal-point accessed 22 July 2015

Bower, J.L. and Gilbert, C.G. (2007), How managers' everyday decisions create or destroy your company's strategy, *Harvard Business Review* available from https://hbr.org/2007/02/how-managers-everyday-decisions-create-or-destroy-your-companys-strategy accessed 5 January 2015

Brammer, S. and Pavelin, S. (2006), Corporate Reputation and Social Performance: the importance of fit, *Journal of Management Studies* 43(3) 435–455 available from http://onlinelibrary.wiley.com/doi/10.1111/j.1467-6486.2006.00597.x/abstract accessed 3 January 2015

Brandeis, L.D. (n.d.), *Justice Louis. D. Brandeis* available from http://www.brandeis.edu/legacyfund/bio.html accessed 29 March 2015

Business in the Community (BiTC) (2014), http://www.bitc.org.uk/ accessed 21 November 2014

Business Social Compliance Initiative (BSCI) (2014), http://www.bsci-intl.org/ accessed 21 November 2014

Cadbury, A. (1992), *Report of the Committee on the Financial Aspects of Corporate Governance* available from http://www.ecgi.org/codes/documents/cadbury.pdf accessed 14 August 2013

Cadbury, A. (2012), *20th Anniversary of the Corporate Governance Code Event – October 2012* available from https://www.frc.org.uk/FRC-Documents/Speeches/Speech-by-Sir-Adrian-Cadbury-at-20th-Anniversary-o.aspx accessed 4 August 2013

CBS News (2009), *Dire predictions for swine flu's future* available from http://www.cbsnews.com/news/dire-predictions-for-swine-flus-future/ accessed 10 June 2016

Centres for Disease Control and Prevention (2012), *First Global Estimates of 2009 H1N1 Pandemic Mortality Released by CDC-Led Collaboration* available from http://www.cdc.gov/flu/spotlights/pandemic-global-estimates.htm accessed 5 November 2014

Cummings, W. (2015), *Airlines ban hunters' big-game 'trophies' after uproar over Cecil the lion* available from http://www.usatoday.com/story/travel/flights/todayinthesky/2015/08/03/american-airlines-animal-trophy-ban/31090331/ accessed 26 August 2015

Delawala, I. (2016), *What is coltan?* available from http://abcnews.go.com/Nightline/story?id=128631&page=1 accessed 20 January 2016

Dorée, A.G. (2004), Collusion in the Dutch construction industry; an industrial organisation perspective, *Building Research and Information* 32(2) available from http://www.tandfonline.com/doi/abs/10.1080/0961321032000172382#.Viy3QX7hC1s accessed 6 April 2014

Dortok, A. (2006), In practice – a managerial look at the interaction between internal communication and corporate reputation, *Corporate Reputation Review* 8(4) 322–338 available from http://www.ingentaconnect.com/content/pal/crr/2006/00000008/00000004/art00005 accessed 3 January 2015

Drucker, P.F. (1974), *Management: tasks, responsibilities, practices*, London, Butterworth-Heinemann

Eaton, D., Akbiyikli, R. and Dickinson, M. (2006), An evaluation of the stimulants and impediments to innovation within PFI/PPP projects, *Construction Innovation* 6(2) 63–77 available from http://www.emeraldinsight.com/doi/abs/10.1108/14714170610710668 accessed 3 January 2015

Economist, The (2005), *British Airways, Catering for Suppliers' Strikes* available from http://www.economist.com/node/4307627 accessed 12 September 2014

Embraer (2014), *Embraer is listed with the Corporate Sustainability Index (ISE) of the BM&FBOVESPA 2015* available from http://www.embraer.com/en-US/Imprensa Eventos/Press-releases/noticias/Pages/Embraer-integra-o-Indice-de-Sustentabilidade-Empresarial-ISE-da-BMFBovespa-2015.aspx accessed 6 December 2014

Ethical Trading Initiative (ETI) (2015), http://www.ethicaltrade.org/ accessed 11 April 2015

Finkelstein, S., Campbell, J. and Whitehead, A. (2008), *Think Again – Why Good Leaders Make Bad Decisions and How to Keep It from Happening to You*, Boston, MA, Harvard Business Press

Fitzsimmons, A. and Haslam, R. (2013), Deconstructing Failure: insights for Boards, *Reputability* available from http://www.reputability.co.uk/files/press/20131001GOVERN ANCEweb1.pdf accessed 14 April 2015

Friedman, M. (1982), *Capitalism and Freedom*, Chicago, IL, Chicago University Press

Gilligan, A. (2009), Copenhagen climate summit: 1,200 limos, 140 private planes and caviar wedges, *The Telegraph*, 5 December available from http://www.telegraph.co.uk/earth/copenhagen-climate-change-confe/6736517/Copenhagen-climate-summit-1200-limos-140-private-planes-and-caviar-wedges.html accessed 28 June 2014

Global Social Compliance Programme (GSCP) (2014), *Welcome to the Global Social Compliance Programme* available from http://www.gscpnet.com/ accessed 25 August 2014

Gosden, E. (2014), *Environmental group campaigns to curb growth in air travel but defends paying a senior executive to commute 250 miles to work by plane* available from http://www.telegraph.co.uk/earth/earthnews/10920198/Greenpeace-executive-flies-250-miles-to-work.html accessed 22 June 2014

Goslett, M. (2014), *Prescott flies 40,000 miles – that's nearly twice around the world – in five months . . . to lecture on climate change* available from http://www.dailymail.co.uk/news/article-2720903/Prescott-flies-40–000-miles-s-nearly-twice-world-five-months-lecture-climate-change.html accessed 16 August 2014

Henderson, D. (2001), *Misguided virtue: false notions of corporate responsibility*, The Institute of Economic Affairs available from http://www.iea.org.uk/publications/research/misguided-virtue-false-notions-of-corporate-social-responsibility accessed 7 October 2014

Hoeken, H. and Renkema, J. (1998), Can corrections repair the damage to a corporate image caused by negative publicity? *Corporate Reputation Review* 2(1) 51–60 available from http://www.palgrave-journals.com/crr/journal/v2/n1/abs/1540066a.html accessed 3 January 2015

International Labour Organisation (ILO) (1998), *Declaration on Fundamental Principles and Rights at Work* available from http://www.ilo.org/declaration/lang–en/index.htm accessed 26 September 2014

Jago, A.G. and Vroom, V.H. (1978), Predicting leader behavior from a measure of behavioral intent, *Academy of Management Journal* 21(4) 715–721 available from http://amj.aom.org/content/21/4/715.full accessed 2 January 2015

Jamieson, A. (2008), *Airlines are akin to arms dealers in ethics stakes* available from http://www.scotsman.com/news/scotland/top-stories/airlines-are-akin-to-arms-dealers-in-ethics-stakes-1-1077010 accessed 14 August 2013

Klein, G. (2007), Performing a Project Pre-mortem, *Harvard Business Review* 85(9) 18–19

Lovallo, D. and Sibony, O. (2010), The case for behavioural strategy, *McKinsey Quarterly* available from http://www.mckinsey.com/insights/strategy/the_case_for_behavioral_strategy accessed 25 September 2014

Massey, R. (2011), *Green activist who stopped Heathrow third runway heads to U.S. to explain how he did it. . . by aeroplane of course* available from http://www.dailymail.co.uk/news/article-2040182/Green-activist-John-Stewart-stopped-Heathrow-3rd-runway-flies-US-explain-.html accessed 16 August 2014

Mendelow, A. (1991), *Stakeholder mapping*, Proceedings of the Second International Conference on Information Systems, Cambridge, MA (cited in Johnson, G., Scholes, K. and Whittington, R., *Exploring Corporate Strategy, 8th ed* 156, Harlow, England, Prentice Hall)

Metro (2016), *Terminated your green ideal, Arnie?* Thursday, 21 January 2016

Mitroff, I., Pearson, C. and Harrington, C. (1996), *The essential guide to managing corporate crises*, Oxford, Oxford University Press

Moore, C. (2013), *This obsession with Ethics is one of the great curses of our time: Paul Flowers and the Co-op Bank thought they were so good they couldn't possibly be bad* available from http://www.telegraph.co.uk/comment/10467982/This-obsession-with-Ethics-is-one-of-the-great-curses-of-our-time.html accessed 25 November 2013

NBC News (2014), *Airlines settle suit in death of 400-lb woman denied a seat* available from http://www.nbcnews.com/news/us-news/airlines-settle-suit-death-400-pound-woman-denied-seat-n198646 accessed 9 September 2104

Nwabueze, U. and Mileski, J. (2008), The challenge of effective governance: the case of Swiss Air, *Corporate Governance* 8(5) 583–594 available from http://www.emeraldinsight.com/doi/abs/10.1108/14720700810913250 accessed 3 January 2015

Omar, M. and Williams, R. (2006), Managing and maintaining corporate reputation and brand identity: Haier Group logo, *Brand Management* 13(4–5) 268–275 available from http://www.palgrave-journals.com/bm/journal/v13/n4/abs/2540270a.html accessed 3 January 2015

Organisation for Economic Cooperation and Development (OECD) (2014), *Anti-bribery Convention* available from http://www.oecd.org/daf/anti-bribery/anti-briberyconvention/ accessed 5 April 2015

Pearson, C.M. and Mitroff, I.I. (1993), From crisis prone to crisis prepared: a framework for crisis management, *Academy of Management Executive* 7(1) 48–59 available from http://amp.aom.org/content/7/1/48.short accessed 3 January 2015

People for the Ethical Treatment of Animals (PETA) (n.d.), www.peta.org.uk accessed 21 November 2014

People for the Ethical Treatment of Animals (PETA) (2015), *Brian Sewell critiques Air France's cruelty to monkeys* available from http://www.peta.org.uk/media/news-releases/brian-sewell-critiques-air-frances-cruelty-to-monkeys/ accessed 23 April 2016

Pfeffer, J. and Sutton, R.I. (2006), Evidence-based management, *Harvard Business Review* (January) 63–74 available from https://hbr.org/2006/01/evidence-based-management accessed 26 September 2014

Poulter, S. (2013), *Why UK passengers pay more on Ryanair: And why this man's victory could open the floodgates* available from http://www.dailymail.co.uk/news/article-2319142/Why-UK-passengers-pay-Ryanair-And-mans-victory-open-floodgates.html accessed 24 August 2014

Radaronline (2015), *'Hypocrite!' Leonardo DiCaprio Took 6 Private Jet Flights In 6 Weeks Sony Emails Reveal – Despite Climate Change Advocacy Work* available from http://radaronline.com/exclusives/2015/04/leonardo-dicaprio-climate-change-hypocrite-sony-emails-wikileaks/ accessed 18 April 2015

Ray, S. (1999), *Strategic communication in crisis management: lessons from the airline industry*, Westport, CT, Quorum Books

Samuelson, W. and Zeckhauser, R. (1988), Status quo bias in decision-making, *Journal of Risk and Uncertainty* 1(1) 7–59 available from http://link.springer.com/article/10.1007%2FBF00055564 accessed 3 January 2015

Schwartz, P. and Gibb, B. (1999), *When good companies do bad things*, New York, John Wiley & Sons, Inc.

Sedex (2014), *Sedex News* available from http://www.sedexglobal.com/news/news/ accessed 21 September 2014

Simon, H.A. (1991), Bounded rationality and organizational learning, *Organization Science* 2(1) 125–134 available from http://pubsonline.informs.org/doi/abs/10.1287/orsc.2.1.125 accessed 3 January 2015

Snowdon, C. (2013), *Euro Puppets: the European Commission's remaking of civil society*, The Institute of Economic Affairs, London available from http://www.iea.org.uk/publications/research/euro-puppets-the-european-commission%E2%80%99s-remaking-of-civil-society accessed 13 December 2014

Social Accountability International (SAI) (2014), *SA 8000 Standard* available from http://www.sa-intl.org/index.cfm?fuseaction=Page.ViewPage&PageID=937 accessed 26 October 2014

Sowell, T. (2003), Corporations promote preferential treatment, *Human Events* 59(6) 16, *ProQuest Political Science* available from http://humanevents.com/2003/02/17/corporations-promote-preferential-treatment/ accessed 3 January 2015

Sternberg, E. (2009), *Corporate social responsibility and corporate governance*, The Institute of Economic Affairs, Oxford, Blackwell available from http://www.iea.org.uk/sites/default/files/publications/files/upldeconomicAffairs342pdfSummary.pdf accessed 30 October 2014

Taylor, B. (2006), Shell Shock: why do good companies do bad things? *Corporate Governance*, 14(3) 181–193 available from http://onlinelibrary.wiley.com/doi/10.1111/j.1467-8683.2006.00498.x/abstract accessed 3 January 2015

Transparency International (2010), *Adequate procedures: guidance to the UK Bribery Act 2010* available from http://www.transparency.org.uk/our-work/bribery-act/adequate-procedures accessed 4 August 2013

United Nations (n.d.), *The 10 principles of the UN Global Compact* available from https://www.unglobalcompact.org/what-is-gc/mission/principles accessed 10 January 2015

United Nations (1948), *Universal Declaration of Human Rights* available from http://www.un.org/en/documents/udhr/ accessed 26 September 2014

United Nations (2011), *Guiding principles on business and human rights* available from http://www.ohchr.org/Documents/Publications/GuidingPrinciplesBusinessHR_EN.pdf accessed 17 June 2016

US Government (2010), *Dodd-Frank Wall Street Reform and Consumer Protection Act* available from https://www.sec.gov/about/laws/wallstreetreform-cpa.pdf accessed 10 January 2015

Williams, R. and Barrett, J. (2000), Corporate philanthropy, criminal activity and firm reputation: is there a link? *Journal of Business Ethics* 2(4) 31–350 available from http://link.springer.com/article/10.1023%2FA%3A1006282312238 accessed 3 January 2015

8 Challenges for sustainability

8.1 COLLATING THE CHALLENGES

Challenges

The activities of privately owned, economically sustainable airlines include flying safely, operating legally, supporting innovation, pursuing competition, creating employment and paying dividends and taxes. Underpinning these objectives is strategic sustainability-thinking (see Figure 7.2 in Chapter 7) supported by tactical activities. Complete sustainability should address the needs of the primary stakeholders (employees, customers and owners) while increasing shareholder value. The decisions taken would, like all economic decisions, require trade-offs. It is the judicious use of resources including time, capital (of all types) and the assembled materials of the natural and manufactured worlds which give an airline its competitive soft and hard edges.

Governments' role in airline economic sustainability

As noted, governments cannot always be relied to act wisely. They frequently waste money and do not always make impartial decisions since they are often reliant on either the unevidenced claims of computer models or asymmetric sources of data and information from CSERplus advocates (see Chapter 1 to Chapter 7). Governments' aviation interventions have alternately supported (through liberalisation) or undermined the industry. An analysis of the ten identified national, multinational and supranational governments' interventions aligned to alleged market inefficiencies and/or failures (see Chapter 1) shows that just one (deregulation which increased competition) has actually benefitted the aviation industry and its passengers whereas the remaining nine could prove detrimental because they lacked comprehensive economic analysis (Table 8.1). Solving the challenges present in the nine (missing markets, negative externalities, imperfect knowledge, principal-agents, government provision, inequalities, free riders, moral hazards and moral panic) has added complexity, confusion and ultimately costs which are borne by the shareholders, employees or passengers.

Table 8.1 Summary of indicators of alleged airline market inefficiency or failure, responses and effects (refer to Chapters 1 to 7)

Indicators of alleged airline market inefficiency and failure	National, multi-national and supranational government responses	Aviation industry's responses to governments' interventions and resultant effects
1. **lack of competition:** occurred when restrictions were placed on airlines through their ownership structures and national protectionist policies	**economic:** deregulation of most of the worldwide aviation industry from around 1970s onwards	**economic:** deregulating enabled growth of the aviation industry and creation of new airport and airline models including no-frills, low-cost carriers creating new industries through outsourcing of services such as aircraft de-icing, catering and fuelling forming alliances or forging mergers, takeovers and acquisitions with other carriers
	social: arrival of low-cost, low-fare carriers	**social:** welcoming the democratisation of air travel and creation of new models for competition
2. **missing markets:** occur where no markets previously existed and goods or services are considered so desirable and necessary that governments often intervene to provide or support them or alternatively regulate for private organisations to fill the gap	**social:** devising and filling missing markets with unfunded mandates and boondoggles often without undertaking the necessary economic impact analyses to examine the effects on the airline industry (missing social markets included PRM regulated provisions) using the intervention of boondoggles and unfunded mandates to support the establishment of formerly missing markets including CSERplus report writing and assurance, environmental advisers and PRM equipment providers	**social:** transporting increasing numbers of qualified and unqualified PRMs with their mobility equipment and service animals to support States' definition of a 'missing market' in order to equalise society for less able citizens supporting the stealth privatisation of UK NHS (and fulfilling formerly unidentified health traveller markets in the process) absorbing the increased costs of security measures (overt and hidden) and the missing markets for negative externalities (e.g. congestion and delay) often caused by statutory bodies

continued . . .

Table 8.1 Continued

Indicators of alleged airline market inefficiency and failure	National, multi-national and supranational government responses	Aviation industry's responses to governments' interventions and resultant effects
		hiring the range of consultants to fulfil the newly identified CSERplus 'missing markets', e.g. CSERplus advisers and report writers
		failing to calculate the future costs of the missing PRM market before the Regulations were implemented has been compounded by lack of corresponding post-implementation economic impact assessment
	environmental: accepting climate alarmists' asymmetric (partisan), myopic concerns and bowing to their solutions for negative externalities and permitting the filling of formerly missing markets for trading negative externalities	**environmental:** investing in software and manpower for voluntary passenger carbon offset schemes needed to fulfil one of the environmental missing markets
	creating a market and ascribing property rights for 'missing' CO_2, CO_2e and other gases which can be monetised and provide a fund for CDMs for advancing-world economies	complying with environmental regulations and hiring the new genre of experts to advise on the newly created environmental markets, e.g. CO_2 fund managers
	supporting emissions trading (a formerly missing market) and peripheral industries	promising to deliver IATA's CNG2020 commitment which has potential for even more still-unidentified missing markets
	subsidising producers of green energy (including biofuels) and taxing consumers to pay for this formerly missing market	

continued . . .

Table 8.1 Continued

Indicators of alleged airline market inefficiency and failure	National, multi-national and supranational government responses	Aviation industry's responses to governments' interventions and resultant effects
	accepting the existence of a new 'market' to support the multiple needs of 'climate change refugees'	
3. **socially and environmentally detrimental (negative) externalities:** affect any stakeholders who were not involved in decisions which could have a negative effect on them; solutions include taxing, issuing permits or regulating (often without undertaking either a preliminary economic impact analysis or a post-implementation assessment)	**environmental:** supporting the use of taxes levied on negative environmental externalities in the advanced-world to fund clean energy and other social projects in the advancing-world formulating assorted regulations to preserve the environment and monetising negative externalities (waste, energy, lighting, noise and emissions) by assigning property rights thereby enabling a market to trade these outputs using the precautionary principle as justification to tax citizens on their emissions ostensibly to prevent possibly natural climate changes requiring emissions trading to offset negative emissions externalities	**environmental:** advanced-world airlines collect and pay environmental taxes to offset emissions which are donated for CDMs in the advancing-world reducing negative aircraft externalities by various means including altering flight paths and angles of aircraft descent; installing aircraft noise reduction measures at source and complimentary noise insulation on qualified dwellings near airports creating voluntary passenger emissions offset schemes to appease the environmental lobby and allow passengers to show their support for the environment participating in emissions trading schemes designed to offset pollutants donating to charities in anticipation of preventing some of the environmental regulations which were eventually established to monetise negative externalities
4. **imperfect knowledge:** national, multi-national and supranational governments did not always give economics	**social:** making decisions influenced by biased inputs from CSERplus' advocates' asymmetric	**social:** managing open-ended, uncontrollable costs for servicing some passenger groups as a result of

continued ...

Table 8.1 Continued

Indicators of alleged airline market inefficiency and failure	National, multi-national and supranational government responses	Aviation industry's responses to governments' interventions and resultant effects
equal weighting with environmental or social factors before they legislated or regulated	information and cherry-picked data which were eventually formed into boondoggles or unfunded mandates failing to undertake pre-regulatory economic impact analyses to support and balance the social or environmental requirements of airlines' obligations	regulations which were implemented on incomplete, cherry-picked knowledge and data and which often lacked pre-implementation economic impact analysis and post-implementation assessment having to obey national, multi-national and supranational legislation, regulations and policies based on CSERplus social advocacy rather than economics or evidence
	environmental: decreeing climate change man-made and dangerous after relying on computer models rather than scientific evidence implementing regulations under the precautionary principle relying on the partisan influence of cronies rather than evidenced knowledge and data to examine any impending environmental disaster imbalanced information and data obtained through providing disproportionate funding volumes to investigate only the AGW-is-harmful issues without providing equivalent funding for investigations into alternative causes for any of Earth's warming or coolings	**environmental:** committing support for governments' aspirations to counter negative emissions externalities which might have been predicated on imperfect knowledge (i.e. asymmetric and incomplete data and information) giving the same weight to unevidenced climate alarmism as to replicable, scientifically obtained data in order to appease national, multi-national and supranational governments and the CSERplus advocates managing the disadvantages derived from the inability to match the national, multi-national and supranational funding for AGW-is-harmful research, services and products which were funded on misinterpreted, misrepresented and distorted knowledge and data

continued . . .

Table 8.1 Continued

Indicators of alleged airline market inefficiency and failure	National, multi-national and supranational government responses	Aviation industry's responses to governments' interventions and resultant effects
	omitting environmental cost–benefit analyses which would assist with improving the level of knowledge and data used in decisions	
5. **principal–agent problem:** agents acting in their own interests rather than those of their principals	**economic, social and environmental:** acting on asymmetric information supplied by self-declared CSERplus 'experts' including NGOs, philanthropists, politicians and others whose self-interest is often prioritised over the national interest because their incomes, employment, status and/or friendships might depend on their continued involvement allowing philanthropists acting in their own interests (altruism and/or egoism) to undermine democracy by donating for national causes which might not have been chosen by the electorate (i.e. democratic deficit)	**environmental:** accepting specific aviation impacts derived from the Kyoto Protocol 1997 and its successors (the UK Climate Change Act 2008, the Environmental Protection Acts of USA, Canada, Australia and other nations) often promoted by agents acting as principals and sometimes undermining democracies
6. **government provision:** governments provide where they consider the market would not supply	**social:** making State provisions for public goods and services for the airline industry including Security, Immigration, Emigration, Police, Aviation Infrastructure Planning and other national requirements supplying subsidies and permits for qualified beneficiaries on local buses, railways and other	**social:** supporting multiple national, multi-national and supranational governments' social objectives without reimbursement (e.g. UK's NHS patient travel) supporting governments by providing airport security including asking security questions and examining passports and visas for validity (among other tasks)

continued . . .

Table 8.1 Continued

Indicators of alleged airline market inefficiency and failure	National, multi-national and supranational government responses	Aviation industry's responses to governments' interventions and resultant effects
	forms of land travel but no equivalent provisions for qualified airline passengers	paying penalties for breach of government regulations (e.g. visa, security etc.) without receiving any offset payments for all the correctly processed transactions
7. **inequalities:** many governments legislate to enable citizens to overcome social inequalities (including in income, health, education, consumption or opportunities) through assorted legislation and regulations to mitigate social deprivations	**social:** legislating and regulating to bridge inequalities caused by age, disability, gender or gender reassignment, religion or belief, sexual orientation, race, culture, language, marriage or civil partnership, pregnancy, maternity and/or paternity, intergenerational obligations, political persuasion or trade union membership or any other criteria provisioning by governments (or generous philanthropists) of goods and services which they deem desirable for citizens' consumption; however, where provided by philanthropists such funding can influence governments to support the donors' views of what they believe is needed for society which might not be what the electorate in democratic nations would have chosen applying higher travel taxes in premium cabins to level out some of the inequality in consumption	**social:** supporting employees who have to implement governments' boondoggles and unfunded mandates, human rights legislation and the deflected corresponding responsibilities in order to make societies more equal supporting inequalities where the travel taxes levied are higher for the more spacious premium cabins (but paradoxically airlines actually increase social inequalities by offering benefits for loyal travellers or those who travel on more expensive tickets in the premium cabins) democratising air travel by forming no-frills, low-cost carriers which means that lesser income earners can afford to travel thereby reducing inequalities providing reduced fares for some socially or economically disadvantaged passenger groups reducing social inequalities between able-bodied and disabled travellers through providing complimentary freight and services for entitled and self-declared but

continued . . .

Table 8.1 Continued

Indicators of alleged airline market inefficiency and failure	National, multi-national and supranational government responses	Aviation industry's responses to governments' interventions and resultant effects
	enacting legislation to level social inequalities by requiring complimentary private provisions to enable consumption by entitled beneficiaries and others who are not entitled (i.e. free riders)	unentitled PRMs and their accompanying service animals donating to charities which benefit disadvantaged populations and offset some inequality
8. **free riders:** members of society who expect others to act on their behalf so they do not have to either pay or take responsibilities	**social:** legislating and regulating for domestic and international PRMs without arranging an appropriate filtering process for entitlement expecting the shareholders, employees and other passengers to subsidise the costs of unentitled free rider air travellers (and possibly their 'service' animals and mobility equipment) who claim to be PRMs	**social:** tolerating passengers' abuses of the PRM provisions because airlines are unable to challenge entitlement which leaves them with open-ended, unbudgeted and unpredictable costs accepting 'assistance animals' which might not be as portrayed by their owners who might want the animals to travel free of charge in the cabin rather than pay for them to be crated in the cargo hold providing un-reimbursable medical assistance and treatments to sick passengers many of whom know they are sick before they travel collecting taxes and checking passports and other services for governments for which there is no corresponding offset cost, i.e. governments are the free riders carrying UK NHS patients at no extra cost for their additional services thereby subsidising their treatment, i.e. NHS is the free rider

continued . . .

Table 8.1 Continued

Indicators of alleged airline market inefficiency and failure	National, multi-national and supranational government responses	Aviation industry's responses to governments' interventions and resultant effects
		assisting with the births of babies on board, i.e. adding to the passenger numbers without payment
		accepting that shareholders do not always vote on matters affecting their investments and thereby accept a free ride
	environmental: providing CDM payments to advancing nations to subsidise clean energy in their homes and energy-hungry industries so that they would not have to change their behaviours thereby allowing them a free ride	**environmental:** collecting non-hypothecated, negative environmental externality and other taxes on behalf of governments thereby giving them a free ride
9. **moral hazards:** risks can be taken because the party undertaking the risk will not bear the costs	**economic and social:** undermining personal responsibility by providing Regulation EC 261/2004 for passengers who have not purchased travel insurance thereby making airlines responsible for risks which might be unforeseen	**economic and social:** claiming damages only on a few occasions from disruptive (e.g. drunk or drugged etc.) passengers who necessitate an aircraft diversion thereby permitting and inadvertently encouraging a moral hazard
		trusting the implicit contract between passengers and airlines that travellers will not disrupt flights, e.g. by threatening behaviour or by travelling with infectious diseases which could contaminate others and trigger a moral hazard
	environmental: appeasing CSERplus advocates and justifying legislation, regulations and policies established on a precautionary basis based on alarmist models	

continued . . .

Table 8.1 Continued

Indicators of alleged airline market inefficiency and failure	National, multi-national and supranational government responses	Aviation industry's responses to governments' interventions and resultant effects
	and donating the money to advancing nations which will not have to change their behaviours as long as the donations continue	
10. **moral panic:** exaggerated importance of an issue despite lack of evidence	**environmental:** funding for AGW–is–harmful research and activities to support the global warming moral panic has been actioned without the equivalent funding for any challenges to the output of computer models that have dictated the expensive application of the 'precautionary principle'	**environmental:** voluntarily developing environmental programmes aimed at appeasing national, multi-national and supranational governments, CSERplus' advocates and NGOs to assuage the AGW–is–harmful moral panic complying with environmental regulations which have been promoted by the CSERplus advocates, celebrities and the media

8.2 ECONOMIC SUSTAINABILITY CHALLENGES

Strategy

CSERplus single-interest stakeholders and NGOs have found that globalised firms – particularly MNEs – respond faster to their pressures than governments because of the impact that civil dissent or consumer boycott can have on commercial operations. Governments change whereas endurable commercial organisations follow the strategic directions set by successive managements in response to economic prompts. As a result, many of the CSERplus-envisioned policies are pursued through commercial organisations as a more expedient route to delivering social and environmental change. Even if corporate managements change, an organisation's mission and vision (see Chapter 3) are still pursued – unlike governments' strategies without explicit visions, missions or core values and which change directions as democracies vote or as dictators churn. Developed world airlines now accept that they are part of the 'social' agenda which has broadened from shareholders, customers and employees to the more encompassing agglomeration of stakeholders.

Airlines' economic sustainability strategies must be integrated with their business strategies and prioritise the most relevant, material issues. There is a tendency for the focus on sustainability to pursue the easy-to-achieve social and environmental goals, to concentrate on unimportant items or the most vocal stakeholders, or to take such a broad approach that, with the limited resources available, the impact could be ineffective (e.g. a high-profile vanity project which delivers minimal airline value).

Once the organisational structure is established, sustainability priorities need to be identified. Sustainability-thinking in which all employees participate (explicitly and naturally) should look to the future and gather information, data and opinions to determine the material issues. Original source materials range from competitors' sustainability reports, patents filed, media reviews and expressed stakeholder concerns, through to predicting national and international legislative plans and risks. Using software that analyses qualitative content can also assess emerging issues including any potential iceberg risks which are not captured in the main risk register. Iceberg risks in the RRR (see Table 7.2 in Chapter 7) could include the economic impacts if global warming is found to be natural rather than man-made (which might take millennia to prove) or the consequences of thinking the 'unthinkables'.

As previous chapters have shown, economics underpins all aviation activities including the social and the environmental dimensions. Economic sustainability-thinking (see Figure 7.2 in Chapter 7) integrates the three dimensions and embeds challenge and innovation in airline DNA. Economic airline sustainability emanates from strategic and tactical decisions which should be formed from comprehensive knowledge (both information and data), balanced discussions and the opinions of the relevant stakeholders (see Chapter 7). Sustainability-thinking must become the way that airlines future-proof their businesses. It involves communicating and converting the language of the specialists so that the Chief Executive can speak with the Finance Director, the Human Resources Manager, the Check-in Agent or the most junior Engineering Apprentice and, in the spirit of openness (using the appropriate core value) they can challenge if they disagree or do not understand.

The airline industry is vulnerable on many issues and it must be able to defend itself which is something it has been slow to do because it lacked economic data and information, and because of the influence of CSERplus' advocates. 'Many people seek to replace your preferences and decisions with their own. They do not necessarily seek material gain. They might simply be overwhelmed by an exaggerated sense of their own morality and wisdom . . . whatever their motivation, such people are always on the lookout for the latest scientific breakthrough that appears to justify their meddling' (Whyte, 2013: 120). Applied to a wider advocate group, this 'organisational narcissism' (Iivonen and Moisander, 2015) describes organisations that want to be perceived as legitimate while exhibiting the characteristics of the narcissist, i.e. 'grandiosity and self-importance, investment in demonstrating one's superiority, excessive need for attention and admiration' (Iivonen and Moisander, 2015: 651). Extreme forms of narcissism can harm organisations and sometimes even destroy them. Economically sustainable airlines need to be wary.

Airlines are trapped between the requirements of numerous external stakeholders and in particular politicians, environmentalists and social interest groups seeking to maximise their views of welfare but the industry lacks the knowledge to counteract these asymmetric influences. As a result it often yields to others promoting their partisan, partial and self-interested views. To paraphrase Whyte (2013) and others: why are these (often unelected) self-selecting private individuals permitted to decide the social good? Politicians create legislation which intervenes in airline markets and increases transaction costs and consumers' prices. Their desire to equalise society pits public benefits against private costs and intervenes in the operation of free markets (Table 8.1). As just one example, the problem of passengers stranded at airports in Europe was resolved with EC 261/2004 with its ill-defined 'extraordinary circumstances' (European Union, 2013) (see also Chapter 1, Chapter 2 and Chapter 5) loosely defined as war, political instability, unlawful act, sabotage, crew or passenger illness, security and meteorological. Under this Regulation passengers can claim assistance during the delay and compensation afterwards. Airlines could be obliged to find accommodation for large numbers of displaced passengers whose personal responsibilities (e.g. lack of travel insurance) have been deflected onto the airlines. Solving one public social problem would have created a much bigger private economic problem. Ultimately, such social legislation could trigger disproportionately increased costs for developed nations' airlines compared to their advancing-world competitors.

Unfair competition

The focus on passengers' human rights and airlines' responsibilities has the potential to undermine the economics of airlines headquartered in countries which have a deluge of such regulation. The cumulative impact of many apparently small, legislated interventions could ultimately lead to airlines headquartering in jurisdictions which are more aviation-friendly with all the implications for bilateral agreements, home-nation employment and national growth.

In developing and emerging nations, inequality has many causes but government economic policies are seen as the most responsible triggers and not wages, education, trade, labour effort or taxes. When surveyed, their citizens tended to support low taxes on wealthy people and corporations as a means of encouraging investment and generating growth (Pew Research, 2014). In contrast, respondents in advanced economies favoured high taxes (Pew Research, 2014). Airlines are part of globalised enterprise and the imposition of higher taxes and more social legislation in developed economies could undermine their airlines' competitiveness. Advanced-world airlines are being asked to break away from their free-market capitalist-based roots and support CSERplus in advancing nations through social and environmental programmes. Carrying this additional overhead could open them to unfair competitive pressures from the airlines of developing and emerging nations with their lower labour costs (see Table 1.1 in Chapter 1) and labour tax and contributions as a proportion of profit (see Table 1.2 in Chapter 1). Those nations might also have the benefits of capital inflows from CDMs (see Chapter 6). This imperfect market (Table 8.1) is uncompetitive and could ultimately be economically unsustainable.

The more prescriptive the regulations, the less freedom there is to act – a constraint which eventually undermines markets. Similarly, the more social legislation similar to EC 261/2004 (see Chapter 1 and Chapter 5) which is pushed towards airlines the greater will be the market impact triggering higher costs and increased airfares. The social responsibility on airlines is, at times, onerous and it is unbalanced. Such regulation needs new thinking so airlines can remain economically sustainable. In future, in order to widen the information base from which policy makers will choose options, airlines need to challenge and 'think the unthinkable' irrespective of how politically incorrect such thoughts might be.

Infrastructure challenges

The fortunes of airlines are symbiotically bound with national infrastructure including airports. Many governments have legislative powers to develop airports as part of national transport infrastructure. Infrastructure (like markets) can be artificially constricted by policies which can have unintended consequences of concern to airlines. National infrastructure must keep pace with the nation's needs or society could crumble (Kilcullen, 2013). In 2012 80% of the world's population lived within 60 miles of the sea (and 75% of large cities were on a coast). Approximately 50% of people now live in cities and by 2050 it is predicted that this could rise to 75% stressing the infrastructure and in particular the ports and airports which connect coastal cities to the outside world (Kilcullen, 2013). When this happens, cities will not be able to cope, leading to:

> violent crime, social and political unrest, and – in severe cases – organized conflict . . . The city's connectedness (via information and money flows, and through transportation hubs such as seaports and airports) allows its population to participate in licit and illicit activities offshore, to influence (and be influenced by) conditions in the rural hinterland, and to connect with global networks including diaspora populations. This set of interactions affects both local and international conflict dynamics.
>
> (Kilcullen, 2013: 45)

This is a grim scenario; however, the future-proofing airline will understand the concept of the city as a complex, open and dynamic system – like the economy – which has to deal with material flows for ecological sustainability. This includes the way cities use and transform inputs of water, air, food and fuel then deal with the resulting wastes (Kilcullen, 2013), all of which can have an impact on economic, social and environmental aviation resource allocations. Economically sustainable airlines will need to be vigilant monitoring the social and environmental impacts of creeping urbanisation at destinations and assess the implications for the safety of their operations and ultimately, their economic survival.

In the UK, despite many legal challenges the government is still planning to build High Speed Rail (HSR). This fast rail network will ultimately join London with the Central Belt of Scotland. It will be in competition with (and a substitute for) domestic air travel. If HSR is not built it is claimed that there will be a pinch-point in the internal transport infrastructure. However, in the planning for HSR the UK government has neglected motorways which are showing increased traffic as the recession recedes. Between 2000 and 2009 only 46 miles of new motorway were opened whereas France opened 850 miles and Germany, 680 miles (*The Economist*, 2014). In the UK (and in other nations) flying provides an alternative to ground transport; however, valuable slots at major airports are frequently used to supplement domestic land travel when they might be more profitably employed for international travel (with increased APD tax take). The UK also has corresponding underinvestment in airport capacity and the extremely long planning inquiries (part of the democratic process) mean that this problem will not be solved in the short-term. This is significant because the UK's nearest international capital city-based rivals have far more airport capacity: Amsterdam has five main runways and Paris and Frankfurt each have four. In contrast (at the time of writing), London Heathrow has two and Gatwick and Stansted have only one each. The UK's constraints affect airline competitiveness and are caused by being so close to urban areas, one of the consequences of development.

Airlines must also interact with other government statutory agencies (including, in the UK, the Home Office; Immigration, Police and Security Agencies; and HM Revenue and Customs). While fully acknowledging the importance of the role of these agencies, they can cause significant flight delays which create costs for the carriers and congestion at airports. These costs are rarely publicly discussed which leaves stakeholders unaware of the impact on punctuality. (This is another item which should go into the airline industries' negotiating toolkits (Table 8.1).) As an example of infrastructure stress, Midway Airport, Chicago, USA has reported that their security line occasionally queues outside the building for over one mile (Moran, 2014). Delays are also caused by unionised authorities such as the French ATC which has been on strike more than 40 times since 2009. The withdrawal of their labour adds considerably to all airlines costs cancelling thousands of flights and hundreds of thousands of passengers enduring cancellations or delays (Ryanair, 2016) and missing holidays, reunions, business meetings and a multitude of other events. It is the airlines which have to handle these disruptions: not the ATC employees.

8.3 SOCIAL SUSTAINABILITY CHALLENGES

Shareholder-owners

Airline shareholders delegate the stewardship of their funds (their risk capital) to the airline management in the anticipation that they would behave responsibly. Shareholders in free-market capitalist democracies have a role to play in governance or they could be undercut by cronies on the Board (see Chapter 1, Chapter 6 and Chapter 7). Shareholders must exercise their democratic rights, hold the Board to account and vote at the AGM. The big investors – pension funds and other financial institutions – are active shareholders and allow the smaller owners a free ride. But by avoiding the exercise of their democratic rights the non-voting shareholders are not using one of the best means for trading-off any weaknesses in free-market capitalism and which could prevent the hiding of irresponsible or reckless management practices (including managements' self-awarded 'rewards for failure').

Other stakeholders

Many airline stakeholders tend to veer towards compassion, which is often easier for them to understand than economics. Socially sustainable airlines comprise many stakeholders (see Table 2.1 in Chapter 2) and while governments are also stakeholders they cannot always be relied upon to support the industry. If an airline is to be economically sustainable it needs to be able to balance the wants of all the relevant stakeholders with the need to make sustainable profits to invest in assets (such as new aircraft), return dividends to risk-taking shareholders, reward employees and keep passengers' fares competitively priced.

Culture

Defining sustainable airlines' social sustainability challenges depends on the perspective of the stakeholder-definer. Employees, shareholders and customers might have one definition while socially motivated CSERplus' advocates and NGOs have another. Economically sustainable airlines' social responsibilities are primarily for the health, safety and well-being of employees and passengers and to provide a return on shareholders' funds because as investors they too have social needs to be met from the rewards of their private investment.

Airlines which do not have sustainability in their veins need to begin by determining their core values and ensuring that they use them for challenging as well as hiring, performance managing, promoting, succession planning, rewarding and firing (see Chapter 3). The core values should be memorable and role-modelled by the Board downwards. From these core values, possibly supported by a Code of Conduct, would emanate the challenge and innovation culture which will keep passengers returning. The search for the problems and creative solutions should be unrelenting.

Economically sustainable airlines are exciting places to work (see Chapter 3). They offer challenge and opportunities for advancement in what should be effective, efficient, adaptable, innovative, open and agile cultures. This should be apparent in low employee turnover coupled with high productivity, creativity and loyalty all of which increase quality, innovation and shareholder returns. Creativity and the innovations it delivers is an important component of airline culture: it identifies problems, provides solutions and opens the airline for new opportunities. From these will flow the profits needed for economic sustainability.

However, culture can be sabotaged by internal enemies including stress, egos and other forces which must be reshaped or removed (see Chapter 3). The Human Resources Department, as the voice of the employees, safeguards the culture by determining and protecting the core values. In today's era of inclusiveness, these values will be lived by the employees as they work towards the common mission, vision and goals of supporting the customers (see Chapter 3 and Chapter 4). The core values operate within an organisation structure in which risk and uncompromising safety are aligned. Actively pursued, they will deliver consistent customer service while being sufficiently flexible and agile to withstand shocks. The Marketing Department, as the voice of the customer, will need to monitor the passengers to ensure that the cultural delivery is exactly what the airline requires for profitable service. If passenger complaints are frequent, consistent and expensive to compensate, the Marketing Department would need to discuss behavioural change programmes with the Human Resources Department (see Chapter 3).

Challenge of biases

Many influencers urge governments to place unfunded mandates onto industry and in doing so are spending private resources which could be better used to improve social welfare for more people. Government intervention in the market-place often pleases a vocal minority at the expense of the majority. Furthermore, governments do not legislate equally and frequently avoid economic impact evaluations but they would almost always launch a social or an environmental assessment under pressure from the CSERplus' lobby. This asymmetric approach introduces biases (see Chapter 7) which could ultimately trigger one or more of the factors in alleged market inefficiency or failure (Table 8.1) and could have a significant impact on any aviation development. Airlines need to consider both internal and external biases when compiling their government and industry negotiating toolkits.

Academics and airlines

Sustainable airlines can revitalise themselves by working with independent research establishments of all types (economic, social and environmental) and using academics to supply intellectual capital. They can use their research skills to assist innovation and solve problems both of which are tactics to keep a sustainable airline ahead of competitors – and if the rewards of their research are somehow linked to the airline's success, they would have 'skin in the game'. For academics, the real reward lies in autonomy and mastery of their skill and acknowledgement of their contribution. As impartial voices, academics can also raise issues which are politically and socially sensitive and which the airline industry is afraid to acknowledge publicly, e.g. solving the free rider PRM and unqualified service animal problems. Academic research can also help the economically sustainable airline to adapt to change. However, there is a caveat to this process: academics often want a research paper but airlines want a product, service or an addition to their negotiating toolkit.

This incompatibility might eventually rupture a working relationship unless the exit strategies are clearly agreed in advance (see Table 3.14 in Chapter 3).

Skewed philanthropy

Economically sustainable airlines need to be wary of becoming enmeshed by stealth in politically inspired causes and avoid any philanthropic diversion of shareholders' funds to charities promoted by biased CSERplus' influencers such as politicians, celebrities or the Chairman (see Chapter 3). When airlines cannot afford dividends for shareholders it can be economically challenging to justify social spending on philanthropy. Airline management are not donating personal funds: they are donating shareholders' funds (see Chapter 3) (another reason why shareholders should vote at the AGM). Lufthansa (*Business Travel News*, 2015) announced that there would be no dividend for Lufthansa shareholders for 2014 at a time when the company had a thriving CSERplus programme and their annual sustainability report comprised 132 pages. What influences did this CSERplus programme have on the employees, customers and owners? Increased sales, improved employees' rewards or uplifts in future investment? Every action and decision must stand scrutiny in order to protect the airlines' reputations and deliver the economic sustainability without which airlines would fail.

Today's philanthropists are likely to be CSERplus advocates and employ a bevy of tax avoidance advisors. By avoiding tax, they will retain more of their wealth to enable them to continue philanthropy, affording them the ear of governments (whose taxes they are avoiding) and advising how they believe national income should be spent. They often appear oblivious to the fact that government money is derived from taxpayers and that not all taxpayers share their recommendations for priority disbursement of national revenues. This new breed of CSERplus philanthropists, like the advocates, perceives 'society's expectations' as homogeneous, given, known and legitimate and take it for granted that corporations now have little choice but to meet them by taking the path of CSR' (Henderson, 2001: 66–67). They also urge or shame other corporations to follow their philanthropic CSERplus lead. Airlines need to be wary of being captured by these organisations.

Inequality and consumption

What was once conspicuous consumption for the rich, such as airline travel, is now considered to be essential and a human right (see Chapter 2) which CSERplus special interest groups believe should be accessible for everybody. This represents yet another example of unbalanced influencing. Anti-poverty campaigners present the slant which suits their agenda and frequently misrepresent free-market capitalism by overlooking the improvements in living standards it has delivered. Entrepreneurialism thrives on inequality and paradoxically, this can make society more unequal as some entrepreneurs create vast, personal wealth. This is the opposite of what so many governments want and set out to neuter through taxation. In doing this, they reduce the incentives and profits made by entrepreneurs (which

– as already noted – some choose to shelter under legal tax avoidance schemes enabling them to retain their fortunes and become altruistic public donors).

With the democratisation of consumption and the widening access to social networks, there is much envy fuelled by CSERplus special interest groups seeking to normalise and democratise the consumption of what were once luxury goods and services such as airline travel. In particular, these CSERplus' advocates have widened philanthropists' and governments' agendas to reduce national and international inequalities in the pursuit of social justice. What they fail to acknowledge is that the democratisation of consumption has been enabled by investor capitalism fuelled by the liberating of markets, risk-taking of entrepreneurs and enforceable regulations to keep the stakeholders honest. Furthermore, definitions of equality of opportunity have changed over decades to the extent that poverty in developed nations has moved from malnourished and homeless to today's UK definition of 'severe material deprivation' which includes not being able to afford one week's annual holiday (ONS, 2013: 7). In emerging nations deprivation is more rudimentary and is defined at the lowest level of Maslow's pyramid (see Chapter 2 and Chapter 3), i.e. food and shelter.

Social sustainability and ITC

Society has benefitted from the airline industry which now relies heavily on ITC as a substitute for personal customer service. However, ITC which was a solution to the problems of complex processes has brought its own complications especially in times of schedule disruption when staff reductions create pinch-points. This is a trade-off: economics vs society.

ITC systems are not low-cost: they represent considerable investment which has to be funded by customers' revenue. Airlines are on the ITC treadmill trying to innovate to get ahead of competitors. The passenger experience could eventually be customised through the use of ITC data packets derived from other industries (Economist Intelligence Unit, 2014). Individualising services would mean gaining more efficiency and producing less waste (including food and time). It could even extend to passengers being re-routed to prevent them becoming stranded at an outstation.

ITC is also useful as a basis for forming internal social networks within the airline which link individuals for problem-solving – much as individuals use social media outside of the workplace. However, if the airline is planning to do this, all employees must be provided with the technology needed and the necessary training including any protocols.

Political responsibility

Politicians urge ethicality and transparency on commercial organisations while many do not exhibit those characteristics themselves (see Chapter 7 and Table 8.1) and perversely, national and supranational governments require higher standards from corporate bodies than they practise in their own bailiwicks. Aviation was one of the industries which ultimately delivered UK Prime Minister Tony Blair's political aspiration of welfare reforms. In his speech to the Labour Party Conference in 1997, he said:

> Our new society will have the same values as ever. It should be a compassionate society, but it is compassion with a hard edge. A strong society cannot be built on soft choices. It means fundamental reform of our welfare state, of the deal between citizen and society.
>
> (Blair, 1997)

In terms of air transport, Prime Minister Blair's idea of reforming the welfare state eventually placed the social costs and responsibilities for less able passengers and free riders onto the privately owned airlines, their employees, shareholders and customers. Governments never have sufficient funds to fulfil their election campaign promises hence the imposition of unfunded mandates to deliver political pledges and to retain power by satisfying the electorate. This solution delivers less than optimal welfare for society as a whole. Legislators in democracies should set policies which reflect the electorate's will; however, they are unlikely to do so if informed by single-interest CSERplus' advocates and if their knowledge sources are asymmetric (one of the triggers for alleged market inefficiency and failure – Table 8.1). As Doganis (2001) (see also Chapter 1) noted, airline privatisation preparations should have identified any social subsidies; however, if they were not identified (by either airlines or government) then those obligations would not have been considered during the privatisation process. The airlines were just as much at fault because they were unprepared. When developed world politicians shift delivery of their social pledges to the airline market, employees' rewards are suppressed and shareholders' returns are reduced. Furthermore, passengers' fares might have to be increased to ensure economic sustainability. These reactions could affect airlines' ability to compete internationally.

Rights and responsibilities

Citizens in democracies have rights and responsibilities. Legislation-passing politicians also have responsibilities including the responsibility to calculate economic impacts before passing legislation and to consider the impartiality of the influential material on which they make laws. Governments have interfered in the marketplace by taxing air travel and extending citizens' rights while ensuring that airlines assume the corresponding responsibilities. In the UK this involves using the airlines to extend the stealthy privatisation of the NHS (see Chapter 4 and Chapter 5) – an outcome opposed by both the UK Coalition Government and the Opposition in 2014. In future, national, multi-national and supranational governments should commit to an economic impact analysis in advance of passing any airline-related legislation otherwise the market distortions could have an even more detrimental impact on the competitiveness and viability of advanced economies' aviation industries.

Political correctness and social responsibility

Airlines are sometimes afraid to defend their businesses for fear of being accused of insensitivity to three of the most influential special interest groups – obesity activists and disability campaigners (see Chapter 5), and environmentalists (see Chapter 6). Not discussing their inflammatory issues will not make the challenges disappear; rather the absence of discussion undermines the openness and transparency that economic sustainability-thinking recommends and democratic governments encourage (*outside* of government). Sensitive topics should be aired and any biases declared (see Chapter 7) so the decision-makers can consider impartial information and data. Airlines must overcome their fear of politically incorrect topics because not discussing them only enforces the closed culture that employing economic sustainability-thinking would dilute. This silence could ultimately lead to market inefficiency or even failure.

8.4 ENVIRONMENTAL SUSTAINABILITY CHALLENGES

Challenges

Airline materiality in environmental issues is extremely broad-based (see Chapter 6). It could involve such diverse issues as the content of food for airline meals, consumption of fossil fuels or production of their biofuel substitutes, recycling of water, promoting public transport over private cars, studying aviation's effects on flora and fauna or reducing the noise footprint of descending aircraft. Each airline needs to assess its own material issues which could possibly vary from destination to destination all of which could add a level of complexity (see Chapter 2).

Aviation environmental sustainability (see Chapter 6) on the ground and in the air is caught between science, politicians, CSERplus advocates, cronies and free-market capitalism. Aviation can adopt common-sense approaches to reduce its energy consumption because doing so saves both fuel costs and emissions taxes. It is also sensible to reduce consumption of consumables and production of wastes. Aviation did not need the CSERplus industry to tell it to do this. There are still many unresolved issues to pursue, e.g. fuels grown at the expense of foodstuffs could necessitate a trade-off between flying and food. These issues must be pursued in a calm, reasoned and level-headed manner as required by the sustainability culture. It should not be mired in hysterical moral panic, asymmetric information, crony-ism and computer models, unlike AGW-is-harmful where the precautionary principle and taxes were applied before balanced debate and confirming scientific evidence.

The speed of atmospheric catastrophe is not occurring as computer models predicted and any climate changes might be attributed to natural variability rather than mankind. The science is unsettled. Temperature increase has been negligible at 0.8°C over the past 150 years (an extremely small timeframe for measuring the planet). Therefore, it is reasonable to reflect on whether AGW is a threat and whether CO_2 is the noxious gas it is ascribed to be. Do temperature rises precede or supersede CO_2 increases or is there no correlation or causal link? Climate variations could be caused by CFCs, cosmic ray flux, clouds, soot, tidal mechanisms, mankind or any other yet-to-be-discovered cause – or they might not even be a problem that man can influence which would mean that the 'AGW-GHG problem' needs to be redefined (see Chapter 6).

Whether or not the computer-predicted 2°C of warming is detrimental to the planet or CO_2 mixed with other gases is harmful rather than life enhancing, national, multi-national and supranational governments and their State-sponsored consensus advisers choose to believe the alarmist views are inevitable and harmful. Environmental debates have not been conducted with contrary views either aired or funded (Table 8.1). Science, which should be in a position to deliver impartial evidence and data, has been skewed by computer models, politicians and vested interests. Although science loses credibility with each unfulfilled computer prediction, legislators have not ceased to create boondoggles to appease the alarmists. Scientific objectivity is needed but the academic peer review process has failed to deliver. Groupthink and consensus have usurped independent thought and scientific evidence. Even though governments had incomplete information and data, they still passed regulations using the precautionary basis as justification.

If there is a problem with aircraft-produced emissions it is possible that it is caused by soot emitted by long-haul aircraft flying at the height of the troposphere. This will not be mitigated by taxing CO_2 as a negative externality. However, as a quantity, soot is minimal. Unravelling the legislation and systems in place for GHG emissions would create many political difficulties, particularly in Europe and the USA. The airlines' challenges are compounded by the stretched targets of their own industry body – IATA – and the increasingly incremental nature of actual improvements to deliver vastly purified emissions. And do the passengers care? It would appear not from the few who subscribe to the voluntary emissions schemes and their concerns are unlikely to impede predicted aviation industry growth.

Sustainable foodstuffs on board

The world of sustainable foodstuffs is evolving. NGOs are forming to guarantee that a particular product is sustainable in the sense that its stocks would not be depleted by being over-harvested (e.g. cod or salmon) or grown by razing forests (e.g. palm oil or soya). Knowing that livestock contributes 9% of anthropogenic CO_2 (i.e. 9% of mankind's share of CO_2's 0.03% of atmosphere) and 37% of methane's 0.0002% of atmosphere (UN FAO, 2006: xxi) raises the spectre of airlines becoming meat/dairy free as one extreme means of partially offsetting their emissions. However, this could undermine competitiveness for omnivore passengers and could be considered hypocritical when vast tracts of forest containing endangered species might have to be felled to grow biofuels for aircraft propulsion (ethical procurement vs environmental preservation?). Instead, sustainable airlines should try to source foods from suppliers who avoid products which are detrimental to the sustainability and welfare of flora or fauna. That is an economic, performance-based, ethical and sensible approach to sensitive environmental issues. Airlines could also avoid carrying beverages infused with CO_2 (e.g. colas) as a (minor) carbon [dioxide] reduction measure which could provide an interesting aspect to the environment debate (see Chapter 6). Do environmentalists drink fizzy beverages infused with CO_2?

8.5 GOVERNANCE AND REPUTATION CHALLENGES

Decision-making and reputation protection

Airlines' reputations are often the focus of the media, NGOs, governments, international bodies and multiple stakeholder groups. Confusion in language often creates its own reputational issues. Aside from the formal requirements of governments, there are also the processes which support decision-making, all of which ultimately protect the airline's reputation. Decision-making taking account of biases (such as misleading pre-judgements and experiences, and inappropriate self-interests and attachments) (see Chapter 7) provides clarity of vision and reputational risk protection. However, the appropriate decision-makers must be involved and be prepared to discuss facts, support challenge and volunteer opinions.

Reporting

From 2017 onwards, the annual reports of large EU-based companies will have to include their impact on society (including human rights) and the environment (see Chapter 7). Sustainability reporting will be integral to annual financial reports but it should not require the additional expense of a specialist team and high-quality publication. The readership will be small and therefore the resources allocated should be appropriate – especially as report production will dispense with more shareholders' funds and employees' rewards to comply with another boondoggle. There is a danger too that with the full disclosure required by the CSERplus proponents commercial confidentiality could be inadvertently breached. The EU is working on proposals to make scope and assurance mandatory for all companies, further increasing bureaucracy for small and medium-sized enterprises (the powerhouses of national economic growth). However, it is to be hoped that there would have been a justifying economic impact analysis and research as to volume of readership before regulation was passed, otherwise it could be a waste of corporate resources. This would suppress entrepreneurship and productivity while offering minimal public benefit. Excessive regulation spawns nothing but a compliance industry. It does, however, give life to a competitive (formerly missing) market for companies wanting to write and assure these reports.

8.6 STEPS TOWARDS ECONOMIC SUSTAINABILITY

Future-proofing activities

Building on managing sustainability (see Chapter 7), airlines need to identify and select appropriate future-proofing activities, one of which involves taking sustainability-thinking to national, multi-national and supranational government negotiations, i.e. sustainability-based negotiating. A comprehensive approach which integrates the three sustainability dimensions and their governance would enable trade-offs. This contrasts with the current situation where negotiations treat the sustainability factors – economic, social and environmental – as separate, distinctive and independent rather than uniting them and offsetting the unreimbursed costs incurred in each dimension with the national social or environmental benefits attained. Unreimbursed social costs from boondoggles or unfunded mandates should be gathered and used in all negotiations because there are economic-social-environmental trade-offs to be discussed for services that add value (e.g. PRM carriage) and those that only add costs (e.g. CSERplus report writing). A comprehensive list of the costs of historic policies implemented without any economic analysis would serve as a foundation for future negotiations. Using sustainability-thinking would mean that before governments implemented any further social or environmental regulations they would consider economics, i.e. employ sustainability-thinking. While this approach might appear naive, it is defendable, whereas ignoring economics in the future is not.

National, multi-national and supranational government negotiations toolkit

The new national, multi-national and supranational government negotiations tool-kit could include:

(a) considering potential trade-offs for any social and environmental airline costs incurred against any national benefits achieved. As noted, the social and environmental dimensions are treated as separate, distinctive, independent and dislocated from economics. In future-proofing terms, and using sustainability-thinking, offsetting the costs incurred in one dimension against the others should be feasible since many governments are keen to pursue social justice which sometimes even involves all three sustainability dimensions. Two examples are (i) carrying outbound UK NHS health tourists (see Chapter 4 and Chapter 5), which involves social, economic and environmental costs and (ii) fuel (energy) consumption and emissions (see Chapter 5 and Chapter 6), which also entwine the three dimensions.

(b) discussing nation-specific activities such as the impact of the UK's APD (or its replacement) on PRMs and the rationale for any rebated taxes available for ground transport but not for airlines

(c) claiming for tax relief for productive hours lost during any government-encouraged volunteering because such activities are a corporate overhead which will eventually reduce national social spending

(d) calculating the hidden costs of health tourists to airlines so that the economic data is available for discussion with governments (particularly UK)

(e) calculating the hidden costs of increasing numbers of flying PRMs which could make airlines eligible for tax relief pending review of PRM legislation

(f) offsetting any delay costs caused by statutory authorities since delays can represent considerable opportunity cost (especially those costs generated by Regulation EC 261/2004)

(g) calibrating the economic impact if aircraft were out of position and passengers needed compensating under EC 261/2004 'extraordinary circumstances' provisions

(h) offsetting the costs of services rendered in place of governments' employees (e.g. visa checking) (governments which expect airlines to do this are taking a free ride)

(i) working through the implications of increasing the number of seats per aircraft to decrease the emissions per seat should governments tax by aircraft capacity (this would align the environmental and social dimensions; developed world airlines need to consider the impact of such legislation on competition from advancing nations' airlines)

(j) monetising the opportunity costs and emissions externalities of shipping airport concession goods free of charge (i.e. a missing market) (this could trigger a new charging regime for passengers and be a source of aggravation for airport concessions)

(k) arranging frequent updates on any unrecovered social costs to be provided to regulators to alert them to the costs of changes

(l) requesting governments deliver consistent consular services in the event of major natural disasters

(m) discussing the likelihood of intergenerational care packages for employees' dependants rather than just nursery-age care

(n) seeking international agency approval for a permit system that acknowledges service animals must be trained and only taken free of charge in the cabin by entitled PRMs.

Further sustainability-supporting activities – strategic, tactical and fanciful – are documented in Table 8.2. This Table is categorised by the CSER dimensions and summarises the suggestions embedded in previous chapters. These suggestions are in no particular order because every airline will have the prioritisation which suits their business.

Table 8.2 Material future-proofing activities (strategic, tactical and fanciful)

Economic

Among the economic future-proofing activities, airlines could:

- cost business cases in terms of amount of profit per seat (or similar measure) to relate costs and profits directly to the number of fare-paying passengers or quantity of freight transported. This gives a benchmark to assess and prioritise any proposal. Using IATA's $US2.56 profit, for example, it could take the profit from approximately 600 passengers to purchase a laptop computer.
- investigate the legality of any regulations (particularly from the EU) for which no preliminary economic impact analysis or post-implementation assessments have ever been undertaken
- ensure the security of shareholders' property (e.g. dividend payments) before making philanthropic donations
- develop a new line in airline-branded luggage, i.e. one which is guaranteed to hold the maximum hand carry weight and being of the correct dimensions
- include PRM costs in philanthropy totals for annual financial accounts
- implement a permit system for trained and qualified service animals
- integrate the lean principles with the appropriate trade-offs for management and operations required for efficient financial stewardship
- invest in 3D printer technology (particularly for aircraft spares when feasible)
- charge deviants for aircraft diversions and/or offer diversion insurance with the sale of seats
- ensure that taxes, suppliers and employees' expenses are paid promptly as agreed
- challenge the appropriateness of costs and budget allocation for attending ego-boosting awards presentations
- save weights on the aircraft by thinking radically and eliminate any on-board items which do not compromise safety in order to economise on fuel consumed and emissions expended, e.g. cutting weight of cutlery, jettisoning underused equipment, changing product specifications
- gauge how far governments could stray in legislation. What new trading blocs could develop or existing trading agreements could unravel? What impact could these have on future travel?
- consider the consequences if the UK withdraws from the political, monetary and economic partnership of the EU (or similar organisations)and the impact on the regulatory boondoggles which could make European airlines uncompetitive
- consider the scale of the impacts if the EU's negotiations on behalf of European aviation dissolve all historic treaties
- assess the potential for performance-based procurement
- consider moving the operation offshore to more business-friendly jurisdictions
- advertise for any sustainability employees in a variety of media including sources used to fulfil economic vacancies, i.e. not (as now) almost exclusively in the press which covers only the social or environmental dimensions
- calculate the cost in fuel consumed and emissions discharged for all PRM items carried free so the owners can understand the opportunity cost of such support; arrange for manufacturers of such equipment to include weights on any of these items
- study competitors' CSER reports for their creativity strategies and to uncover what bothers them; search for relevant comparative indicators such as low employee turnover, health and safety statistics (e.g. accidents), water consumption, research and development spend
- start an RRR (see Table 7.1 in Chapter 7) and begin the process of horizon-scanning for future risks of all types and determine the relevant CSFs and KPIs

---

continued . . .

Table 8.2 Continued

- form partnerships with universities worldwide alongside the existing and proposed international route network to gather market insights and access cutting-edge research (see Appendix)
- uncover evolving CSERplus special interest groups and add to the RRR for monitoring for likelihood of political influence
- assess the future travellers for their ITC requirements and the potential impact on productivity, costs and employee numbers
- allocate research and development resources to all departments (resources could include building in some costed 'slack' time for employees to use for thinking)
- embed sustainability-thinking in the day-to-day activities of every employee
- assess the impact of increased ITC on the airline organisation structure
- consider the allocation of research and development monies to ensure all SBUs get funded to seek the 'golden nugget'
- take control and develop the airline industry's sustainability index (AISI) rather than wait for the CSERplus' advocates to impose their CSFs and KPIs
- consider the implications of a world headed for another economic recession
- develop comprehensive business cases for material economic sustainability spending which must include risks and payback, e.g. mid-seat armrests must be fully retractable to enable obese passengers purchasing two seats to travel in comfort and CRS must be able to process these double-seat sales

Social

Employees

Airlines could support their employees by:

- developing a culture which is open, accepts challenge and encourages innovation
- devising a method to capture innovation and harness its potential possibly by establishing an innovation centre (either virtual or real) or a Research and Development hub and ensuring that the members have sufficient authority to deliver any projects
- widening the search for innovation including using open forums, e.g. www.innocentive.com
- determining whether CSERplus activities over and above what is economically justifiable actually encourage increased seat or freight sales (and the research must be conducted by independent observers – not advocacy organisations)
- ensuring Human Resources Department check whether rewards are team-focussed or individually awarded when the airline's emphasis is on teams
- using core values for hiring, performance managing, promoting, succession planning, rewarding and firing in preparation for the changing roles of the Strategic Corporal in all its guises
- monitoring and measuring the impact of any philanthropic donations by devising appropriate CSFs and KPIs before donating
- thinking the 'unthinkable' in all three sustainability dimensions (e.g. regulatory recognition that GHGs are actually naturally occurring 'infrared-absorbing' gases and not significantly influenced by mankind); place the 'unthinkables' on the RRR (see Table 7.2 in Chapter 7) or on the master risk register
- considering making maximum body weight a condition of crew employment (for health, safety and evacuation purposes) and ensure it complies with equalities legislation
- investigating whether cutting current crew numbers to save costs is compatible with the safe carriage of increasing numbers of ageing, obese and medically incapacitated PRMs; note any additional costs and impact on flight economics (and add this to the agenda for government discussions)

continued . . .

Table 8.2 Continued

- increasing employers' insurance for cabin crew so they can assist growing numbers of PRMs to lift their hand baggage into overhead lockers or alternatively, ensuring that passengers are aware that cabin crew are not permitted to assist with lifting of any type
- facilitating regular creativity sessions for all employees on the ground or in the air to prompt airline-focussed innovations
- asking the metaphor questions and extrapolate answers from other industries (including hospitality, logistics, facilities management, vehicle valeting, furniture manufacturers and hospital management)
- training employees in lean processes
- offering language training opportunities to all employees (not just cabin crew) during working hours to prepare for market expansions (especially those prospects available after a normalisation of diplomatic relations: after Iran and Cuba, maybe even North Korea?)
- considering awards for employees who exemplify the core values
- treating stakeholders fairly (including paying invoices on time)
- considering which stakeholder groups have the ability to disrupt operations (to be recorded in the RRR)
- avoiding biases (including political, religious and Chairman's whim) in decision-making and donations by ensuring the decision-makers declare their allegiances
- keeping employee turnover low thereby retaining the corporate memory (to avoid repeating mistakes)
- arranging for PRMs with physical, intellectual, mental or hidden disabilities to address all staff (including baggage loaders) so there is a common understanding of the difficulties encountered by both parties
- bringing employees (and the Human Resources Department) into the brand-building processes
- increasing formal and informal employee education opportunities making sure that the recipients are not over-developed and that they are able to use their knowledge
- establishing a web-based system for staff when travelling as passengers to record their reviews of their flight experience on any airline
- ensuring that employees who have to interact with other stakeholders (e.g. neighbours) have the training required so that in the event of a crisis, the key contacts are known
- facilitating social media for creativity and problem-solving for the airline
- considering ideas to enforce on-board safety messages, e.g. competitions to find the passengers who can tie the dummy life jacket the quickest; quiz on safety procedures etc.

Passengers

Potential actions to economically acquire, retain and manage passengers include:

- future-proofing the contentious passenger issues including (i) charging by emissions or by weight to make future travel fair (in an altered definition of 'social justice' those who create the greatest emissions should have an increased and proportionate share of the additional costs and those who create the least emissions should pay a lower proportion); (ii) developing an on-board telephone protocol (as currently exists in UK trains) including use of mobile phones on board during sleep times; (iii) developing (and publicising) a policy on knee defenders
- forming a partnership with diet food suppliers for on-board meals (especially the low-calorie selections) and advising diners how far they would have to walk to work off the calories consumed (particularly important for sedentary passengers on long-haul flights)

continued . . .

Table 8.2 Continued

- considering adopting the default position of serving low-calorie meals on board to everyone – or serving smaller portions – to increase social awareness of obesity and to reduce waste and emissions
- encouraging healthy eating habits by, e.g. removing the sugar packets on meal trays and replacing the dessert sweet with fruit; notifying calorie count on all foodstuffs available on board in a typeface which is readable by the ageing passengers as well as the young
- catering to a calorie budget per meal rather than (or as well as) a financial budget
- considering marking waist measurements on lap belts for weight conscious passengers
- removing items which are either not consumed or never used on meal trays
- avoiding genteel extortion from large corporate customers who request conformance with their CSERplus policies
- opening the debate about the definition of 'social justice' for airline passengers so that it includes standard or lightweight, low-income and able-bodied passengers; involve employees, philosophers, economists, CSERplus' advocates, charities, NGOs, industry groups and any other appropriate stakeholders
- ensuring passengers are aware of the implicit contract not to travel with infectious diseases
- researching the commercial impact of airlines' philanthropic, social and environmental programmes to determine whether they have any influence on seat or freight sales
- allowing passengers to practice safety in advance of flight by uploading the on-board safety video to the internet and provide the relevant web links with the issue of the ticketing information or boarding pass
- increasing passenger customisation using data packets if the outputs pass the lean test
- examining the passenger trade-offs in disruption, i.e. employees vs ITC
- ensuring that on-board factual programmes (e.g. news broadcasts) are balanced and accurate to avoid exposing passengers to asymmetric and distorting influences which can be detrimental to the airline industry
- installing an allergy tick-box on the booking form to alert the carrier to potential operational challenges and subsequent litigation
- inviting representatives from specific passenger groups for discussions (including learning-disabled, orthopaedic, epileptic and others with a different perspective on airline travel)
- informing passengers as to what proportion of their purchase supports airline CSERplus activities above those required by regulations
- ensuring that current and future aircraft can accommodate qualified service animals' requirements
- ensuring that current and future aircraft can accommodate the PRM requirements for an ageing and increasingly obese population
- offering discounted fares (as part of any commercial or philanthropic strategy) to members of the armed forces (past and present) as a sign of solidarity and recognition of those who protect the aviation industry
- examining the on-board needs of families travelling together in the 21st century, e.g. crèche for babies? breakout areas for children? intergenerational mixing areas?

Shareholders/owners

Airline shareholders could be:

- encouraged to participate in the democratic processes associated with responsible share ownership in a free-market, capitalist democracy

continued . . .

Table 8.2 Continued

- invited to assist with choosing the recipients of any affordable philanthropic disbursements, the selections of which must be transparent and included in discussions for approval by the voting majority of shareholders (since it is their funds which are being donated)

Other influential stakeholders

In solving the *real* problems (see Chapter 7) airlines must also identify, evaluate and prioritise secondary stakeholders and decide whether and how to engage with them including:

- local airport residents: evaluate their role in undermining or supporting industry expansion; support neighbourhood social enterprises which could develop future employees, reduce crime or build support for airline growth
- politicians: influence the lawmakers to legislate based on impartial information with any biases declared (*i.e. open and transparent governance to be practised by governments*); undertake appropriate economic impact analyses before legislation and assessments after implementation
- special interest groups/charities/NGOs: invite prioritised groups to pitch for airline philanthropic support if there is a strategic fit (and in recognition that their resources are scarce these applicants should be offered compensation for the time and effort for unsuccessful pitches, e.g. complimentary, subject-to-load seats, freight space or appropriate consultancy fees as a donation); conduct due diligence before supporting a charity in order to avoid any reputational risk associated with failed ventures
- suppliers: examine supply chains (including airports, financiers, insurers, outsourced suppliers) for biases, potential iceberg issues for the RRR and vested interests including 'economic protection' (i.e. 'genteel extortion'); pay suppliers according to contracts

Environment

Airlines could consider:

- illustrating the imbalance in influencing by highlighting the disproportionate national, multi-national and supranational funds which are placed into AGW-is-harmful causes
- removing all beverages with infused CO_2 (or justify their inclusion) when this life-giving gas is promoted by AGW-is-harmful advocates to be dangerous and is treated as a negative and taxable externality
- ensuring that the airlines' economic voice is heard when environmental protection proposals are promoted by national-, multi-national- or supranational-funded, partisan environmental organisations or CSERplus' advocates
- including environmental items in the on-board entertainment offerings to educate passengers and provide balance in the environmental debate (e.g. *Nobel Laureate Smashes the Global Warming Hoax* (Giaever, 2015) or *Confessions of a Greenpeace Dropout* (Moore, 2014)).
- discovering (sometimes uncovering) and including any relevant environmental factors into supply contracts but always remembering that some emissions might be natural and not an environmental problem that mankind can alter
- exploring the legislated monetisation of actual, evidenced negative environmental externalities
- including any potential negative externalities as part of new business case preparation. Although the information/data revealed might not be active it would increase knowledge around which the decision can be made, flag any non-financial barriers and identify potential reputational risks for the RRR. It could also indicate what various governments might tax next.

continued . . .

Table 8.2 Continued

- avoiding wastes: refuse, reduce, reuse, recycle (or safe disposal if necessary)
- using square cardboard containers on board for non-carbonated beverages to reduce wasted space and weight
- considering support for the research and development of new fuels (including algae)
- debating biofuels for aviation vs growing foodstuffs and being aware of the wider social and environmental impacts of new biofuels
- determining the environmental impact of each product before inclusion in the on-board menu
- considering serving vegetarian- or fish-based menus to reduce total airline meal-attributed emissions (since environmentally warming methane is a by-product of meat production) and avoid controversies over animal killing methods and exploitation
- determining the importance of GM foods, animal welfare and related issues to passengers and any effect (positive or negative) on seat or freight sales
- discovering whether airline environmental credentials have any real impact on passenger purchasing (the lean principle)
- ensuring due diligence is conducted on any CDM projects associated with the airline because association with projects in corrupt destinations could undermine the airline's reputation
- inviting NGOs such as Global Action Plan to advise on common-sense energy saving measures

Governance

Airlines should consider:

- ensuring that the Board role models the core values
- formalising full sustainability-thinking in decision-making by including a tick-box on every business case to ensure the issues are examined under the three sustainability dimensions of economic, social and environmental factors before approval
- ensuring that the culture accepts challenge and is as free from bias as is humanly possible
- ensuring the NEDs are not 'friends of the Board' and that they are truly independent and able to provide the challenge needed
- employing informal governance processes to complement the formal processes and ensure that decisions take account of the economic, social and environmental dimensions (see Figure 7.2 in Chapter 7)
- encouraging shareholders to vote

8.7 FUTURE CHALLENGES FOR ECONOMICALLY SUSTAINABLE AIRLINES

Current assessment

Through the economic lens of market inefficiency and failure, it has been possible to examine whether in exchange for liberating airlines and limited tax-free concessions, national, multi-national and supranational governments are extracting what might be disproportionate payback (Table 8.1). Their interventions have included identifying missing markets, assigning property rights to negative externalities, using imperfect knowledge to sway legislators and reduce social inequalities, fuelling the moral panic of anthropogenic-induced climate change, supporting free riders and endorsing agents who might not always act for their principals. These interventions add costs.

It was free-market capitalism – through contestable markets and innovation – which reduced so many social inequalities and allowed less privileged citizens to enjoy the goods and services (such as air travel) which were once only available to the very wealthy. However, from time to time, free-market capitalism has been skyjacked by cronyism and CSERplus activists wielding considerable economic, social and environmental power. Airlines try to appease the CSERplus' advocates by donating towards vanity projects or social or environmental activities (beyond those required by regulation) in order to retain the 'licence to operate'; however, in doing so, they confiscate shareholders' dividends and employees' rewards. Business owners support the State by paying taxes which ultimately underpin national economic, social and environmental programmes. However, if these entrepreneurs are not rewarded they are worse off and any incentive to invest and contribute to national prosperity is removed.

Future economic sustainability challenges

Economic-based sustainability-thinking and activities are not bandages for reputational haemorrhages (see Chapter 7). They are strategic tools to provide confidence in the airline industry, to support sustainable growth and minimise all types of risks. Sustainability-thinking must become a mainstream activity for economically sustainable airlines and is to be similarly encouraged in the stakeholders (many of whom could have diametrically opposed concerns requiring trade-offs). Sustainability-thinking is not complicated: it uses every-day language, applies common sense, welcomes challenge, encourages innovation, increases competitiveness, seeks wide-ranging and informed opinions under the three intertwined dimensions, and should underpin the airline's business strategy. Most importantly, it delivers balance in decision-making. Economically sustainable airlines are vibrant, creative, innovative, energetic, customer-responsive organisations, value-driven by the employees whose behaviours encourage customers to return. Employees build the airlines' reputations by staying within the law and ensuring continuance of the implicit 'licence to operate'.

Airlines can be defensive (i.e. reactive) in their economic sustainability activities by waiting for events to unfold or they can be offensive (i.e. proactive) by stretching their enterprise and innovation. Reactive and tactical actions would ensure that airline resources could provide the best defence against competition but they could waste opportunities. In contrast, strategically offensive economic thinking in an open, challenge culture allows competitively focussed airlines to seize opportunities ahead of their rivals. Such offensive activity delivers reputational risk management, trumps competitors and delivers the cost-side balance to offset the benefits-only focus of CSERplus mono-topic interest groups. Thinking and reacting offensively can save shareholders' funds, cut waste and avoid groupthink, legal actions and public embarrassment as well as encouraging a culture of doing more with less – all of which are sound economics. The only constant is, paradoxically, that the world of airlines and consumers is changing. Offensive economic thinking is needed to prepare for the impacts of unexpected social and environmental interventions lest airlines are again caught unaware.

The need to reduce airline overheads in the face of more deflected government social costs could have a deleterious effect on developed nations' employment. In order to remain competitive, social cost deflection onto airlines could lead to them seeking more offshore suppliers in lower-labour-cost nations, using more ITC instead of manpower or relocating the airline headquarters to countries with lower overheads in order to remain competitive. Developed nations' airlines are being asked to assume some of the social responsibility mantle of their own (and some advancing nations') governments. The result is that the competitiveness of air passenger markets is weakened by political influences which could eventually reduce home-nation welfare.

Democratising the consumption of airline travel has transformed it from luxury good to being perceived as almost a necessity. The process has been facilitated by entrepreneurialism, innovation and deregulation of the industry. With a widening choice of location for airports and air carriers, more people can take more flights at prices to suit almost every aspirational traveller. Furthermore, the extension of budget airline routes and the political loosening of Europe allowed many families to purchase holiday homes abroad and transform working lives by being able to commute creating even more new markets. Markets, however, are not perfect because the users (producers and consumers) are not always either honest or rational. Markets could perform inefficiently or fail for many reasons (Table 8.1) particularly if influential decisions to prevent inefficiencies or failures are not taken with openness and transparency. Interventions by national, multi-national and supranational governments to either prevent or 'mop up' market inefficiencies or failures should not trigger the very consequences they were trying to prevent. Upon liberalisation the airline market was subjected to significant government social and environmental interventions with regulations and policies which were formulated on only partial (and often partisan) knowledge and which, in the absence of cost-benefit analyses, it is possible have added disproportionately to overheads. Airlines whose governments practice sustainability-thinking impacts on the marketplace will prosper at the expense of those carriers whose governments do not. Increased costs will result in increased fares and possibly eventually excluding income-deprived citizens from travel. So, in the interests of openness and honest disclosure as recommended by best-practice economic sustainability governance, airlines should in future challenge governments as to exactly which problem their interventions are trying to solve, i.e. airline economics vs politics, society and environment.

As long as CSERplus advocacy continues influencing in the background, national, multi-national and supranational government organisations will legislate tightening the rights for passengers and the responsibilities for airlines. At times it almost seems that some governments are anti-airline and yet trading nations need air connections to succeed. However, the airline industry has also been at fault for not insisting that legislators produce economic impact analyses (see e.g. Table 5.2 in Chapter 5) before ruling. The airline industry does not voice all the challenges forced upon it for fear of public repudiation in an age of politically correct CSERplus capitalism and social media. And yet so much of the aviation research on which legislators rule is actually advocacy and asymmetric in origin and could eventually lead to international airline market inefficiency or ultimately even failure.

In order to pursue social agendas, governments have used negative aviation externalities as a cause for non-hypothecated taxation while simultaneously acknowledging some and ignoring other triggers of alleged airline market inefficiency and failure (Table 8.1). Consequently they have precipitated the misallocation of resources and fettered regional airline competition against those carriers from nations with minimal social and environmental legislation. In one of the most international of industries, airlines from the developed world are competing with considerable restrictions on their competitive potential. The CSERplus' advocates in the airline marketplace have inadvertently provoked unintended economic consequences in the pursuit of human rights and social equality and equity. Those who inflict their own view of social justice are rarely affected by any of the negative consequences of their influence. Many of these influencers avoid taxes of all types (including income taxes), fly in private jets (which did not attract UK APD until 2013) and might not personally contribute to airlines' emissions offset programmes. Without strong and viable markets there can be no privately provided social interventions because industries will eventually become economically unsustainable and relocate to more hospitable nations (i.e. society vs environment vs governments' goals vs airline economics).

In the UK APD is a regressive tax which affects the more economically deprived travellers hardest and is contrary to the concept of low-cost, low-fare carriers with their enabling of equality of opportunity. The more social responsibility is placed onto airlines, the less affordable flying could become. Paradoxically, this might achieve the opposite of what governments and CSERplus interest groups advocate and could even return full-service flying to the domain of the luxury good. Abolition of the UK's APD is possible if the four nations (England, Scotland, Wales and Northern Ireland) decide to act independently and competitively to determine their own air tax regimes. However, APD could be replaced with another tax (because these governments need the revenues) and it would be logical at that time for any 'green' tax to be applied on a known negative (and measurable) externality such as soot and not life-enabling CO_2. Whichever is chosen, it should only be implemented after an open and well-informed debate and not reliant on asymmetric information or the sway of vested interests.

Bigger subsonic aircraft with longer ranges are in development and might eventually fly the ultra-long distance from The Netherlands to Australia without refuelling (see Chapter 1). This could reduce the pressure on the mid-point or transit airports and might also change the operating structures and markets of airlines based there. Supersonic long-range aircraft are under development and could transform long-haul passenger experiences if stakeholders (including those who might be affected by any noise) were willing to allow it. Further developments include pilotless aircraft with their virtual travel experience and vulnerability to computer hacking as well as the Dragon Dream airship – a rigid frame, lighter-than-air freighter fuelled by helium (Trimble, 2013). All of these technological developments could improve connectedness but in the meantime, fossil fuels are a constraint and biofuels, with their encroachment on nutritional land space and virgin forests, might not be able to provide sufficient substitute energy sources. While innovative technology solves some problems (e.g. knee defenders (see Chapter 4)) it sometimes creates others (e.g. the same knee defenders' impact on other passengers' human rights). ITC (including wireless internet connections and mobile phones) could eventually be used in the cabin during flight. Protests are already forming from those who value the status quo silence away from the noise of voice technology (which is ironic given that aircraft manufacturers have now made interiors far quieter than previous generations). This development could eventually require 'phone-free' cabins (as currently happens on UK trains – the forerunner of which was the smoke-free carriage). Eventually there might even be a ban on using mobile phones on board, especially during night flights when many passengers prefer to sleep.

Increasing use of mobile ITC can also affect future-proof thinking. Much future connectivity might be by non-flying means such as hand-held communications devices. There are an estimated six billion mobile phone handsets worldwide and the increasing use of technologies such as digital conferencing might mean reduced travel for business or VFR. However, in support of the airline industry, many observers believe that the tourism experience would still be much sought after.

Future social sustainability challenges

Airlines have stakeholders, the most important of whom are the employees, passengers and owners (see Chapter 3). They all have human rights but occasionally some stakeholders' rights encroach on other peoples' rights and the corresponding responsibilities (along with the liabilities) are transferred to the airlines. Employee stakeholders should maintain the airline's high reputation and competitiveness while practising the core values and generating innovations. The most responsible activity for the employees of an economically sustainable airline is to manage the business well. Airline employees working in their role as hosts could evolve into Strategic Corporals (Krulak, 1999) (see Chapter 2 and Chapter 3) taking them beyond their current paygrade with potential for error and/or subsequent litigation. Future airline customer hosts could be required to make more decisions on a greater number of topics all of which would previously have been made by their leaders or managers. This increases the vicarious liability risks of the airline as the hosts' responsibilities widen beyond their potential competence. They must therefore be recruited on core values, trained, empowered and trusted to act (see Chapter 3).

On the other hand, some passenger stakeholders (in pursuit of satisfying their own needs) activate the tyranny of the minority by holding airlines and fellow passengers to ransom. Whether they have a nut allergy, suffer a heart attack, are drunk or drugged or are one of the exported elderly, these outliers could trigger disruptions, disorder, delays, diversions, moral hazards and increased costs (Table 8.1). While many airlines have returned to profitability, the changing passenger mix with more service-dependent passengers could affect the future competitiveness of developed nations' airlines and increase their costs. The combination of State-inflicted social costs plus increased operating costs derived from the CSERplus advocates could place these airlines under pressure from carriers of advancing nations with lower-cost structures and the benefits of CDM capital inflows (i.e. politics and society vs airline economics).

In the UK necessities such as public ground transport are perceived as a social equality issue and are often subsidised by the State; however, airlines are not afforded the same consideration. In a perplexing double standard, the UK government considers air travel as a luxury for the purpose of taxation, but a necessity for social justice without allocating any form of subsidy equivalent to that granted to land transport providers. Furthermore, airlines are unique among disabled people's product and service providers in not being able to recover specialised PRM costs from the users or from their governments. In a juxtaposition, low-weight, low-income, able-bodied people might not be able to afford to fly (and to exercise their 'human rights') and yet if they received a proportional subsidy (like unentitled PRMs who abuse the system) their economic circumstances might change and enable them to travel. Would this be social justice for them? Who defines social justice? What is social justice? Is it based on income, consumption, health, physical ability, social equality or equity – or even other criteria?

Advanced-world airlines have to manage the signals arising from potential legislated market inefficiencies or failures by thinking creatively about the most efficient use of resources. Layering social costs (including labour taxes (see Table 1.2 in Chapter 1)) onto private airlines means that passengers' fares would have to increase. Globalisation, on which airlines thrive, is actually an enabler not a barrier to egalitarian social ideals. Entrepreneurialism chases markets seeking opportunities where costs can be competitive, market share increased and profits realised (Sanandaji and Sanandaji, 2014). It is therefore in every nation's interest that airline globalisation continues competing successfully to provide profits, employment and socially beneficial economic growth.

The airlines' socio-economic sustainability-thinking needs to stretch beyond the aviation industry as a future-proof measure. Future trends include a burgeoning global population with rising affluence accompanied by globalisation and growth of travel, tourism, migration and business (see Chapter 1). However, these will take place against a background of changing threats and risks. The four biggest threats to the West are population-linked: unchecked growth, littoralisation (movements towards the coast), urbanisation (occupation of urban areas) and connectivity (increased trade, commerce and communications) (Kilcullen, 2013). In the future, security threats will change. Wars will no longer be fought at sea or in the desert but rather in the urban areas. The cities with their own cultures will become the unit of analysis rather than nation states and will sprout new social problems. The increased connectivity will allow criminal networks to flourish more easily. Crime and war will intertwine and cities will be under stress from social and resource pressures and the virtual and real worlds will collide (Kilcullen, 2013). The UN Department of Economic and Social Affairs predicted a world population of 9.6 billion by 2050 (United Nations, 2013) which will not be evenly spread. There will be vast population expansion in cities particularly in current low-income countries and many of the inhabitants will be elderly, ill and/or obese and unable to afford the medical treatment they require for healthy longevity. (These nations could possibly have the largest number of potentially eligible climate change refugees (see Chapter 6).) Many of these citizens could be attracted to fly to countries where medical treatment is lower cost or free (or, in the case of UK citizens, reimbursed by the NHS) (see Chapter 5). Such travel could place the airlines at economic risk and increase carriers' social responsibilities. The increasing population in cities means that there could be more protests about airport expansion because of land take and negative externalities emanating from 24-hour airport connectivity. There is also the very real possibility of self-appointed CSERplus experts and vested interests increasing the number of moral panics and growing the specialists to manage them.

The rising middle class in advancing nations have aspirations to fly since the right to fly is already becoming the new 'normal' pushed by social equality and equity advocates in the developing world. However, advancing-world airports might become sites of extreme vulnerability since they are often near or in densely populated urban areas with a tendency to high crime.

Governments have tackled the threats to aircraft security with a raft of tactics which have often inefficiently increased security queues beyond those ever computer-modelled during airport design. Safety and security must be 'hygiene' issues for aviation. However, in the sustainability spirit of openness, transparency and challenge, the effectiveness of these costs too must be fully assessed before they are incurred. Saving the Euro distracted funding and attention from long-term security costs for the Eurozone. It meant less European supranational government monies available for deflecting terrorism in the lawless states from where terrorism originates. In the UK, the recession of 2008 to 2013 resulted in State funding cuts, which contributed to a significant reduction in the border police and the armed forces (the protector of airports and airlines when the nation is under threat) in order for the Coalition Government to maintain welfare payments and increase its foreign aid spending to 0.7% of GDP *ad infinitum*. This is an example of the tensions between politicians and economics, and politicians and society.

Future environment sustainability challenges

Airline environmental issues are awash with complication and misinformation. Firstly, the evidenced negative externalities (including soot, noise and lighting pollution) are being managed within the regulations and the technologies available while the aviation industry (including aircraft and fuel manufacturers) is always seeking innovative improvements. Secondly, the atmospheric science is incomplete. Climate warming alarmists claim that there are threats posed by mankind without understanding how all gases (including CO_2 and clouds of H_2O) behave in the atmosphere. Their rationale for limiting mankind-influenced climate warming to 2°C and CO_2 to 350 ppm (most of which occurs naturally) is also inadequately evidenced and the vast precautionary costs are so far unjustified. Furthermore, if the IPCC is correct, the unilaterally imposed regulations would only hurt advanced-world competitiveness. Mother Nature works on millennia; mankind can work on time measurements as small as nano-seconds. How does mankind intend to control nature's timetable and activities so changes can be measured? When would this measurement start and for how long? The precautionary principle is enriching too many environmental stakeholders to make them impartial in a debate in which (contrary to sustainability-thinking) challenges are ignored. Non-hypothecated taxes charged to neutralise unproven detrimental externalities are being donated to CDM social and environmental projects in the advancing-world. Their airlines have neither the overheads of such projects nor the high national social costs of their advanced-world competitors. This amounts to a subsidy from developed world airlines to their competitors in the advancing-world and undermines the working of a competitive international market. Was developed world competitiveness considered when the CSERplus' advocates promoted CDMs? Such interventions lacked economic assessment but epitomised the confluence of social and environmental ambitions. The airline industry needs to adopt an offensive (i.e. proactive) stance to pre-empt future moves by national, multi-national and supra-national governments which might ultimately restrict any of the developed world's airlines' current activities. Such threats must be deflected with comprehensive and impartial economic-based environmental impact analyses before implementation of any new legislation or regulations.

In coming decades, there might be more definitive scientific measurement to determine whether the changes in the climate are a short-term fluctuation or a long-term trend, whether they are natural or man-made and their effect on migration. The environmental implications of populations living by water are significant for transport hubs. Because so many people will be living near water they are more likely to experience flooding – and therefore believe in the threat of 'global warming'. Even without the threat or non-threat of climate changing, water levels rise and fall. Access to water also has implications for freight. The most expensive means of moving perishable freight is by air so improvements in product deterioration technology and easier access to water ports might mean that more freight is shipped by sea. Exporters of perishable shipments could therefore use shipping over air freight with an even greater increase in emissions (unless cleaner ocean technology becomes available).

Conclusion: So . . . what now?

End game?

When will the CSERplus advocates' myopic, economics-deficient challenges end? When their definition of a socially just world has been fulfilled by CDM payments?

When the advancing-world pollutes with impunity because the advanced-world energy-consuming industries have closed? When advanced-world airlines (unable to compete internationally because of high CSERplus costs) have relocated to advancing nations? Or when inefficient international airline markets have finally failed? Furthermore, does airline participation in economically deficient CSERplus activities encourage the increased seat and freight sales which are so essential for economic sustainability?

Reflecting

The lack of economic assessment caught airlines unprepared for many policies, regulations, boondoggles and unfunded mandates. They were out-manoeuvred by politicians persuaded by CSERplus advocates. Being unprepared for PRMs' costs was almost understandable given that regulations were implemented before airlines understood the long-term implications of an increasingly ageing and obese society. However, to be caught by the AGW-is-harmful advocates was perplexing since the science was incomplete and sometimes even misinterpreted, misrepresented and distorted. In the short-term, the CSERplus' advocates' social and environmental demands were largely unchallenged by the aviation industry because, focussed on economic sustainability, it lacked the resources (data, knowledge, time and funds) to match the national, multi-national and supranational subsidies given to the lobby groups. The industry also conceded to the 'unobjectionable doctrines' with 'superficial plausibility' which, because of their 'apparent generosity', have encouraged uncritical acceptance. However, the potential outcome for long-term market inefficiency and/or failure should concern every industry which either supports the CSERplus' advocates' ideals or which, in contrast, failed to launch, could not compete or closed down because of boondoggles and unfunded mandates. In this battle of ideologies free-market capitalist, democratic voices are often undermined by vested interests whose livelihoods, affiliations, altruism and/or egoism are derived from promoting just one or two of CSER's four dimensions. CSERplus' advocates discuss the social and environmental dimensions as if they are separate, distinctive and dislocated from economics and governance rather than being intertwined and dependent. Any future government-industry negotiations must be sure to consider the economic, social and environmental domains simultaneously supported by governance in the form of comprehensive sustainability-thinking. This would deliver a trade-off of private costs incurred in one dimension against the public benefits delivered in the others.

The opinions of many CSERplus observers and participants have provided the context for investigating potential airline market inefficiencies and failures. Airlines are part of civil society and act responsibly to preserve their reputations for safe and secure operations, customer service and environmental conformance. Any failings could be corrected by regulators terminating licences, shareholders divesting their holdings or customers ceasing to purchase seats or freight space. Airlines did not need advice from CSERplus' advocates, particularly those who failed to declare their biases or allegiances or who used incomplete, partisan information and data to sway politicians, legislators and regulators. Their failure – contrary to sustainability-thinking – has compromised decision-making governance and undermined developed world airlines' economic viability.

Market inefficiency or failure

Expensive public (social) programmes need either funding from high taxes (which are contrary to entrepreneurial cultures) or corporately provided, mandated provisions. In some developed nations, governments have required airlines to support national social programmes both at home and perversely, in their competitor airlines' advancing nations with lower tax rates and businesses unfettered by the same obligations. The only means by which developed world airlines can cover these costs is to close routes, cut overheads, cancel dividends, reduce employee numbers and/or raise ticket prices. Since price is the most important factor in customer choice, this could make developed world airlines uncompetitive. Furthermore, by reducing the competitiveness of international businesses like airlines, home-nation welfare could eventually be reduced. CSERplus requirements applied universally would be competition levellers but when applied unevenly, like many of the boondoggles and unfunded mandates, they could generate unpredictable, detrimental market consequences.

Future-proofing

Airlines must practice sustainability-thinking in order to anticipate whatever challenges regulators and CSERplus' advocates are contemplating and remind governments that they have a duty to undertake economic analysis before legislating. The lack of impartial, factual detail on which many CSERplus-inspired statutory interventions were made compromises the spirit of openness and transparency that the advocates espouse for commercial organisations (including airlines). Furthermore, many of these interventions could at least trigger market inefficiency or at worst, failure. The CSERplus principles sound reasonable until it is realised that the enabling economics are absent. Economically deficient social and environmental programmes will lead to increased airline costs and customer prices.

The refusal of many CSERplus' advocates to be challenged should signal a warning to advanced-world airlines. They need to be alert to the unintended consequences of national, multi-national or supranational governments' interventions. Any more economically deficient interventions could force advanced-world airlines to relocate to more entrepreneurial, advancing nations which benefit from lower social costs and CDM capital inflows. Relocation would make advanced nations worse off but would ensure their airlines did not become the 21st century's equivalent of 'canaries in the coal mines'. Could the omission of economics from the CSERplus, advocates' demands make airline markets inefficient or could it eventually result in their failure?

References

Blair, Tony (1997), *Speech to Labour Party Conference, 1997* available from http://www. guardian.co.uk/politics/1997/oct/01/speeches1 accessed 2 March 2013

Business Travel News (2015), *No dividend at Lufthansa* available from http://www.btnews. co.uk/article/8465 accessed 23 February 2015

Doganis, R. (2001), *The airline business in the 21st century*, London, Routledge

Economist Intelligence Unit (2014), *The future of air travel: the air traveller as 'data packet'* available from http://www.atn.aero/print_analysis.pl?id=1538 accessed 22 November 2014

Economist, The (2014), *Roadrunners: rather tardily, the government is championing motorways* available from http://www.economist.com/news/britain/21603475-rather-tardily-govern ment-championing-motorways-roadrunners accessed 31 August 2014

European Union (2013), *Draft list of extraordinary circumstances following the National Enforcement Bodies (NEB) meeting held on 12 April 2013* available from http://ec.europa.eu/transport/ themes/passengers/air/doc/neb-extraordinary-circumstances-list.pdf accessed 5 January 2015

Giaever, I. (2015), *Nobel Laureate Smashes the Global Warming Hoax* available from https:// www.youtube.com/watch?v=TCy_UOjEir0 accessed 12 November 2015

Henderson, D. (2001), *Misguided virtue: false notions of corporate responsibility*, The Institute of Economic Affairs available from http://www.iea.org.uk/publications/research/misguided-virtue-false-notions-of-corporate-social-responsibility accessed 7 October 2014

Iivonen, K. and Moisander, J. (2015), Rhetorical construction of narcissistic CSR orientation, *Journal of Business Ethics* 131: 649–664

Kilcullen, D. (2013), *Out of the mountains: the coming age of the urban guerrilla*, London, C. Hurst and Co. (Publishers) Ltd

Krulak, C. (1999), The Strategic Corporal: Leadership in the Three Block War, *Marines Magazine*, January available from http://www.au.af.mil/au/awc/awcgate/usmc/strategic_corporal.htm accessed 29 August 2014

Moore, P. (2014), *Confessions of a Greenpeace dropout* available from https://www.youtube. com/watch?v=dCrkqLaYjnc accessed 20 December 2015

Moran, L. (2014), *Passengers deal with mile-long security lines in Chicago airport, TSA blamed for dozens of missed flights* available from http://www.nydailynews.com/news/national/ passengers-deal-mile-long-tsa-lines-chicago-airport-article-1.2028687 accessed 6 December 2014

Office of National Statistics (ONS) (2013), *Poverty and Social Exclusion in the UK and EU, 2005–2011* available from http://www.ons.gov.uk/ons/dcp171776_295020.pdf accessed 26 October 2014

Pew Research (2014), *Emerging and developing economies much more optimistic than rich countries about the future* available from http://www.pewglobal.org/2014/10/09/emerging-and-developing-economies-much-more-optimistic-than-rich-countries-about-the-future/ accessed 28 October 2014

Ryanair (2016), *Ryanair Calls For Immediate Action as French ATC Workers Call 40th Strike Since 2009* available from http://www.atn.aero/article.pl?mcateg=&id=57538&member= 642E6A2E616E63656C6C40676F6F676C656D61696C2E636F6D7C333036357C32303 1362D30312D3235 accessed 26 January 2015

Sanandaji, T. and Sanandaji, N. (2014), *Superentrepreneurs and how your country can get them*, Centre for Policy Studies available from http://www.cps.org.uk/files/reports/original/ 140429115046-superentrepreneursandhowyourcountrycangetthemupdate.pdf accessed 14 December 2014

Trimble, S. (2013), *Aeros gains airworthiness certificate for new hybrid airship* available from http://www.flightglobal.com/news/articles/aeros-gains-airworthiness-certificate-for-new-hybrid-390293/ accessed 23 August 2015

United Nations (2013), *World population projected to reach 9.6 billion by 2050* available from http://www.un.org/en/development/desa/news/population/un-report-world-popula tion-projected-to-reach-9–6-billion-by-2050.html accessed 23 November 2014

United Nations Food and Agricultural Organisation (UN FAO) (2006), *Livestock's Long Shadow* available from ftp://ftp.fao.org/docrep/fao/010/a0701e/a0701e00.pdf accessed 14 August 2013

Whyte, J. (2013), *Quack policy: abusing science in the causes of paternalism*, The Institute of Economic Affairs available from http://www.iea.org.uk/publications/research/quack-policy-%E2%80%93-abusing-science-in-the-cause-of-paternalism accessed 4 October 2014

Appendix

Future research and some unresolved issues

The pursuit of complete sustainability should uncover many knowledge gaps, pose many challenges and offer solutions, i.e. the natural output of full sustainability-thinking. Filling these gaps or meeting these challenges using research (whether internally or externally commissioned) can lead to that much-prized golden nugget of competitive advantage. Unresolved issues included:

- why did legislators and regulators omit economic impact analyses and assessments? (industry failure? regulatory failure?)
- where do CDM payments go and which nations and their airlines could benefit the most?
- is there an economic trade-off between ITC and customer complaints?
- where are the rights and responsibilities when one passenger has a service animal and another has an animal allergy? or when one passenger has stiff knees and the passenger in front uses knee defenders? or when one passenger makes a mobile phone call and disturbs sleeping fellow passengers?
- what training would the future Strategic Corporals require for 2020 and beyond?
- is there any relationship during disruptions between the amount of ITC used in operations and the number of customer complaints?
- does the airline organisation structure need to change to cope with innovations?
- how can an ageing workforce be managed particularly on the frontline including the Aircraft Loaders, PRM Mobility Assistants and Check-in Agents?
- does internet or social network chatter have any real effect on intentions to purchase or repurchase?
- what parts of 'reputation' really matters to customers? just safety? philanthropy?
- to what extent is the ageing passenger population comfortable with ITC? what proportion of offline bookings is simply because of age-related disabilities?
- where does innovation *really* happen in the organisation?
- are passengers influenced by an airline's sustainability credentials? and can these credentials overrule price as a concern?
- for which stakeholders are the CSERplus activities beneficial and which activities contribute positively to the profitability of the airline?

- do social sustainability activities (including philanthropy) really contribute to seat or freight sales? would customers pay more to increase philanthropic activities?
- what, if any, is the relationship between core value dissonance, employee burnout and performance, work engagement, and safety in the air and on the ground?

Index

 # Taylor & Francis eBooks

Helping you to choose the right eBooks for your Library

Add Routledge titles to your library's digital collection today. Taylor and Francis ebooks contains over 50,000 titles in the Humanities, Social Sciences, Behavioural Sciences, Built Environment and Law.

Choose from a range of subject packages or create your own!

Benefits for you

» Free MARC records
» COUNTER-compliant usage statistics
» Flexible purchase and pricing options
» All titles DRM-free.

 Free Trials Available
We offer free trials to qualifying academic, corporate and government customers.

Benefits for your user

» Off-site, anytime access via Athens or referring URL
» Print or copy pages or chapters
» Full content search
» Bookmark, highlight and annotate text
» Access to thousands of pages of quality research at the click of a button.

eCollections – Choose from over 30 subject eCollections, including:

Archaeology	Language Learning
Architecture	Law
Asian Studies	Literature
Business & Management	Media & Communication
Classical Studies	Middle East Studies
Construction	Music
Creative & Media Arts	Philosophy
Criminology & Criminal Justice	Planning
Economics	Politics
Education	Psychology & Mental Health
Energy	Religion
Engineering	Security
English Language & Linguistics	Social Work
Environment & Sustainability	Sociology
Geography	Sport
Health Studies	Theatre & Performance
History	Tourism, Hospitality & Events

For more information, pricing enquiries or to order a free trial, please contact your local sales team: www.tandfebooks.com/page/sales